Irelandhotels
Guide 2
formerly the Be Our G

Featuring the largest choice of Hotels and Guesthouses
including sections on Golf, Angling, Conferences & Meetings, Spa & Leisure Facilities as well as extensive Touring Maps

Produced by

IRISH HOTELS FEDERATION
13 Northbrook Road, Dublin 6, Ireland
Tel +353 1 497 6459 **Fax** +353 1 497 4613

or visit www.irelandhotels.com/onlineguide

Telephone Code for dialling Northern Ireland from the Republic of Ireland:
replace the prefix +44 48 with 048 followed by the 8 digit number

The Irish Hotels Federation does not accept any responsibility for errors, omissions or any information whatsoever in the Guide and members and users of the Guide are requested to consult page 11 hereof for further information.

Design & Database published by NeoGen, www.neogen.ie

Hotels and Guesthouses Listing   GUINNESS

Maamturk Mountains, Co. Galway

Ireland West

		Page Nos.
1.	Clare	35-45
2.	Donegal	45-54
3.	Galway	54-76
4.	Leitrim	77-78
5.	Limerick	79-82
6.	Mayo	82-93
7.	Roscommon	94
8.	Sligo	94-97

Northern Ireland

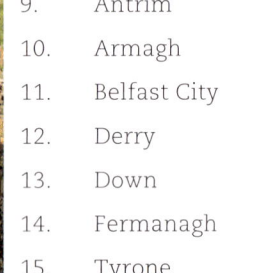
Giants Causeway, Co. Antrim

9.	Antrim	103-105
10.	Armagh	—
11.	Belfast City	105-106
12.	Derry	107-108
13.	Down	108-109
14.	Fermanagh	109-110
15.	Tyrone	111

Dublin & Ireland East

Ha'Penny Bridge, Dublin

16.	Cavan	117-119
17.	Dublin	119-150
18.	Kildare	151-156
19.	Laois	156-157
20.	Longford	158-159
21.	Louth	159-161
22.	Meath	162-165
23.	Monaghan	166-167
24.	Offaly	168-170
25.	Westmeath	170-173
26.	Wicklow	174-178

Ireland South

Loop Head Lighthouse, Co. Wexford

27.	Carlow	183-184
28.	Cork	185-208
29.	Kerry	208-237
30.	Kilkenny	238-245
31.	Tipperary	245-250
32.	Waterford	251-261
33.	Wexford	261-269

We've got it covered!

Contents, Map & Layout of Guide

Contents

Layout of Guide & Map	2-3
Explanation of Facilities - Key to Symbols	4
Sample Entry	6
Explanation of B&B/Room/Suite Rates	8
Explanation of Classifications	9
Access for Persons with Disabilities	10
GPS - Global Positioning System Co-Ordinates	10
Necessary Information & Irelandhotels.com Online	11
Spa Categories	12
Healthy Food for Kids	13
Index to Locations	14-15
IHF President's Welcome Message	16-17
Irelandhotels.com Online	18 & 27
General Tourist Information	20
Map of Ireland	24-25
Local Tourist Information Offices	26 & 28
Ireland's Tourist Boards - Home & Abroad	29
Introduction to Ireland's 4 Regions	30

Illustrated Guide to Hotels & Guesthouses

Ireland West	31-97
Northern Ireland	99-111
Dublin & Ireland East	113-178
Ireland South	179-269

Activities

	Golf	271-282
	Angling	283-287
	Conferences & Meetings	289-307
	Spa & Leisure	309-323

Maps of Ireland	325-340
Index of Hotels & Guesthouses	341-351

Regions
Begin by selecting the **Region(s)** you wish to visit. This guide divides into **4 separate Regions – Ireland West, Northern Ireland, Dublin & Ireland East, Ireland South** – and they are represented in that order.

Counties
Within each Region, Counties are presented alphabetically.

Locations – Cities, Towns, Villages
Within Counties, Locations are also presented alphabetically, see **Index to Locations** on Pages 14 & 15.

Hotels & Guesthouses
Within Locations, Hotels and Guesthouses are also presented in alphabetical order, see **Index of Hotels and Guesthouses** on Pages 341 to 351.

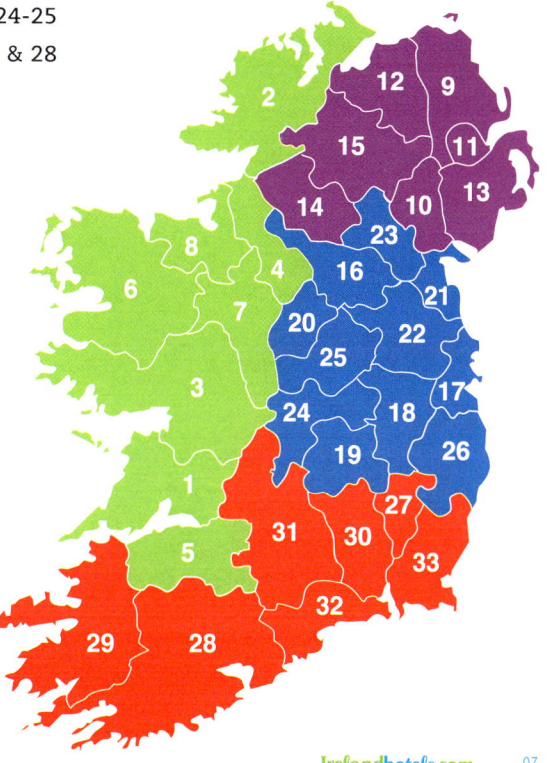

Facilities - Keys to Symbols

GUINNESS

For further details on any of these symbols please contact the premises

 Number of Beds

 Lift/Elevator

 Can be Booked Through Travel Agent / Tourist Office and Commission Paid

 Child Friendly

 Leisure Facilities

 Golf Course on Site

 Angling on Site or Nearby

 Car Parking

 Facilities for Pets

 Tea/Coffee Making Facilities in Bedroom

 Restaurant

 Wine Licence Only **or**

 Licensed to Sell All Alcoholic Drink

 Internet Access

 Air Conditioned Bedrooms

 Guide Dogs Welcome

 Access for Persons with Disabilities - **See also page 10**

 Healthy Food For Kids - For details see page 13

 Eco Label Flower
European standard recognising exceptional environmental managment and performance

Green symbols illustrated above & opposite denote that the hotel or guesthouse is included in a particular Activity Section. Detailed information on these Activities is shown on pages: **271** to **323**.

Activity Sections

271 — Golf

283 — Angling

289 — Conferences & Meetings

309 — Spa & Leisure

04 *We've got it covered!*

Enjoy GUINNESS Sensibly. Visit

GUINNESS cork jazz festival
28TH - 31ST OCT'11

IT'S ALIVE INSIDE

The GUINNESS word and associated logos are trade marks. © Guinness & Co. 2011.

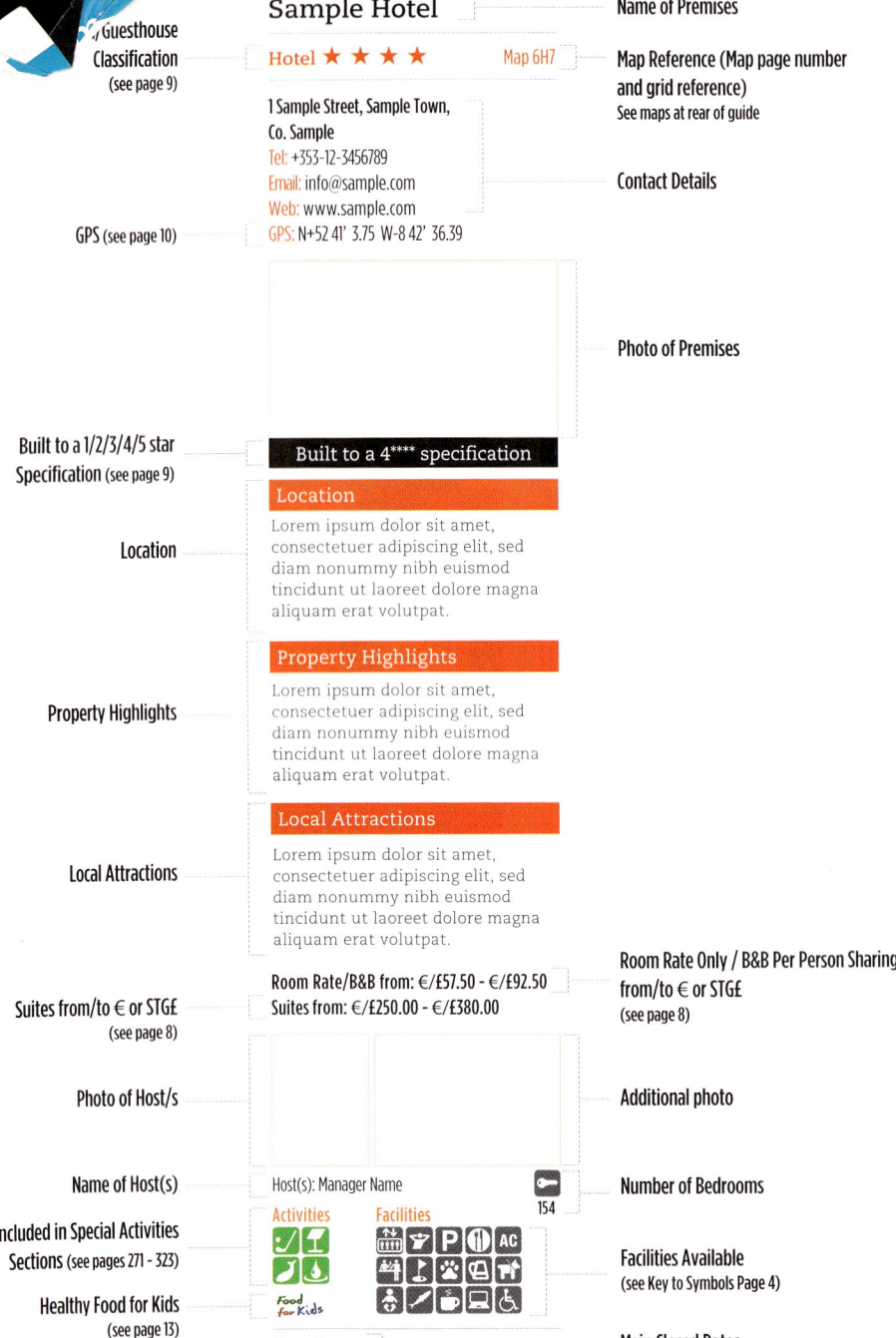

Enjoy SMITHWICK'S Sensibly. Visit drinkaware.ie

Judge it for yourself.

During its rich history of brewing Smithwick's Superior Irish Ale has been awarded seven gold medals for quality by an independent international jury.

Why not judge it for yourself?

SMITHWICK'S

300 YEARS

Explanation of B&B/Room/Suite Rates   GUINNESS

It is essential that, when booking your accommodation, you request the IrelandHotels.com Guide 2011 Rate

Our Guide features a broad selection of Irish Hotels and Guesthouses, from ultra modern buildings to stately Country Houses, luxurious Castles and old-world Inns. The majority of these Hotels and Guesthouses are members of the Irish Hotels Federation or the Northern Ireland Hotels Federation and we hope that the illustrations and descriptions of these premises and the amenities they offer will help you to choose the most suitable premises for your needs. All of the Hotels and Guesthouses featured in the Guide at the time of going to print (9th October 2010) have been registered, or are in the process of applying for registration by Fáilte Ireland or by the Northern Ireland Tourist Board, in accordance with the Statutory Registration Regulations which they administer.

B&B, Room Only And Suite Rates*

The only rates featured in this publication relate to either a **Bed & Breakfast Per Person Sharing, a Room Rate only or a Suite Rate.** These are **Guideline Rates:** Please ensure that you contact the premises to verify the rates applicable to your reservation.

Supplements may be payable for suites* (see below) or superior/de luxe rooms. Also, where single or double/twin bedded rooms are occupied by one person, a supplement may be payable. Correspondingly, if more than two persons share a family room, special reduced rates may be available.

*The definition of a Suite or Half Suite, broadly speaking, is: The bedroom area must be either separate from the living area or clearly defined by an obvious divide i.e. a door or arch or different floor coverings e.g. carpet, tiles or wooden flooring. Please contact each premises to ascertain the exact definition of their suite(s).

Per Person Sharing: relates to the cost of Bed & Full Breakfast per Person per Night, on the basis of two persons occupying a Standard Double/Twin Bedded Room, most having private bath/shower.

Room Rate: relates to the cost of a Standard Room per Night. There may be a restriction on the number of persons allowed to share the room. It is advisable to check this when making your reservation.

Suites: relates to the cost of a Suite per Night. There may be a restriction on the number of persons allowed to share the suite. It is advisable to check this when making your reservation.

The rates range from minimum to maximum and are those generally in operation throughout the year, but may not apply during special occasions such as Public Holiday Weekends, Christmas and New Year, International Events, Major Festivals and Sporting Fixtures, or on such other occasions as individual premises may decide.

Rates are inclusive of Value Added Taxes at current (2010) rates and Services Charges (if any). In the case of Hotels and Guesthouses in the Republic of Ireland, rates are quoted in € **(Euro)**, whereas in Northern Ireland rates are quoted in **STG£**.

Special Offers: Many of the Hotels & Guesthouses featured in this guide offer great special value on our website. For full details, please visit **www.irelandhotels.com/offers.**

Opening Dates For Premises Under Construction Or Refurbishment
Some of the premises featured in the guide were not open at the guide print date (9th October 2010). The planned date of opening as supplied by these premises is displayed on the premises photograph.

Explanation of Classifications

Explanation of Classification (Star Rating) Scheme

Republic of Ireland

A mandatory **Hotel and Guesthouse Classification Scheme**, introduced during 2007, was developed by Fáilte Ireland, in conjunction with the Irish Hotels Federation (IHF). This new classification scheme has been in place since 2009.

Hotels are rated from 1 Star to 5 Stars and Guesthouses are rated from 1 Star to 4 Stars. The stars are indicated on each entry under the Name of the Hotel or Guesthouse.

If the star rating is not shown, this means that the premises is perhaps undergoing a period of renovation or refurbishment and is awaiting its assessment for grading or, it was a late addition to the guide and missed the deadline for the inspection process. Where this is the case, the premises should be contacted directly for a classification update.

"Built to a 1/2/3/4/5 star specification": This is shown in the first line of description where premises are Under Construction and not yet opened at the time of going to print, but are due to open during 2011

or

where premises have not yet been registered by Fáilte Ireland

or

where premises have been registered prior to printing this guide, but have not yet been classified. This means that, although not yet formally inspected for their star grading, the premises has been built to the standards set out in the classification criteria and it is expected to reach this standard during the inspection visit.

As the new classification system is mandatory for all premises in the Republic of Ireland, their classification details must be displayed as outlined above.

The new classification criteria for each grade can be viewed and downloaded from
http://www.failteireland.ie/Business-Supports/Quality-and-Standards

Please refer to Page **4** for the Explanation of Facilities/Key to Symbols shown at the end of each entry in order to review the services and facilities offered by individual premises. Further details of facilities and services available in each premises can be viewed on **www.discoverireland.ie**

Northern Ireland

All premises listed in the Northern Ireland section of this guide have been inspected and classified by Northern Ireland Tourist Board. Some premises are not currently classified. Please see page **29** for contact details.

Access For Persons with Disabilities   GUINNESS

♿ Access For Persons with Disabilities
In all cases where this symbol is shown, **we strongly advise** you to contact the premises for full information.

Republic of Ireland
The **ABLE Tourism Awards** scheme has been developed by Rehab and EIQA in conjunction with Fáilte Ireland and ensures an accessible environment for customers and staff with disabilities. **Contact Details:**
Rehab - Tel: 01 205 7306   **Email:** ableawards@rehab.ie   **Web:** www.able.ie

Northern Ireland
No official approval system is currently in place. Therefore, we would advise that you contact the Hotel or Guesthouse directly in order to confirm the status of their accessibility for persons with disabilities.

Further information may also be available from:
Northern Ireland Tourist Board, 59 North Street, Belfast, BT1 1NB
Tel: +44 28 9023 1221   **Fax:** +44 28 9024 0960
or
Disability Action Northern Ireland
Tel: +44 28 9029 7880   **Fax:** +44 28 9029 7881   **Email:** hq@disabilityaction.org
Web: www.disabilityaction.org

GLOBAL POSITIONING SYSTEM

GPS in the **IrelandHotels.com Guide** is measured in Degrees Minutes and Seconds. An example of this would be:

N -53 17' 14.59"   W -6 21' 58.97"

(LONG) where N=North and W=West

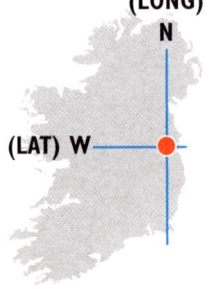

Input the co-ordinates shown for any hotel or guesthouse within the guide (shown above photo) into your SATNAV (satellite navigation system) to locate that property.

Necessary Information

Reservations

Courtesy Onward Reservations
If you are moving around the country, the premises in which you are staying will be delighted to help you select your next accommodation from the IrelandHotels.com Guide and make your reservation.

The following are other ways in which a booking can be made:

1 Advance enquiries and reservations may be made directly to the premises by phone, fax, e-mail or letter and details of the reservation should be confirmed by both parties. A deposit should be forwarded if requested.

2 Book your accommodation online at:

Irelandhotels.com features all premises listed in this Guide and contains the best rates and special offers.

3 Some hotels and guesthouses show a Central Reservations Number in their entry.

4 Travel Agent - your travel agent will normally make a booking on your behalf without extra charge where the premises pays travel agents' commission (this is indicated by the symbol in the Guide). In other cases, agents will usually charge a small fee to cover the cost of telephone calls and administration.

5 Some local tourist information offices listed in this guide (see pages **26 & 28**) operate an enquiry and booking service and will make an accommodation reservation on your behalf.

Complaints

Should there be cause for complaint, the matter should be brought to the notice of the Management of the premises in the first instance. Failing satisfaction, the matter should be referred to the Tourist Information Office concerned (see list on pages **26 & 28**) or Fáilte Ireland, Amiens Street, Dublin 1. In the case of Northern Ireland premises, complaints should be addressed to the Customer Relations Section, Northern Ireland Tourist Board, 59 North Street, Belfast BT1 1NB.

Errors And Omissions

The information contained in the accommodation section has been supplied by individual premises. While reasonable care has been taken in compiling the information supplied and ensuring its accuracy and compliance with consumer protection laws, the Irish Hotels Federation cannot accept any responsibility for any errors, omissions or misinformation regarding accommodation, facilities, prices, services, classification or any other information whatsoever in the Guide and shall have no liability whatsoever and howsoever arising to any person for any loss, whether direct, indirect, economic or consequential, or damages, actions, proceedings, costs, claims, expenses or demands arising therefrom. The listing of any premises in this guide is not and should not be taken as a recommendation from the IHF or a representation that the premises will be suitable for your purposes.

Think About Insurance

We strongly advise you to take out an insurance policy against accidents, cancellations, delays, loss of property and medical expenses. Such travel and holiday insurance policies are available quite cheaply and are worth every penny for peace of mind alone.

Cancellations

Should it be necessary to amend or cancel your reservation, please advise the premises immediately, as there may be a cancellation penalty. **Please establish, when making a reservation, the cancellation policy which applies.**

Spa Categories

Spa & Wellness Categories - www.discoverireland.ie/spa

New Health & Wellness categorisation system launched by Failte Ireland. It is designed to help customers to better understand the variety of spa and wellness offerings available to them.

Destination Spas provide a total immersion in the spa experience, in an environment dedicated to health, fitness and relaxation. Here you will feel at ease walking around in your robe and slippers, dining in a robe, or lounging around the pool or garden because everyone else will be doing the same thing!

Resort Spas offer recreational activities alongside spa treatments, workshops and fitness facilities, in a scenic hotel resort environment to leave you feeling both pampered and invigorated. Other activities typically include golf, horse-riding, fishing, walking, cycling and tennis.

Hotel Spas are divided into four categories:
Comprehensive
Extensive
Selective
Leisure Club

Specialised Retreats also feature.

Hotel with Comprehensive Spa offers a wide variety of spa treatments and rituals in a dedicated spa facility that is an integral part of a wider hotel complex.

Hotel with Extensive Spa offers a carefully selected menu of spa services and treatments in a spa environment that is part of a wider hotel offering.

Hotel with Selective Spa offers a small but carefully selected variety of spa services and treatments in a spa environment that is part of a wider hotel offering. The primary focus is on treatments rather than thermal experiences.

Hotel with Leisure Club Spa offers carefully selected spa treatments within a leisure club facility, in or close to the hotel.

Specialised Retreats including **Thalassotherapy Resorts**, are dedicated to creating a well-being experience of a specialised nature combining the best of rejuvenating treatments and therapies in beautiful country settings. Immerse yourself in healing algae, explore the benefits of thalassotherapy and be pummelled, exfoliated, massaged and pampered into a state of utter relaxation.

You can find all the best deals in all of these places

Website | Mobile App | Printed Guide | facebook.com/irelandhotels | irelandhotels.com/onlineguide

Healthy Food For Kids

Healthy Food For Kids Initiative

The Irish Hotels Federation's Healthy Food for Kids initiative was developed to guide and encourage hotels and guesthouses to provide healthier menu options for young diners. The initiative was launched in March 2008 by the then IHF President, Matthew Ryan, and has generated great interest and support from the Irish Hotels Federation members. In excess of 187 establishments have committed to the programme and customer feedback has been excellent.

According to the current IHF President, Paul Gallagher, everyone has a role to play in encouraging the promotion of healthy food to young people to assist in reducing the prevalence of obesity. This has been the first national hospitality programme of its kind which has aimed to constructively highlight the problems of childhood obesity. Feedback has been very positive and parents are enjoying the experience of seeing their children eating a tasty and healthy meal when dining in participating hotels and guesthouses.

The guidelines, which were compiled in conjunction with a prominent dietician, contain the correct balance of proteins and carbohydrates as deemed appropriate for an optimum healthy children's meal. The IHF guidelines also recommend cooking methods to ensure that whilst the food is nutritious, it remains tasty, attractive and fun for children.

Hotels and Guesthouses which are taking part in the programme are identifiable in the IrelandHotels.com Guide with the following logo

If you would like further details, please log on to **www.ihf.ie**

Index to Locations

GUINNESS

LOCATION	COUNTY	PAGE NO.
A		
Achill Island	Co. Mayo	82
Adare	Co. Limerick	79
Aghadowey	Co. Derry	107
Allihies	Co. Cork	185
Annalong	Co. Down	108
Aran Islands	Co. Galway	54
Ardara	Co. Donegal	45
Ardmore	Co. Waterford	251
Arklow	Co. Wicklow	174
Ashbourne	Co. Meath	162
Ashford	Co. Wicklow	174
Athenry	Co. Galway	55
Athlone	Co. Westmeath	170
Athy	Co. Kildare	151
B		
Bailieborough	Co. Cavan	117
Balbriggan	Co. Dublin	119
Ballina	Co. Mayo	83
Ballinamore	Co. Leitrim	77
Ballinasloe	Co. Galway	56
Ballincollig	Co. Cork	185
Ballybofey	Co. Donegal	45
Ballybunion	Co. Kerry	208
Ballycastle	Co. Antrim	103
Ballyconnell	Co. Cavan	117
Ballycotton	Co. Cork	185
Ballyfarnon	Co. Roscommon	94
Ballygawley	Co. Sligo	94
Ballyhaunis	Co. Mayo	85
Ballylickey	Co. Cork	186
Ballymacarbry	Co. Waterford	252
Ballymena	Co. Antrim	103
Ballynahinch	Co. Galway	56
Ballyshannon	Co. Donegal	46
Ballyvaughan	Co. Clare	35
Ballyvourney	Co. Cork	186
Baltimore	Co. Cork	186
Bandon	Co. Cork	187
Bantry	Co. Cork	187
Barntown	Co. Wexford	261
Belfast City	Belfast City	105
Belmullet	Co. Mayo	85
Birr	Co. Offaly	168
Blarney	Co. Cork	188
Bray	Co. Wicklow	175
Bunclody	Co. Wexford	261
Bundoran	Co. Donegal	47
Bunratty	Co. Clare	35
Bushmills	Co. Antrim	103
C		
Caherdaniel	Co. Kerry	209
Caherlistrane	Co. Galway	56
Cahir	Co. Tipperary	245
Cappoquin	Co. Waterford	252
Caragh Lake	Co. Kerry	209
Carlingford	Co. Louth	159
Carlow Town	Co. Carlow	183
Carna	Co. Galway	57
Carnlough	Co. Antrim	104
Carrickmacross	Co. Monaghan	166
Carrick-on-Shannon	Co. Leitrim	77
Carrick-on-Suir	Co. Tipperary	246
Carrigaline	Co. Cork	189
Cashel	Co. Galway	57
Cashel	Co. Tipperary	246
Castlebar	Co. Mayo	86
Castleconnell	Co. Limerick	79
Castlegregory	Co. Kerry	210
Castlemartyr	Co. Cork	190
Castletownshend	Co. Cork	190
Cavan Town	Co. Cavan	118
Charlestown	Co. Mayo	87
Charleville	Co. Cork	191
Clane	Co. Kildare	152
Claremorris	Co. Mayo	87
Clifden	Co. Galway	57
Cloghane	Co. Kerry	210
Clonakilty	Co. Cork	191
Clonbur (An Fháirche)	Co. Galway	61
Clonmel	Co. Tipperary	247
Cloondara	Co. Longford	158
Cobh	Co. Cork	192
Coleraine	Co. Derry	107
Collooney	Co. Sligo	95
Cong	Co. Mayo	87
Cookstown	Co. Tyrone	111
Cork City	Co. Cork	193
Courtmacsherry	Co. Cork	199
Curracloe	Co. Wexford	262
D		
Derry City	Co. Derry	107
Dingle (An Daingean)	Co. Kerry	210
Donabate	Co. Dublin	119
Donegal Town	Co. Donegal	47
Doolin	Co. Clare	36
Downings	Co. Donegal	49
Drogheda	Co. Louth	160
Dublin Airport	Co. Dublin	120
Dublin City	Co. Dublin	121
Dun Laoghaire	Co. Dublin	147
Dunboyne	Co. Meath	162
Dundalk	Co. Louth	161
Dunfanaghy	Co. Donegal	49
Dungarvan	Co. Waterford	252
Dunkineely	Co. Donegal	50
Dunmore East	Co. Waterford	253
Durrow	Co. Laois	156
E		
Ennis	Co. Clare	37
Enniscorthy	Co. Wexford	262
Enniscrone	Co. Sligo	95
Enniskerry	Co. Wicklow	176
Enniskillen	Co. Fermanagh	109
Ennistymon	Co. Clare	40
F		
Faithlegg	Co. Waterford	254
Fota Island	Co. Cork	200
Foulksmills	Co. Wexford	262
Furbo	Co. Galway	61
G		
Galway City	Co. Galway	61
Glaslough	Co. Monaghan	166
Glen of Aherlow	Co. Tipperary	248
Glendalough	Co. Wicklow	176
Glengarriff	Co. Cork	200
Glen-O-The-Downs	Co. Wicklow	177
Glenties	Co. Donegal	50
Gorey	Co. Wexford	263
Gormanston	Co. Meath	163
Gort	Co. Galway	70
Gougane Barra	Co. Cork	201
Graiguenamanagh	Co. Kilkenny	238
Gweedore	Co. Donegal	51

14 *We've got it covered!*

Index to Locations

LOCATION	COUNTY	PAGE NO.
H		
Headford	Co. Galway	71
Horse and Jockey	Co. Tipperary	249
Howth	Co. Dublin	147
I		
Inishbofin Island	Co. Galway	71
Innishannon	Co. Cork	201
Irvinestown	Co. Fermanagh	110
K		
Kells	Co. Meath	164
Kenmare	Co. Kerry	215
Kildare Town	Co. Kildare	152
Kilkee	Co. Clare	40
Kilkenny City	Co. Kilkenny	238
Killarney	Co. Kerry	217
Killenard	Co. Laois	157
Killiney	Co. Dublin	148
Killorglin	Co. Kerry	233
Killybegs	Co. Donegal	51
Kilmallock	Co. Limerick	80
Kilmessan	Co. Meath	164
Kiltimagh	Co. Mayo	88
Kinsale	Co. Cork	202
Kinvara	Co. Galway	72
Knock	Co. Mayo	88
Knocktopher	Co. Kilkenny	244
L		
Laghey	Co. Donegal	51
Lahinch	Co. Clare	42
Leenane	Co. Galway	72
Leighlinbridge	Co. Carlow	184
Leixlip	Co. Kildare	152
Letterfrack	Co. Galway	73
Letterkenny	Co. Donegal	52
Limavady	Co. Derry	108
Limerick City	Co. Limerick	80
Lisdoonvarna	Co. Clare	44
Lismore	Co. Waterford	254
Longford Town	Co. Longford	158
Loughrea	Co. Galway	73
Lucan	Co. Dublin	148
Lusk	Co. Dublin	149
M		
Macroom	Co. Cork	204
Malahide	Co. Dublin	149
Malin	Co. Donegal	53
Mallow	Co. Cork	205
Mitchelstown	Co. Cork	205
Moate	Co. Westmeath	172
Mohill	Co. Leitrim	78
Monaghan Town	Co. Monaghan	167
Monasterevin	Co. Kildare	153
Mountnugent	Co. Cavan	118
Moville	Co. Donegal	53
Mullaghmore	Co. Sligo	96
Mullinavat	Co. Kilkenny	245
Mullingar	Co. Westmeath	173
Mulranny	Co. Mayo	89
N		
Naas	Co. Kildare	154
Navan	Co. Meath	164
Nenagh	Co. Tipperary	249
New Ross	Co. Wexford	264
Newbawn	Co. Wexford	264
Newbridge	Co. Kildare	154
Newcastle	Co. Down	109
Newmarket-on-Fergus	Co. Clare	45
Newry	Co. Down	109
O		
Omagh	Co. Tyrone	111
Oughterard	Co. Galway	74
P		
Pontoon	Co. Mayo	89
Portlaoise	Co. Laois	157
Portmagee	Co. Kerry	233
Portrush	Co. Antrim	104
Portumna	Co. Galway	75
R		
Rathmullan	Co. Donegal	54
Rathnew	Co. Wicklow	178
Renvyle	Co. Galway	75
Roscommon Town	Co. Roscommon	94
Rosscarbery	Co. Cork	206
Rosses Point	Co. Sligo	96
Rosslare	Co. Wexford	264
Rosslare Harbour	Co. Wexford	265
Roundstone	Co. Galway	76
S		
Schull	Co. Cork	206
Shanagarry	Co. Cork	206
Skerries	Co. Dublin	149
Skibbereen	Co. Cork	207
Sligo Town	Co. Sligo	96
Sneem	Co. Kerry	233
Spiddal	Co. Galway	76
Straffan	Co. Kildare	156
Sutton	Co. Dublin	150
Swords	Co. Dublin	150
T		
Tahilla	Co. Kerry	234
Tarbert	Co. Kerry	234
Templemore	Co. Tipperary	249
Templepatrick	Co. Antrim	105
Thurles	Co. Tipperary	250
Tipperary Town	Co. Tipperary	250
Tralee	Co. Kerry	235
Tramore	Co. Waterford	254
Trim	Co. Meath	165
Tubbercurry	Co. Sligo	97
Tullamore	Co. Offaly	168
Tullow	Co. Carlow	184
V		
Virginia	Co. Cavan	119
W		
Waterford City	Co. Waterford	256
Waterville	Co. Kerry	237
Westport	Co. Mayo	89
Wexford Town	Co. Wexford	266
Wicklow Town	Co. Wicklow	178
Woodenbridge	Co. Wicklow	178
Y		
Youghal	Co. Cork	208

IHF President's Welcome Message

Paul Gallagher
President

Ní haon ní coitianta é an Óstlann nó an Teach Lóistín in Éirinn. Is i seilbh teaghlaigh iad a bhformhór acu agus bíonn an t-úinéir agus baill den teaghlach romhat chun fáilte Uí Cheallaigh a chur romhat. Fiú nuair is le comhlacht iad, nó is cuid de ghrúpa iad, baineann meon agus atmaisféar áitreabh teaghlaigh leo – áiteanna ina gcuirfí fíorchaoin fáilte romhat.

Rud ar leith is ea an óstlann in Éirinn agus is dócha ná a mhalairt go bhfeidhmíonn sí mar lárionad sóisialta don phobal. Cuireann an óstlann i bhfad níos mó ná leaba agus béile ar fáil - is lárionad sóisialta, a siamsaíochta, gnó agus pobail ar fheabhas í chomh maith agus gach aon áis faoin spéir aici, a chuireann bia, lóistín, imeachtaí spóirt, áiseanna siamsíochta agus só agus tarraingtí nach iad ar fáil.

Agus tú ag taisteal timpeall na tíre gheobhaidh tú amach go mbeidh "IrelandHotel.com" an-áisiúil agus an chéad suíomh eile á roghnú agat. Is mian le hóstlannaithe agus le lucht tithe lóistín na hÉireann fáilte a chur romhat agus a bheith in ann a dheimhniú go mbainfidh tú sult as do sheal in Éirinn. Tá súil againn go bhfanfaidh tú linn agus go mbainfidh tú leas as an treoir seo chun do rogha óstlann nó teach lóistín a aimsiú.

Hotels and Guesthouses in Ireland are very special. The majority are family owned with the proprietor and members of the family there to welcome guests and to extend to them renowned Irish hospitality. Even when they are owned by a company, or are part of a group, they still retain the character and ambience of a family premises - a place where you will be truly welcome.

The Irish hotel is unique, in that more often than not, it acts as a social centre for the community. Hotels offer a lot more than just a bed and a meal - they are fully fledged social, leisure, business and community centres with every imaginable facility and amenity, providing food, accommodation, sports, leisure facilities, entertainment and other attractions.

If you are moving around the country, you'll find that the "IrelandHotels.com" guide is an invaluable help in choosing your next location.

Ireland's hoteliers and guesthouse owners want to welcome you and want to play their part in ensuring that your stay in Ireland is a happy one. We hope that you will stay with us and that you will use this guide to select the hotel or guesthouse of your choice.

Les hôtels et les pensions en Irlande sont d'un caractère particulier. Ils sont très souvent gérés par le propriétaire et des membres de sa famille, présents pour accueillir les visiteurs et leur faire découvrir la célèbre hospitalité irlandaise. Même s'ils appartiennent à une entreprise ou font partie d'un groupe de sociétés, ils possèdent toujours ce caractère et cette ambiance des lieux familiaux - un endroit où vous serez sincèrement bien accueillis.

L'hôtel irlandais est unique en ce qu'il joue très souvent le rôle de centre social pour la communauté. Les hôtels offrent beaucoup plus qu'un lit et un repas - ce sont, pour la communauté, de véritables centres sociaux, de loisirs et d'affaires, équipés de toutes les infrastructures et installations imaginables. Ils vous proposent le gîte et le couvert, mais aussi activités sportives et de loisir, divertissements et autres attractions.

Si vous voyagez dans le pays, vous trouverez que le guide "IrelandHotels.com" est d'une aide précieuse pour vous aider à choisir votre prochaine destination.

Les hôteliers et les propriétaires de pensions irlandais veulent vous accueillir et être là pour vous assurer un séjour agréable en Irlande. Nous espérons que vous resterez avec nous et que vous utiliserez ce guide pour sélectionner l'hôtel ou la pension de votre choix.

IHF President's Welcome Message

🇩🇪

Die Hotels und Pensionen in Irland sind von ganz besonderer Art. Zum größten Teil handelt es sich dabei um private Familienbetriebe, in denen der Besitzer und die Familienmitglieder ihre Gäste mit der vielgerühmten irischen Gastfreundschaft willkommen heißen. Aber auch wenn sich diese Häuser in Unternehmensbesitz befinden oder einer Kette angehören, strahlen sie dennoch den Charakter und die Atmosphäre von Familienbetrieben aus - ein Ort, an dem Sie immer herzlich willkommen sind.

Hotels in Irland sind einzig in ihrer Art und dienen oftmals als Mittelpunkt geselliger Treffen. Hotels haben viel mehr zu bieten als nur ein Bett und eine Mahlzeit - sie sind Gesellschafts-, Freizeit-, Geschäfts- und öffentlicher Treffpunkt mit allen nur erdenklichen Einrichtungen und Annehmlichkeiten, angefangen bei Essen, Unterkunft, Sport und Freizeitmöglichkeiten bis zur Unterhaltung und anderen Anziehungspunkten.

Auf Ihren Reisen im Land werden Sie feststellen, daß Ihnen der "IrelandHotels.com"-Führer eine wertvolle Hilfe bei der Suche nach der nächstgelegenen Unterkunft leistet.

Irlands Hotel und Pensionsbesitzer heißen Sie gerne willkommen und möchten ihren Anteil dazu beitragen, daß Ihnen Ihr Aufenthalt in Irland in angenehmer Erinnerung bleibt. Wir hoffen, daß Sie uns besuchen werden und diesen Führer bei der Auswahl Ihres Hotels oder Ihrer Pension zu Rate ziehen.

🇪🇸

Los hoteles y las pensiones en Irlanda son muy especiales. La mayoría son propiedades familiares habitadas por el mismo propietario junto a los miembros de su familia que se encuentran predispuestos a dar la bienvenida a los huéspedes y, de este modo, contribuir a ampliar su reconocida hospitalidad irlandesa. Incluso si pertecen a una compañía o forman parte de un grupo, siempre mantendrán el carácter y ambiente de las propiedades familiares, un lugar donde siempre serás bienvenido de corazón.

El hotel irlandés es único y se comporta bastante a menudo como el mismo centro social de la comunidad. Estos hoteles ofrecen algo más que una cama y comida, rebozan de centros sociales comunitarios de ocio y negocios con una amplia gama de servicios inimaginables. Ofrece comida, alojamiento, deportes, actividades de ocio, entretenimiento y todo tipo de atracciones.

Si te encuentras viajando por nuestro país, te darás cuenta que la ayuda que te ofrece "IrelandHotels.com", a la hora de elegir tu próximo destino, no tiene precio. Los hoteleros y propietarios de pensiones de Irlanda quieren darte la bienvenida y quieren contribuir a que tu estancia en Irlanda sea una estancia feliz. Esperamos que te quedes con nosotros y que utilices esta guía para elegir el hotel o pensión que tú elijas.

🇮🇹

Gli hotel e le pensioni in Irlanda sono davvero speciali. Molti sono a conduzione familiare, e gli ospiti vengono accolti dai proprietari e le loro famiglie secondo le famose tradizioni di ospitalità irlandesi. Il calore e l'ambiente intimo e accogliente si ritrovano persino negli hotel delle grandi compagnie e catene alberghiere: avrete sempre la sensazione di essere ospiti graditi.

Una caratteristica unica degli hotel irlandesi è che, molto spesso, fungono anche da centro di aggregazione della comunità. Gli alberghi offrono molto di più di un letto e dei pasti: sono centri per socializzare, divertirsi, fare affari e vivere la dimensione locale. Qui si può trovare ogni attrezzatura e comfort immaginabile: ristoranti, alloggi, impianti sportivi, attività ricreative, divertimento e tante altre attrazioni.

Se prevedete molti spostamenti, scoprirete in "IrelandHotels.com" uno strumento di valore inestimabile per la scelta delle prossime mete. Gli albergatori e i proprietari delle pensioni irlandesi vi aspettano per darvi il benvenuto e fare la loro parte per rendere piacevole il vostro soggiorno in Irlanda. Ci auguriamo che vogliate viaggiare con noi, usando la nostra guida per scegliere un hotel o una pensione di vostro gusto.

Direct low rates and great special offers guaranteed

Irelandhotels.com
We've got it covered

You can find all the best deals in all of these places

Website | Mobile App | Printed Guide |
facebook.com/irelandhotels | irelandhotels.com/onlineguide

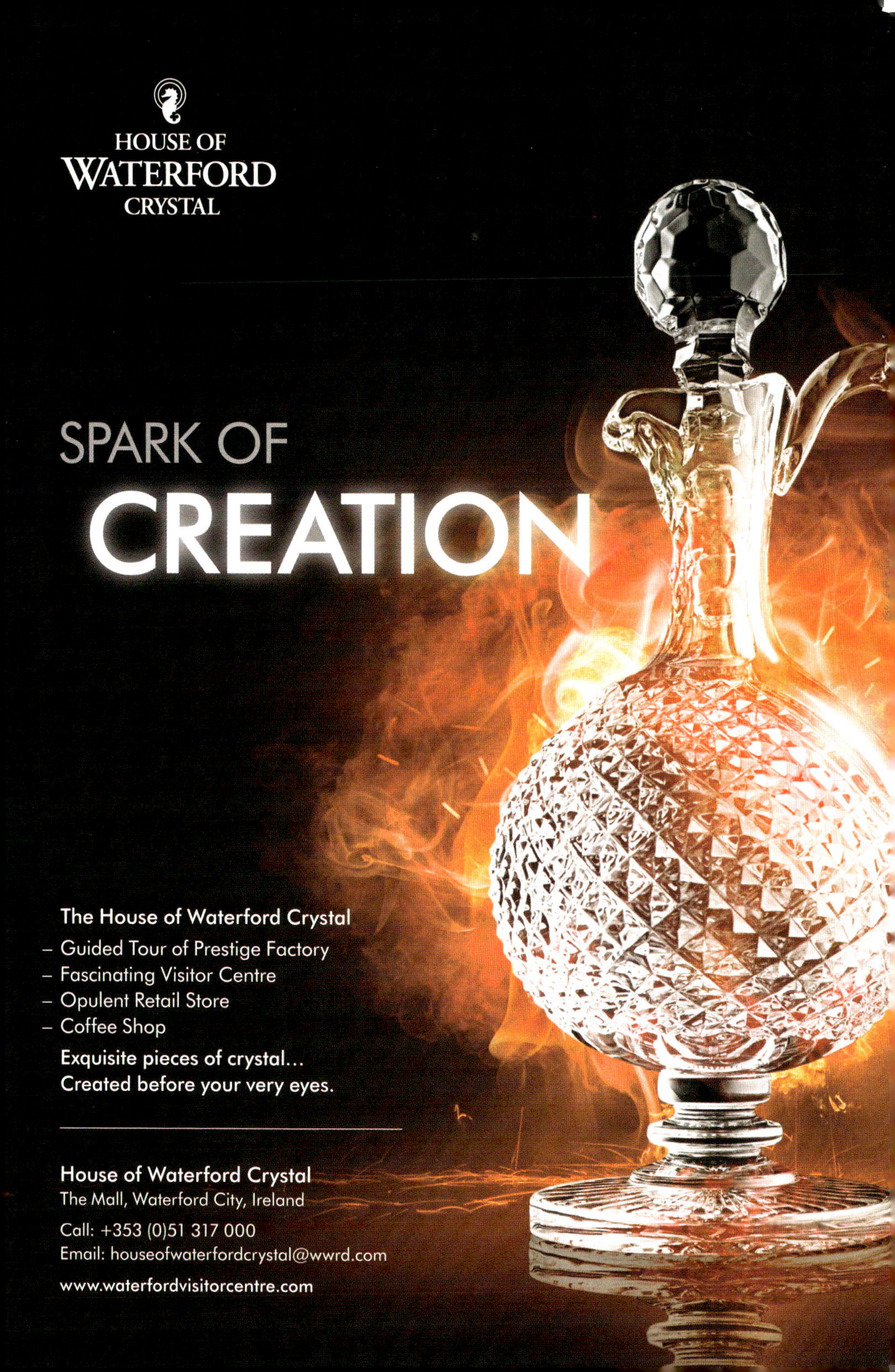

HOUSE OF WATERFORD CRYSTAL

SPARK OF
CREATION

The House of Waterford Crystal
- Guided Tour of Prestige Factory
- Fascinating Visitor Centre
- Opulent Retail Store
- Coffee Shop

Exquisite pieces of crystal…
Created before your very eyes.

House of Waterford Crystal
The Mall, Waterford City, Ireland
Call: +353 (0)51 317 000
Email: houseofwaterfordcrystal@wwrd.com

www.waterfordvisitorcentre.com

General Tourist Information   GUINNESS

Language

Irish (Gaelic) and English are the two official languages of the Republic of Ireland and street and road signs are all bilingual. In Gaeltacht areas Irish is spoken daily, however English is spoken by everyone. In Northern Ireland, English is the official language. The Irish Language, Gaelic, is also taught in many schools and summer schools. Ulster Scots, spoken in Northern Ireland, is on the increase and is being taught to those who are keen to explore another facet of their national identity.

Currency

The Euro € is the local currency of the Republic of Ireland. One Euro consists of 100 cent. Notes are €5, €10, €20, €50, €100, €200 and €500. Coins are 1c, 2c, 5c, 10c, 20c, 50c, €1 and €2.

In Northern Ireland (as in the rest of the United Kingdom), Sterling is the local currency. Stg£1 consists of 100 pence. The notes consist of £5, £10, £20, £50 and £100. The coins are 1p, 2p, 5p, 10p, 20p, 50p, £1 & £2.

The Currencies of the Republic of Ireland and Northern Ireland are not interchangeable.

Regulations for under 21 year olds in bars

In the Republic of Ireland the Liquor Licensing Hours provide that persons under the age of 18 are not allowed in the bar areas of licensed premises (including hotels and guesthouses) after 9.00 p.m. (10.00 p.m. May to September). Persons aged 18 – 21 are required to produce evidence of age in order to be allowed enter or remain in the bar area of licensed premises (including hotels) after 9.00 pm. The acceptable evidence of age may be one of the following: Garda Age Card, a Passport or Identity Card of a EU Member State, a Driver's Licence.

Emergency numbers

In case of emergency, please ring 999 or 112. The Irish Tourist Assistance Service (ITAS) is a free nationwide service offering support and assistance to tourists who experience any crime or traumatic incidents while visiting the Republic of Ireland. Tel: 1890 365 700. Website: www.itas.ie and email: info@itas.ie. ITAS is also contactable via Garda (police) stations.

Prohibition on smoking

In order to combat the damage to health caused by tobacco smoke and to provide an environment of smoke free air, the Government of the Republic of Ireland introduced, early in 2004, a total ban on smoking in the workplace (indoors). This means that smoking is not permitted in all enclosed areas of hotels and guesthouses with the exception of hotel and guesthouse bedrooms. However the proprietor is not legally obliged to offer any smoking bedrooms and may choose to provide a totally smoke-free environment.

Driving

Visitors should be in possession of **either**: a valid full national driving licence, **or** an international driving permit issued abroad. These are readily available from motoring organisations in the country of origin. If planning to bring your car to Ireland, advise your insurance company before travelling.

Driving in Ireland is on the left and seat belts must be worn at all times in the front and the back of the vehicle. Likewise, motorcyclists and their passengers must wear helmets. There are very strict laws on drinking and driving and the best advise is simply 'don't drink and drive'.

In both the Republic of Ireland and Northern Ireland, speed limits are 30-50kmph/20-30mph in built-up urban areas, 100kmph/60mph on the open road and 120kmph/75mph on the motorway.

In the Republic of Ireland, the majority of signposts denoting distance are now in kilometres and speed limits are denoted in kilometres per hour. All signposts and place names are displayed bilingually in both Irish (Gaelic) and English.

In Northern Ireland, all signposts and speed limits are in miles and place names are displayed in the English language.

Driving Association in Ireland:
The Automobile Association (AA),
Tel: 01 617 9977 or visit www.aaireland.ie

We've got it covered!

 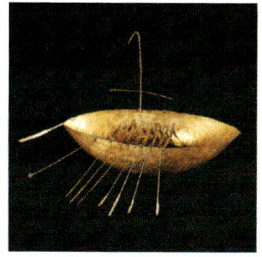  

Priceless treasures that belong to everyone.

Free admission to the greatest collections of Irish heritage, culture and history in the world.

museum
National Museum of Ireland
Ard-Mhúsaem na hÉireann

- Archaeology
- Natural History
- Decorative Arts & History
- Country Life

Family programmes & events for people of all ages.
Guided Tours & Lectures. Museum Shops & Cafes. For further information - Telephone (01) 6777 444
Open: Tuesday to Saturday 10am to 5pm. Sunday 2pm to 5pm. **Closed Mondays incl. Bank Holidays.**

Free Admission - *For further details please visit www.museum.ie*

KILLIMER TARBERT FERRY

From Killimer, Co. Clare Sailing on the hour

		First	Last
Apr to Sept	Monday–Saturday	07.00H	21.00H
	Sundays	09.00H	21.00H
Oct to Mar	Monday–Saturday	07.00H	19.00H
	Sundays	09.00H	19.00H

From Tarbert, Co. Kerry Sailing on the half hour

		First	Last
Apr to Sept	Monday–Saturday	07.30H	21.30H
	Sundays	09.30H	21.30H
Oct to Mar	Monday–Saturday	07.30H	19.30H
	Sundays	09.30H	19.30H

Bridging the best of Ireland's West
- Over 30 sailings a day
- Sailings everyday of the year except Christmas Day
- The direct route to and from Kerry and Clare
- Visitor Centre, Shop, Restaurant

June to September, Two ferries operate between 10.00 & 18.00 from Killimer and 10.30 & 18.30 from Tarbert, providing additional half-hourly service.

☎ 065-905 3124. 📠 065-905 3125. ✉ enquiries@shannonferries.com www.shannonferries.com

SHANNON**FERRY** GROUP

Ordnance Survey Ireland
National Mapping Agency

The New Discovery Series Maps

- All forestry data is updated from OSi's large scale data capture.

- The National Trails Office (NTO) are providing updates on all the waymarked walks. This data will include looped walks and Trail heads managed by Fáilte Ireland and Coillte outdoors trails managed by Coillte Teoranta (Irish Forestry Board).

- OSi will present summit information in three different categories based on information supplied by members of the MountainViews.ie community

The maps are fully GPS compatible so the paper map will act as a companion to users of any GPS device.

We are also delighted to announce that Irish Grid is being retained.

Now with some exciting band new features...

Available from www.irishmaps.ie or all good book stores

We've got it covered!

THE ARTHUR GUINNESS FUND

FROM ONE TO MANY

BENEFITING LOCAL COMMUNITIES

For more information on
the Arthur Guinness Fund visit www.guinness.com

In association with **social entrepreneurs** IRELAND

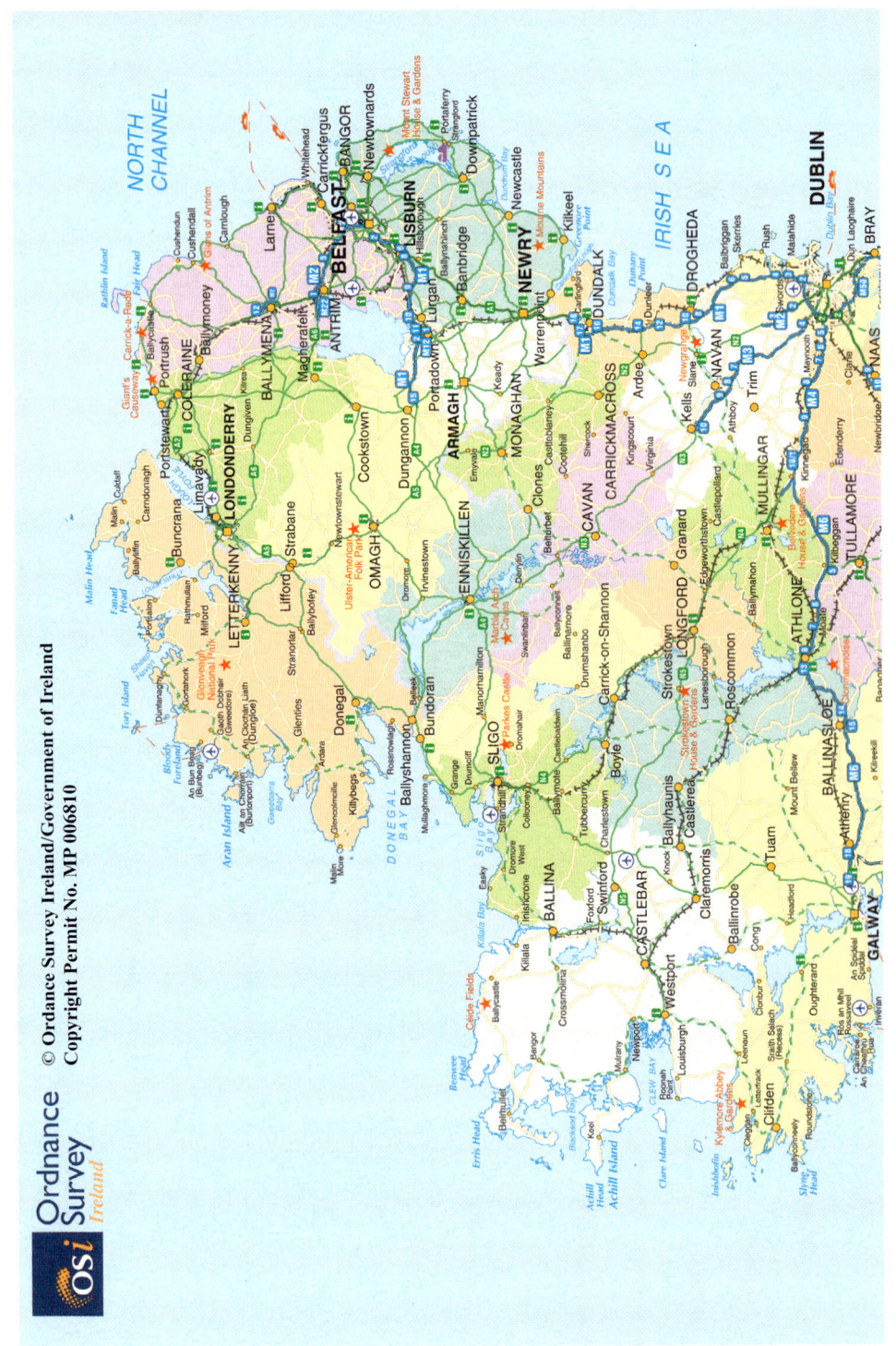

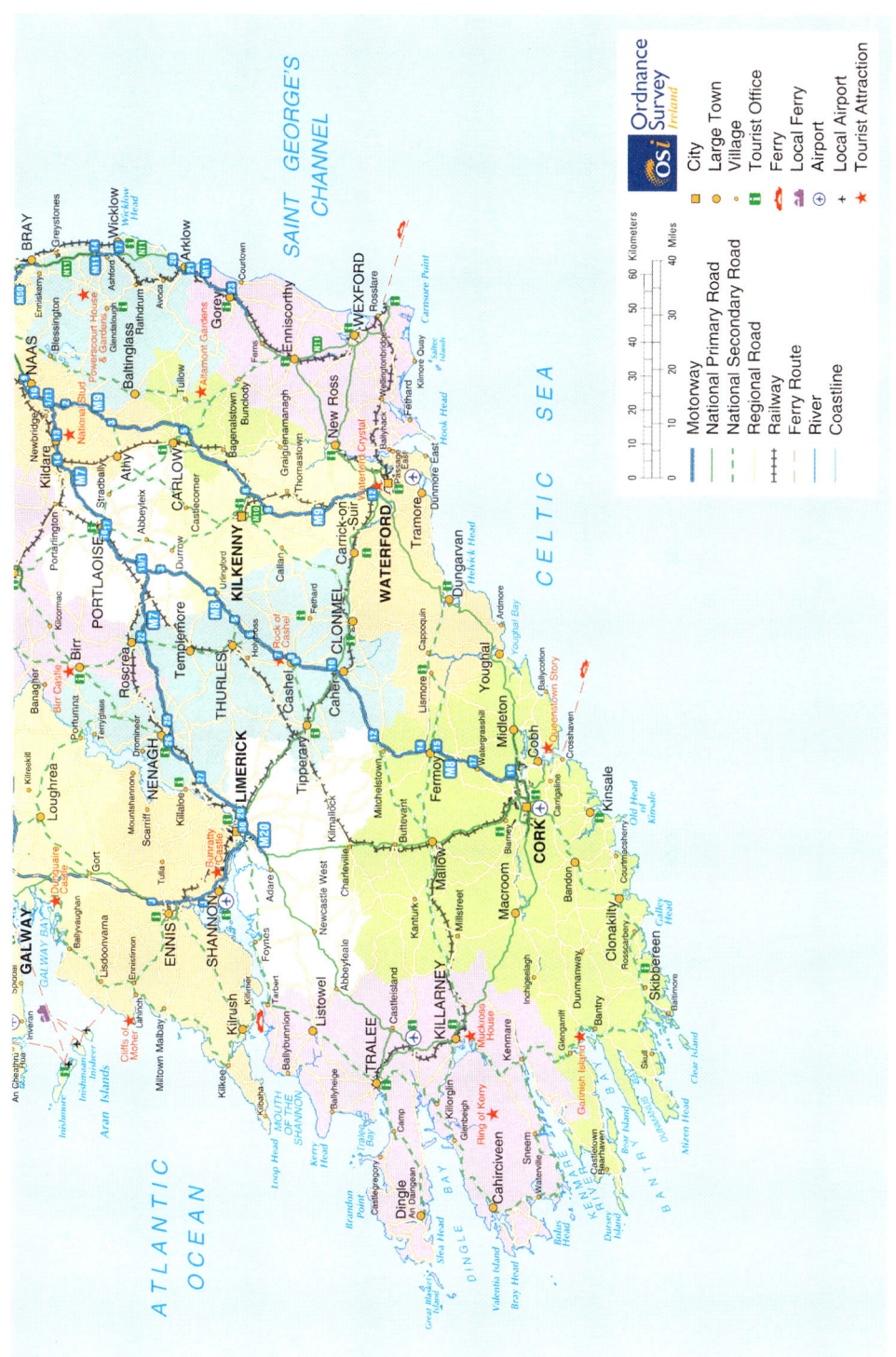

Discover Ireland Centres (Tourist Offices)   GUINNESS

Adare
The Heritage Centre
Tel: 061-396255
Email:
touristofficeadare@shannondevelopment.ie

Antrim
The Old Courthouse, Market Sq.
Tel: 028-9442 8331
Email: info@antrim.gov.uk

Aran Islands
Oifig Fáilte, Kilronan,
Inis Mór, Co. Na Gaillimhe
Tel: 099-61263
Fax: 099-61420
Email: aran@failteireland.ie

Armagh
40 English Street, BT61 7BA
Tel: 028-3752 1800
Email: info@armagh.gov.uk

Ballycastle
Sheskburn House
7 Mary Street, BT54 6QH
Tel: 028-2076 2024
Email: tourism@moyle-council.org

Ballymena
1-29 Bridge Street, BT43 5EJ
Tel: 028-2563 5900
Email:
tourist.information@ballymena.gov.uk

Ballymoney
Ballymoney Town Hall
1 Townhead Street, BT53 6BE
Tel: 028-2766 0230
Email: touristinfo@ballymoney.gov.uk

Banbridge
FE McWilliam Gallery & Studio
200 Newry Road, BT32 3NB
Tel: 028-4062 3322
Email: tic@banbridge.gov.uk

Bangor
34 Quay Street, BT20 5ED
Tel: 028-9127 0069
Email: tic@northdown.gov.uk

Belfast City
47 Donegall Place, BT1 5AD
Tel: 028-9024 6609
Email:
welcomecentre@belfastvisitor.com

Belfast Airports
George Best Belfast City Airport
Sydenham Bypass, BT3 9JH
T: 028-9093 5372
Email:
welcomecentre@belfastvisitor.com

Belfast International Airport
Arrivals Hall, BT29 4AB
Tel: 028-9448 4677
Email:
welcomecentre@belfastvisitor.com

Carlow
College Street
Tel: 059-913 1554
Fax: 059-917 0776
Email: carlow@failteireland.ie

Carrickfergus
11 Antrim Street,
BT38 7DG
Tel: 028-9335 8049
Email: touristinfo@carrickfergus.org

Clonakilty
Ashe Street
Tel: 023-883 3226
Email:
clonakiltytio@failteireland.ie

Coleraine
25 Railway Road, BT52 1PE
Tel: 028-7034 4723
Email: colerainetic@btconnect.com

Cookstown
The Burnavon, Burn Road,
BT80 8DN
Tel: 028-8676 9949
Email: tic@cookstown.gov.uk

Cork City
Grand Parade
Tel: 021-425 5100
Fax: 021-425 5199
Email:
corkkerryinfo@failteireland.ie

Derry
44 Foyle Street, BT48 6AT
Tel: 028-7126 7284
Email: info@derryvisitor.com

Dingle
The Quay
Tel: 066-915 1188
Fax: 066-915 1270
Email: dingletio@failteireland.ie

Donegal Town
The Quay
Tel: 074-972 1148
Fax: 074-972 2762
Email: donegal@failteireland.ie

Downpatrick
The St. Patrick Centre,
53a Market Street, BT30 6LZ
Tel: 028-4461 2233
Email: downpatrick.tic@downdc.gov.uk

Dublin
Dublin City -
Suffolk Street,
O'Connell Street
Dublin Airport - Arrivals Hall,
Dun Laoghaire - Ferry Terminal
For information and reservations
please visit www.visitdublin.com
or contact Dublin Reservations
Freephone
Tel: 1850 230 330 / 1800 363 626

Dungannon / Killymaddy
190, Ballygawley Road (off A4),
Dungannon, BT70 1TF
Tel: 028-8776 7259
Email:
killymaddy.reception@dungannon.gov.uk

Dundalk
Jocelyn Street
Tel: 042-933 5484
Fax: 042-933 8070
Email: dundalk@failteireland.ie

Dungarvan
The Courthouse
Tel: 058-41741
Email:
info@dungarvantourism.com

Ennis
Arthur's Row
Tel: 065-682 8366
Email:
touristofficeennis@shannondevelopment.ie

Enniskillen
Wellington Road, BT74 7EF
Tel: 028-6632 3110
Email: tic@fermanagh.gov.uk

Galway
Aras Fáilte, Forster Street
Galway City
Tel: 091-537700
Fax: 091-537733
Email:
irelandwestinfo@failteireland.ie

Giant's Causeway
44 Causeway Road,
Bushmills, BT57 8SU
Tel: 028-2073 1855
Email:
info@giantscausewaycentre.com

We've got it covered!

Direct low rates and great special offers guaranteed

Irelandhotels.com
We've got it covered

You can find all the best deals in all of these places

Website | Mobile App | Printed Guide |
facebook.com/irelandhotels | irelandhotels.com/onlineguide

 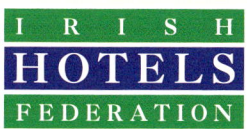

Discover Ireland Centres (Tourist Offices) GUINNESS

Hillsborough
The Courthouse, The Square,
BT26 6AG
Tel: 028-9268 9717
Email:
tic.hillsborough@lisburn.gov.uk

Kildare Town
Heritage Centre, Market Square
Tel: 045-521240

Kilkeel
The Nautilus Centre,
Rooney Road, BT34 4AG
Tel: 028-4176 2525
Email: kdakilkeel@hotmail.com

Kilkenny
Shee Alms House
Tel: 056-775 1500
Fax: 056-776 3955
Email: kilkenny@failteireland.ie

Killarney
Beech Road
Tel: 064-663 1633
Fax: 064-663 4506
Email: killarneytio@failteireland.ie

Kinsale
Pier Road
Tel: 021-477 2234
Email: kinsaletio@failteireland.ie

Larne
Narrow Gauge Road, BT40 1XB
Tel: 028-2826 0088
Email: larnetourism@btconnect.com

Letterkenny
Neil T Blaney Road
Tel: 074-912 1160
Fax: 074-912 5180
Email: letterkenny@failteireland.ie

Limavady
Council Offices
7 Connell Street, BT49 0HA
Tel: 028-7776 0307
Email: tourism@limavady.gov.uk

Limerick City
Arthur's Quay
Tel: 061-317 522
Email:
touristofficelimerick@shannondevelopment.ie

Lisburn
15 Lisburn Square, BT28 1AN
Tel: 028-9266 0038
Email: tic.lisburn@lisburn.gov.uk

Magherafelt
The Bridewell,
6 Church Street, BT45 6AN
Tel: 028-7963 1510
Email:
thebridewell@magherafelt.gov.uk

Mullingar
Market Square
Tel: 044-934 8650
Fax: 044-934 7890
Email: mullingar@failteireland.ie

Newcastle
10-14 Central Promenade,
BT33 0AA
Tel: 028-4372 2222
Email:
newcastle.tic@downdc.gov.uk

Newgrange
Bru na Boinne Visitor Centre,
Donore, Co. Meath
Tel: 041-988 0305
Fax: 041-988 0310
Email:
brunaboinne@failteireland.ie

Newry
Bagenal's Castle,
Castle Street, BT34 2DA
Tel: 028-3031 3170
Email:
newrytic@newryandmourne.gov.uk

Newtownards
31 Regent Street, BT23 4AD
Tel: 028-9182 6846
Email: tourism@ards-council.gov.uk

Omagh
Strule Arts Centre,
Townhall Square, BT78 1BL
Tel: 028-8224 7831
Email: info@struleartscentre.co.uk

Oranmore
Co. Galway
Tel: 091-790811
Fax: 091-790187
Email: oranmore@eircom.net

Oughterard
Main Street, Oughterard,
Co. Galway
Tel: 091-552808
Fax: 091-552811
Email:
info@connemarabegins.com
www.connemarabegins.com

Shannon Airport
Arrivals Hall
Tel: 061-471 664
Email:
touristofficeshannon@shannondevelopment.ie

Skibbereen
North Street
Tel: 028-21766
Fax: 028-21353
Email:
skibbereen@failteireland.ie

Sligo
Temple Street
Tel: 071-916 1201
Fax: 071-916 0360
Email:
northwestinfo@failteireland.ie

Strabane
The Alley Arts and Conference
Centre, 1a Railway Street,
BT82 8EF
Tel: 028-7138 4444
Email: alleytheatre@strabanedc.com

Tralee
Ashe Memorial Hall
Tel: 066-712 1288
Fax: 066-712 1700
Email: traleetio@failteireland.ie

Waterford City
The Quay
Tel: 051-875823
Fax: 051-876720
Email: waterford@failteireland.ie

Westport
James Street, Westport
Co. Mayo
Tel: 098-25711
Fax: 098-26709
Email: westport@failteireland.ie

Wexford
The Quay Front
Tel: 053-9123111
Fax: 053-9141743
Email: wexford@failteireland.ie

Wicklow
Fitzwilliam Square
Tel: 0404-69117
Fax: 0404-69118
Email: wicklow@failteireland.ie

We've got it covered!

GUINNESS — Ireland's Tourists Boards - Home & Abroad

**FÁILTE IRELAND
NATIONAL TOURISM
DEVELOPMENT AUTHORITY**
www.discoverireland.ie

IRELAND
Dublin
Fáilte Ireland,
Amiens Street, Dublin 1
Tel: 01 - 884 7700
Fax: 01 - 855 6821

NORTHERN IRELAND
Belfast
Belfast Visitor & Convention Centre
47 Donegall Place, Belfast BT1 5AD
Tel: 028 - 9031 2345
Email: infob@failteireland.ie

Derry
Fáilte Ireland,
44 Foyle Street, Derry BT48 6AT
Tel: 028 - 7136 9501
Email: failteireland@derryvisitor.com

Northern Ireland Tourist Board
www.discovernorthernireland.com
Belfast
Northern Ireland Tourist Board,
59 North Street, Belfast BT1 1NB
Tel: 028 - 9023 1221
Fax: 028 - 9024 0960

Dublin
Northern Ireland Tourist Board,
Tourist Information Centre,
Suffolk Steet, Dublin 2
Tel: 01 - 605 7732
Fax: 01 - 605 7725

TOURISM IRELAND – EUROPE
www.discoverireland.com

Austria
Simone Korb, Tourism Ireland
Tel: 581 89 22 70
Email: skorb@tourismireland.com
Web: www.discoverireland.com

Belgium
Tourism Ireland,
Avenue Louise 66, Louizalaan,
1050 Brussels
Tel: 02 - 275 0171
Email: info.be@tourismireland.com
Web: www.discoverireland.com/be-fr
       www.discoverireland.com/be-nl

Britain-London
Tourism Ireland
Tel: 0800 039 7000 (Call Centre)
Email: info.gb@tourismireland.com
Web: www.discoverireland.com

Britain-Glasgow
Tourism Ireland
Tel: 0800 039 7000 (Call Centre)
Email: info.gb@tourismireland.com
Web: www.discoverireland.com

France
Tourisme Irlandais
Tel: 01 - 70 20 00 20
Email: info.fr@tourismireland.com
Web: www.irlande-tourisme.fr

Germany
Tourism Ireland
Gutleutstrasse 32, D-60329
Frankfurt am Main
Tel: 069 668 00950
Email: info.de@tourismireland.com
Web: www.discoverireland.com/de

Italy
Turismo Irlandese
Piazza Cantore 4, 20123 Milano
Tel: 02 - 4829 6060
Email: info.it@tourismireland.com
Web: www.irlanda-travel.com

The Netherlands
Tourism Ireland, Spuistraat 104,
1012 VA Amsterdam
Tel: 020 - 504 0689
Email: info@ierland.nl
Web: www.ierland.nl

Nordic Region
Tourism Ireland,
Store Kongensgade3, 1,
1264 Copenhagen K, Denmark
Tel: 80 60 15 18
Email: info.nordic@tourismireland.com
Web: www.discoverireland.com

Finland   Tel: 0800 41 969
Norway   Tel: 800 35 018
Sweden   Tel: 02 0015 9101

Poland
Tourism Ireland
Kramarska 1/7. 61-765, Poznan
Tel: +48 (0) 61 855 32 26
Fax: +48 (0) 61 855 32 36
Email: jschramm@tourismireland.com
Web: www.tourismireland.com/pl

Spain
Turismo de Irlanda,
Paseo de la Castellana 46, 2°
28046 Madrid
Tel: 91-745 6420
Email: info.es@tourismireland.com
Web: www.turismodeirlanda.com

Switzerland
Tourism Ireland
Email: ggregori@tourismireland.com
Web: www.discoverireland.com

TOURISM IRELAND – REST OF THE WORLD

Australia
Tourism Ireland,
Level 5, 36 Carrington Street,
Sydney, NSW 2000
Tel: 02 - 9964 6900
Email: info@tourismireland.com.au
Web: www.tourismireland.com.au

Canada
Tourism Ireland,
2 Bloor St. West, Suite 3403
Toronto, M4W 3E2
Tel: 1800 - 7426 7625
Email: info.ca@tourismireland.com
Web: www.discoverireland.com

USA
Tourism Ireland, 345 Park Avenue,
17th Floor, New York NY 10154
Tel: 1800 - 7426 7625
Email: info.us@tourismireland.com
Web: www.discoverireland.com

China
Tourism Ireland,
Suite 728, Shanghai Centre,
1376 Nanjing Road West,
Shanghai 200040
Tel: +86 (0) 21 6279 8788
Fax: +86 (0) 21 6279 8799
Email: sli@tourismireland.com
Web: www.discoverireland.com/cn

India
Tourism Ireland,
Beautiful Planet, Grants Building
Annexure, Office No. 46, 1st Floor,
Opposite Strand Cinema, Colaba,
Mumbai 400 005
Tel: +91 (0) 22 3096 1624
Fax: +91 (0) 22 2218 0489
Email: hfraser@tourismirelandindia.com
Web: www.discoverireland.com/in

Japan
Tourism Ireland,
International Place, 26-3, Sanei-cho,
Shinjuku-ku, Tokyo 160-0008
Tel: +81 (0) 3 5367 6525
Fax: +81 (0) 3 5363 1118
Email: kasano@aviareps.com
Web: www.discoverireland.com/jp

South Africa
Tourism Ireland,
c/o Development Promotions
62 Hume Road, Dunkeld,
P.O. Box 30615, Braamfontein 2017,
Johannesberg
Tel: +27 (0) 11 442 0824
Fax: +27 (0) 11 442 0821
Email: tourismireland@dpgsa.co.za
Web: www.discoverireland.com/za

U.A.E.
Gulf Reps Ltd., Mezzanine Level,
Dnata Travel Centre Building,
Sh Zayed Road, PO Box 75142,
Dubai, United Arab Emirates
Tel: +971 (0) 43 166 170
Fax: +971 (0) 43 166 565
Email: aiveen@tourismireland.ae
Web: www.discoverireland.com/ae

Introduction To Ireland's 4 Regions   GUINNESS

The wonderful, diverse country of Ireland is divided into **four regions** each with its own charm, attractions and appealing characteristics. They are **Ireland West, Northern Ireland, Dublin & Ireland East and Ireland South.** Together, they form a very special island, full to bursting with dramatic landscapes, idyllic lakes, beaches, cosmopolitan towns and vibrant city life. Most of all, Ireland's regions are renowned for their rich cultural heritage, historical treasures and warm hospitality.

Discover a spectacular rural landscape of rich colour, an enchanted countryside dotted with reminders of a colourful past, a coastline etched out by the mighty Atlantic, great activities, ancient sites and city lights. Experience the renowned welcome for yourself.

Access has never been easier, either through the major ports or via airports. Many local airports offer an increasing range of flights from the UK, Europe and the USA, making it easier than ever to reach this wonderful island. Internal flights from Dublin make reaching other parts of the country straightforward.

Ireland West   31

Ireland West covers the mighty Atlantic coastline from the northernmost tip of Donegal right down to Limerick, an unspoiled and pristine countryside proudly maintaining the traditions and cultures of yesteryear.

Dublin & Ireland East   113

Dublin & Ireland East incorporates the capital city as well as the East Coast and Midlands. Dublin itself is a fascinating city, energetic and youthful with a compelling mix of history, culture, architecture, pubs and shopping. The surrounding region offers so much for the visitor to see and do, all within easy reach.

Northern Ireland   99

The six counties of Northern Ireland are just waiting to be explored, and welcome visitors with an enticing combination of history, culture, magnificent landscapes and vibrant festivals.

Ireland South   179

Discover food as fresh as the air in picturesque Ireland South with Cork and Kerry and encompassing the South East. From farmers markets and pub grub, to restaurants and fine dining, the South is fast acquiring a reputation as Ireland's gourmet region.

...small enough for easy travelling, yet full of contrasts and contradictions, Ireland is waiting here for you!

We've got it covered!

Ireland West

For Detailed Maps of this Region See Pages 325-340. Each Hotel or Guesthouse has a Map Reference to these detailed maps below the premises name.

See page 325 for map with access points and driving distances

Co. Clare
Ballyvaughan 35
Bunratty 35
Doolin 36
Ennis 37
Ennistymon 40
Kilkee 40
Lahinch 42
Lisdoonvarna 44
Newmarket-on-Fergus 45

Co. Donegal
Ardara 45
Ballybofey 45
Ballyshannon 46
Bundoran 47
Donegal Town 47
Downings 49
Dunfanaghy 49
Dunkineely 50
Glenties 50
Gweedore 51
Killybegs 51
Laghey 51

Letterkenny 52
Malin 53
Moville 53
Rathmullan 54

Co. Galway
Aran Islands 54
Athenry 55
Ballinasloe 56
Ballynahinch 56
Caherlistrane 56
Carna 57
Cashel 57
Clifden 57
Clonbur (An Fháirche) 61
Furbo 61
Galway City 61
Gort 70
Headford 71
Inishbofin Island 71
Kinvara 72
Leenane 72
Letterfrack 73
Loughrea 73

Oughterard 74
Portumna 75
Renvyle 75
Roundstone 76
Spiddal 76

Co. Leitrim
Ballinamore 77
Carrick-on-Shannon 77
Mohill 78

Co. Limerick
Adare 79
Castleconnell 79
Kilmallock 80
Limerick City 80

Co. Mayo
Achill Island 82
Ballina 83
Ballyhaunis 85
Belmullet 85
Castlebar 86
Charlestown 87

Claremorris 87
Cong 87
Kiltimagh 88
Knock 88
Mulranny 89
Pontoon 89
Westport 89

Co. Roscommon
Ballyfarnon 94
Roscommon Town 94

Co. Sligo
Ballygawley 94
Collooney 95
Enniscrone 95
Mullaghmore 96
Rosses Point 96
Sligo Town 96
Tubbercurry 97

Ireland West

Clare, Donegal, Galway, Leitrim, Limerick, Mayo, Roscommon, Sligo
(see pages 2 & 3 for full County listing)

The Green Carpet is out and ready for you ... in Ireland's Western Regions.

Ireland's Western Regions are a beautiful part of a magical island. Come to Ireland's North West, West and Shannon Regions and discover a special place, rich in history and wild in spirit.

This is the Ireland made famous in poetry, song and film. It's the essence of Ireland and the part you can't miss if you want to see the real country. Come to the Western Regions where the best of the past mingles effortlessly with a pulsating, contemporary present. The magic is all in the blend.

The scenery might be just the beginning, but what a way to start! A dramatic Atlantic coastline running from Donegal to Clare. Towering cliffs contrast with golden sandy beaches; Sliabh Liag, the Cliffs of Moher, Keem Bay and Black Head. Inland, nature offers lakes and mountains, the splendour of Connemara, the fragile beauty of the Burren and a series of beautiful National Parks.

No matter when you visit, you'll find a festival in full swing somewhere. It could be traditional music at the Willie Clancy Festival, matchmaking in Lisdoonvarna, arts or oysters in Galway, perhaps a salmon festival in Ballina or the time honoured Mary from Dungloe, or rounding off the year in October at the intimate event with headline acts that is Sligo Live. Learn to play the Bodhran on the Aran Islands, join in the fun at the South Sligo Summer School or in one of the many summer schools scattered throughout the region.

We have so many places to visit and attractions to see. Ancient castles, forts and abbeys; sea life centres, waterworlds, folk parks, museums, raptor research centre, show caves, steam trains, pet farms, island and dolphin watching boat trips, island safaris, river boat tours and much more.

Doolough Pass, Co. Mayo

We've got it covered!

Adare Cottage, Co. Limerick

Poulnabrone Dolmen, Co Clare

Achill Island, Co. Mayo

Some are world famous - Bunratty, Dun Aenghus, Cong and the Quiet Man Cottage. A host of others are just waiting to be discovered, by you.

It's a playground for sports - on dry land or in the water. Over 80 golf links and parkland courses compete for attention, so golfers will be in their element. Challenge yourself on some of the top championship courses in the country and be pleasantly surprised at the green fees. Fishermen find their utopia. Casting a line in Ballina, the Salmon Capital, is almost a rite of passage for the game fisherman. The Great Western Lakes teem with trout and coarse fishermen will find healthy fishing waters all around the region. The best sea angling waters in the country tempt everyone from the novice to the expert. Watch out for competitions throughout the year to test yourself against the best.

The geography of the region lends itself perfectly to walking trails and paths. Beaches, woodland, mountains, drumlin and lakeland compete for attention. Marked long distance walks criss-cross the country and many towns and communities have their own shorter walks for visitors to enjoy. Take only pictures, leave only footprints.

Sailors plot courses through picturesque islands, and a growing supply of visitor moorings and marinas. The great River Shannon offers idyllic cruising waters with delightful stop off villages and pubs along the banks. Wind surfers, snorkellers, surfers, body boarders, kite boarders, canoeists and swimmers can take their choice of a hundred beaches, many with EU Blue Flag status. Deep sea divers revel in pristine waters of perfect clarity. It's no wonder the West is known as the Adventure Capital of Ireland.

Don't feel obliged to take part, try some spectator sports. Come horse racing and join in the fun at the big Galway Race Festival or at one of the smaller racecourses. It's the heart of real Ireland. Go to the dogs at a greyhound track or catch a rugby match. The West is home to the mighty red army of Munster and Connaught Rugby Teams.

The West is the home of traditional music and melodies spill from pubs and sessions every night of the week. Music is an intrinsic part of the culture and spontaneous singing or playing are part of every event all year around. Festivals abound and visitors are enthusiastically welcomed into the celebrations.

Don't forget our cities and towns. Sligo, Letterkenny, Galway and Limerick are great centres for shopping, dining and nightlife. They're full of character, colour and life and they're just waiting here for you.

Wherever you visit, you'll always remember the West.

Ireland West

Equestrian

Whether you are looking for an exhilarating beach ride, a leisurely trek or a week long trail across some of Ireland's most famous landscapes, the West has it all. Trail riding is very popular on the west coast and the more experienced rider will enjoy getting out and about and off the beaten track across varied terrain.
Check out www.discoverireland.ie/equestrian

Family Fun

You and your family will have a great holiday in Bundoran. Perched on wonderful Donegal Bay, this town offers great family friendly accommodation as well as an impressive natural playground. Why not plan your trip to coincide with something from Bundoran's impressive and eclectic calendar of free events? Choose from sand sculpting competitions, street carnivals, or music sessions. For more information visit
www.discoverireland.ie/family

Traditionally Irish

Take in some traditional music in one of the many venues in the West, be it an intimate music session in a cosy pub or a spectacular music and dance show in a theatre setting. Engage in the traditions of old, Irish music, song and dance at Cnoc Suain, Spiddal, Co. Galway a pre-famine hill village set in 200 acres of pristine wilderness or the Coleman Traditional Irish Music Centre, Gurteen, Co. Sligo. Or reconnect with the Gaelic language at Oideas Gael, Glencolumcille, Co. Donegal. For more information check out www.discoverireland.ie

Angling

Ireland's western landscape is heavily punctuated by the large limestone lakes of Loughs Corrib, Mask and Carra. These superb wild brown trout lakes provide a quality of game fishing hard to equal anywhere in Europe. Co. Mayo boasts the most prolific salmon river in Ireland. The River Drowes which flows through the counties of Leitrim and Donegal regularly produces the first salmon of the year, usually right on January 1st! Or cast your line on Lough Gill in Sligo if lake fishing is your thing. For more information and the lists of towns that are part of our anglers welcome initiative visit www.discoverireland.ie/angling

Adventure

Wherever you go, you'll find spectacular opportunities to discover the great outdoors with scenic cycling on quiet, twisty roads, magnificent walking on dramatic hills, bracing horse riding on pristine beaches, and a range of adrenaline-fuelled adventure activities that make the most of dramatic surroundings. Surfers gravitate towards the West Coast and especially the seaside villages of Strandhill, Enniscrone, Easkey, Streedagh, Bundoran and Achill. For more information visit www.discoverireland.ie/adventure

Top Attractions

1. Dun Aenghus, Aran Islands, Co. Galway
2. Kylemore Abbey & Gardens, Co. Galway
3. Galway City Museum, Galway
4. Connemara National Park, Co. Galway
5. Glenveagh National Park, Co. Donegal
6. National Museum of Country Life, Castlebar, Co. Mayo
7. Cliffs of Moher, Co. Clare
8. Bunratty Castle & Folk Park, Co. Clare
9. Strokestown House & Famine Museum, Co. Roscommon
10. Ceide Fields, Co. Mayo
11. Burren National Park, Co. Clare
12. Yeats Grave, Drumcliff, Co. Sligo
13. Benbulben, Co. Sligo
14. Sliabh Liag, Co. Donegal
15. Glencar Waterfall, Co. Leitrim

10 Key Walks

1. Diamond Hill Loops, Co. Galway
2. Inishbofin Island, Co. Galway
3. Carrateigue Loops, Co. Mayo
4. Croagh Patrick, Co. Mayo
5. Lough Key Forest, Co. Roscommon
6. Mullaghmore, Ben Bulben & Rosses Point, Co. Sligo
7. Glencolmcille Loops, Co. Donegal
8. Glenveagh National Park, Co. Donegal
9. The Burren, Co. Clare
10. Ballyhoura, Co. Limerick

Maps for these walks and 200 looped walks across Ireland and the many Coillte forest trails all can be downloaded on www.discoverireland.ie/walking

Ireland's Islands

Get away from it all to the rugged islands off the coast of Galway, Mayo and Donegal. Be it a yoga weekend on Clare Island (Mayo), diving off Tory Island (Donegal), or walking on Inishbofin (Galway), taking in some of the historic sites on Coney Island (off Sligo) or a trip to Innismurray monastic Island off Mullaghmore in County Sligo, there's something there for everyone. For more information on Ireland's islands, including how to get there check out www.discoverireland.ie

We've got it covered!

To Book Call **+353-1-8084419** or www.irelandhotels.com

Co. Clare

Ballyvaughan / Bunratty

Ballyvaughan Lodge

Guesthouse ★ ★ ★ Map 6 F 10

Ballyvaughan,
Co. Clare
Tel: +353-65-707 7292
Email: ballyvau@iol.ie
Web: www.ballyvaughanlodge.com
GPS: N +53° 6' 57.96" W -9° 8' 47.15"

Location
Located in the heart of Ballyvaughan Village adjacent to all eateries, public houses, local craft fairs and shops.

Property Highlights
Renowned for our breakfasts using locally produced foods as well as our warm hospitality. Comfortable individually decorated bedrooms, parking on site, sun deck, gallery.

Local Attractions
In the unique Burren landscape, overlooking Galway Bay, close to Cliffs of Moher, Aran Islands, Connemara, hill walking, horse riding, cycling nearby.

B&B from: €35.00 - €40.00

Host(s): Pauline Burke

11

Facilities

Closed 25 - 26 December

Hyland's Burren Hotel

Hotel ★ ★ ★ Map 6 F 10

Ballyvaughan,
Co. Clare
Tel: +353-65-707 7037
Email: info@hylandsburren.com
Web: www.hylandsburren.com
GPS: N +53° 6' 54.99" W -9° 8' 57.39"

Location
Located in the picturesque village of Ballyvaughan, nestling in the unique Burren landscape of Co. Clare.

Property Highlights
Experience bygone charm, open turf fires, informal bars & restaurants specialising in the finest local seafood.

Local Attractions
The Burren limestone area has unusual features that make it unique in Europe. Aillwee Cave is located nearby. An artist's haven. Many great links and parkland golf courses close by. Fishing locally.

B&B from: €50.00 - €80.00

Host(s): Tony McDermott

30

Facilities

Closed 24 - 27 December

Bunratty Castle Hotel

Hotel ★ ★ ★ Map 6 G 7

Bunratty,
Co. Clare
Tel: +353-61-478700
Email: info@bunrattycastlehotel.com
Web: www.bunrattycastlehotel.com
GPS: N +52° 41' 46.58" W -8° 48' 54.18"

Location
Nestled in the historic Village of Bunratty within easy access to Shannon Airport. Ideal base for touring Galway, Connemara and Killarney.

Property Highlights
Bunratty Castle Hotel operates a complimentary Airport shuttle 7 days a week.

Local Attractions
The hotel is a short stroll away from the famous 15th century Bunratty Castle & Folk Park.

B&B from: €75.00 - €90.00
Suites from: €160.00 - €200.00

Host(s): Lee Gregson

144

Activities   Facilities

Closed 24 - 26 December

B&B Rates are per Person Sharing per Night incl. Breakfast. Room/Suite Rates are per Room per Night. See also page 08

Co. Clare

Bunratty / Doolin

Bunratty Grove

Guesthouse ★ ★ ★   Map 6 G 7

Low Road, Bunratty,
Co. Clare
Tel: +353-61-369579
Email: bunrattygrove@eircom.net
Web: www.bunrattygrove.com
GPS: N +52° 42' 36.56"   W -8° 48' 30.77"

Location
Conveniently located just 10 mins. from Shannon Airport, 15 mins. from Limerick and just 3 mins. from the scenic village of Bunratty in Co. Clare.

Property Highlights
Bunratty Grove is a purpose built luxurious guesthouse. All rooms are en suite with multi-channel TV, hairdryer, tea/coffee facilities and direct dial phone. Free Internet access.

Local Attractions
Bunratty Medieval Castle Banquet, Bunratty Castle and Folk Park, The Burren, Fishing, golfing and historical interests are within a short distance. Prime gateway to the West and South of Ireland.

B&B from: €30.00 - €35.00

Host(s): Joe & Maura Brodie

Facilities

6

Open All Year

Aran View House Hotel & Restaurant

Hotel ★ ★ ★   Map 5 E 9

Coast Road, Doolin,
Co. Clare
Tel: +353-65-707 4061
Email: info@aranview.com
Web: www.aranview.com
GPS: N +53° 1' 40.55"   W -9° 21' 57.90"

Location
Doolin is easily reached by road or rail or via Shannon International Airport. 78km from Galway City, 164km from Cork, 263km from Dublin.

Property Highlights
Aran View House Hotel was built in the Georgian period in 1736, on a hill overlooking the Aran Islands & Cliffs of Moher. Highly rated restaurant with idyllic views. Rooms decorated in Georgian style.

Local Attractions
Near Doolin Cave, home to the great Stalactite of Doolin. To our left are the beautiful Cliffs of Moher. Trips can be taken to the Islands, Inisheer, Inishmore & Inishmaan. To the north is the Burren.

B&B from: €50.00 - €60.00
Suites from: €120.00 - €160.00

Host(s): Theresa & Sharon Linnane

19

Facilities

Closed 16 October - 22 April

Ballinalacken Castle Country House & Restaurant

Hotel ★ ★ ★ ★   Map 5 E 9

Coast Road, Doolin,
Co. Clare
Tel: +353-65-707 4025
Email: ballinalackencastle@eircom.net
Web: www.ballinalackencastle.com
GPS: N +53° 2' 47.02"   W -9° 20' 16.29"

Location
We are located on the coast near Doolin on the R477, 1 hour from Shannon Airport & Galway.

Property Highlights
4**** hotel with award-winning restaurant. The ruins of a castle built in 1390 stand beside the hotel. Most rooms have excellent views of the Cliffs of Moher, Aran Islands & Connemara Hills.

Local Attractions
Ideal base from which to tour this historic & interesting region of the west coast of Ireland; Doolin Caves, Cliffs of Moher 15 mins., Burren 25 mins., trips to Aran Islands from Doolin.

B&B from: €65.00 - €120.00
Suites from: €200.00 - €300.00

Host(s): Mary & Denis O'Callaghan

12

Facilities

Closed 26 October - 16 April

See also page 08

To Book Call **+353-1-8084419** or www.irelandhotels.com

Co. Clare
Doolin / Ennis

Cullinan's Seafood Restaurant & Guesthouse

Guesthouse ★ ★ ★   Map 5 E 9

**Doolin,
Co. Clare**
Tel: +353-65-707 4183
Email: cullinans@eircom.net
Web: www.cullinansdoolin.com
GPS: N +53° 0' 59.03"   W -9° 22' 38.37"

Location
We are centrally located in the heart of Doolin, overlooking Aille River, within walking distance of all amenities. Shannon Airport - 64km.

Property Highlights
Chef / Owner awarded AA Dining Rosette & Breakfast Award 2010, Bridgestone 100 Best Places to Stay, Spacious bedrooms all en suite, Flatscreen TVs, Complimentary WiFi.

Local Attractions
Traditional music nightly in all pubs. Other attractions include the Cliffs of Moher, the Burren, Doolin Cave and the Aran Islands.

B&B from: €35.00 - €50.00

Host(s): Carol & James Cullinan

8

Facilities

Closed 01 December - 10 February

O'Connors Guesthouse

Guesthouse ★ ★ ★   Map 5 E 9

**Doolin,
Co. Clare**
Tel: +353-65-707 4498
Email: joan@oconnorsdoolin.com
Web: www.oconnorsdoolin.com
GPS: N +53° 0' 15.64"   W -9° 37' 89.3"

Location
In the centre of Doolin, 1 hrs drive to Shannon Airport, 30 minutes drive to train station. 1.5 hrs drive to Galway & Limerick Cities, 10 minutes to Cliffs of Moher.

Property Highlights
High standard of accommodation in comfortable bedrooms. All are en suite with telephone, TV, tea/coffee making facilities & hairdryer. 2 purpose-built bathrooms for people with disabilities. WiFi.

Local Attractions
Cliffs of Moher, Doolin Cave, The Burren, Trips to the Aran Islands, Lahinch & Doonbeg Golf Courses, Aillwee Caves, Burren Smokehouse.

B&B from: €35.00 - €45.00

Host(s): Joan O'Connor

10

Facilities

Closed 30 November - 01 February

Ardilaun Guesthouse

Guesthouse ★ ★ ★   Map 6 F 8

**Galway Road, Ennis,
Co. Clare**
Tel: +353-65-682 2311
Email: purcells.ennis@eircom.net
Web: www.ardilaun.com
GPS: N +52° 52' 8.23"   W -8° 58' 34.90"

Location
Ardilaun is located on the N18 approx. 3 minutes drive from Ennis Town centre, 20 minutes drive from Shannon Airport.

Property Highlights
All rooms en suite with TV, tea/coffee, hairdryers, free WiFi. Most rooms have panoramic views over the River Fergus, as does our gym's sauna facility.

Local Attractions
Our guesthouse is an ideal base for touring Clare, Limerick and Galway. The Burren and Cliffs of Moher are located nearby. Adjacent to Ballyalia Amenity Area.

B&B from: €35.00 - €40.00

Host(s): Anne Purcell

10

Activities   **Facilities**

Closed 23 - 29 December

B&B Rates are per Person Sharing per Night incl. Breakfast. Room/Suite Rates are per Room per Night. **See also page 08**

Co. Clare

To Book Call **+353-1-8084419** or www.irelandhotels.com

Ennis

Ashford Court Boutique Hotel

Hotel ★ ★ ★ Map 6 F 8

No 1 Old Mill Road, Ennis,
Co. Clare
Tel: +353-65-689 4444
Email: info@ashfordcourt.ie
Web: www.ashfordcourt.ie
GPS: N +52° 50' 42.23"   W -8° 59' 23.19"

Location
Ashford Court Boutique Hotel is ideally situated in Ennis Town Centre. Just off the main road from Galway and Shannon, Ashford Court is easily accessed by car.

Property Highlights
Ashford Court is a new 'boutique' style hotel. A small charming hotel with an emphasis on style, comfort, and friendliness. Beside Leisure Centre, Meeting rooms, Restaurant, Free WiFi & parking.

Local Attractions
Cliffs of Moher, Bunratty Castle, The Burren. Beside theatres, nightlife and pubs. One of Ashford Court's greatest attractions is the town itself, great for shopping & nightlife.

B&B from: €30.00 - €60.00
Suites from: €100.00 - €160.00

Host(s): Corinne Mannion

28

Facilities

Open All Year

Auburn Lodge Hotel & Leisure Centre

Hotel ★ ★ ★ Map 6 F 8

Galway Road, Ennis,
Co. Clare
Tel: +353-65-682 1247
Email: stay@irishcourthotels.com
Web: www.auburnlodge.com
GPS: N +52° 51' 54.83"   W -8° 58' 51.27"

Location
Located 2km outside Ennis Town Centre on the Galway Road. Shannon Airport 15km.

Property Highlights
Full leisure facilities including swimming pool, gym, jacuzzi, sauna, steam room & 4 beauty treatment rooms. Full car parking facilities. WiFi throughout entire hotel. Conference & banqueting suites.

Local Attractions
Cloister Bar & Restaurant adjoins the Friary. Nearby all local golf clubs, Bunratty Folk Park, near the famous Durty Nelly's Pub & Restaurant, Cliffs of Moher, The Burren, Ailwee Caves.

B&B from: €50.00 - €99.00
Suites from: €120.00 - €280.00

Host(s): Angela Lyne

108

Facilities

Closed 24 - 26 December

Old Ground Hotel

Hotel ★ ★ ★ ★ Map 6 F 8

O'Connell Street, Ennis,
Co. Clare
Tel: +353-65-682 8127
Email: reservations@oldgroundhotel.ie
Web: www.flynnhotels.com
GPS: N +52° 50' 32.50"   W -8° 58' 59.41"

Location
The Old Ground Hotel is in the centre of Ennis Town, 5 minutes walk from railway station, 20 minutes drive from Shannon International Airport.

Property Highlights
De luxe rooms with king beds and spacious suites in soft restful colour schemes. Elegant dining room and Town Hall Bistro renowned for excellent cuisine.

Local Attractions
Ennis is an attractive town with a myriad of unique shopping opportunities. The Gateway to the spectacular beauty of Ireland's West Coast. Golf at Doonbeg & Lahinch. Bunratty Castle within easy reach.

B&B from: €50.00 - €85.00

Host(s): Allen Flynn & Mary Gleeson

83

Facilities

Closed 24 - 25 December

38 Ireland West   B&B Rates are per Person Sharing per Night incl. Breakfast. Room/Suite Rates are per Room per Night. See also page 08

To Book Call **+353-1-8084419** or www.irelandhotels.com

Co. Clare
Ennis

Temple Gate Hotel

Hotel ★ ★ ★ Map 6 F 8

The Square, Ennis,
Co. Clare
Tel: +353-65-682 3300
Email: info@templegatehotel.com
Web: www.templegatehotel.com
GPS: N +52° 50' 36.72" W -8° 58' 54.16"

Location
Located just off Ennis Town Centre and within 2 minutes drive of Ennis Train & Bus Station. It is located within 15km of Shannon Airport.

Property Highlights
Charming town house hotel, family owned & managed. Preachers Pub features live music & acclaimed bar menu. Legends Restaurant – awarded the AA Rosette every year since the hotel opened in 1996.

Local Attractions
Just a short distance from Bunratty Castle, Cliffs of Moher, The Burren, Clare County Museum and Lahinch & Doonbeg Golf courses. Many sandy beaches in close proximity.

B&B from: €39.50 - €99.50
Suites from: €129.00 - €219.00

Host(s): Paul Madden

70

Activities

Facilities

Closed 25 - 27 December

B&B Rates are per Person Sharing per Night incl. Breakfast. Room/Suite Rates are per Room per Night. See also page 08

Co. Clare

To Book Call **+353-1-8084419** or www.irelandhotels.com

Ennistymon / Kilkee

Falls Hotel & Spa

Hotel ★ ★ ★   Map 5 E 9

Ennistymon,
Co. Clare
Tel: +353-65-707 1004
Email: reservations@fallshotel.ie
Web: www.fallshotel.ie
GPS: N +52° 56' 26.20" W -9° 17' 55.53"

Location
The Hotel is conveniently located in the centre of Ennistymon, 50km from Shannon Airport & only 2km from Lahinch Beach.

Property Highlights
The hotel has 9 duplex apartments, bar, Thai River & the Cascades Restaurants, Leisure Club & River Spa.

Local Attractions
Cliffs of Moher, Burren Region, Aran Ferry, Doolin Cave & much more are only a few minutes drive from the hotel.

B&B from: €45.00 - €85.00
Suites from: €140.00 - €280.00

Host(s): John & Michael McCarthy

140

Activities
Facilities

Open All Year

Grovemount House

Guesthouse ★ ★ ★   Map 5 E 9

Lahinch Road, Ennistymon,
Co. Clare
Tel: +353-65-707 1431
Email: grovmnt@eircom.net
Web: www.grovemount-ennistymon.com
GPS: N +52° 56' 22.91" W -9° 18' 13.00"

Location
Grovemount House is situated on the outskirts of Ennistymon Town. It is approximately 1 hour's drive from Shannon Airport.

Property Highlights
We are a family-run business available to assist you at all times while still allowing you the privacy to relax in peace & tranquillity & enjoy our unique setting overlooking the Inagh River.

Local Attractions
The Cliffs of Moher & the world famous Burren are within close proximity. Lahinch Golf & Beach just 2 miles away. Traditional music & great restaurants are in abundance.

B&B from: €35.00 - €40.00

Host(s): Sheila Linnane

6

Facilities

Closed 31 October - 01 April

Halpin's Townhouse Hotel

Hotel ★ ★ ★   Map 5 D 7

2 Erin Street, Kilkee,
Co. Clare
Tel: +353-65-905 6032
Email: halpinshotel@iol.ie
Web: www.halpinshotel.com
GPS: N +52° 40' 49.76" W -9° 38' 46.86"

Location
Highly acclaimed townhouse hotel overlooking Victorian Kilkee, near Shannon Airport & Killimer Car Ferry. Situated midway between Connemara and Ring of Kerry.

Property Highlights
A combination of old world charm, fine food, vintage wines & modern comforts. Accolades: Times, Best Loved Hotels.USA Toll Free: 1800 617 3178. Car Parking.

Local Attractions
Ideal base for touring Cliffs of Moher, Bunratty, the Burren & Loop Drive. Nearby Major Golf Courses: Lahinch, Doonbeg, Ballybunion.

B&B from: €49.00 - €99.00

Host(s): Pat Halpin & Ann Keane

10

Activities
Facilities

Closed 15 November - 15 March

B&B Rates are per Person Sharing per Night incl. Breakfast. Room/Suite Rates are per Room per Night. See also page 08

Discover The Wonders Of Ireland's Shannon Region

A journey through the Shannon Region is more than just a holiday, it is the starting point for priceless memories. Whether on your own, with a partner or with family, whether you are driving, cycling or walking, in the Shannon Region fun and adventure is just around the corner. Your journey throughout the Region will take you on a magical ride through South Offaly's rugged landscape, North Tipperary's fertile pastures, Limerick's medieval past and Clare's sandy beaches and award winning golf courses.

Limerick City is a cocktail of modern and medieval, a combination of old and new. You can marvel at the medieval city and soak up the atmosphere from Viking time and the Siege of Limerick and experience what it would be like to live in King John's 13th century castle.

If city life isn't for you why not revel in the delectable delights that are on offer in the countryside, from Limerick's Ballyhoura Mountain walkways to the Slieve Bloom Mountains' trials in the unspoilt backdrop that is County Offaly. Adare, winner of the much-coveted title of 'the Prettiest Village in Ireland' is an extraordinary village. A drive along the Shannon Estuary will surprise you with delights of all kind - the forest park with the most astounding walking trials; a visitor farm; adventure centre and the Flying Boat Museum in the portside village of Foynes, home of the Irish Coffee.

Why not take a cruise along the River Shannon and help us celebrate the renaissance of Limerick's Riverside city, and if you are lucky you may even see a dolphin or two. Or go north along the Shannon and journey through the spectacular Lough Derg.

While cruising along the lake why not try your hand at a spot of fishing. Fish in the lake are plentiful; brown trout, pike and coarse fish. Or why not stop off in Tipperary's Ballina and let the rolling pastures be the setting for a luscious meal or continue on to Terryglass for a bit of craic and ceol, you could even learn to Irish dance!!! Whilst in Tipperary, a stop in Thurles to 'Clash the Ash' and a visit to Lar na Pairce, an intriguing museum where the history of the Gaelic Games comes alive, are a must.

A trip to the Shannon Region would not be complete without a visit to County Clare, from the lunar like terrain of the world famous Burren National Park to the stunning Cliffs of Moher, now in the running to become one of the 7 Wonders of the World. While in the area a visit to Doolin Cave is a must. The cave boasts one of the world's largest Stalactites.

Clare is also said to be home of traditional Irish music and Ennis is most certainly the musical hub of Clare. Ennis has an array of pubs that has Traditional Irish Music every night where a good 'seisun' is always guaranteed. Clare has so much to offer from the many fishing lakes of East Clare to the scenic drives and water based activities of the West Coast from Kilkee to Ballyvaughan. Why not stop off in any of the towns and villages with rustic charm and character like Lahinch, Miltown Malbay, and Doonbeg. A visit to Clare however would not be complete without a stop at Bunratty Castle and Folk Park. The park boasts a majestic 15th century castle alongside its folk park that recreates 19th century Irish life over 26 acres.

For fantastic value and great holiday choice visit

Festival & Events

March
4th - 6th Ennis Book Club Festival, Co. Clare

May
Apr 29th - May 2nd Riverfest, Limerick City

August
5th - 12th Birr Vintage Week, Birr, Co. Offaly
17th - 21st Terryglass Arts Festival, Co. Tipperary

For further information contact:
Tourist Information Office
Arthur's Quay, Limerick
Tel 061 317522
Fax 061 317939
www.shortbreaksireland.ie

Co. Clare

To Book Call **+353-1-8084419** or www.irelandhotels.com

Kilkee / Lahinch

Kilkee Thalassotherapy Centre & Guesthouse

Guesthouse ★ ★ ★   Map 5 D 7

Grattan Street, Kilkee,
Co. Clare
Tel: +353-65-905 6742
Email: info@kilkeethalasso.com
Web: www.kilkeethalasso.com
GPS: N +52° 40' 51.45"   W -9° 38' 41.55"

Location
Close to bus stop. 2 minutes from beach. 1 hr from Shannon Airport. 45 minutes from Ennis Railway Station. 1 hr from Cliffs of Moher. Ideal touring base.

Property Highlights
5 en suite rooms, orthopaedic beds, WiFi. Quiet location. Award-winning spa. Natural seaweed baths a speciality.

Local Attractions
Dolphin Watching, Scuba Diving, Scenic Cliff Walks, Spectacular Running Routes. Golf Courses include Kilkee, Kilrush, Doonbeg, Ballybunion.

B&B from: €40.00 - €60.00

Host(s): Eileen Mulcahy

Activities   Facilities

Open All Year

Strand Guest House

Guesthouse ★ ★ ★   Map 5 O 7

The Strand Line, Kilkee,
Co. Clare
Tel: +353-65-905 6177
Email: thestrandkilkee@eircom.net
Web: www.thestrandkilkee.com
GPS: N +52° 40' 49.95"   W -9° 38' 49.21"

Location
Overlooking the beautiful cresent shaped beach in the centre of Kilkee, only 45 miles from Shannon Airport.

Property Highlights
Warm welcome, magnificent sea views, central location, freshly home cooked food, fully licensed restaurant. WiFi. TV. Tea and coffee.

Local Attractions
European Destination of Excellence Award 2010 "Loophead Peninsula". Diving, Water Sports, Waterworld, Horse Riding, Golf (5 courses within 35km), Dolphin Watching all available locally. Fishing.

B&B from: €37.00 - €59.00

Host(s): Johnny Redmond

Facilities

Open All Year

Dough Mor Lodge

Guesthouse ★ ★ ★   Map 5 E 9

Station Road, Lahinch,
Co. Clare
Tel: +353-65-708 2063
Email: dough@gofree.indigo.ie
Web: www.doughmorlodge.com
GPS: N +52° 56' 0.16"   W -9° 20' 2.77"

Location
30 miles - Shannon Airport, 40 miles - Limerick & Galway, 180 miles - Dublin. Train Station is 20 miles away in Ennis. On Station Road up main street, left at church.

Property Highlights
Quiet location, set back from road, private off road parking. Internet access, residents' lounge, power showers, big garden and excellent breakfast.

Local Attractions
Golf 36 holes in village, surfing .5 mile, heated indoor pool .5 mile. Excellent walks, Doonbeg Golf Club 30 mins. drive. Cliffs of Moher 5 miles Burren 30 mins. drive. Restaurant/Pubs 10 mins. walk.

B&B from: €40.00 - €65.00

Host(s): Jim Foley

Activities   Facilities

Closed 01 November - 28 February

See also page 08

To Book Call **+353-1-8084419** or www.irelandhotels.com

Co. Clare
Lahinch

Lahinch Golf & Leisure Hotel

Hotel ★ ★ ★   Map 5 E 9

Lahinch,
Co. Clare
Tel: +353-65-708 1100
Email: info@lahinchgolfhotel.com
Web: www.lahinchgolfhotel.com
GPS: N +52° 55' 54.25"   W -9° 20' 43.44"

Location
Lahinch Golf & Leisure Hotel is located in the seaside village of Lahinch. Just a stroll from the beach & an hour from Shannon Airport.

Property Highlights
The hotel offers luxurious accommodation & excellent leisure facilities. The Aberdeen Bar offers an inviting atmosphere which our residents can enjoy.

Local Attractions
Located close to all local amenities & attractions - including Lahinch Golf Club, Cliffs of Moher, The Burren & Aillwee Caves.

B&B from: €50.00 - €85.00
Suites from: €180.00 - €300.00

Host(s): John O' Meara

144

Moy House

Guesthouse ★ ★ ★ ★   Map 5 E 9

Lahinch,
Co. Clare
Tel: +353-65-708 2800
Email: moyhouse@eircom.net
Web: www.moyhouse.com
GPS: N +52° 55' 5.15"   W -9° 20' 56.53"

Location
Member of Ireland's Blue Book. Prevailing over the breathtaking seascape of Lahinch Bay, this 18th century house is set on 15 acres of ground. Adorned by mature woodland & picturesque river.

Property Highlights
Dining at Moyhouse is a truly memorable experience in the new classical conservatory restaurant overlooking the Atlantic. Personal attention & outstanding service make for an unforgettable experience.

Local Attractions
An ideal base from which to visit Cliffs of Moher, The Burren or play the famous Lahinch Golf Links.

B&B from: €95.00 - €140.00
Suites from: €270.00 - €360.00

Host(s): Brid O'Meara

9

Sancta Maria Hotel

Hotel ★ ★   Map 5 E 9

Lahinch,
Co. Clare
Tel: +353-65-708 1041
Email: info@sancta-maria.ie
Web: www.sancta-maria.ie
GPS: N +52° 56' 1.41"   W -9° 20' 36.86"

Location
The Sancta Maria is in the village of Lahinch, within 100 yards of Lahinch Golf Club and 30 miles from Shannon Airport.

Property Highlights
The McInerney Family has operated the Sancta Maria for 60 years. We place special emphasis on personal service.

Local Attractions
Lahinch is a surfer's paradise. The hotel is an ideal base for visiting the Cliffs of Moher, the Aran Islands and the Burren.

B&B from: €45.00 - €60.00

Host(s): Thomas McInerney

24

Closed 01 November - 28 February

Closed 01 January - 14 February

Closed 01 November - 01 March

B&B Rates are per Person Sharing per Night incl. Breakfast. Room/Suite Rates are per Room per Night. See also page 08

Co. Clare

To Book Call **+353-1-8084419** or www.irelandhotels.com

Lahinch / Lisdoonvarna

Vaughan Lodge and Seafood Restaurant

Hotel ★ ★ ★ ★   Map 5 E 9

Ennistymon Road, Lahinch,
Co Clare
Tel: +353-65-708 1111
Email: info@vaughanlodge.ie
Web: www.vaughanlodge.ie
GPS: N +52° 56' 0.73"   W -9° 20' 28.11"

Location
Situated in Lahinch Village on the west coast of Clare. 45 minutes from Shannon Airport.

Property Highlights
Smart 4 star lodge where traditional values still abound. Spacious rooms, power showers, free broadband & WiFi. Award-winning seafood restaurant. Library Lounge.

Local Attractions
Enjoy glorious scenery & fabulous attractions. Links golf at Lahinch & Doonbeg, surfing, Cliffs of Moher, The Burren, Aillwee Cave, Corcomroe Abbey, Bunratty, walking & cycling.

B&B from: €70.00 - €100.00

Host(s): Maria & Michael Vaughan   20

Activities
Facilities

Closed 01 January - 01 April

44   Ireland West

Rathbaun Hotel

Hotel ★ ★   Map 5 E 9

Main Street, Lisdoonvarna,
Co. Clare
Tel: +353-65-707 4009
Email: rathbaunhotel@eircom.net
Web: www.rathbaunhotel.com
GPS: N +53° 1' 43.43"   W -9° 17' 22.77"

Location
A welcoming and friendly atmosphere awaits you at the Rathbaun Hotel. In the Burren region, 10km from Cliffs of Moher, 60km from Shannon & Galway Airports.

Property Highlights
Our hotel is the most renowned venue in Co. Clare for live Irish Music - played nightly from June to September inclusive.

Local Attractions
The best value for money in accommodation is our attraction. Quality is always on the menu. Céad Míle Fáilte, Welcome, Bienvenue, Willkommen.

B&B from: €30.00 - €70.00

Host(s): Lynn and John Connolly   10

Facilities

Closed 06 October - 28 April

Sheedy's Country House Hotel

Hotel ★ ★ ★ ★   Map 5 E 9

Lisdoonvarna,
Co. Clare
Tel: +353-65-707 4026
Email: info@sheedys.com
Web: www.sheedys.com
GPS: N +53° 1' 48.09"   W -9° 17' 22.21"

Location
On the edge of the town of Lisdoonvarna, two minutes walk from Traditional Irish Music Pubs. 45 minutes drive from Shannon Airport.

Property Highlights
4* family run hotel. 2 AA Rosettes for Food. Also awarded Georgina Campbell Host of the Year 2008, listed in Bridgestone 100 Best Places to Stay. Michelin recommended. "Best breakfast in Munster".

Local Attractions
Famous Cliffs of Moher - 10km drive. Doolin and Ferry to Aran Islands just 5km away. Aillwee Caves, Kilfenora, Burren National Park.

B&B from: €55.00 - €85.00
Suites from: €150.00 - €200.00

Host(s): John & Martina Sheedy   11

Facilities

Closed 01 October - 01 April

B&B Rates are per Person Sharing per Night incl. Breakfast. Room/Suite Rates are per Room per Night.   See also page 08

To Book Call **+353-1-8084419** or www.irelandhotels.com

Co. Clare - Co. Donegal
Newmarket-on-Fergus / Ardara / Ballybofey

Dromoland Castle

Hotel ★ ★ ★ ★ ★   Map 6 G 8

**Newmarket-on-Fergus,
Co. Clare**
Tel: +353-61-368144
Email: sales@dromoland.ie
Web: www.dromoland.ie
GPS: N +52° 46' 57.44"   W -8° 54' 23.63"

Location
Located 16km from Shannon Airport, take M18 at Junction 11, follow signposts for Dromoland.

Property Highlights
18 Hole championship Golf Course. Fully automated Golf Academy. Luxurious health spa, hydro pool & hair salon. Fully equipped leisure centre & 18m swimming pool. Award-winning restaurant.

Local Attractions
Bunratty Castle & Folk Park, Cliffs of Moher, The Burren & Aillwee Caves, King John's Castle, Hunt Museum. Close proximity to Galway & Limerick shopping destinations. Proximity to Shannon Airport.

Room Rate from: €238.00 - €607.00
Suites from: €499.00 - €1,365.00

Host(s): Mark Nolan

99

Facilities

Closed 24 - 27 December

Woodhill House

Guesthouse ★ ★ ★   Map 13 H 18

**Wood Road, Ardara,
Co. Donegal**
Tel: +353-74-954 1112
Email: yates@iol.ie
Web: www.woodhillhouse.com
GPS: N +54° 45' 30.10"   W -8° 24' 10.80"

Location
On the coast, west of the Blue Stacks, just outside Ardara. 20 minutes from Donegal Town, Killybegs & Slieve League.

Property Highlights
A coastal Manor House set in its own grounds & walled garden. Fully licensed bar & French style restaurant.

Local Attractions
Slieve League Cliffs, Maghera Caves & Waterfall, Glengesh Pass, Naran Beach, Glenveagh National Park & Ardara's lively musical bars.

B&B from: €45.00 - €65.00

Host(s): Yates Family

13

Facilities

Closed 20 - 26 December

Jackson's Hotel, Conference & Leisure Centre

Hotel ★ ★ ★ ★   Map 13 J 19

**Ballybofey,
Co. Donegal**
Tel: +353-74-913 1021
Email: enquiry@jacksons-hotel.ie
Web: www.jacksons-hotel.ie
GPS: N +54° 47' 59.90"   W -7° 47' 4.83"

Location
At centre of Donegal. 27 miles from Derry and 58 miles from Sligo.

Property Highlights
Situated on the banks of the River Finn & Drumboe Woods. Relax in our award-winning "Glue Pot" Bar & enjoy breathtaking views from our garden. Ideal touring centre for Donegal. Family-run since 1945.

Local Attractions
Ballybofey & Stranorlar Golf Club 1 mile, Isaac Butt Museum, Glenveagh Castle, Slieve League 40m.

B&B from: €60.00 - €75.00
Suites from: €100.00 - €140.00

Host(s): Barry Jackson

137

Activities   Facilities

Open All Year

B&B Rates are per Person Sharing per Night incl. Breakfast. Room/Suite Rates are per Room per Night.   See also page 08

Co. Donegal

To Book Call +353-1-8084419 or www.irelandhotels.com

Ballybofey / Ballyshannon

Kee's Hotel, Leisure & Wellness Centre

Hotel ★ ★ ★   Map 13 J 19

Stranorlar, Ballybofey,
Co. Donegal
Tel: +353-74-913 1018
Email: info@keeshotel.ie
Web: www.keeshotel.ie
GPS: N +54° 48' 16.68"   W -7° 46' 8.54"

Location
Kee's Hotel is within easy reach from all major airports, approx. 2 hours from Belfast and under 3 hours from Dublin.

Property Highlights
Family-run for 5 generations. Established 1845, historical coaching inn. Overall excellence awards 10 consecutive years. In-House wellness centre.

Local Attractions
Glenveagh National Park is a wildlife reserve with castle and gardens. Oakfield Park, woodland gardens with miniature railway. Dunlewey Centre.

B&B from: €40.00 - €75.00
Suites from: €95.00 - €165.00

Host(s): Richard, Jayne & Vicky Kee   53

Activities   Facilities

Open All Year

Creevy Pier Hotel

Hotel ★   Map 13 I 17

Kildoney Glebe, Creevy, Ballyshannon,
Co. Donegal
Tel: +353-71-985 8355
Email: info@creevy.ie
Web: www.creevy.ie
GPS: N +54° 31' 33.66"   W -8° 15' 9.68"

Location
Charming, family-run hotel, set in the picturesque village of Creevy. The hotel itself offers breathtaking views of Donegal Bay & the wild Atlantic Ocean.

Property Highlights
We at Creevy Pier Hotel pride ourselves on offering only the highest standard of food, beverage & accommodation, with genuine Irish hospitality.

Local Attractions
The hotel is ideally located for any activity break, whether it be walking, fishing, surfing, or golfing - we have it all on our doorstep.

B&B from: €35.00 - €50.00

Host(s): Jason Horkan & McBride Family   10

Activities   Facilities

Open All Year

Dorrians Imperial Hotel

Hotel ★ ★ ★   Map 13 I 17

Main Street, Ballyshannon,
Co. Donegal
Tel: +353-71-985 1147
Email: info@dorriansimperialhotel.com
Web: www.dorriansimperialhotel.com
GPS: N +54° 30' 7.88"   W -8° 11' 29.61"

Location
Town Centre Hotel. Sligo 40 minutes, Knock 90 minutes, Dublin 3 hours, Belfast 3 hours, Donegal 15 minutes, Belleek / Bundoran 10 minutes.

Property Highlights
Traditional (1781) family-run hotel since 1937 by the Dorrian Family. Excellent home-cooked food, friendly, warm atmosphere.

Local Attractions
Golfing, Fishing, Horse Riding, Walking Tours, Beaches, Surfing, Theatre, Traditional Thatch Pub.

B&B from: €50.00 - €80.00

Host(s): Mary & Ben Dorrian   47

Facilities

Closed 23 December - 15 January

See also page 08

To Book Call **+353-1-8084419** or www.irelandhotels.com

Co. Donegal
Bundoran / Donegal Town

Grand Central Hotel

Hotel ★ ★ ★   Map 13 | 17

Main Street, Bundoran,
Co. Donegal
Tel: +353-71-984 2722
Email: info@grandcentralbundoran.com
Web: www.grandcentralbundoran.com
GPS: N +54° 28' 47.48"   W -8° 16' 35.63"

Location
Located in the heart of Bundoran, recognised as its best value 3* hotel. 2.5 hours from Dublin via the M3. From Galway take the N17 to Sligo & N15 to Bundoran.

Property Highlights
Along with our 63 bedrooms, we have sea views, a Féile Bia approved restaurant, Bar, free WiFi, Broadband & music every weekend.

Local Attractions
Golf, Angling, Surfing, Horse Riding and Hill Walking all nearby, all of which can be arranged by the hotel.

B&B from: €29.00 - €39.00

Host(s): Andrew Thomas

63

Facilities

Closed 01 December - 01 February

Great Northern Hotel

Hotel ★ ★ ★ ★   Map 13 | 17

Bundoran,
Co. Donegal
Tel: +353-71-984 1204
Email: reservations@greatnorthernhotel.com
Web: www.greatnorthernhotel.com
GPS: N +54° 29' 7.40"   W -8° 16' 36.15"

Location
Located in Bundoran. 215km from Dublin, 187km from Sligo Train Station, 100km from Knock Airport.

Property Highlights
24hr room service. 18 hole Championship Golf Course. Leisure centre, swimming pool, childrens' pool, gym, sauna, steam room, jacuzzi. Childrens' playroom and outdoor play area. Grill Room. Kids' Club.

Local Attractions
6 Screen Cinema, Waterworld Indoor Swimming Park, Outdoor Theme Park, Go Karting, Horse Riding, Surf Schools, Donegal Adventure Centre, Bingo Hall.

B&B from: €70.00 - €125.00
Suites from: €250.00 - €350.00

Host(s): Philip McGlynn

96

Activities   Facilities

Closed 16 - 27 December

Ard Na Breátha

Guesthouse ★ ★ ★   Map 13 | 18

Drumrooske Middle, Donegal Town,
Co. Donegal
Tel: +353-74-972 2288
Email: info@ardnabreatha.com
Web: www.ardnabreatha.com
GPS: N +54° 39' 46.24"   W -8° 6' 4.31"

Location
Located in a quiet country area. We are a 3 minute drive on the Lough Eske Road from Donegal Town and a 10 minute walk to the town centre.

Property Highlights
On site Restaurant with Bar, offering organically grown produce from our farm. Private residents' lounge. Lovely views of Barnes Mountains. "Georgina Campbell Guesthouse of the Year 2009".

Local Attractions
Slieve League, the highest sea cliffs in Europe, Glenveagh National Park, Marble Arch Caves are all under 1 hour drive from us. Also, Donegal Castle & Donegal Waterbus a must see.

B&B from: €35.00 - €55.00

Host(s): Theresa & Albert Morrow

6

Facilities

Closed 24 - 26 December

B&B Rates are per Person Sharing per Night incl. Breakfast. Room/Suite Rates are per Room per Night. See also page 08

Ireland West   47

Co. Donegal

To Book Call **+353-1-8084419** or www.irelandhotels.com

Donegal Town

Atlantic Guesthouse

Guesthouse ★ ★ Map 13 | 18

Main Street, Donegal Town,
Co. Donegal
Tel: +353-74-972 1187
Email: atlanticguesthouse@yahoo.ie
Web: www.atlanticguesthouse.ie
GPS: N +54° 39' 22.2"   W -8° 6' 47.9"

Location
We are in the town centre beside bus stop, sea food restaurants, live Irish traditional music.

Property Highlights
Our rooms have TVs, tea and coffee facilities. Free WiFi and private car park.

Local Attractions
Sandy beaches just 5 minutes drive. Donegal Bay Waterbus, Slieve League less than an hour away.

B&B from: €30.00 - €40.00

Host(s): Lorraine Browne
16

Facilities

Open All Year

Harvey's Point Hotel

Hotel ★ ★ ★ ★ Map 13 | 18

Lough Eske, Donegal Town,
Co. Donegal
Tel: +353-74-972 2208
Email: stay@harveyspoint.com
Web: www.harveyspoint.com
GPS: N +54° 41' 45.29"   W -8° 3' 13.31"

Location
Harvey's Point is situated 6km from Donegal Town, on the shores of Lough Eske & at the foot of the Blue Stack Mountains.

Property Highlights
Palatial bedrooms, gourmet cuisine & a warm Donegal welcome are just some of the unique selling points of this Swiss family-run hotel.

Local Attractions
Glenveagh National Park, Slieve League, The Blue Stack Mountains, Donegal Castle, Donegal Waterbus, miles of sandy beaches, great golf courses.

B&B from: €79.00 - €99.00
Suites from: €198.00 - €640.00

Host(s): Marc Gysling & Deirdre McGlone
70

Facilities

Open All Year

Mill Park Hotel, Conference Centre & Leisure Club

Hotel ★ ★ ★ ★ Map 13 | 18

The Mullins, Donegal Town,
Co. Donegal
Tel: +353-74-972 2880
Email: info@millparkhotel.com
Web: www.millparkhotel.com
GPS: N +54° 39' 32.83"   W -8° 7' 5.52"

Location
Located a few minutes stroll from Donegal Town.

Property Highlights
Interior design is a fusion of traditional & contemporary. Enjoy a choice of restaurants & leisure facilities, including swimming pool & jacuzzi.

Local Attractions
Enjoy a cruise of Donegal Bay, one of the most historical areas of Ireland. Visit Deane's Farm & Equestrian Centre, Salthill Gardens, Mountcharles & Donegal Castle. Golf courses & local fishing.

B&B from: €45.00 - €115.00
Suites from: €170.00 - €320.00

Host(s): Tony McDermott
110

Activities Facilities

Closed 24 - 27 December

B&B Rates are per Person Sharing per Night incl. Breakfast. Room/Suite Rates are per Room per Night. See also page 08

To Book Call **+353-1-8084419** or www.irelandhotels.com

Co. Donegal

Donegal Town / Downings / Dunfanaghy

Solis Lough Eske Castle

Hotel ★ ★ ★ ★ ★   Map 12 I 18

Lough Eske, Donegal Town, Co. Donegal
Tel: +353-74-972 5100
Email: reservations.lougheske@solishotels.com
Web: www.solisougheskecastle.ie
GPS: N +54° 41' 18.02"   W -8° 3' 57.77"

Location
A 43 acre estate hugging the shores of Lough Eske, near the Blue Stack Mountains and only 5km from Donegal Town.

Property Highlights
Winner of the World's Best Luxury Country Hotel Award, this is Donegal's only 5 star hotel and spa resort. Wedding venue of the year in Ireland 2009.

Local Attractions
Fishing on Lough Eske, hiking and biking through the Blue Stack Mountains, Donegal's waterbus, Slieve League, local villages for crafts and culture.

B&B from: €87.50 - €212.50
Suites from: €225.00 - €1,650.00

Host(s): Jeroen Quint

95

Activities / Facilities

Open All Year

Downings Bay Hotel

Hotel ★ ★ ★   Map 13 J 19

Downings, Letterkenny, Co. Donegal
Tel: +353-74-915 5586
Email: info@downingsbayhotel.com
Web: www.downingsbayhotel.com
GPS: N +55° 11' 40.42"   W -7° 50' 8.36"

Location
Situated on Sheephaven Bay & the Atlantic Drive. 22 miles North of Letterkenny, approximately 1 hour from Derry Airport.

Property Highlights
Especially renowned for our delicious food. Complimentary use of our nearby Magherabeg Leisure Centre & Kids Kingdom Play Centre.

Local Attractions
Right beside 2 beautiful beaches, 2 golf courses & a comfortable drive to Glenveagh National Park & Horn Head.

B&B from: €35.00 - €70.00

Host(s): Eileen Rock

40

Activities / Facilities

Closed 24 - 26 December

Arnolds Hotel

Hotel ★ ★ ★   Map 13 J 21

Dunfanaghy, Co. Donegal
Tel: +353-74-913 6208
Email: enquiries@arnoldshotel.com
Web: www.arnoldshotel.com
GPS: N +55° 10' 59.77"   W -7° 58' 11.86"

Location
23 miles north west of Letterkenny & situated at the entrance to the village of Dunfanaghy overlooking Sheephaven Bay and Horn Head.

Property Highlights
Managed by the 3rd & 4th generations of the Arnold family. Activity holidays include horse riding, painting, photography & quilting.

Local Attractions
Glenveagh National Park, Horn Head. Scenic Drive & Walks, Workhouse Heritage Centre, Glebe Gallery, Bloody Foreland & Atlantic Drive.

B&B from: €49.00 - €69.00

Host(s): Arnold Family

30

Activities / Facilities

Closed 31 October - 15 April

B&B Rates are per Person Sharing per Night incl. Breakfast. Room/Suite Rates are per Room per Night. **See also page 08**

Co. Donegal

To Book Call **+353-1-8084419** or www.irelandhotels.com

Dunfanaghy / Dunkineely / Glenties

Shandon Hotel Spa and Wellness

Hotel ★ ★ ★ ★   Map 13 J 21

Marble Hill Strand, Port-na-Blagh, Dunfanaghy,
Co. Donegal
Tel: +353-74-913 6137
Email: info@shandonhotel.com
Web: www.shandonhotel.com
GPS: N +55° 10' 47.56"   W -7° 54' 24.32"

Location
33km to Letterkenny (N56) between villages of Creeslough & Dunfanaghy. Airports - Dublin (M1/N2) 3.5 hrs, Belfast (M2/A6/N13) 2.5hrs, Derry (N13/N56) 1 hr.

Property Highlights
Panoramic view of Marble Hill Strand, excellent "Ocean Resort Spa" with outdoor hot tub. "the Den" childrens' playhouse with tennis courts, basketball, pool & gym. Family-run, rooms with sea views.

Local Attractions
Marble Hill Strand, Ocean Spa, Golf, Surfing, Horse Riding, Glenveagh National Park, Ards Forest Park.

B&B from: €50.00 - €120.00
Suites from: €160.00 - €400.00

Host(s): Dermot & Catherine McGlade

50

Activities   Facilities

Closed 19 December - 12 February

Castlemurray House Hotel

Hotel ★ ★   Map 13 H 18

St John's Point, Dunkineely,
Co. Donegal
Tel: +353-74-973 7022
Email: info@castlemurray.com
Web: www.castlemurray.com
GPS: N +54° 37' 4.12"   W -8° 22' 29.75"

Location
Situated on the N56, 8km from Killybegs, 20km from Donegal Town on the coast road to St. John's Point. Take the first left outside Dunkineely village.

Property Highlights
10 individually decorated sea view rooms. Fine dining restaurant serving the very best in local seafood and Irish meat with amazing view overlooking the sea & mountains.

Local Attractions
Horse riding centre, Killybegs - Largest fishing port in Ireland, Slieve League - Highest sea cliffs in Europe.

B&B from: €40.00 - €50.00

Host(s): Marguerite Howley

10

Facilities

Closed 03 January - 11 February

Highlands Hotel

Hotel ★ ★   Map 13 I 19

Main Street, Glenties,
Co. Donegal
Tel: +353-74-955 1111
Email: highlandhotel@eircom.net
Web: www.highlandshotel.ie
GPS: N +54° 47' 45.09"   W -8° 16' 54.07"

Location
Glenveagh National Park, Sliabh League, Fintown Heritage Railway, The Ancient Dolmen, Kilcooney & the fantastic beaches for which Donegal is famous all close by.

Property Highlights
"It embodies with a special ease and grace what we hope is the very essence of Irishness" - Brian Friel

Local Attractions
Golfing, Hill Walking, Surfing, Kayaking, Scuba Diving...there is no shortage of activities in Glenties and the surrounding area.

B&B from: €45.00 - €55.00

Host(s): The Boyle Family

24

Facilities

Open All Year

B&B Rates are per Person Sharing per Night incl. Breakfast. Room/Suite Rates are per Room per Night. See also page 08

To Book Call **+353-1-8084419** or www.irelandhotels.com

Co. Donegal

Gweedore / Killybegs / Laghey

An Chúirt, (Gweedore Court Hotel) & Earagail Health Club

Hotel ★★★★   Map 13 I 20

Gaoth Dobhair, Gweedore,
Co. Donegal
Tel: +353-74-953 2900
Email: info@gweedorecourthotel.com
Web: www.gweedorecourthotel.com
GPS: N +55° 2' 55.10"   W -8° 13' 20.27"

Location
Spectacularly situated overlooking the Clady River on the N56. Close to Glenveagh National Park & the villages of Dunlewey & Bunbeg. 35 mins. drive from Letterkenny & 10 mins. from Donegal Airport.

Property Highlights
Irish cuisine daily in our restaurant. Conferencing/banqueting facilities. Award-winning health club, Serenity Hair & Beauty, Marina Kids Adventure Centre, Arts & Crafts Centre. Parking & WiFi.

Local Attractions
Enjoy hill walking, golf, mountain climbing, angling, surfing. Day trips to Tory & Gola Islands. Dunlewey Lakeside Centre & Glenveagh National Park.

B&B from: €65.00 - €85.00
Suites from: €170.00 - €200.00

Host(s): Lewis Connon   69

Closed 24 - 25 December

Bay View Hotel & Leisure Centre

Hotel ★★★   Map 13 H 18

Main Street, Killybegs,
Co. Donegal
Tel: +353-74-973 1950
Email: info@bayviewhotel.ie
Web: www.bayviewhotel.ie
GPS: N +54° 38' 12.49"   W -8° 26' 31.92"

Location
Derry Airport approx 2 hours away. Sligo is the nearest train station, with trains to Dublin & Belfast. Regular bus service from Sligo to Donegal (1.5 hrs away).

Property Highlights
The Bay View Hotel is a delightful 3 star hotel offering guests a high standard of comfort. With 40 en suite rooms, Leisure & Fitness Centre & Swimming Pool.

Local Attractions
Donegal boasts many Blue Flag beaches including Fintra Beach which is located 5 minutes drive from Killybegs. Other popular attractions include guided walks, boat trips and water sports.

B&B from: €35.00 - €65.00

Host(s): Philip McBride   40

Closed 24 - 27 December

Moorland Guesthouse

Guesthouse ★★★   Map 13 I 18

Laghey, R.232, Donegal Town,
Co. Donegal
Tel: +353-74-973 4319
Email: moorland@eircom.net
Web: www.moorland-guesthouse.com
GPS: N +54° 35' 58.24"   W -8° 0' 20.46"

Location
Quiet & relaxed countryside atmosphere, near Donegal Town.

Property Highlights
Health & Beauty Clinic, Restaurant, Sauna, Lounge. German spoken.

Local Attractions
Near sandy beaches and golf links. Set in a landscape of mountains & high moor/hill. Lake & sea fishing nearby.

B&B from: €38.00 - €45.00

Host(s): Rosemarie & Walter Schaffner   8

Closed 01 November - 31 March

B&B Rates are per Person Sharing per Night incl. Breakfast. Room/Suite Rates are per Room per Night. See also page 08

Co. Donegal

To Book Call **+353-1-8084419** or www.irelandhotels.com

Letterkenny

Best Western Milford Inn Hotel & Natural Wellness

Hotel ★ ★ ★ Map 13 J 20

Letterkenny Road, Milford,
Co. Donegal
Tel: +353-74-915 3313
Email: info@milfordinnhotel.com
Web: www.milfordinnhotel.com
GPS: N +55° 4' 36.07"   W -7° 40' 51.17"

Location
Hotel is a 10 minute drive from the busy town of Letterkenny on the R245 between the village of Letterkenny and the Heritage Town of Ramelton.

Property Highlights
Famed for the 'Blaney' hospitality, food, drink and a warm welcome. No matter the occasion, be it wedding, business or a romantic weekend break, the Milford Inn Hotel is that special place for you.

Local Attractions
A short drive to Glenveagh National Park. Nearby we have fishing, surfing and clay pigeon shooting or enjoy one of our many walking routes like the Colmcille Trail.

B&B from: €35.00 - €80.00

Host(s): Mandy & Neil Blaney

33

Activities / Facilities

Closed 24 - 26 December

Castle Grove Country House Hotel

Hotel ★ ★ ★ ★ Map 13 J 19

Castle Grove (off the R245), Letterkenny,
Co. Donegal
Tel: +353-74-915 1118
Email: reservations@castlegrove.com
Web: www.castlegrove.com
GPS: N +54° 59' 13.15"   W -7° 38' 53.62"

Location
From Dublin take the N2 & A5 through Northern Ireland which is approx. a 3.5 hour journey. From Belfast take the A6 which is approx. a 2 hour journey.

Property Highlights
This beautiful Georgian House overlooking Lough Swilly has established a strong reputation of excellence for food, accommodation and service. Recognised by Georgina Campbell, AA & Michelin.

Local Attractions
In a very central location for golf at any of the local Golf Clubs, also for River & Sea Angling, winter sports of shooting & deer stalking. An ideal location for a garden trail or mountain climbing.

B&B from: €60.00 - €95.00
Suites from: €200.00 - €350.00

Host(s): Raymond & Mary T. Sweeney

15

Activities / Facilities

Closed 18 - 28 December

Clanree Hotel Conference & Leisure Centre

Hotel ★ ★ ★ Map 13 J 19

Derry Road, Letterkenny,
Co. Donegal
Tel: +353-74-912 4369
Email: info@clanreehotel.com
Web: www.clanreehotel.com
GPS: N +54° 56' 38.37"   W -7° 41' 52.44"

Location
Conveniently located on the outskirts of Letterkenny town centre, the Clanree Hotel offers luxury accommodation in an elegant setting.

Property Highlights
Full health & fitness club, gym, pool & beauty salon. Award-winning Aileach Restaurant offers excellent à la carte, carvery & early bird menu. Oscar's Bar offers a bar food menu & entertainment.

Local Attractions
Close by you'll find Glenveagh National Park, Grianan of Aileach, Inishowen & Derry City as well as Blue Flag beaches, golf courses, hills and lakes.

B&B from: €40.00 - €80.00

Host(s): Michael Naughton

119

Facilities

Closed 23 - 27 December

B&B Rates are per Person Sharing per Night incl. Breakfast. Room/Suite Rates are per Room per Night. See also page 08

To Book Call **+353-1-8084419** or www.irelandhotels.com

Co. Donegal
Letterkenny / Malin / Moville

Silver Tassie Hotel & Spa

Hotel ★ ★ ★ ★ Map 13 J 19

Ramelton Road, Letterkenny,
Co. Donegal
Tel: +353-74-912 5619
Email: info@silvertassiehotel.ie
Web: www.silvertassiehotel.com
GPS: N +54° 59' 9.82"   W -7° 40' 13.89"

Location
Only 5 mins. drive from the bustling town of Letterkenny on the Ramelton Rd. Bus station located in town centre. 60km to Donegal Airport, 33km to Derry Airport.

Property Highlights
Our Seascape Spa & Atomic Hair Salon are perfect pamper options. Afternoon tea or our delicious food tickle your taste buds. Your home from home experience will leave you wanting to come back again.

Local Attractions
Ideal countryside location. Ramelton, Milford & Rathmullan offer plenty of choice for day trips as well as Glenveagh National Park. Ideal for visiting Derry or the North West Coast.

B&B from: €40.00 - €85.00
Suites from: €120.00 - €200.00

Host(s): Rose & Ciaran Blaney

Activities / Facilities

Closed 24 - 26 December

Malin Hotel

Hotel ★ ★ Map 14 L 21

Malin Town, Inishowen,
Co. Donegal
Tel: +353-74-937 0606
Email: info@malinhotel.ie
Web: www.malinhotel.ie
GPS: N +55° 17' 43.05"   W -7° 15' 40.66"

Location
Situated at the tip of the beautiful Inishowen Peninsula. 40 mins. from Derry Airport, 30 mins. from Derry, 50 mins. from Letterkenny, 120 mins. from Belfast.

Property Highlights
Boutique style bedrooms, warm friendly bar & bistro, award-winning restaurant and champion of local produce.

Local Attractions
Malin Hotel is the perfect base to explore local attractions. Malin Head, Malin Equestrian Centre, Ballyliffin Golf Club, Culdaff Beach, Derry City, Glenveagh National Park, Doagh Famine Village.

B&B from: €65.00 - €85.00

Host(s): Madeline McLaughlin

Facilities

Open All Year

Carlton Redcastle Hotel

Hotel ★ ★ ★ ★ Map 14 L 21

Inishowen Peninsula, Moville,
Co. Donegal
Tel: +353-74-938 5555
Email: reservations.redcastle@carlton.ie
Web: www.carlton.ie/redcastle
GPS: N +55° 9' 31.43"   W -7° 7' 21.90"

Location
Waterfront location overlooking Lough Foyle on the stunning Inishowen Peninsula. 30 minutes from Derry City & Airport. Ideal location to explore the north west.

Property Highlights
93 luxury rooms & suites all with spectacular views; fine dining Waters Edge Restaurant, Captains Bar, spacious banqueting & conference Ocean Suite with panoramic views. C-Spa offers Thalassotherapy.

Local Attractions
Blue Flag Beaches of Stove & Culdaff nearby. Visit Malin Head, most northern point in Ireland, Derry City Walls, Giant's Causeway, Glenveagh National Park & Castle, Bushmills Distillery.

B&B from: €49.00 - €129.00
Suites from: €170.00 - €510.00

Host(s): Matt Doherty

Facilities

Closed 23 - 26 December

B&B Rates are per Person Sharing per Night incl. Breakfast. Room/Suite Rates are per Room per Night. **See also page 08**

Co. Donegal - Co. Galway

To Book Call **+353-1-8084419** or www.irelandhotels.com

Rathmullan / Aran Islands

Fort Royal Country House

Hotel ★ ★ ★   Map 14 K 20

Rathmullan,
Co. Donegal
Tel: +353-74-915 8100
Email: fortroyal@eircom.net
Web: www.fortroyal.ie
GPS: N +55° 6' 14.14"   W -7° 31' 40.90"

Location
Beautifully situated country house hotel located half a mile from the small town of Rathmullan.

Property Highlights
Surrounded by 7 hectares of magnificent grounds and gardens. Renowned for good food and a home from home atmosphere.

Local Attractions
Close to several top golf courses & ideal base to explore north Donegal coastline & beaches as well as the famous Glenveagh National Park.

B&B from: €70.00 - €80.00

Host(s): Tim & Tina Fletcher

11

Facilities

Closed 30 September - 01 April

54   Ireland West

Waters Edge (The)

Hotel ★ ★ ★   Map 14 K 20

Rathmullan,
Co. Donegal
Tel: +353-74-915 8182
Email: info@thewatersedge.ie
Web: www.watersedgedonegal.com
GPS: N +55° 5' 32.08"   W -7° 33' 1.12"

Location
Located in the idyllic village of Rathmullan. Set on the edge of Lough Swilly with stunning views over the lough.

Property Highlights
Gaze out of our glass front restaurant at the finest views & enjoy award-winning food. Enjoy a night cap in a dreamy setting, sleep with the sound of water lapping & awaken to the spectacular sunrise.

Local Attractions
Rathmullan, famous for its long, sandy beach. Charter boats to fish on Lough Swilly.

B&B from: €40.00 - €80.00

Host(s): Mandy & Neil Blaney

10

Activities

Facilities

Closed 24 - 26 December

Árd Einne Guesthouse

Guesthouse ★ ★ ★   Map 5 D 10

Inis Mór, Aran Islands,
Co. Galway
Tel: +353-99-61126
Email: ardeinne@eircom.net
Web: www.ardeinne.com
GPS: N +53° 6' 0.55"   W -9° 39' 20.04"

Location
Unspoilt area of Inis Mór, Aran Islands. By air - Aer Arann Inverin, guesthouse 300m from airfield. By sea - Ros a Mhíle/ Doolin, 2km from Cillronan Harbour.

Property Highlights
Family-run, ideal base to explore Aran Islands. High standard accommodation, non-smoking, all rooms offer sea views. Overlooking own beach, Árd Einne is located in peaceful atmosphere on Inis Mór.

Local Attractions
Near prehistoric forts (Black Fort), Cliffs & monastic ruins (St Enda & Bennan Churches). Ideal to explore flora & fauna, sand dunes. Walk/bike to other historic sites on island. Dún Aonghusa (5km).

B&B from: €45.00 - €60.00

Host(s): Clodagh Ní Ghoill-Mullin

8

Facilities

Closed 30 November - 01 February

B&B Rates are per Person Sharing per Night incl. Breakfast. Room/Suite Rates are per Room per Night.   See also page 08

To Book Call **+353-1-8084419** or www.irelandhotels.com

Co. Galway

Aran Islands / Athenry

Pier House

Guesthouse ★ ★ ★   Map 5 D 10

Kilronan, Aran Islands,
Co. Galway
Tel: +353-99-61417
Email: pierhousearan@gmail.com
Web: www.pierhousearan.com
GPS: N +53° 7' 11.99"   W -9° 39' 56.51"

Location
Overlooking Kilronan Harbour, 2 minutes walk from the ferry, located in the village of Kilronan.

Property Highlights
All bedrooms are en suite, comfortable house, very central location. TV, telephone, WiFi, a café and restaurant, visitors lounge.

Local Attractions
Neolithic Dun Aengus and Black Fort within walking distance, close to the local pubs in the village.

B&B from: €45.00 - €60.00

Host(s): Maura Joyce

12

Facilities

Closed 01 November - 17 March

Tigh Fitz

Guesthouse ★ ★ ★   Map 5 D 10

Killeany, Kilronan, Inishmore, Aran Islands,
Co. Galway
Tel: +353-99-61213
Email: penny@tighfitz.com
Web: www.tighfitz.com
GPS: N +53° 6' 20.07"   W -9° 39' 51.01"

Location
Tigh Fitz is 1 mile from the ferry port and 10 minutes walk from the airport.

Property Highlights
3 star guesthouse with a beautiful sea view from most bedrooms. All rooms en suite with tea/coffee facilities, TV, DD, & WiFi. Walking distance from all amenities, bars, restaurants & beaches.

Local Attractions
Guesthouse looks out to Teampall Bheanain dated 846AD. Smallest church in Europe. Arkin Castle to the left of the house & the Black Fort to the right of Tigh Fitz, 45 minutes walk.

B&B from: €40.00 - €60.00

Host(s): Penny Fitzpatrick

10

Facilities

Closed 01 - 28 December

Raheen Woods Hotel
Tranquillity Spa & Kardio Kidz

Hotel ★ ★ ★   Map 6 G 10

Athenry,
Co. Galway
Tel: +353-91-875888
Email: info@raheenwoodshotel.ie
Web: www.raheenwoodshotel.ie
GPS: N +53° 18' 2.31"   W -8° 45' 42.29"

Location
Conveniently located 1km off M6 Motorway in historic Athenry.

Property Highlights
50 bright, well-appointed spacious bedrooms & suites. All areas wheelchair accessible. Excellent food in McHale's Bar & Grill.

Local Attractions
Golf at Athenry & Cregmore. Visit Connemara & Cliffs of Moher. Stroll leisurely through Athenry's shops & King John's Castle.

B&B from: €45.00 - €120.00
Suites from: €190.00 - €245.00

Host(s): Frank Corby

50

Activities   Facilities

Closed 23 - 26 December

B&B Rates are per Person Sharing per Night incl. Breakfast. Room/Suite Rates are per Room per Night. **See also page 08**

Co. Galway

To Book Call **+353-1-8084419** or www.irelandhotels.com

Ballinasloe / Ballynahinch / Caherlistrane

Carlton Shearwater Hotel & C-Spa

Hotel ★ ★ ★ ★   Map 6 I 11

Marina Point, Ballinasloe,
Co. Galway
Tel: +353-909-630400
Email: info.shearwater@carlton.ie
Web: www.carlton.ie/shearwater
GPS: N +53° 19' 35.35" W -8° 13' 12.23"

Location
Located off the N6, 90 minutes from Dublin (Exit 14). 25 minutes from Galway, on main Galway - Dublin Rail, beside the River Suck.

Property Highlights
De luxe rooms, Marengo's Restaurant offers the best in fine dining, a contemporary style bar, C-Spa & leisure centre, 20m pool, Kids Club, free WiFi & parking, roof top garden suite ideal for BBQs.

Local Attractions
Zorbing Ballinasloe, Ballinasloe Golf Course, Turoe Pet Farm, International Horse Fair, The Bog Rail, Rathcroghan Tours, Silverline Cruisers, Clonmacnoise Monastic Settlement, golfing & fishing.

B&B from: €49.00 - €119.00
Suites from: €180.00 - €298.00

Host(s): Jacinta Naughton
104

Facilities

Closed 23 - 26 December

Ballynahinch Castle Hotel

Hotel ★ ★ ★ ★   Map 5 D 11

Ballinafad, Recess, Connemara,
Co. Galway
Tel: +353-95-31006
Email: bhinch@iol.ie
Web: www.ballynahinch-castle.com
GPS: N +53° 27' 36.68" W -9° 51' 44.51"

Location
Set on a 450 acre estate, among river and lakes and overlooked by mountains, only one hour west of Galway City in Connemara.

Property Highlights
Country sporting estate with fly-fishing, gardens and professional guided walking. Award-winning restaurant & atmospheric pub.

Local Attractions
Kylemore Abbey, Roundstone Connemara Golf Club, Inis Bofin Island and Clifden are all nearby.

B&B from: €70.00 - €175.00
Suites from: €215.00 - €400.00

Host(s): Patrick O'Flaherty

40

Activities Facilities

Closed Christmas Week & February

Lisdonagh House

Guesthouse ★ ★ ★ ★   Map 10 F 12

Caherlistrane,
Co. Galway
Tel: +353-93-31163
Email: cooke@lisdonagh.com
Web: www.lisdonagh.com
GPS: N +53° 29' 30.65" W -9° 3' 20.84"

Location
Lisdonagh House is an early Georgian Heritage House, located 20 minutes from Galway City in a glorious tranquil setting.

Property Highlights
Elegantly restored house retaining the classical proportions. The oval entrance hall has murals depicting four virtues dating from 1790. Cooking is superb, innovatively using local ingredients.

Local Attractions
Over 100 acres of woodland on the estate where guests can meander on country walks. Fishing & horse riding can be arranged.

B&B from: €70.00 - €90.00
Suites from: €180.00 - €240.00

Host(s): John & Finola Cooke

9

Facilities

Closed 01 Novemeber - 01 May

56   Ireland West   B&B Rates are per Person Sharing per Night incl. Breakfast. Room/Suite Rates are per Room per Night.   See also page 08

To Book Call **+353-1-8084419** or www.irelandhotels.com

Co. Galway

Carna / Cashel / Clifden

Carna Bay Hotel

Hotel ★ ★ ★   Map 9 D 11

Carna, Connemara,
Co. Galway
Tel: +353-95-32255
Email: carnabay@iol.ie
Web: www.carnabay.com
GPS: N +53° 19' 35.10"   W -9° 50' 19.75"

Location
The hotel is located in the heart of the West Connemara Gaeltacht, surrounded by beautiful scenery & rugged coastline.

Property Highlights
Family owned & managed hotel, our friendly Irish speaking staff will ensure your stay is a memorable one.

Local Attractions
Kylemore Abbey, Connemara National Park, Aran & Inish Bofin Islands, Killary Cruise, Western Way Walking Route. Outdoor pursuit & water sports available from hotel.

B&B from: €45.00 - €130.00

Host(s): Michael & Sheamus Cloherty

24

Facilities

Closed 22 - 27 December

Cashel House Hotel

Hotel ★ ★ ★ ★   Map 5 D 11

Cashel, Connemara,
Co. Galway
Tel: +353-95-31001
Email: res@cashel-house-hotel.com
Web: www.cashel-house-hotel.com
GPS: N +53° 25' 10.37"   W -9° 48' 28.62"

Location
In countryside beside sea. 40 miles to train station, 45 miles to Airport (Galway).

Property Highlights
Large gardens & woodland walks, garden school, stud farm, small private beach, vegetable & fruit gardens.

Local Attractions
Aran Island, Inish Bofin, Kylemore Abbey, 3 Golf Courses within 25 miles, Deep Sea Fishing & Lake Fishing by arrangement.

B&B from: €75.00 - €170.00
Suites from: €290.00 - €380.00

Host(s): Ray Doorley & Frank McEvilly

30

Facilities

Closed 04 January - 11 February

Abbeyglen Castle Hotel

Hotel ★ ★ ★ ★   Map 9 C 12

Sky Road, Clifden,
Co. Galway
Tel: +353-95-21201
Email: info@abbeyglen.ie
Web: www.abbeyglen.ie
GPS: N +53° 29' 17.88"   W -10° 1' 53.85"

Location
Abbeyglen is a ten minute walk from the village of Clifden on the Sky Road.

Property Highlights
Abbeyglen has great food, atmosphere, a mini spa, great gardens, tennis court, snooker, pitch & putt, luxury rooms & turf fires.

Local Attractions
Connemara Golf Club, Kylemore Abbey, National Park, great beaches, Inishbofin, Sky Road, Aran Islands, Killary Harbour, great walking, fishing, cycling and pony trekking.

B&B from: €99.00 - €125.00

Host(s): Brian / Paul Hughes

45

Activities Facilities

Closed 09 January - 04 February

B&B Rates are per Person Sharing per Night incl. Breakfast. Room/Suite Rates are per Room per Night. **See also page 08**

Co. Galway

To Book Call **+353-1-8084419** or www.irelandhotels.com

Clifden

All The Twos Guesthouse

Guesthouse   Map 9 C 12

Galway Road, Clifden, Connemara,
Co. Galway
Tel: +353-95-22222
Email: allthetwos@gmail.com
Web: www.clifden-allthetwos-connemara.com
GPS: N +53° 29' 17.99"   W -10° 0' 44.20"

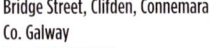

Location
Close to Clifden Town Centre (1km). A lot of off-road parking back & front, room for horseboxes, etc.

Property Highlights
Large luxurious bedrooms, king size beds, LCD TV, radio, DD phone, hospitality tray, hairdryer, free WiFi, power showers. Most rooms separate baths & walk in showers. Safe storage for bikes.

Local Attractions
Championship Links Golf, Pony-Trekking, Fishing, Theatre, Music Venue, Cinema, Museum, Connemara National Park, Inishbofin Island, Kylemore Abbey.

B&B from: €45.00 - €60.00

Host(s): Brendan & Maureen Lavin

12

Facilities

Open All Year

Ben View House

Guesthouse ★ ★   Map 9 C 12

Bridge Street, Clifden, Connemara,
Co. Galway
Tel: +353-95-21256
Email: benviewhouse@ireland.com
Web: www.benviewhouse.com
GPS: N +53° 29' 19.51"   W -10° 1' 14.87"

Location
Close to seaside, shops, etc. Galway 75km, Shannon & Knock Airports 2 hrs drive. Free overnight street parking.

Property Highlights
Est. 1926. Recommended by Frommer, Guide du Routard, Le Petit Futé Guide, AA 3 star, antique furnishing, storage for motorcycles, etc.

Local Attractions
Safe Beaches, Fishing, Scenic Drives, National Park, Hill Walking, Kylemore Abbey, First Trans-Atlantic landing site, Irish Music / Dance Concerts.

B&B from: €35.00 - €45.00

Host(s): Eileen Morris

9

Activities   Facilities

Closed 06 - 26 December

Buttermilk Lodge

Guesthouse ★ ★ ★   Map 9 C 12

Westport Road, Clifden, Connemara,
Co. Galway
Tel: +353-95-21951
Email: info@buttermilklodge.com
Web: www.buttermilklodge.com
GPS: N +53° 29' 31.53"   W -10° 1' 24.83"

Location
Located on N59 Clifden to Westport Road. 5 minutes walk to Clifden Town Centre, can collect from bus stop.

Property Highlights
Extensive breakfast menu all freshly cooked to order. Home baking. Free WiFi and parking. Connemara ponies & sheep to visit on our farm nearby. Warm & friendly.

Local Attractions
Connemara National Park, Inishbofin Island, Alcock & Brown Memorial, Sky Road, Marconi Station, Kylemore Abbey, etc.

B&B from: €35.00 - €50.00

Host(s): Patrick & Cathriona O'Toole

11

Facilities

Closed 03 January - 04 February

B&B Rates are per Person Sharing per Night incl. Breakfast. Room/Suite Rates are per Room per Night. See also page 08

To Book Call **+353-1-8084419** or www.irelandhotels.com

Co. Galway

Clifden

Clifden Station House Hotel

Hotel ★ ★ ★ Map 9 C 12

Clifden, Connemara,
Co. Galway
Tel: +353-95-21699
Email: info@clifdenstationhouse.com
Web: www.clifdenstationhouse.com
GPS: N +53° 29' 19.63"   W -10° 1' 3.70"

Location
Located in the heart of Clifden, Connemara. Only 1 hour's drive from Galway or Westport.

Property Highlights
Hotel with spa, leisure centre, theatre, cinema and courtyard shopping.

Local Attractions
Kylemore Abbey, Killary Cruises, Roundstone Village, Leenane Village & Dan O'Hara Homestead.

B&B from: €40.00 - €120.00
Suites from: €200.00 - €300.00

Host(s): Wilson Bird

78

Activities

Facilities

Open All Year

Connemara Country Lodge

Guesthouse ★ ★ ★ Map 9 C 12

Westport Road, Clifden,
Co. Galway
Tel: +353-87-992 5777 / 095-22122
Email: connemara@unison.ie
Web: www.connemaracountrylodge.com
GPS: N +53° 29' 28.90"   W -10° 1' 16.29"

Location
Located at the edge of Clifden Town (only 2 minutes walk) on 2 acres of grounds with large private car park.

Property Highlights
The hostess speaks fluent French and German and also speaks Italian & Irish. She sings an Irish Ballad during breakfast & has musical evenings singing & playing the violin & whistle. Free WiFi.

Local Attractions
Horse riding on beaches, mountain climbing, beautiful walks, Connemara National Park, Kylemore Abbey, Connemara Golf Course, Roundstone, fishing & cycling.

B&B from: €35.00 - €45.00

Host(s): Mary Corbett

10

Facilities

Open All Year

Kylemore Abbey & Victorian Walled Garden

Nestled in the heart of Connemara... Learn about the romance that started it all, the tragedy that befell it and the restoration to its former glory.

Enjoy a range of attractions including:

- 6 acre Victorian Walled Garden
- Restored Rooms of the Abbey
- Gothic Church
- Craft Shop
- Art Exhibitions & Choral Performances
- Guided Tours / Self Guided Tours
- Pottery Studio
- Set in a 1000 acre estate

Home to the Benedictine Order of Nuns since 1820

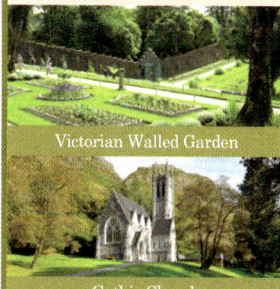

Victorian Walled Garden

Gothic Church

For more information contact
T: +353 95 41146
E: bookings@kylemoreabbeytourism.ie
www.kylemoreabbeytourism.ie

B&B Rates are per Person Sharing per Night incl. Breakfast. Room/Suite Rates are per Room per Night. **See also page 08**

Ireland West 59

Co. Galway

To Book Call **+353-1-8084419** or www.irelandhotels.com

Clifden

Dun Ri Guesthouse

Foyles Hotel

Quay House (The)

Guesthouse ★ ★ ★   Map 9 C 12

Hotel ★ ★ ★   Map 9 C 12

Guesthouse ★ ★ ★   Map 9 C 12

Hulk Street, Clifden,
Co. Galway
Tel: +353-95-21625
Email: info@dunri.ie
Web: www.dunri.ie
GPS: N +53° 29' 16.35"   W -10° 1' 6.37"

Main Street, Clifden,
Co. Galway
Tel: +353-95-21801
Email: info@foyleshotel.com
Web: www.foyleshotel.com
GPS: N +53° 29' 19.06"   W -10° 1' 22.06"

Beach Road, Clifden,
Co. Galway
Tel: +353-95-21369
Email: thequay@iol.ie
Web: www.thequayhouse.com
GPS: N +53° 29' 8.59"   W -10° 1' 48.14"

Location
Centrally located on a quiet street just 2 minutes walk from Clifden Town Centre.

Location
Foyles Hotel is situated in the centre of Clifden and is an ideal base for exploring Connemara.

Location
7/8 minutes walk or 2 minutes drive from Clifden Town centre overlooking the quay. 80km NW of Galway City (N59).

Property Highlights
The only guesthouse in Clifden Town centre with private parking and secure bike / motorcycle parking. Spacious rooms. Free WiFi. Complimentary tea / coffee.

Property Highlights
Charming hotel managed personally by the Foyles for over a century with each room individually decorated by the family. Our award-winning Marconi Restaurant offers local produce with a creative twist.

Property Highlights
Antique furnishings, original artwork, comfortable sitting rooms, private courtyard.

Local Attractions
An ideal base to explore all Connemara has to offer. Kylemore Abbey, National Park, Golf, Fishing, Hiking and close to Restaurants and Pubs.

Local Attractions
Connemara Golf Club, Kylemore. Connemara Lakes, Mountains & Beaches offer fishing, walking, cycling and an abundance of water sports.

Local Attractions
Sea-fishing on the doorstep, golf, horse riding, angling, hill-walking, lovely beaches.

B&B from: €35.00 - €50.00

B&B from: €40.00 - €75.00

B&B from: €65.00 - €80.00

Host(s): Michael & Aileen King

Host(s): Edmund Foyle

Host(s): Paddy & Julia Foyle

13

25

14

Facilities

Facilities

Facilities

Closed 23 - 27 December

Closed 10 January - 10 February

Closed 1 November - 14 March

To Book Call **+353-1-8084419** or www.irelandhotels.com

Co. Galway

Clonbur (An Fháirche) / Furbo / Galway City

Fairhill House Hotel

Hotel ★ ★ ★   Map 9 E 12

Clonbur, Connemara,
Co. Galway
Tel: +353-94-954 6176
Email: info@fairhillhouse.com
Web: www.fairhillhouse.com
GPS: N +53° 32' 39.89"   W -9° 21' 52.19"

Location
35 minutes to Galway Airport, 40 minutes to Knock Airport. 2.5 hours from Dublin City. 40 minutes to Galway City. 3 minutes from Cong.

Property Highlights
Famous traditional bar, 3 star service. Known for high standard in trad & folk music. Seafood, steak a speciality. 180+ different malt whiskeys. Mentioned on Pat Kenny show as great place to stay.

Local Attractions
Huge location for all levels of Hill Walking. Maps & Guide available on request. Perfect centre for touring Connemara, Lough Corrib, Lough Mask only 2 minute drive. Anglers paradise.

B&B from: €45.00 - €75.00

Host(s): Edward Lynch

20

Activities   Facilities

Closed 24 - 26 December

Connemara Coast Hotel

Hotel ★ ★ ★ ★   Map 6 F 10

Furbo,
Galway
Tel: +353-91-592108
Email: info@connemaracoast.ie
Web: www.sinnotthotels.com
GPS: N +53° 14' 55.03"   W -9° 12' 1.64"

Location
Spectacularly set with grounds that sweep down to the shores of Galway Bay, yet just 10 minutes from Galway City centre.

Property Highlights
Ideal base when visiting Galway/Connemara, with dedicated staff providing a warm welcome. The hotel boasts restful lounges, restaurants, extensive grounds, award winning leisure centre & free parking.

Local Attractions
Galway City, museum & shops, Spiddal Ceardlann Craft Village, Aran Islands, Kylemore Abbey, Brigit's Gardens, Oughterard Mines, cruising Lough Corrib or Killary. Many festivals & Galway Race Track.

B&B from: €70.00 - €175.00
Suites from: €300.00 - €600.00

Host(s): Ann Downey

141

Activities   Facilities

Closed 23 - 26 December

Ardilaun Hotel Conference Centre & Leisure Club

Hotel ★ ★ ★ ★   Map 6 F 10

Taylor's Hill,
Galway City, Co. Galway
Tel: +353-91-521433
Email: info@theardilaunhotel.ie
Web: www.theardilaunhotel.ie
GPS: N +53° 16' 3.30"   W -9° 4' 51.15"

Location
Nestled in the leafy suburb of Taylor's Hill on its own landscaped grounds, 1 mile from the city & Galway Bay.

Property Highlights
Facilities include 125 luxurious bedrooms, beautiful gardens with terrace patio, spacious lounges, award-winning Camilaun Restaurant, Blazers Bar & Bistro, leisure club with pool, sauna, steam room.

Local Attractions
The Ardilaun is situated 1km from Galway City & close to Salthill. Driving distance to Connemara, The Burren & close to ferry access to the Aran Islands.

B&B from: €55.00 - €135.00
Suites from: €105.00 - €185.00

Host(s): John Ryan

125

Facilities

Closed 22 - 26 December

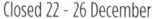

B&B Rates are per Person Sharing per Night incl. Breakfast. Room/Suite Rates are per Room per Night. See also page 08

Ireland West 61

Co. Galway

Galway City

To Book Call **+353-1-8084419** or www.irelandhotels.com

Atlantic View Guesthouse

Guesthouse ★ ★ ★ Map 6 F 10

4 Ocean Wave, Dr. Colohan Road,
Galway City, Co. Galway
Tel: +353-91-582109
Email: atlanticbandb@hotmail.com
Web: www.atlanticbandb.com
GPS: N +53° 15' 50.64"   W -9° 4' 9.18"

Carlton Hotel Galway

Hotel ★ ★ ★ Map 6 F 10

Dublin Road, Galway City East,
Co. Galway
Tel: +353-91-381200
Email: reservations.galwaycity@carlton.ie
Web: www.carltonhotelgalwaycity.com
GPS: N +53° 16' 48.13"   W -9° 1' 18.17"

Claregalway Hotel (The)

Hotel ★ ★ ★ Map 6 11 G

Claregalway,
Galway City, Co. Galway
Tel: +353-91-738300
Email: stay@claregalwayhotel.ie
Web: www.claregalwayhotel.ie
GPS: N +53° 20' 37.13"   W -8° 56' 38.31"

Location
Located in Galway City on road to Salthill on R336 which leads to Connemara and Seafront. Mobile 086 852 4579.

Location
Carlton Hotel Galway is located 9km from Galway Airport & 4km from train station & city centre.

Location
Just 10 minutes from Galway City Centre off the N17/18 road, 5 minutes from Galway Airport & the new M6.

Property Highlights
Overlooking the sea. Large sun balcony, great views of the sea. We are an ideal base from which to explore Connemara, Cliffs of Moher and the Burren. Free WiFi and computer available for guests use.

Property Highlights
Superior rooms & suite facilities. Bar & restaurant serve food daily. Excellent leisure facilities.

Property Highlights
Family-run hotel boasting comfortable bedrooms, 3 funky bars, a contemporary restaurant, a modern luxurious leisure centre, swimming pool & spa suites incorporating seaweed baths. Award-winning team.

Local Attractions
Beach across the road, surfing, sailing, snorkelling. All water sports. Golf & horse riding nearby. Also tennis & fishing.

Local Attractions
Close to Connemara, Aran Islands, Hills of Clare & vibrant Galway City. Salthill is only a short drive. 8 Blue Flag beaches in close proximity.

Local Attractions
Stunning nature walks along the River Clare with an 11th century Abbey & 13th century Castle.

B&B from: €30.00 - €90.00

B&B from: €49.00 - €139.00
Suites from: €129.00 - €329.00

B&B from: €50.00 - €200.00
Suites from: €100.00 - €300.00

Host(s): Tara Treacy

Host(s): Siobhán Burke

Host(s): Paul & Nora Gill

5

363

45

Activities

Facilities

Activities

Facilities

Activities

Facilities

Closed 23 - 26 December

Closed 22 - 26 December

Closed 24 - 26 December

Co. Galway
Galway City

To Book Call **+353-1-8084419** or www.irelandhotels.com

Clayton Hotel Galway

Hotel ★ ★ ★ ★   Map 6 F 10

**Ballybrit,
Galway City, Co. Galway**
Tel: +353-91-721900
Email: info@clayton.ie
Web: www.claytonhotelgalway.ie
GPS: N +53° 17' 29.51"   W -8° 59' 18.88"

Location
The Clayton Hotel Galway is located on the Lynch Roundabout next to the M6 exit, minutes from Galway City centre, Galway Airport and Ballybrit Racecourse, home to the Galway Races.

Property Highlights
Spacious luxury hotel accommodation & leisure centre. Tribes Restaurant serves the finest cuisine or you can relax in the Enclosure Bar & Bistro and enjoy a delectable & varied bar menu. Free parking.

Local Attractions
Bowling. Horse Riding. Golf. Art Galleries & Theatres. Culture & Heritage and plenty of shopping.

Room Rate from: €99.00 - €350.00
Suites from: €250.00 - €350.00

Host(s): Edward Sweeney

195

Facilities

Closed 23 - 26 December

Corrib Haven Guest House

Guesthouse ★ ★ ★   Map 6 F 10

**107 Upper Newcastle,
Galway City, Co. Galway**
Tel: +353-91-524171
Email: corribhaven@eircom.net
Web: www.corribhaven.net
GPS: N +53° 17' 12.94"   W -9° 4' 11.40"

Location
Located in Galway City on N59 to Clifden, walking distance to University Hospital, 20 minutes walk to city centre. Free Private Parking.

Property Highlights
Tea/Coffee in rooms, WiFi, Free Parking. Ideal for University, Regional Hospital, close to Westwood Hotel, Glenlo Abbey. 25 minutes drive to Galway Airport, 80 minutes to Shannon.

Local Attractions
University College Hospital, University, Beach, Golf at Salthill & Glenlo Abbey Hotel, Fishing, Angling, Horse Riding, Walking, Mountain Trekking, Surfing.

B&B from: €35.00 - €60.00

Host(s): Angela & Tom Hillary

9

Facilities

Closed 15 December - 10 January

webpostit

No Stamps
No Paper
No Hassle

✓ We Print it
✓ We Package it
✓ We Stamp it
✓ We Post it

Mailed on the same day for next day delivery

**A one page letter costs €1.50
All inclusive**
A minimum of €5.00 credit is required

**First letter is FREE just sign up and enter the coupon code
IRELAND HOTEL 287**
N.B one coupon per new client

You don't have to leave your hotel, you can send from anywhere in the world, we do the work, you enjoy your stay.

www.webpostit.ie

B&B Rates are per Person Sharing per Night incl. Breakfast. Room/Suite Rates are per Room per Night. See also page 08

Co. Galway

To Book Call +353-1-8084419 or www.irelandhotels.com

Galway City

Courtyard Marriott Galway

Hotel ★ ★ ★ ★ Map 6 F 10

Headford Point, Headford Road,
Galway City, Co. Galway
Tel: +353-91-513200
Email: galway.reservations@courtyardgalway.com
Web: www.courtyardgalway.ie
GPS: N +53° 17' 8.56" W -9° 2' 42.49"

Location
Located within walking distance of Eyre Square and Shop Street, with Galway Airport less than 5 minutes away.

Property Highlights
Guest rooms are spacious & comfortable featuring high speed internet access, air conditioning, built in mini fridge & safe. Facilities include Point Bar, Spa, fitness suite, business centre, parking.

Local Attractions
Galway City is host to many sites of historic interest. Also ideal for touring Connemara and the Burren.

Room Rate from: €99.00 - €350.00
Suites from: €150.00 - €500.00

Host(s): Cian Landers   104

Activities   Facilities

Open All Year

Eyre Square Hotel

Hotel ★ ★ ★ Map 6 F 10

Forster Street, Eyre Square,
Galway City, Co. Galway
Tel: +353-91-569633
Email: eyresquarehotel@eircom.net
Web: www.eyresquarehotel.com
GPS: N +53° 16' 27.34" W -9° 2' 50.60"

Location
Forster Street in the heart of the city, just off Eyre Square. 2 minutes from Shop Street and bus and train station.

Property Highlights
Music at weekends. Excellent food and service. First class location. Comfortable rooms. Complimentary WiFi. En suite rooms. Restaurant and bar menu.

Local Attractions
Connaught Rugby, Greyhound Stadium, Terryland Park, Pearse Stadium, Spanish Arch, NUIG, UHG 2 minute walk from the main shopping area, theatres & nightlife.

B&B from: €35.00 - €150.00

Host(s): Roger Carey   52

Facilities

Closed 19 - 27 December

Flannery's Hotel

Hotel ★ ★ ★ Map 6 F 10

Dublin Road,
Galway City, Co. Galway
Tel: +353-91-755111
Email: reservations@flanneryshotel.net
Web: www.flanneryshotel.net
GPS: N +53° 16' 41.71" W -9° 0' 53.73"

Location
Galway City East, 2km from Eyre Square.

Property Highlights
134 bedrooms, award-winning Galwegian Restaurant and Frankie's Bar & Bistro. 4 conference suites, free WiFi, free car parking.

Local Attractions
Galway City Centre, Galway Irish Crystal, Royal Tara China, Ballyloughane Beach.

Room Rate from: €49.00 - €299.00

Host(s): Mary Flannery   134

Activities   Facilities

Closed 19 - 29 December

To Book Call **+353-1-8084419** or www.irelandhotels.com

Co. Galway
Galway City

g Hotel (The)

Hotel ★ ★ ★ ★ ★   Map 6 F 10

Wellpark,
Galway
Tel: +353-91-865200
Email: info@theg.ie
Web: www.theghotel.ie
GPS: N +53° 16' 55.25" W -9° 1' 55.75"

Location
The g hotel is located close to the heart of Galway City, along the majestic coastline of Galway Bay. The g is a luxurious escape that combines comfort & lavishness in a totally original fashion.

Property Highlights
Designed by renowned milliner, Philip Treacy, the g boasts extravagant rooms, luxury spa designed by ESPA, delectable dining options, state of the art conference facilities & bespoke wedding venue.

Local Attractions
Explore one of Ireland's most magical regions: visit the Spanish Arch, Galway City Museum, Galway Cathedral or enjoy a daytrip to the Aran Islands, Cliffs of Moher or Connemara National Park.

Room Rate from: €150.00 - €630.00
Suites from: €310.00 - €2,500.00

Host(s): Damien O'Riordan

101

Activities   **Facilities**

Closed 23 - 27 December

Galway Bay Hotel, Conference & Leisure Centre

Hotel ★ ★ ★ ★   Map 6 F 10

The Promenade, Salthill,
Galway City, Co. Galway
Tel: +353-91-520520
Email: info@galwaybayhotel.com
Web: www.galwaybayhotel.com
GPS: N +53° 15' 31.37" W -9° 5' 5.94"

Location
On the famous Salthill Promenade, overlooking Clare Hills, Atlantic Ocean, & just 2 hours from Dublin - one of Ireland's finest locations.

Property Highlights
The 153 bedroom stunning Galway Bay Hotel, awarded best 4* Hotel 2010, is Galway's premier Leisure & Conferencing destination.

Local Attractions
Cruising, walking, golfing, heritage, angling, legendary festivals & nightlife, combined with luxury accommodation, exquisite fine dining & exceptional service.

B&B from: €65.00 - €115.00
Suites from: €170.00 - €460.00

Host(s): Dan Murphy

153

Facilities

Food for Kids

Open All Year

Glenlo Abbey Hotel

Hotel ★ ★ ★ ★ ★   Map 6 F 10

Kentfield, Bushypark,
Galway City, Co. Galway
Tel: +353-91-526666
Email: info@glenloabbey.ie
Web: www.glenlo.com
GPS: N +53° 18' 0.70" W -9° 5' 53.13"

Location
Glenlo Abbey Hotel is located on its own 138 acre golf estate, 5 minutes from Galway City Cathedral in the centre of the city.

Property Highlights
Glenlo Abbey Hotel is a Manor House dating back to 1740. Highlights include the Abbey, The Pullman Restaurant and serene privacy of the estate.

Local Attractions
Galway City, Connemara, The Burren, Cliffs of Moher, The Aran Islands.

Room Rate from: €130.00 - €400.00
Suites from: €350.00 - €700.00

Host(s): Bourke Family

46

Facilities

Food for Kids

Closed 23 - 27 December

B&B Rates are per Person Sharing per Night incl. Breakfast. Room/Suite Rates are per Room per Night. **See also page 08**

Ireland West   65

Co. Galway

To Book Call **+353-1-8084419** or www.irelandhotels.com

Galway City

Hotel Meyrick

Hotel ★ ★ ★ ★ Map 6 F 10

Eyre Square,
Galway City, Co. Galway
Tel: +353-91-564041
Email: reshm@hotelmeyrick.ie
Web: www.hotelmeyrick.ie
GPS: N +53° 16' 25.80"   W -9° 2' 52.73"

Location
Ideally located in the centre of Galway City, overlooking Eyre Square. Adjacent to train station and coach station.

Property Highlights
Since 1852, Hotel Meyrick has been the meeting place in Galway with four dining and bar options, beautiful bedrooms and extensive spa.

Local Attractions
The shops, bars, cafés, theatres and sights of Galway are all on the doorstep. Druid Theatre, Town Hall Theatre, Eyre Square, Quay Street & Spanish Arch, Connaught Rugby Grounds.

B&B from: €57.50 - €178.00
Suites from: €215.00 - €650.00

Host(s): Cian O'Broin

97

Activities

Facilities

Closed 24 - 26 December

House Hotel (The)

Hotel ★ ★ ★ ★ Map 6 F 10

Spanish Parade,
Galway City, Co. Galway
Tel: +353-91-538900
Email: info@thehousehotel.ie
Web: www.thehousehotel.ie
GPS: N +53° 16' 12.02"   W -9° 3' 11.65"

Location
In the heart of the Latin Quarter, based just off Quay St. in a quiet haven. 5 minutes from train, bus & coach stations. 20 minutes from Galway Airport.

Property Highlights
The House Hotel is a stylish, boutique hotel with an unbeatable location. The Hotel oozes personality and charm. The House Bistro boasts brasserie-style food & a distinctive wine list.

Local Attractions
The House Hotel is the perfect hotel for a city shopping break, only 1 minutes walk from the Spanish Arch. 13 minutes walk from Salthill's famous promenade.

B&B from: €55.00 - €120.00
Suites from: €160.00 - €450.00

Host(s): Margaret Jenkins

40

Facilities

Closed 24 - 27 December

Huntsman Inn

Hotel ★ ★ ★ Map 6 F 10

164 College Road,
Galway City, Co. Galway
Tel: +353-91-562849
Email: info@huntsmaninn.com
Web: www.huntsmaninn.com
GPS: N +53° 16' 52.77"   W -9° 2' 2.06"

Location
We are located 5 minutes from city centre and train/bus station. 5 miles from Galway Airport. 2 hours from Dublin.

Property Highlights
Food served 7.30am to 9.30am Monday to Saturday, 12 noon to 9.00pm Sundays in our award-winning bars and restaurants.

Local Attractions
Health Spas, Golf Courses, Salthill, The Burren, Connemara, Galway City - Bars, Restaurants, Night Clubs & Shopping.

B&B from: €40.00 - €80.00
Suites from: €100.00 - €180.00

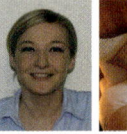

Host(s): Cathrina McManamon

12

Facilities

Closed 24 - 28 December

66 Ireland West   B&B Rates are per Person Sharing per Night incl. Breakfast. Room/Suite Rates are per Room per Night. See also page 08

To Book Call **+353-1-8084419** or www.irelandhotels.com

Co. Galway

Galway City

You can find all the best deals in all of these places

Website

Mobile App

Printed Guide

facebook.com/irelandhotels

irelandhotels.com/onlineguide

Inishmore House

Guesthouse ★ ★ ★　　　　Map 6 F 10

109 Fr. Griffin Road, Lower Salthill,
Galway City, Co. Galway
Tel: +353-91-582639
Email: inishmorehouse@eircom.net
Web: www.inishmoreguesthouse.com
GPS: N +53° 16' 1.61"　W -9° 4' 1.03"

Location
Centrally located between Galway City and Salthill and within five minutes walk of beach.

Property Highlights
Charming family owned guesthouse with secure car park. Complimentary tea/coffee, breakfast menu, 8 en suite bedrooms, phone & multi-channel TV in all rooms, German spoken. Free WiFi.

Local Attractions
An ideal base for touring the Aran Islands, Burren, Cliffs of Moher and Connemara. Golfing/Fishing holidays can be arranged. B&B and transport to golf course included.

B&B from: €35.00 - €70.00

Host(s): Marie & Peter

8

Facilities

Open All Year

Maldron Hotel Galway

Hotel ★ ★ ★　　　　Map 6 F 10

Oranmore, Galway,
Co. Galway
Tel: +353-91-792244
Email: info.galway@maldronhotels.com
Web: www.maldronhotels.com
GPS: N +53° 16' 40.27"　W -8° 55' 38.63"

Location
The Maldron Hotel Galway is superbly located in Oranmore on the N6 just a 10 minute drive from Galway City & 5 minute drive from Galway Airport.

Property Highlights
Free car parking, playroom & leisure centre with 20m Pool. All 113 bedrooms have free WiFi & broadband, as well as fantastic meeting rooms.

Local Attractions
Adjacent to hotel is an Omniplex Cinema & City Limits Entertainment Centre. Fishing, golf, shopping & much more available nearby.

B&B from: €39.00 - €119.00

Host(s): Dermot Comerford

113

Facilities

Closed 24 - 26 December

Ireland West　67

Co. Galway

To Book Call **+353-1-8084419** or www.irelandhotels.com

Galway City

Marian Lodge Guesthouse

Guesthouse ★ ★ ★   Map 6 F 10

Knocknacarra Road, Upper Salthill,
Co. Galway
Tel: +353-91-521678
Email: celine@iol.ie
Web: www.marian-lodge.com
GPS: N +53° 15' 33.34"   W -9° 6' 9.21"

Menlo Park Hotel

Hotel ★ ★ ★ ★   Map 6 F 10

Terryland, Headford Road,
Galway City, Co. Galway
Tel: +353-91-761122
Email: info@menloparkhotel.com
Web: www.menloparkhotel.com
GPS: N +53° 17' 16.40"   W -9° 2' 48.73"

Oranmore Lodge Hotel, Conference & Leisure Centre

Hotel ★ ★ ★ ★   Map 6 G 10

Oranmore, Galway City,
Co. Galway
Tel: +353-91-794400
Email: info@oranmorelodge.ie
Web: www.oranmorelodgehotel.ie
GPS: N +53° 16' 33.63"   W -8° 55' 51.28"

Location
Adjacent to promenade/beach in Upper Salthill. Galway Airport 7 miles, Shannon 60 miles, Dublin Airport 2 hours, Galway City 2 miles, train station 2 miles.

Location
Conveniently located only half a mile from the city centre and ten minutes from the airport.

Location
Located 2km from M6 (exit 19), 5km from Airport, 7km from Galway City, bus/train station. 5 mins. walk to the village of Oranmore. Ideal base to explore Galway.

Property Highlights
Large rooms en suite, DD phone, TV, orthopaedic beds, hairdryer, tea/coffee facilities, iron trouser press, children welcome, free internet access, tours arranged for Connemara/Burren, Aran Islands.

Property Highlights
70 luxury rooms with 14 superior rooms, WiFi, free parking, weekend entertainment, food served all day, Irish Accommodation Services Institute Award 2010, Optimus Service Excellence Award 2010/2011.

Property Highlights
4 star family-run hotel with full leisure centre, superb dining facilities, WiFi & complimentary car parking. Comprises of 68 well appointed rooms, excellent conference facilities & spacious ballroom.

Local Attractions
Close to nightly entertainment. Leisureland, tennis, fishing, wind surfing, horse riding, Galway Bay, Ardilaun, Clybaun, Salthill Hotels, Aquarium, golf driving range, restaurants, pubs & shops.

Local Attractions
Tours to Connemara and to the Burren direct from the hotel, city sightseeing tours, close to Art Gallery, City Museum, Town Hall theatre, Black Box theatre, Terryland Stadium, Shopping Centres.

Local Attractions
3km to Galway Bay Sailing Club & Renville Park. 5 mins. to City Limits Entertainment Centre for families. Turoe Pet Farm & Horse Museum 25 mins. Galway City 10 mins. Drive with bus route 5 mins. Walk.

B&B from: €39.00 - €60.00

B&B from: €60.00 - €180.00

Room Rate from: €69.00 - €229.00
Suites from: €109.00 - €259.00

Host(s): Celine Molloy

Host(s): Elaine Brennan

Host(s): Brian J. O'Higgins

6

70

68

Facilities

Facilities

Facilities

Closed 23 - 28 December

Closed 24 - 26 December

Closed 20 - 28 December

B&B Rates are per Person Sharing per Night incl. Breakfast. Room/Suite Rates are per Room per Night.   See also page 08

To Book Call **+353-1-8084419** or www.irelandhotels.com

Co. Galway
Galway City

Salthill Hotel

Hotel ★ ★ ★ Map 6 F 10

The Promenade, Salthill, Galway City,
Co. Galway
Tel: +353-91-522711
Email: reservations@salthillhotel.com
Web: www.salthillhotel.com
GPS: N +53° 15' 31.38"   W -9° 5' 14.56"

Location
On the spectacular Salthill Galway Promenade, with panoramic views of Galway Bay & the Clare hills.

Property Highlights
Rooms en suite, DD phone, tea/coffee facilities. Excellent cuisine & service. Ocean Fitness & Leisure Centre. Live entertainment nightly. Car park.

Local Attractions
Enjoy the charm of Galway City & the west of Ireland landscape, heritage & culture. Galway Bay & sandy beaches, Burren, Aran Islands & Dun Aongasa, Oughterard, Kinvara, Coole Park, Salthill Golf Club.

B&B from: €75.00 - €150.00

Host(s): Pauline Griffin

161

Facilities

Closed 23 - 27 December

Skeffington Arms Hotel

Hotel ★ ★ ★ Map 6 F 10

Eyre Square,
Galway City, Co. Galway
Tel: +353-91-563173
Email: reception@skeffington.ie
Web: www.skeffington.ie
GPS: N +53° 16' 26.64"   W -9° 3' 0.52"

Location
Overlooking Eyre Square, The Skeffington Arms is at an enviable position close to rail & bus terminals. Just a short stroll from an array of shops & theatres.

Property Highlights
Boutique style hotel boasting 24 refurbished, modern bedrooms oozing style & comfort. The hotel boasts the famous Skeff Bar & Restaurant. Please enquire about facilities for Persons with Disabilities.

Local Attractions
Tour buses to Aran Islands, Connemara and Cliffs are but a 3 minute walk form our hotel. Close to some of Ireland's most renowned golf courses and beaches.

B&B from: €50.00 - €190.00

Host(s): Lisa Moore

24

Facilities

Closed 24 - 26 December

Twelve (The)

Hotel ★ ★ ★ Map 6 F 10

Barna Coast Road,
Galway City, Co. Galway
Tel: +353-91-597000
Email: enquire@thetwelvehotel.ie
Web: www.thetwelvehotel.ie
GPS: N +53° 15' 5.04"   W -9° 9' 9.76"

Location
Just 10 minutes from Galway City on the Connemara Coast Road. The Twelve is located in the picturesque village of Barna.

Property Highlights
Two award-winning restaurants and one of Ireland's finest wine collections. A beautifully designed boutique hotel.

Local Attractions
Gateway to Connemara, Blue Flag beaches, Barna Woods, Salthill and Galway City's nightlife. Barna has it all.

B&B from: €50.00 - €80.00
Suites from: €130.00 - €190.00

Host(s): Fergus O'Halloran

48

Activities **Facilities**

Open All Year

B&B Rates are per Person Sharing per Night incl. Breakfast. Room/Suite Rates are per Room per Night. See also page 08

Co. Galway

Galway City / Gort

To Book Call **+353-1-8084419** or www.irelandhotels.com

Victoria Hotel

Hotel ★ ★ ★   Map 6 F 10

Victoria Place, Eyre Square,
Galway City, Co. Galway
Tel: +353-91-567433
Email: victoriahotel@eircom.net
Web: www.victoriahotelgalway.com
GPS: N +53° 16' 23.06"   W -9° 2' 52.12"

Location
The Victoria Hotel is located in the heart of Galway City, just 100 yards off Eyre Square.

Property Highlights
Each of the spacious en suite rooms has DD phone, TV, tea/coffee making facilities & hairdryer. Enjoy excellent cuisine in our restaurant or visit our lively bar.

Local Attractions
The Victoria Hotel is withing walking distance of all shops, theatres, pubs & cinema.

B&B from: €30.00 - €150.00

Host(s): Mary T.Cullinane

57

Facilities

Open All Year

Westwood Hotel (The)

Hotel ★ ★ ★ ★   Map 6 F 10

Dangan, Upper Newcastle,
Galway City, Co. Galway
Tel: +353-91-521442
Email: resmanager@westwoodhotel.com
Web: www.westwoodhousehotel.com
GPS: N +53° 17' 21.22"   W -9° 4' 30.44"

Location
On the west side of Galway City in the university district, close to University College Hospital. Ideal for exploring Galway City & the beauty of Connemara.

Property Highlights
The Westwood stands amidst a rural landscape & combines a mellow taste of the countryside with the city's cutting edge. Luxurious guestrooms, Bar, Restaurant, Meeting & Banqueting facilities, Air-Con.

Local Attractions
The Claddagh, Spanish Arch, Salthill, Shopping, Boating, Fishing, Golf, Hill-walking, Connemara, Galway Races, Arts Festival & Oyster Festivals.

B&B from: €49.50 - €169.50
Suites from: €139.00 - €339.00

Host(s): David Kelly

58

Facilities

Food for Kids

Closed 24 - 26 December

Lady Gregory Hotel, Conference & Leisure Club

Hotel ★ ★ ★   Map 6 G 9

Ennis Road, Gort,
Co. Galway
Tel: +353-91-632333
Email: manager@ladygregoryhotel.ie
Web: www.ladygregoryhotel.ie
GPS: N +53° 3' 40.38"   W -8° 48' 53.74"

Location
Just 5 minutes from Gort Railway Station, 30 minutes from Galway City, 40 minutes from Limerick City & 30 minutes from Shannon & Galway Airports.

Property Highlights
A renowned warm friendly welcome awaits you from our friendly & efficient staff as you enter the architectural splendour of the Lady Gregory Hotel whether as a corporate, leisure or business client.

Local Attractions
A Heritage Town with many local attractions to offer, from golf to the historical former homes of WB Yeats at Thoor Ballylee & Lady Gregory at Coole Park, now a National Forest & Wildlife Park.

B&B from: €45.00 - €85.00

Host(s): Brian Morrissey

87

Activities   Facilities

Closed 24 - 27 December

To Book Call **+353-1-8084419** or www.irelandhotels.com

Co. Galway

Gort / Headford / Inishbofin Island

Sullivan's Royal Hotel

Hotel ★ ★   Map 6 G 9

The Square, Gort,
Co. Galway
Tel: +353-91-631257/401
Email: sullivanslhotel@eircom.net
GPS: N +53° 4' 2.84"   W -8° 49' 10.65"

Location
On main road from Cork to Donegal, 30 minutes from Shannon Airport and Galway City. In the town centre of Gort.

Property Highlights
Family run business. 12 newly refurbished rooms, excellent food and service. Dining Pub of the Year Award 2009.

Local Attractions
Christy O'Connor designed Golf Course, The Burren, Coole Park, W.B. Yeats Castle, Irish Music Sessions.

B&B from: €30.00 - €60.00

Host(s): John Sullivan

12

Activities
Facilities

Open All Year

Anglers Rest Hotel

Hotel ★ ★   Map 10 F 12

Headford,
Co. Galway
Tel: +353-93-35528
Email: anglersresthotel@eircom.net
GPS: N +53° 28' 10.13"   W -9° 6' 24.08"

Location
In the heart of Headford Village on the N84 main Galway to Castlebar Road.

Property Highlights
Owned and managed by the Heneghan family since 1905, Anglers Rest has a warm and comfortable interior to wind away the evening.

Local Attractions
Close to Lough Corrib and many historical sites and ruins in the area.

B&B from: €45.00 - €65.00

Host(s): Frank Heneghan

16

Activities

Facilities

Closed 25 26 December

Doonmore Hotel

Hotel ★ ★   Map 9 C 12

Inishbofin Island,
Co. Galway
Tel: +353-95-45814
Email: info@doonmorehotel.com
Web: www.doonmorehotel.com
GPS: N +53° 36' 50.48"   W -10° 13' 41.56"

Location
Doonmore Hotel is ideally situated overlooking the entrance to the island's beautiful natural harbour. The hotel is owned and managed by The Murray Family.

Property Highlights
All rooms are en suite, some with panoramic sea views. The Doonmore welcomes individual boarding, families and groups and provides excellent packages for weddings, parties and small conferences.

Local Attractions
Safe swimming and snorkelling from shell-strewn beaches. Walking and cycling are among some of the activities on offer. A haven for bird watchers and artists.

B&B from: €40.00 - €65.00

Host(s): Aileen Murray

20

Activities

Facilities

Closed 27 September - 15 April

B&B Rates are per Person Sharing per Night incl. Breakfast. Room/Suite Rates are per Room per Night. **See also page 08**

Co. Galway

To Book Call **+353-1-8084419** or www.irelandhotels.com

Inishbofin Island / Kinvara / Leenane

Inishbofin House Hotel

Hotel ★ ★ ★   Map 9 C 12

Inishbofin Island, Connemara,
Co. Galway
Tel: +353-95-45809
Email: info@inishbofinhouse.com
Web: www.inishbofinhouse.com
GPS: N +53° 36' 49.38"   W -10° 12' 21.96"

Location
From Galway head north on the N59 towards Clifden, follow sign for Cleggan to board the Island Discovery Ferry.

Property Highlights
Inishbofin House is a de luxe hotel with a Marine Spa which commands exquisite views of the beautiful harbour. Family owned hotel offers a warm welcome, friendly & efficient service & excellent food.

Local Attractions
Fishing, cycling, hill walking, boating, archaeology & exploring, painting, scuba diving, swimming, horse riding.

B&B from: €50.00 - €90.00

Host(s): Reception

34

Activities | Facilities

Closed 30 November - 01 March

Merriman Inn & Restaurant

Hotel ★ ★ ★   Map 6 G 10

Main Street, Kinvara,
Co. Galway
Tel: +353-91-638222
Email: merrimanhotel@eircom.net
Web: www.merrimanhotel.com
GPS: N +53° 8' 21.47"   W -8° 56' 23.67"

Location
Located in the picturesque village of Kinvara, on the shores of Galway Bay. Less than 1 hour from Shannon International Airport & half an hour from Galway City.

Property Highlights
Our "Quilty Room" Restaurant offers local & international flavours. "M'Asal Beag Dubh" Bar offers a mouth watering Bistro Menu, excellent Guinness & local country & traditional music.

Local Attractions
The largest "Thatched Hotel" in Ireland. Medieval Dunguaire Castle. Gateway to the Burren Limestone Moonscape in Co Clare. Discover rugged Connemara or watch the "sun go down on Galway Bay".

B&B from: €40.00 - €70.00
Suites from: €120.00 - €180.00

Host(s): Leonard Murphy

32

Facilities

Open All Year

Delphi Mountain Resort

Hotel ★ ★ ★ ★   Map 9 D 12

Leenane,
Co. Galway
Tel: +353-95-42208
Email: info@delphiescape.com
Web: www.delphimountainresort.com
GPS: N +53° 37' 21.62"   W -9° 45' 16.59"

Location
Located in the stunningly beautiful Delphi Valley, Delphi Mountain Resort is 1.5 hrs from both Knock and Galway Airports & 40 mins. from Westport Train Station.

Property Highlights
Award-winning Spa, stunning accommodation, exceptional restaurant, outdoors adventure centre. Natural spring water and locally sourced food used throughout hotel.

Local Attractions
Kylemore Abbey, Connemara National Park, Westport House, Aisleigh Falls, Leenane Village, Mweelrea, Croagh Patrick, Clare Island.

B&B from: €69.00 - €79.00
Suites from: €158.00 - €198.00

Host(s): Jackie Lydon

36

Activities | Facilities

Closed 31 December - 01 February

B&B Rates are per Person Sharing per Night incl. Breakfast. Room/Suite Rates are per Room per Night. See also page 08

Co. Galway

Leenane / Letterfrack / Loughrea

Leenane Hotel

Hotel ★ ★ ★   Map 9 D 12

Leenane, Connemara,
Co. Galway
Tel: +353-95-42249
Email: info@leenanehotel.com
Web: www.leenanehotel.com
GPS: N +53° 35' 40.35"   W -9° 42' 17.79"

Location
Situated overlooking stunning Killary Harbour, Ireland's only Fjord. In North Connemara, 7 miles from Kylemore Abbey.

Property Highlights
Restaurant serving fresh seafood caught daily in Killary Harbour. Steam room, sauna & the only natural saltwater seaweed baths in Connemara.

Local Attractions
Kylemore Abbey 7 miles, Killary Cruises 1 mile, Killary Adventure Centre 3 miles, Delphi Adventure Centre 6 miles, Western Way walking route 400 metres, Ashleigh Falls 2 miles.

B&B from: €39.00 - €65.00

Host(s): Conor Foyle

29

Facilities

Closed 15 November - 15 March

Rosleague Manor

Hotel ★ ★ ★ ★   Map 9 C 12

Letterfrack,
Co. Galway
Tel: +353-95-41101
Email: info@rosleague.com
Web: www.rosleague.com
GPS: N +53° 32' 55.56"   W -9° 58' 27.59"

Location
Ideally located in the heart of Connemara overlooking Ballinakill Bay and Connemara National Park. Letterfrack Village - 1 mile, Clifden - 8 miles.

Property Highlights
Historic House run by the Foyle family for 3 generations. Renowned for good food - Good Hotel Guide, Bridgestone 100 Best, Michelin, etc.

Local Attractions
National Park 1 mile, Kylemore Abbey 3 miles, Boat to Inishbofin 4 miles, Killary Fjord 7 miles, Great Walking & Cycling from front door.

B&B from: €70.00 - €105.00
Suites from: €170.00 - €250.00

Host(s): Mark Foyle

20

Facilities

Closed 31 October - 15 March

Lough Rea Hotel & Spa

Hotel ★ ★ ★ ★   Map 6 H 10

Galway Road, Loughrea,
Co. Galway
Tel: +353-91-880088
Email: sales@loughreahotelandspa.com
Web: www.loughreahotelandspa.com
GPS: N +53° 12' 17.17"   W -8° 35' 52.80"

Location
20 minutes from Galway City Centre, 2 hours from Dublin on the M6, Athenry train station is 10 minutes away.

Property Highlights
New hotel with state of the art facilities, kids area, Shore Island Spa, 7 meeting rooms and 400 seater conference centre.

Local Attractions
Loughrea Lake, Dartfield Horse Museum, Golf Courses, Galway City, Pallas Karting.

B&B from: €59.00 - €150.00
Suites from: €198.00 - €500.00

Host(s): Barry Kilroy

91

Activities   Facilities

Closed 24 - 26 December

B&B Rates are per Person Sharing per Night incl. Breakfast. Room/Suite Rates are per Room per Night. See also page 08

Ireland West   73

Co. Galway

To Book Call **+353-1-8084419** or www.irelandhotels.com

Loughrea / Oughterard

Meadow Court Hotel

Hotel ★ ★ ★ ★   Map 6 H 10

Clostoken, Loughrea,
Co. Galway
Tel: +353-91-841051
Email: meadowcourthotel@eircom.net
Web: www.meadowcourthotel.com
GPS: N +53° 12' 37.00"   W -8° 38' 10.37"

Location
Two miles west of Loughrea town on the main Dublin/Galway road (N6). 20 miles from Galway Airport, Shannon and Knock Airports 1 hour 25 minute drive.

Property Highlights
Charming boutique hotel tucked into the tranquil West of Ireland countryside. Family-run hotel, proudly offers first class service & an award-winning restaurant. Flat screen plasma TVs in all rooms.

Local Attractions
Within easy reach of vibrant Galway City and provides an ideal base from which to explore many hidden gems.

B&B from: €40.00 - €80.00
Suites from: €160.00 - €160.00

Host(s): Tommy & Margaret Corbett
21

Closed 24 - 27 December

Corrib Wave Guest House

Guesthouse ★ ★ ★   Map 5 E 11

Portacarron, Oughterard, Connemara,
Co. Galway
Tel: +353-91-552147
Email: cwh@gofree.indigo.ie
Web: www.corribwave.com
GPS: N +53° 25' 55.95"   W -9° 17' 19.56"

Location
Panoramic lakeside guesthouse on shore of Lough Corrib, overlooking Connemara Mountains. Galway City 25km, Oughterard Town 3km.

Property Highlights
Excellent Home Cooking. Spectacular views. Turf fire, peace & tranquillity. WiFi available. Recommended Le Guide Routard & Georgina Campbell. Best Places to Stay.

Local Attractions
Own private Jetty, Boats, Engines for Hire, Angling Specialists, Lakeside Walks, 18 hole golf 1km. Mountain Bike Trail 4km. See website for more info.

B&B from: €33.00 - €40.00

Host(s): Maria & Michael Healy
10

Closed 01 November - 01 February

Mountain View Guest House

Guesthouse ★ ★ ★   Map 5 E 11

Aughnanure, Oughterard,
Co. Galway
Tel: +353-91-550306
Email: tricia.oconnor@eircom.net
Web: www.mountainviewgalway.com
GPS: N +53° 24' 43.49"   W -9° 16' 39.77"

Location
Situated just off the N59, 24kms from Galway City & within 2.4km of Oughterard, with Connemara Mountains & Lough Corrib nearby.

Property Highlights
All bedrooms en suite, with TV, DD phones, tea/coffee making facilities & hair dryers. Free WiFi. Private garden for guest use.

Local Attractions
Local attractions within a 5 minute drive include golf, walking, Aughnanure Castle, St. Brigit's Gardens, Glengowla Mines, boating & fishing on Lough Corrib.

B&B from: €32.00 - €40.00

Host(s): Patricia & Richard O'Connor
10

Closed 22 - 28 December

74   Ireland West   B&B Rates are per Person Sharing per Night incl. Breakfast. Room/Suite Rates are per Room per Night.   See also page 08

Co. Galway

Oughterard / Portumna / Renvyle

Ross Lake House Hotel

Hotel ★★★★ Map 5 E 11

Rosscahill, Oughterard,
Co. Galway
Tel: +353-91-550109
Email: rosslake@iol.ie
Web: www.rosslakehotel.com
GPS: N +53° 23' 31.73" W -9° 16' 50.75"

Location
Ross Lake House Hotel is situated 22km from Galway City on route N59, the main Galway/Clifden Road. Turn left after Rosscahill Village.

Property Highlights
This Georgian Country House is surrounded by acres of mature trees & rolling lawns creating a quiet heaven.

Local Attractions
Fishing on Lough Corrib & Ross Lake. Golfing at Oughterard Golf Club, Aughnanure Castle, home to the ferocious O' Flahertys. Also explore Aran Islands, Burren, Cliffs of Moher & magical Connemara.

B&B from: €70.00 - €85.00
Suites from: €200.00 - €300.00

Host(s): Elaine & Henry Reid

13

Facilities

Closed 31 October - 15 March

Shannon Oaks Hotel & Country Club

Hotel ★★★ Map 6 I 9

Portumna,
Co. Galway
Tel: +353-90-974 1777
Email: sales@shannonoaks.ie
Web: www.shannonoaks.ie
GPS: N +53° 5' 24.77" W -8° 13' 25.78"

Location
Parkland setting on the edge of the bustling town of Portumna. 1 hour from Galway, 2 hours from Dublin.

Property Highlights
Family friendly destination, with a choice of hotel, suites or lodges. Award-winning Leisure Centre, gym, pool, jacuzzi & treatment rooms.

Local Attractions
Portumna Forest Park, 17th century Portumna Castle & Gardens, Lough Derg, angling, water sports, golf, pet farms, Dartfield Horse and Vintage Car Museums, equestrian centres.

B&B from: €35.00 - €80.00

Host(s): Karl Reinhardt

63

Activities

Facilities

Open All Year

Renvyle House Hotel

Hotel ★★★ Map 9 C 12

Renvyle, Connemara,
Co. Galway
Tel: +353-95-43511
Email: info@renvyle.com
Web: www.renvyle.com
GPS: N +53° 36' 32.41" W -10° 0' 6.04"

Location
Renvyle House is set on 200 acres in Connemara, nestled between mountains, sea and lake.

Property Highlights
Family friendly hotel, award-winning food, seasonal wine tasting and drama play and some great walks.

Local Attractions
Kylemore Abbey, Connemara National Park, Ocean's Alive, Killary Fjord, Day Trip to Inishbofin.

B&B from: €30.00 - €125.00

Host(s): Ronnie Counihan

70

Facilities

Closed 02 January - 10 February

B&B Rates are per Person Sharing per Night incl. Breakfast. Room/Suite Rates are per Room per Night. See also page 08

Co. Galway
Roundstone / Spiddal

Roundstone House Hotel

Hotel ★ ★   Map 9 C 11

**Roundstone, Connemara,
Co. Galway**
Tel: +353-95-35864
Email: vaughanshotel@eircom.net
Web: www.irishcountryhotels.com
GPS: N +53° 23' 42.46"   W -9° 55' 8.82"

Location
Hotel located on the Western Seaboard, 52 miles from Galway Airport, 48 miles from the train station & Galway City.

Property Highlights
A family hotel situated in the picturesque village of Roundstone. A fascinating place for a holiday offering a wide range of interests for holidaymakers.

Local Attractions
Beaches safe for swimming & windsurfing. Close to Connemara golf course. Watch musical instruments being made, visit Connemara National Park or the Heritage & History Centre. Hill walking is popular.

B&B from: €50.00 - €60.00

Host(s): Maureen, Diarmuid & Siobhan Vaughan

12

Facilities

Closed 01 November - 01 April

An Crúiscín Lán Hotel

Hotel ★ ★   Map 5 E 10

**Spiddal,
Co. Galway**
Tel: +353-91-553148
Email: ancruiscinlanhotel@gmail.com
Web: www.ancruiscinlan.com
GPS: N +53° 14' 38.34"   W -9° 18' 23.52"

Location
In the heart of the Irish speaking Spiddal village, 14km from Galway Airport and 12km from Galway City on the scenic coast road. Bus stop at hotel.

Property Highlights
Family-run. A warm welcome awaits you. It boasts a snug bar showing your fav. sports events & a lounge bar for meeting friends. A dining conservatory has views of the Burren, Galway Bay & the Islands.

Local Attractions
Beach 200m from hotel. Visit the Aran Islands. Oughterard & Barna Golf Courses nearby. Sea fishing, bus tours of Connemara, horse riding all close by.

B&B from: €45.00 - €60.00

Host(s): John Foye

14

Facilities

Closed 25 -26 December

Park Lodge Hotel

Hotel ★ ★ ★   Map 5 E 10

**Park, Spiddal,
Co. Galway**
Tel: +353-91-553159
Email: parklodgehotel@eircom.net
Web: www.parklodgehotel.ie
GPS: N +53° 14' 49.35"   W -9° 15' 52.31"

Location
Park Lodge Hotel is 15km from Galway train / bus station and 22km from Galway Airport.

Property Highlights
We are a family-run business. Home cooked food is the hallmark of the Park Lodge Hotel.

Local Attractions
We are ideally situated for visiting the Aran Islands and Connemara.

B&B from: €40.00 - €55.00

Host(s): Jane Marie Foyle

23

Activities   **Facilities**

Closed 01 October - 31 May

To Book Call **+353-1-8084419** or www.irelandhotels.com

Co. Leitrim
Ballinamore / Carrick-on-Shannon

Glenview Guesthouse

Guesthouse ★ ★ — Map 11 J 15

Aughoo, Ballinamore,
Co. Leitrim
Tel: +353-71-964 4157
Email: glenvhse@iol.ie
Web: www.glenview-house.com
GPS: N +54° 1' 37.70"   W -7° 47' 50.75"

Location
3km from Ballinamore. Dublin & Belfast Airports 2 hours. Knock Airport 1 hour.

Property Highlights
Long established guesthouse. Beside Shannon-Erne Waterway. On site folk museum, restaurant & tennis court. Self catering also available.

Local Attractions
Arigna Mining Experience, horse riding, angling, golf, Lough Rynn House & gardens, Discover Lough Allen, Famine Museum.

B&B from: €40.00 - €45.00

Host(s): Teresa Kennedy

Facilities

Open All Year

Aisleigh Guest House

Guesthouse ★ ★ ★ — Map 10 I 14

Dublin Road, Carrick-on-Shannon,
Co. Leitrim
Tel: +353-71-962 0313
Email: aisleigh@eircom.net
Web: www.aisleighguesthouse.com
GPS: N +53° 56' 33.14"   W -8° 4' 11.55"

Location
Located on the N4. 40 mins. from Knock Airport, 2 hrs from Dublin. Situated 1km from the picturesque town of Carrick-on-Shannon, Ireland's best kept secret.

Property Highlights
Free WiFi & Broadband Internet Access, private car parking. Tastefully decorated en suite bedrooms with TV, DD phones, power shower, sauna. Ideal base for touring the North West. CCTV monitored.

Local Attractions
Arigna Mining Museum, Leitrim Design House, Dock Theatre, Lough Key Forest Park, Aura Leisure Centre, River Cruising, 41 Fishing Lakes, Hill Walking & Golfing.

B&B from: €35.00 - €50.00

Host(s): Charlotte & Sean

Facilities

Open All Year

Bush Hotel

Hotel ★ ★ ★ — Map 10 I 14

Town Centre, Carrick-on-Shannon,
Co. Leitrim
Tel: +353-71-967 1000
Email: info@bushhotel.com
Web: www.bushhotel.com
GPS: N +53° 56' 45.94"   W -8° 5' 38.40"

Location
Town Centre location adjacent to River Shannon. Ireland's oldest hotel, steeped in tradition with many memorabilia from the past.

Property Highlights
Boutique Hotel with open fire, theme lounges, bistro and coffee shop. Free WiFi. Conferencing and banqueting. Ireland's first Ecolabel hotel.

Local Attractions
Arigna Mining Museum, Strokestown House & Famine Museum. Lough Key National Park. Arts, Theatre, History and Culture at our doorstep.

B&B from: €45.00 - €89.00
Suites from: €159.00 - €199.00

Host(s): Joseph Dolan

Activities

Facilities

Open All Year

B&B Rates are per Person Sharing per Night incl. Breakfast. Room/Suite Rates are per Room per Night. See also page 08

Co. Leitrim

To Book Call **+353-1-8084419** or www.irelandhotels.com

Carrick-on-Shannon / Mohill

Ciúin House & Chungs Asian Restaurant

Guesthouse ★ ★ ★ ★   Map 10 I 4

Hartley, Carrick-on-Shannon,
Co. Leitrim
Tel: +353-71-967 1488
Email: info@ciuinhouse.com
Web: www.ciuinhouse.com
GPS: N +53° 57' 15.02"   W -8° 5' 22.67"

Location
Ciúin House is a 4**** luxury guesthouse & restaurant, situated in a quiet residential area close to the town centre & family run. A non-smoking house. Free WiFi.

Property Highlights
15 de luxe rooms with en suite bathrooms, DD phone, Internet access, orthopaedic beds, tea/coffee making facilities. Private car parking, lounge with plasma screen, fully licensed Asian Restaurant.

Local Attractions
Lough Key Forest Park, Dock Theatre & Gallery. Arigna Mining Museum, golf club, cruising, Aura Leisure Centre. Activity/play centre, horse riding.

B&B from: €40.00 - €55.00

Host(s): Nelson Chung
15

Facilities

Open All Year

Landmark Hotel

Hotel ★ ★ ★ ★   Map 10 I 14

Carrick-on-Shannon,
Co. Leitrim
Tel: +353-71-962 2222
Email: reservations@thelandmarkhotel.com
Web: www.thelandmarkhotel.com
GPS: N +53° 56' 36.73"   W -8° 5' 34.33"

Location
Ideally located on the Dublin to Sligo (N4) Road, overlooking the River Shannon. 1 hour 40 mins. to Dublin, just 30 mins. to Sligo & 1 hour to Knock International Airport. Train station 5 mins. walk.

Property Highlights
Breathtaking views of the River Shannon. Free WiFi throughout the hotel. Free car parking. A choice of restaurants with diverse menu selection. A warm welcome awaits you at the Landmark.

Local Attractions
Within 10 mins. drive of 18 hole Carrick Golf Club. Beautiful riverside walks & river cruising. There is plenty to enjoy in this charming town; quaint bars, cafes, shops, theatres & new 4plex cinema.

B&B from: €55.00 - €95.00
Suites from: €160.00 - €240.00

Host(s): John Rowe
49

Activities

Facilities

Closed 24 - 25 December

Lough Rynn Castle

Hotel ★ ★ ★ ★   Map 11 J 14

Mohill,
Co. Leitrim
Tel: +353-71-963 2700
Email: enquiries@loughrynn.ie
Web: www.loughrynn.ie
GPS: N +53° 53' 37.55"   W -7° 50' 50.05"

Location
Lough Rynn is located 90 minutes from Dublin on the N4 Sligo route. 10km from Dublin Sligo rail connection. 45 minutes from Knock Airport.

Property Highlights
300 acre private estate. Largest Victorian walled gardens in North West. Conference facilities for 450 persons. Grand Ballroom. 18th century Castle. Wedding Venue of the Year finalist 2010.

Local Attractions
Angling. Horse Riding. Boating at Carrick-on-Shannon. Arigna Mines.

B&B from: €49.50 - €92.50
Suites from: €175.00 - €255.00

Host(s): Ciaran Reidy
40

Activities

Facilities

Open All Year

78 Ireland West   B&B Rates are per Person Sharing per Night incl. Breakfast. Room/Suite Rates are per Room per Night. See also page 08

To Book Call **+353-1-8084419** or www.irelandhotels.com

Co. Limerick
Adare / Castleconnell

Dunraven Arms Hotel

Hotel ★ ★ ★ ★   Map 6 G 7

Adare,
Co. Limerick
Tel: +353-61-605900
Email: reservations@dunravenhotel.com
Web: www.dunravenhotel.com
GPS: N +52° 33′ 54.68″   W -8° 47′ 13.74″

Location
Located 20 minutes drive from Shannon Airport and a 1 hour drive from Cork & Kerry Airports. 2 hours from Dublin Airport.

Property Highlights
Two 18 hole golf courses in the village of Adare. Equestrian facilities at Clonshire Equestrian Centre. Fishing & Clay Pigeon facilities. New Conference Centre.

Local Attractions
Limerick Racecourse, Thomond Park, Adare Heritage Centre, Curraghchase Forest Park, Bunratty Castle, The Hunt Museum, Limerick University Concert Hall.

B&B from: €65.00 - €80.00
Suites from: €220.00 - €295.00

Host(s): Hugh Murphy

86

Activities   Facilities

Open All Year

Fitzgeralds Woodlands House Hotel & Spa

Hotel ★ ★ ★   Map 6 G 7

Knockanes, Adare,
Co. Limerick
Tel: +353-61-605100
Email: reservations@woodlands-hotel.ie
Web: www.woodlands-hotel.ie
GPS: N +52° 33′ 46.90″   W -8° 45′ 57.32″

Location
Situated on 44 private acres of Golden Vale countryside on the edge of Adare village, 15 minutes Limerick City, 30 minutes Shannon Airport. An ideal location for visit

Property Highlights
Timmy Mac's Irish Bistro. Award-winning Revas Spa. Fitzy's Piano Bar. Extensive Leisure Club, Woodie's Kids Club, Brennan Room Restaurant.

Local Attractions
Desmond Castle, Adare Heritage Centre, Adare Manor GC, Stonehall Farm, Ballyhoura Mountain Biking, Lough Gur Centre, Bleach Lough Angling, Bunratty Castle, Clonshire Equestrian Centre, Stonehall Farm.

B&B from: €29.50 - €89.50

Host(s): Mary & David Fitzgerald

93

Activities   Facilities

Closed 24 - 25 December

Castle Oaks House Hotel & Country Club

Hotel ★ ★ ★   Map 6 H 7

Castleconnell,
Co. Limerick
Tel: +353-61-377666
Email: info@castleoaks.ie
Web: www.castleoaks.ie
GPS: N +52° 42′ 34.28″   W -8° 30′ 30.60″

Location
Castle Oaks House Hotel & Holiday Village is set on 26 acres of landscaped garden in a tranquil setting on the banks of the River Shannon, only 10 minutes from Limerick City.

Property Highlights
20 bedrooms in the main house plus 22 two bedroom garden suites with private living room. 19 4 star Holiday homes. Full leisure centre, tennis courts, playground, on site salon and riverside walks.

Local Attractions
Fishing, lakeside activities, equestrian & golfing holidays our speciality. Visit nearby Thomond Park "Home of Munster Rugby", King John's Castle or Bunratty Castle and Folk Park.

B&B from: €39.00 - €85.00
Suites from: €120.00 - €300.00

Host(s): Gobnait O'Connell

64

Facilities

Closed 23 - 26 December

Co. Limerick

To Book Call **+353-1-8084419** or www.irelandhotels.com

Kilmallock / Limerick City

Deebert House Hotel

Hotel ★ ★ ★   Map 6 H 6

Deebert, Kilmallock,
Co. Limerick
Tel: +353-63-31200
Email: info@deeberthousehotel.com
Web: www.deeberthousehotel.com
GPS: N +52° 24' 2.96"   W -8° 34' 14.23"

Location
Nestled at the foot of the Ballyhoura Mountains. 35km from Limerick, 60km from Shannon Airport, 70km from Cork Airport.

Property Highlights
Intimate, family-run hotel with 20 bedrooms, bar, restaurant, function room & meeting room. Drying room & storage areas. Packed lunches provided.

Local Attractions
10 minutes from Ballyhoura Bike Park, in historic Kilmallock. Near Lough Gur, Limerick Race Course & Adare.

B&B from: €37.50 - €55.00

Host(s): Margaret Atalla

20

Facilities

Closed 24 - 28 December

Absolute Hotel & Spa

Hotel ★ ★ ★ ★   Map 6 H 7

Sir Harry's Mall,
Limerick
Tel: +353-61-463600
Email: info@absolutehotel.com
Web: www.absolutehotel.com
GPS: N +52° 40' 2.27"   W -8° 37' 11.07"

Location
Located in city centre overlooking Abbey River on a quiet street. Easy access to Shannon Airport and all major routes.

Property Highlights
Modern, chic, 4 star hotel, free WiFi & internet. Escape Spa and Vanilla Brown's hairdresser. Great value menus in Riverbank Restaurant. Car parking spaces available.

Local Attractions
Walking distance to Thomond Park, King John's Castle, Hunt Museum, Milk Market, Treaty Stone and Shopping District.

B&B from: €49.50 - €99.50
Suites from: €149.00 - €299.00

Host(s): Donnacha Hurley

99

Activities   Facilities

Open All Year

Best Western Pery's Hotel

Hotel ★ ★ ★   Map 6 H 7

Glentworth Street,
Limerick
Tel: +353-61-413822
Email: info@perys.ie
Web: www.perys.ie
GPS: N +52° 39' 37.95"   W -8° 37' 40.52"

Location
Less than 5 minutes walk from Limerick's bus & railway station. Excellent city centre location. 20 minutes drive from Shannon Airport.

Property Highlights
Complimentary parking facilities, free Wifi access throughout the hotel. Gym & sauna. Bar, restaurant & coffee shop.

Local Attractions
Excellently situated, within walking distance of Thomond Park, King John's Castle, Hunt Museum, Gallery of Art, Georgian House & Gardens & much more.

Room Rate from: €49.00 - €160.00

Host(s): Marie Tynan

62

Facilities

Closed 24 - 25 December

80   Ireland West   B&B Rates are per Person Sharing per Night incl. Breakfast. Room/Suite Rates are per Room per Night. See also page 08

To Book Call **+353-1-8084419** or www.irelandhotels.com

Co. Limerick
Limerick City

Carlton Castletroy Park Hotel

Hotel ★ ★ ★ Map 6 H 7

Dublin Road,
Limerick
Tel: +353-61-335566
Email: reservations.castletroy@carlton.ie
Web: www.carlton.ie/castletroy
GPS: N +52° 40' 0.69"   W -8° 34' 36.94"

Location
Just 3 miles from the city & opposite UL, 25 minutes from Shannon, 20 minutes from Bunratty, 20 minutes from Thomond Park, 2 hours from Kerry & 1 hour from Clare.

Property Highlights
Limerick's finest hotel, award-winning restaurant, free car parking, WiFi throughout hotel, C - Salon, 20m pool, jacuzzi, sauna & steam room, dedicated sports team room, Carlton Kids Club.

Local Attractions
UL Activity Centre, Thomond Park, University Concert Hall, Castletroy Golf Club, Limerick Race Course, Bunratty Folk Park, Foynes Flying Boat Museum, Archery, Dry Fly Fishing & dolphin watching.

B&B from: €59.00 - €189.00
Suites from: €200.00 - €320.00

Host(s): Denis Deery

107

Closed 23 - 26 December

Clifton House

Guesthouse ★ ★ ★ Map 6 H 7

Ennis Road,
Limerick
Tel: +353-61-451166
Email: cliftonhouse@eircom.net
Web: www.cliftonhouse.ie
GPS: N +52° 40' 6.60"   W -8° 39' 1.23"

Location
We are situated on the main Limerick/Shannon Road. Within walking distance of city centre, famous Thomond Park and close to Gaelic Grounds. Private car parking.

Property Highlights
Family run quiet guesthouse, situated on its own grounds. Spacious TV lounge where complimentary tea/coffee is served. Free web access.

Local Attractions
Easy access to city centre, Hunt Museum, St. John's Castle, St. Mary's Cathedral. Bunratty Castle & Folk Park are just a 15 minute drive.

B&B from: €35.00 - €45.00

Host(s): Michael & Mary Powell

16

Closed 24 January - 13 February

Kilmurry Lodge Hotel

Hotel ★ ★ ★ Map 6 H 7

Dublin Road, Castletroy,
Limerick
Tel: +353-61-331133
Email: info@kilmurrylodge.com
Web: www.kilmurrylodge.com
GPS: N +52° 40' 7.20"   W -8° 33' 11.67"

Location
Located on the Dublin Road (N7) in Castletroy. Adjacent to the University of Limerick and National Technology Park.

Property Highlights
Our bedrooms are comfortable and spacious with an extensive breakfast buffet in Flanagan's Restaurant. Nelligan's Bar offers an authentic Irish welcome and friendly service.

Local Attractions
The University Sports Arena and Concert Hall are located close to the hotel. Thomond Park, the Home of Munster Rugby, is 5km away.

Room Rate from: €59.00 - €99.00

Host(s): Siobhan Hoare

102

Closed 24 - 27 December

B&B Rates are per Person Sharing per Night incl. Breakfast. Room/Suite Rates are per Room per Night. See also page 08

Ireland West   81

Co. Limerick - Co. Mayo

To Book Call **+353-1-8084419** or www.irelandhotels.com

Limerick City / Achill Island

Maldron Hotel Limerick

Hotel ★ ★ ★   Map 6 H 7

Southern Ring Road, Roxboro,
Limerick
Tel: +353-61-436100
Email: info.limerick@maldronhotels.com
Web: www.maldronhotels.com
GPS: N +52° 38' 50.44"   W -8° 37' 6.97"

Location
Conveniently located just off the newly opened southern ring road and just 5 minutes drive from Limerick City Centre.

Property Highlights
The hotel boasts well appointed accommodation, superb leisure club, extensive dining options, as well as 12 state of the art meeting rooms which include WiFi & broadband accommodating up to 60 pax.

Local Attractions
Dolans pub & restaurant with traditional Irish music seven nights a week. University Concert Hall. Belltable Arts Centre, art and culture.

Room Rate from: €59.00 - €199.00

Host(s): Emma Dalton
199

Facilities

Closed 23 - 27 December

No 1 Pery Square, Hotel & Spa

Hotel ★ ★ ★ ★   Map 6 H 7

Pery Square, Georgian Quarter,
Limerick City
Tel: +353-61-402402
Email: info@oneperysquare.com
Web: www.oneperysquare.com
GPS: N +52° 39' 29.67"   W -8° 37' 47.72"

Location
City centre location (Limerick) only 20 minutes from Shannon Int. Airport. 5 minutes walk from train & bus station. Located close to main shopping district.

Property Highlights
Best Irish Boutique Hotel Spa awarded by Tatler Magazine. Award-winning restaurant, heavenly beds in each individually designed room.

Local Attractions
Bunratty Castle, Hunt Museum, People's Park, Medieval Quarter in Limerick, Adare Village, King John's Castle.

Room Rate from: €135.00 - €195.00
Suites from: €250.00 - €350.00

Host(s): Patricia Roberts
20

Activities   Facilities

Closed 24 - 28 December

Achill Cliff House Hotel

Hotel ★ ★ ★   Map 9 C 14

Keel, Achill Island,
Co. Mayo
Tel: +353-98-43400
Email: info@achillcliff.com
Web: www.achillcliff.com
GPS: N +53° 58' 33.90"   W -10° 4' 52.44"

Location
Superbly located in Keel, beside the beach, looks out at Minaun Cliffs & Atlantic Ocean with Slieve Mor Mountain in the background.

Property Highlights
Panoramic views. Excellent restaurant, wonderful home baking, freshly caught fish carefully prepared daily. Delicious breakfast, spacious rooms, sauna, wireless internet, reading room.

Local Attractions
Ideal for a walking holiday, maps available, surfing and water sports, golf, deserted village, scenic drives, beside beach, fishing.

B&B from: €35.00 - €60.00

Host(s): Teresa McNamara
10

Facilities

Closed 10 January - 10 February

B&B Rates are per Person Sharing per Night incl. Breakfast. Room/Suite Rates are per Room per Night. See also page 08

To Book Call **+353-1-8084419** or www.irelandhotels.com

Co. Mayo

Achill Island / Ballina

Óstán Oileán Acla

Hotel ★ ★ ★   Map 9 C 14

Achill Sound, Achill,
Co. Mayo
Tel: +353-98-45138
Email: reservations@achillislandhotel.com
Web: www.achillislandhotel.com
GPS: N +53° 55' 58.55"   W -9° 55' 10.05"

Location

Close to Knock Airport. 40 minutes from Castlebar, Co. Mayo.

Property Highlights

Situated on an island joined to the mainland by a bridge. 5 Blue Flag Beaches. Exceptional walking & cycling routes throughout the island.

Local Attractions

Gráinne Mhaol's (Pirate Queen) Castle, historic sites - Kildavnet Graveyard & the Deserted Village. Surfer's paradise. Highest sea cliffs in Europe.

B&B from: €35.00 - €60.00

Host(s): Una McLoughlin   26

Facilities

Closed 25 December

Ballina Manor Hotel

Hotel   Map 10 F 15

Barrett Street, Ballina,
Co. Mayo
Tel: +353-96-80900
Email: info@ballinamanorhotel.com
Web: www.ballinamanorhotel.com
GPS: N +54° 6' 41.76"   W -9° 9' 17.32"

Location

Located in the heart of Ballina Town overlooking the River Moy & the Ridgepool - world famous for salmon fishing. An ideal base for guests touring the West & North West of Ireland.

Property Highlights

Re-opening Jan '11, refurbished to the highest standard with Leisure Centre. The Restaurant uses only the freshest locally sourced ingredients & has spectacular views overlooking the River Moy.

Local Attractions

Céide Fields, Jackie Clarke Library & Archives, Foxford Woollen Mills Visitor Centre, Michael Davitt Museum, Tom Ruane Park, The Cloghgle Portal Dolmen, Belleek Woods, Ballina Golf Course.

Room Rate from: €69.00 - €189.00

Host(s): Sinéad Costello   69

Activities

Facilities

Closed 24 - 27 December

Belleek Castle

Hotel ★ ★ ★   Map 10 F 15

Belleek, Ballina,
Co. Mayo
Tel: +353-96-22400
Email: belleekcastlehotel@eircom.net
Web: www.belleekcastle.com
GPS: N +54° 7' 59.79"   W -9° 8' 42.08"

Location

1 hour from Knock Airport, 1 hour from Sligo Airport, 10 minutes from Train & Bus Station, 5 minutes from town.

Property Highlights

Lovely walks in woods. Armada Bar, Restaurant. Rooms with 4 poster beds. Set in a quiet location, ideal for relaxing.

Local Attractions

River Moy fishing, Enniscrone Beach, Ballina Golf Club, Foxford Woollen Mills, Ceide Fields.

B&B from: €80.00 - €95.00

Host(s): Jacqueline Doran   10

Facilities

Closed 30 September   22 April

B&B Rates are per Person Sharing per Night incl. Breakfast. Room/Suite Rates are per Room per Night. See also page 08

Co. Mayo

To Book Call **+353-1-8084419** or www.irelandhotels.com

Ballina

Downhill House Hotel & Eagles Leisure Club

Hotel ★ ★ ★ Map 10 F 15

Ballina,
Co. Mayo
Tel: +353-96-21033
Email: info@downhillhotel.ie
Web: www.downhillhotel.ie
GPS: N +54° 7' 2.79"   W -9° 8' 8.41"

Location
Located on the periphery of Ballina, the Salmon capital of Ireland. Close to Ballina Train Station, Knock Airport & Sligo Airport.

Property Highlights
Celebrated 75 years in business & managed by the Moylett Family in 2010. Landscaped gardens, delicious home produced & cooked foods.

Local Attractions
Foxford Woollen Mills, Ceide Fields, Davitt Museum, National Museum of Country Life, Fr. Peyton Centre, Knock Shrine, Hennigan's Heritage Farm. River, lake, deep sea fishing. Six 18 hole golf courses.

B&B from: €85.00 - €99.00
Suites from: €250.00 - €350.00

Host(s): Karen Moylett

Closed 22 - 26 December

Downhill Inn

Hotel ★ ★ ★ Map 10 F 15

Sligo Road, Ballina,
Co. Mayo
Tel: +353-96-73444
Email: info@downhillinn.ie
Web: www.downhillinn.com
GPS: N +54° 7' 9.90"   W -9° 8' 6.19"

Location
Located 1.5km from Ballina on the N59 (Sligo Rd). Near the town's Bus or Train station or within 40 minutes from Ireland West Airport (Knock) or Sligo Airport.

Property Highlights
Family-owned 3* contemporary hotel with well appointed en suite rooms to suit both business & leisure guests alike. The Bar & Restaurant menus offer a selection of fresh local produce for all tastes.

Local Attractions
Superb fishing on nearby River Moy, Lough Conn or Killala Bay. In the midst of excellent links golf courses - Enniscrone, Rosses Point or Carne. Surrounded by magnificent scenery & historical sites.

B&B from: €45.00 - €70.00

Host(s): John Raftery / Nicola Moylett

Closed 21 - 28 December

Mount Falcon

Hotel ★ ★ ★ ★ Map 10 F 15

Foxford Road, Ballina,
Co. Mayo
Tel: +353-96-74472
Email: info@mountfalcon.com
Web: www.mountfalcon.com
GPS: N +54° 3' 24.74"   W -9° 9' 25.37"

Location
Located between Foxford & Ballina, 10 minutes from train & bus, 35 minutes from Knock Airport.

Property Highlights
Family-run with self catering options. Fishing on the River Moy. Spa with leisure facilities. 2 AA Rosettes, AA Hotel of the Year 2010.

Local Attractions
Fishing, Childrens' Play area, Golf - 12 courses within 1 hours drive, Foxford Woollen Mills, Ceide Fields, Enniscrone Seaweed Baths.

B&B from: €130.00 - €300.00
Suites from: €480.00 - €480.00

Host(s): Alan Maloney

Closed 23 - 28 December

Ireland West

B&B Rates are per Person Sharing per Night incl. Breakfast. Room/Suite Rates are per Room per Night. **See also page 08**

Co. Mayo

Ballyhaunis / Belmullet

Website

Mobile App

Printed Guide

facebook.com/irelandhotels

irelandhotels.com/onlineguide

Courthouse (The)

Guesthouse — Map 10 G 13

Main Street, Ballyhaunis,
Co. Mayo
Tel: +353-94-963 0068
Email: info@courthouse.ie
Web: www.courthouse.ie
GPS: N +53° 45' 49.32"   W -8° 45' 59.47"

Built to a 3*** specification

Location
Located 10 minutes from Knock Airport, with daily flights to Dublin & the UK. 5 minutes walk from train station servicing Dublin Heuston in 2 hours 30 minutes.

Property Highlights
All rooms en suite with flat screen TV & broadband. An Lochán Bar shows all major sporting events on Sky Sports & ESPN.

Local Attractions
Variety of local top class golf courses as well as angling in many of the surrounding lakes.

B&B from: €35.00 - €45.00

Host(s): Tommy Leonard

10

Facilities

Closed Christmas Day

Sea Rod Inn

Guesthouse ★ ★ — Map 9 C 16

Doohoma, Belmullet,
Co. Mayo
Tel: +353-97-86767
Email: info@thesearodinn.ie
Web: www.thesearodinn.ie
GPS: N +54° 4' 12.38"   W -9° 57' 8.40"

Location
Beside sea, overlooking Achill Island. 90 minutes from Knock Airport, 45 minutes from train station in Ballina.

Property Highlights
Located on the southern shore of Doohoma Peninsula. Stunning, panoramic views of Achill Island and the Atlantic Ocean. Peaceful. Friendly. Family-owned and run.

Local Attractions
9 Hole Golf Courses, Sandy Beaches, Walks, Fishing, Tennis, Squash, Pitch & Putt.

B&B from: €40.00 - €60.00

Host(s): Bernie Barrett

9

Activities   Facilities

Closed 25 December

Ireland West

Co. Mayo

To Book Call **+353-1-8084419** or www.irelandhotels.com

Castlebar

Harlequin Hotel

Hotel ★ ★ ★ ★ Map 9 E 14

Lannagh Road, Castlebar,
Co. Mayo
Tel: +353-94-928 6200
Email: info@harlequin.ie
Web: www.harlequinhotel.ie
GPS: N +53° 51' 12.51"   W -9° 18' 20.37"

Location
Located beside shopping & theatre district in Castlebar town centre. 5 minutes from train station & 1 minutes walk to bus. Adjacent to Royal Theatre Castlebar.

Property Highlights
Business hotel, contemporary & chic in design. Castlebar's only 4* hotel. Award-winning Harlequin Restaurant is open daily serving the best Irish & local cuisine. Complimentary broadband in all rooms.

Local Attractions
Nat. Museum of Country Life, Mayo Peace Park, Royal Theatre Castlebar, Foxford Woollen Mills, Westport House, Ballintubber Abbey, Ceide Fields, Croagh Patrick. Some on our doorstep /a few mins drive.

Room Rate from: €69.00 - €139.00
Suites from: €99.00 - €169.00

Host(s): Lynda Foley

90

Activities   Facilities

Closed 22 - 27 December

Kennys Guest House

Guesthouse ★ ★ ★ Map 9 E 14

Lucan Street, Castlebar,
Co. Mayo
Tel: +353-94-902 3091
Email: info@kennysguesthouse.com
Web: www.kennysguesthouse.com
GPS: N +53° 51' 28.52"   W -9° 17' 47.16"

Location
Situated in the town centre. Close to the theatre, hospitals & art gallery.

Property Highlights
Freshly cooked breakfast by owner chef. WiFi when you need it. Secure off street lock up parking. Free range eggs from our farm.

Local Attractions
Walking distance to all activities. Golf course, Museum of Country Life, Knock, Ballintubber Abbey, Foxford Woollen Mills, Ceide Fields and many more beautiful attractions.

B&B from: €35.00 - €45.00

Host(s): Susanna Kenny

8

Facilities

Open All Year

TF Royal Hotel & Royal Theatre

Hotel ★ ★ ★ Map 9 E 14

Old Westport Road, Castlebar,
Co. Mayo
Tel: +353-94-902 3111
Email: info@tfroyalhotel.com
Web: www.tfroyalhotel.com
GPS: N +53° 51' 11.50"   W -9° 18' 14.48"

Location
Castlebar Town Centre, close to Mayo General Hospital, GMIT 3rd Level College, train & bus station, 40 minutes from Knock International Airport.

Property Highlights
Royal Theatre hosts major Acts. WiFi, modern Conference Centre, Café Bar, Restaurant & Carvery, Harlequin Shopping Centre, in house Hairdresser & Beauty Therapist.

Local Attractions
The Royal Theatre. National Museum, Ballintubber Abbey, Golf Course, Tennis Club, Angling, Leisure Complex, walking routes. Ideal for touring. Harlequin Shopping Centre.

B&B from: €55.00 - €85.00

Host(s): Pat & Mary Jennings

27

Activities   Facilities

Closed 24 - 26 December

Ireland West   B&B Rates are per Person Sharing per Night incl. Breakfast. Room/Suite Rates are per Room per Night.   See also page 08

To Book Call **+353-1-8084419** or www.irelandhotels.com

Co. Mayo

Charlestown / Claremorris / Cong

Riverside Guesthouse

| Guesthouse ★ ★ | Map 10 G 14 |

**Church Street, Charlestown,
Co. Mayo**
Tel: +353-94-925 4200
Email: riversiderestaurant@eircom.net
Web: www.riversiderest.com
GPS: N +53° 57' 49.09" W -8° 47' 46.47"

Location
In town centre. Situated off bypass on intersection of N17 & N5 primary routes. 6km to Knock Airport. 25 minutes from Sligo.

Property Highlights
Charming, family-run guesthouse, all rooms en suite. Good central location in town. Award-winning chef owner.

Local Attractions
Ideal base for touring the west of Ireland. 15 minutes from the Museum of Country Life. Turlough Golf Course 7km. Foxford Woollen Mills, Céide Fields & Croagh Patrick all in close proximity.

B&B from: €36.00 - €38.00

Host(s): Anthony & Anne Kelly

8

Facilities

Closed 23 - 27 December

McWilliam Park Hotel (The)

| Hotel ★ ★ ★ ★ | Map 10 F 13 |

**Claremorris,
Co. Mayo**
Tel: +353-94-937 8000
Email: info@mcwilliamparkhotel.ie
Web: www.mcwilliampark.ie
GPS: N +53° 43' 31.51" W -8° 59' 22.26"

Location
Claremorris in the heart of the West. Direct rail link from Dublin and 20 minutes from Ireland West Airport (Knock).

Property Highlights
4**** Luxury Hotel offering superb dining & accommodation and leisure facilities including 18m pool jacuzzi and Karma Health & Beauty Studios.

Local Attractions
Knock Marian Shrine, Cong, Ballintubber Abbey, Museum of Country Life, Foxford Woollen Mills, Leenane, Fr. Peyton Memorial Centre, Ceide Fields.

B&B from: €55.00 - €130.00
Suites from: €190.00 - €340.00

Host(s): Fergal Ryan

103

Activities   Facilities

Open All Year

Ashford Castle

| Hotel ★ ★ ★ ★ ★ | Map 9 E 12 |

**Cong,
Co. Mayo**
Tel: +353-94-954 6003
Email: ashford@ashford.ie
Web: www.ashford.ie
GPS: N +53° 32' 4.23" W -9° 17' 7.12"

Location
Situated on the shores of Lough Corrib, 30 mins. from Galway City. 2 hours 30 mins. from Dublin Airport, 2 hours from Shannon Airport & 45 mins. from Knock Airport

Property Highlights
13th Century Castle with 83 bedrooms, all individually designed with stunning views. Two dining options, a spa and a host of activities.

Local Attractions
Situated near the village of Cong which was made famous by the making of the film "The Quiet Man" in 1952 and 30 minutes from Medieval Galway City.

B&B from: €87.50 - €212.50
Suites from: €450.00 - €950.00

Host(s): Niall Rochford

83

Activities   Facilities

Open All Year

B&B Rates are per Person Sharing per Night incl. Breakfast. Room/Suite Rates are per Room per Night. See also page 08   Ireland West   87

Co. Mayo

To Book Call **+353-1-8084419** or www.irelandhotels.com

Cong / Kiltimagh / Knock

Lisloughrey Lodge

Hotel ★ ★ ★ ★   Map 9 E 12

The Quay, Cong,
Co. Mayo
Tel: +353-94- 954 5400
Email: lodge@lisloughrey.ie
Web: www.lisloughrey.ie
GPS: N +53° 31' 56.82"   W -9° 16' 54.70"

Location
Close to Galway & Connemara. Overlooking Lough Corrib next to the village of Cong and Ashford Estate.

Property Highlights
Award-winning Salt Restaurant, Sundari Treatment Rooms, lakeside setting with mature woodlands. Hot tub & sauna outdoors.

Local Attractions
Beautiful walks in the woods, cruising & fishing on Lough Corrib, golf, falconry & horse riding, Connemara & Westport.

B&B from: €75.00 - €100.00

Host(s): Marc MacCloskey
50

Facilities

Closed 23 - 26 December

Park Hotel Kiltimagh

Hotel ★ ★ ★   Map 10 F 14

Swinford Road, Kiltimagh,
Mayo
Tel: +353-94-937 4922
Email: info@parkhotelmayo.com
Web: www.parkhotelmayo.com
GPS: N +53° 51' 26.15"   W -8° 59' 35.91"

Location
Located only a few minutes stroll from Kiltimagh town. Minutes from Ireland West Airport Knock.

Property Highlights
A warm welcome awaits you & it is an ideal base for touring the West. Enjoy our individually decorated de luxe or executive rooms, full fitness centre. Dine in our café bar or à la carte restaurant.

Local Attractions
Sporting & outdoor opportunities, fishing of all sorts. Watersports, hiking and walking, golf links & courses, horse riding & cycling. Sandy EU Blue Flag beaches, clear waters & beautiful islands.

B&B from: €50.00 - €90.00
Suites from: €170.00 - €270.00

Host(s): Noel Lafferty
45

Activities

Facilities

Closed 24 - 27 December

Knock House Hotel

Hotel ★ ★ ★   Map 10 G 13

Ballyhaunis Road, Knock,
Co. Mayo
Tel: +353-94-938 8088
Email: info@knockhousehotel.ie
Web: www.knockhousehotel.ie
GPS: N +53° 47' 27.68"   W -8° 54' 51.63"

Location
The Hotel is located in the tranquil village of Knock. Close by is Claremorris Train Station and Ireland West Airport Knock.

Property Highlights
68 superb bedrooms, 6 designed for limited mobility users. Four Seasons Restaurant and Glazed Lounge offer superb food all day.

Local Attractions
Located in 100 acres and situated adjacent to the hotel are The Basilica, Museum, Bookshop and numerous chapels, with beautiful walks.

B&B from: €55.00 - €75.00

Host(s): Brian Crowley
68

Activities   **Facilities**

Food for Kids

Open All Year

88   Ireland West   B&B Rates are per Person Sharing per Night incl. Breakfast. Room/Suite Rates are per Room per Night. **See also page 08**

To Book Call **+353-1-8084419** or www.irelandhotels.com

Co. Mayo

Mulranny / Pontoon / Westport

Mulranny Park Hotel

Hotel ★ ★ ★ ★   Map 9 D 14

**Mulranny, Westport,
Co. Mayo**
Tel: +353-98-36000
Email: info@mulrannyparkhotel.ie
Web: www.mulrannyparkhotel.ie
GPS: N +53° 54' 21.63"   W -9° 46' 57.55"

Location
Perched above the glittering waters of the Atlantic Ocean, this is a stunning destination. Only minutes from Achill Island and a short drive to Westport.

Property Highlights
This historical hotel has retained its original charm and character. Superb cuisine in the elegant Nephin Restaurant and Waterfront Bar. Extensive leisure facilities.

Local Attractions
Overlooks the Blue Flag beach. Activities on our doorstep include supervised kayaking, surfing, sailing, biking, walking and golf. Uniquely located on the Great Western Greenway walk and cycle trail.

B&B from: €55.00 - €89.00

Host(s): Dermot Madigan
41

Activities   Facilities

Closed 03 - 29 January

Healys Restaurant & Fishing Lodge

Hotel ★ ★   Map 9 F 14

**Pontoon, Foxford,
Co. Mayo**
Tel: +353-94-925 6443
Email: info@healyspontoon.com
Web: www.healyspontoon.com
GPS: N +53° 58' 37.90"   W -9° 12' 44.00"

Location
10 minutes from Foxford Station, 20 minutes Castlebar Station, 20 minutes Ballina Station, 30 minutes Knock Airport, Bus stop outside hotel.

Property Highlights
Food is 60% of our turnover - that speaks for ourselves. Fishing / golf / walking - We can arrange all your needs. "Probably the best food in the west".

Local Attractions
River Moy, Lough Conn & Cullen, Golf: Enniscrone, Carne, Ballina, Castlebar, Westport & Swinford, Horse Riding, Museum of Country Life, Foxford Woolen Mills. We can arrange all your needs.

B&B from: €35.00 - €35.00

Host(s): John Dever & Josette Maurer
14

Activities   Facilities

Open All Year

Augusta Lodge

Guesthouse ★ ★ ★   Map 9 E 13

**Golf Links Road, Westport,
Co. Mayo**
Tel: +353-98-28900
Email: info@augustalodge.ie
Web: www.augustalodge.ie
GPS: N +53° 48' 23.43"   W -9° 31' 40.35"

Location
Augusta Lodge is a 10 minute stroll from the picturesque, award-winning, Heritage Town of Westport, on the golf course road.

Property Highlights
Augusta Lodge has its own private all-weather 9 hole synthetic putting/chipping green for guests' use. Sharpen your game before your round.

Local Attractions
Local attractions include golf, horse riding, kayaking, cycling, fishing and numerous scenic drives and walks, including Ireland's Holy Mountain Croagh Patrick.

B&B from: €30.00 - €50.00

Host(s): Dave O'Regan
9

Facilities

Closed 23 27 December

B&B Rates are per Person Sharing per Night incl. Breakfast. Room/Suite Rates are per Room per Night. See also page 08

Co. Mayo

To Book Call +353-1-8084419 or www.irelandhotels.com

Westport

Boffin Lodge

Guesthouse ★ ★ ★ Map 9 E 13

The Quay, Westport,
Co. Mayo
Tel: +353-98-26092
Email: info@boffinlodge.com
Web: www.boffinlodge.com
GPS: N +53° 47' 54.64" W -9° 32' 33.78"

Location
In Harbour Area of Westport Town close to many pubs, hotels & restaurants.

Property Highlights
Quiet location with off street parking. Some rooms have additional features such as 4 poster beds or steam room.

Local Attractions
Located close to Westport House & Country Estate. Plus all the amenities of Westport Harbour/Quay Area.

B&B from: €35.00 - €45.00

Host(s): Patrick Aylward

10

Facilities

Open All Year

Carlton Atlantic Coast Hotel & Ayurveda C Spa

Hotel ★ ★ ★ ★ Map 9 E 13

The Quay, Westport,
Co. Mayo
Tel: +353-98-29000
Email: info@atlanticcoasthotel.com
Web: www.carlton.ie/atlantic
GPS: N +53° 47' 58.41" W -9° 32' 59.65"

Location
Hotel is over looking Clew Bay. 40 minutes from Knock Airport. 90 minutes from Galway & Sligo. 5 minutes from the train station.

Property Highlights
One of Westport's finest & most popular hotels, received Failte Ireland Gold Medal. Blue Wave Restaurant - AA Rosette, Fishworks Cafe, WiFi, Ayurveda C-Spa, free cycle hire, pool, secure/free parking.

Local Attractions
Plenty to do and see in & around Westport including Croagh Patrick, Clew Bay, Clare Island, Westport House, Achill Island, Bertra Bay, Killary Adventure, Foxford Woollen Mills, Deep Sea Fishing.

B&B from: €59.00 - €129.00
Suites from: €180.00 - €310.00

Host(s): Garrett McGuinness

85

Facilities

Closed 23 - 26 December

Castlecourt Hotel
Spa, Leisure, Conference

Hotel ★ ★ ★ Map 9 E 13

Castlebar Street, Westport,
Co. Mayo
Tel: +353-98-55088
Email: info@castlecourthotel.ie
Web: www.castlecourthotel.ie
GPS: N +53° 48' 4.54" W -9° 31' 6.99"

Location
Located in the heart of Westport Town, within 5 minutes walk of Train Station & 60km from Ireland West Airport.

Property Highlights
Family-run hotel, we have earned our reputation as a home away from home as well as being one of the largest hotels in the West of Ireland. Leisure Centre and Resort Spa.

Local Attractions
Croagh Patrick, Blue Flag Beaches, Golf, Tennis, Horse Riding, Cycle and Walking Routes, Surfing, Sailing, Fishing, Angling, Westport House and National Museum of Country Life located nearby.

B&B from: €45.00 - €119.00
Suites from: €130.00 - €340.00

Host(s): Anne Corcoran / Joseph Corcoran

148

Activities Facilities

Closed 24 - 26 December

B&B Rates are per Person Sharing per Night incl. Breakfast. Room/Suite Rates are per Room per Night. See also page 08

Co. Mayo
Westport

Clew Bay Hotel

Hotel ★★★ Map 9 E 13

James Street, Westport,
Co. Mayo
Tel: +353-98-28088
Email: info@clewbayhotel.com
Web: www.clewbayhotel.com
GPS: N +53° 48' 1.77"   W -9° 31' 24.05"

Location
Westport town centre location, ideal base for touring the West Coast, Achill Island and Connemara. Ireland West Airport transfers available.

Property Highlights
A beautifully appointed, family-run hotel with genuine Irish hospitality. All guests have complimentary access to Westport Leisure Park, located next door. Rooms have complimentary internet access.

Local Attractions
Westport House, Croagh Patrick. We specialise in organising all activities, e.g. Hill Walking, Surfing, Golf, Kayaking, Boat Trips, Cycling & Angling.

B&B from: €50.00 - €95.00

Host(s): Maria Ruddy & Darren Madden

40

Facilities

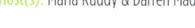

Closed 20 - 27 December

Hotel Westport

Hotel ★★★★ Map 9 E 13

Newport Road, Westport,
Co. Mayo
Tel: +353-98-25122
Email: reservations@hotelwestport.ie
Web: www.hotelwestport.ie
GPS: N +53° 48' 3.44"   W -9° 31' 42.79"

Location
4* Hotel Westport is located in the heart of Westport, 5 minutes from Westport Train Station, 50 minutes from Knock Airport & 3 hours drive from Dublin.

Property Highlights
Secluded in beautiful woodland, facilities include Maple Bar, Islands Restaurant, Ocean Spirit Spa & Leisure, Hair Salon, Children's Club, Free Car Parking.

Local Attractions
Local Attractions include Croagh Patrick, Blue Flag Beaches, Fishing, Golf, Horse Riding, Surfing, Cycling, Walking, Westport House, National Museum of Country Life.

B&B from: €55.00 - €95.00
Suites from: €160.00 - €240.00

Host(s): Declan Heneghan

129

Activities

Facilities

Open All Year

WESTPORT HOUSE & PIRATE ADVENTURE PARK

The Home of Great Experiences

Westport House & Pirate Adventure Park is one of Ireland's most popular days out for the entire family. One of those rare attractions, it appeals to everyone with its extraordinary mixture of history and heritage blended with the thrills of the theme park.

Visit **www.WestportHouse.ie** for more information. Buy tickets online - up to **10%** off!

Co. Mayo

To Book Call **+353-1-8084419** or www.irelandhotels.com

Westport

Knockranny House Hotel & Spa

Hotel ★ ★ ★ ★   Map 9 E 13

Westport,
Co. Mayo
Tel: +353-98-28600
Email: info@khh.ie
Web: www.khh.ie
GPS: N +53° 48' 7.68"   W -9° 30' 28.52"

Location
Set in secluded grounds overlooking the picturesque town of Westport, with breathtaking views of Croagh Patrick and Clew Bay.

Property Highlights
The fine dining restaurant La Fougère, awarded Best Hotel Restaurant in Ireland, has also achieved two AA Rosettes for culinary excellence.

Local Attractions
Westport boasts an almost endless range of activities suitable for every taste including golf, fishing, equestrian stables. Tourist attractions include Westport House & Kylemore Abbey.

B&B from: €70.00 - €145.00
Suites from: €230.00 - €590.00

Host(s): Geraldine & Adrian Noonan

97

Facilities

Closed 23 - 27 December

Mill Times Hotel Westport

Hotel ★ ★ ★   Map 9 E 13

Town Centre, Mill Street, Westport,
Co. Mayo
Tel: +353-98-29200
Email: info@milltimeshotel.ie
Web: www.milltimeshotel.ie
GPS: N +53° 47' 54.57"   W -9° 31' 20.40"

Location
Westport Town Centre, close to all amenities, walking distance to train station, 1 minute from bus stop.

Property Highlights
Recently refurbished, friendly & welcoming, family-run boutique hotel, award-winning chefs specialising in seafood & steak, relaxing atmosphere in hotel.

Local Attractions
Ireland's tidiest town 2009 & 2008, bike hire, sea fishing, beach & hill walks, Croagh Patrick, Blue Flag Beaches.

Room Rate from: €59.00 - €199.00
Suites from: €89.00 - €249.00

Host(s): Tony Conneely

34

Activities   Facilities

Closed 24 - 25 December

Quay West

Guesthouse ★ ★   Map 9 E 13

Quay Road, Westport,
Co. Mayo
Tel: +353-98-27863
Email: quaywest@eircom.net
Web: www.quaywestport.com
GPS: N +53° 47' 55.00"   W -9° 32' 23.19"

Location
Quay West is just 10 minutes away from Westport town and 5 minutes from the harbour and directly opposite the Westport Woods Hotel.

Property Highlights
Guests can enjoy the superb leisure facilities at Westport Woods Hotel at discounted rates. Rooms have power showers & orthopaedic beds. TV lounge for guests' comfort.

Local Attractions
Quay West is the perfect base for touring beautiful Mayo, Connemara & relaxing in some of Westport's most famous pubs & restaurants.

B&B from: €32.00 - €40.00

Host(s): David Kelly

6

Facilities

Closed 23 - 28 December

To Book Call +353-1-8084419 or www.irelandhotels.com

Co. Mayo
Westport

Westport Plaza Hotel
Spa, Leisure, Conference

Hotel ★ ★ ★ ★ Map 9 E 13

Castlebar Street, Westport,
Co. Mayo
Tel: +353-98-51166
Email: info@westportplazahotel.ie
Web: www.westportplazahotel.ie
GPS: N +53° 48' 3.73" W -9° 31' 9.96"

Location
Located in the heart of Westport town, within 5 minutes walk of train station and 60km from Ireland West Airport.

Property Highlights
A fusion of contemporary chic and classic elegance awaits you as you unwind and relax in ultimate luxury. Sophisticated dining in Restaurant Merlot, Spa Sula & Resort Leisure Centre.

Local Attractions
Croagh Patrick, Blue Flag Beaches, Golf, Tennis, Horse Riding, Cycle & Walking Routes, Surfing, Sailing, Fishing, Angling, Westport House & National Museum of Country Life located nearby.

B&B from: €65.00 - €129.00
Suites from: €150.00 - €358.00

Host(s): Anne Corcoran, Joseph Corcoran

88

Activities
Facilities

Open All Year

Westport Woods Hotel & Spa

Hotel ★ ★ ★ Map 9 E 13

Quay Road, Westport,
Co. Mayo
Tel: +353-98-25811
Email: info@westportwoodshotel.com
Web: www.westportwoodshotel.com
GPS: N +53° 47' 57.42" W -9° 32' 26.07"

Location
Ideally located - halfway between the town centre of Westport and the Quay, on private woodlands.

Property Highlights
We have got a lot more than you'd expect - Equestrian Centre, Go!Kids! Club, Leisure Centre and Spa, plus all the usual facilities.

Local Attractions
Westport has lots to do and plenty to see... Mountains, horse riding, museums, watersports, golf, fishing... Where do you start?

B&B from: €35.00 - €110.00

Host(s): Michael Lennon & Joanne McEniff

122

Activities

Facilities

Open All Year

Wyatt Hotel

Hotel ★ ★ ★ Map 9 E 13

The Octagon, Westport,
Co. Mayo
Tel: +353-98-25027
Email: info@wyatthotel.com
Web: www.wyatthotel.com
GPS: N +53° 47' 57.06" W -9° 31' 31.03"

Location
A charming boutique hotel in the heart of Westport, Co. Mayo, nestled between the peaks of Croagh Patrick and the deep blue seas of Clew Bay & the Atlantic Ocean.

Property Highlights
Named after famed Georgian architect James Wyatt, credited with the design of picturesque Westport. Enjoy tea/coffee at JW's Brasserie or a relaxing drink in the traditional Cobblers Bar & Courtyard.

Local Attractions
Within short drives from Westport are the most beautiful, biggest and safest beaches in Europe, many of which are Blue Flag. Westport Golf Course 18 Hole Championship Course. Westport Leisure Park.

B&B from: €49.00 - €130.00
Suites from: €150.00 - €300.00

Host(s): Barney Clarke

52

Activities
Facilities

Closed 20 - 28 December

B&B Rates are per Person Sharing per Night incl. Breakfast. Room/Suite Rates are per Room per Night. See also page 08

Co. Roscommon - Co. Sligo   To Book Call **+353-1-8084419** or www.irelandhotels.com

Ballyfarnon / Roscommon Town / Ballygawley

Kilronan Castle Estate & Spa

Hotel ★ ★ ★ ★   Map 10 I 15

Ballyfarnon,
Co. Roscommon
Tel: +353-71-961 8000
Email: enquiries@kilronancastle.ie
Web: www.kilronancastle.ie
GPS: N +54° 3' 50.90"   W -8° 10' 39.23"

Location
This secluded, luxury, Roscommon Castle Hotel is majestically set on the shores of Lough Meelagh. 35km from Sligo & 20km from both Carrick-on-Shannon & Boyle.

Property Highlights
We provide the highest level of comfort & service with a world class spa & thermal suite; leisure, conference & wedding facilities; pool; fine dining restaurant. Designed with your desires in mind.

Local Attractions
Step back in time when you tour the Arigna Coal Mines & Museum, enjoy a stroll & boat ride in Lough Key Forest Park. Hike or bike around the area. Horse riding, fishing & adventure centre all close.

B&B from: €49.50 - €110.00
Suites from: €149.00 - €270.00

Host(s): Michelle Coghlan

84

Activities Facilities

Open All Year

Gleesons Townhouse & Restaurant

Guesthouse ★ ★ ★   Map 10 I 12

Market Square, Roscommon Town,
Co. Roscommon
Tel: +353-90-662 6954
Email: info@gleesonstownhouse.com
Web: www.gleesonstownhouse.com
GPS: N +53° 37' 51.31"   W -8° 11' 29.31"

Location
Town Centre.
Railway & Bus Station 5 minutes.
Galway 60 minutes.
Dublin 90 minutes.
Knock 60 minutes.
Shannon 90 minutes.

Property Highlights
Family Run.
Town Centre Location.
Bridgestone Guide.
Artisan Food & Wine Shop.
Customer Carpark. Euro/Toques Chef.
In-House Bakery. Locally Sourced Food.

Local Attractions
Roscommon Golf Club. Equestrian centre. Suck Valley walking. Coarse fishing. Viking boat tours. Heritage sites - Roscommon Castle/Abbey, Cruacla Aí, Rathcrogh. Famine Museum.

B&B from: €50.00 - €75.00
Suites from: €150.00 - €195.00

Host(s): Mary & Eamonn Gleeson

19

Facilities

Closed 25 - 26 December

Castle Dargan Golf Hotel Wellness

Hotel ★ ★ ★ ★   Map 10 H 15

Ballygawley,
Co. Sligo
Tel: +353-71-911 8080
Email: info@castledargan.com
Web: www.castledargan.com
GPS: N +54° 11' 50.64"   W -8° 26' 11.90"

Location
8 minutes from Sligo Town Centre, just off the N4 Sligo to Dublin Road. 12km from Sligo Airport, 2 hours from Dublin and only 40 minutes to Ireland West Airport Knock.

Property Highlights
Luxury abounds! Visited by WB Yeats. Resort includes Contemporary Hotel, Period House, Castle Ruins, Darren Clarke Golf Course & Icon Spa. Exquisite cuisine, accommodation & relaxation awaits.

Local Attractions
Yeats Memorial, Sligo Abbey, Sligo Folk Park, Inishmurray Island, Carrowmore Megalithic Tomb. Castle Dargan Activities: Golfing, Surfing, Hill Walking, Angling, Horse Riding, Theatre.

B&B from: €65.00 - €150.00
Suites from: €199.00 - €400.00

Host(s): Francis Breslin

22

Activities  Facilities

Closed 24 - 26 December

B&B Rates are per Person Sharing per Night incl. Breakfast. Room/Suite Rates are per Room per Night. See also page 08

To Book Call **+353-1-8084419** or www.irelandhotels.com   **Co. Sligo**

Collooney / Enniscrone

Markree Castle

Hotel ★ ★ ★   Map 10 H 15

Collooney,
Co. Sligo
Tel: +353-71-916 7800
Email: info@markreecastle.ie
Web: www.markreecastle.ie
GPS: N +54° 10' 26.63"   W -8° 27' 42.14"

Location
Near Collooney, just 8 miles from Sligo off N4. Sligo Airport 10 miles. Train Station 1.5 miles.

Property Highlights
A unique country house hotel with old world charm, excellent food and a warm, friendly welcome.

Local Attractions
Yeats' Country, Megalithic Tombs, Horse Riding, Golf, Fishing, Surfing, Archery, Falconry.

B&B from: €49.00 - €130.00

Host(s): Charles & Mary Cooper

30

Facilities

Closed 24 - 27 December

Diamond Coast Hotel

Hotel ★ ★ ★ ★   Map 10 F 15

Bartragh, Enniscrone,
Co. Sligo
Tel: +353-96-26000
Email: info@diamondcoast.ie
Web: www.diamondcoast.ie
GPS: N +54° 12' 17.21"   W -9° 6' 10.78"

Location
Located in Enniscrone, a seaside village situated along the Atlantic Ocean on the North West coast, 7km from Ballina, Co. Mayo & 64km from Sligo town.

Property Highlights
92 spacious guestrooms & an exclusive suite, facilities include a banqueting suite ideal for weddings, catering for up to 450 guests, meeting rooms, Stir Bistro & Coral Restaurant.

Local Attractions
Excellent angling available nearby on lakes such as the River Moy & Lough Conn. Situated on the eastern shore of historic Killala Bay, Enniscrone is suitable for all water sports.

B&B from: €39.00 - €119.00

Host(s): Brian Pierson

92

Activities

Facilities

Closed 23 - 27 December

Arigna Mining Experience

Discover and Experience...

the fascinating life of a Coal Miner

A Unique Underground Tour in what was Ireland's last working Coal Mine at:
Derreenavoggy,
Arigna, Co. Roscommon.

Only 12 Miles From Carrick-on-Shannon.
Tel: 071 9646466
Web: www.arignaminingexperience.ie

B&B Rates are per Person Sharing per Night incl. Breakfast. Room/Suite Rates are per Room per Night. See also page 08   Ireland West   95

Co. Sligo

To Book Call **+353-1-8084419** or www.irelandhotels.com

Mullaghmore / Rosses Point / Sligo Town

Pier Head Hotel, Spa and Leisure Centre

Hotel ★ ★ ★ Map 13 H 17

Mullaghmore,
Co. Sligo
Tel: +353-71-916 6171
Email: reception@pierheadhotel.ie
Web: www.pierheadhotel.ie
GPS: N +54° 28' 0.75" W -8° 26' 51.41"

Location
Situated in the picturesque harbour village of Mullaghmore, on the West Coast of Ireland. Turn off N15 Sligo/Bundoran Rd at Cliffoney. Sligo 20km. Strandhill Airport 30km.

Property Highlights
Pier Head Hotel features seaweed baths, outdoor Canadian hot tub, swimming pool, Pier Perfection Salon & treatment rooms. Weekend entertainment. Magnificent views from bedrooms, restaurant & bar.

Local Attractions
Mullaghmore Beach, Classiebawn Castle, Creevykeel Court Cairn, Lissadell House, Yeats Country, Glencar Waterfall, Benbulben, Surfing, Hill Walking, Horse Riding, Scuba Diving

B&B from: €50.00 - €70.00

Host(s): John McHugh 40

Activities   Facilities

Closed 24 - 26 December

Yeats Country Hotel, Spa & Leisure Club

Hotel ★ ★ ★ Map 10 H 16

Rosses Point,
Co. Sligo
Tel: +353-71-917 7211
Email: reception@yeatscountryhotel.com
Web: www.yeatscountryhotel.com
GPS: N +54° 18' 22.18" W -8° 33' 54.72"

Location
In Rosses Point Village, just 5 miles from Sligo Town Centre. 15 minutes to Strandhill Airport & 50 minutes to Knock Airport. Opposite Rosses Point Blue Flag Beach.

Property Highlights
Family run, all rooms en suite. 2 bars, 3 restaurants, 18m pool, 34 station gym, steamroom, sauna, jacuzzi. Adjacent to Rosses Point, Co. Sligo's Championship Golf course.

Local Attractions
Co. Sligo Golf Club, Lissadell House, Yeat's Burial Grave, Glencar Waterfall, Parkes Castle, Mullaghmore, Wild Rose Waterbus, fishing charters, Yacht Club.

B&B from: €49.00 - €90.00

Host(s): Fiona McEniff 98

Activities   Facilities

Closed 20 - 27 Dec & 10 - 28 Jan

Radisson Blu Hotel & Spa Sligo

Hotel ★ ★ ★ ★ Map 10 H 16

Ballincar, Rosses Point,
Sligo
Tel: +353-71-914 0008
Email: info.sligo@radissonblu.com
Web: www.radissonblu.ie/hotel-sligo
GPS: N +54° 17' 56.76" W -8° 30' 0.21"

Location
Located near Rosses Point with stunning views of Sligo Bay. 132 luxurious bedrooms. Classiebawn Restaurant offering local and international cuisine. Benwiskin Bar offering extensive menu. Solas Spa

Property Highlights
Healthstyles offering 18m swimming pool, steam room, jacuzzi, sauna, outdoor Canadian hot tub and gym. Solas Spa offers 7 treatment rooms, thermal suite incl. razul. Stunning sea and mountain views.

Local Attractions
Located only 2km from renowned Co. Sligo Golf Club and only 5 minutes drive from Sligo City Centre - best of both worlds. Horseriding, angling and historical sites close by.

B&B from: €45.00 - €125.00

Host(s): Fergus O'Donovan 132

Activities   Facilities

Open All Year

B&B Rates are per Person Sharing per Night incl. Breakfast. Room/Suite Rates are per Room per Night. See also page 08

To Book Call **+353-1-8084419** or www.irelandhotels.com

Co. Sligo

Sligo Town / Tubbercurry

Sligo City Hotel

Hotel ★★★ Map 10 H 16

Quay Street,
Sligo
Tel: +353-71-914 4000
Email: info@sligocityhotel.com
Web: www.sligocityhotel.com
GPS: N +54° 16' 23.48"   W -8° 28' 34.47"

Location
Town centre location, Sligo Airport 8 minutes drive, Ireland West Airport Knock 45 minutes drive, walking distance from train/bus station.

Property Highlights
Offers a warm welcome to all our guests & prides itself on delivering service excellence. Bedrooms en suite with cable TV & DD phone, broadband and tea/coffee making facilities.

Local Attractions
Within 5 mile radius of 2 links golf courses. Surfing, fishing & horse riding centres locally. In the heart of Yeat's Country with spectacular scenery.

Room Rate from: €79.00 - €180.00
Suites from: €89.00 - €190.00

Host(s): Bernard Mullen & Michael Mulholland

60

Facilities

Closed 24 December - 02 January

Sligo Park Hotel & Leisure Club

Hotel ★★★★ Map 10 H 16

Pearse Road,
Sligo
Tel: +353-71-919 0400
Email: sligo@leehotels.com
Web: www.leehotels.com
GPS: N +54° 15' 16.7"   W -8° 28' 18.5"

Location
Just off the N4 on the old Dublin Road, set in private parkland and within walking distance or short suburban bus ride of Sligo town centre.

Property Highlights
Bright spacious rooms with some stunning views. Warm and welcoming lobby with open fire. Professional service where guest enjoyment is everything.

Local Attractions
Nearby beaches, woodland, lakes, the delights of Yeats Country, Lough Gill and Glencar Waterfall. Enjoy golf, water sports, shopping and the nightlife of Sligo Town.

B&B from: €37.50 - €97.50

Host(s): Gerard Moore

137

Activities

Facilities

Open All Year

Cawley's Guesthouse

Guesthouse ★★ Map 10 G 15

Emmet Street, Tubbercurry,
Co. Sligo
Tel: +353-71-918 5025
Email: cawleysguesthouse@eircom.net
Web: www.cawleysguesthouse.com
GPS: N +54° 3' 14.01"   W -8° 43' 40.98"

Location
In town centre off N17, 25 minutes from Knock and Sligo Airports, Bus Service - Derry, Sligo, Galway. 10 minutes from Ballymote train station.

Property Highlights
Friendly family-run guesthouse with bar, restaurant, banqueting, garden, parking, comfortable bedrooms with TV, tea facilities, telephone, free lobby WiFi.

Local Attractions
Wonderfully central for golf courses, mountain walks, local beaches, angling at Moy River, Lough Talt, horse trekking and Eagles Centre.

B&B from: €35.00 - €45.00

Host(s): Teresa Cawley & Pierre Krebs

14

Facilities

Closed 25 December - 02 January

B&B Rates are per Person Sharing per Night incl. Breakfast. Room/Suite Rates are per Room per Night. See also page 08

Ireland West 97

Direct low rates and great special offers guaranteed

Irelandhotels.com
We've got it covered

You can find all the best deals in all of these places

Website | Mobile App | Printed Guide |
facebook.com/irelandhotels | irelandhotels.com/onlineguide

Northern Ireland

For Detailed Maps of this Region See Pages **325-340**. Each Hotel or Guesthouse has a Map Reference to these detailed maps below the premises name.

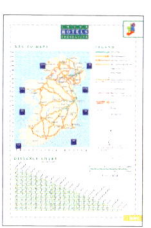

See page **325** for map with access points and driving distances

Co. Antrim
Ballycastle 103
Ballymena 103
Bushmills 103
Carnlough 104
Portrush 104
Templepatrick 105

Belfast City
Belfast City 105

Co. Derry
Aghadowey 107
Coleraine 107
Derry City 107
Limavady 108

Co. Down
Annalong 108
Newcastle 109
Newry 109

Co. Fermanagh
Enniskillen 109
Irvinestown 110

Co. Tyrone
Cookstown 111
Omagh 111

Irelandhotels.com
We've got it covered

Find your journey... in Northern Ireland.

Northern Ireland is full of fascinating gems. All you have to do is go find them.

With stunning coastal drives, cool attractions and mythical legends, it's the perfect place to get away for a few days – no matter what time of the year you visit.

northernireland
Explore More

There's the **Giant's Causeway** – an unbelievable sight to behold with its 40,000 interlocking basalt columns leading into the sea. The result of millions of years of volcanic activity? Or the work of legendary giant Finn McCool? We'll let you decide.

Then there's **Carrick-a-rede rope bridge**; dangling 80 feet high above the sea. Walk it. Then steady your nerves with a tipple at Bushmills, Ireland's oldest distillery.

That's the beauty of Northern Ireland. Everything is close by. Travel from rugged coastline to **Belfast, Northern Ireland's capital**, in minutes.

Visit the city's rejuvenated **Cathedral Quarter**. Marvel at the magnificent examples of Victorian architecture. Or pick up a bargain in one of Belfast's leading high street stores or designer boutiques.

Follow the **Saint Patrick's Trail** through **Counties Armagh and Down**. Go walking in the majestic **Mountains of Mourne**, the inspiration behind C.S. Lewis's 'The Chronicles of Narnia'. Or visit **Lough Neagh** and **Strangford Lough** – a haven for wildlife, birdlife and a wide range of outdoor activities.

Take to the lakes in **Fermanagh**. A 70km stretch of water dotted with islands and ancient ruins. Linked to the River Shannon, it's the longest navigable inland waterway in Europe.

For myth and magic, come to **County Tyrone**; home to the **Sperrins**. A mountain range dating back 500 million years. Legend has it that there's gold in the hills. And a ghost called Murphy.

Make your way to **Londonderry**; the first ever UK City of Culture and the only completely walled city in Ireland. Get the full story of Derry at the **Tower Museum**. Then climb to the top of the tower for spectacular panoramic views of the city.

Wherever you visit in **Northern Ireland**, there's a range of accommodation to make you feel right at home. Be it a family-run B&B, a quaint guesthouse, a quiet country retreat or a 5-star luxury hotel. With the renowned Northern Irish warmth and hospitality, you'll want to stay forever.

There's so much more to explore in Northern Ireland. Come and discover it all for yourself.

Call us on +44 (0) 28 9024 6609.

discover**northernireland**.com

To Book Call **+353-1-8084419** or www.irelandhotels.com

Co. Antrim

Ballycastle / Ballymena / Bushmills

Glenluce Lodge

Guesthouse ★ ★　　　　Map 15 O 21

42 Quay Road, Ballycastle,
Co. Antrim BT54 6BH
Tel: +44-28-2076 2914
Email: enquires@glenluce.com
Web: www.glenluce.com
GPS: N +55° 12' 13.95"　W -6° 14' 37.39"

Location
Located in the North-East corner of Ireland, Glenluce Lodge is in the picturesque town of Ballycastle, half way between the town centre and the seafront.

Property Highlights
Glenluce Lodge has a teahouse for daytime refreshments, WiFi, trampoline and table tennis for guest use. Packed lunches available.

Local Attractions
Giant's Causeway, Carrick-a-Rede Bridge, Rathlin Island, grass tennis courts, sea fishing and walks & cycle routes can be recommended.

Room Rate from: £30.00 - £120.00

Host(s): Clarie White

8

Facilities

Galgorm Resort & Spa

Hotel ★ ★ ★ ★　　　　Map 15 O 19

136 Fenaghy Road, Ballymena,
Co. Antrim BT42 1EA
Tel: +44-28-2588 1001
Email: sales@galgorm.com
Web: www.galgorm.com
GPS: N +54° 52' 37.61"　W -6° 20' 46.01"

Location
30 mins. to Belfast City, 20 mins. to Belfast International Airport, 35 mins. to Belfast City Airport. Giant's Causeway & stunning North Coast less than 1 hr away.

Property Highlights
Our facilities include 88 bedrooms & suites, self catering cottages & cabins, 2 restaurants & an award-winning Spa.

Local Attractions
The 163 acre parkland estate sits on the banks of the River Maine, perfect for a spot of fishing or a leisurely walk. Great shopping, world class golf & cultural attractions are all within easy reach.

B&B from: £52.50 - £102.50
Suites from: £195.00 - £245.00

Host(s): Yvonne Smyth

88

Facilities

Bayview Hotel

Hotel ★ ★ ★　　　　Map 14 N 21

2 Bayhead Road, Portballintrae, Bushmills,
Co. Antrim BT57 8RZ
Tel: +44-28-2073 4100
Email: info@bayviewhotelni.com
Web: www.bayviewhotelni.com
GPS: N +55° 12' 56.22"　W -6° 32' 41.68"

Location
On North Antrim's Giant's Causeway Coast overlooking the Atlantic Ocean in the picturesque harbour village of Portballintrae.

Property Highlights
Stunning ocean views from bedrooms & restaurant. Family-owned and operated, homely and relaxed. Real turf & log fire in the Porthole Bar.

Local Attractions
Giant's Causeway, Bushmills Distillery, Carrick-A-Rede Rope Bridge, Dunluce Castle, Downhill, Royal Portrush Golf Club.

B&B from: £40.00 - £85.00

Host(s): Steven Kane/Louise Dobbin

25

Activities　**Facilities**

Open All Year　　　　　Open All Year　　　　　Open All Year

B&B Rates are per Person Sharing per Night incl. Breakfast. Room/Suite Rates are per Room per Night. **See also page 08**

Northern Ireland　　103

Co. Antrim

To Book Call **+353-1-8084419** or www.irelandhotels.com

Bushmills / Carnlough / Portrush

Bushmills Inn Hotel

Hotel ★ ★ ★ ★   Map 14 N 21

9 Dunluce Road, Bushmills,
Co. Antrim BT57 8QG
Tel: +44-28-2073 3000
Email: mail@bushmillsinn.com
Web: www.bushmillsinn.com
GPS: N +55° 12' 25.64"   W -6° 31' 26.63"

Location
On the A2, the Antrim Coast Road, as you cross the River Bush. Follow the Giant's Causeway signs.

Property Highlights
Hotel boasts intriguing bedrooms, an atmospheric restaurant, a turf-fired old kitchen and a Victorian bar still lit by gas light. AA Rosette Restaurant, NITB Accommodation of the Year 2010.

Local Attractions
Giant's Causeway, Royal Portrush Golf Club, Carrick-a-Rede Rope Bridge, Dunluce Castle, Antrim Coast Road, Bushmills Distillery.

Room Rate from: £128.00 - £268.00
Suites from: £398.00 - £398.00

Host(s): Alan Walls

41

Activities   Facilities

Open All Year

Londonderry Arms Hotel

Hotel ★ ★ ★   Map 15 P 20

Glens of Antrim, 20 Harbour Road, Carnlough,
Co. Antrim BT44 0EU
Tel: +44-28-2888 5255
Email: lda@glensofantrim.com
Web: www.glensofantrim.com
GPS: N +54° 59' 33.31"   W -5° 59' 24.95"

Location
Close to Larne Harbour. 1 hour to Belfast City & International Airports. Ideal for exploring Glens of Antrim. Situated halfway between Belfast & Giant's Causeway.

Property Highlights
Sumptous dining in our Georgian Frances Anne & Tapestry Room Restaurant. Once owned by Winston Churchhill. Full conference and wedding facilities available. Registered for civil marriages.

Local Attractions
Carnfunnock Park 20 minutes drive, Giant's Causeway 1 hour drive, Carrick-a-Rede Rope Bridge 1 hour drive, Bushmills Distillery 1 hour drive, Belfast 1 hour drive.

B&B from: £40.00 - £85.00

Host(s): Frank O'Neill

35

Activities   Facilities

Closed 24 - 25 December

Ramada Portrush

Hotel ★ ★ ★   Map 14 N 21

73 Main Street, Portrush,
Co. Antrim BT56 8BN
Tel: +44-28-7082 6100
Email: info@ramadaportrush.com
Web: www.ramadaportrush.com
GPS: N +55° 12' 28.32"   W -6° 39' 19.13"

Location
Situated in the centre of town overlooking the Atlantic Ocean on the causeway coastal route. Close to the Giant's Causeway.

Property Highlights
Counties Cafe Bar & Restaurant, local food, 69 bedrooms, lift, room safe, internet access, TV with in-house movies, hospitality tray.

Local Attractions
Giant's Causeway, Old Bushmills Distillery, Carrick-a-Rede Rope Bridge, Dunluce Castle, Royal Portrush & Portstewart Golf Courses and many more.

B&B from: £37.50 - £90.00

Host(s): Ann Donaghy

69

Activities   Facilities

Open All Year

Northern Ireland   B&B Rates are per Person Sharing per Night incl. Breakfast. Room/Suite Rates are per Room per Night. **See also page 08**

To Book Call **+353-1-8084419** or www.irelandhotels.com

Co. Antrim - Belfast City

Templepatrick / Belfast City

Hilton Templepatrick

Hotel ★ ★ ★ ★   Map 15 O 18

Castle Upton Estate, Templepatrick,
Co. Antrim BT39 0DD
Tel: +44-28-9443 5500
Email: reservations.templepatrick@hilton.com
Web: www.hilton.co.uk/templepatrick
GPS: N +54° 42' 35.41"   W -6° 5' 39.22"

Location
10 minutes from Belfast International Airport. Located in the Castle Upton Estate. 20 minutes drive from Belast.

Property Highlights
Livingwell Gym, Spa & Beauty. Swimming pool. 18 hole championship golf course. Driving range.

Local Attractions
Castle Upton Gallery, Ballyrobert Cottage Garden and Nursery, Belfast Zoo, Odyssey Arena, Ulster Musem.

B&B from: £39.50 - £84.50

Host(s): Mark Walker

129

Activities   Facilities

Open All Year

Fitzwilliam Hotel Belfast (The)

Hotel   Map 15 P 18

Great Victoria Street,
Belfast BT2 7HR
Tel: +44-28-9044 2080
Email: enq@fitzwilliamhotelbelfast.com
Web: www.fitzwilliamhotelbelfast.com
GPS: N +54° 35' 44.10"   W -5° 56' 2.73"

Built to a 5***** specification

Location
In the heart of Belfast City centre. 5 minutes from main train station & 10 minutes drive from Belfast City Airport. Prime location.

Property Highlights
New hotel opened in March 2009, awaiting grading. Beautifully designed, contemporary hotel, right beside the glorious Grand Opera House. Great restaurant with menu by Kevin Thornton.

Local Attractions
Ulster Museum, City Hall, Belfast Zoo, Giant's Causeway, Carrick-a-Rede Rope Bridge, Bushmills Distillery.

Room Rate from: £125.00 - £200.00
Suites from: £215.00 - £280.00

Host(s): Vincent O'Gorman

130

Activities   Facilities

Open All Year

Hilton Belfast

Hotel ★ ★ ★ ★   Map 15 P 18

4 Lanyon Place,
Belfast BT1 3LP
Tel: +44-28-9027 7000
Email: reservations.belfast@hilton.com
Web: www.hilton.co.uk/belfast
GPS: N +54° 35' 46.89"   W -5° 55' 8.89"

Location
City Centre location, 2 minutes walk from Central Station. 5 minutes taxi to Belfast City Airport. Banks of the River Lagan.

Property Highlights
City Centre location, 2 minutes walk from Victoria Square shopping centre. Executive lounge.

Local Attractions
City Hall, Odyssey Arena, Titanic Quarter, Stormont, city tours.

B&B from: £47.50 - £104.50

Host(s): Mark Walker

198

Activities   Facilities

Open All Year

B&B Rates are per Person Sharing per Night incl. Breakfast. Room/Suite Rates are per Room per Night. **See also page 08**

Belfast City

To Book Call **+353-1-8084419** or www.irelandhotels.com

Belfast City

La Mon Hotel & Country Club

Hotel ★ ★ ★ ★   Map 15 P 18

41 Gransha Road, Castlereagh,
Belfast BT23 5RF
Tel: +44-28-9044 8631
Email: info@lamon.co.uk
Web: www.lamon.co.uk
GPS: N +54° 32' 51.04"   W -5° 49' 8.09"

Location
20 minutes from Belfast City Centre & George Best City Airport via Outer Ring/A55, right onto Ballygowan Rd, then signposted.

Property Highlights
We are family friendly with a warm welcome. Great facilities include Country Club, Tennis Court, free parking & internet access.

Local Attractions
15 minutes drive to 4 quality golf courses, family adventure centre, Belfast City Centre and Co. Down National Trust Estates.

B&B from: £35.00 - £50.00

Malone Lodge Hotel & Apartments

Hotel ★ ★ ★ ★   Map 15 P 18

60 Eglantine Avenue, Malone Road,
Belfast BT9 6DY
Tel: +44-28-9038 8000
Email: info@malonelodgehotel.com
Web: www.malonelodgehotelbelfast.com
GPS: N +54° 34' 54.36"   W -5° 56' 33.66"

Location
City Centre 1.5 miles, M1/M2 1 mile, Train 0.5 mile, City Airport 6 miles, Situated in tree lined terraces of the University Quarter.

Property Highlights
Accommodation - Bedrooms, Suite & Apartments. Restaurant - AA Rosette & Taste of Ulster Awards. NITB Highly Commended Hotel.

Local Attractions
Kings Hall 1 mile, Odyssey Arena 1.5 miles, Ulster Museum/QUB 0.25 mile, Waterfront 1 mile, Malone Golf Club 2 miles, City Hall 1 mile, Stormont 5 miles.

B&B from: £37.50 - £60.00
Suites from: £120.00 - £200.00

Ten Square Hotel

Hotel ★ ★ ★ ★   Map 15 P 18

10 Donegall Square South,
Belfast BT1 5JD
Tel: +44-28-9024 1001
Email: reservations@tensquare.co.uk
Web: wwww.tensquare.co.uk
GPS: N +54° 35' 44.64"   W -5° 55' 49.12"

Location
Centrally located behind City Hall in close proximity to Central Station and George Best Belfast City Airport.

Property Highlights
Grill Room & Bar. Conference & Wedding facilities. Business and Concierge facilities available.

Local Attractions
City Hall, Titanic Dock & Pumphouse, Ulster Museum, W5, Belfast Zoo, Lagan Boat Tours.

B&B from: £40.00 - £75.00
Suites from: £85.00 - £132.50

Host(s): Francis Brady
120

Host(s): Mary & Brian Macklin
46

Host(s): Kevin Smyth
22

Activities   Facilities

Activities   Facilities

Facilities

Closed 24 - 26 December

Open All Year

Closed 24 - 26 December

106   Northern Ireland   B&B Rates are per Person Sharing per Night incl. Breakfast. Room/Suite Rates are per Room per Night. See also page 08

To Book Call **+353-1-8084419** or www.irelandhotels.com

Co. Derry

Aghadowey / Coleraine / Derry City

Brown Trout Golf & Country Inn

Hotel ★ ★ ★   Map 14 N 20

209 Agivey Road, Aghadowey,
Co. Derry BT51 4AD
Tel: +44-28-7086 8209
Email: jane@browntroutinn.com
Web: www.browntroutinn.com
GPS: N +55° 2' 13.71"   W -6° 36' 9.25"

Location
Within 45 minutes of Belfast City, International and Derry Airports and under 10 minutes to Ballymoney train station. We are 7 miles south of Coleraine on A54.

Property Highlights
Original family-run hotel on its own golf course. Great food with breakfast served until lunchtime and where customers become our friends.

Local Attractions
20 minutes drive to Royal Portrush, Portstewart & Castlerock Golf Clubs. Giant's Causeway, North Coast and Glens of Antrim all within half an hour. Derry's walled city 45 minutes.

B&B from: £40.00 - £55.00

Host(s): Jane O'Hara

15

Facilities

Open All Year

Bushtown Hotel

Hotel ★ ★ ★   Map 14 N 20

283 Drumcroone Road, Coleraine,
Co. Derry BT51 3QT
Tel: +44-28-7035 8367
Email: bushtownhotel@btinternet.com
Web: www.bushtownhotel.co.uk
GPS: N +55° 6' 13.97"   W -6° 41' 23.32"

Location
Set amidst mature woodland just 1 mile from Coleraine town centre and close to the Causeway Coast, this is the perfect place to relax and indulge.

Property Highlights
The hotel had 2 award-winning restaurants, The Bay's Bistro and The Stables Restaurant. We have an indoor heated swimming pool, sauna, full fitness gym and beauty room.

Local Attractions
Close to Royal Portrush Golf Course, Beaches, The Bushmills Distillery and Carrick-a-Rede Rope Bridge.

B&B from: £35.00 - £55.00
Suites from: £130.00 - £170.00

Host(s): Dermot Friel & Kieran McGilligan

37

Facilities

Open All Year

Beech Hill Country House Hotel

Hotel ★ ★ ★ ★   Map 14 L 20

32 Ardmore Road, Londonderry,
Co. Derry BT47 3QP
Tel: +44-28-7134 9279
Email: info@beech-hill.com
Web: www.beech-hill.com
GPS: N +54° 58' 10.02"   W -7° 16' 11.90"

Location
Beech Hill is a privately owned country house hotel, situated on 32 acres, 2 miles from Londonderry.

Property Highlights
Retains the elegance of country living, restored to create a hotel of charm, character & style. Superb cuisine using local produce & homemade specialties. Ardmore Golf Club & Stables next to hotel.

Local Attractions
Harbour Museum, Museum of Free Derry, Riverwatch Aquarium, St. Columb's Cathedral, The Amelia Earhart Centre, Ulster American Folk Park, Pony Trekking Centre, Carrick-a-Rede Bridge, Derry City Walls.

B&B from: £57.50 - £67.50
Suites from: £190.00 - £230.00

Host(s): Seamus Donnelly

27

Facilities

Closed 24 - 26 December

B&B Rates are per Person Sharing per Night incl. Breakfast. Room/Suite Rates are per Room per Night. **See also page 08**

Co. Derry - Co. Down

To Book Call **+353-1-8084419** or www.irelandhotels.com

Derry City / Limavady / Annalong

Best Western White Horse Hotel

Hotel ★ ★ ★　　　　　　　　　Map 14 L 20

68 Clooney Road,
Derry BT47 3PA
Tel: +44-28-7186 0606
Email: reservations@whitehorsehotel.biz
Web: www.whitehorsehotel.biz
GPS: N +55° 1' 49.12"　W -7° 13' 6.19"

Location
Situated just 6km from the city centre & just 1km from the City of Derry Airport on the main route to the famous Giant's Causeway.

Property Highlights
Superb leisure centre comprising of 20m swimming pool, sauna, steam room & gymnasium. The hotel also boasts a salon on site.

Local Attractions
Our hotel is perfectly positioned to experience both the vibrancy of the historic walled city (UK City of Culture 2008) and the stunning North Coast.

B&B from: £30.00 - £45.00

Host(s): Keith Baldrick

57

Activities　　Facilities

Open All Year

Radisson Blu Roe Park Resort

Hotel ★ ★ ★ ★　　　　　　　　Map 14 M 20

40 Drumrane Road, Limavady,
Co. Londonderry BT49 9LB
Tel: +44-28-7772 2222
Email: limavady.reservations@radissonsas.com
Web: www.radissonroepark.com
GPS: N +55° 2' 19.58"　W -6° 57' 17.97"

Location
The resort is located 45 minutes from Belfast International Airport & 10 miles from the City of Derry Airport.

Property Highlights
Surrounded by enchanting countryside, just waiting to be explored, our resort offers spa, golf & leisure facilities and two restaurants.

Local Attractions
Roe Valley Country Park is just on our doorstep, the fascinating Giant's Causeway & the award-winning Benone Beach.

B&B from: £55.00 - £70.00

Host(s): George Graham

118

Activities　　Facilities

Open All Year

Glassdrumman Lodge

Guesthouse ★ ★ ★　　　　　　Map 12 P 15

85 Mill Road, Annalong,
Co. Down, BT34 4RH
Tel: +44-28-4376 8451
Email: info@glassdrummanlodge.com
Web: www.glassdrummanlodge.com
GPS: N +54° 7' 10.38"　W -5° 54' 48.35"

Location
Set in the heart of the Mourne Mountains only 6 miles from Newcastle, 40 miles from Belfast, 90 miles from Dublin.

Property Highlights
Log fires, beautiful gardens, sea views, mountain views, our own fishing lake, award-winning food.

Local Attractions
Mourne Mountains, Royal County Down Golf Course, Tollymore Forest Park, Silent Valley, Kilkeel Golf Course, Annalong Harbour & Work Mill.

B&B from: £35.00 - £90.00

Host(s): Ben & Jonny Hall

10

Facilities

Open All Year

Northern Ireland　　B&B Rates are per Person Sharing per Night incl. Breakfast. Room/Suite Rates are per Room per Night. See also page 08

To Book Call **+353-1-8084419** or www.irelandhotels.com

Co. Down - Co. Fermanagh
Newcastle / Newry / Enniskillen

Burrendale Hotel, Country Club & Spa

Hotel ★ ★ ★ Map 12 P 16

51 Castlewellan Road, Newcastle,
Co. Down BT33 0JY
Tel: +44-28-4372 2599
Email: reservations@burrendale.com
Web: www.burrendale.com
GPS: N +54° 13' 32.38" W -5° 53' 40.51"

Location
Located 45 minutes from Belfast or Newry, 90 minutes from Dublin & a 10 minute walk from the seaside town of Newcastle.

Property Highlights
Rejuvenate in the Country Club, pamper yourself in the Spa & Hair Salon. Excellent à la carte & bistro dining. Authentic cottage bar.

Local Attractions
At the foot of the Mourne Mountains, it is the perfect location for business, pleasure or leisure. Close to RCD, horse riding & beach/forest parks.

B&B from: £70.00 - £80.00
Suites from: £170.00 - £170.00

Host(s): Denis Orr
68

Activities Facilities

Open All Year

Canal Court Hotel

Hotel ★ ★ ★ ★ Map 12 O 15

Merchants Quay, Newry,
Co. Down BT35 8HF
Tel: +44-28-3025 1234
Email: manager@canalcourthotel.com
Web: www.canalcourthotel.com
GPS: N +54° 10' 34.52" W -6° 20' 25.70"

Location
Perfect location at the heart of Newry City, which is within walking distance of the hotel. Courtesy transport available from train station to hotel.

Property Highlights
Leisure facilities with full gym, sauna, jacuzzi, steam room, 20m pool, plunge & childrens' pool.

Local Attractions
Excellent shopping in Newry City. Complimentary transfer to Serenity Spa at our sister hotel.

B&B from: £65.00 - £150.00
Suites from: £150.00 - £300.00

Host(s): Deborah Ferguson
112

Activities Facilities

Closed 25 December

Glendarragh Valley Inn

Guesthouse ★ ★ ★ Map 11 K 16

9 Castlederg Road, Ederney, Near Enniskillen,
Co. Fermanagh BT93 0AL
Tel: +44-28-6863 2777
Email: enquiries@glendarraghvalleyinn.com
Web: www.glendarraghvalleyinn.com
GPS: N +54° 32' 8.93" W -7° 39' 32.60"

Location
Road to Donegal conveniently situated to the main town of Co. Fermanagh, Enniskillen. Easily accessible to Derry Airport.

Property Highlights
Private car parking, en suite bedrooms, WiFi. Ideal rural location for a quiet break.

Local Attractions
Townlands displayed at the Inn, historical landmarks such as Drumskinny Stone Circle, Famine Pit, Janus Figure & the Wishing Well and local beauty spots, Muckross, Drummoney Falls & Castle Archdale.

B&B from: £35.00 - £40.00

Host(s): John F Maguire
6

Facilities

Open All Year

B&B Rates are per Person Sharing per Night incl. Breakfast. Room/Suite Rates are per Room per Night. **See also page 08**

Co. Fermanagh

To Book Call **+353-1-8084419** or www.irelandhotels.com

Enniskillen / Irvinestown

Killyhevlin Hotel

Hotel ★ ★ ★ ★   Map 11 K 16

Killyhevlin, Enniskillen,
Co. Fermanagh BT74 6RW
Tel: +44-28-6632 3481
Email: info@killyhevlin.com
Web: www.killyhevlin.com
GPS: N +54° 19' 47.16"   W -7° 37' 11.55"

Location
The Killyhevlin Hotel is located only 1km from Enniskillen Town on the main A4 road. 130km from Belfast Airport. 165km from Dublin Airport.

Property Highlights
70 Guest Rooms & Suites, 13 Lakeside Chalets, Luxury Health Club with Swimming Pool & Outdoor Hot Tub, Elemis Spa with 4 Treatment Rooms, Boathouse Grill & Bar, Silks Restaurant.

Local Attractions
Belleek Pottery, Culcagh Mountain Park, Marble Arch Caves, 3 National Trust Properties, Lough Navar Forest, Enniskillen Castle Museums, The Buttermarket, Lough Erne.

B&B from: £70.00 - £80.00

Host(s): Mr. Rodney Watson

70

Activities   Facilities

Closed 24 - 26 December

Manor House Resort Hotel

Hotel ★ ★ ★ ★   Map 14 K 16

Killadeas, Enniskillen,
Co. Fermanagh BT94 1NY
Tel: +44-28-6862 2200
Email: info@manorhouseresorthotel.com
Web: www.manorhousecountryhotel.com
GPS: N +54° 25' 46.31"   W -7° 40' 43.54"

Location
On the edge of Lower Lough Erne. 7 miles from Enniskillen.

Property Highlights
This 19th century Manor is a first class hotel offering luxury accommodation, comfort & services. It commands magnificent views of Lough Erne. Leisure complex with pool, steamroom, jacuzzi & sauna.

Local Attractions
The Erne Waterway & its mountains for beautiful scenic drives & boat trips, Marble Arch Caves, Enniskillen Town Hall, Castle Archdale Islands.

B&B from: £37.50 - £65.00
Suites from: £325.00 - £325.00

Host(s): David Begley

81

Activities   Facilities

Open All Year

Mahon's Hotel

Hotel ★ ★ ★   Map 13 K 17

Enniskillen Road, Irvinestown,
Co. Fermanagh BT94 1GS
Tel: +44-28-6862 1656
Email: info@mahonshotel.co.uk
Web: www.mahonshotel.co.uk
GPS: N +54° 28' 24.33"   W -7° 37' 35.85"

Location
In the heart of the Fermanagh Lakeland. Belleek Pottery 20 minutes, Marble Arch Caves 30 minutes, Equestrian Centre 5 minutes, Lough Erne 5 minutes, Donegal 20 minutes.

Property Highlights
Bushmills Bar of the Year winner, entertainment at weekends, private car park. Family-run since 1883. Hotel upgraded to three star NITB & AA. Bedrooms have modem access, DVD & WiFi.

Local Attractions
Cycling, horse riding, tennis & golf all available.

B&B from: £40.00 - £52.50

Host(s): Joe Mahon

19

Activities   Facilities

Closed 25 - 27 December

110   Northern Ireland   B&B Rates are per Person Sharing per Night incl. Breakfast. Room/Suite Rates are per Room per Night. See also page 08

To Book Call **+353-1-8084419** or www.irelandhotels.com

Co. Tyrone
Cookstown / Omagh

Tullylagan Country House Hotel

Hotel ★ ★ Map 14 M 18

40b Tullylagan Road, Cookstown,
Co. Tyrone BT80 9AZ
Tel: +44-28-8676 5100
Email: info@tullylagan.com
Web: www.tullylagan.com
GPS: N +54° 35' 38.70" W -6° 46' 31.84"

Location
Tullylagan Country House is in the heart of Mid-Ulster, at the foot of the Sperrins, 35 mins. from Belfast and 45 mins. from anywhere else in Northern Ireland.

Property Highlights
Set on 30 acres of mature grounds. 2 award-winning restaurants, Wedding Venue of the Year 2009. Variety of private suites for 15 to 140 guests in our medieval banqueting hall.

Local Attractions
Close to Ballyronan Marina, Lough Neagh, Sperrin Mountains, Springhill House, Wellbrook Beetling Mill, Beaghmore Stone Circles, An Creagan Visitors Centre, Drum Manor Forest Park.

B&B from: £45.00 - £47.50
Suites from: £100.00 - £130.00

Host(s): Mr. Adrian Martin

15

Facilities

Closed 24 - 27 December

Silverbirch Hotel

Hotel ★ ★ ★ Map 14 L 18

5 Gortin Road, Omagh,
Co. Tyrone BT79 7DH
Tel: +44-28-8224 2520
Email: info@silverbirchhotel.com
Web: www.silverbirchhotel.com
GPS: N +54° 36' 37.04" W -7° 17' 58.94"

Location
Silverbirch Hotel is located on the outskirts of Omagh on the B48 leading to the Gortin Glens, Sperrins and the Ulster American Folk Park.

Property Highlights
Set in its own spacious & mature grounds, the hotel has 64 bedrooms furnished to a 3* standard. Other facilities include a newly refurbished Bar & Restaurant & also a new Business Centre.

Local Attractions
Ulster American Folk Park, Sperrin Mountains, An Creagan Visitor Centre, Gortin Glen Forest Park, Gortin Lakes, Clay Pigeon Shooting, Coarse Angling, Cycling, Golf, Horse Riding.

B&B from: £46.00 - £75.00

Host(s): Allan Duncan

64

Facilities

Closed 25 December

BELLEEK POTTERY VISITOR CENTRE

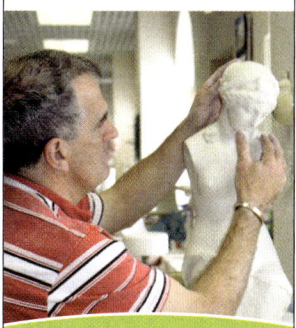

Treasure the memories of Irelands Oldest Working Pottery Discover the secrets that have made the Belleek name famous the world over, Take a personally guided tour through all stages of production and see how our craftspeople delicately apply their creativity to each handmade piece. Marvel at the skill and attention to detail that makes every product bearing the distinctive Belleek back stamp a collectors item to cherish.

The Centre is open all year round and guided tours run every 30 minutes Mon - Fri.

EMAIL visitorcentre@belleek.ie
TEL +44(0)28 6865 9300
        +44(0)28 6865 8501
WEB www.belleek.ie

B&B Rates are per Person Sharing per Night incl. Breakfast. Room/Suite Rates are per Room per Night. See also page 08

Direct low rates and great special offers guaranteed

Irelandhotels.com
We've got it covered

You can find all the best deals in all of these places

Website | Mobile App | Printed Guide |
facebook.com/irelandhotels | irelandhotels.com/onlineguide

Dublin & Ireland East

For Detailed Maps of this Region See Pages **325-340**. Each Hotel or Guesthouse has a Map Reference to these detailed maps below the premises name.

See page **325** for map with access points and driving distances

Co. Cavan
Bailieborough	117
Ballyconnell	117
Cavan Town	118
Mountnugent	118
Virginia	119

Co. Dublin
Balbriggan	119
Donabate	119
Dublin Airport	120
Dublin City	121
Dun Laoghaire	147
Howth	147
Killiney	148
Lucan	148
Lusk	149
Malahide	149
Skerries	149
Sutton	150
Swords	150

Co. Kildare
Athy	151
Clane	152
Kildare Town	152
Leixlip	152
Monasterevin	153
Naas	154
Newbridge	154
Straffan	156

Co. Laois
Durrow	156
Killenard	157
Portlaoise	157

Co. Longford
Cloondara	158
Longford Town	158

Co. Louth
Carlingford	159
Drogheda	160
Dundalk	161

Co. Meath
Ashbourne	162
Dunboyne	162
Gormanston	163
Kells	164
Kilmessan	164
Navan	164
Trim	165

Co. Monaghan
Carrickmacross	166
Glaslough	166
Monaghan Town	167

Co. Offaly
Birr	168
Tullamore	168

Co. Westmeath
Athlone	170
Moate	172
Mullingar	173

Co. Wicklow
Arklow	174
Ashford	174
Bray	175
Enniskerry	176
Glendalough	176
Glen-O-The-Downs	177
Rathnew	178
Wicklow Town	178
Woodenbridge	178

Dublin & Ireland East

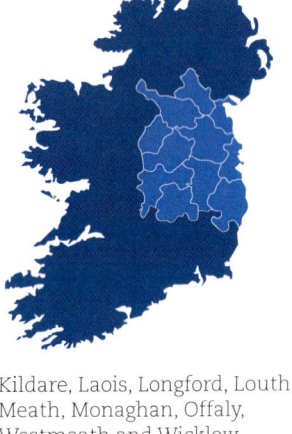

Cavan, Dublin, Kildare, Laois, Longford, Louth Meath, Monaghan, Offaly, Westmeath, Wicklow
(see pages 2 & 3 for full County listing)

Feast your senses on bewitching scenery, fantastic city life, sensational sporting events and compelling historical sights.

The republic's capital city **Dublin** lies at the heart of a region that enchants the visitor with a selection of lakes, rivers and stretches of coastline. Dublin is usually the first port of call for visitors and this energetic, youthful city pulsates with a compelling mix of history, culture, hip bars and pubs, elegant architecture, great shopping and some of the country's most sophisticated restaurants. Cosmopolitan and diverse, Dublin is now one of Europe's top urban hotspots.

Ireland's capital is steeped in history and youthful energy. Dublin is a city where the charming and cosmopolitan converge in delightful diversity. Medieval, Georgian and modern architecture provide a backdrop to this friendly bustling port. Attractions are many, from castles, museums and art galleries to the lively spirit of Temple Bar. As one of the oldest cities in Europe, Dublin provides you with a multitude of cultural riches from the ancient to the ultra-modern and from history, architecture and literature to the performing arts. Dublin has lively pedestrian shopping streets at the heart of the city, alive with buskers and street performers, and there is a number of huge shopping centres in the outskirts offering excellent choice all under one roof, or go further a field to the surrounding towns and villages where you'll find boutiques and craft shops. Rich culture, gourmet cuisine, lively pubs, fabulous shopping, music for all and plenty of sport are just some of the experiences Dublin has to offer. There has never been a better time to visit Dublin! Visit the official online tourist office for Dublin **www.visitdublin.com**. The Dublin Pass offers the visitor the best in attraction, sightseeing, shopping, service and restaurant offers, all in one complete package. The purchase price of the pass covers entrance to over thirty of Dublin's top attractions and gives access to over twenty five special offers, added value and preferential rates at selected venues, theatres, retail outlets, restaurants, transport and tours. For more information see **www.dublinpass.ie**

Ireland East & Dublin will shower you with friendship and unforgettable memories and your adventures begin now...

Beyond Dublin, the east of Ireland tells a different story with the counties of Cavan, Kildare, Laois, Longford, Louth, Meath, Monaghan, Offaly, Westmeath and Wicklow offering a contrasting slice of life. This region is famed for its rich natural charms, ancient sites of Newgrange and Clonmacnoise, top golfing and world-renowned horseracing. The county of Kildare, in particular, is home to some of the world's finest thoroughbreds and of course the 2006 Ryder Cup.

But what really defines the east is the unspoilt countryside. With glistening lakes, tranquil rivers, authentic rural life, scenic pastureland, rolling hills and forest parks, this area is a haven for outdoors enthusiasts with cycling, watersports, walking, angling, golfing, horseriding and cruising in plentiful supply.

Cruising, fishing, golfing and equestrian enthusiasts should look no further than **Laois** and **Offaly**. The town of Tullamore has put Offaly firmly on the map as a short break location and from here the ancient monastic site of Clonmacnoise, and of course the famous Tullamore Dew Heritage Centre, can be visited. For those who enjoy country walks and visiting gardens, Laois provides both. Tranquillity reigns along the banks of the Grand Canal at Vicarstown or the walking

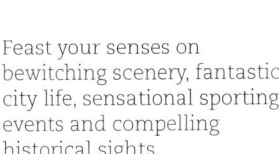

We've got it covered!

Belvedere House & Gardens, Co. Westmeath Newgrange, Co. Meath Glendalough, Co. Wicklow

routes of the Slieve Blooms. Splendid gardens surround the Gandon House at Emo or the Lutyens Gardens at Heywood.

Kildare, host of the prestigious international Ryder Cup, is also home of the Irish horse. The county boasts three of the country's premier race courses as well as the Irish National Stud, Japanese and St. Fiachra's Gardens. Other attractions include Castletown House, Leixlip Castle, Ballindoolin Gardens and Mondello International Motor Race Course.

Neighbouring **Wicklow**, known as the Garden of Ireland, contains outstanding scenery of mountains, valleys, lakes and coastlines. Renowned for its walking trails, The Wicklow Way is one of the most famous. The ancient monastic site of Glendalough, Powerscourt Gardens, Mount Usher Gardens, Wicklow Gaol and Parnell's Avondale House are some of the many attractions well worth a visit.

The royal county of **Meath** has some of the most spectacular attractions in the country including the passage Graves at Newgrange, the historic Trim Castle and the famous Hills of Tara and Slane. The vibrant towns of Navan, Trim and Kells provide the ideal base for touring. **Louth** also has a rich medieval past. The town of Dundalk has connections with the mythical hero Cuchulainn. It is a vibrant shopping town and has a newly refurbished Town Hall & Basement Gallery, an award-winning County Museum and the magnificent St. Patrick's Cathedral that dates back to 1837. Drogheda, on the River Boyne, has many fascinating buildings including St. Laurence's Gate, Milmount Motte and Martello Tower. The relics of St. Oliver Plunkett, martyred in 1681, are preserved in St. Peter's Church. The heritage town of Carlingford displays its past in King John's Castle and the interpretive centre.

Cavan is known as the Lake County with an ancient and colourful heritage. Discover that Cavan is a fun and vibrant place to visit. Cavan is buzzing with friendly people, lively towns and villages, spectacular scenery, a vibrant arts and theatre scene, walks, cycle routes, museums, heritage centres, sparkling lakes, fishing, cruising and activities. Ireland's longest river – the mighty River Shannon rises in Dowra, Co. Cavan and forms part of the Shannon Erne Waterway. Why not hire a cruiser and meander your way through the longest navigable waterway in Europe. There is no better place to start than Cavan…

Monaghan landscape resounds with the poetry of Patrick Kavanagh. The renowned poet is celebrated in the Patrick Kavanagh Rural and Literary Resource Centre in Inniskeen – a must for anyone interested in the poet's life and work. Monaghan has long been known as an angler's paradise and with several walking routes in the Sliabh Beagh area; it is well worth a visit. In addition, there are 36 looped walks, throughout the Sliabh Beagh region, all of which are way marked and vary in length from 4km – 15km.

Counties **Longford** and **Westmeath** with their rivers, lakes and canal ensure many watersports are enjoyed here as well as top class angling with all species of coarse fish and brown trout. An area noted for its history and varied heritage, visitor attractions include the Corlea Trackway near Kenagh, the Bog Oak Sculptures in Newtowncashel, the magnificent Belvedere House and Gardens outside Mullingar, Athlone Castle and Locke's Distillery situated in the town of Kilbeggan which also hosts horse racing during the summer months. Literary associations include Maria Edgeworth, Padraic Colum, Oliver Goldsmith, James Joyce and Jonathan Swift.

Irelandhotels.com 115

Dublin & Ireland East

Equestrian

Ireland's East Coast offers some extraordinary equestrian experiences from horse racing, to horse riding, museums and studs to horse drawn caravan holidays.

The region is most famous for its horse racing so after a visit to the National Museum and Stud in Kildare why not take in one of our famous racing festivals like those at the Curragh or Punchestown. Ireland has over 300 race meetings every year across its many racecourses so finding a fixture that suits you is never a problem.

To find one near you, check out
www.discoverireland.ie/equestrian

10 Key Walks

1. Howth Looped Walks, Co. Dublin
2. Bailieborough, Co. Cavan
3. Glendalough, Co. Wicklow
4. Crone Woods, Co. Wicklow
5. Tinahely, Co. Wicklow
6. Glenbarrow Looped Walks, Co. Laois
7. Kinnitty Looped Walks, Co. Offaly
8. Slieve Foye Looped Walks, Carlingford, Co. Louth
9. Donadea Forest Park, Co. Kildare
10. Drewstown Woods, Co. Meath

Maps for these walks and the other 200 looped walks across Ireland can be downloaded on
www.discoverireland.ie/walking

Or why not get on your bike and follow one of 3 cycling trails surrounding Mullingar?

Top Attractions

1. National Museum of Ireland Kildare Street, Dublin (Archaeology)
2. Guinness Storehouse, Dublin
3. National Museum of Ireland Collins Barracks, Dublin (Decorative Art & History)
4. Kilmainham Gaol, Dublin
5. Dublinia, Dublin
6. Glendalough, Co. Wicklow
7. Belvedere House & Gardens Mullingar, Co. Westmeath
8. Clonmacnoise, Co. Offaly
9. Castletown House, Co. Kildare
10. Newgrange & Bru na Boinne, Co. Meath
11. Mellifont Abbey, Drogheda, Co. Louth
12. Japanese Gardens & National Stud, Co. Kildare
13. GAA Museum, Dublin

Angling

The mighty pike is most prevalent in the counties of Monaghan and Cavan. County Cavan boasts 365 lakes alone! Major pike fisheries on the River Shannon include Loughs Allen, Ree, Derravaragh and Derg. Coarse anglers will find easily accessible stretches on the Grand and Royal canal systems running though the towns of Edenderry, Prosperous, Enfield and Leixlip. The River Fane in County Louth has a deservedly fine reputation for its wild brown trout as has the River Boyne in the adjoining county of Meath.

For more information and the lists of towns that are part of our anglers welcome initiative visit
www.discoverireland.ie/angling

Cruising

What better way to enjoy Ireland's dramatic unspoilt inland lakes and rivers than to take a boat trip. This, for the less experienced sailors, is the best way to sit back and relax and take in what Ireland has to offer.

Dotted with lakes, and criss-crossed by lovely rivers and historic canals, Ireland is a watery paradise for those looking to relax and go with the flow on a cruising holiday. But taking a cruising trip in Ireland – where no experience or license is required – goes far beyond the boat.

Take the mighty River Shannon. Once a major route through the country, it was used by Viking invaders to attack monastic settlements along its banks like Clonmacnoise. Surging from Yeats Country through the brimming bowl of Lough Derg – it is now a haven for anglers, water sports enthusiasts, golfers, historians and foodies. While the Shannon may be the jewel in the crown, you might prefer to choose your own personal gem from the many other scenic rivers, lakes and canals. And if our inland waterways aren't enough to float your boat, maybe you'll be tempted by an excursion to one of our many rugged islands.

For more information on where to hire a boat visit
www.discoverireland.ie

Historic Boyne Valley

Discover the ancient splendor of Ireland's heritage from the Battle of the Boyne to Cuchulainn – within a landscape which is abundant with history & tradition. For more information check out
www.discoverireland.ie

We've got it covered!

Co. Cavan

Bailieborough / Ballyconnell

Bailie Hotel

Hotel ★ ★   Map 11 M 14

Main Street, Bailieborough,
Co. Cavan
Tel: +353-42-966 5334
Email: hotelbailie@eircom.net
Web: www.bailiehotel.com
GPS: N +53° 54' 57.86" W -6° 58' 10.69"

Location

Located in the centre of Bailieborough Town. Only 1 hour 30 minutes from Dublin on the N3 road.

Property Highlights

Family run, with a reputation for superb quality foods. Our cosy Tailor Lounge boasts live music every weekend. All en suite bedrooms furnished with TV, DD phone & tea/coffee making facilities.

Local Attractions

Local attractions include leisure centre with fully equipped gym, pool, steam room, sauna & Jacuzzi, golf, fishing & horse riding.

B&B from: €40.00 - €45.00

Host(s): McEnaney family

18

Facilities

Closed 25 - 27 December

Keepers Arms

Guesthouse ★ ★   Map 11 K 15

Bridge Street, Bawnboy, Ballyconnell,
Co. Cavan
Tel: +353-49-952 3318
Email: info@keepersarms.com
Web: www.keepersarms.com
GPS: N +54° 7' 13.56" W -7° 40' 36.16"

Location

The Keepers Arms in Bawnboy is 6km from Ballyconnell, 30km from Cavan Town, 2 hours from both Dublin & Belfast Airports.

Property Highlights

9 en suite bedrooms with tea, coffee making facilities, multichannel TV. Family run, with delicious home cooking. Fully licensed bar, private parking, family run & garden for visitors use.

Local Attractions

Angling, Outdoors & Dirty Adventure Centre, UNESCO Geopark/Marble Arch Caves, museum, craft shops, Irish Arts Centre, pet farm, equestrian centre.

B&B from: €70.00 - €70.00

Host(s): Sheila McKiernan

9

Activities   Facilities

Closed 23 December - 01 January

Slieve Russell Hotel Golf & Country Club

Hotel ★ ★ ★ ★   Map 11 K 15

Ballyconnell,
Co. Cavan
Tel: +353-49-952 6444
Email: enquiries@slieverussell.ie
Web: www.slieverussell.ie
GPS: N +54° 5' 46.44" W -7° 33' 30.13"

Location

Located 90 miles from Belfast & Dublin, travel time from Dublin now under 90 minutes via M3!

Property Highlights

This quality four star hotel includes a world class spa, magnificent leisure centre & superb 18 hole championship golf course.

Local Attractions

Angling, boat hire, canoeing, extreme activity centre, Shannon Erne waterway cruising, forest parks, equestrian, bowling, cinema & open farm.

B&B from: €65.00 - €79.00
Suites from: €230.00 - €259.00

Host(s): Tony Walker

222

Activities   Facilities

Open All Year

Co. Cavan

To Book Call **+353-1-8084419** or www.irelandhotels.com

Cavan Town / Mountnugent

Hotel Kilmore

Hotel ★ ★ ★ Map 11 L 14

Dublin Road, Cavan Town,
Co. Cavan
Tel: +353-49-433 2288
Email: info@hotelkilmore.ie
Web: www.hotelkilmore.ie
GPS: N +53° 59' 12.93" W -7° 19' 21.36"

Location
Located on main Dublin Road, just a few km from Cavan Town and only 1 hour and 30 minutes from Dublin on the M3.

Property Highlights
38 beautifully appointed bedrooms. Two spectacular wedding/function rooms and conference facilities. The hotel offers guests a blend of old world charm and contemporary design.

Local Attractions
Golfing, angling, forest parks close by suitable for walking.

B&B from: €75.00 - €95.00
Suites from: €120.00 - €160.00

38

Host(s): Paul Henry

Activities **Facilities**

Closed 24 - 26 December

Radisson Blu Farnham Estate Hotel

Hotel ★ ★ ★ ★ Map 11 L 14

Farnham Estate, Cavan,
Co. Cavan
Tel: +353-49-437 7700
Email: info@farnhamestate.com
Web: www.farnhamestate.com
GPS: N +54° 0' 6.97" W -7° 24' 1.35"

Location
Located approx 3km outside Cavan Town. Less than 90 minutes from Dublin City and 2 hours from Belfast.

Property Highlights
Set on a 1300 acre estate, the Radisson Blu Farnham Estate boasts 158 guest rooms & suites, a 40,000 sq ft Health Spa, 18 hole golf course & 7km of walking trails.

Local Attractions
Farnham Lake for fishing, Florence Court House & Gardens, Marble Arch Caves & Geopark, Killykeen Forest Park. Enjoy walking through ancient woodland, biking, fishing and golf.

B&B from: €65.00 - €120.00
Suites from: €180.00 - €340.00

158

Host(s): Clodagh Pryce

Activities **Facilities**

Open All Year

Crover House Hotel & Golf Club

Hotel ★ ★ ★ Map 11 L 13

Lough Sheelin, Mountnugent,
Co. Cavan
Tel: +353-49-854 0206
Email: crover@iol.ie
Web: www.croverhousehotel.ie
GPS: N +53° 49' 36.03" W -7° 17' 43.03"

Location
Crover House Hotel & Golf Club is a luxurious destination situated on the shores of Lough Sheelin. We are only 1.5 hours from Dublin and 2 hours from Belfast.

Property Highlights
Enjoy a superb bar menu in our intimate Sailor's Bar & in the contemporary Lakeview Bar or fine dining in our elegant Sheelin Room. Enjoy a round of golf or a stroll in our beautiful scenic gardens.

Local Attractions
9 hole golf course & angling on site. Pony trekking, Loughcrew Gardens, Cavan County Museum & Ramour Theatre all in locality.

B&B from: €65.00 - €80.00

37

Host(s): Gabrielle Leahy

Activities **Facilities**

Closed 25 - 27 December

Dublin & Ireland East   B&B Rates are per Person Sharing per Night incl. Breakfast. Room/Suite Rates are per Room per Night. See also page 08

To Book Call **+353-1-8084419** or www.irelandhotels.com

Co. Cavan - Co. Dublin
Virginia / Balbriggan / Donabate

Lakeside Manor Hotel

Hotel ★ ★ ★   Map 11 L 13

**Dublin Road, Virginia,
Co. Cavan**
Tel: +353-49-854 8200
Email: info@lakesidemanor.ie
Web: www.lakesidemanor.ie
GPS: N +53° 49' 7.37"   W -7° 3' 12.66"

Location
The Lakeside Manor Hotel at the end of the new M3 Motorway, less than 1 hour from Dublin.

Property Highlights
This family run, homely 30 bedroom hotel is a prefect location for weddings & all celebrations, with breath taking views.

Local Attractions
Lots of activities on the lake right on our doorstep. Local golf clubs. Big Pumpkin Festival in October. Fleadh Ceoil in August.

B&B from: €45.00 - €55.00
Suites from: €110.00 - €130.00

Host(s): Meabh & Jim Brady
30

Activities   Facilities

Closed 24 - 26 December

Bracken Court Hotel

Hotel ★ ★ ★ ★   Map 12 O 12

**Bridge Street, Balbriggan,
Co. Dublin**
Tel: +353-1-841 3333
Email: info@brackencourt.ie
Web: www.brackencourt.ie
GPS: N +53° 36' 32.12"   W -6° 10' 58.74"

Location
15 minutes from Dublin Airport, beside train station & bus, centre of the town.

Property Highlights
A boutique style hotel of timeless elegance & underestimated luxury. Home to Jack Doyle's Bar & Laveer Restaurant.

Local Attractions
Ardgillan Castle, Wildlife Parks, Museums, Galleries, Beautiful Beaches, Newgrange.

B&B from: €49.50 - €49.50
Suites from: €150.00 - €150.00

Host(s): Luke Moriarty
66

Activities   Facilities

Open All Year

Waterside House Hotel & Signal Restaurant

Hotel ★ ★ ★   Map 12 O 12

**Balcarrick Road, Donabate,
Co. Dublin**
Tel: +353-1-843 6153
Email: info@watersidehousehotel.ie
Web: www.watersidehousehotel.ie
GPS: N +53° 28' 44.08"   W -6° 6' 55.74"

Location
Situated in North County Dublin. Dublin Airport 15 minutes, City Centre 20 minutes, Train 3 minutes, M1 5 minutes, M50 8 minutes.

Property Highlights
Stunning views of the Irish Sea, Lambay Island & Howth Head. 12 golf courses within 12 minutes and the award-winning Signal Restaurant. Tower Bar & Bistro serves food from 7am-8.30pm.

Local Attractions
12 golf courses in the surrounding area & Corballis Golf Links & Donabate Beach on its doorstep. Historic Newbridge House & Farm nearby. Dublin City Centre 20 minutes away.

B&B from: €30.00 - €140.00
Suites from: €100.00 - €250.00

Host(s): Chris & Thelma Slattery
35

Activities   Facilities

Open All Year

B&B Rates are per Person Sharing per Night incl. Breakfast. Room/Suite Rates are per Room per Night. See also page 08   Dublin & Ireland East   119

Co. Dublin

To Book Call **+353-1-8084419** or www.irelandhotels.com

Dublin Airport

Bewley's Hotel Dublin Airport

Hotel ★ ★ ★   Map 12 O 12

Stockhole Lane (N32 Junction), Swords,
Co. Dublin
Tel: +353-1-871 1000
Email: dublinairport@bewleyshotels.com
Web: www.bewleyshotels.com
GPS: N +53° 24' 41.32"   W -6° 13' 0.25"

Location
Located just off the M50/M1. Close to Dublin Airport, courtesy coach available to Dublin Airport.

Property Highlights
Oversized bedrooms, fluffy duvets, hypo-allergic pillows, tea/coffee making facilities, internet access, multi-channel TV, 24hr courtesy coach to airport terminal. Brasserie Restaurant & Lounge Bar.

Local Attractions
Malahide Castle, National Showcentre, North County Dublin coastline.

Room Rate from: €69.00 - €199.00

Host(s): Tom Moran

466

Activities

Facilities

Closed 24 - 26 December

Carlton Dublin Airport Hotel

Hotel ★ ★ ★ ★   Map 12 O 11

Old Airport Road, Dublin Airport,
Co. Dublin
Tel: +353-1-866 7500
Email: info.dublin@carlton.ie
Web: www.carlton.ie/dublinairport
GPS: N +53° 24' 55.23"   W -6° 14' 25.22"

Location
Next to Dublin Airport Terminal, 15 minutes from city centre, 10 minutes from Croke Park, 2 hours from Belfast, 20 minutes from train station, beside bus stop.

Property Highlights
Elegantly built, offers every facility for business & leisure. Award-winning Kitty Hawks Bar & Bistro, Clouds Rooftop Conference Centre, fitness gym, free 24hr shuttle bus, free internet & parking.

Local Attractions
Guinness Storehouse, Trinity College, historic cathedrals, Croke Park, museums, concert hall, Malahide Marina, Newbridge House & all other attractions Dublin City has to offer.

Room Rate from: €89.00 - €250.00
Suites from: €225.00 - €450.00

Host(s): Declan Meagher

100

Facilities

Closed 24 - 27 December

Hilton Dublin Airport

Hotel ★ ★ ★ ★   Map 12 O 12

Northern Cross, Malahide Road,
Dublin 17
Tel: +353-1-866 1800
Email: reservations.dublinairport@hilton.com
Web: www.dublinairport.hilton.com
GPS: N +53° 24' 13.16"   W -6° 10' 48.21"

Location
The Hilton Dublin Airport is located just a short distance from Dublin Airport by shuttle bus.

Property Highlights
De-stress in the gym or sample delicious steaks at the Burnell Bars Grill. Wind down listening to live music every Friday and Saturday.

Local Attractions
Take an evening shuttle to Howth (views of Dublin Bay & finest seafood). Visit Malahide, a picturesque seaside village, with boutiques, restaurants & Malahide Castle.

Room Rate from: €65.00 - €150.00
Suites from: €105.00 - €190.00

Host(s): Paul Flavin

166

Activities

Facilities

Closed 24 - 29 December

Dublin & Ireland East   B&B Rates are per Person Sharing per Night incl. Breakfast. Room/Suite Rates are per Room per Night.   See also page 08

To Book Call **+353-1-8084419** or www.irelandhotels.com

Co. Dublin
Dublin Airport / Dublin City

Metro Hotel Dublin Airport

Hotel ★ ★ ★   Map 8 O 11

Santry Cross, Ballymun Road,
Dublin 9
Tel: +353-1-866 9500
Email: info@metrohoteldublin.com
Web: www.metrohoteldublinairport.com
GPS: N +53° 24' 3.30"   W -6° 15' 50.30"

Location
Located within 7 minutes of Dublin Airport & 20 minutes from the city centre. The M50 Motorway is 1 minute away.

Property Highlights
88 superb bedrooms, with TV, tea/coffee facilities & safe. Excellent meeting & conference facilities. Rueben's Restautant and Bar. Free WiFi. Free parking. Airport shuttle available. Suites available.

Local Attractions
Malahide Castle, IKEA, Omni Shopping Centre, Dublin City University, Dublin Airport, Botanic Gardens.

Room Rate from: €49.00 - €199.00
Suites from: €69.00 - €229.00

Host(s): Mark Williams

88

Open All Year

Abbott Lodge

Guesthouse ★ ★   Map 8 O 11

87/88 Lower Gardiner Street,
Dublin 1
Tel: +353-1-836 5548
Email: info@abbottlodge.com
Web: www.abbottlodge.com
GPS: N +53° 21' 7.86"   W -6° 15' 21.09"

Location
10 miles from Airport, 10 minutes walk Trinity College, 5 minutes walk to city centre, 5 minutes walk to Busáras Bus Station, 5 minutes walk to Connolly DART Station.

Property Highlights
All rooms en suite with toilet & shower, coffee/tea facilities, full breakfast, 24 hour reception, clean towels.

Local Attractions
Trinity College, Temple Bar, Grafton Street 15 minutes, O2 Arena 25 minutes, Croke Park 15 minutes walk.

B&B from: €30.00 - €60.00

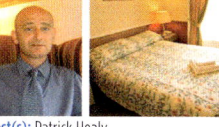

Host(s): Patrick Healy

29

Open All Year

SKERRIES MILLS

Located in the coastal town of Skerries just 30km north of Dublin off the M1

Two Windmills & a Watermill - Guided Tour.
Watermill Café all in - house Baking & Cooking
Crafts Council of Ireland recommended Craft - Shop

**Open 7 days throughout the year from 10.00am
Closed 24th - 27th Dec
& 30th Dec - 1st Jan (Inclusive)**

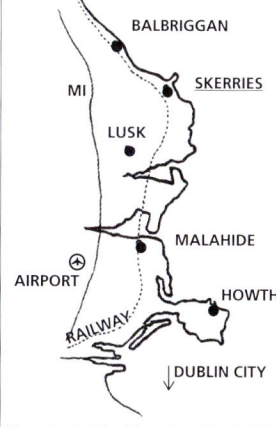

Skerries Mills, Skerries, Co. Dublin
Tel: 353 1 8495208
Fax: 353 1 8495213
Email: skerriesmills@indigo.ie
Web: www.skerriesmills.org

B&B Rates are per Person Sharing per Night incl. Breakfast. Room/Suite Rates are per Room per Night. **See also page 08**   Dublin & Ireland East   121

Co. Dublin

To Book Call **+353-1-8084419** or www.irelandhotels.com

Dublin City

Aberdeen Lodge

Guesthouse ★ ★ ★ ★   Map 8 O 11

53 Park Avenue, Off Ailesbury Road,
Ballsbridge, Dublin 4
Tel: +353-1-283 8155
Email: aberdeen@iol.ie
Web: www.aberdeen-lodge.com
GPS: N +53° 19' 30.06"   W -6° 12' 47.69"

An Glen Guesthouse

Guesthouse ★ ★   Map 8 O 11

84 Lower Gardiner Street,
Dublin 1
Tel: +353-1-855 1374
Email: theglen@eircom.net
Web: www.glenguesthouse.com
GPS: N +53° 21' 5.89"   W -6° 15' 17.33"

Ardagh House

Guesthouse ★ ★ ★   Map 8 O 11

No.1 Highfield Road, Rathgar,
Dublin 6
Tel: +353-1-497 7068
Email: enquiries@ardagh-house.ie
Web: www.ardagh-house.ie
GPS: N +53° 18' 46.66"   W -6° 15' 50.84"

Location
One of Dublin's gems, ideally located in the exclusive embassy district of Ballsbridge. South city centre. Near Airport, Ferry Terminals, DART & Bus.

Location
Beside Connolly Train Station, Bus Áras, 3 minutes walk to the spire. Approx 15 minutes to Dublin Airport and docks.

Location
Located south of city centre. At the cross road with Rathmines Road Upper / Palmerstown Park / Dartry Road. Bus 128 & 14A, Luas close by.

Property Highlights
The perfect balance of luxury, privacy and location. Elegant bedrooms, several with four poster beds, spa baths, complimentary WiFi, garden & car park. USA Toll Free: 1800 617 3178

Property Highlights
Set in Dublin's City Centre, avail of our public bar at our sister hotel. Convenient to all shopping districts. Beside Croke Park and on DART line for new Aviva Stadium.

Property Highlights
Warm family welcome to gracious & spacious Victorian property (1898). Updated & modernised to provide comfortable accommodation. On 1/2 acre with free parking.

Local Attractions
Close to RDS, O2 Theatre, Aviva Stadium, Convention Centre, Grand Canal Theatre, Dublin Airport Coach Link 20 minutes

Local Attractions
Trinity College, Temple Bar, Dublin Zoo, Dublin Arts Museum, Kilmainham Gaol, new Aviva Stadium, Croke Park.

Local Attractions
Perfectly positioned for all the city attractions - historical & entertainment, RDS, Aviva etc. Convenient to M50 Motorway for countrywide access.

B&B from: €69.00 - €99.00
Suites from: €220.00 - €300.00

B&B from: €25.00 - €125.00

B&B from: €35.00 - €55.00

Host(s): Pat Halpin & Ann Keane   20

Host(s): Martin Tynan & Rossi Borisova   13

Host(s): Willie & Mary Doyle   19

Activities   **Facilities**

Facilities

Facilities

Open All Year

Closed 24 - 27 December

Closed 21 December - 03 January

122   Dublin & Ireland East   B&B Rates are per Person Sharing per Night incl. Breakfast. Room/Suite Rates are per Room per Night.   **See also page 08**

To Book Call **+353-1-8084419** or www.irelandhotels.com

Co. Dublin

Dublin City

Ashling Hotel

Hotel ★ ★ ★ ★   Map 8 O 11

**Parkgate Street,
Dublin 8**
Tel: +353-1-677 2324
Email: info@ashlinghotel.ie
Web: www.ashlinghotel.ie
GPS: N +53° 20' 53.00"   W -6° 17' 28.04"

Location

Excellent city location, adjacent to Heuston Railway Station, on Luas Red Line, easy access to M50 Motorway and major routes.

Property Highlights

225 en suite bedrooms. Chesterfields Brassiere and Iveagh Bar. Free car-parking for residents, free WiFi available. Wide range of meeting rooms.

Local Attractions

Phoenix Park, Dublin Zoo, Guinness Brewery, National Museum, Jameson Distillery, Kilmainham Gaol, Temple Bar, The O2, Croke Park, Aviva Stadium.

Room Rate from: €79.00 - €310.00
Suites from: €150.00 - €350.00

Host(s): Alan Moody

225

Activities   **Facilities**

Closed 24 - 26 December

Belvedere Hotel Parnell Square

Hotel ★ ★ ★   Map 8 O 11

**Great Denmark Street, Parnell Square,
Dublin 1**
Tel: +353-1-873 7700
Email: info@belvederehotel.ie
Web: www.belvederehoteldublin.com
GPS: N +53° 21' 18.03"   W -6° 15' 44.25"

Location

City centre location - minutes walk from O'Connell St, retail centres & Croke Park Stadium. 9km from Dublin Airport & 1km from Connolly Train Station.

Property Highlights

Spacious family rooms. Free Wi-Fi access. Traditional Dublin pub feel, all day menu, live music, big screen for sports and events and friendly surroundings.

Local Attractions

James Joyce Centre, Hugh Lane Gallery, Dublin Writers Museum, Gate Theatre. Croke Park, Trinity College, Temple Bar, and Grafton St. Dublin's O2 Arena & Convention Centre.

Room Rate from: €79.00 - €299.00

Host(s): Niamh Fitzpatrick

92

Facilities

Closed 23 - 26 December

Best Western Dublin Skylon Hotel

Hotel ★ ★ ★   Map 8 O 11

**Upper Drumcondra Road,
Dublin 9**
Tel: +353-1-884 3900
Email: reservations@dublinskylonhotel.com
Web: www.dublinskylonhotel.com
GPS: N +53° 22' 21.81"   W -6° 15' 12.07"

Location

A smart hotel on the northern approach of Dublin City, ten minutes from the airport and five from the city centre.

Property Highlights

Dublin Skylon Hotel has just the right blend of style and informality to make your stay special. Its restaurant and bar are welcoming and just as popular in the neighbourhood as with guests.

Local Attractions

Botanic Gardens, Croke Park, O2 Arena, Trinity College, Guinness Storehouse, Temple Bar, Dublin Zoo, National Museums & the many other attractions Dublin City has to offer.

Room Rate from: €49.00 - €499.00
Suites from: €99.00 - €499.00

Host(s): Brian McEniff / Andrew Hyland

126

Activities   **Facilities**

Closed 24 - 26 December

B&B Rates are per Person Sharing per Night incl. Breakfast. Room/Suite Rates are per Room per Night. **See also page 08**

Co. Dublin

To Book Call **+353-1-8084419** or www.irelandhotels.com

Dublin City

Bewley's Hotel Ballsbridge

Hotel ★ ★ ★　　　　　　　　Map 8 0 11

Merrion Road, Ballsbridge,
Dublin 4
Tel: +353-1-668 1111
Email: ballsbridge@bewleyshotels.com
Web: www.bewleyshotels.com
GPS: N +53° 19' 32.41"　W -6° 13' 30.54"

Location
Located adjacent to the RDS grounds in the heart of Dublin's exclusive embassy belt. Situated close to many of the city's tourist attractions.

Property Highlights
Beautifully restored building, originally a Monastic school. Large rooms boast fluffy duvets, tea & coffee facilities, in room safe, internet access, TV. The Brasserie & Tom's Bar for delicious food.

Local Attractions
Situated minutes from Dublin City Centre, the hotel is the ideal base for visiting many of the city's tourist attractions including Trinity College, Guinness Storehouse & many more.

Room Rate from: €69.00 - €199.00

Host(s): Tom Moran
304

Activities　Facilities

Food for Kids

Open All Year

Bewley's Hotel Leopardstown

Hotel ★ ★ ★　　　　　　　　Map 8 0 11

Central Park, Leopardstown,
Dublin 18
Tel: +353-1-293 5000
Email: leopardstown@bewleyshotels.com
Web: www.bewleyshotels.com
GPS: N +53° 16' 16.73"　W -6° 12' 21.91"

Location
Located off M50 and N11. Easy access to city centre via Luas Lite Rail system. Close proximity to Dublin Airport.

Property Highlights
Oversized bedrooms, fluffy duvets & hypo-allergenic pillows. Tea/coffee making facilities, high speed internet access, in-room safe, multi-channel TV. Brasserie Restaurant, Lounge Bar.

Local Attractions
Leopardstown Racecourse, Sandyford Industrial Estate & business Parks.

Room Rate from: €69.00 - €199.00

Host(s): Tom Moran
352

Activities　Facilities

Closed 24 - 26 December

Bewley's Hotel Newlands Cross

Hotel ★ ★ ★　　　　　　　　Map 8 0 11

Newlands Cross, Naas Road (N7),
Dublin 22
Tel: +353-1-464 0140
Email: newlandscross@bewleyshotels.com
Web: www.bewleyshotels.com
GPS: N +53° 18' 48.94"　W -6° 23' 33.41"

Location
Located at Dublin's gateway to the provinces (M50/N7 junction) and convenient to Dublin City Centre via Luas lite rail system.

Property Highlights
Oversized bedrooms, fluffy duvets, hypoallergenic pillows, tea/coffee making facilities, high speed internet access, multi-channel TV, Brasserie Restaurant, Lounge Bar.

Local Attractions
Dublin City Centre, Dublin Zoo, Guinness Storehouse, Croke Park Stadium, Punchestown Racecourse, Grand Canal Theatre.

Room Rate from: €69.00 - €199.00

Host(s): Tom Moran
299

Activities　Facilities

Closed 24 - 27 December

Dublin & Ireland East　　B&B Rates are per Person Sharing per Night incl. Breakfast. Room/Suite Rates are per Room per Night. **See also page 08**

'Sine Metu' www.tours.jamesonwhiskey.com

VISIT JAMESON DISTILLERY TOURS IRELAND

Enjoy JAMESON Sensibly
Visit drinkaware.ie

Open 7 days all year

Guided Tours, Tutored Whiskey Tastings, Restaurant & Jameson Gift Shop.

Book online to receive a 10% discount on adult admission

The Old Jameson Distillery, Bow Street, Smithfield, Dublin 7. e: reservations@ojd.ie, t: 00353 (0)1 807 2355, f: 00353 0(1) 807 2369.

The Jameson Experience, The Old Distillery, Midleton, Co.Cork. e:bookings@omd.ie, t: 00353 (0)21 461 3594, f: 00353 (0)21 461 3704.

Co. Dublin

To Book Call **+353-1-8084419** or www.irelandhotels.com

Dublin City

Blakes Hotel & Spa

Hotel   Map 8 O 11

50-56 Merrion Road, Ballsbridge,
Dublin 4
Tel: +353-1-668 8324
Email: info@blakeshotelandspa.com
Web: www.blakeshotelandspa.com
GPS: N +53° 19' 39.92"   W -6° 13' 32.61"

Built to a 5***** specification

Location
New hotel & spa concept for Dublin. Located in the south city centre embassy district. 20 minutes by Aircoach to Dublin Airport. Near DART & Bus. Car parking.

Property Highlights
Built to a 5 star specification. A sleek urban hotel, Blakes is quickly making its mark as a first class spa hotel in Dublin. USA toll free: 1800 617 3178.

Local Attractions
Near RDS, Aviva Stadium/Lansdowne Road, O2 Arena, Convention Centre, Grafton Street, city centre, Grand Canal Theatre, ferry terminals.

B&B from: €79.00 - €149.00
Suites from: €229.00 - €399.00

Host(s): Pat Halpin & Ann Keane

30

Activities   **Facilities**

Open All Year

Brooks Hotel

Hotel ★ ★ ★ ★   Map 8 O 11

Drury Street,
Dublin 2
Tel: +353-1-670 4000
Email: reservations@brookshotel.ie
Web: www.sinnotthotels.com
GPS: N +53° 20' 29.58"   W -6° 15' 49.09"

Location
In the fashionable heart of Dublin City Centre, 3 minutes from Grafton Street, St. Stephen's Green, Trinity College, Convention Centre. Train & airport easily accessed.

Property Highlights
Award-winning hotel with high standards of customer care, great attention to detail, and a warm welcome second to none.

Local Attractions
Ideal base to explore the city. Local attractions: Guinness Storehouse, Dublin Castle, Trinity College, The O2, Grand Canal Theatre, Gaeity Theatre, The National Museum, Dublin's famous Grafton St.

Room Rate from: €150.00 - €300.00
Suites from: €350.00 - €650.00

Host(s): Anne McKiernan

98

Activities   **Facilities**

Open All Year

Burlington (The)

Hotel ★ ★ ★   Map 8 O 11

Upper Leeson Street,
Dublin 4
Tel: +353-1-618 5600
Email: info@burlingtonhotel.ie
Web: www.burlingtonhotel.ie
GPS: N +53° 19' 49.89"   W -6° 14' 56.55"

Location
Short stroll to city centre with RDS, Aviva Stadium & CCD within quick access by car, bus or taxi. 12km to Dublin Airport with Aircoach stop outside the hotel. Situated in the leafy Embassy Belt.

Property Highlights
Fully refurbished ground floor. 2 bars & 2 restaurants. Renowned conference facilities for up to 1,200 pax. 500 rooms, car parking, free internet access. An ideal choice for business or leisure.

Local Attractions
Grafton Street, St. Stephen's Green, Trinity College, RDS, Grand Canal Theatre, The O2 & CCD.

Room Rate from: €99.00 - €250.00
Suites from: €199.00 - €350.00

Host(s): John Clifton

500

Activities   **Facilities**

Open All Year

B&B Rates are per Person Sharing per Night incl. Breakfast. Room/Suite Rates are per Room per Night. **See also page 08**

To Book Call **+353-1-8084419** or **www.irelandhotels.com**

Co. Dublin
Dublin City

Buswells Hotel

Hotel ★ ★ ★   Map 8 O 11

23/25 Molesworth Street,
Dublin 2
Tel: +353-1-614 6500
Email: enquiries@buswells.ie
Web: www.buswells.ie
GPS: N +53° 20' 26.71"   W -6° 15' 20.93"

Location
City centre location, short distance from Grafton St and major attractions including the Aviva Stadium, The O2 & Convention Centre. Aircoach stop beside hotel.

Property Highlights
A warm friendly welcome awaits you where we offer value for money. Complimentary WiFi in selected bedrooms.

Local Attractions
A short stroll from Book of Kells, National Museum, Galleries & St. Stephen's Green, a choice of theatres including the new Grand Canal Theatre & shops at your doorstep.

B&B from: €49.00 - €150.00

Host(s): Paul Gallagher
67

Activities
Facilities

Closed 24 - 27 December

Butlers Town House

Guesthouse ★ ★ ★ ★   Map 8 O 11

44 Lansdowne Road, Ballsbridge,
Dublin 4
Tel: +353-1-667 4022
Email: info@butlers-hotel.com
Web: www.butlers-hotel.com
GPS: N +53° 20' 2.56"   W -6° 13' 56.32"

Location
Located beside Aviva Stadium - Lansdowne Road, 2 minutes walk from RDS & DART Station. Situated in Dublin's embassy district.

Property Highlights
20 en suite bedrooms, wonderful afternoon tea, gourmet Irish breakfast, free access to leisure club around corner, 24 hour service.

Local Attractions
2 minutes walk from RDS, behind Aviva Stadium, 10 minutes walk from O2 and Grand Canal Theatre.

B&B from: €70.00 - €90.00

Host(s): Cecilia Farrell
20

Facilities

Open All Year

The Book of Kells
'Turning Darkness into Light'

Exhibition and Library Shop open seven days a week

Admission Times

Monday-Saturday
09.30 - 17.00

Sunday (October to April)
12.00 - 16.30

Sunday (May to September)
09.30 - 16.30

Tel: +353 1 896 2320
Fax: +353 1 896 2690

www.bookofkells.ie
bookofkells@tcd.ie

Trinity College Library Dublin

Co. Dublin

To Book Call **+353-1-8084419** or www.irelandhotels.com

Dublin City

Camden Court Hotel

Hotel ★ ★ ★   Map 8 O 11

**Camden Street,
Dublin 2**
Tel: +353-1-475 9666
Email: sales@camdencourthotel.com
Web: www.camdencourthotel.com
GPS: N +53° 19' 59.15"   W -6° 15' 52.32"

Location
Located in Dublin City, within a 5 minute walk from St. Stephen's Green/Grafton Street, close to Luas Green line on Harcourt Street.

Property Highlights
Superb Iveagh Restaurant & C-Central Bar, 12 State of the art conference rooms, Leisure Centre including 16 metre pool, complimentary car parking, Free WiFi.

Local Attractions
Within walking distance to many of Dublin's top attractions - such as Trinity College, National Concert Hall, Christ Church Cathedral, Temple Bar.

Room Rate from: €79.00 - €200.00
Suites from: €155.00 - €250.00

Host(s): Stephen Hanna

246

Activities   **Facilities**

Closed 23 - 28 December

Cassidys Hotel

Hotel ★ ★ ★   Map 8 O 11

**Cavendish Row, Upper O'Connell Street,
Dublin 1**
Tel: +353-1-878 0555
Email: stay@cassidyshotel.com
Web: www.cassidyshotel.com
GPS: N +53° 21' 11.43"   W -6° 15' 41.76"

Location
"A little Gem in the Heart of Dublin". Cassidys is a comfortable, boutique-styled hotel located in Dublin's City Centre opposite the famous Gate Theatre.

Property Highlights
Groomes Bar & Bistro adds a relaxing air and offers character and comfort. Complimentary WiFi and access to fitness suite.

Local Attractions
Within a 10 minute stroll of Trinity College, Temple bar, Theatres, Jameson Distillery.

B&B from: €69.00 - €199.00

Host(s): Martin Cassidy

113

Activities   **Facilities**

Closed 24 - 29 December

Castle Hotel

Hotel ★ ★ ★   Map 8 O 11

**2-4 Gardiner Row,
Dublin 1**
Tel: +353-1-874 6920
Email: info@castle-hotel.ie
Web: www.castle-hotel.ie
GPS: N +53° 21' 17.41"   W -6° 15' 48.06"

Location
Elegant Georgian hotel close to Dublin's main shopping, just 2 minutes from O'Connell Street, close to Temple Bar, Croke Park & Shopping.

Property Highlights
One of Dublin's oldest hotels. The individually decorated rooms are all en suite, with TV, DD phone, hairdryers and tea/coffee making facilities. The hotel has a restaurant, bar and private parking.

Local Attractions
Just 2 minutes walk from O'Connell Street and within walking distance of Croke Park, Temple bar and Dublin's finest Tourist attractions.

Room Rate from: €69.00 - €189.00
Suites from: €150.00 - €300.00

Host(s): Yvonne O' Keeffe

120

Facilities

Closed 24 - 27 December

B&B Rates are per Person Sharing per Night incl. Breakfast. Room/Suite Rates are per Room per Night. See also page 08

To Book Call **+353-1-8084419** or www.irelandhotels.com

Co. Dublin
Dublin City

Castleknock Hotel and Country Club

Hotel ★ ★ ★ ★   Map 8 0 11

Porterstown Road, Castleknock,
Dublin 15
Tel: +353-1-640 6300
Email: reservations@chcc.ie
Web: www.castleknockhotel.com
GPS: N +53° 21' 57.50"   W -6° 23' 23.34"

Location
Located in Castleknock, 9km from Dublin City Centre & 13km from Dublin Airport. Just minutes from the M50 Motorway.

Property Highlights
Leisure centre, Day Spa, golf course, 2 bars, AA Rosette "Park Restaurant", Brassiere Restaurant, children's playground, extensive conference & banqueting facilities.

Local Attractions
Phoenix Park, Dublin Zoo, National Aquatic Centre, Blanchardstown Shopping Centre, Museum of Modern Art, Guinness Storehouse, St. Patrick's Cathedral.

Room Rate from: €69.00 - €300.00
Suites from: €160.00 - €330.00

Host(s): Guy Thompson

138

Activities

Facilities

Closed 24 - 27 December

Celtic Lodge Guesthouse

Guesthouse ★ ★   Map 8 0 11

81/82 Talbot Street,
Dublin 1
Tel: +353-1-878 8732
Email: info@celticlodge.ie
Web: www.celticlodge.ie
GPS: N +53° 21' 1.77"   W -6° 15' 18.21"

Location
Celtic Lodge is located in the heart of the city centre, just minutes walk from the train, bus and Luas.

Property Highlights
Perfect spot for a city break, comprising of a bed and breakfast, traditional Irish pub and an award winning restaurant. Airport transfer available.

Local Attractions
A stroll from our door is the vibrant Temple Bar district. Trinity College, Dublin Castle, National Gallery, Gaiety Theatre etc. are all within a stone's throw.

B&B from: €24.50 - €75.00

Host(s): Brian Moloney

29

Facilities

Closed 23 - 27 December

The National Wax Museum Plus
Foster Place, Temple Bar
Dublin 2
Tel: 01 6718373
Fax: 01 6779140

Now taking bookings for School Tours.
Teachers are FREE!

Email: hello@waxmuseumplus.ie
Web: www.waxmuseumplus.ie

The National Wax Museum Plus is Dublin's most exciting interactive visitor attraction. The museum offers an in site in to Irish history while entertaining through music and dance. Boasting an interactive science gallery, an enchanted children's world and all your favourite superstars immortalized in Wax.

B&B Rates are per Person Sharing per Night incl. Breakfast. Room/Suite Rates are per Room per Night. See also page 08   Dublin & Ireland East   129

Co. Dublin

To Book Call **+353-1-8084419** or www.irelandhotels.com

Dublin City

Charleville Lodge

Guesthouse ★ ★ ★   Map 8 0 11

268-272 North Circular Road, Phibsborough,
Dublin 7
Tel: +353-1-838 6633
Email: info@charlevillelodge.ie
Web: www.charlevillelodge.ie
GPS: N +53° 21' 32.92"   W -6° 16' 47.51"

Location
Ideally located within walking distance of Temple Bar, Trinity College, Phoenix Park. Within easy reach of Dublin Airport, Car Ferries & many historical sites.

Property Highlights
Boutique accommodation, beautifully restored & tastefully refurbished in a traditional manner. Offers guests imitable service & comfort in an atmosphere that is welcoming, attentive & personal.

Local Attractions
Dublin City Tour Bus, can be taken from nearby Parnell Square. This is a great means of seeing the city as one can hop on and off as they please. Close to Croke Park, Mater Hospital & Grangegorman.

B&B from: €17.50 - €75.00

Host(s): Paul Stenson

30

Activities   **Facilities**

Closed 20 - 27 December

Clarence (The)

Hotel ★ ★ ★ ★   Map 8 0 11

6-8 Wellington Quay,
Dublin 2
Tel: +353-1-407 0800
Email: reservations@theclarence.ie
Web: www.theclarence.ie
GPS: N +53° 20' 42.90"   W -6° 16' 0.28"

Location
The Clarence is located in the heart of the city centre. The front of the hotel overlooks the River Liffey and the back overlooks Temple Bar.

Property Highlights
The Clarence, owned by Bono & The Edge of U2, houses the famous Tea Room Restaurant & Octagon Bar.

Local Attractions
Temple Bar, Christchurch, Trinity College, Dublin Castle, Guinness Storehouse, Grafton Street.

Room Rate from: €139.00 - €459.00
Suites from: €349.00 - €2,800.00

Host(s): Clinton Attwell

49

Facilities

Closed 24 - 27 December

Clifden Guesthouse

Guesthouse ★ ★ ★   Map 8 0 11

32 Gardiner Place, (off middle Gardiner Street),
Dublin 1
Tel: +353-1-874 6364
Email: info@clifdenhouse.com
Web: www.clifdenhouse.com
GPS: N +53° 21' 21.30"   W -6° 15' 37.47"

Location
32 Gardiner Place Dublin 1. Located off the top of O'Connell Street. 10 minute walk to O'Connell Bridge.

Property Highlights
All rooms are en suite with telephone, TV, tea & coffee facilities, WiFi access. Walking distance to city centre. Convenient access to all modes of public transport.

Local Attractions
5 minute walk from O'Connell Street. 10 minute walk to Temple Bar, 5 minute walk to Croke Park, restaurants, theatres, gallery's, museums and public swimming pool.

B&B from: €25.00 - €80.00

Host(s): Jack & Mary Lalor

15

Facilities

Open All Year

Co. Dublin
Dublin City

Cliff Town House (The)

Guesthouse ★ ★ ★ ★　　Map 12 O 11

22 St. Stephens Green,
Dublin 2
Tel: +353-1-638 3939
Email: info@theclifftownhouse.com
Web: www.theclifftownhouse.com
GPS: N +53° 20' 21.22"   W -6° 15' 26.19"

Location
St. Stephen's Green, close to buses, LUAS and all major train stations. All Dublin's tourist attractions are a short walk away.

Property Highlights
The restaurant at the Cliff Town House is one of the most talked about, stylish dining venues in Dublin. The bedrooms are luxuriously decorated & are one of Dublin's best kept secrets.

Local Attractions
Close by to the fashionable Grafton Street, right on St. Stephen's Green, all of Dublin's theatres, event and sporting venues are within walking distance.

B&B from: €65.00 - €95.00

Host(s): Drew Flood

10

Activities　Facilities

Closed 25 - 26 December

Clontarf Castle Hotel

Hotel ★ ★ ★ ★　　Map 8 O 11

Castle Avenue, Clontarf,
Dublin 3
Tel: +353-1-833 2321
Email: info@clontarfcastle.ie
Web: www.clontarfcastle.ie
GPS: N +53° 21' 53.32"   W -6° 12' 25.25"

Location
Located in the picturesque coastal suburb of Clontarf, 2 miles from Dublin City, 5 miles from Dublin Airport.

Property Highlights
12th Century castle offering a blend of contemporary & traditional. 111 bedrooms, conference catering for 600, unique restaurants & bars, car parking.

Local Attractions
Experience Dublin City & the Clontarf area. Bull Island Nature Reserve, Clontarf Village, St. Anne's Park, Royal Dublin Golf Club.

Room Rate from: €100.00 - €400.00
Suites from: €140.00 - €420.00

Host(s): Mark Long

111

Activities　Facilities

Open All Year

---

webpostit

No Stamps
No Paper
No Hassle

✓ We Print it
✓ We Package it
✓ We Stamp it
✓ We Post it

Mailed on the same day for next day delivery

A one page letter costs €1.50 All inclusive
A minimum of €5.00 credit is required

First letter is FREE just sign up and enter the coupon code
IRELAND HOTEL 287
N.B one coupon per new client

You don't have to leave your hotel, you can send from anywhere in the world, we do the work, you enjoy your stay.

www.webpostit.ie

To Book Call **+353-1-8084419** or www.irelandhotels.com

B&B Rates are per Person Sharing per Night incl. Breakfast. Room/Suite Rates are per Room per Night. See also page 08

Co. Dublin

To Book Call **+353-1-8084419** or www.irelandhotels.com

Dublin City

Conrad Dublin

Hotel ★ ★ ★ ★ ★   Map 8 O 11

**Earlsfort Terrace,
Dublin 2**
Tel: +353-1-602 8900
Email: dublininfo@conradhotels.com
Web: www.conraddublin.com
GPS: N +53° 20' 5.79"   W -6° 15' 26.17"

Location
In the heart of Dublin, opposite the National Concert Hall. Just off St. Stephen's Green, only minutes walk from fashionable Grafton Street.

Property Highlights
Spacious guest rooms with all mod cons, ergonomic work stations, broadband internet & bathrobes. Restaurant, 2 bars, business centre, fitness centre & extensive conference & events facilities.

Local Attractions
Across the road from the National Concert Hall, around the corner from St. Stephen's Green, only minutes walk from Grafton Street, Trinity College, National Gallery & Georgian Dublin.

Room Rate from: €149.00 - €339.00
Suites from: €239.00 - €1,239.00

Host(s): Martin Mangan

191

Activities
Facilities

Open All Year

Croke Park Hotel (The)

Hotel ★ ★ ★   Map 8 O 11

**Jones's Road,
Dublin 3**
Tel: +353-1-871 4444
Email: crokepark@doylecollection.com
Web: www.doylecollection.com
GPS: N +53° 21' 38.88"   W -6° 15' 14.04"

Location
A short distance from the city centre & in easy reach of retail, entertainment, business districts & the airport, the perfect base for business / leisure trips.

Property Highlights
With its spacious, contemporary interiors, luxurious bedrooms and buzzing bistro and bar, The Croke Park Hotel makes every occasion special.

Local Attractions
Situated directly opposite Croke Park Stadium, the GAA Museum & Stadium are a must-see. Perfect, whether you're in Dublin for a match, concert, conference or that important business meeting.

Room Rate from: €79.00 - €399.00

Host(s): Alan Smullen

232

Facilities

Closed 25 - 28 December

Dergvale Hotel

Hotel ★ ★   Map 8 O 11

**4 Gardiner Place,
Dublin 1**
Tel: +353-1-874 4753
Email: dergvale@indigo.ie
Web: www.dergvalehotel.com
GPS: N +53° 21' 21.99"   W -6° 15' 38.69"

Location
Excellent city centre location, close proximity to O'Connell Street, Airport buses, LUAS Rail System and many of Dublin City's top attractions.

Property Highlights
Family-run Georgian hotel, comprising 20 individually decorated bedrooms with en suite shower bathrooms, direct dial telephone, TV and hairdryer. Fully licensed bar.

Local Attractions
Perfect base from which to explore Dublin Castle, Trinity College, Christchurch Cathedral, Guinness Storehouse, Croke Park, Temple Bar, shopping and much more.

B&B from: €25.00 - €80.00

Host(s): Gerard Nolan

20

Facilities

Closed 23 December - 05 January

---

132   Dublin & Ireland East   B&B Rates are per Person Sharing per Night incl. Breakfast. Room/Suite Rates are per Room per Night. **See also page 08**

To Book Call **+353-1-8084419** or www.irelandhotels.com

Co. Dublin

Dublin City

Drury Court Hotel

Hotel ★ ★ ★   Map 8 0 11

28-30 Lower Stephen Street,
Dublin 2
Tel: +353-1-475 1988
Email: reservations@drurycourthotel.com
Web: www.drurycourthotel.com
GPS: N +53° 20' 28.13"   W -6° 15' 51.80"

Location
Located in the heart of the city, a 2 minute walk to Grafton Street, St. Stephen's Green, Temple Bar and many other visitor attractions.

Property Highlights
42 en suite bedrooms with complimentary WiFi, multi-channel TV/radio & tea/coffee making facilities. Bia Bar provides food, beverages & cocktails.

Local Attractions
Dublin Castle, Chester Beatty Library, Christ Church Cathedral, St. Patrick's Cathedral, Trinity College, National Library and theatres.

Room Rate from: €55.00 - €190.00

Host(s): Paul Hand

42

Facilities

Closed 23 - 28 December

Dylan Hotel

Hotel ★ ★ ★ ★ ★   Map 8 0 11

Eastmoreland Place,
Dublin 2
Tel: +353-1-660 3000
Email: justask@dylan.ie
Web: www.dylan.ie
GPS: N +53° 20' 1.92"   W -6° 14' 32.06"

Location
Just off Baggot St in Dublin's south city centre, minutes from St. Stephen's Green & the main shopping area of Grafton Street. 30 minutes from Dublin Airport.

Property Highlights
44 bespoke rooms offering luxury, style, charm & comfort. Impeccable service. Fine dining in the restaurant, excellent cocktail bar & free internet. The experience at our 5* hotel is worth repeating.

Local Attractions
Dublin's nightlife, shops, bars & restaurants, theatres, museums & a host of local secrets & world famous attractions & landmarks closeby. RDS, Aviva Stadium, The 02, Croke Park & Grand Canal Theatre.

Room Rate from: €169.00 - €395.00
Suites from: €395.00 - €800.00

Host(s): Grainne Ross

44

Facilities

Closed 24 - 26 December

Egan's Guesthouse

Guesthouse ★ ★ ★   Map 8 0 11

7 Iona Park, Glasnevin,
Dublin 9
Tel: +353-1-830 3611
Email: info@eganshouse.com
Web: www.eganshouse.com
GPS: N +53° 22' 1.18"   W -6° 15' 59.59"

Location
Dublin Airport 10km, city centre 2km, bus stop 0.5km, train station 1km, O2 3km, Aviva Stadium 6km, RDS 6km, Mater Hospital 1km.

Property Highlights
Superb staff. WiFi in all rooms. Free games & toys. On-site parking. Free newspapers. Private garden. 10% discount in local restaurants & bars.

Local Attractions
Croke Park 2km, Botanic Gardens 1km, Glasnevin Cemetery & Museum 1km, Griffith Park (includes playground), Royal Canal Walks.

Room Rate from: €20.00 - €80.00

Host(s): Monica & Pat Finn

23

Facilities

Open All Year

B&B Rates are per Person Sharing per Night incl. Breakfast. Room/Suite Rates are per Room per Night. **See also page 08**

Co. Dublin

To Book Call +353-1-8084419 or www.irelandhotels.com

Dublin City

Ferryview Guesthouse

Guesthouse ★ ★ ★   Map 8 O 11

**96 Clontarf Road, Clontarf,
Dublin 3**
Tel: +353-1-833 5893
Email: ferryview@oceanfree.net
Web: www.ferryviewhouse.com
GPS: N +53° 21' 37.54"   W -6° 12' 25.48"

Location
Ferryview Guesthouse is located 2.5 miles from the city centre on the coast road in Clontarf. It is close to the O2 Theatre, Grand Canal Theatre & Croke Park.

Property Highlights
All rooms are en suite with TV, telephone and tea/coffee facilities. WiFi is also available in guest lounge. Free off-street parking.

Local Attractions
Attractions include Clontarf Golf Club, St Anne's Links, and Royal Dublin Golf Course. The Bull Island nature reserve and St Anne's International Rose Garden are also close by.

B&B from: €35.00 - €45.00

Host(s): Margaret Allister

8

Facilities

Open All Year

Fitzsimons Hotel

Hotel ★ ★ ★   Map 8 O 11

**21-22 Wellington Quay, Temple Bar,
Dublin 2**
Tel: +353-1-677 9315
Email: info@fitzsimonshotel.com
Web: www.fitzsimonshotel.com
GPS: N +53° 20' 44.09"   W -6° 15' 55.15"

Location
Fitzsimons is located in the heart of Temple Bar on the banks of the River Liffey. Within walking distance of the major shopping areas and local attractions.

Property Highlights
In the heart of Temple Bar, on the banks of the River Liffey, we are within walking distance of theatres, music venues, restaurants, Trinity College, Dublin Castle, Guinness Brewery & Stephen's Green.

Local Attractions
5 floors of bars incl. a roof terrace where you can dine alfresco or just relax with a drink and watch the many plasma screens. Free live entertainment every night and the night club is open 7 nights.

B&B from: €45.00 - €100.00

Host(s): Darina Howard

22

Facilities

Closed 24 - 25 December

Four Seasons Hotel Dublin

Hotel ★ ★ ★ ★ ★   Map 8 O 11

**Simmonscourt Road,
Dublin 4**
Tel: +353-1-665 4000
Email: reservations.dublin@fourseasons.com
Web: www.fourseasons.com/dublin
GPS: N +53° 19' 35.76"   W -6° 13' 33.86"

Location
In a location of cosmopolitan convenience, a short walk from vibrant shopping and local restaurants. 25 minutes from Dublin International Airport.

Property Highlights
Authentic Irish character blends with chic contemporary style. Enjoy Dublin's only full-service hotel spa, and service that anticipates your every wish.

Local Attractions
Minutes from the cultural and entertainment options of the city centre, easy access to explore Dublin Bay and the Wicklow Mountains.

Room Rate from: €199.00 - €305.00
Suites from: €390.00 - €800.00

Host(s): Jose Soriano

197

Facilities

Open All Year

Dublin & Ireland East | B&B Rates are per Person Sharing per Night incl. Breakfast. Room/Suite Rates are per Room per Night. See also page 08

To Book Call **+353-1-8084419** or www.irelandhotels.com

Co. Dublin

Dublin City

Glenogra House

Guesthouse ★ ★ ★   Map 8 O 11

64 Merrion Road, Ballsbridge,
Dublin 4
Tel: +353-1-668 3661
Email: info@glenogra.com
Web: www.glenogra.com
GPS: N +53° 19' 38.67"   W -6° 13' 29.20"

Location
Close to the RDS, Aviva Stadium, British & American Embassies, Dublin Port, Dun Laoghaire Stena Line, St. Vincent's and Blackrock Hospital.

Property Highlights
Luxurious accommodation in Ballsbridge, set inside an Edwardian House. Relaxed & informal ambiance makes Glengora the perfect place to stay for business & pleasure. Close to Aircoach, Dart & buses.

Local Attractions
Within walking distance you will find a cosmopolitan blend of restaurants & pubs. Herbert Park, Aviva Stadium & seafronts walks.

B&B from: €39.00 - €99.00

Host(s): Joseph Donohoe

13

Facilities

Closed 23 - 28 December

Gresham (The)

Hotel ★ ★ ★ ★   Map 8 O 11

23 Upper O'Connell Street,
Dublin 1
Tel: +353-1-874 6881
Email: info@thegresham.com
Web: www.gresham-hotels.com
GPS: N +53° 21' 5.96"   W -6° 15' 37.17"

Location
Located on O'Connell Street in the city centre of Dublin, easy access from the airport and all other major routes.

Property Highlights
Elegant, sophisticated, tasteful & classic, with 288 bedrooms, excellent conference facilities, Clefs d'Or concierge service, 2 bars, 2 restaurants and a fitness suite. Complimentary WiFi throughout.

Local Attractions
Close to Theatres, Shopping Areas, Cultural Attractions and Temple Bar. The Convention Centre, O2, Croke Park and Aviva Stadium are in walking distance.

B&B from: €60.00 - €300.00
Suites from: €1,500.00 - €2,200.00

Host(s): Paul McCracken

288

Activities

Facilities

Open All Year

Hampton Hotel

Hotel ★ ★ ★ ★   Map 8 O 11

19-29 Morehampton Road,
Dublin 4
Tel: +353-1-668 0995
Email: info@hamptonhotel.ie
Web: www.hamptonhotel.ie
GPS: N +53° 19' 32.94"   W -6° 14' 34.53"

Location
Hampton Hotel is located in Donnybrook, an easy stroll from Dublin City Centre.

Property Highlights
At Hampton Hotel, each of our 24 rooms showcases the charm of the original Georgian architecture combined with bold colours & stylish interior.

Local Attractions
With the city centre, the RDS, Aviva Stadium & The National Concert Hall all within walking distance, Hampton Hotel is the perfect setting to experience Dublin.

Room Rate from: €99.00 - €319.00
Suites from: €189.00 - €479.00

Host(s): Bruno Gorisch

24

Facilities

Open All Year

B&B Rates are per Person Sharing per Night incl. Breakfast. Room/Suite Rates are per Room per Night. See also page 08

Co. Dublin

To Book Call **+353-1-8084419** or www.irelandhotels.com

Dublin City

Harcourt Hotel

Hotel ★ ★ ★   Map 8 0 11

60-65 Harcourt Street,
Dublin 2
Tel: +353-1-478 3677
Email: reservations@harcourthotel.ie
Web: www.harcourthotel.ie
GPS: N +53° 20' 3.91"   W -6° 15' 45.97"

Location
Fashionable city centre location, just off St. Stephen's Green. On Luas Green Line serving Dundrum Town Centre. Grafton St. just a short walk away.

Property Highlights
The Harcourt Hotel is well known for its lively bar & D2 nightclub. An all weather beer garden is a popular feature. Little Caesars' Restaurant takes orders until midnight nightly.

Local Attractions
Dublin Castle, Trinity College, St. Stephen's Green, Iveagh Gardens, The National Art Gallery & all national museums are close by.

Room Rate from: €49.00 - €249.00

Host(s): Danielle McGill

52

Facilities

Closed 24 - 26 December

Harrington Hall

Guesthouse ★ ★ ★ ★   Map 8 0 11

69-70 Harcourt Street,
Dublin 2
Tel: +353-1-475 3497
Email: harringtonhall@eircom.net
Web: www.harringtonhall.com
GPS: N +53° 20' 5.90"   W -6° 15' 46.92"

Location
Fashionable city centre location on Harcourt St, just off St. Stephen's Green. Just a stroll to Grafton St. On Luas Green Line which serves Dundrum Town centre.

Property Highlights
A member of Manor House Hotels. AA 5* rating. Georgian elegance in the heart of the city. Free parking on site.

Local Attractions
Iveagh Gardens at rear of property. Trinity College, Grafton Street. All museums & National Art Gallery are close by, O2 (venue) transfers close by on Stephen's Green.

Room Rate from: €69.00 - €200.00
Suites from: €199.00 - €259.00

Host(s): Paul Glynn

28

Facilities

Open All Year

Harvey's Guest House

Guesthouse ★ ★ ★   Map 8 0 11

11 Upper Gardiner Street,
Dublin 1
Tel: +353-1-874 8384
Email: info@harveysguesthouse.com
Web: www.harveysguesthouse.com
GPS: N +53° 21' 26.45"   W -6° 15' 35.96"

Location
Close to Bus Aras, Connolly Train Station, O'Connell Street and minutes from Dublin City Centre.

Property Highlights
A family-run Georgian guesthouse with a household atmosphere, and we have time to chat with you.

Local Attractions
Close to the Abbey & Gate Theatres, the Writers Museum, Hugh Lane Art Gallery and James Joyce Centre. In close proximity to Croke Park, Temple Bar & Cobblestone Park.

B&B from: €30.00 - €70.00

Host(s): Elizabeth Flood

16

Facilities

Closed 03 January - 03 February

136 Dublin & Ireland East   B&B Rates are per Person Sharing per Night incl. Breakfast. Room/Suite Rates are per Room per Night. See also page 08

To Book Call **+353-1-8084419** or www.irelandhotels.com

Co. Dublin
Dublin City

Website

Mobile App

Printed Guide

facebook.com/irelandhotels

irelandhotels.com/onlineguide

Hilton Dublin

Hotel ★ ★ ★ ★   Map 8 0 11

**Charlemont Place,
Dublin 2**
Tel: +353-1-402 9988
Email: reservations.dublin@hilton.com
Web: www.hilton.com/dublin
GPS: N +53° 19' 52.25" W -6° 15' 33.69"

Location
The Hilton Dublin is ideally situated within walking distance of the main shopping and cultural centre of Dublin.

Property Highlights
We offer Uisce Restaurant and lively Stil Bar, along with an on site fitness centre and LUAS tram stop right outside.

Local Attractions
Perfectly placed to visit Dublin City's most famous landmarks, such as Trinity College, Guinness Storehouse and Christchurch Cathedral to name but a few.

Room Rate from: €99.00 - €290.00

Host(s): Erwin Verhoog

193

Activities

Facilities

Closed 24 - 27 December

Hotel Isaacs

Hotel ★ ★ ★   Map 8 0 11

**Store Street,
Dublin 1**
Tel: +353-1-813 4700
Email: hotel@isaacs.ie
Web: www.hotelisaacs.com
GPS: N +53° 21' 0.32" W -6° 15' 10.05"

Location
City centre, adjacent to Busaras, 200 metres to Connolly Station, DART, Luas. Short walk to Croke Park and the O2 Arena.

Property Highlights
Direct Airport shuttle. Renowned friendly relaxed atmosphere. Superb Italian restaurant, cool cafe bar, gym, unrivalled location. The best breakfast in Dublin.

Local Attractions
Temple Bar, Croke Park, Docklands area, the O2 Arena, the Aviva Stadium, O' Connell Street, river boardwalk, shopping, theatres, museums.

Room Rate from: €50.00 - €280.00
Suites from: €80.00 - €350.00

Host(s): Justin Lowry

103

Activities

Facilities

Open All Year

B&B Rates are per Person Sharing per Night incl. Breakfast. Room/Suite Rates are per Room per Night. **See also page 08**   Dublin & Ireland East

Co. Dublin

To Book Call **+353-1-8084419** or www.irelandhotels.com

Dublin City

La Stampa Hotel

Hotel ★ ★ ★ ★   Map 8 O 11

35/36 Dawson Street,
Dublin 2
Tel: +353-1-677 4444
Email: hotel@lastampa.ie
Web: www.lastampa.ie
GPS: N +53° 20' 25.34"   W -6° 15' 31.48"

Location
Situated in the heart of Dublin City Centre, overlooking the Mansion House.

Property Highlights
This hip boutique hotel features the outstanding Balzac Restuarant and Samsara Café-Bar, while the unique Mandala Spa offers a sanctuary within the bustling city centre.

Local Attractions
Perfect for all Dublin has to offer: shopping, theatres, museums and business.

Room Rate from: €110.00 - €350.00
Suites from: €150.00 - €350.00

Host(s): Daniel Fodor

30

Facilities

Closed 25 - 27 December

Lansdowne Hotel

Hotel ★ ★ ★   Map 8 O 11

27 / 29 Pembroke Road, Ballsbridge,
Dublin 4
Tel: +353-1-668 2522
Email: reception@lansdownehotel.ie
Web: www.lansdownehotel.ie
GPS: N +53° 19' 58.31"   W -6° 14' 28.32"

Location
Located beside Aviva Stadium / DART and main shopping area. Aircoach 5 minutes away.

Property Highlights
Delicious bar food served Mon-Sat in our Den Bar. Hosts the Irish House Party (Traditional Irish Music & Dancing). Weddings - Raglan Function Room & Druids for smaller groups. Family run.

Local Attractions
Newly opened Aviva Stadium is 10 minutes walk, close to RDS. Embassy belt of Ballsbridge, Grafton Street, Trinity College & all major attractions in city centre. Guided walking tours available.

Room Rate from: €49.00 - €230.00

Host(s): Frank Quinn

38

Activities

Facilities

Closed 23 - 30 December

Maldron Hotel Cardiff Lane

Hotel ★ ★ ★ ★   Map 8 O 11

Cardiff Lane, Sir John Rogerson's Quay,
Dublin 2
Tel: +353-1-643 9500
Email: info.cardifflane@maldronhotels.com
Web: www.maldronhotels.com
GPS: N +53° 20' 42.91"   W -6° 14' 28.16"

Location
Conveniently located in the heart of the city off the River Liffey with many nearby attractions.

Property Highlights
Spacious guestrooms with complimentary broadband, Health & Fitness Club offering 22m pool.

Local Attractions
Adjacent to Grand Canal Theatre, one of the closest hotels to The o2, Convention Centre Dublin and Grand Canal Theatre.

Room Rate from: €99.00 - €359.00

Host(s): Conor O'Kane

304

Facilities

Open All Year

To Book Call **+353-1-8084419** or www.irelandhotels.com

Co. Dublin
Dublin City

Maldron Hotel Citywest

Hotel ★ ★ ★   Map 8 O 11

Kingswood Village, Naas Road,
Dublin 22
Tel: +353-1-461 9900
Email: info.citywest@maldronhotels.com
Web: www.maldronhotels.com
GPS: N +53° 18' 4.37"   W -6° 25' 6.24"

Location
The Maldron Hotel Citywest is located at Exit 2 on the N7 (Naas Road). Just 9 miles from Dublin City and less than ten minutes drive to the nearest Luas Station.

Property Highlights
Tastefully decorated rooms, Stir Café, 24 hour reception, complimentary car parking, free WiFi, a choice of meeting rooms & Kingswood Bar & Grill located on site.

Local Attractions
Easy access to all the famous attractions that Dublin City offers, Guinness Storehouse, Trinity College & The Book of Kells, The Old Jameson Distillery, Dublin Castle, National Gallery of Ireland.

Room Rate from: €59.00 - €229.00

Host(s): Ann Marie Traynor

129

Maldron Hotel Parnell Square

Hotel ★ ★ ★   Map 8 o 11

Parnell Square West,
Dublin 1
Tel: +353-1-871 6800
Email: info.parnellsquare@maldronhotels.com
Web: www.maldronhotels.com
GPS: N +53° 21' 18.03"   W -6° 15' 44.25"

Location
Located in Dublin 1 City Centre, a 5 minute walk to Dublin's retail centres. 9km from Dublin Airport. Easy access to Croke Park Stadium & Trinity College Dublin.

Property Highlights
Guest rooms offer stylish décor, free internet access & in-room air-con. Secure parking available at discounted rates for hotel guests. Varied room types available. Ideal city centre base.

Local Attractions
Hugh Lane Gallery, Dublin Writers Museum, Gate Theatre. Within 10 minutes walk of the hotel is Croke Park, Trinity College, Temple Bar, Old Jameson Distillery & Grafton St.

Room Rate from: €79.00 - €299.00

Host(s): Philip Uzice

126

Maldron Hotel Smithfield

Hotel ★ ★ ★   Map 8 O 11

Smithfield,
Dublin 7
Tel: +353-1-485 0900
Email: info.smithfield@maldronhotels.com
Web: www.maldronhotels.com
GPS: N +53° 20' 57.72"   W -6° 16' 43.04"

Location
City centre location. Adjacent to Luas Smithfield. Heuston/Connolly Stations nearby. Walking distance to many tourist attractions, shopping & legal districts.

Property Highlights
Contemporary spacious en-suite rooms, balconies or full length windows with panoramic views. Suites ideal for families or long stay guests.

Local Attractions
Prime city attractions: Dublin Zoo, Jameson Distillery, Guinness Storehouse, Christchurch, Temple Bar, Trinity College, O2, Grand Canal Theatre, Convention Centre Dublin & shopping districts.

Room Rate from: €59.00 - €299.00
Suites from: €79.00 - €299.00

Host(s): Gemma Lucey

92

Closed 21 - 29 December | Closed 23 - 26 December | Closed 23 - 26 December

B&B Rates are per Person Sharing per Night incl. Breakfast. Room/Suite Rates are per Room per Night. **See also page 08**

Dublin & Ireland East   139

Co. Dublin

To Book Call **+353-1-8084419** or www.irelandhotels.com

Dublin City

Maldron Hotel Tallaght

Hotel ★ ★ ★   Map 8 I1 O

Whitestown Way, Tallaght,
Dublin 24
Tel: +353-1-468 5400
Email: info.tallaght@maldronhotels.com
Web: www.maldronhotels.com
GPS: N +53° 17' 2.21"   W -6° 22' 34.69"

Location
In the heart of South Dublin, the perfect base for business or leisure. Located on N81, exit 11 off the M50 & accessible to city centre via Luas, bus or taxi.

Property Highlights
Complimentary secure underground parking. Arena leisure centre incl. 20 metre indoor heated pool, sauna, steam room, jacuzzi, kids pool & fully equipped gymnasium.

Local Attractions
Close to Dublin Mountains & the Square Shopping Centre. Luas is only 5 mins. walk from the hotel providing easy access to Dublin City Centre, Croke Park, Trinity College, O'Connell Street & much more.

B&B from: €35.00 - €139.00

Host(s): Rishnoor Kaur

119

Facilities

Closed 23 - 25 December

Maple Hotel

Hotel ★ ★   Map 8 O 11

74/75 Lower Gardiner Street,
Dublin 1
Tel: +353-1-855 5442
Email: info@maplehotel.com
Web: www.maplehotel.com
GPS: N +53° 21' 4.00"   W -6° 15' 15.95"

Location
We are located in the heart of the city centre with Bus Áras, Connolly Train Station and Temple Bar all within a few minutes of our front door.

Property Highlights
Located beside Temple Bar and within walking distance to Croke Park. Maple Hotel features Ned Keenan's Irish Music Bar, with live music 7 nights a week. Helpful staff, tours organised.

Local Attractions
Temple Bar, Trinity College, O2 Arena, Dublin Castle. O'Connell Street, Grafton Street, Croke Park Stadium, Aviva Stadium.

B&B from: €20.00 - €150.00

Host(s): Martin Tynan

37

Facilities

Closed 24 - 27 December

Marian Guest House

Guesthouse ★   Map 8 O 11

21 Upper Gardiner Street,
Dublin 1
Tel: +353-1-874 4129
Email: info@marianguesthouse.ie
Web: www.marianguesthouse.ie
GPS: N +53° 21' 28.13"   W -6° 15' 37.95"

Location
The Marian Guesthouse is located in Dublin City Centre. Close to Connolly Station, buses to & from the Airport are nearby.

Property Highlights
We offer full Irish breakfast, tea and coffee making facilities available in kitchen area at all times. There is a nice, comfortable lounge to relax in.

Local Attractions
We are ten minutes walk to O'Connell Street, walking distance to Temple Bar, all cinemas and theatres & all main shopping areas. Close to Croke Park and the O2.

B&B from: €30.00 - €45.00

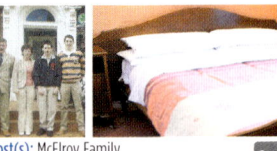

Host(s): McElroy Family

6

Facilities

Open All Year

B&B Rates are per Person Sharing per Night incl. Breakfast. Room/Suite Rates are per Room per Night. See also page 08

To Book Call **+353-1-8084419** or www.irelandhotels.com

Co. Dublin
Dublin City

Mercer Hotel

Hotel ★ ★ ★ Map 8 O 11

Lower Mercer Street,
Dublin 2
Tel: +353-1-478 2179
Email: reception@mercerhotel.ie
Web: www.mercerhotel.ie
GPS: N +53° 20' 22.03"   W -6° 15' 50.58"

Location
Located in Dublin City Centre close to Stephen's Green, we are an ideal base for leisure & corporate guests.

Property Highlights
Friendly, welcoming staff ensure our guests stay is comfortable & enjoyable where all requests are dealt with professionally.

Local Attractions
Close by: St. Stephen's Green Park, Gaiety Theatre, Grafton Street's many shops, 5 mins to Temple Bar Cultural Quarter, Luas Tram stops nearby, Trinity College, Museums, Art Galleries.

B&B from: €65.00 - €140.00

Host(s): Ann O'Doherty

Activities **Facilities**

Closed 23 - 30 December

Merrion Hotel (The)

Hotel ★ ★ ★ ★ ★ Map 8 O 11

Upper Merrion Street,
Dublin 2
Tel: +353-1-603 0600
Email: info@merrionhotel.com
Web: www.merrionhotel.com
GPS: N +53° 20' 18.72"   W -6° 15' 10.34"

Location
The Merrion stands directly opposite government buildings in the heart of Dublin City Centre.

Property Highlights
Home of Ireland's largest private art collection. 1/2 acre of private landscaped gardens. Ireland's only 2 Michelin star restaurant. 18 m pool & spa facilities.

Local Attractions
Merrion Square, National Gallery, National History Museum are located on the Merrion's doorstep. A short walk leads to the adjacent "Golden Mile" of lively pubs, shops & restaurants.

Room Rate from: €480.00 - €510.00
Suites from: €960.00 - €3,000.00

Host(s): Peter MacCann

Facilities

Open All Year

Mespil Hotel

Hotel ★ ★ ★ Map 8 O 11

Mespil Road,
Dublin 4
Tel: +353-1-488 4600
Email: mespil@leehotels.com
Web: www.mespil.com
GPS: N +53° 20' 0.17"   W -6° 14' 47.05"

Location
City centre hotel located in the heart of Georgian Dublin, at Baggot Street Bridge, overlooking the banks of the Grand Canal.

Property Highlights
All guest bedrooms are bright, modern & spacious to ensure a relaxing stay. The Terrace Bar & Glaze Bistro offer many dining options. Free WiFi available. Two meeting rooms.

Local Attractions
Aviva Stadium, Grand Canal Theatre, RDS Ballsbridge, Trinity College, Merrion Square, St. Stephen's Green & Grafton Street are all within walking distance.

Room Rate from: €75.00 - €205.00

Host(s): Martin Holohan

Facilities

Closed 23 - 28 December

B&B Rates are per Person Sharing per Night incl. Breakfast. Room/Suite Rates are per Room per Night. **See also page 08**

Co. Dublin

To Book Call **+353-1-8084419** or www.irelandhotels.com

Dublin City

Number 31

Guesthouse ★★★★ Map 8 O 11

31 Leeson Close,
Dublin 2
Tel: +353-1-676 5011
Email: info@number31.ie
Web: www.number31.ie
GPS: N +53° 20' 0.26" W -6° 15' 13.15"

Location
Right in the heart of Georgian Dublin a few minutes walk from St. Stephen's Green and the main shopping district of Dublin.

Property Highlights
An award-winning guesthouse recommended by the Good Hotel Guide, Egon Ronay, Bridgestone 100 Best Places, Fodors & awarded Georgina Campbell's Irish Breakfast Award 2008.

Local Attractions
Just a few minutes walk from St. Stephen's Green, Grafton Street, museums and galleries.

B&B from: €70.00 - €140.00

Host(s): Noel Comer 21

Facilities

Open All Year

O'Sheas Hotel

Hotel ★ Map 8 O 11

19 Talbot Street,
Dublin 1
Tel: +353-1-836 5670
Email: osheashotel@eircom.net
Web: www.osheashotel.com
GPS: N +53° 21' 2.76" W -6° 15' 17.90"

Location
Located in the city centre, only 5 minutes from O'Connell Street, 20 minutes from Dublin Airport and 5 minutes from train and bus stations.

Property Highlights
O'Sheas Hotel has 34 recently refurbished en suite bedrooms. The hotel also has conference facilities for up to 180 people. Known for food, service, room quality, cost and location.

Local Attractions
5 minutes walk from city centre, 10 minutes walk from Temple Bar. Close to all main attractions.

B&B from: €35.00 - €80.00

Host(s): John McCormack 34

Facilities

Closed 25 - 26 December

Palmerstown Lodge

Guesthouse ★★★ Map 8 O 11

Palmerstown Village,
Dublin 20
Tel: +353-1-623 5494
Email: info@palmerstownlodge.ie
Web: www.palmerstownlodge.ie
GPS: N +53° 21' 19.01" W -6° 22' 17.25"

Location
Prime location, this superb purpose-built property adjoins the N4/M50 motorway. It is minutes from the city centre and a mere 12 minutes drive to the airport.

Property Highlights
Offering all the features & standards of a hotel. Each en suite bedroom has individual temperature control, ambient lighting, phone, TV, separate tea/coffee & free internet area. Private car park.

Local Attractions
Short distance from Dublin City & all it has to offer. Local golf courses, National Aquatic Centre & Phoenix Park. Shopping facilities including Blanchardstown & Liffey Valley Shopping Centres.

B&B from: €30.00 - €50.00

Host(s): Gerry O'Connor 19

Facilities

Open All Year

142 Dublin & Ireland East   B&B Rates are per Person Sharing per Night incl. Breakfast. Room/Suite Rates are per Room per Night. **See also page 08**

To Book Call **+353-1-8084419** or www.irelandhotels.com   Co. Dublin

Dublin City

You can find all the best deals in all of these places

Website

Mobile App

Printed Guide

facebook.com/irelandhotels

irelandhotels.com/onlineguide

Radisson Blu St Helen's Hotel

Hotel ★ ★ ★ ★   Map 8 0 11

Stillorgan Road, Blackrock,
Dublin 4
Tel: +353-1-218 6000
Email: info.dublin@radissonblu.com
Web: www.radissonblu.ie/sthelenshotel-dublin
GPS: N +53° 18' 17.25"   W -6° 12' 20.43"

Location
Located 3.5 miles south of city centre, with easy access to the N11 & M50, DART, Air Coach, dedicated bus corridor to the city centre, Port Tunnel to airport.

Property Highlights
151 luxurious rooms & suites, also Talavera authentic Italian restaurant, The Orangerie Bar & Ballroom Lounge, Fitness Room & Beauty Salon. Complimentary Car Parking & WiFi.

Local Attractions
Dundrum Town Centre is 10 minutes away, also nearby is Dun Laoghaire, the Wicklow Mountains, RDS, Aviva Stadium & Grand Canal Theatre.

**Room Rate from: €109.00 - €500.00
Suites from: €159.00 - €550.00**

Host(s): Neil Lane

151

Activities   Facilities

Food for Kids

Open All Year

Red Cow Moran Hotel

Hotel ★ ★ ★ ★   Map 8 0 11

Red Cow Complex, Naas Road,
Dublin 22
Tel: +353-1-459 3650
Email: redcowres@moranhotels.com
Web: www.moranhotels.com
GPS: N +53° 19' 7.95"   W -6° 21' 50.21"

Location
Gateway to the provinces, Red Cow Moran Hotel is a short distance from Dublin International Airport. Easy access to the city centre via Luas Lite Rail service.

Property Highlights
Air conditioned rooms, TV, fluffy duvets, DD phone, WiFi, hair dryer, tea/coffee making facilities, boasts 2 restaurants, choice of lively bars, conference facilities & business centre. Free parking.

Local Attractions
Dublin Zoo, Dublin City Centre, Guinness Storehouse.

**B&B from: €49.00 - €195.00
Suites from: €150.00 - €500.00**

Host(s): Tom Moran

123

Activities   Facilities

Food for Kids

Closed 24 - 27 December

B&B Rates are per Person Sharing per Night incl. Breakfast. Room/Suite Rates are per Room per Night. **See also page 08**   Dublin & Ireland East   143

Co. Dublin

To Book Call **+353-1-8084419** or www.irelandhotels.com

Dublin City

Sandymount Hotel (formerly Mount Herbert Hotel)

Hotel ★ ★ ★   Map 8 O 11

Herbert Road, Lansdowne Road,
Dublin 4
Tel: +353-1-614 2000
Email: info@sandymounthotel.ie
Web: www.sandymounthotel.ie
GPS: N +53° 20' 0.26"   W -6° 13' 28.09"

Location
In exclusive Dublin 4, only 2 stops from city centre by DART rail, with easy access to the Airport & Ferry.

Property Highlights
Renowned over 50 years for excellent & friendly service. Private Gardens, Free Parking, Restaurant, Bar, Business Centre, free WiFi.

Local Attractions
At Aviva Stadium, near RDS, The O2, Grand Canal Theatre, The CCD, City Centre, Temple Bar & Trinity College.

Room Rate from: €59.00 - €240.00
Suites from: €130.00 - €320.00

Host(s): Michelle Sweeney

168

Closed 23 - 26 December

Shelbourne Hotel (The)

Hotel ★ ★ ★ ★ ★   Map 8 O 11

27 St. Stephen's Green,
Dublin 2
Tel: +353-1-663 4500
Email: rhi.dubbr.reservations@renaissancehotels.com
Web: www.theshelbourne.ie
GPS: N +53° 20' 20.58"   W -6° 15' 21.94"

Location
Located right in the heart of Dublin on St. Stephen's green. 9km from Dublin Airport, footsteps from the sights and sounds of Georgian Dublin.

Property Highlights
13 Historic Conference & Banqueting Suites, Afternoon Tea in the Lord Mayors Lounge, No. 27 Lounge & Bar, The Horseshoe Bar, The Saddle Room Restaurant.

Local Attractions
Trinity College, shopping on Grafton Street, Dublin Castle, National Gallery, National Concert Hall.

B&B from: €99.00 - €145.00
Suites from: €330.00 - €2,500.00

Host(s): Liam Doyle

265

Open All Year

Stillorgan Park Hotel

Hotel ★ ★ ★ ★   Map 8 O 11

Stillorgan Road, Stillorgan,
Dublin 18
Tel: +353-1-200 1800
Email: reservations@stillorganpark.com
Web: www.stillorganpark.com
GPS: N +53° 17' 41.93"   W -6° 12' 10.08"

Location
Excellent location on the N11, close to M50, Dublin City Centre, the O2, Aviva Stadium, RDS & public transport routes. An ideal base from which to explore Dublin City and its surroundings.

Property Highlights
150 air conditioned, modern rooms. Award-winning restaurant & bar. White Pebble Day Spa & gym. Complimentary WiFi. Free parking. Complimentary courtesy bus service locally to city centre.

Local Attractions
Dundrum Shopping Centre, O2 Arena, Aviva Stadium, RDS, Dun Laoghaire Port, Leopardstown Racecourse & Grand Canal Theatre all a short distance from the hotel.

Room Rate from: €79.00 - €189.00
Suites from: €129.00 - €239.00

Host(s): Daragh O'Neill

150

Closed 24 - 26 December

B&B Rates are per Person Sharing per Night incl. Breakfast. Room/Suite Rates are per Room per Night. See also page 08

To Book Call **+353-1-8084419** or www.irelandhotels.com

Co. Dublin
Dublin City

Tara Towers Hotel

Hotel ★ ★ ★   Map 8 O 11

**Merrion Road,
Dublin 4**
Tel: +353-1-269 4666
Email: reservations@taratowers.com
Web: www.taratowers.com
GPS: N +53° 18' 44.44"   W -6° 12' 8.86"

Location
19km from Dublin International Airport & 7km from Dublin City Centre & only 0.5km from Booterstown Train Station.

Property Highlights
Free car parking for all guests of the hotel, views of Dublin Bay and Dublin Mountains. All 111 rooms with en suite facilities, bar, restaurant & lounge facilities.

Local Attractions
RDS, Aviva Stadium, Blackrock Village, 5 minutes from the beach. Dun Laoghaire 10 minutes drive, 5km from Dundrum Shopping Centre.

B&B from: €45.00 - €150.00
Suites from: €150.00 - €150.00

Host(s): Catherine McGrath
111

Activities   Facilities

Closed 20 - 31 December

Temple Bar Hotel

Hotel ★ ★ ★   Map 8 O 11

**Fleet Street, Temple Bar,
Dublin 2**
Tel: +353-1-677 3333
Email: reservations@tbh.ie
Web: www.TempleBarHotel.com
GPS: N +53° 20' 45.00"   W -6° 15' 37.49"

Location
Located in the heart of Dublin City, Temple Bar is in walking distance of all major transport links and attractions.

Property Highlights
We have 129 de luxe rooms right in the middle of Dublin City Centre. Our famous Busker's Bar is always lively & a visit to our Alchemy Club & Venue is a must.

Local Attractions
We are within walking distance of all of Dublin's attractions, shopping areas & the best pubs & clubs in the city.

Room Rate from: €70.00 - €180.00

Host(s): Olive Santry
129

Activities   Facilities

Closed 23 - 25 December

Trinity Capital Hotel

Hotel ★ ★ ★   Map 8 O 11

**Pearse Street,
Dublin 2**
Tel: +353-1-648 1000
Email: info@trinitycapital-hotel.com
Web: www.trinitycapitalhotel.com
GPS: N +53° 20' 42.70"   W -6° 15' 15.04"

Location
Beside Trinity College, Grafton Street, Temple Bar, O2 Arena, Grand Canal Theatre, The IFSC & The Convention Centre.

Property Highlights
Our beautifully designed boutique style guestrooms offer all the modern conveniences to make your stay memorable. Ask about the luxurious upgrade options.

Local Attractions
All entertainment & cultural attractions are close by, including Trinity College, Temple Bar, Dublin Castle, St. Patrick's Cathedral & Guinness Storehouse.

Room Rate from: €89.00 - €275.00
Suites from: €129.00 - €325.00

Host(s): Denyse Campbell
195

Facilities

Closed 24 - 27 December

B&B Rates are per Person Sharing per Night incl. Breakfast. Room/Suite Rates are per Room per Night. **See also page 08**

Co. Dublin

To Book Call **+353-1-8084419** or www.irelandhotels.com

Dublin City

Uppercross House

Hotel ★ ★ ★   Map 8 O 11

26-30 Upper Rathmines Road, Rathmiines,
Dublin 6
Tel: +353-1-497 5486
Email: enquiries@uppercrosshousehotel.com
Web: www.uppercrosshousehotel.com
GPS: N +53° 19' 15.00" W -6° 15' 54.82"

Location
Rathmines - 2km south of city centre. 1.5km RDS / Aviva Stadium. 1km Harold's Cross Greyhound Stadium.

Property Highlights
Family run hotel, great food & drink, live music, 24 hour reception service. Pet friendly.

Local Attractions
Jameson Distillery, Guinness Brewery, Grand Canal Theatre, RDS, Harolds Cross Races, Aviva Stadium & St. Stephen's Green.

B&B from: €34.50 - €65.00

Host(s): David Mahon

50

Facilities

Closed 23 - 29 December

Waterloo House

Guesthouse ★ ★ ★ ★   Map 8 O 11

8-10 Waterloo Road, Ballsbridge,
Dublin 4
Tel: +353-1-660 1888
Email: waterloohouse@eircom.net
Web: www.waterloohouse.ie
GPS: N +53° 19' 53.67" W -6° 14' 36.62"

Location
Ballsbridge, minutes from the city centre, RDS, Aviva Stadium, Stephen's Green, Grafton Street, Grand Canal Theatre, Lansdowne Road DART.

Property Highlights
Georgian house, refurbished to superb standard with a unique atmosphere, style & elegance. Breakfast served on garden level. Lift & car park. Courtesy Irish Times & WiFi free of charge.

Local Attractions
RDS, Aviva Stadium, city centre, St. Stephen's Green.

B&B from: €49.00 - €100.00
Suites from: €110.00 - €220.00

Host(s): Evelyn Corcoran

17

Facilities

Closed 23 - 28 December

Westbury Hotel (The)

Hotel ★ ★ ★ ★ ★   Map 8 O 11

Grafton Street,
Dublin 2
Tel: +353-1-679 1122
Email: westbury@doylecollection.com
Web: www.doylecollection.com
GPS: N +53° 20' 29.25" W -6° 15' 42.02"

Location
The Westbury Hotel, a member of The Leading Hotels of the World is located in Dublin's City Centre, just off Grafton St.

Property Highlights
The Westbury Hotel offers a genuine welcome whether you're relaxing in The Gallery, dining in either of our superb restaurants or doing business in our superbly equipped conference suites.

Local Attractions
Located half-way between historic Trinity College and Stephen's Green, The Westbury Hotel is at the very heart of Dublin's premier retail and cultural quarter.

Room Rate from: €179.00 - €499.00

Host(s): Edward Stephenson

205

Facilities

Open All Year

146   Dublin & Ireland East   B&B Rates are per Person Sharing per Night incl. Breakfast. Room/Suite Rates are per Room per Night. See also page 08

To Book Call **+353-1-8084419** or www.irelandhotels.com

Co. Dublin

Dublin City / Dun Laoghaire / Howth

Westin Dublin

Hotel ★ ★ ★ ★ ★   Map 8 O 11

At College Green, Westmoreland Street,
Dublin 2
Tel: +353-1-645 1000
Email: reservations.dublin@westin.com
Web: www.thewestindublin.com
GPS: N +53° 20' 44.31" W -6° 15' 32.05"

Location
Situated in the heart of Dublin City centre, follow all signs for Dublin City centre, and contact our concierge team on 01-6451000 for further directions.

Property Highlights
Behind the historic, listed facade of the former Allied Irish Bank built in 1863, the 5 star Westin Dublin has become a landmark in Ireland's capital.

Local Attractions
Opposite Trinity College. The exclusive shops of Grafton Street and Dublin's business & financial districts all within walking distance. Dublin's cultural quarter, Temple Bar is a stones throw away.

Room Rate from: €169.00 - €489.00

Host(s): Andrew R. Henning

163

Activities   Facilities

Open All Year

Royal Marine Hotel

Hotel ★ ★ ★ ★   Map 8 O 11

Marine Road, Dun Laoghaire,
Co. Dublin
Tel: +353-1-230 0030
Email: sales@royalmarine.ie
Web: www.royalmarine.ie
GPS: N +53° 17' 32.07" W -6° 8' 2.13"

Location
Dun Laoghaire, overlooking Dublin Bay. 15 minutes south of the city, accessible via DART line, buses & taxi service.

Property Highlights
Sea view suites & bedrooms, 1863 built historic building. 14 dedicated meeting rooms, Carlisle Conference Centre, Sansana Spa & Pier Health Club.

Local Attractions
Dun Laoghaire Harbour, Pavilion Theatre, Maritime Museum, James Joyce Martello Towers & Museum, Dalkey Castle, Killiney Hill, sailing, golf.

Room Rate from: €99.00 - €379.00
Suites from: €199.00 - €1,999.00

Host(s): Aidan Ryan

228

Activities   Facilities

Open All Year

Deer Park Hotel Golf & Spa

Hotel ★ ★ ★   Map 12 P 11

Howth,
Co. Dublin
Tel: +353-1-832 2624
Email: sales@deerpark.iol.ie
Web: www.deerpark-hotel.ie
GPS: N +53° 22' 49.93" W -6° 4' 41.36"

Location
Set in the magnificent grounds of Howth Castle overlooking the sea, just 14km from Dublin City, Airport & Ferry Port.

Property Highlights
4 golf courses, leisure centre, cookery school and magnificent woodland and hill walks, all within the 600 acre grounds.

Local Attractions
Howth Harbour with its seal colony, cliff walks, traditional pubs and restaurants, sandy beaches, numerous loop walks and the DART.

B&B from: €40.00 - €80.00

Host(s): David & Antoinette Tighe

69

Activities   Facilities

Closed 23 - 27 December

B&B Rates are per Person Sharing per Night incl. Breakfast. Room/Suite Rates are per Room per Night. See also page 08   Dublin & Ireland East   147

Co. Dublin

To Book Call **+353-1-8084419** or www.irelandhotels.com

Killiney / Lucan

Fitzpatrick Castle Hotel

Hotel ★ ★ ★ ★   Map 8 P 10

Killiney,
Co. Dublin
Tel: +353-1-230 5400
Email: info@fitzpatricks.com
Web: www.fitzpatrickcastle.com
GPS: N +53° 16' 9.62"   W -6° 6' 47.10"

Location
Hotel is 18 miles from Dublin Airport, 9 miles from city centre. Dun Laoghaire Ferry Port is 3 miles from the hotel & Dalkey DART/train station is just 1/2 mile.

Property Highlights
Original castle with car parking complimentary. Rooms with sea views and original castle suites. Award-winning AA rosette restaurant. 20m swimming pool, jacuzzi, sauna, steam room & gym.

Local Attractions
Killiney Hill, Dun Laoghaire Harbour, James Joyce Tower, Powerscourt Gardens, Dalkey Castle & Heritage Centre, Leopardstown Racecourse.

Room Rate from: €120.00 - €360.00
Suites from: €200.00 - €500.00

Host(s): Nicholas Logue

Activities **Facilities**

Open All Year

Finnstown Country House Hotel

Hotel ★ ★ ★   Map 8 N 11

Newcastle Road, Lucan,
Co. Dublin
Tel: +353-1-601 0700
Email: manager@finnstown-hotel.ie
Web: www.finnstown-hotel.ie
GPS: N +53° 20' 22.75"   W -6° 27' 41.05"

Location
8 miles from airport, 12km from Dublin City. The hotel is located off the N4 in the direction of Adamstown & Newcastle, past Superquinn Shopping Centre in Lucan.

Property Highlights
45 acres of private grounds. 18th Century building, original fire places. Old world charm. AA Rosette Restaurant. Real Irish welcome. Private, intimate, relaxing.

Local Attractions
Castletown House Parkland, Liffey Valley Shopping & Cinema, Dublin Zoo, Kildare Village, Irish National Stud, Japanese Gardens, Butterfly Farm, Pet Farm, Dublin Mountains.

B&B from: €79.00 - €250.00

Host(s): Barry Maher

Activities **Facilities**

Closed 24 - 26 December

Moat Lodge

Guesthouse ★ ★   Map 8 N 11

Adamstown Road, Lucan,
Co. Dublin
Tel: +353-1-624 1584
Email: info@moatlodge.ie
Web: www.moatlodge.ie
GPS: N +53° 21' 16.29"   W -6° 26' 58.89"

Location
In the heart of Lucan village, just off N4. Close to Liffey Valley Shopping Centre, Hermitage & Lucan Golf Courses.

Property Highlights
17th century house, overlooked by wooded area. Award winning small garden. Private secure car park.

Local Attractions
Quaint Lucan village. Lovely walks through St. Catherine's Park beside River Liffey. Historic Castletown House nearby.

B&B from: €30.00 - €35.00

Host(s): Astrid Scott

Facilities

Open All Year

To Book Call **+353-1-8084419** or www.irelandhotels.com

Co. Dublin

Lusk / Malahide / Skerries

Hillview House

Guesthouse ★ ★ ★   Map 12 O 12

Ballaghstown, Lusk,
Co. Dublin
Tel: +353-1-843 8218
Email: lfynes@indigo.ie
Web: www.hillviewhouselusk.com
GPS: N +53° 32' 31.46"   W -6° 8' 53.55"

Location
Hillview House is situated between Lusk & seaside town of Skerries, yet only 15 minutes away from Dublin Airport and 30 minutes from Dublin City.

Property Highlights
Hillview is a purpose-built family-run guesthouse with residence lounge. Large and spacious rooms offering similar facilities to those of quality hotels. Set in a peaceful and tranquil area.

Local Attractions
Hillview House is situated minutes from the fishing village of Skerries, Ardgillan Castle, Skerries Mills, sandy beaches, golf courses, horseriding and clay pigeon shooting.

B&B from: €40.00 - €50.00

Host(s): Leo & Kay Fynes

10

Facilities

Closed 20 December - 03 January

Grand Hotel

Hotel ★ ★ ★ ★   Map 12 O 12

Malahide,
Co. Dublin
Tel: +353-1-845 0000
Email: booking@thegrand.ie
Web: www.thegrand.ie
GPS: N +53° 27' 2.71"   W -6° 8' 50.73"

Location
The Grand Hotel is located by the sea in the village of Malahide, 10 minutes drive from Dublin Airport & 30 mins. from the city centre. The DART 15 mins. away.

Property Highlights
203 bedrooms, most rooms have spectacular sea views. Leisure centre includes 21 metre swimming pool, jacuzzi, fully equipped gymnasium, sauna & steam room.

Local Attractions
Surrounded by excellent golf courses, visitor attractions include Malahide Castle & Demesne.

B&B from: €57.50 - €125.00
Suites from: €130.00 - €800.00

Host(s): Matthew Ryan

203

Activities   Facilities

Closed 24 - 26 December

Carroll's Pierhouse Hotel

Hotel ★ ★   Map 12 P 12

The Harbour, Skerries,
Co. Dublin
Tel: +353-1-849 1033
Email: info@pierhousehotel.ie
Web: www.pierhousehotel.ie
GPS: N +53° 35' 6.83"   W -6° 6' 18.23"

Location
Located in the quiet fishing village of Skerries in North County Dublin, close to Dublin Airport, Train Station & Buses & 30 minutes from Dublin City Centre.

Property Highlights
Family-run hotel, delightfully furnished & elegant in style. The idyllic location provides its guests with a wonderful panoramic view of the Irish Sea. Free WiFi.

Local Attractions
Shooting, fishing, horseriding, sea swimming, golfing, tennis, cricket & rugby.

B&B from: €35.00 - €65.00

Host(s): Mary & Michael Carroll

10

Facilities

Closed 24 - 26 December

B&B Rates are per Person Sharing per Night incl. Breakfast. Room/Suite Rates are per Room per Night. *See also page 08*   Dublin & Ireland East   149

Co. Dublin

To Book Call **+353-1-8084419** or www.irelandhotels.com

Skerries / Sutton / Swords

Redbank House Guesthouse & Restaurant

Guesthouse ★ ★ ★ Map 12 P 12

5 - 7 Church Street, Skerries,
Co. Dublin
Tel: +353-1-849 1005
Email: info@redbank.ie
Web: www.redbank.ie
GPS: N +53° 34' 47.24" W -6° 6' 33.35"

Location
Located on Church St, Skerries, short walk to station on the main rail line between Dublin & Belfast with frequent commuter service. 20 minutes on N1 to Airport.

Property Highlights
We have one of Ireland's premier seafood restaurants with TV Chef Proprietor cooking the catch of the day landed each evening at Skerries Pier. A retired bank, the vault is now the wine cellar.

Local Attractions
The Historic Boyne Valley, medieval Carlingford, Malahide Castle just a short drive. The commuter train/bus service to Dublin is the way to go & avoid gridlock & frustration.

B&B from: €40.00 - €75.00

Host(s): Terry McCoy

18

Activities

Facilities

Open All Year

Marine Hotel

Hotel ★ ★ ★ Map 12 P 11

Sutton Cross,
Dublin 13
Tel: +353-1-839 0000
Email: info@marinehotel.ie
Web: www.marinehotel.ie
GPS: N +53° 23' 19.42" W -6° 6' 37.63"

Location
The Marine Hotel overlooking the shore of Dublin Bay with its lawns sweeping down to the sea. The city centre is 6km away and airport 25 minutes. DART closeby.

Property Highlights
Indoor, heated swimming pool and sauna. All bedrooms are en suite and have trouser press, TV, direct dial phone and tea/coffee facilities.

Local Attractions
Nearby are the Royal Dublin and Portmarnock Championship Golf Courses. The charming old fishing village of Howth is just minutes away with several excellent restaurants, bars, coastal walks.

Room Rate from: €50.00 - €200.00

Host(s): Matthew Ryan

48

Facilities

Closed 24 - 26 December

Roganstown Hotel & Country Club

Hotel ★ ★ ★ ★ Map 12 O 12

Roganstown, Naul Road, Swords,
Co. Dublin
Tel: +353-1-843 3118
Email: info@roganstown.com
Web: www.roganstown.com
GPS: N +53° 29' 12.33" W -6° 16' 23.67"

Location
Located approx. 5 minutes from Dublin Airport & just 5 minutes from Swords Village. 25 minutes from Dublin City Centre & 15 minutes from Malahide Train Station.

Property Highlights
With ample complimentary car parking & a convenient location to Dublin Airport, a stay at Roganstown Hotel & Country Club is the perfect place to relax & unwind. Full leisure centre & indoor pool.

Local Attractions
Complimentary shuttle to and from Dublin Airport, on site golf course, kids' camps, pilates, restaurant, spa.

Room Rate from: €49.50 - €147.80

Host(s): Ian McGuinness

52

Facilities

Closed 24 - 26 December

Dublin & Ireland East B&B Rates are per Person Sharing per Night incl. Breakfast. Room/Suite Rates are per Room per Night. See also page 08

To Book Call **+353-1-8084419** or www.irelandhotels.com

Co. Kildare

Athy

Carlton Abbey Hotel & C-Spa

Hotel ★ ★ ★ ★   Map 7 M 9

**Town Centre, Athy,
Co. Kildare**
Tel: +353-59-863 0100
Email: reservations.abbey@carlton.ie
Web: www.carlton.ie/abbey
GPS: N +52° 59' 37.74" W -6° 58' 56.96"

Location
Carlton Abbey Hotel is situated in the heart of Athy, Co. Kildare. 45 minutes from Dublin 1 hour from Dublin Airport and 5 minutes from Athy Train Station.

Property Highlights
Luxurious bedrooms, conference & banqueting facilities, Abbey Bar, formerly a church, leisure club, pool, sauna, jacuzzi, steam room & modern gym, luxury C-Spa, Residents Lounge in original convent.

Local Attractions
The bustling Heritage Town of Athy, Japanese Gardens, Irish National Stud, Curragh Racecourse, Punchestown, Kildare Village, Newbridge Silverware, golfing, shopping, fishing & walking.

B&B from: €49.00 - €129.00

Host(s): Ted Egan

49

Facilities

Closed 23 - 26 December

Clanard Court Hotel

Hotel ★ ★ ★ ★   Map 7 M 9

**Dublin Road N78, Athy,
Co. Kildare**
Tel: +353-59-864 0666
Email: sales@clanardcourt.ie
Web: www.clanardcourt.ie
GPS: N +52° 59' 55.48" W -6° 57' 35.58"

Location
Set in beautiful gardens in the rolling countryside of the midlands, 1 mile from the Heritage Town of Athy. Close to Kildare, Carlow, Laois, Kildare and Dublin.

Property Highlights
Family-run with strong emphasis on customer service. Boasting 38 spacious rooms with all modern conveniences to make your stay comfortable. We specialise in tailor-made banqueting & events.

Local Attractions
Guests have complimentary use of our affiliated K Leisure Centre. Enjoy a day trip to Japanese Gardens & National Stud, Kildare Village Shopping Outlet, the races in The Curragh, Punchestown or golf.

B&B from: €45.00 - €130.00

Host(s): Liam Corr

38

Activities

Food for Kids

Facilities

Closed 23 - 26 December

Castletown House & Parklands
- Celbridge, Co. Kildare -

Castletown House is the most celebrated and magnificent Palladian style mansion in Ireland. The house was built in the 1720's for William Conolly who from humble origins became an important political figure in early 18th century Ireland. His architectural legacy, Castletown, was re-invigorated by his grand nephew Tom and his wife Lady Louisa Lennox. The extraordinary scale, decoration, plasterwork and collections at Castletown as presented today continue to bring to life this unique period in Ireland's history.

House Opening Times:
Mid Mar - End Oct Tues - Sunday & B.H. Mon 10am with the last tour at 4.45pm. Access to the house is by guided tour. Unfortunately there is currently no wheelchair access to the main house.

Price: Adult €4.50, Senior & Student €3.50, Family €12.50. O.P.W Heritage Cards accepted. Groups +12 by prior appointment *See Web for Open for Winter Programme.*

18th Century parkland - Open Daily during daylight hours. Free admission.

Claire Hanley Restaurant - located in the West Wing - Tel:+353-1-627-9498 or Email castletown@clairehanley.ie for their opening times and bookings.

Vehicle Access - Located 20km from Dublin City - Exit 6 on M4 at Celbridge West.

Dublin Bus - 67/67A to Celbridge Main Street. Castletown House is approx. a 10 minute walk through parkland.

B&B Rates are per Person Sharing per Night incl. Breakfast. Room/Suite Rates are per Room per Night. **See also page 08**

Co. Kildare

To Book Call **+353-1-8084419** or www.irelandhotels.com

Clane / Kildare Town / Leixlip

Westgrove Hotel

Hotel ★ ★ ★ ★   Map 8 N 11

Clane,
Co. Kildare
Tel: +353-45-989900
Email: reservations@westgrovehotel.com
Web: www.westgrovehotel.com
GPS: N +53° 17' 25.01"   W -6° 40' 53.70"

Location
Easily accessible whilst offering an oasis from the bustle of the city, situated on the fringes of Clane Village, 10 minutes from M4 & M7, under 40 minutes from Dublin City.

Property Highlights
Boasting 99 well appointed rooms, an extensive conference centre, a choice of restaurants & bars, an award-winning leisure centre & dedicated Spa. A genuinely warm welcome awaits you.

Local Attractions
Kildare Village Outlet, Irish National Stud & Japanese Gardens, Mondello Park, Punchestown, Naas & The Curragh Racecourse, Castletown House, an array of golf courses on our doorstep.

B&B from: €59.00 - €100.00
Suites from: €200.00 - €470.00

Host(s): Ian Hyland

99

Closed 24 - 27 December

Derby House Hotel

Hotel ★ ★   Map 7 M 10

Dublin Road, Kildare Town,
Co. Kildare
Tel: +353-45-522144
Email: enquiries@derbyhousehotel.ie
Web: www.derbyhousehotel.ie
GPS: N +53° 9' 19.95"   W -6° 54' 26.24"

Location
Centre of Kildare Town, 2 minutes walk to Kildare Village Outlet, 5 minutes drive to the Curragh Racecourse, 10 minutes walk to train station, 35 minutes drive to Dublin.

Property Highlights
The Kingsland Restaurant has one of the finest Chinese Cuisine in Kildare sine 1983. The Diamond Suite, our grand ballroom, is ideal for wedding, dinner dances, conferences & parties.

Local Attractions
Close to Irish National Stud and Horse Museum, The Japanese Gardens, St. Brigit's Well & the Kildare Village Outlet Shopping Mall.

B&B from: €35.00 - €85.00
Suites from: €120.00 - €150.00

Host(s): Sarah Chan

20

Open All Year

Courtyard Hotel Leixlip

Hotel ★ ★ ★ ★   Map 8 N 11

Main Street, Leixlip,
Co. Kildare
Tel: +353-1-629 5100
Email: info@courtyard.ie
Web: www.courtyard.ie
GPS: N +53° 21' 50.48"   W -6° 29' 19.78"

Location
Just off the N4, 20 minutes from the Airport, on both the train and the bus routes to Dublin City Centre (25 minutes).

Property Highlights
Award-winning restaurant, five bars including cocktail bar, live music 5 nights a week, 10ft outdoor screen for all sporting events. Built upon the original home of the Guinness Brewery.

Local Attractions
Guinness' Castle, Arthur Guinness Grave, Leixlip Spa, River Liffey Walks, Largest Beer Garden in Kildare.

B&B from: €49.50 - €49.50
Suites from: €139.00 - €139.00

Host(s): Luke Moriarty

40

Open All Year

To Book Call **+353-1-8084419** or www.irelandhotels.com

Co. Kildare
Monasterevin

Hazel Hotel

Hotel ★ ★ ★   Map 7 N 10

Dublin Road, Monasterevin,
Co. Kildare
Tel: +353-45-525373
Email: sales@hazelhotel.com
Web: www.hazelhotel.com
GPS: N +53° 8' 9.22"   W -7° 4' 11.13"

Location
Located 1 hour from Dublin Airport, Kildare, Portarlington, close to train stations. 5 minutes drive off M7 motorway.

Property Highlights
Food all day. Weekend entertainment. Wheelchair accessible.

Local Attractions
Japanese Gardens, Irish National Stud, Kildare Village Outlet, Curragh Racecourse.

B&B from: €50.00 - €70.00
Suites from: €130.00 - €150.00

Host(s): Margaret Kelly

24

Facilities

Closed 24 - 26 December

Opening times:
12th February to Christmas
7 days a week
9 a.m. - 5 p.m.

The Irish National Stud

Japanese Gardens, St. Fiachra's Garden & Horse Museum

- **Location:** 45 mins South of Dublin off the M7 Exit 13 onto R 415
- **Access** By Road, By Bus from Dublin or Rail to Kildare Town (Shuttle Bus from Rail station to Kildare Village Chic outlet shopping & Irish National Stud)
- The only Stud farm in Ireland open to the public offering daily guided tours
- World Famous Japanese Gardens
- Award winning St. Fiachra's Garden
- Horse Museum
- Gift shop and Restaurant
- Free car and coach park

Tel: **+353 (0)45 521617**

Irish National Stud,
Tully, Kildare, Ireland.
Email: japanesegardens@instourism.net

ONE ADMISSION CHARGE COVERS ALL 4 ATTRACTIONS
Bookable on line at: www.irish-national-stud.ie

Co. Kildare

To Book Call **+353-1-8084419** or www.irelandhotels.com

Naas / Newbridge

Harbour Hotel & Restaurant

Hotel ★ ★ Map 8 N 10

**Newbridge Road, Naas,
Co. Kildare**
Tel: +353-45-879145
Email: mary@harbourhotel.ie
Web: www.harbourhotel.ie
GPS: N +53° 12' 58.36"   W -6° 40' 4.02"

Location
15 minutes from Sallins Railway Station. Conveniently situated for Dublin, the Airport and Ferryport.

Property Highlights
Looking after the needs of guests and providing quality service is a priority in this family-run hotel. Restaurant serving the finest in traditional Irish cuisine & Indian cuisine.

Local Attractions
Punchestown, Naas Racecourse, Mondello Park, Japanese Garden, Goff's Sails, Curragh Racecourse, K-Club, Kildare shopping village.

B&B from: €60.00 - €110.00

Host(s): Mary Monaghan

10

Facilities

Closed 24 - 27 December

Maudlins House Hotel

Hotel ★ ★ ★ ★ Map 8 N 10

**Exit 9, M7, Dublin Road, Naas,
Co. Kildare**
Tel: +353-45-896999
Email: info@maudlinshousehotel.ie
Web: www.maudlinshousehotel.ie
GPS: N +53° 13' 54.01"   W -6° 38' 25.13"

Location
3 minutes from Naas Town Centre, located off the M7 at exit 9. 30 minutes from Dublin Airport & Dublin City Centre. Close proximity to Naas Racecourse, Punchestown.

Property Highlights
4**** luxury country house hotel, 2 AA Rosettes-winning Virginia Restaurant, Cinema complex on site, Maudlins Bar, conference & banqueting facilities. A place to indulge yourself.

Local Attractions
Local amenities include golf, horse racing, Goffs Horse Sales, Curragh & Naas Racecourse, Japanese Gardens and National Stud, Whitewater Shopping Centre & Kildare Village Outlet Centre.

Room Rate from: €79.00 - €99.00
Suites from: €175.00 - €250.00

Host(s): David Fagan

25

Activities   **Facilities**

Closed 25 - 26 December

Gables Guesthouse & Leisure Centre

Guesthouse ★ ★ ★ Map 7 M 10

**Ryston, Kilcullen Road, Newbridge,
Co. Kildare**
Tel: +353-45-435330
Email: gablesguesthse@ireland.com
Web: www.gablesguesthouseandleisurecentre.com
GPS: N +53° 10' 30.15"   W -6° 47' 34.95"

Location
Situated on the banks of the Liffey, our family-run guesthouse is 35 minutes from Dublin Airport, 5 minutes walk to Train Station. Off M7.

Property Highlights
New 20m Swimming Pool, 2 Jacuzzis, Sauna, Steam Room, Thermium, Kiddie's Pool, Plunge Pool, Water Cannons, Fully Equipped Gym & Studio.

Local Attractions
Punchestown, The Curragh & Naas Racecourses, Goffs Sales, Newbridge Greyhound Track, National Stud & Japanese Gardens, Great Shopping Location, Whitewater Mall, Kildare Outlet, Newbridge Silverware.

B&B from: €45.00 - €80.00

Host(s): Ray & Jackie Cribbin

25

Facilities

Closed 24 - 27 December

---

154   Dublin & Ireland East   B&B Rates are per Person Sharing per Night incl. Breakfast. Room/Suite Rates are per Room per Night. See also page 08

NEWBRIDGE SILVERWARE VISITOR CENTRE

VISIT THE MICHAEL JACKSON COLLECTION

IRELAND'S MOST UNIQUE VISITOR DESTINATION

VISIT THE MARILYN MONROE COLLECTION

MUSEUM OF STYLE ICONS

THE HEPBURN ROOM

SHOWROOMS AND SILVER RESTAURANT

Visit the Newbridge Silverware Visitor Centre, Ireland's most unique visitor destination. Home to the Museum of Style Icons with memorabilia from Michael Jackson, Marilyn Monroe, Audrey Hepburn, the Beatles and many more. With great shopping, great food and the museum's outstanding permament collection, this is an incredible experience for all visitors.

Open 7 days, Free entry.
Parking facilities onsite.

Directions: Take the M7 from Dublin. Leave M7 at Junction 12 signed CURRAGH / NEWBRIDGE and follow the signs into town. Turn right at shopping center. The Newbridge Silverware Visitor Centre is 600 metres on the right.

MASTERCRAFTSMAN AT WORK

NEWBRIDGE silverware®
Est. 1934

PRESENT THIS AD FOR A 10% DISCOUNT IN THE NEWBRIDGE SILVERWARE VISITORS CENTRE ONLY
WWW.NEWBRIDGESILVERWARE.COM

Co. Kildare - Co. Laois

To Book Call **+353-1-8084419** or www.irelandhotels.com

Newbridge / Straffan / Durrow

Keadeen Hotel

Hotel ★ ★ ★ ★   Map 7 M 10

**Curragh Road, Newbridge,
Co. Kildare**
Tel: +353-45-431666
Email: info@keadeenhotel.ie
Web: www.keadeenhotel.ie
GPS: N +53° 10' 13.65" W -6° 48' 51.70"

Location
Kildare's longest family-run hotel is located 35 minutes from Dublin, exit 12 off M7 motorway.

Property Highlights
75 luxurious & spacious bedrooms. Health & fitness complex, extensive conference & banqueting suites. Fine dining in our bar & restaurant.

Local Attractions
Local attractions include Kildare Village Outlet, Whitewater Shopping Centre, Newbridge Silverware, Curragh Racecourse, Japanese Gardens, Golf, Lullymore Heritage Park.

B&B from: €62.50 - €84.50

Host(s): Rose O'Loughlin

75

Activities

Facilities

Closed 24 December - 26 December

K Club (The)

Hotel ★ ★ ★ ★ ★   Map 8 N 11

**The Kildare Hotel, Spa and Country Club,
Straffan,
Co. Kildare**
Tel: +353-1-601 7200
Email: sales@kclub.ie
Web: www.kclub.ie

Location
The K Club is situated 30 minutes from Dublin City Centre, approximately 35 minutes from the airport & is 15 minutes from the nearest train station.

Property Highlights
The K Club has 2 Arnold Palmer designed golf courses, hosted the 2006 Ryder Cup, has a world class Spa & an exceptional fine dining restaurant, The Byerley Turk. All rates include breakfast.

Local Attractions
Irish National Stud, Butterfly Farm, Dublin Zoo, Japanese Gardens, The Curragh, Castletown House, Punchestown Racecourse.

**Room Rate from: €295.00 - €395.00
Suites from: €795.00 - €7,950.00**

Host(s): Mick Casey

69

Activities

Facilities

Open All Year

Castle Arms Hotel

Hotel ★   Map 7 L 8

**The Square, Durrow,
Co. Laois**
Tel: +353-57-873 6117
Email: info@castlearmshotel.ie
Web: www.castlearmshotel.ie
GPS: N +52° 50' 43.25" W -7° 23' 46.33"

Location
Situated in the award-winning picturesque village of Durrow. 1.5 hours from Dublin, two hours from Cork and three hours from Belfast.

Property Highlights
Family-run hotel, our reputation is for good food, service & friendliness. Granstown Lake is described as being the best coarse fishing lake in Europe.

Local Attractions
Local amenities include fishing, horse trekking & many golf courses within easy reach. Brand Central designer outlet is 10 minutes drive away. Ideal for a weekend away shopping.

B&B from: €50.00 - €60.00

Host(s): Seosamh Murphy

14

Facilities

Open All Year

B&B Rates are per Person Sharing per Night incl. Breakfast. Room/Suite Rates are per Room per Night. **See also page 08**

To Book Call **+353-1-8084419** or www.irelandhotels.com

Co. Laois

Killenard / Portlaoise

Heritage Golf & Spa Resort (The)

Hotel ★ ★ ★ ★ ★   Map 7 L 10

Killenard,
Co. Laois
Tel: +353-57-864 5500
Email: info@theheritage.com
Web: www.theheritage.com
GPS: N +53° 7' 59.39"   W -7° 9' 5.98"

Location
Situated south west of Dublin City Centre & Airport, just off the M7 Motorway. Portarlington Town Train Station is located 3 miles from the resort.

Property Highlights
A 98 guestroom Hotel, Resort Spa & Health Club, 18 hole golf course & golf school, as well as a variety of restaurants & bars.

Local Attractions
Slieve Bloom Mountains, The Curragh Racecourse, Kildare Village - chic outlet shopping, Irish National Stud & Gardens.

B&B from: €60.00 - €115.00
Suites from: €220.00 - €500.00

Host(s): Struan Craig

98

Activities
Facilities

Closed 23 - 28 December

Maldron Hotel Portlaoise

Hotel ★ ★ ★   Map 7 L 9

Midway, Abbeyleix Road, Portlaoise,
Co. Laois
Tel: +353-57-869 5900
Email: info.portlaoise@maldronhotels.com
Web: www.maldronhotels.com
GPS: N +53° 0' 55.99"   W -7° 18' 3.50"

Location
The Maldron Hotel Portlaoise is located just 1 hour from Dublin at Junction 17 of the M7 motorway (Durrow exit).

Property Highlights
Spacious bedrooms, free car parking, free broadband, WiFi, Club Vitae Health and Fitness Club & Stir Bar & Restaurant.

Local Attractions
Golf, fishing, pony trekking, walking & cycling tours, museums, gardens, shopping, barge cruise, paintballing.

Room Rate from: €49.00 - €249.00

Host(s): Michael Lally

90

Closed 20 - 28 December

Portlaoise Heritage Hotel

Hotel ★ ★ ★ ★   Map 7 L 9

Town Centre, Portlaoise,
Co. Laois
Tel: +353-57-867 8588
Email: info@theheritagehotel.com
Web: www.theheritagehotel.com
GPS: N +53° 2' 5.68"   W -7° 18' 11.02"

Location
The hotel is located in the town centre on Jessop Street, just 5 minutes walk from the train station.

Property Highlights
110 de luxe bedrooms, beautiful spacious lobby. 13 meeting rooms, Maryborough Suite accom. 300 pax. White Flag leisure centre, 20 m pool. Kelly's Foundry Grillhouse. Spago's Italian Bistro, Ealu Spa.

Local Attractions
Rock of Dunamaise, Emo Court & Gardens. Slieve Bloom Mountains, Dunamaise Arts Centre. Roll & Bowl for the kids, Kilvahan Adventure Farm. Heritage Golf & Spa Resort, Kildare Village, Heywood Gardens.

Room Rate from: €59.00 - €220.00
Suites from: €109.00 - €270.00

Host(s): Jerry Russell

110

Activities
Facilities

Closed 23 - 27 December

B&B Rates are per Person Sharing per Night incl. Breakfast. Room/Suite Rates are per Room per Night. See also page 08

Dublin & Ireland East   157

Co. Longford

To Book Call **+353-1-8084419** or www.irelandhotels.com

Cloondara / Longford Town

Richmond Inn Guesthouse

Guesthouse ★ ★ ★   Map 11 J 13

Cloondara,
Co. Longford
Tel: +353-43-332 6126
Email: therichmondinn@eircom.net
Web: www.richmondinnireland.com
GPS: N +53° 43' 52.78"   W -7° 54' 17.20"

Location
The Richmond Inn licensed guesthouse overlooks Richmond Harbour in the picturesque village of Cloondara, 5km from Longford Town.

Property Highlights
All bedrooms are en suite, tastefully decorated & equipped to a high standard. Excellent cuisine, friendly service with a personal touch makes this a favourite with home & overseas visitors.

Local Attractions
Fishing, walking, cycling, indoor & outdoor swimming, 18 hole golf courses, pitch & putt, horse riding & greyhound racing, Kenagh Interpretative Centre & Ardagh, the tidiest village in Ireland.

B&B from: €40.00 - €70.00

Host(s): Des & Frances McPartland

5

Facilities

Closed 12 December - 12 January

Annaly Hotel

Hotel ★ ★   Map 11 J 13

57 Main Street, Longford Town,
Co. Longford
Tel: +353-43-334 3690
Email: info@annalyhotel.ie
Web: www.annalyhotel.ie
GPS: N +53° 43' 42.65"   W -7° 48' 3.18"

Location
The hotel offers modern surroundings in the heart of Longford. Equidistant from east & west coasts, the hotel is superbly serviced by train & bus & with its own in-house taxi service for guests.

Property Highlights
Stunning contemporary bar & restaurant. Access to our sister hotel's leisure facilities is complimentary, 22m indoor pool, sauna, steam room, jacuzzi & gymnasium. Superb Spa facilities at this hotel.

Local Attractions
River Shannon excellent for angling, cruising & water pursuits. Corlea Trackway Ctr for archaeology enthusiasts. Longford provides superb entertainment, Back Stage Theatre, cinema, bars & restaurants.

B&B from: €40.00 - €120.00

Host(s): Jim Reynolds

32

Activities   Facilities

Open All Year

Longford Arms Hotel, Spa & Leisure Centre

Hotel ★ ★ ★   Map 11 J 13

24 Main Street, Longford Town,
Co. Longford
Tel: +353-43-334 6296
Email: longfordarms@eircom.net
Web: www.longfordarms.ie
GPS: N +53° 43' 43.46"   W -7° 48' 6.34"

Location
Equidistant from east & west coasts, it is superbly serviced by train & bus & with its own in-house taxi service for guests. Base for social life in the town.

Property Highlights
Leisure facilities at hotel are extensive & feature-rich. A 22m indoor heated pool with lifeguard supervision, sauna, steam room, jacuzzi & gymnasium. Superb Spa facilities.

Local Attractions
River Shannon excellent for angling, cruising & water pursuits. Corlea Trackway Ctr for archaeology enthusiasts. Longford provides superb entertainment, Back Stage Theatre, cinema, bars & restaurants.

B&B from: €40.00 - €100.00

57

Host(s): Jim Reynolds

Activities   Facilities

Open All Year

To Book Call **+353-1-8084419** or www.irelandhotels.com

Co. Longford - Co. Louth

Longford Town / Carlingford

Viewmount House

Guesthouse — Map 11 J 13

**Dublin Road, Longford Town,
Co. Longford**
Tel: +353-43-334 1919
Email: info@viewmounthouse.com
Web: www.viewmounthouse.com
GPS: N +53° 43' 17.26"   W -7° 46' 14.83"

Built to a 4**** specification

Location
From town centre, take R393, 1km, slip road on right. 1 mile from Longford Train Station.

Property Highlights
Magnificent Georgian House set in 4 acres of stunning gardens adjoining Longford Golf Course, individually styled bedrooms. Dining is truly memorable, winner of Best Hotel Restaurant in Leinster 2010.

Local Attractions
Adjoined to Longford Golf Course, Corlea Trackway Centre, Strokestown House & Famine Museum, Tullynally Castle, Belvedere House & Gardens, Close to Shannon River & Lough Gowna

B&B from: €60.00 - €75.00
Suites from: €150.00 - €200.00

Host(s): James & Beryl Kearney

13

Facilities

Open All Year

Beaufort House

Guesthouse ★ ★ ★ ★ — Map 12 O 15

**Ghan Road, Carlingford,
Co. Louth**
Tel: +353-42-937 3879
Email: michaelcaine@beauforthouse.net
Web: www.beauforthouse.net
GPS: N +54° 2' 25.77"   W -6° 10' 35.88"

Location
Beaufort House is beautifully located on the sea shore, with spectacular sea & mountain views, just a short walk from the village centre.

Property Highlights
Beaufort House has a national reputation for the high quality of its food and accommodation. Fáilte Ireland Award-Winners of Excellence. In-house activities include sailing school & yacht charter.

Local Attractions
Located close to 5 championship golf courses, fishing, horse riding, hill walking, swimming & tennis are all on our doorstep.

B&B from: €45.00 - €60.00

Host(s): Michael & Glynnis Caine

5

Facilities

Open All Year

Website

Mobile App

Printed Guide

facebook.com/irelandhotels

irelandhotels.com/onlineguide

Co. Louth
Carlingford / Drogheda

McKevitt's Village Hotel

Hotel ★ ★   Map 12 O 15

**Market Square, Carlingford,
Co. Louth**
Tel: +353-42-937 3116
Email: mckevittshotel@yahoo.com
Web: www.mckevittshotel.com
GPS: N +54° 2' 25.41"   W -6° 11' 13.98"

Location
The hotel is situated on the shore of Carlingford Lough, 1 hour's drive from Dublin or Belfast. Buses run daily from Newry & Dundalk.

Property Highlights
The hotel is home to the famous Schooner's Steakhouse / Restaurant, known for its fresh local produce & friendly local staff. The hotel is found in the centre of Carlingford.

Local Attractions
Carlingford is a Medieval village with cobbled streets, castles & Heritage Centre. There are fantastic hill walks, fishing, sailing and outdoor pursuits. There are Bistros and Traditional Pubs.

B&B from: €50.00 - €80.00

Host(s): Dermot O'Farrell
13

Activities   **Facilities**

Closed 25 December

d (The)

Hotel ★ ★ ★ ★   Map 12 O 13

**Scotch Hall, Drogheda,
Co. Louth**
Tel: +353-41-987 7700
Email: info@thedhotel.com
Web: www.thedhotel.com
GPS: N +53° 42' 50.39"   W -6° 20' 42.39"

Location
The d Hotel is located on the banks of the River Boyne in Drogheda. 25 minutes from Dublin Airport and 40 minutes from Dublin using the Port Tunnel.

Property Highlights
The d Hotel has 104 bedrooms, many with superb views over the River and Town.

Local Attractions
The d Hotel is located close to the Battle of the Boyne site, Newgrange and Monasterboice High Crosses, Beaulieu House & Gardens.

Room Rate from: €79.00 - €299.00
Suites from: €250.00 - €1,000.00

Host(s): Rory Scott
104

Activities   **Facilities**

Closed 24 - 29 December

Westcourt Hotel

Hotel ★ ★ ★   Map 12 O 13

**West Street, Drogheda,
Co. Louth**
Tel: +353-41-983 0965
Email: reservations@westcourt.ie
Web: www.westcourt.ie
GPS: N +53° 42' 53.74"   W -6° 21' 13.88"

Location
Westcourt Hotel is situated on the main street in the heart of historical Drogheda and the Boyne Valley.

Property Highlights
Stylish refurbishment - Lively Barocco Bar, Earth Nightclub, our entertainment emporium, banqueting facilities & West29 RestoLounge, a new concept in dining. Backed by friendly & efficient staff.

Local Attractions
Many local attractions Millmount Museum & Martello Tower, Shrine of St Oliver Plunkett in St. Peter's Church, Newgrange, Brú na Boinne, Battle of the Boyne site & Visitor Centre, Beaulieu House.

B&B from: €50.00 - €65.00

Host(s): Valerie Sherlock
27

Activities   **Facilities**

Closed 25 - 26 December

To Book Call **+353-1-8084419** or www.irelandhotels.com

Co. Louth
Dundalk

Ballymascanlon House Hotel

Hotel ★ ★ ★ ★   Map 12 O 14

Carlingford Road (R173), Dundalk,
Co. Louth
Tel: +353-42-935 8200
Email: info@ballymascanlon.com
Web: www.ballymascanlon.com
GPS: N +54° 1' 52.82"   W -6° 21' 8.14"

Location
2 miles north of Dundalk, Exit 18 on M1. 50 minutes from Dublin & Belfast. 40 minutes to Dublin Airport.

Property Highlights
Fáilte Ireland AA 4 star Country House Hotel Golf & Leisure Centre set on 130 acres of mature parkland estate.

Local Attractions
8 miles to Mediaeval Carlingford Village. Close to Dundalk Horse / Dog Racing Stadium. 2 miles to Dundalk, 8 miles to Newry.

B&B from: €80.00 - €95.00

Host(s): Oliver Quinn

90

Activities **Facilities**

Open All Year

Lismar Guesthouse

Guesthouse ★ ★ ★   Map 12 O 14

8 Stapleton Place, Dundalk,
Co. Louth
Tel: +353-42-935 7246
Email: lismar@iol.ie
Web: www.lismar.ie
GPS: N +53° 59' 55.66"   W -6° 24' 24.98"

Location
Only an hour from major airports & ferries, easily accessible from the M1 & within walking distance of bus & train stations.

Property Highlights
Superb family-run guesthouse. Situated on a quiet street, only minutes walk to Dundalk town centre & all amenities.

Local Attractions
The ideal base for trips to the Cooley Peninsula, Carlingford, the Mournes, the Tain Trail, golf and race courses. Guesthouse is only minutes from restaurants, pubs, shops & Marshes shopping centre.

B&B from: €32.50 - €42.50

Host(s): Michael & Elizabeth Smyth

8

Facilities

Open All Year

BEAULIEU HOUSE, GARDEN & CAR MUSEUM

Enjoy tranquil surroundings and views over the river Boyne whilst savouring this gem of Irish Architecture. The one hour guided tour brings you into the house, home to the same family since 1650. Learn of the present family involvement in local and famous world history.

OPEN 2ND MAY UNTIL MID SEPTEMBER
Weekdays 11am-5pm
Weekends (open Jul & Aug only) 1-5pm

Phone: 00353 (0)41 983 8557
Email: info@beaulieuhouse.ie
www.beaulieu.ie
Sat Nav Lat 53° 43.7N / Long 6° 17.7W

Dublin & Ireland East

Co. Meath

To Book Call **+353-1-8084419** or www.irelandhotels.com

Ashbourne / Dunboyne

Aisling Guest House

Guesthouse ★ ★   Map 12 O 12

**Dublin Road, Baltrasna, Ashbourne,
Co. Meath**
Tel: +353-1-835 0359
Email: info@aislingguesthouse.ie
Web: www.aislingguesthouse.ie
GPS: N +53° 29' 49.96"   W -6° 23' 4.67"

Location
Exit 3 M2 (Ashbourne - Ratoath exit) and then 3rd exit at roundabout (R135, signposted on roundabout) 50 metres after roundabout on right hand side.

Property Highlights
Free internet & WiFi, Sky TV on plasma screen TV, fridge (customer use) in all rooms. All rooms en suite. Breakfast from 6am. 24hr continental breakfast, free car parking. Free park & ride to Airport.

Local Attractions
3 mins. from M50 exit N2. 5 mins. to Fairyhouse Racecourse & Tattersalls. Newgrange, Hill of Tara, Slane Castle, Bective Abbey are close by. 15 mins. to Killeen Castle (site of 2011 Ladies Ryder Cup).

**B&B from: €29.00 - €35.00
Suites from: €80.00 - €100.00**

Host(s): Rod Cosgrave

20

Facilities

Open All Year

Ashbourne Marriott Hotel

Hotel ★ ★ ★ ★   Map 12 O 12

**The Rath, Ashbourne,
Co. Meath**
Tel: +353-1-835 0800
Email: info@marriottashbourne.com
Web: www.marriottashbourne.com
GPS: N +53° 31' 38.35"   W -6° 24' 55.04"

Location
Located in Ashbourne Co. Meath, 25 minutes from Dublin International Airport. Minutes from Fairyhouse Racecourse and other famous landmarks.

Property Highlights
4 star Marriott property, with complimentary WiFi throughout hotel. Clann Fitness and Leisure Club, Red Bar and Lounge, Grill Twenty One Restaurant, Jule Beauty and Therapy Spa.

Local Attractions
Fairyhouse Racecourse, Newgrange, Hill of Tara, Tattersalls, Pudden-Hill Activity Centre, Showtime Cinemas, Slane Castle, Killeen Castle Golf Club.

**Room Rate from: €80.00 - €150.00
Suites from: €180.00 - €400.00**

Host(s): Gabriele Molari

148

Facilities

Closed 24 - 26 December

Dunboyne Castle Hotel & Spa

Hotel ★ ★ ★ ★   Map 12 N 11

**Dunboyne,
Co. Meath**
Tel: +353-1-801 3500
Email: info@dunboynecastlehotel.com
Web: www.dunboynecastlehotel.com
GPS: N +53° 25' 1.73"   W -6° 28' 38.88"

Location
Only 8 miles from Dublin Airport and 11 miles from city centre. Train station located in Dunboyne Village.

Property Highlights
State of the art Seoid Spa, with 18 treatment rooms & thermal suite. Conference & banqueting facilities for up to 400.

Local Attractions
Blanchardstown Shopping Centre, National Aquatic Centre, Phoenix Park, Fairyhouse Racecourse, Hill of Tara, Newgrange.

B&B from: €50.00 - €170.00

Host(s): Christopher Carson

145

Activities
Facilities

Open All Year

Dublin & Ireland East   B&B Rates are per Person Sharing per Night incl. Breakfast. Room/Suite Rates are per Room per Night.   See also page 08

To Book Call **+353-1-8084419** or www.irelandhotels.com

Co. Meath

Gormanston

CityNorth Hotel

Hotel ★ ★ ★ ★ Map 12 O 13

**Gormanston,
Co. Meath**
Tel: +353-1-690 6666
Email: info@citynorthhotel.com
Web: www.citynorthhotel.com
GPS: N +53° 38' 17.90" W -6° 15' 26.14"

Location
Located off Junction 7 on the M1, 20 minutes transfer to Dublin Airport, free 24hr shuttle bus & close to surrounding towns such as Balbriggan, Drogheda, Swords & Boyne Valley.

Property Highlights
125 de luxe guestrooms, fitness suite, kids games room, beauty & massage, delicious carvery & formal restaurant. Live music at weekends. Public transport to Drogheda & Dublin from hotel entrance.

Local Attractions
Midway between Dublin City & the Boyne Valley, near the coast. Newgrange, Funtasia, Ardgillan Castle within easy reach. Walk/cycle to quaint village of Stamullen. Exclusive deals in local retailers.

Room Rate from: €59.00 - €129.00
Suites from: €99.00 - €129.00

 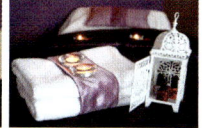

Host(s): Aogan Dunne

125

Activities **Facilities**

Open All Year

from ancient castles to future battles... Meath is the stuff of legends!

catch all the drama of the battle for the Solheim Cup at Killeen Castle, Co. Meath
23-25 September 2011

check **www.meathtourism.ie** today for great accommodation deals and a host of special offers

Once the territory of the High Kings of Ireland, today Meath is home to heart pulsing horse racing, fun family activities, great value golf and a packed calendar of cultural events & festivals. Contact us now for your free brochure.

+353 (0) 46 909 7060 or info@meathtourism.ie

Meath
Ireland's Heritage Capital

B&B Rates are per Person Sharing per Night incl. Breakfast. Room/Suite Rates are per Room per Night. **See also page 08**

Co. Meath

To Book Call **+353-1-8084419** or www.irelandhotels.com

Kells / Kilmessan / Navan

Headfort Arms

Station House Hotel and Signal Restaurant

Newgrange Hotel

Hotel ★ ★ ★   Map 11 M 13

Hotel ★ ★ ★   Map 12 N 12

Hotel ★ ★ ★   Map 12 N 13

Headfort Place, Kells,
Co. Meath
Tel: +353-818-222800
Email: info@headfortarms.ie
Web: www.headfortarms.ie
GPS: N +53° 43' 37.20" W -6° 52' 29.23"

Kilmessan,
Co. Meath
Tel: +353-46-902 5239
Email: info@thestationhousehotel.com
Web: www.thestationhousehotel.com
GPS: N +53° 33' 50.03" W -6° 40' 1.17"

Bridge Street, Navan,
Co. Meath
Tel: +353-46-907 4100
Email: info@newgrangehotel.ie
Web: www.newgrangehotel.ie
GPS: N +53° 39' 6.79" W -6° 40' 58.70"

Location
Located in the Heritage Town of Kells, in the heart of the Boyne Valley. 30 minutes from Dublin on the M3, 45 minutes from Dublin Airport, 1 hour from ferry service.

Location
20 miles from Dublin, 6 miles from Trim, Navan & Dunshaughlin, The Station House Hotel is surrounded by archaeological treasures and ancient legends.

Location
Centrally located in Navan Town in the heart of the Royal County, Newgrange is only 30 minutes from Dublin. Easily accessible from Dublin Airport & City Centre.

Property Highlights
The Headfort offers true Irish hospitality & family-run atmosphere. Hosting so much under one roof, including an award-winning restaurant & traditional Irish pub.

Property Highlights
Once a train station connecting Dublin to Kingscourt, original buildings and reminders of a forgotten time are still present. Each en suite bedroom equipped with TV, DD phone, tea/coffee facilities.

Property Highlights
A modern hotel designed & inspired by the ancient history of the area. In addition to 62 elegantly decorated en suite bedrooms the hotel boasts extensive conference & banqueting facilities.

Local Attractions
Visit the town where the Book of Kells was written; High Crosses, St. Colmcilles House, country walks, Loughcrew Cairns, 36 hole golfing complex & many family attractions.

Local Attractions
Unspoilt rural village steeped in history and folklore, with castles like the 800 year old Dunsany noted for its beauty & romance & Killeen Castle which will host the prestigious Solheim Cup in 2011.

Local Attractions
Local attractions & activities include The Hill of Tara, Newgrange & Trim Castle, Salmon Fishing, Golfing, Horse Racing & Horse Riding. Championship Golf available at Knightsbrook.

B&B from: €49.00 - €89.00
Suites from: €178.00 - €198.00

B&B from: €30.00 - €140.00
Suites from: €100.00 - €250.00

B&B from: €35.00 - €95.00

Host(s): The Duff Family

Host(s): Denise Slattery

Host(s): Jim Carlton

45

20

62

Closed 25 December

Open All Year

Closed 24 - 26 December

To Book Call +353-1-8084419 or www.irelandhotels.com

Co. Meath

Trim

You can find all the best deals in all of these places

Website

Mobile App

Printed Guide

facebook.com/irelandhotels

irelandhotels.com/onlineguide

Knightsbrook Hotel, Spa & Golf Resort

Hotel ★ ★ ★ ★ Map 11 M 12

Dublin Road, Trim,
Co. Meath
Tel: +353-46-948 2100
Email: info@knightsbrook.com
Web: www.knightsbrook.com
GPS: N +53° 32' 55.87" W -6° 45' 55.48"

Location
Located a mere 35 minutes from Dublin in the picturesque Heritage Town of Trim, County Meath, situated at the heart of 186 acres of rolling parkland.

Property Highlights
Built to an exceptionally high 4 star standard, we offer luxury & opulence combined with modern sophistication. Boasts 131 De luxe rooms with all the facilities a discerning guest requires.

Local Attractions
On site 18 Hole Championship Golf Course designed by Christy O'Connor Jr. Nearby: Trim Castle, Hill of Slane, Hill of Tara, The Zone - 24000sq ft extreme activity centre with paintball, carting, etc.

B&B from: €55.00 - €100.00
Suites from: €185.00 - €370.00

Host(s): Patrick Curran
131

Activities

Facilities

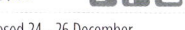

Closed 24 - 26 December

Trim Castle Hotel

Hotel ★ ★ ★ ★ Map 11 M 12

Trim,
Co. Meath
Tel: +353-46-948 3000
Email: info@trimcastlehotel.com
Web: www.trimcastlehotel.com
GPS: N +53° 33' 14.05" W -6° 47' 27.90"

Location
Overlooking the mystical Trim Castle in the beautiful Royal County, the hotel is just 40 minutes from Dublin.

Property Highlights
The hotel has 68 luxury guest rooms, the Bailey Bar, Barista Cafe, Jules Restaurant and a tranquil rooftop garden.

Local Attractions
We are an ideal touring base for the Boyne Valley. Golf, angling and equestrian activities together with a wonderful heritage tour can be booked at the hotel.

B&B from: €55.00 - €100.00
Suites from: €125.00 - €200.00

Host(s): Noel Comer
68

Activities

Facilities

Closed 24 - 26 December

B&B Rates are per Person Sharing per Night incl. Breakfast. Room/Suite Rates are per Room per Night. See also page 08   Dublin & Ireland East

Co. Monaghan

To Book Call **+353-1-8084419** or www.irelandhotels.com

Carrickmacross / Glaslough

Shirley Arms Hotel

Hotel ★ ★ ★ ★   Map 12 N 14

**Lower Main Street, Carrickmacross,
Co. Monaghan**
Tel: +353-42-967 3100
Email: reception@shirleyarmshotel.ie
Web: www.shirleyarmshotel.ie
GPS: N +53° 58' 40.59"   W -6° 43' 11.96"

Location
Approximately 1 hour from Belfast & Dublin. Located in close proximity to Dundalk, Monaghan Town, Ardee and Cavan.

Property Highlights
Chic manor house hotel constructed in the early 19th century. An important part of architectural heritage of Carrickmacross. We offer 25 luxurious bedrooms & banqueting facilities for 150 guests.

Local Attractions
Centrally located in the busy market town of Carrickmacross, famous for its lace & where Patrick Kavanagh penned his famous poetry. Located near Concra Wood & Irish quad biking.

B&B from: €60.00 - €90.00
Suites from: €150.00 - €250.00

Host(s): Jim & Colm McBride

25

Facilities

Closed 24 - 26 December

Castle (The) at Castle Leslie Estate

Guesthouse ★ ★ ★ ★   Map 11 M 16

**Glaslough,
Co. Monaghan**
Tel: +353-47-88100
Email: info@castleleslie.com
Web: www.castleleslie.com
GPS: N +54° 19' 05"   W -6° 53' 44"

Location
Glaslough, Co. Monaghan, 80 minutes from Dublin and 60 minutes from Belfast.

Property Highlights
Nestled on 1,000 acres of undulating Irish countryside, dotted with ancient woodland & glittering lakes. Offers a variety of activities, an Equestrian Centre, coarse fishing & organic Spa Treatments.

Local Attractions
Patrick Kavanagh Centre, Carrickmacross Lace, Navan Fort, Armagh Planetarium, Ulster American Folk Park.

B&B from: €85.00 - €120.00
Suites from: €250.00 - €300.00

Host(s): Brian Baldwin

20

Activities **Facilities**

Closed 24 - 26 December

Lodge (The) at Castle Leslie Estate

Hotel ★ ★ ★ ★   Map 11 M 16

**Glaslough,
Co. Monaghan**
Tel: +353-47-88100
Email: info@castleleslie.com
Web: www.castleleslie.com
GPS: N +54° 19' 05"   W -6° 53' 44"

Location
Glaslough, Co. Monaghan, 80 minutes from Dublin and 60 minutes from Belfast.

Property Highlights
Nestled on 1,000 acres of undulating Irish countryside, dotted with ancient woodland & glittering lakes. Offers a variety of activities, including equestrian, coarse fishing & organic Spa Treatments.

Local Attractions
Patrick Kavanagh Centre, Carrickmacross Lace, Navan Fort, Armagh Planetarium, Ulster American Folk Park.

B&B from: €65.00 - €95.00

Host(s): Brian Baldwin

30

Facilities

Closed 23 - 27 December

B&B Rates are per Person Sharing per Night incl. Breakfast. Room/Suite Rates are per Room per Night. **See also page 08**

To Book Call **+353-1-8084419** or www.irelandhotels.com   **Co. Monaghan**

Monaghan Town

You can find all the best deals in all of these places

Website

Mobile App

Printed Guide

facebook.com/irelandhotels

irelandhotels.com/onlineguide

Four Seasons Hotel & Leisure Club

Hotel ★ ★ ★   Map 11 M 16

Coolshannagh, Monaghan Town, Co. Monaghan
Tel: +353-47-81888
Email: info@4seasonshotel.ie
Web: www.4seasonshotel.ie
GPS: N +54° 14' 57.54"   W -6° 10' 21.09"

Location
1km from northern side of Monaghan Town Centre. Equidistant from Dublin & Belfast. Halfway between Donegal & Dublin, located on the Monaghan Town bypass on N2.

Property Highlights
We pride ourselves on the quality of our food & service. Relax in the Still Bar & Range Restaurant. Award-winning leisure facilities - 18m pool, sauna, jacuzzi, steamroom, outdoor hot tub & gymnasium.

Local Attractions
Monaghan County Museum, Patrick Kavanagh Centre, Sam More Open Farm, Equestrian Centres, Ballybay Wetlands Centre, Rally School Ireland, Muckno Water Sports Centre, Clay Shooting.

B&B from: €49.50 - €95.00

Host(s): Frank McKenna

59

Facilities

Food for Kids

Open All Year

Hillgrove Hotel Leisure & Spa

Hotel ★ ★ ★ ★   Map 11 M 16

Old Armagh Road, Monaghan, Co. Monaghan
Tel: +353-47-81288
Email: info@hillgrovehotel.com
Web: www.hillgrovehotel.com
GPS: N +54° 14' 47.35"   W -6° 57' 18.13"

Location
A majestic & magical setting awaits you. Minutes walk from Monaghan Town. 1 hour from Dublin and 1 hour from Belfast.

Property Highlights
Suites with Jacuzzi. Restaurant, Bars, Leisure Club, Pool, Jacuzzi, Steam Room, Sauna, Hot Tub, Spa, Hair Salon, Games Room, Bouncy Castle.

Local Attractions
Murder Mysteries, CSI Packages, Spa Pamper & Girlie Packages on site. Locally Rally School, Horseriding, Golf, Outdoor Pursuits, Cinema, Theatre, Bowling.

B&B from: €35.00 - €75.00
Suites from: €90.00 - €190.00

Host(s): Audri & Colm Herron

87

Activities   **Facilities**

Food for Kids

Open All Year

B&B Rates are per Person Sharing per Night incl. Breakfast. Room/Suite Rates are per Room per Night. **See also page 08**   Dublin & Ireland East   167

Co. Offaly

Birr / Tullamore

Aaron House

Guesthouse ★ ★ ★   Map 7 J 9

Kinnitty, Birr,
Offaly
Tel: +353-57-913 7040
Email: mail@aaronhouse.ie
Web: www.aaronhouse.ie
GPS: N +53° 5' 58.09"   W -7° 42' 49.02"

Location
Welcome to our home! Close to the Slieve Bloom Mountains in the beautiful village of Kinnitty. Within walking distance of Kinnitty Castle. 10 minutes from Birr.

Property Highlights
Purpose built, spacious rooms, king size beds, DD phones, TV, hairdryer, iron/ironing board, guest TV lounge, tea/coffee making facilities, free WiFi, breakfast menu. Easy to find, hard to leave!

Local Attractions
Slieve Bloom Mountains just outside our front door! Walking Trails, Kinnitty Castle, Heritage Town of Birr with its giant telescope, Clonmacnoise Heritage Site, Leap Castle all close by.

B&B from: €40.00 - €40.00

Host(s): Betty Grimes

5

Facilities

Open All Year

County Arms Hotel & Leisure Club

Hotel ★ ★ ★ ★   Map 7 J 9

Moorpark, Birr,
Co. Offaly
Tel: +353-57-912 0791
Email: info@countyarmshotel.com
Web: www.countyarmshotel.com
GPS: N +53° 5' 26.33"   W -7° 54' 21.30"

Location
Country House setting, 5 minutes walk from centre of Birr Georgian Heritage Town. Within 2 hours of Dublin & major cities.

Property Highlights
Family-run since 1962. Leisure Club, Spa treatments, award-winning Food, genuine service, private dining. Family friendly, extensive gardens, spacious bedrooms.

Local Attractions
Birr Castle & Gardens, Birr Theatre, Lough Boora Parklands, Clonmacnoise, Slieve Bloom Mountains, Tullamore Dew Heritage Centre, Craft Village, Playground.

B&B from: €39.00 - €99.00
Suites from: €169.00 - €499.00

Host(s): Loughnane Family Since 1962

70

Facilities

Open All Year

Bridge House Hotel

Hotel ★ ★ ★ ★   Map 7 K 10

Tullamore,
Co. Offaly
Tel: +353-57-932 5600
Email: info@bridgehouse.com
Web: www.bridgehouse.com
GPS: N +53° 16' 29.85"   W -7° 29' 39.96"

Location
Located in the heart of Tullamore town centre, less than 90 minutes from train station. Just over an hour's drive to Dublin Airport.

Property Highlights
Excellent customer service, with over 40 years experience. 3rd consecutive Michelin Guide Recommendation. White Flag Award Leisure Club, Sanctuary Spa. Host of live entertainment.

Local Attractions
Fourteen 18 hole Championship Golf Courses, Tullamore Dew Heritage Centre, Clonmacnoise Monastic Ruins, Slieve Bloom Mountains, Large range of Canals/Walkways, Historic Castles.

B&B from: €65.00 - €175.00
Suites from: €140.00 - €500.00

Host(s): Denise Brereton

70

Activities   Facilities

Open All Year

Dublin & Ireland East   B&B Rates are per Person Sharing per Night incl. Breakfast. Room/Suite Rates are per Room per Night. See also page 08

Co. Offaly
Tullamore

Grennans Country House & Cottages

Guesthouse ★ ★ ★ ★   Map 7 K 10

**Aharney, Tullamore,
Co. Offaly**
Tel: +353-57-935 5893
Email: deirdregrennan5@eircom.net
Web: www.grennanscountryhouse.ie
GPS: N +53° 18' 13.02"   W -7° 34' 7.72"

Location
Situated in the heart of the highlands, 1 mile off the N80. 1 hour from Dublin & Galway, 2 hours from Belfast. Mobiles: Pat: +353 86 335 1821 / Deirdre: +353 86 382 5148.

Property Highlights
Rural setting, ample car parking, 2 luxury 4 star cottages. All rooms en suite, TV, WiFi. 6 en suite rooms in guesthouse, DD phone, tea/coffee facilities, guest lounge, access for wheelchair users.

Local Attractions
Ideal local touring base. 10 golf courses within 0.5 hours of the property. Golfing, fishing, equestrian, walking, your choice is our pleasure.

B&B from: €35.00 - €45.00

Host(s): Deirdre & Pat Grennan

6

Facilities

Open All Year

Castle Barna Golf Club.

Daingean, Tullamore,
Co Offaly
Tel: 057 935 3384
Fax: 057 935 3077
Email: info@castlebarna.ie
Web: www.castlebarna.ie

A fantastic 18 hole parkland course built on the banks of the Grand Canal, in the heart of the Midlands, renowned for its excellent greens, lush fairways, mature trees and beautiful lakes. It is a course that suits all levels of golfers. Castle Barna was host to the G.U.I. Pierce Purcell Shield in 2000, 2002 and 2004, Junior Cup 2008 and Jimmy Bruen Shield 2010.

Members, Green Fees & Societies always welcome.

Located near Tullamore and just off the Dublin to Galway M6 motorway at junction 3. GPS Coordinates N53.17.908 W.07.16.840

The 19th hole is an old stone clubhouse with full bar, catering facilities & modern changing rooms.

Castle Barna is a course you would love to play again.

Tullamore Dew HERITAGE CENTRE

Visit the home of
Tullamore Dew
& Irish Mist Liqueur

Tullamore Dew Heritage Centre

- Open 7 days a week, all year
- Audiovisual, guided & self guided tours available
- Gift Shop & Café Bar
- Tourist Office
- Meeting rooms
- Children's fun trail
- Wheel chair accessible

Special Hotel Discount of €5 (usual rate €6) on presentation of this Guide

Bury Quay, Tullamore,
Co. Offaly
Tel: +353 (0)57 9325015
Fax: +353 (0)57 9325106
info@tullamore-dew.org
www.tullamore-dew.org

Co. Offaly - Co. Westmeath

To Book Call **+353-1-8084419** or www.irelandhotels.com

Tullamore / Athlone

Sea Dew Guesthouse

Guesthouse ★ ★ ★   Map 7 K 10

Clonminch Road, Tullamore,
Co. Offaly
Tel: +353-57-935 2054
Email: enquiries@seadewguesthouse.com
Web: www.seadewguesthouse.com
GPS: N +53° 16' 6.96"   W -7° 29' 19.46"

Location
Located in Tullamore town, close to hotels, restaurants, bars, shops & train station. 1 hour 10 minutes drive to Dublin/Galway. 2 hours to Shannon and Northern Ireland.

Property Highlights
A family-run, purpose built, luxury guesthouse. enjoy home baking & fresh local produce. Private car park, peaceful setting, complimentary broadband.

Local Attractions
10 golf courses within 5 - 40km. Swimming pool, leisure centre, athletic stadium, heritage sites, hill walking nearby. Check our webiste for things to do.

B&B from: €35.00 - €60.00

Host(s): Frank & Claire Gilsenan

10

Facilities

Closed 22 - 27 December

Tullamore Court Hotel

Hotel ★ ★ ★ ★   Map 7 K 10

O'Moore Street, Tullamore,
Co. Offaly
Tel: +353-57-934 6666
Email: info@tullamorecourthotel.ie
Web: www.tullamorecourthotel.ie
GPS: N +53° 16' 11.58"   W -7° 29' 32.73"

Location
A contemporary 4 star hotel in the heart of the Midlands. Less than 90 minutes from Dublin, Galway & Limerick & 2 hours from 50% of the rest of the country.

Property Highlights
Class leading conference facilities, unrivalled level of service for the conference organiser. 14 meeting suites accommodating conferences from 5-750 delegates. Award-winning 280 seater restaurant.

Local Attractions
Located in the Ryder Cup region, Tullamore is ideal for golf. Or for those looking for something more extreme - skydiving in the nearby Irish Parachute Club. Also - clay pigeon shooting, horse riding.

B&B from: €45.00 - €75.00
Suites from: €180.00 - €280.00

Host(s): Philip O'Brien

104

Activities   Facilities

Closed 24 - 26 December

Creggan Court Hotel

Hotel ★ ★ ★   Map 7 J 11

N6 Centre, Dublin Road, Athlone,
Co. Westmeath
Tel: +353-90-647 7777
Email: info@creggancourt.com
Web: www.creggancourt.com
GPS: N +53° 24' 37.21"   W -7° 53' 39.13"

Location
Junction 8, off N6 Motorway, midway between Dublin and Galway.

Property Highlights
An ideal base to explore the Midlands. The Creggan Court offers spacious en suite rooms and free ample car parking. Carvery food all day. Meeting rooms. 24 hour reception.

Local Attractions
Clonmacnoise. Glendeer Pet Farm. Athlone is a golfer's paradise, surrounded by championship golf courses - 5 golf courses within 10 miles.

B&B from: €35.00 - €60.00

Host(s): Catherine Daly

70

Facilities

Closed 25 - 26 December

B&B Rates are per Person Sharing per Night incl. Breakfast. Room/Suite Rates are per Room per Night. **See also page 08**

To Book Call **+353-1-8084419** or www.irelandhotels.com

Co. Westmeath

Athlone

Glasson Country House Hotel and Golf Club

Hotel ★ ★ ★ ★   Map 11 J 11

Glasson, Athlone,
Co. Westmeath
Tel: +353-90-648 5120
Email: info@glassongolf.ie
Web: www.glassongolfhotel.ie
GPS: N +53° 28' 32.38"   W -7° 54' 2.68"

Location
Situated on the beautiful shores of Lough Ree, Glasson is centrally located, less than 1 hour 15 minutes from Dublin Airport and 1 hour from Galway.

Property Highlights
Fantastic panoramic views of the Golf Course and the Lake await at Glasson. With its Sauna & Steam Room, Fitness Suite and Treatment Room as well as Private Jetty and on site Golf Course.

Local Attractions
With its lakeside setting, Glasson is ideally placed for a range of boat trips on the lake, is 30 minutes from the monastic site Clonmacnoise and close to a wide range of other attractions/activities.

B&B from: €45.00 - €100.00
Suites from: €150.00 - €300.00

Host(s): Tom & Breda Reid & Family

65

Open All Year

Hodson Bay Hotel

Hotel ★ ★ ★ ★   Map 11 J 11

Athlone,
Co. Westmeath
Tel: +353-90-644 2000
Email: info@hodsonbayhotel.com
Web: www.hodsonbayhotel.com
GPS: N +53° 28' 4.25"   W -7° 59' 20.67"

Location
Surrounded by the spectacular lake and golf course, accessibility to Hodson Bay via rail, road and boat makes it truly unique.

Property Highlights
The 182 bedroom Hodson Bay Hotel & Spa Resort is one of Ireland's most impressive leisure & conferencing destinations.

Local Attractions
Kayaking, sailing, cruising, golfing, walking, heritage, angling, equestrian, combined with luxury accommodation, exquisite fine dining & 5* Spa.

B&B from: €65.00 - €115.00
Suites from: €170.00 - €460.00

Host(s): Timothy Hayes

182

Open All Year

Prince of Wales Hotel

Hotel ★ ★ ★ ★   Map 11 J 11

Church Street, Athlone,
Co. Westmeath
Tel: +353-90-647 6666
Email: info@theprinceofwales.ie
Web: www.theprinceofwales.ie
GPS: N +53° 25' 26.16"   W -7° 56' 18.49"

Location
Located in the heart of Athlone, near the Athlone Town Centre shops, the Shannon River, the Deane Crowe Theatre and all the best pubs and restaurants.

Property Highlights
Incorporating 46 well appointed bedrooms with free internet access & the famous Prince Bar, with excellent food & the best cocktails in town!

Local Attractions
Boating on the Shannon, Clonmacnoise, golf, walking, angling, great shopping, access to Ireland's Lake Lands.

B&B from: €44.50 - €105.00

Host(s): Chris Vos

46

Closed 24 - 27 December

B&B Rates are per Person Sharing per Night incl. Breakfast. Room/Suite Rates are per Room per Night. **See also page 08**

Co. Westmeath

To Book Call **+353-1-8084419** or www.irelandhotels.com

Athlone / Moate

Radisson Blu Hotel Athlone

Hotel ★ ★ ★ ★   Map 11 J 11

**Northgate Street, Athlone,
Co. Westmeath**
Tel: +353-90-644 2600
Email: info.athlone@radissonblu.com
Web: www.radissonblu.ie/hotel-athlone
GPS: N +53° 25' 28.37"   W -7° 56' 28.89"

Location
The hotel is situated in the Town Centre, overlooking the River Shannon. Within walking distance of the train and bus station.

Property Highlights
The hotel stands out among Ireland hotels with a relaxing outdoor riverside terrace and meeting rooms perfect for events along the marina.

Local Attractions
Explore attractions nearby the hotel including Ireland's oldest pub - Sean's Bar, Clonmacnoise monastic site or Athlone Castle.

B&B from: €49.00 - €105.00
Suites from: €139.00 - €259.00

Host(s): Declan Sweeney

128

Activities   Facilities

Open All Year

Sheraton Athlone Hotel

Hotel ★ ★ ★ ★   Map 11 J 11

**Athlone,
Co. Westmeath**
Tel: +353-90-645 1000
Email: reservations@sheratonathlonehotel.com
Web: www.sheratonathlonehotel.com
GPS: N +53° 25' 25.64"   W -7° 56' 5.82"

Location
The spectacular 12 storey Sheraton Tower with views over the majestic River Shannon & Athlone Town is just 1 hour from Dublin and 900m from M6.

Property Highlights
The beautiful, stylish 167 bedroom Sheraton Athlone boasts luxury Urban Spa, Leisure Complex, comprehensive conferencing centre & 3 exceptional dining options.

Local Attractions
Cruising, golfing, walking, heritage & neighbouring Athlone town centre - it's Ireland's only shop, stop & Spa all under one roof!

B&B from: €59.00 - €199.00
Suites from: €139.00 - €279.00

Host(s): Johnny O'Sullivan

167

Activities   Facilities

Closed 25 - 26 December

Temple Country Retreat & Spa

Guesthouse ★ ★ ★ ★   Map 11 J 11

**Horseleap, Moate,
Co. Westmeath**
Tel: +353-57-933 5118
Email: reservations@templespa.ie
Web: www.templespa.ie
GPS: N +53° 24' 20.76"   W -7° 36' 9.79"

Location
Rural setting, 5 minutes from the M6 Dublin - Galway Motorway. Convenient to Athlone, Tullamore & Mullingar.

Property Highlights
Temple is a Destination Spa, a calm retreat to relax & unwind, to take part in an activity programme or just do nothing at all.

Local Attractions
Lockes Distillery Museum, Belvedere House & Gardens, Clonmacnoise & Clara Bog.

B&B from: €75.00 - €175.00
Suites from: €250.00 - €400.00

Host(s): Declan & Bernadette Fagan

23

Activities   Facilities

Closed 20 - 28 December

172   Dublin & Ireland East   B&B Rates are per Person Sharing per Night incl. Breakfast. Room/Suite Rates are per Room per Night. **See also page 08**

To Book Call **+353-1-8084419** or www.irelandhotels.com

Co. Westmeath
Mullingar

Bloomfield House Hotel

Hotel ★ ★ ★ Map 11 L 12

Belvedere, Mullingar,
Co. Westmeath
Tel: +353-44-934 0894
Email: info@bloomfieldhouse.com
Web: www.bloomfieldhousehotel.ie
GPS: N +53° 29' 15.47" W -7° 21' 44.96"

Location
Located on the shores of Lough Ennell just 3km south of Mullingar town. Easily accessible from M50, M6, M4.

Property Highlights
Combining 30 years tradition with outdoor dining, kids club, a friendly atmosphere & excellent leisure and spa facilities.

Local Attractions
A perfect location with many great activities on site & in the surrounding area including greyhound racing, horseracing, fishing and golf.

B&B from: €50.00 - €100.00
Suites from: €100.00 - €250.00

Host(s): Ronan Byrne

111

Facilities

Closed 25 December

Greville Arms Hotel

Hotel ★ ★ ★ Map 11 L 12

Mullingar,
Co. Westmeath
Tel: +353-44-934 8563
Email: info@grevillearmshotel.ie
Web: www.grevillearms.ie
GPS: N +53° 31' 32.62" W -7° 20' 27.50"

Location
Located off N4. Tour Centre. Close to bus & train terminal. Private car parking.

Property Highlights
In the heart of Mullingar, recently refurbished. The Greville Restaurant is renowned for its cuisine. The hotel includes Ulysses Bar with its life size figure of James Joyce.

Local Attractions
Belvedere House & Garden. Tullynally Castle. Village of Fore. Fishing on lakes. Greyhound stadium. Joe Dolan Mullingar Tours.

B&B from: €40.00 - €80.00

Host(s): John Cochrane

40

Activities Facilities

Closed 25 - 26 December

McCormack's Guesthouse

Guesthouse ★ ★ ★ Map 11 L 12

Old Dublin Road, Mullingar,
Co. Westmeath
Tel: +353-44-934 1483
Email: info@mccormacksbandb.com
Web: www.mccormacksbandb.com
GPS: N +53° 31' 9" W -7° 17' 50"

Location
Located at the junction of N4 & N52, close to Mullingar Park Hotel. On Old Dublin Road to Mullingar. Approximately 45 minutes from Dublin Airport.

Property Highlights
Located in peaceful farm setting approximately 20 minutes walk from Mullingar Town. Log cabin with sauna & hot tub on site. Tennis court & games room with pool table, etc. Free WiFi.

Local Attractions
Close by we have Belvedere House & Gardens, Mullingar Golf Club, Greyhound Stadium & all the visitor attractions of Mullingar & Westmeath.

B&B from: €35.00 - €70.00

Host(s): Tom & Margaret Mc Cormack

10

Facilities

Open All Year

B&B Rates are per Person Sharing per Night incl. Breakfast. Room/Suite Rates are per Room per Night. **See also page 08**

Co. Wicklow

To Book Call **+353-1-8084419** or www.irelandhotels.com

Arklow / Ashford

Arklow Bay Conference, Leisure & Spa Hotel

Hotel ★ ★ ★   Map 8 O 8

Arklow,
Co. Wicklow
Tel: +353-402-32309
Email: reservations@arklowbay.com
Web: www.arklowbay.com
GPS: N +52° 48' 11.04" W -6° 8' 36.47"

Location
The hotel is within walking distance of the town. Only 40 minutes from Dublin. Accessible by train & bus.

Property Highlights
Full leisure centre & Spa on site. Free Kids Club during school holidays. Free parking. Kids share free B&B.

Local Attractions
Glendalough, Wicklow Gaol, Avoca, Golf courses including European, Seafield, Powerscourt, Woodenbridge. Extensive walks.

B&B from: €40.00 - €95.00

Host(s): Tina O'Sullivan

92

Facilities

Open All Year

Bridge Hotel

Hotel ★ ★   Map 8 O 8

Bridge Street, Arklow,
Co. Wicklow
Tel: +353-402-31666
Email: bridgearklow@gmail.com
Web: www.arklowbridgehotel.com
GPS: N +52° 47' 53.39" W -6° 9' 8.88"

Location
Situated in Arklow Town beside the shopping centre, approximately 1 hour from Dublin & Rosslare. Bus & train services are just a 5 minute walk.

Property Highlights
Small family-run hotel of character offering friendly personal service with home cooked food in our relaxing lounge.

Local Attractions
Beside the seaside, close to swimming pool, leisure centre, cinema & major golf clubs of Arklow, Woodenbridge & European. Hill walking, fishing, archery & horse riding.

B&B from: €45.00 - €60.00

Host(s): Jim Hoey

14

Facilities

Closed 25 December & Good Friday

Ballyknocken House & Cookery School

Guesthouse ★ ★ ★ ★   Map 8 P 9

Glenealy, Ashford,
Co. Wicklow
Tel: +353-404-44627
Email: reservations@ballyknocken.com
Web: www.ballyknocken.com
GPS: N +52° 58' 37.47" W -6° 8' 35.32"

Location
29 miles south of Dublin, close to ferry ports. 350 acre farm with pretty gardens and a mountain backdrop, ideal for walking and golfing.

Property Highlights
Cookery school with TV chef Catherine Fulvio, use of organic produce. 1850s farmhouse, Victorian style bedrooms, cooking, walking, golf, holidays.

Local Attractions
Close to Glendalough, Powerscourt, Mount Usher Gardens, Sally Gap and Guinness Lake (location of "PS I Love You" and "Braveheart").

B&B from: €49.00 - €59.00

Host(s): Catherine Fulvio

7

Facilities

Closed 13 December - 07 January

B&B Rates are per Person Sharing per Night incl. Breakfast. Room/Suite Rates are per Room per Night. See also page 08

Co. Wicklow
Ashford / Bray

Bel-Air Hotel

Hotel ★   Map 8 P 9

**Ashford,
Co. Wicklow**
Tel: +353-404-40109
Email: belairhotel@eircom.net
Web: www.belairhotelequestrian.com
GPS: N +53° 0' 5.49" W -6° 7' 18.61"

Location
Situated in the centre of 81 hectares of parklands just outside the village of Ashford in Co. Wicklow, which is 45 kilometres south of Dublin just off the N11.

Property Highlights
Family-run since 1937, featuring lovely gardens with a breathtaking view of the sea. Traditional family atmosphere & rich history make for a popular venue, rooms en suite with tea/coffee facilities.

Local Attractions
Adjacent to Equestrian Centre specialising in cross country riding and jumping, Hill Walking in Wicklow Mountains, Beach and Cliff Walks, Forest Walks, Mount Usher Gardens, Ashford. 30+ Golf Courses.

B&B from: €60.00 - €60.00

Host(s): William Freeman

10

Facilities

Closed 23 December - 15 January

Yew Tree @ The Chester Beatty

Hotel ★ ★   Map 8 P 9

**Ashford Village,
Co. Wicklow**
Tel: +353-404-40206
Email: hotelchesterbeatty@eircom.net
Web: www.theyewtree.ie
GPS: N +53° 0' 39.91" W -6° 6' 31.68"

Location
Located in Ashford Village, Co. Wicklow at junction 15/16 on the N11. 30 minutes to Dublin City.

Property Highlights
12 Luxury en suite bedrooms, award-winning restaurant, open fires, traditional Irish bar with live music every weekend, entertainment & themed events, located amidst The Garden of Ireland.

Local Attractions
Exceptional golf courses, horse riding, heritage sites, Brittas Bay, The Wicklow Way.

B&B from: €40.00 - €70.00

Host(s): Anne Burgess & George Smullen

12

Activities

Facilities

Closed 23 - 26 December

Crofton Bray Head Inn

Guesthouse ★ ★   Map 8 P 10

**Strand Road, Bray,
Co. Wicklow**
Tel: +353-1-286 7182
Email: croftonbrayheadinn@hotmail.com
GPS: N +53° 11' 46.81" W -6° 5' 34.50"

Location
We are ideally located for touring Wicklow and a 10 minute walk from an excellent commuter train to Dublin.

Property Highlights
Crofton Bay Head Inn is 150 years old, with original Victorian fixtures still intact. It has glorious sea views, all bedrooms en suite with TV and telephone.

Local Attractions
Swimming, all sea activities and walking are recommended. Golf, Fishing, Bowling & Horse Riding nearby. A great favourite with film directors. The Commitments, Breakfast on Pluto were filmed here.

B&B from: €50.00 - €50.00

Host(s): Ena Regan Cummins

30

Facilities

Closed 01 October - 01 June

B&B Rates are per Person Sharing per Night incl. Breakfast. Room/Suite Rates are per Room per Night. **See also page 08**

Co. Wicklow

To Book Call **+353-1-8084419** or www.irelandhotels.com

Bray / Enniskerry / Glendalough

Martello Hotel (The)

Hotel ★ ★   Map 8 P 10

**Strand Road, Bray,
Co. Wicklow**
Tel: +353-1-286 8000
Email: info@themartello.ie
Web: www.themartello.ie
GPS: N +53° 12' 7.18"   W -6° 5' 54.07"

Location
Located 5 minutes to both Aircoach & DART terminals. 30 minutes to City Centre. 20 minutes to Glendalough, 10 minutes to Dundrum Town Centre.

Property Highlights
Martello Bar food and Tower Bistro early bird menu. Terrace Bar with stunning sea views, Adams Room functions. Friendly staff.

Local Attractions
Powerscourt House, Gardens & Waterfall, Glendalough, Clara Lara Fun Park adjacent. 15 Golf Courses including Druids Glen, Avondale House & Forest Walks.

Room Rate from: €50.00 - €140.00

Host(s): John Duggan

25

Activities   **Facilities**

Closed 24 - 26 December

The Ritz-Carlton, Powerscourt

Hotel ★ ★ ★ ★ ★   Map 8 O 10

**Powerscourt Estate, Enniskerry,
Co. Wicklow**
Tel: +353-1-274 8888
Email: powerscourtreservations@ritzcarlton.com
Web: www.ritzcarlton.com
GPS: N +53° 11' 10.22"   W -6° 10' 51.20"

Location
At the centre of the historic Powerscourt Estate beside the picturesque village of Enniskerry. 30 mins. from Dublin City Centre & 45 mins. from Dublin Airport.

Property Highlights
Ireland's only Gordon Ramsay Restaurant, stunning views of the Wicklow countryside & 124 extensive & luxurious suites.

Local Attractions
Powerscourt House & Gardens, Glendalough, The Wicklow Way, Dublin City & all it has to offer.

Room Rate from: €255.00 - €315.00
Suites from: €295.00 - €5,000.00

Host(s): Max Zanardi

200

Activities   **Facilities**

Open All Year

Glendalough Hotel

Hotel ★ ★ ★   Map 8 O 9

**Glendalough,
Co. Wicklow**
Tel: +353-404-45135
Email: info@glendaloughhotel.ie
Web: www.glendaloughhotel.ie
GPS: N +53° 0' 41.01"   W -6° 19' 32.79"

Location
The Glendalough Hotel is family owned & run, with 37 bedrooms, only 45km from Dublin's City Centre.

Property Highlights
The hotel backs onto Glendalough National Park. Our Glendasan Restaurant, renowned for its fine cuisine using local produce, overhangs the Glendasan River.

Local Attractions
We are in the heart of Ireland's most famous National park and an easy drive from some of Ireland's best golf courses and walking trails.

B&B from: €60.00 - €95.00

Host(s): Pat Casey

37

Activities   **Facilities**

Closed 01 December - 31 January

176 Dublin & Ireland East   B&B Rates are per Person Sharing per Night incl. Breakfast. Room/Suite Rates are per Room per Night. See also page 08

To Book Call **+353-1-8084419** or www.irelandhotels.com

Co. Wicklow
Glendalough / Glen-O-The-Downs

Lynham's Hotel

Hotel ★ ★ ★ Map 8 0 9

Laragh, Glendalough,
Co. Wicklow
Tel: +353-404-45345
Email: info@lynhamsoflaragh.ie
Web: www.lynhamsoflaragh.ie
GPS: N +53° 0' 28.88"   W -6° 17' 50.02"

Location
Family-owned Lynham's Hotel is situated in the heart of Wicklow National Park, just minutes from the beautiful, historic Glendalough.

Property Highlights
The warm, welcoming atmosphere and superb food in Jake's Bar & Old World Restaurant lends a traditional air to Lynham's.

Local Attractions
Local attractions include walking routes in Wicklow National Park, Glendalough 12th century Monastic City, Golf, Horse Riding, Fishing & many more.

B&B from: €50.00 - €105.00

Host(s): John & Anne Lynham

14

Facilities

Closed 21 - 28 December

Glenview Hotel & Leisure Cub

Hotel ★ ★ ★ ★ Map 8 0 10

Glen of The Downs, Delgany,
Co. Wicklow
Tel: +353-1-287 3399
Email: sales@glenviewhotel.com
Web: www.glenviewhotel.com
GPS: N +53° 8' 31.89"   W -6° 7' 38.66"

Location
Just off the M50 Motorway on N11. Located in Glen of the Downs, 30 miles from Dublin Airport & 23 miles from Dublin City Centre.

Property Highlights
Stunning views, extensive leisure club, beauty treatment rooms, woodland walks & gardens, ample car parking & complimentary WiFi throughout the hotel.

Local Attractions
Powerscourt Gardens & Waterfall, Mount Usher Gardens, Avoca Handweavers, Killruddery House, Dundrum Shopping Centre, Silver Strand Beaches.

B&B from: €55.00 - €95.00

Host(s): Pat Hevey

70

Activities   **Facilities**

Open All Year

RUSSBOROUGH

Russborough is the finest house in Ireland open to the public. The house which is beautifully maintained and lavishly furnished is home to the Beit collections of paintings and also contains fine furniture, tapestries, carpets, porcelain and silver. The Maze is open every day throughout the season, as is the souvenir & craft shop and the new 'kitchen garden cafe' for lunches etc. Craft workshops now open including blacksmith, weaver & wood turner.
Free parking at all times.

OPENING TIMES
Mid April to End Sept - Daily
10.00 - 18.00
(last tour admission 17.00)
All year around for Groups by appointment.

PRICE
Adult €10.00
Senior & Student €8.00
Under 16 €5.00
Family €25.00
(2 adults + 4 children under 16)

Russborough
Blessington, Co. Wicklow
Tel: +353 (0)45 865239
Email: russborough@eircom.net
Web: www.russborough.ie

B&B Rates are per Person Sharing per Night incl. Breakfast. Room/Suite Rates are per Room per Night. See also page 08

Co. Wicklow

To Book Call **+353-1-8084419** or www.irelandhotels.com

Rathnew / Wicklow Town / Woodenbridge

Tinakilly House Hotel

Hotel ★ ★ ★ ★   Map 8 P 9

Wicklow, (Rathnew),
Co. Wicklow
Tel: +353-404-69274
Email: reservations@tinakilly.ie
Web: www.tinakilly.ie
GPS: N +52° 59' 46.61" W -6° 4' 1.56"

Location
Tinakilly House is an elegant Victorian Mansion set in 7 acres of beautifully landscaped gardens overlooking the Irish Sea.

Property Highlights
Tinakilly is the ideal venue for weddings, private functions & conferences. Bedrooms are furnished in period style & most overlook the Irish Sea. Award-winning cuisine, with food sourced locally.

Local Attractions
Golf, horse riding, Powerscourt, Mount Usher Gardens, Glendalough, Dublin 46km.

B&B from: €40.00 - €125.00
Suites from: €100.00 - €320.00

Host(s): Ian Finnan

51

Facilities

Open All Year

Grand Hotel

Hotel ★ ★ ★   Map 8 P 9

Abbey Street, Wicklow Town,
Co. Wicklow
Tel: +353-404-67337
Email: reservations@grandhotel.ie
Web: www.grandhotel.ie
GPS: N +52° 58' 50.28" W -6° 2' 51.92"

Location
Located 15 mins. from the Wicklow Train Station. Dublin Bus right outside the hotel. 40 mins. drive from Dublin City Centre, 50 mins. from Dublin Airport.

Property Highlights
Complimentary car parking. Full bar menu from 12 - 9:30pm. Breakfast served from 7 - 11am. Coach parking at the front of hotel. 4 conference rooms. Catering for weddings 30 - 250 guests.

Local Attractions
The Wicklow Gaol, Bowling Alley, Glendalough, Hill Walking, Wicklow Beaches, 20 minutes from Kilruddery House, sailing, fishing, horse riding & bike riding are all available.

B&B from: €45.00 - €70.00

Host(s): Veronica Timlin

33

Activities Facilities

Closed 25 - 26 December

Woodenbridge Hotel & Lodge

Hotel ★ ★ ★   Map 8 O 8

Vale Of Avoca, Arklow,
Co. Wicklow
Tel: +353-402-35146
Email: reservations@woodenbridgehotel.com
Web: www.woodenbridgehotel.com
GPS: N +52° 49' 55.95" W -6° 14' 6.62"

Location
Located in Vale of Avoca, 4.5 miles from Arklow on R747, 4.5 miles off N11, just 1 hour from Dublin.

Property Highlights
Oldest hotel in Ireland. Historic hotel overlooking Woodenbridge Golf Course. Near Avoca film location for Ballykissangel & Avoca Hand Weavers. Our restaurant & bar serve quality Irish food.

Local Attractions
Golf Courses, Meeting of Waters, Avondale Forest Park, Aughrim Fishing Centre, Glendalough, Open farms & Historic Gardens. There are lots of local walks & beaches.

B&B from: €35.00 - €60.00

Host(s): Esther & Bill O'Brien

62

Facilities

Open All Year

178 Dublin & Ireland East   B&B Rates are per Person Sharing per Night incl. Breakfast. Room/Suite Rates are per Room per Night. **See also page 08**

Ireland South

For Detailed Maps of this Region See Pages **325-340**. Each Hotel or Guesthouse has a Map Reference to these detailed maps below the premises name.

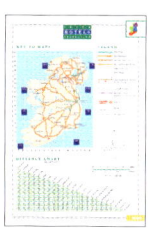

See page **325** for map with access points and driving distances

Co. Carlow
Carlow Town 183
Leighlinbridge 184
Tullow 184

Co. Cork
Allihies 185
Ballincollig 185
Ballycotton 185
Ballylickey 186
Ballyvourney 186
Baltimore 186
Bandon 187
Bantry 187
Blarney 188
Carrigaline 189
Castlemartyr 190
Castletownshend 190
Charleville 191
Clonakilty 191
Cobh 192
Cork City 193
Courtmacsherry 199
Fota Island 200

Glengarriff 200
Gougane Barra 201
Innishannon 201
Kinsale 202
Macroom 204
Mallow 205
Mitchelstown 205
Rosscarbery 206
Schull 206
Shanagarry 206
Skibbereen 207
Youghal 208

Co. Kerry
Ballybunion 208
Caherdaniel 209
Caragh Lake 209
Castlegregory 210
Cloghane 210
Dingle (An Daingean) 210
Kenmare 215
Killarney 217
Killorglin 233
Portmagee 233

Sneem 233
Tahilla 234
Tarbert 234
Tralee 235
Waterville 237

Co. Kilkenny
Graiguenamanagh 238
Kilkenny City 238
Knocktopher 244
Mullinavat 245

Co. Tipperary
Cahir 245
Carrick-on-Suir 246
Cashel 246
Clonmel 247
Glen of Aherlow 248
Horse and Jockey 249
Nenagh 249
Templemore 249
Thurles 250
Tipperary Town 250

Co. Waterford
Ardmore 251
Ballymacarbry 252
Cappoquin 252
Dungarvan 252
Dunmore East 253
Faithlegg 254
Lismore 254
Tramore 254
Waterford City 256

Co. Wexford
Barntown 261
Bunclody 261
Curracloe 262
Enniscorthy 262
Foulksmills 262
Gorey 263
New Ross 264
Newbawn 264
Rosslare 264
Rosslare Harbour 265
Wexford Town 266

Ireland South

Carlow, Cork, Kerry, Kilkenny, Tipperary, Waterford, Wexford
(see pages 2 & 3 for full County listing)

Welcome to Ireland South. Seven counties, like jewels adorning Ireland's southern shores.

Welcome to a land of unparalleled scenic beauty, picturesque valleys and ancient roadways, vibrant streets and spectacular coastline. Where the lilt of a fiddler's tune entwined with peat smoke and conversation in a city bar, is as eloquent an expression of its beauty as are the run of its waters, the vaunt of its peaks, or the glint of a leaping salmon in the fading evening light. Ireland South is special for so many reasons – the drama of its diverse yet spectacular landscapes, the naturally sculpted beauty of its award-winning beaches, the mystical charms of its past, the quality and variety of its world-class visitor attractions, the unique personalities of its many famous cities, towns and villages and the open warmth and creative spirit of its extraordinary people. All of this is waiting for you, to explore, to discover, to fall in love with.

Carlow, framed by the River Barrow to the west and the River Slaney to the east, is a county defined by its rivers. The Barrow Navigation is popular for pleasure boating, angling and walking, one of the best ways to get to know this beautiful river. Carlow is steeped in history and among its top visitor attractions are Altamont Gardens, The Visual Centre for Contemporary Art and the George Bernard Shaw Theatre, Huntingdon Castle, Saint Lazerian's Cathedral and Duckett's Grove. The Carlow Garden Trail with its 16 locations and the Carlow – Trails of the Saints, Christian Heritage Drive.

Cork, perhaps no other corner of Ireland contains so much to see, do and experience as County Cork. Cork City is a thriving metropolis with a continental air. The east of the county is ripe with fertile farmlands, verdant river valleys and picturesque towns and villages while the west boasts a long, magnificent coastline, which stretches 200 miles from Youghal to Ardgroom on the Beara Peninsula.

Cork is also brimming with must see visitor attractions, like the world famous island garden of Ilnacullin-(Garinish Island), Bantry House and Gardens, Blarney Castle, the Old Midleton Distillery, the Michael Collins Centre at Clonakilty and Fota Arboretum and Gardens.

Kerry, perhaps the most popular tourist destination in Ireland, is also considered by many to be the most beautiful. From the spectacular Ring of Kerry, to the extraordinary 25,000 acre Killarney National Park – home to Muckross House, to beauty spots like the Gap of Dunloe and Torc Waterfall, Kerry is replete in awe inspiring natural beauty. The county is rich in archaeological treasures too, none more famous than the 6th century Skelligs UNESCO World Heritage Site, 12km off the southwest coast of Ireland. Among the many world class visitor attractions that have been developed recently are The Geraldine Experience and the Kerry County Museum in Tralee, Derrynane House, The Old Barracks Heritage Centre, Cahersiveen, the Skellig Experience and the Great Blasket Island Interpretative Centre.

Kilkenny, whether you're fishing for trout on the Nore, sinking a putt at Mount Juliet, or driving through pretty towns and villages like Thomastown and Inistioge, you'll be struck by the peaceful beauty of Kilkenny. The county has a wealth of visitor attractions, from the wonders of Dunmore Cave and Jerpoint Abbey, to the magnificently restored Kilkenny Castle or the newly opened St. Francis Abbey Brewery Tours...the home of Smithwick's beer since 1710. The ancient medieval city of Kilkenny is today a thriving, modern capital that has protected its precious heritage and crafts whilst evolving as one of Ireland's most vibrant and enjoyable cities in which to stay.

Tipperary, there's probably no livelier a collection of market towns in all Ireland than Carrick-on-Suir, Clonmel, Cahir, Tipperary and Cashel. Nor a more distinctive set of landmarks than Cahir Castle on its island in the middle of the River Suir and the great Rock of Cashel, rising above the Golden Vale and the Glen of Aherlow. Tipperary has some fascinating visitor attractions, like Mitchelstown Cave, one of Europe's most spectacular, and the captivating Brú Ború Cultural Centre, commemorating Brian Boru, the Last of the High Kings, with a 'cultural village' dedicated to the study and celebration of native Irish music, song, dance and theatre.

Waterford, famous the world over for the beauty and craftsmanship of its master glass cutters at the newly opened House of Waterford Crystal Centre located in the city centre. This includes a factory tour where you see glass being blown, cut and engraved. The tour finishes in the show room / retail area which houses the largest collection of Waterford Crystal in the World. Enjoy the Viking Triangle Walking Tour in Irelands oldest city...1,000 years history in 1,000 paces. Opening in 2011 is the Bishops Palace – Museum of Modern Waterford 1700-2000. Waterford also offers visitors a choice between a cosmopolitan vibrant city, charming seaside resorts with miles of sandy beaches and countryside getaway locations set against the backdrop of the Comeragh Mountains. From the charm of rural towns and villages like Dungarvan, Lismore, Cappoquin and Ballymacarbry to the resort villages of Ardmore, Dunmore and Tramore there is something to appeal to all tastes. With an excellent choice of world-class visitor attractions to enjoy including The Museum of Treasures and Edmund Rice Heritage Centre which are complemented by Jack Burtchaell Walking Tour all of which tell the story of Waterford. For families, the newly restored Waterford to Kilmeaden narrow gauge railway is a fabulous way to take in the sweep of the Suir Valley and to go back 450 million years you can take a tour of the spectacular Copper Coast UNESCO Geopark.

Wexford, located in the sunny South East of Ireland is fast becoming the spa capital of Ireland and is the ideal location for a restful and rejuvenating break. But long before the arrival of 'spas', Wexford was famous for its rich history, the story of which is told through the numerous visitor attractions in the county. The most fascinating include the remarkable Irish National Heritage Park at Wexford – which will take you on a tour of how the Irish lived, worshipped and died from the stone age to the 12th Century; the Dunbrody Heritage Ship in New Ross - a replica of a 19th Century famine ship that transported the Irish to the new world; the medieval Hook Lighthouse – where monks kept the fire alight as far back as the 5th Century; add to these the National 1798 Rebellion Centre in Enniscorthy, Ireland's premier wildfowl sanctuary, the Wexford Wildfowl Reserve and the JFK Arboretum and you get the finest array of quality visitor attractions. The South East has 56 gardens that welcome visitors and offer a great variety of designs and styles of gardens to those who simply appreciate good gardens and want to enjoy the natural environment. Given the higher than average sunshine and better weather in the region many of the gardens are unique in Ireland and the world such as Mount Congreve Gardens in Waterford and Altamont Gardens in Carlow.

Heritage
With a rich cultural tapestry of towering castles, magnificent stately homes, ancient Celtic monuments, early Christian ecclesiastical sites, fascinating museums and intriguing city architecture, Ireland South boasts a wealth of world-class cultural and heritage visitor centres.

In every corner of these counties you'll find a thread of ancient times so alive it seems still woven to the present day; captivating history brought to life through enthralling tales, working museums, and state-of-the-art interpretative centres.

Discover the medieval splendour of the Rock of Cashel, boost your powers of eloquence by kissing the famous Blarney Stone, or take an easy wander round the magnificent Kilkenny Castle. There's also the fully restored elegance of Ross Castle in Kerry, and the fascinating war-entangled history of Charles Fort at Kinsale to explore.

Ireland South

Equestrian

Horse riding in Ireland is very popular and is an accessible pursuit for all ages, abilities and budgets. There are numerous riding centres in the region that would be happy to provide you with anything from an hour's riding, to trekking/trail riding or even beach riding. To find one near to you, check out **www.discoverireland.ie/equestrian**

Or why not try your luck on the horses and spend a day at the races?

10 Key Walks

1. Barrow Valley, Co. Carlow
2. Castlemorris, Co. Kilkenny
3. Glen of Aherlow, Co. Tipperary
4. Sheeps Head Peninsula, Co. Cork
5. Beara Peninsula, Co. Cork
6. Killarney National Park, Co. Kerry
7. Glenbeigh Loops, Co. Kerry
8. Dingle Peninsula, Co. Kerry
9. Coastal Walks, Co. Wexford
10. Comeragh Mountains, Co. Waterford

Maps for these walks and the other 200 Looped Walks across Ireland can be downloaded on **www.discoverireland.ie/walking**

Or why not try your hand at mountain biking in the Ballyhoura Mountains in East Limerick and North Cork?

Top Attractions

1. Crawford Art Gallery, Cork
2. Lewis Glucksman Gallery, Cork
3. Cork City Gaol, Cork
4. Fota House & Gardens, Cork
5. Killarney National Park, Co. Kerry
6. Muckross House & Gardens, Killarney, Co. Kerry
7. Skellig Islands, Co. Kerry
8. Kilkenny Castle, Kilkenny
9. Dunbrody Famine Ship, New Ross, Co. Wexford
10. Altamont Gardens, Tullow, Co. Carlow
11. Rock of Cashel, Co. Tipperary
12. Waterford Museum of Treasures, Waterford
13. House of Waterford Crystal Centre
14. Kilkenny St. Francis Abbey Brewery Tours (Smithwick's)

Angling

The counties of Cork, Kerry, Waterford and Wexford offer spectacular deep sea fishing. There are numerous charter boat operators dotted along the coastline offering fishing over offshore wreck and reefs. The variety of species in Irish waters is impressive; turbot, pollock, cod, tope, skate, bass and shark to name but a few. Serious anglers and the less experienced are always welcome. And don't worry if you don't have any equipment with you as tackle is available to hire on board. Kilmore Quay is a centre of excellence for sea angling and Cahir is a centre of excellence for brown trout.

For more information and the lists of towns that are part of our anglers welcome initiative visit **www.discoverireland.ie/angling**

Family Fun

Ireland South is ideal for families from Ballybunion all along the coast to North Wexford, taking in Tramore, Dunmore East and the Hook. There is loads to keep the family entertained- endless water sports, horse riding, quad biking and fishing, or get involved in history and tradition at the many heritage sites and museums. Your biggest challenge will be deciding what to do.

For more information visit **www.discoverireland.ie/familyfun**

Adventure

If you long for adventure, let the Ireland South Region extend you a gilt-edged adrenalin-charged invitation. It is a paradise for sea kayakers, as well as windsurfers, kitesurfers and surfers who are hell bent on harnessing the swells that the North Atlantic sends pounding in, depending on her mood.

The mountains too boast their own adventures. For some it will be riding a horse or a mountain bike through the rugged territory. For others, the mountaineering challenges of the MacGillycuddy's Reeks, home to Ireland's highest peak, Carrantouhill. Tramore has four Surf Schools and why not try your hand at Watersports/ Rock climbing in Dunmore East or take on the challenge of the famous Comeragh Mountains from the Rathgormack Hiking Centre.

But don't let a lack of experience or skill put you off. If you like what you hear but don't know where to start, there are plenty of qualified instructors and guides ready to make your adrenalin dreams a reality.

For more information visit **www.discoverireland.ie/adventure**

Ireland's Islands

Visit the magnificent islands off the coast of West Cork. Take in a looped walk on Bere Island, experience the thrill in Ireland's only cable car across to Dursey Island, do some sailing on Heir Island or just get away from it all on Cape Clear.

For more information on Ireland's islands, including how to get there check out **www.discoverireland.ie**

To Book Call **+353-1-8084419** or www.irelandhotels.com

Co. Carlow
Carlow Town

Barrowville Town House

Guesthouse ★ ★ ★ Map 7 M 8

Kilkenny Road, Carlow Town,
Co. Carlow
Tel: +353-59-914 3324
Email: barrowvilletownhouse@eircom.net
Web: www.barrowville.com
GPS: N +52° 49' 57.84" W -6° 56' 2.99"

Location
Just 5 minutes walk to Carlow Town Centre on the Kilkenny Road. Close to bus park, train station & Carlow Institute of Technology.

Property Highlights
Regency Town House built circa 1790, the townhouse contains antique furniture with well appointed bedrooms. Breakfast served in the conservatory overlooking mature gardens.

Local Attractions
Carlow Golf Club, River Barrow for fishing & walks. Visual Centre for Contemporary Art. Only a 30 minute drive to Kilkenny City.

B&B from: €35.00 - €70.00

Host(s): Anna & Dermot Smyth

7

Facilities

Closed 24 - 26 December

Seven Oaks Hotel

Hotel ★ ★ ★ Map 7 M 8

Athy Road, Carlow Town,
Co. Carlow
Tel: +353-59-913 1308
Email: info@sevenoakshotel.com
Web: www.sevenoakshotel.com
GPS: N +52° 50' 27.63" W -6° 55' 44.14"

Location
Ideally located just 3 minutes walk from Carlow town centre and bus/train station. Now only 45 minutes drive to Dublin via the new M9 motorway.

Property Highlights
We specialise in the best of Irish foods in our Oaks Bar carvery & intimate TD Molloy's Restaurant. Individually designed rooms and executive suites, conference and leisure facilities.

Local Attractions
Located beside VISUAL & the George Bernard Shaw Theatre - a dynamic new multi-disciplinary arts facility presenting the best of local, national and international work in the visual & performing arts.

B&B from: €50.00 - €80.00

Host(s): Michael Murphy & Michael Walsh

89

Facilities

Closed 25 - 26 December

With soaring mountains, verdant river valleys and rich rolling countryside, Co. Carlow in Ireland's Sunny South-East, offers the perfect backdrop for golf, walking, angling, horse riding, canoeing and quading. Take a trip & discover mystical pre-christian monuments, ancient ecclesiastical sites, grand country houses & gardens & picturesque award winning villages. Against this timeless landscape visitors will discover excellent shopping, great food & accommodation.

For all your tourism needs contact
CARLOW TOURISM
The Foresters Hall,
College Street, Carlow.

Phone: +353 (0) 59 9130411
Email: info@carlowtourism.com
Website: www.carlowtourism.com

B&B Rates are per Person Sharing per Night incl. Breakfast. Room/Suite Rates are per Room per Night. *See also page 08*

Co. Carlow

To Book Call **+353-1-8084419** or www.irelandhotels.com

Carlow Town / Leighlinbridge / Tullow

Talbot Hotel Carlow

Hotel ★ ★ ★ ★   Map 7 M 8

**Portlaoise Road, Carlow Town,
Co. Carlow**
Tel: +353-59-915 3000
Email: sales@talbothotelcarlow.ie
Web: www.talbotcarlow.ie
GPS: N +52° 50' 47.00"   W -6° 56' 37.26"

Location
Conveniently located close to Carlow Town and just 1 hour from Dublin and within easy access of bus & train stations.

Property Highlights
4th floor Liberty Tree Restaurant with stunning views. Hotel leisure club with pool, sauna, steam room & hotel spa. Talbot Tigers supervised kids' club. Corries Bar & Bistro.

Local Attractions
Dome Family Entertainment Centre, Oak Forest Park, Delta Sensory Gardens Visual Centre & The George Bernard Shaw Theatre.

B&B from: €50.00 - €120.00
Suites from: €140.00 - €290.00

Host(s): Larry Bowe

84

Activities   Facilities

Closed 24 - 26 December

Lord Bagenal Inn

Hotel ★ ★ ★ ★   Map 7 M 8

**Main Street, Leighlinbridge,
Co. Carlow**
Tel: +353-59-977 4000
Email: info@lordbagenal.com
Web: www.lordbagenal.com
GPS: N +52° 44' 10.36"   W -6° 58' 36.38"

Location
Situated on the banks of the River Barrow in the picturesque village of Leighlinbridge, only 8 miles from Carlow and 12 miles from Kilkenny.

Property Highlights
New luxurious bedrooms, private marina. Award-winning Lord Bagenal Restaurant. Wedding, conferences, banquets catered for.

Local Attractions
Arboretum Garden Centre, Walking Leinster Mountains, Fishing on the River Barrow, Bernard Shaw Theatre Carlow.

B&B from: €55.00 - €75.00

Host(s): James & Mary Kehoe

39

Activities   Facilities

Closed 25 - 26 December

Mount Wolseley Hotel, Spa & Country Club

Hotel ★ ★ ★ ★   Map 8 N 8

**Tullow,
Co. Carlow**
Tel: +353-59-918 0100
Email: info@mountwolseley.ie
Web: www.mountwolseley.ie
GPS: N +52° 47' 27.67"   W -6° 43' 53.05"

Location
Located just over an hours drive from Dublin & Dublin Airport & Rosslare Port. 2 hours from Belfast & 2.5 hours from Cork City, 1 hour from Kilkenny.

Property Highlights
Luxurious 4**** resort boasting 18 hole championship golf course, leisure centre, award-winning Resort Spa, tennis courts, kids club & Fredericks award-winning restaurant.

Local Attractions
Altamount Gardens, Duckett's Grove, Carlow Brewing Company, Kilkenny Castle, Huntington Castle, Horse Racing, Fishing, Kildare Village, National Stud & Japanese Gardens.

B&B from: €75.00 - €110.00
Suites from: €240.00 - €295.00

Host(s): Odhran Lawlor

143

Activities   Facilities

Closed 24 - 26 December

184   Ireland South   B&B Rates are per Person Sharing per Night incl. Breakfast. Room/Suite Rates are per Room per Night. See also page 08

To Book Call **+353-1-8084419** or www.irelandhotels.com

Co. Cork

Allihies / Ballincollig / Ballycotton

Sea View Guest House

Guesthouse ★ ★ ★ Map 1 C 2

Cluin Village, Allihies, Beara,
Co. Cork
Tel: +353-27-73004
Email: seaviewg@iol.ie
Web: www.allihiesseaview.com
GPS: N +51° 38' 26.44"   W -10° 2' 38.51"

Location
Allihies is a charming village on the very south west tip of Ireland, on the end of the Beara peninsula and 70km from Bantry, Co. Cork.

Property Highlights
A wonderful 3 star guesthouse, personally managed by Mary O'Sullivan & her family. En suite rooms with TV, DD phone & tea/coffee making facilities. Reputation for comfort and relaxed style.

Local Attractions
Natural stone arches, mountain walks and a cable car visit to Dursey island are some of the many things a visitor can do. Old Cornish Copper Mine buildings, Allihies Copper Mine Museum.

B&B from: €35.00 - €45.00

Host(s): John & Mary O'Sullivan

10

Facilities

Closed 30 November - 01 March

Oriel House Hotel, Leisure Club & Spa

Hotel ★ ★ ★ ★ Map 2 H 3

Ballincollig,
Co. Cork
Tel: +353-21-420 8400
Email: info@orielhousehotel.ie
Web: www.orielhousehotel.ie
GPS: N +51° 53' 16.72"   W -8° 36' 5.08"

Location
Located on the west side of Cork City. In close proximity to Cork Airport, Train Station & Blarney. A gateway to explore Kerry.

Property Highlights
Newly extended leisure centre, 25m pool, kiddies pool, sauna, jacuzzi, Oriel Spa & Treatment Rooms, Thermal Suite, Aroma Steam Rooms, relaxation area.

Local Attractions
Ballincollig Powdermills Heritage Centre, Fota Wildlife Park, Ballincollig Regional Park, Cobh The Queenstown Story, Blarney Castle & Gardens, Farran Woods & Inniscarra Lakes.

B&B from: €65.00 - €75.00
Suites from: €180.00 - €230.00

Host(s): Breda Keane Shortt

78

Activities   **Facilities**

Closed 24 - 28 December

Bayview Hotel

Hotel ★ ★ ★ ★ Map 3 J 3

Ballycotton,
Co. Cork
Tel: +353-21-464 6746
Email: res@thebayviewhotel.com
Web: www.thebayviewhotel.com
GPS: N +51° 49' 40.11"   W -8° 0' 16.47"

Location
Nestled in the unspoilt fishing village of Ballycotton, the Bayview Hotel directly overlooks miles of spectacular coastline. 40 minutes east from Cork City.

Property Highlights
35 luxurious bedrooms overlooking the bay. Gardens step down to our own bathing area. Capricho Restaurant promises dishes from the cold, crystal depths of Atlantic Ocean to your plate.

Local Attractions
East Cork abounds with things to do while on holiday - Cobh, Queenstown, Fota Wildlife Park & House, Midleton Jameson Distillery experience, Ballymaloe Cookery School & Gardens, Youghal Walking Tours.

B&B from: €69.00 - €145.00
Suites from: €220.00 - €300.00

Host(s): Stephen Belton

35

Facilities

Closed 31 October - 1 April

B&B Rates are per Person Sharing per Night incl. Breakfast. Room/Suite Rates are per Room per Night. See also page 08

Co. Cork

To Book Call **+353-1-8084419** or www.irelandhotels.com

Ballylickey / Ballyvourney / Baltimore

Seaview House Hotel

Hotel ★ ★ ★ ★ Map 2 E 2

**Ballylickey, Bantry,
Co. Cork**
Tel: +353-27-50073
Email: info@seaviewhousehotel.com
Web: www.seaviewhousehotel.com
GPS: N +51° 43' 19.93"   W -9° 26' 11.45"

Location
On main N71, 3 miles from Bantry, 7 miles from Glengariff. Cork Airport, Kerry Airport, Cork City Train Station all approx 1.5 hours travel.

Property Highlights
4* Country House Hotel. An award-winning restaurant. Very comfortable, large bedrooms. Recipient of a number of prestigious awards.

Local Attractions
Garnish Island, Gougane Barra, Sheeps Head, Beara Peninsula, Bantry House, Mizen Head - all are within easy reach of the hotel.

B&B from: €55.00 - €70.00
Suites from: €140.00 - €165.00

Host(s): Kathleen O'Sullivan

25

Facilities

Closed 15 November - 15 March

Abbey Hotel

Hotel ★ ★ ★ Map 2 F 3

**Ballyvourney, Macroom,
Co. Cork**
Tel: +353-26-45324
Email: abbeyhotel@eircom.net
Web: www.theabbeyhotel.ie
GPS: N +51° 56' 22.03"   W -9° 9' 28.74"

Location
Situated on the border of Cork & Kerry on the main Cork/Killarney road (N22).

Property Highlights
Ballyvourney is a Gaeltacht area (native Irish speaking). Traditional Irish music & set dancing are the order of the day in the hotel bar.

Local Attractions
Killarney only 20 mins. drive, a great start to the Ring of Kerry. Overlooking the village is St. Gobnait's Shrine. Gougane Barra is 20 mins. drive. Cork City 40 mins. drive. Kenmare 30 mins. drive.

B&B from: €35.00 - €55.00

Host(s): Micheal & Mary Creedon

39

Activities

Facilities

Closed 30 October - 01 March

Casey's of Baltimore

Hotel ★ ★ ★ Map 2 E 1

**Baltimore,
Co. Cork**
Tel: +353-28-20197
Email: info@caseysofbaltimore.com
Web: www.caseysofbaltimore.com
GPS: N +51° 29' 4.81"   W -9° 21' 44.99"

Location
90km from Cork. From Cork, follow N71 to Skibbereen and from Skibbereen, take R595 to Baltimore.

Property Highlights
3 star family run hotel with en suite bedrooms. Situated overlooking the Ilen River. All have tea & coffee facilities, TV, hairdryer, telephone. Traditional pub & seafood restaurant on site.

Local Attractions
Local attractions include Ferries to the islands, Lough Ine Nature Reserve, Country Walks and all the different water sports such as sailing, diving, canoeing, angling, whale watching.

B&B from: €77.00 - €91.00

Host(s): Ann & Michael Casey

14

Facilities

Closed 20 - 27 December

B&B Rates are per Person Sharing per Night incl. Breakfast. Room/Suite Rates are per Room per Night. **See also page 08**

To Book Call **+353-1-8084419** or www.irelandhotels.com

Co. Cork

Baltimore / Bandon / Bantry

Waterfront (The)

Guesthouse ★ ★ ★   Map 2 E 1

The Square, Baltimore,
Co. Cork
Tel: +353-28-20600
Email: info@waterfrontbaltimore.ie
Web: www.waterfrontbaltimore.ie
GPS: N +51° 28' 58.21"   W -9° 22' 23.85"

Location
On the square, in the heart of Baltimore Village overlooking Baltimore Bay & the islands.

Property Highlights
3 restaurants and bar. All budgets - pizzas to shellfish platters. Bright spacious standard & superior rooms. Most with sea views.

Local Attractions
On the water, gateway to the islands. Watersports, Diving, Walking. People-watching on the square with a pint and oysters.

B&B from: €40.00 - €80.00

Host(s): Youen & Kate Jacob

13

Facilities

Closed 24 - 25 December

Munster Arms Hotel

Hotel ★ ★   Map 2 G 2

Oliver Plunkett Street, Bandon,
Co. Cork
Tel: +353-23-884 1562
Email: info@munsterarmshotel.com
Web: www.munsterarmshotel.com
GPS: N +51° 44' 42.64"   W -8° 44' 3.24"

Location
We are located on the N71, 20 minutes from Cork Airport & City. Ideal base for touring the West Cork area.

Property Highlights
Renowned for its friendly atmosphere, excellent food and value for money. Top class night club at weekends. All amenities close by.

Local Attractions
Ideal touring base for Kinsale, Cork City, Blarney, Killarney and West Cork. Close to Blarney Castle, Fota Wildlife Park, Old Head of Kinsale, Model Village, Clonakility & Beal na Bláth.

B&B from: €50.00 - €50.00

Host(s): Don O'Sullivan

30

Activities   Facilities

Closed 24 - 27 December

Westlodge Hotel

Hotel ★ ★ ★   Map 2 E 2

Bantry,
Co. Cork
Tel: +353-27-50360
Email: reservations@westlodgehotel.ie
Web: www.westlodgehotel.ie
GPS: N +51° 40' 20.88"   W -9° 28' 29.58"

Location
Situated on the edge of the Beautiful town of Bantry in the heart of West Cork. Close to Cork Airport, Cork City, Bantry Town, Cork Ferry Port.

Property Highlights
Ideal base to reach numerous tourist attractions. Provide a warm, friendly service to all our guests. Boasts 20 acres of landscaped gardens. Family friendly. Self catering cottages. Free car parking.

Local Attractions
Local attractions include Bantry House & Gardens, The Sheep's Head Walking and Cycling Tours, Bantry Market, Bantry Bay Golf Club, Mizen Head, Garnish Island, Glengarriff.

Room Rate from: €79.00 - €129.00
Suites from: €159.00 - €189.00

Host(s): Eileen M O'Shea

90

Activities   Facilities

Closed 21 - 27 December

B&B Rates are per Person Sharing per Night incl. Breakfast. Room/Suite Rates are per Room per Night. **See also page 08**   Ireland South

Co. Cork

To Book Call **+353-1-8084419** or www.irelandhotels.com

Blarney

Ashlee Lodge

Guesthouse ★ ★ ★ ★ Map 2 H 3

Tower, Blarney,
Co. Cork
Tel: +353-21-438 5346
Email: info@ashleelodge.com
Web: www.ashleelodge.com
GPS: N +51° 55' 27.58"   W -8° 36' 44.04"

Location
A quiet setting in a residential area called Tower, minutes from Blarney village. 10 minutes to Cork city centre, 20 mins. To Airport, situated on the R617.

Property Highlights
Owned & personally managed boutique property striking the perfect balance. Traditional comfort and contemporary atmosphere. King beds, Air-con, Hot tub, Sauna, Luxurious Rooms & Suites, Wifi.

Local Attractions
Blarney Castle, Blarney Woollen Mills, Fota Wildlife Park, Cobh Titanic Trail, Jameson Distillery, Cork City Gaol, Cork City Tour, Charles Fort & the perfect location for touring the South West.

B&B from: €50.00 - €85.00
Suites from: €150.00 - €250.00

Host(s): John O'Leary

10

Facilities

Closed 20 December - 20 January

Blarney Castle Hotel

Hotel ★ ★ ★   Map 2 H 3

Blarney,
Co. Cork
Tel: +353-21-438 5116
Email: info@blarneycastlehotel.com
Web: www.blarneycastlehotel.com
GPS: N +51° 55' 52.73"   W -8° 34' 6.58"

Location
Picturesque village inn on peaceful village green, beside the entrance to Blarney Castle. Five miles (8km) northwest of Ireland's Second City, Cork.

Property Highlights
Tastefully appointed spacious bedrooms. Unspoilt traditional bar. Kitchen specialising in finest local produce. Quality local entertainment regularly in bar.

Local Attractions
Killarney, Kenmare, Kinsale, Cobh, Waterford & numerous Golf Courses all an easy drive. Immediately to the left are the Blarney Castle Grounds & Gardens and to the right Blarney Woollen Mills.

B&B from: €40.00 - €75.00

Host(s): Ian & Una Forrest

13

Activities

Facilities

Closed 24 - 25 December

Blarney Golf Resort

Hotel ★ ★ ★ ★ Map 2 H 3

Tower, Blarney,
Co. Cork
Tel: +353-21-438 4477
Email: reservations@blarneygolfresort.com
Web: www.blarneygolfresort.com
GPS: N +51° 56' 16.41"   W -8° 37' 45.00"

Location
Located 20 minutes from Cork Airport, 9 miles from Cork City Centre, 9 miles from Train Station.

Property Highlights
The Resort's impressive signature championship golf course was co-designed by two-time major winner John Daly. Golf Lodges catering for families in comfort and style.

Local Attractions
The historic town of Blarney is steeped in history, legend & rugged natural beauty, with Blarney Castle and Inniscarra Sailing & Kayaking Club nearby.

B&B from: €45.00 - €85.00
Suites from: €115.00 - €150.00

Host(s): Conor O'Toole

62

Activities

Facilities

Open All Year

To Book Call **+353-1-8084419** or www.irelandhotels.com

Co. Cork

Blarney / Carrigaline

Blarney Woollen Mills Hotel

Hotel ★ ★ ★   Map 2 H 3

Blarney,
Co. Cork
Tel: +353-21-438 5011
Email: info@blarneywoollenmillshotel.com
Web: www.blarneywoollenmillshotel.com
GPS: N +51° 55' 59.65"   W -8° 33' 54.95"

Location
Our hotel is nestled in the picturesque village of Blarney and located in one of the most legendary places in Ireland, yet only minutes from Cork City centre.

Property Highlights
Famous as a great shopping experience with a fantastic choice of dining options in the Mill Restaurant or Christy's Grill Bar & boasting luxury accommodation, many rooms with a view of Blarney Castle.

Local Attractions
The world famous Blarney Woollen Mills and Meadows & Byrne is situated under the same roof. Get the gift of eloquence by kissing the Blarney Stone, located only minutes from our hotel.

B&B from: €69.00 - €109.00

Host(s): Neil Grant

48

Facilities

Open All Year

Muskerry Arms

Guesthouse ★ ★ ★   Map 2 H 3

The Square, Blarney,
Co. Cork
Tel: +353-21-438 5200
Email: jerome@muskerryarms.com
Web: www.muskerryarms.com
GPS: N +51° 55' 59.35"   W -8° 34' 4.05"

Location
With all the attributes of a small hotel, the Muskerry Arms is ideally located for your stay in Blarney.

Property Highlights
Stylish, spacious guest rooms & family suites. Live music is a regular feature in the popular Muskerry Bar & two delicious menus are available in the bar & restaurant.

Local Attractions
Within walking distance of Blarney Castle and Woollen Mills.

B&B from: €39.00 - €49.00

Host(s): Nell O'Connor

11

Facilities

Open All Year

Carrigaline Court Hotel & Leisure Centre

Hotel ★ ★ ★ ★   Map 3 H 3

Carrigaline,
Co. Cork
Tel: +353-21-485 2100
Email: reception@carrigcourt.com
Web: www.carrigcourt.com
GPS: N +51° 48' 58.06"   W -8° 23' 31.69"

Location
Located in Carrigaline Town, 15 minutes from Cork City and 10 minutes from Cork Airport. 10 minutes from Ringaskiddy Ferry Port.

Property Highlights
91 spacious, bright guestrooms. Collins Bar has great food & lively atmosphere. Bistro with outdoor terrace serving sumptuous evening meals. Leisure centre with 20m pool, treatment rooms & Kids Club.

Local Attractions
Crosshaven, home to Royal Cork Yacht Club, is just minutes away. Kinsale, Fota, Cobh & Blarney are within a 20 minute drive.

B&B from: €55.00 - €70.00
Suites from: €200.00 - €300.00

Host(s): Jerry Healy

91

Facilities

Closed 20 - 27 December

B&B Rates are per Person Sharing per Night incl. Breakfast. Room/Suite Rates are per Room per Night. See also page 08

Co. Cork

To Book Call +353-1-8084419 or www.irelandhotels.com

Carrigaline / Castlemartyr / Castletownshend

Glenwood House | Castlemartyr Resort | Castle (The)

Glenwood House	Castlemartyr Resort	Castle (The)
Guesthouse ★ ★ ★ ★ Map 3 H 3	Hotel ★ ★ ★ ★ ★ Map 3 I 3	Guesthouse ★ Map 2 F 1
Ballinrea Road, Carrigaline, **Co. Cork** Tel: +353-21-437 3878 Email: info@glenwoodguesthouse.com Web: www.glenwoodguesthouse.com GPS: N +51° 49' 17.08" W -8° 23' 42.03"	**Castlemartyr,** **Co. Cork** Tel: +353-21-421 9000 Email: reception@castlemartyrresort.ie Web: www.castlemartyrresort.ie GPS: N +51° 54' 40.59" W -8° 3' 45.06"	**Castletownshend, Near Skibbereen,** **Co. Cork** Tel: +353-28-36100 Email: castle_townshend@hotmail.com Web: www.castle-townshend.com GPS: N +51° 31' 46.41" W -9° 10' 21.46"

Location

Glenwood House is located 10 minutes south of Cork City, within easy reach of the airport and car ferry in Ringaskiddy. Ideally located for touring the south coast.

Location

Located 20 mins. from Cork City, 30 mins. from Cork Airport & 10 mins. from Midleton Train Station. 2 hours from Shannon Airport & 3 hours from Dublin Airport.

Location

Castletownshend Village is on the south west coast of Cork County. Cork Airport 80km. Ferry port 90km. Bus 9km.

Property Highlights

A purpose built guesthouse offering exceptional comfort, with private parking in a quiet residential area. Facilities for disabled guests. We run cookery courses which can be tailored to suit groups.

Property Highlights

Extensive gardens, indoor pool, sauna, plunge pool, fitness suite, croquet, heli-pad, 18 hole golf course, carriage tours, exclusive wedding venue.

Property Highlights

Bedrooms and terrace overlooking sea. Extensive private grounds. Access to beach boats.

Local Attractions

We are ideally located for golf and fishing breaks and only 10 minutes from the coast.

Local Attractions

Cork City, Kinsale, Blarney Castle, Lismore Castle & Gardens, Ballymaloe House, Gardens & Cookery School, Cobh Harbour, Ballycotton & Youghal Fishing Villages.

Local Attractions

Whale Watching, Fishing Trips, Kayaking, Rowing Boat, Golf Course, Horse Riding, Playground.

B&B from: €35.00 - €55.00

B&B from: €97.50 - €275.00
Suites from: €375.00 - €3,250.00

B&B from: €50.00 - €80.00

Host(s): Adrian Sheedy, Noelle Morrison

14

Host(s): Andrew Phelan
109

Host(s): Anne & Malcolm Cochrane Townshend
7

Facilities

Facilities

Facilities

Closed 15 December - 12 January

Closed 25 December - 26 December

Closed 15 December - 15 January

B&B Rates are per Person Sharing per Night incl. Breakfast. Room/Suite Rates are per Room per Night. *See also page 08*

To Book Call **+353-1-8084419** or www.irelandhotels.com

Co. Cork

Charleville / Clonakilty

Charleville Park Hotel & Leisure Club

Hotel ★★★★ Map 2 G 5

Limerick Road, Charleville,
Co. Cork
Tel: +353-63-33700
Email: info@charlevilleparkhotel.com
Web: www.charlevilleparkhotel.com
GPS: N +52° 21' 38.14" W -8° 40' 59.08"

Dunmore House Hotel

Hotel ★★★ Map 2 G 2

Muckross, Clonakilty,
Co. Cork
Tel: +353-23-883 3352
Email: enq@dunmorehousehotel.ie
Web: www.dunmorehousehotel.ie
GPS: N +51° 35' 24.91" W -8° 52' 3.51"

Inchydoney Island Lodge & Spa

Hotel ★★★★ Map 2 G 2

Clonakilty,
West Cork
Tel: +353-23-883 3143
Email: reservations@inchydoneyisland.com
Web: www.inchydoneyisland.com
GPS: N +51° 35' 50.55" W -8° 51' 44.20"

Location
Located in Charleville, north Cork, in the heart of Munster. Only 5 minutes from Charleville Train Station. Charleville also operates a regular bus service.

Location
Seaside location situated on the South West coast of Ireland, 3km outside Clonakilty Town, 30km from Cork City.

Location
Overlooking two stunning beaches with views of the ocean. 3 miles from Clonakility Town in the heart of West Cork.

Property Highlights
91 luxurious bedrooms & full leisure club including 25m pool. Greenfinch Bistro, Ed's Bar & The Osprey Lounge serving modern Irish food daily. WiFi available.

Property Highlights
Family-owned hotel, with beautifully decorated rooms featuring spectacular views of the Atlantic Ocean overlooking Clonakilty Bay. Magnificent patio area. Sample our home-cooked local produce.

Property Highlights
Luxurious accommodation with private beachfront balconies, fine dining & unique seawater therapies.

Local Attractions
For the kids: Buttercup Farm, Donkey Sanctuary & much more. Golf, mountain biking, angling, kayaking all nearby with preferred rates throughout the hotel.

Local Attractions
Free Golf onsite for residents. Horse riding, angling, surfing, walking, magnificent beaches. Private foreshore available for sea angling. Clonakilty Town for restaurants, traditional pubs & shopping.

Local Attractions
Enjoy surfing, whale watching, golf, beach walks, fishing & paragliding.

B&B from: €45.00 - €90.00
Suites from: €140.00 - €200.00

B&B from: €95.00 - €105.00

B&B from: €95.00 - €125.00

Host(s): Brendan Comerford 91

Host(s): Derry & Mary O'Donovan 29

Host(s): The Team at Inchydoney 67

Activities Facilities

Activities Facilities

Activities Facilities

Closed 24 - 26 December

Closed 17 January - 11 March

Closed 23 - 27 December

B&B Rates are per Person Sharing per Night incl. Breakfast. Room/Suite Rates are per Room per Night. See also page 08

Ireland South 191

Co. Cork

To Book Call **+353-1-8084419** or www.irelandhotels.com

Clonakilty / Cobh

O'Donovan's Hotel

Hotel ★★ Map 2 G 2

**Pearse Street, Clonakilty,
West Cork**
Tel: +353-23-883 3250
Email: info@odonovanshotel.com
Web: www.odonovanshotel.com
GPS: N +51° 37' 22.74" W -8° 53' 23.83"

Location
Located in the centre of the town. 45 minutes to Airport/Ferry/Train. Bus Stop at front door.

Property Highlights
Lock up off-street car park. Elevator to all floors. Historic & family-run.

Local Attractions
Beach 10 minutes in the car. Shopping, pubs & restaurants on adjoining streets. Model Railway Village, Michael Collins Centre, Museum & live music venue all close by.

B&B from: €45.00 - €60.00

Host(s): O'Donovan Family

21

Facilities

Closed 25 - 27 December

Commodore Hotel

Hotel ★★ Map 3 I 3

**Westbourne Place, Cobh,
Co. Cork**
Tel: +353-21-481 1277
Email: commodorehotel@eircom.net
Web: www.commodorehotel.ie
GPS: N +51° 50' 59.46" W -8° 17' 46.59"

Location
Located in Cobh Town Centre, East Cork, overlooking the world's 2nd largest harbour. 25 minutes to Cork City via regular train service. 40 minutes Cork Airport.

Property Highlights
Historic, family-owned hotel renowned for its home-grown hospitality, as well as its sea view rooms, roof garden and Maritime Bar. Personal service given to all in a family-friendly environment.

Local Attractions
Queenstown Heritage, Titanic Trail, Cobh Museum, Fota Wildlife Park, House & Gardens, Golf - Cobh 18 Hole Golf Course, Cork City, Jameson Heritage, Blarney.

B&B from: €35.00 - €57.00

Host(s): Patrick O'Shea

40

Activities   **Facilities**

Closed 24 - 25 December

WatersEdge Hotel

Hotel ★★★ Map 3 I 3

**(Next To Cobh Heritage Centre), Cobh,
Co. Cork**
Tel: +353-21-481 5566
Email: info@watersedgehotel.ie
Web: www.watersedgehotel.ie
GPS: N +51° 50' 56.50" W -8° 17' 52.47"

Location
Next to Heritage Centre on the waterfront in the town centre. Overlooking the beautiful Cork Harbour.

Property Highlights
Sea view rooms some with balconies. Satellite TV, WiFi, bistro restaurant, tea making facilities, hairdryer, direct dial phones.

Local Attractions
Cathedral, Titanic Trail, Spike Island Tour, Fota Wildlife Park, angling, golf, sailing, horseriding, Heritage Centre, walking tours.

B&B from: €40.00 - €85.00
Suites from: €110.00 - €150.00

Host(s): David Ruttle

19

Facilities

Closed 24 - 26 December

B&B Rates are per Person Sharing per Night incl. Breakfast. Room/Suite Rates are per Room per Night. See also page 08

To Book Call **+353-1-8084419** or www.irelandhotels.com

Co. Cork
Cork City

Achill House

Guesthouse ★ ★ ★ Map 2 H 3

Western Road,
Cork City
Tel: +353-21-427 9447
Email: info@achillhouse.com
Web: www.achillhouse.com
GPS: N +51° 53' 45.40"   W -8° 29' 16.83"

Location
Located within a short walk of the city centre. Close to train station & bus station making Achill House an ideal base for touring Cork & Kerry.

Property Highlights
A truly unique guesthouse where our guests can rest, relax & enjoy our delicious home cooking. Achill House provides free WiFi for guests.

Local Attractions
Close to the many shopping & cultural facilities of Cork City, including universities, galleries & cathedrals. Located on the Western Road it is close to Blarney & Kinsale.

B&B from: €40.00 - €60.00

Host(s): Helena McSweeney

6

Facilities

Closed 24 - 27 December

Ambassador Hotel & Health Club

Hotel ★ ★ ★ ★ Map 2 H 3

Military Hill, St. Lukes,
Cork City
Tel: +353-21-453 9000
Email: info@ambassadorhotel.ie
Web: www.ambassadorhotelcork.ie
GPS: N +51° 54' 18.49"   W -8° 27' 33.83"

Location
Located close to all attractions and public transport. Airport 15 minutes, Train Station 5 minutes, Bus Station 5 mins, Ferryport 20 minutes, Cork City 3 minutes.

Property Highlights
Located on a hilltop, the Ambassador Hotel commands spectacular panoramic views of Cork City. Full health centre. Balcony rooms, luxuriously decorated to the highest standards.

Local Attractions
Fota Wildlife, Kartworld, Mardyke Entertainment Complex, Blarney Castle, Shandon Bells, Butter Exchange, Midleton Distillery, Opera Lane Shopping, Mahon Point Shopping.

B&B from: €49.00 - €89.00
Suites from: €150.00 - €260.00

Host(s): Chris Crowley

70

Facilities

Closed 24 - 27 December

Explore Cobh's Fascinating history and the towns' direct links with Titanic! The original Titanic Trail guided walking tour takes place every day all year. Leaving at **11am daily** (time varies off - season) from the Commodore Hotel this famous tour is educational, interesting and fun. Cost is €9.50 per person. Duration is 60 minutes. In June, July, and August additional tours also run at 11am and 2pm.
(Oct to May booking required)

Contact: Michael Martin Author and Creator Titanic Trail

Tel: +353 (21) 481 5211
Mobile: +353 (87) 276 7218
Email: info@titanic.ie
www.titanic.ie

Co. Cork

Cork City

Ashley Hotel

Hotel ★ ★   Map 2 H 3

Coburg Street,
Cork City
Tel: +353-21-450 1518
Email: info@ashleyhotel.com
Web: www.ashleyhotel.com
GPS: N +51° 54' 7.03"   W -8° 28' 14.93"

Location
City Centre on the Dublin Road and Limerick side of the River Lee (do not cross any bridge), minutes walk to bus and train station.

Property Highlights
On site private car park, locked at night with CCTV security. Kennels, Wifi, Child Friendly Hotel, Airport Shuttle nearby.

Local Attractions
University College Cork, City Gaol, English market, Fota Wildlife Park, Cobh Titanic Story and a choice of 16 golf courses.

B&B from: €55.00 - €100.00

Host(s): Anita Coughlan
                                             27

Facilities

Closed 22 December - 05 January

Blarney Stone

Guesthouse ★ ★ ★   Map 2 H 3

Western Road,
Cork City
Tel: +353-21-427 0083
Email: bsgh@eircom.net
Web: www.blarneystoneguesthouse.ie
GPS: N +51° 53' 45.36"   W -8° 29' 17.14"

Location
Located in the city centre, opposite the University Complex. In close proximity to airport, ferry, train or bus.

Property Highlights
Victorian residence, which has been recently refurbished, has character & charm and offers luxurious accommodation. All rooms en suite & tastefully decorated to high standard.

Local Attractions
Close proximity to a selection of restaurants, bars and entertainment venues. 5 minute walk from St. Finbarr's Cathedral. Blarney Stone & Castle 15 minute drive/bus journey.

B&B from: €42.50 - €59.50

Host(s): Angela Hartnett
                                             8

Facilities

Open All Year

Commons Inn Hotel

Hotel ★ ★ ★   Map 3 H 3

New Mallow Road,
Cork City
Tel: +353-21-421 0300
Email: info@commonsinn.com
Web: www.commonsinn.com
GPS: N +51° 55' 18.65"   W -8° 29' 15.43"

Location
Close to Cork city on the main Cork/Blarney road. Ideal for people travelling to/from Limerick/West of Ireland.

Property Highlights
The Commons Inn has one of the busiest bars and cavery in Cork. Entertainment on a regular basis. Free WiFi in all rooms and public areas.

Local Attractions
Close to world famous Blarney Castle and all of Cork's attractions. Blackpool Shopping Centre is just 5 minutes walk and includes a cinema.

B&B from: €30.00 - €50.00

Host(s): Ashley Colson
                                             40

Activities   Facilities

Closed 24 December - 02 January

B&B Rates are per Person Sharing per Night incl. Breakfast. Room/Suite Rates are per Room per Night. See also page 08

To Book Call **+353-1-8084419** or www.irelandhotels.com

Co. Cork
Cork City

Fitzgeralds Vienna Woods Hotel Cork

Hotel ★★★ Map 3 H 3

Dunkettle, Glanmire,
Cork City
Tel: +353-21-455 6800
Email: josie@viennawoodshotel.com
Web: www.viennawoodshotel.com
GPS: N +51° 54' 43.11"   W -8° 24' 10.74"

Location
Located outside the village of Glanmire just after the Jack Lynch Tunnel. We are located only 3.8km from Cork City with motorway access to rail, sea & airports.

Property Highlights
Family owner operated hotel with the combined warmth of the traditional Irish welcome with 1st class hospitality. All staff have a service promise to "meet", "exceed" & "wow" customer expectations.

Local Attractions
Only minutes drive from Mahon Point Shopping Centre, Cork City Centre, multiple Golf Courses, Local Beaches & Fota Wildlife Park. Midelton & Traboyne are only a 20 minute drive from the hotel.

B&B from: €25.00 - €85.00
Suites from: €110.00 - €198.00

Host(s): Michael Magner & David Fitzgerald

47

Activities

Facilities

Closed 23 - 27 December

Garnish House

Guesthouse ★★★ Map 3 H 3

Western Road,
Cork City
Tel: +353-21-427 5111
Email: garnish@iol.ie
Web: www.garnish.ie
GPS: N +51° 53' 45.23"   W -8° 29' 18.50"

Location
Central to the city and opposite Cork University. Train station & airport in close proximity.

Property Highlights
We serve an amazing breakfast, 30 choices & free welcome tea on arrival. Being Lonely Planet's Pick and Bridgestone's Place to Stay - rest in the knowledge you have picked the best.

Local Attractions
Universtity across the street, Fitzgeralds Park, Cork City Gaol, St. Finbarr's Cathedral, Blarney, Kinsale, Fota Wildlife Park, Shandon Cathedral.

B&B from: €49.00 - €69.00

Host(s): Johanna Lucey

21

Facilities

Open All Year

CORK CITY GAOL

Step back in time to see what 19th & early 20th Century life was like in Cork - inside & outside prison walls! Amazingly lifelike figures, furnished cells, sound effects and fascinating exhibitions.

OPEN 7 DAYS
Throughout the year.
At same location the
RADIO MUSEUM

Sunday's Well, Cork City
Tel: 021-430 50 22
Email: corkgaol@indigo.ie
www.corkcitygaol.com

B&B Rates are per Person Sharing per Night incl. Breakfast. Room/Suite Rates are per Room per Night. See also page 08

Co. Cork

To Book Call **+353-1-8084419** or www.irelandhotels.com

Cork City

Gresham Metropole

Hotel ★ ★ ★   Map 3 H 3

MacCurtain Street,
Cork City
Tel: +353-21-464 3700
Email: info@gresham-metropolehotel.com
Web: www.gresham-hotels.com
GPS: N +51° 54' 4.52"   W -8° 28' 3.97"

Location
Located in the heart of Cork City, just a short walk from the excellent shops, boutiques, theatres and galleries.

Property Highlights
Spacious and elegant with 112 tastefully decorated bedrooms, superb conference facilities and award-winning leisure centre.

Local Attractions
Fota Wildlife Park, Blarney Castle, Cork City Gaol, Blackrock Castle Observatory, St. Anne's of Shandon, Crawford Art Gallery.

B&B from: €45.00 - €130.00
Suites from: €199.00 - €350.00

Host(s): Roger Russell

112

Activities   Facilities

Open All Year

Hayfield Manor Hotel

Hotel ★ ★ ★ ★ ★   Map 2 H 3

Perrott Avenue, College Road,
Cork City
Tel: +353-21-484 5900
Email: enquiries@hayfieldmanor.ie
Web: www.hayfieldmanor.ie
GPS: N +51° 53' 27.57"   W -8° 29' 24.58"

Location
Located within a 10 minute walk to Cork City, alongside UCC and 6 miles to Cork Airport.

Property Highlights
Let calmness envelope you as Hayfield Manor becomes your home away from home: luxurious accommodation, 2 restaurants, spa & leisure facilities, exceptional service, Les Clef d'Or Concierge.

Local Attractions
Highlights & attractions of Cork City on our doorstep, popular tourist areas such as Blarney a short drive away. Golf available locally.

B&B from: €79.00 - €190.00
Suites from: €590.00 - €1,030.00

Host(s): Ettienne van Vrede

88

Activities   Facilities

Open All Year

Hotel Isaacs

Hotel ★ ★ ★   Map 3 H 3

48 MacCurtain Street,
Cork City
Tel: +353-21-450 0011
Email: cork@isaacs.ie
Web: www.isaacs.com
GPS: N +51° 54' 5.75"   W -8° 28' 5.13"

Location
Located in Cork City centre close to bus and train stations, with airport shuttle stop at gate. Car parking nearby at a nightly charge.

Property Highlights
Greenes Restaurant, a fish & seafood dining destination with its floodlit waterfall.

Local Attractions
Cork City, English Market, Cork City Gaol, Shandon, Fota Wildlife Park, golf, go karting and sea kayaking nearby.

Room Rate from: €59.00 - €150.00

Host(s): Paula Lynch

50

Activities   Facilities

Closed 24 - 27 December

---

196   Ireland South   B&B Rates are per Person Sharing per Night incl. Breakfast. Room/Suite Rates are per Room per Night.   See also page 08

Co. Cork
Cork City

Imperial Hotel with Escape Salon and Spa

Hotel ★★★★ — Map 3 H 3

South Mall,
Cork City
Tel: +353-21-427 4040
Email: reservations@imperialhotelcork.ie
Web: www.flynnhotels.com
GPS: N +51° 53' 49.80" W -8° 28' 12.66"

Location
In the heart of Cork City, walking distance from shopping district & many fine restaurants. 5 minutes from airport. 5 minutes walk from bus & 10 minutes from train station.

Property Highlights
Rooms individually designed & supremely comfortable. Delicious dining in the Pembroke Seafood Bar & Grill, Lafayette's Food Hall, South's Bar. Award-winning Spa "Escape", Aveda Lifestyle Salon & Spa.

Local Attractions
A cultural & historic city with the Shandon Bells, UCC, art galleries, St. Finbarr's Cathedral & many more. Visit Cobh, Midleton, Kinsale & Blarney.

Room Rate from: €79.00 - €200.00
Suites from: €250.00 - €750.00

Host(s): Joe Kennedy   130

Facilities

Closed 24 - 26 December

Killarney Guest House

Guesthouse ★★★ — Map 2 H 3

Western Road, (Opp. UCC),
Cork City
Tel: +353-21-427 0290
Email: killarneyhouse@iol.ie
Web: www.killarneyguesthouse.com
GPS: N +51° 53' 43.27" W -8° 29' 30.71"

Location
A close walk to the city centre and opposite the University College Cork.

Property Highlights
This charming & distinctive guesthouse is renowned for its unique blend of comfort & hospitality. Its sumptuous breakfast menu includes a buffet table laden with fresh produce & home baking.

Local Attractions
Walking distance to Museum in Fitzgeralds Public Park, University College Cork, many shops, cafes, art galleries and superb restaurants in the vibrant and bustling centre of Cork City.

Room Rate from: €40.00 - €60.00

Host(s): Margaret O'Leary   19

Facilities

Closed 12 December - 01 January

webpostit

No Stamps
No Paper
No Hassle

✓ We Print it
✓ We Package it
✓ We Stamp it
✓ We Post it

Mailed on the same day for next day delivery

A one page letter costs €1.50 All inclusive
A minimum of €5.00 credit is required

First letter is FREE just sign up and enter the coupon code
IRELAND HOTEL 287
N.B one coupon per new client

You don't have to leave your hotel, you can send from anywhere in the world, we do the work, you enjoy your stay.

www.webpostit.ie

Co. Cork

To Book Call +353-1-8084419 or www.irelandhotels.com

Cork City

Maldron Hotel Cork

Hotel ★ ★ ★ Map 2 H 3

John Redmond Street, Shandon,
Cork City
Tel: +353-21-452 9200
Email: info.cork@maldronhotels.com
Web: www.maldronhotels.com
GPS: N +51° 54' 9.93"   W -8° 28' 28.56"

Location
Nestled beneath the Shandon Bells in Cork City Centre and only a 5 minute walk from Patrick Street, Cork's main thoroughfare.

Property Highlights
Full leisure facilities: 20 metre pool, gymnasium, sauna, jacuzzi. Complimentary WiFi and internet access, Bells Bar & Stir Restaurant.

Local Attractions
Fota Wildlife Park, Blarney Castle, Cork Opera House, Cork City Gaol, Jameson Midleton Distillery, Kartworld, Cork Butter Museum, Blackrock Castle Observatory.

Room Rate from: €65.00 - €139.00

Host(s): Aidan Moynihan

101

Facilities

Closed 24 - 27 December

Maryborough Hotel & Spa

Hotel ★ ★ ★ Map 3 H 3

Douglas,
Cork City
Tel: +353-21-436 5555
Email: info@maryborough.ie
Web: www.maryborough.com
GPS: N +51° 52' 25.68"   W -8° 25' 13.02"

Location
10 minutes from city centre & Cork International Airport. 4 minutes from Lee Tunnel & adjacent to South City Link Road.

Property Highlights
300 year old gardens, 18 acres of grounds, EFQM Business Excellence Award, ESPA Spa, Full Leisure Club, AA Rosette in Restaurant, On site pet farm.

Local Attractions
Mahon Point Shopping Centre, Douglas Golf Club, Fota Wildlife Park, Sailing, Fishing, Horse Riding, Whale Watching, Cycling, City Gaol. Ideal gateway to East & West Cork.

B&B from: €55.00 - €125.00
Suites from: €190.00 - €400.00

Host(s): Justin McCarthy

93

Activities   Facilities

Closed 24 - 26 December

Redclyffe Guest House

Guesthouse Map 2 H 3

Western Road,
Cork City
Tel: +353-21-427 3220
Email: info@redclyffe.com
Web: www.redclyffe.com
GPS: N +51° 53' 43.65"   W -8° 29' 38.01"

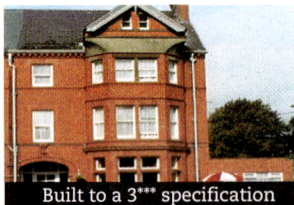

Built to a 3*** specification

Location
Located 10 minutes walk from city centre overlooking Fitzgeralds Park and opposite UCC. On N71 & N22 to West Cork & Killarney.

Property Highlights
Free WiFi & car parking. Traditional Irish breakfast served.

Local Attractions
Adjacent to airport, St. Finbarr's Cathedral, English Market and Blarney Castle.

B&B from: €30.00 - €40.00

Host(s): Michael & Maura Sheehan

16

Facilities

Open All Year

---

198 Ireland South   B&B Rates are per Person Sharing per Night incl. Breakfast. Room/Suite Rates are per Room per Night. See also page 08

To Book Call **+353-1-8084419** or www.irelandhotels.com

Co. Cork

Cork City / Courtmacsherry

River Lee Hotel (The)

Hotel ★★★★   Map 2 H 3

Western Road,
Cork City
Tel: +353-21-425 2700
Email: riverlee@doylecollection.com
Web: www.doylecollection.com
GPS: N +51° 53' 45.05" W -8° 29' 5.95"

Location
On the banks of the River Lee, Cork's beautiful city centre is laid out before you. The city's treasures are waiting to be discovered, all within easy reach.

Property Highlights
Steeped in luxury, with the superb Urban Escape Day Spa leisure facilities, complimentary car parking, light-filled Weir Restaurant & Bar with riverside terrace to compliment its 182 stylish bedrooms.

Local Attractions
St. Finbarr's Cathedral, the English Market, Glucksman Gallery, UCC, Cork City Gaol.

Room Rate from: €99.00 - €299.00

Host(s): Ruairi O'Connor

182

Facilities

Closed 23 - 27 December

Silver Springs Moran Hotel

Hotel ★★★★   Map 3 H 3

Tivoli,
Cork City
Tel: +353-21-450 7533
Email: silverspringsinfo@moranhotels.com
Web: www.moranhotels.com
GPS: N +51° 54' 15.19" W -8° 25' 24.39"

Location
Located just a few minutes from Cork City & 7 miles from Cork International Airport.

Property Highlights
Wide screen multi-channel TVs, fluffy duvet's & hypoallergenic pillows, in-room safe, high speed WiFi. Full leisure facilities including 25m pool.

Local Attractions
Fota Wildlife Park, Cork City Centre, Monkey Maze, Midleton Distillery, Cobh Heritage Centre, Ballymaloe House, Blarney Castle.

B&B from: €50.00 - €150.00
Suites from: €160.00 - €250.00

Host(s): Tom Moran

109

Activities   Facilities

Closed 25 - 27 December

Courtmacsherry Hotel & Coastal Cottages

Hotel ★★   Map 2 G 2

Courtmacsherry, Bandon,
Co. Cork
Tel: +353-23-884 6198
Email: courtmacsherryhotel@eircom.net
Web: www.courtmacsherryhotel.ie
GPS: N +51° 37' 57.87" W -8° 41' 55.94"

Location
Located 40 minutes from Cork Airport. 50 minutes from Cork City train Station.

Property Highlights
Exquisite mansion, rooms designed to add to the Victorian theme that is evident throughout this unique hotel. Rooms are en suite with all of the basic commodities. Award-winning Cork Tree Restaurant.

Local Attractions
Timoleague Abbey, Micheal Collins Heritage Centre. Horse riding, canoeing, falconry, river/deep sea fishing, beautiful scenic walks, sighting of rare birds.

B&B from: €40.00 - €60.00

Host(s): Billy Adams

10

Facilities

Closed 01 - 31 Nov & 01 - 31 Jan

B&B Rates are per Person Sharing per Night incl. Breakfast. Room/Suite Rates are per Room per Night. See also page 08

Ireland South   199

Co. Cork

To Book Call **+353-1-8084419** or www.irelandhotels.com

Fota Island / Glengarriff

Fota Island Resort

Hotel ★ ★ ★ ★ ★ Map 3 I 3

Fota Island Resort, Fota Island,
Co. Cork
Tel: +353-21-488 3700
Email: reservations@fotaisland.ie
Web: www.fotaisland.ie
GPS: N +51° 54' 0.68"   W -8° 17' 28.69"

Location
A short drive to Cork City Centre, Ringaskiddy, Ferry Port & Cork Airport. The resort is situated in the peaceful surroundings of 780 acres of woodlands.

Property Highlights
Kids' Camps, Lodges, Spa, Irish Open Golf Course, Golf Academy Bootcamp & Fitness Camps. 3 dining options; fine dining in Fota, casual dining in the Amber Lounge, bistro style in the Spike Bar.

Local Attractions
Fota Island Wildlife Park, Fota House & Gardens, Midleton Distillery, Cobh Heritage Centre, Spike Island, Cork City, Ballymaloe House, Blarney Castle.

Room Rate from: €109.00 - €300.00
Suites from: €174.00 - €700.00

Host(s): John O'Flynn

131

Activities **Facilities**

Closed 24 - 26 December

Casey's Hotel

Hotel ★ ★ ★ Map 1 D 2

The Village, Glengarriff,
Co. Cork
Tel: +353-27-63010
Email: info@caseyshotelglengarriff.ie
Web: www.caseyshotelglengarriff.com
GPS: N +51° 45' 0.06"   W -9° 33' 3.86"

Location
On the shores of Bantry Bay nestled in the heart of the picturesque village of Glengarriff. 87km on the N71 from Cork City Airport/ferry port, train and bus stations.

Property Highlights
"Famous for our Food", our motto is "Value, Comfort & Care". Enjoy friendly, personal service. Rooms renovated to the highest standard. Private parking. Visit our website for Seasonal Special Offers.

Local Attractions
Glengarriff (The Rugged Glen), gateway to the little-known and unspoiled Ring of Beara. Extensive forest and hill walking, world famous Garnish Island and so much more!

B&B from: €47.00 - €55.00

Host(s): Donal & Eileen Deasy

10

Facilities

Closed 20 December - 12 February

Glengarriff Park Hotel

Hotel ★ ★ ★ Map 1 D 2

The Village, Glengarriff,
West Cork
Tel: +353-27-63000
Email: info@glengarriffpark.com
Web: www.glengarriffpark.com
GPS: N +51° 45' 1.29"   W -9° 32' 58.74"

Location
We are located in the heart of the beautiful village of Glengarriff. At the entrance of the Blue Pool Park & Garnish Island.

Property Highlights
Our hotel offers the unique opportunity to relax & unwind with a range of luxurious bedrooms & suites. Share a drink with locals in our warm, friendly bar or enjoy superior dining in the Park Bistro.

Local Attractions
We are perfectly situated to tour the Beara Peninsula and the Ring of Kerry or take a walk through the 60 acres of parks, botanical gardens and nature reserve right on our doorstep.

B&B from: €49.00 - €79.00
Suites from: €170.00 - €240.00

Host(s): Maureen MacCarthy

26

Facilities

Open All Year

200   Ireland South   B&B Rates are per Person Sharing per Night incl. Breakfast. Room/Suite Rates are per Room per Night. See also page 08

To Book Call **+353-1-8084419** or www.irelandhotels.com

Co. Cork

Gougane Barra / Innishannon

Gougane Barra Hotel

Hotel ★ ★ ★   Map 2 E 3

Gougane Barra, Ballingeary,
Co. Cork
Tel: +353-26-47069
Email: gouganebarrahotel@eircom.net
Web: www.gouganebarrahotel.com
GPS: N +51° 50' 19.99"   W -9° 19' 0.94"

Location
Gougane Barra Hotel is located in West Cork, between the towns of Macroom and Bantry. Only one hour from the airports of Cork & Kerry.

Property Highlights
Located in a spectacular scenic valley in among the hills of Cork & Kerry. A magical location, for walking and cycling. Gougane Barra is also a special wedding destination with a chapel on the lake.

Local Attractions
We are centrally located for touring Cork & Kerry. We are a country lakeside location, excellent for fishing, boating, walking & cycling. Our guests spend time here without ever needing to travel out.

B&B from: €49.50 - €65.00

Host(s): Katy & Neil Lucey

26

Facilities

Closed 17 October - 09 April

Innishannon House Hotel

Hotel ★ ★ ★   Map 2 G 2

Innishannon,
Co. Cork
Tel: +353-21-477 5121
Email: info@innishannon-hotel.ie
Web: www.innishannon-hotel.ie
GPS: N +51° 45' 34.71"   W -8° 38' 53.55"

Location
Ideally located for visiting many of the beautiful sights Cork has to offer. Only 15 mins. from Cork City, 10 mins. from Kinsale, 10 mins. from Cork Airport.

Property Highlights
A romantic hotel built in 1720 in the Petit Château style on the banks of the River Bandon. All rooms are en suite with TV, DD phone, radio. Al fresco dining in our award-winning restaurant.

Local Attractions
Fishing on the Bandon River, Charles Fort Kinsale, The Market Square Kinsale, The Church of St Anne, excellent golf courses, Cork City Hall & Cobh are just some of the many attractions nearby.

Room Rate from: €55.00 - €130.00

Host(s): David Roche

12

Facilities

Open All Year

Co. Cork

To Book Call **+353-1-8084419** or www.irelandhotels.com

Kinsale

Actons Hotel

Hotel ★ ★ ★   Map 2 H 2

Pier Road, Kinsale,
Co. Cork
Tel: +353-21-477 9900
Email: res@actonshotelkinsale.com
Web: www.actonshotelkinsale.com
GPS: N +51° 42' 11.95"   W -8° 31' 16.31"

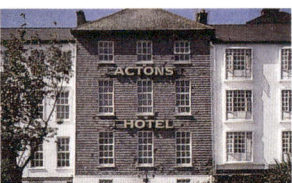

Location
Located in landscaped gardens overlooking the marina. Five minutes walk to town centre. 30 minutes from Cork Airport, 35 minutes to city centre.

Property Highlights
Landscaped gardens overlooking the beautiful harbour of Kinsale. Friendly service. Great leisure centre. Great food.

Local Attractions
5 minutes from town centre pubs and restaurants. Sailing, angling and golf. History on our doorstep. The Old Head of Kinsale, Charles Fort.

B&B from: €45.00 - €85.00

Host(s): Mr. Jack Walsh

73

Activities Facilities

Closed 22 - 27 December

Blue Haven Kinsale (The)

Hotel ★ ★ ★   Map 2 H 3

3-4 Pearse Street, Kinsale,
Co. Cork
Tel: +353-21-477 2209
Email: info@bluehavenkinsale.com
Web: www.bluehavenkinsale.com
GPS: N +51° 42' 23.15"   W -8° 31' 22.53"

Location
Located 20 minutes from Cork Airport, 30 minutes from Cork Train Station. Hotel located in centre of Kinsale Town.

Property Highlights
Property steeped in history, renowned for great food, service, style & music 7 nights a week. Friendly staff.

Local Attractions
Local attractions include historical walks, sailing, walks, gourmet restaurants, ghost tours, superb golf courses, tours on cruise boats, fishing, bike hire, sea sports.

B&B from: €40.00 - €97.50

Host(s): Declan Delaney

17

Activities Facilities

Open All Year

Carlton Hotel & C-Spa Kinsale

Hotel ★ ★ ★ ★   Map 2 H 2

Rathmore Road, Kinsale,
Co. Cork
Tel: +353-21-470 6000
Email: info@carltonkinsalehotel.com
Web: www.carlton.ie/kinsale
GPS: N +51° 41' 56.62"   W -8° 27' 52.86"

Location
20 miles from Cork City, follow R600 (Kinsale), turn off Charles Fort, continue 1.5 miles. 5 minutes from Kinsale Town Centre.

Property Highlights
Set on 90 acres of parkland, with views overlooking Oysterhaven Bay. On site highlights include Kinsale C Spa and Captain's Bar & Bistro. An ideal wedding venue.

Local Attractions
Charles Fort, Desmond Castle, Old Head Golf Course, James Fort, Scenic Harbour Coast, Ghost Tour, Guided Historical Walking Tour, Kinsale Museum.

B&B from: €49.00 - €169.00
Suites from: €258.00 - €420.00

Host(s): John McGrath

90

Facilities

Closed 23 - 26 December

202 Ireland South   B&B Rates are per Person Sharing per Night incl. Breakfast. Room/Suite Rates are per Room per Night. See also page 08

To Book Call **+353-1-8084419** or www.irelandhotels.com

Co. Cork
Kinsale

Friar's Lodge

Guesthouse ★ ★ ★ ★ Map 2 H 2

Friar's Street, Kinsale,
Co. Cork
Tel: +353-21-477 7384
Email: mtierney@indigo.ie
Web: www.friars-lodge.com
GPS: N +51° 42' 25.74"   W -8° 31' 36.31"

Location
Set in the heart of the picturesque town of Kinsale, famous for its gourmet restaurants and lively character bars with a wide range of quality food and music.

Property Highlights
We have 18 Non Smoking rooms in total consisting of 2 suites, 8 triple rooms and 8 double rooms. All our bedrooms are spacious and fitted out to the highest of standards, all with en suite bathrooms.

Local Attractions
On our doorstep is the town museum, new wine museum & "Art Hub" in the renovated Old Mill, Desmond Castle, Charles and James Forts, spectacular scenery with wonderful walks & award-winning beaches.

B&B from: €40.00 - €65.00
Suites from: €110.00 - €150.00

Host(s): Maureen Tierney

18

Facilities

Closed 22 - 28 December

Jim Edwards

Guesthouse ★ ★ Map 2 H 2

Market Quay, Kinsale,
Co. Cork
Tel: +353-21-477 2541
Email: info@jimedwardskinsale.com
Web: www.jimedwardskinsale.com
GPS: N +51° 42' 21.04"   W -8° 31' 22.77"

Location
We are a 20 minute drive from the airport and 30 minutes from both the ferry and train services.

Property Highlights
Family-run since 1971, Jim Edwards has a tradition of a warm, friendly welcome with an exceptional restaurant on site, providing guests with great local seafood.

Local Attractions
We are located in the centre of Kinsale which is the most beautiful seaside town in Ireland.

B&B from: €30.00 - €45.00

Host(s): Jim Edwards

7

Facilities

Open All Year

Old Bank House Kinsale (The)

Guesthouse ★ ★ ★ ★ Map 2 H 2

10/11 Pearse Street, Kinsale,
Co. Cork
Tel: +353-21-477 4075
Email: info@oldbankhousekinsale.com
Web: www.oldbankhousekinsale.com
GPS: N +51° 42' 21.55"   W -8° 31' 18.82"

Location
20 minutes from Cork Airport. 30 minutes from Cork Train Station. Located in the heart of Kinsale.

Property Highlights
Beautiful Georgian house, with stylish café and gourmet food store. Centrally located, friendly service, many rooms enjoy harbour views.

Local Attractions
Historical walk, gourmet restaurants, superb golf courses, fishing, bike hire, sailing, sea sports, music in most pubs during the summer.

B&B from: €60.00 - €115.00
Suites from: €190.00 - €350.00

Host(s): Louise O'Donnell

17

Activities

Facilities

Closed 24 - 26 December

B&B Rates are per Person Sharing per Night incl. Breakfast. Room/Suite Rates are per Room per Night. See also page 08

Co. Cork

To Book Call **+353-1-8084419** or www.irelandhotels.com

Kinsale / Macroom

Tierney's Guest House

Guesthouse ★ ★   Map 2 H 2

70 Main Street, Kinsale,
Co. Cork
Tel: +353-21-477 2205
Email: info@tierneys-kinsale.com
Web: www.tierneys-kinsale.com
GPS: N +51° 42' 19.90"   W -8° 31' 26.14"

Location
Tierney's is superbly located in the centre of Main St., Kinsale. 20 minutes to Cork Airport. Within walking distance of all restaurants and entertainment.

Property Highlights
Free WiFi, TVs in all rooms. Tea/coffee facilities. All rooms have been refurbished & all bedrooms en suite. Enjoy breakfast in our courtyard conservatory.

Local Attractions
3 large golf courses, water sports, river & sea fishing, surfing lessons & pony trekking all nearby.

B&B from: €34.00 - €44.00

Host(s): Fiona O'Mahony

9

Facilities

Open All Year

White House

Guesthouse ★ ★ ★   Map 2 H 2

Pearse St. & The Glen, Kinsale,
Co. Cork
Tel: +353-21-477 2125
Email: whitehse@indigo.ie
Web: www.whitehouse-kinsale.ie
GPS: N +51° 42' 23.79"   W -8° 31' 24.05"

Location
The White House is situated in the heart of Kinsale Town. 20 minutes from Cork Airport, Cork City, train station & ferry port.

Property Highlights
Long-standing tradition in friendliness, hospitality and good food both in bar and Restaurant d'Antibes, with spacious and modern accommodation.

Local Attractions
Historic Kinsale offers: fishing, 18 hole golf courses, sailing and walking & guided town walks, harbour cruises, museums, art galleries shopping or a leisurely stroll through narrow winding streets.

B&B from: €55.00 - €100.00

Host(s): Rose & Michael Frawley

10

Activities   **Facilities**

Closed 24 - 26 December

Coolcower House

Guesthouse ★ ★   Map 2 F 3

Coolcower, Macroom,
Co. Cork
Tel: +353-26-41695
Email: info@coolcowerhouse.ie
Web: www.coolcowerhouse.ie
GPS: N +51° 53' 14.97"   W -8° 56' 33.11"

Location
Situated on the N22 Cork/Macroom Killarney Road. 40 minutes from Cork Airport & Ferryport. Within 1 hour of Killarney, Kenmare, Kinsale, Blarney, Bantry, Cobh.

Property Highlights
Large Country House on picturesque grounds surrounded by woods & parkland. Magical lakeside setting with coarse fishing on waters edge. Licensed bar & restaurant by arrangment.

Local Attractions
The town square is dominated by the remains of a 13th Century castle. Only 5 minutes drive from the town. Very impressive town hall. 18 hole golf course, restaurants & shops.

B&B from: €40.00 - €48.00

Host(s): Evelyn Casey

10

Facilities

Closed 30 November - 14 March

To Book Call **+353-1-8084419** or www.irelandhotels.com

Co. Cork
Mallow / Mitchelstown

Springfort Hall Hotel

Hotel ★ ★ ★   Map 2 G 4

Mallow,
Co. Cork
Tel: +353-22-21278
Email: stay@springfort-hall.com
Web: www.springfort-hall.com
GPS: N +52° 11' 7.20"   W -8° 39' 24.72"

Location
Springfort Hall Hotel is located just 5 minutes outside Mallow, Co. Cork, 25 minutes from Cork City and 30 minutes from Cork International Airport.

Property Highlights
This 18th Century Manor House, hidden away in the tranquil ancient woodlands, offers unique beauty, charm, great country cooking and a sincere family welcome.

Local Attractions
Ballyhass Lakes & Adventure Centre, Blarney Castle, The Donkey Sanctuary, Doneraile Park, 30 minutes from all Cork City attractions.

B&B from: €55.00 - €90.00

Host(s): Margaret Corbett & The Walsh Family

49

Activities   Facilities

Closed 24 - 27 December

Fir Grove Hotel

Hotel ★ ★   Map 3 I 5

Cahir Hill, Mitchelstown,
Co. Cork
Tel: +353-25-24111
Email: info@firgrovehotel.com
Web: www.firgrovehotel.com
GPS: N +52° 16' 27.72"   W -8° 16' 20.02"

Location
Located on the outskirts of Mitchelstown, exit 12 or 13 off the M8, 45 minutes from Cork Airport.

Property Highlights
Carvery lunches and bar food, Mulberry Restaurant, private gardens, wedding and conference venue. WiFi available.

Local Attractions
Ballyhoura Biking Range, Mitchelstown Caves, Galtee Mountains, Golf, Fishing, Pony Trekking, Touring Base.

B&B from: €50.00 - €65.00

Host(s): Brenda & Pat Tangney

14

Facilities

Closed 23 - 26 December

Irelandhotels.com
We've got it covered

You can find all the best deals in all of these places

Website

Mobile App

Printed Guide

facebook.com/irelandhotels

irelandhotels.com/onlineguide

B&B Rates are per Person Sharing per Night incl. Breakfast. Room/Suite Rates are per Room per Night. See also page 08

Ireland South

Co. Cork

To Book Call +353-1-8084419 or www.irelandhotels.com

Rosscarbery / Schull / Shanagarry

Celtic Ross Hotel

Hotel ★ ★ ★   Map 2 F 1

**Rosscarbery,
West Cork**
Tel: +353-23-884 8722
Email: info@celticross.com
Web: www.celticrosshotel.com
GPS: N +51° 34' 33.18"   W -9° 1' 44.17"

Location
Located 67km south of Cork City. 50 mins. to Cork Airport on the South Ring Road West N71. Cork Train Station 5 mins. walk from city centre. Nearest port: Ringaskiddy.

Property Highlights
3 star property located in the heart of West Cork overlooking Rosscarbery Bay. Many rooms with sea views.

Local Attractions
Local children's playground 5 mins. walk from hotel. Lagoon Activity Centre 5 mins. from hotel - canoe, pedal & row boat hire. Warren Beach 10 mins. walk from hotel.

B&B from: €45.00 - €100.00

Host(s): Christopher Byrnes

66

Facilities

Closed 01 January - 20 February

Corthna-Lodge Guesthouse

Guesthouse ★ ★ ★   Map 1 D 1

**Airhill, Schull,
Co. Cork**
Tel: +353-28-28517
Email: info@corthna-lodge.net
Web: www.corthna-lodge.net
GPS: N +51° 31' 32.61"   W -9° 33' 37.27"

Location
Dublin Airport by car 4.5 hours, Cork Airport 2 hours, Shannon Airport 4 hours.

Property Highlights
Charming high standard guesthouse in a quiet setting. Our beautifully landscaped gardens, with an outdoor Hot Tub, Sauna House, Swiss Chalet & gym are the perfect place to relax and dream.

Local Attractions
Within walking distance of lovely Schull Village & harbour. Ideal location for touring West Cork. Ferry to Cape Clear, Mizen Head Lighthouse, Barley Cove Beaches. Water sports, sailing & golf clubs.

Room Rate from: €80.00 - €95.00

Host(s): Andrea & Martin Mueller

6

Facilities

Closed 01 October - 30 April

Garryvoe Hotel

Hotel ★ ★ ★ ★   Map 3 J 3

**Ballycotton Bay, Shanagarry,
Co. Cork**
Tel: +353-21-464 6718
Email: res@garryvoehotel.com
Web: www.garryvoehotel.com
GPS: N +51° 51' 33.90"   W -8° 0' 13.97"

Location
Coastal location overlooking 5km of one of Ireland's finest beaches, an ideal holiday destination. 40 minutes drive to Cork City and right in the heart of East Cork.

Property Highlights
Family owned, boasts luxurious rooms & sincere, friendly service. Lighthouse Bar & Grill & The Sapphire Restaurant serve the finest in local cuisine. New Health Club with extensive leisure facilities.

Local Attractions
East Cork abounds with things to do while on holiday. Cobh/Queenstown, Fota Wildlife Park, Fota House, Jameson Midleton Distillery, Ballymaloe Cookery School & Gardens, historic Youghal.

Room Rate from: €69.00 - €145.00
Suites from: €220.00 - €300.00

Host(s): Anthony Moloney

68

Activities   **Facilities**

Closed 24 - 26 December

206   Ireland South   B&B Rates are per Person Sharing per Night incl. Breakfast. Room/Suite Rates are per Room per Night. **See also page 08**

To Book Call **+353-1-8084419** or www.irelandhotels.com

Co. Cork
Skibbereen

West Cork Hotel

Hotel ★ ★ ★ Map 2 E 1

Ilen Street, Skibbereen,
Co. Cork
Tel: +353-28-21277
Email: info@westcorkhotel.com
Web: www.westcorkhotel.com
GPS: N +51° 33' 2.89"   W -9° 16' 13.97"

Location
The West Cork Hotel is located in Skibbereen, on Ilen River, 1 hour 30 minutes west of Cork Airport, Cork City and the train station (N71).

Property Highlights
Breakfast served until 12. Extensive à la carte menus in Ilen Bar and Kennedy's Restaurant. WiFi in bedrooms. Dog kennels available.

Local Attractions
Laid back charm, colourful market town. Award-winning restaurants, lively traditional pubs, bustling farmers markets. Whale watching, dining, fishing available. Heritage centre for genealogy services.

B&B from: €30.00 - €60.00

Host(s): Charlie Costelloe

30

Activities
Facilities

Closed 24 - 28 December

AWARD WINNING
MIZEN HEAD SIGNAL STATION

Ireland's most Southwesterly Point!
Near Goleen, West Cork

Mizen Cafe
Shop @ the Mizen
World class must-see location
Come and Experience
The New Arched Bridge
The 99 Steps
Navigational Aids
Simulator, Fastnet Rock
Lighthouse model.
If you miss the Mizen, you haven't done Ireland

**Open daily mid Mar - May, Oct 10.30am - 5pm
June - Sept 10 am - 6pm
Nov - mid March
Weekends 11am - 4pm**

Tel: 028-35115
028-35225
info@mizenhead.ie
www.mizenhead.ie
www.mizenhead.net

B&B Rates are per Person Sharing per Night incl. Breakfast. Room/Suite Rates are per Room per Night. See also page 08

Co. Cork - Co. Kerry

To Book Call **+353-1-8084419** or www.irelandhotels.com

Youghal / Ballybunion

Aherne's Townhouse & Seafood Restaurant

Guesthouse ★ ★ ★ ★   Map 3 J 3

163 North Main Street, Youghal,
Co. Cork
Tel: +353-24-92424
Email: ahernes@eircom.net
Web: www.ahernes.com
GPS: N +51° 57' 25.44"   W -7° 51' 6.51"

Location
Located between Cork and Waterford, Youghal is on the N25, 35 minutes from Cork Airport. Directions see www.ahernes.net/directions.html.

Property Highlights
Our restaurant and bar food menus specialise in the freshest of locally landed seafood. Open turf fires and the warmest of welcomes await you. Private parking.

Local Attractions
Youghal is a heritage town steeped in history with a wonderful 5 mile long beach. Youghal, and the surrounding area, are a year round holiday destination for families & friends.

B&B from: €65.00 - €90.00
Suites from: €150.00 - €210.00

Host(s): The Fitzgibbon Family

12

Facilities

Closed 23 - 26 December

Quality Hotel & Leisure Centre Youghal

Hotel ★ ★ ★   Map 3 J 3

Redbarn Beach, Youghal,
Co. Cork
Tel: +353-24-93050
Email: info@qualityhotelyoughal.com
Web: www.qualityhotelyoughal.com
GPS: N +51° 55' 29.99"   W -7° 52' 21.51"

Location
Located directly on a Blue Flag beach along East Cork coastline, 4 miles outside of Youghal. Just off N25 Cork-Waterford.

Property Highlights
Directly on beach. Self-catering options available. Leisure Club. Children's facilities. Spa treatments.

Local Attractions
Fota Wildlife Park, Ballymaloe, Jameson Old Distillery, Perks indoor entertainment centre, Trabolgan.

Room Rate from: €89.00 - €109.00
Suites from: €99.00 - €119.00

Host(s): Allen McEnery

25

Facilities

Closed 14 - 27 December

Eagle Lodge

Guesthouse ★   Map 5 D 6

Town Centre, Ballybunion,
Co. Kerry
Tel: +353-68-27224
Email: eaglelodgeballybunion@gmail.com
GPS: N +52° 30' 42.08"   W -9° 40' 20.62"

Location
Situated in town centre. Farranfore Aiport 45 minutes, Shannon Airport 90 minutes.

Property Highlights
Warm relaxed atmosphere in this owner managed guesthouse. All bedrooms with bathrooms and central heating throughout. A beautiful lounge and private car park for guests.

Local Attractions
Ballybunion world famous golf club (green fee concessions October - June). Miles of sandy beaches. Ballybunion Health & Leisure Centre nearby.

B&B from: €40.00 - €60.00

Host(s): Mildred Gleasure

8

Facilities

Open all Year

208 Ireland South   B&B Rates are per Person Sharing per Night incl. Breakfast. Room/Suite Rates are per Room per Night. See also page 08

To Book Call **+353-1-8084419** or www.irelandhotels.com

Co. Kerry

Caherdaniel / Caragh Lake

Derrynane Hotel & Holiday Homes

Hotel ★ ★ ★   Map 1 C 2

Caherdaniel, Ring of Kerry,
Co. Kerry
Tel: +353-66-947 5136
Email: info@derrynane.com
Web: www.derrynane.com
GPS: N +51° 45' 27.46"   W -10° 5' 24.24"

Location
In the heart of the Iveragh Peninsula beside the beautiful village of Catherdaniel. On The Ring of Kerry, overlooking the Atlantic Ocean. The perfect place to explore the Ring of Kerry. (On the N70).

Property Highlights
Family run-hotel. 50 bedrooms with 8 de luxe holiday homes. 15m outdoor pool. Fabulous new steam room, sauna & gym. Luxurious Seaweed Therapy Bath, meeting room, wedding venue, children's games room.

Local Attractions
Horse riding on the beach, surfing, waterskiing, learn to windsurf, visit Daniel O'Connell's home & National Park, Staigue Fort, angling, bird watching, boat trip to Skelligs Rock.

B&B from: €49.00 - €69.00

Host(s): Mary O'Connor

50

Facilities

Closed 03 October - 21 April

Ard-Na-Sidhe Country House

Hotel ★ ★ ★ ★   Map 1 D 4

Caragh Lake, Killorglin,
Co. Kerry
Tel: +353-66-976 9105
Email: reservations@ardnasidhe.com
Web: www.ardnasidhe.com
GPS: N +52° 3' 36.87"   W -9° 50' 28.80"

Location
5 miles from Killorglin on the Ring of Kerry. Easily accessible from Kerry, Cork and Shannon Airports. Ample free car parking.

Property Highlights
Charming country house set on 32 acres of gardens. Feather beds and fairytale views, delicious dinners and afternoon teas plus complimentary boating & fishing make this a tranquil & relaxing idyll.

Local Attractions
On the shores of Caragh Lake along the Ring of Kerry, nearby bustling market town of Killorglin famed for traditional Irish music.

B&B from: €85.00 - €150.00

Host(s): Michael W. Brennan

18

Facilities

Closed 01 October - 30 April

Carrig Country House

Guesthouse ★ ★ ★ ★   Map 1 D 4

Caragh Lake, Killorglin,
Co. Kerry
Tel: +353-66-976 9100
Email: info@carrighouse.com
Web: www.carrighouse.com
GPS: N +52° 4' 26.23"   W -9° 51' 0.58"

Location
On the renowned Ring of Kerry, also central for Dingle & Beara Peninsulas & World Heritage Site "Skellig Micheal". Only 10 minutes drive from Killorglin or Glenbeigh. Member of Ireland's Blue Book.

Property Highlights
Charming Victorian Manor with antique period furnishings. On acres of lakeside gardens. AA Rosette Restaurant. Recommended by: Good Hotel Guide, Michelin Guide, Georgina Campbell Hideaway of the Year.

Local Attractions
Central to: 12 superb golf courses, links & parkland. Kerry Way walking trail 5 mins. horseriding on Rossbeigh Beach. Fishing, water sports & hill walking popular. Dingle, Killarney National Park.

B&B from: €75.00 - €125.00

Host(s): Frank & Mary Slattery

17

Facilities

Closed 01 December - 04 March

Co. Kerry

To Book Call **+353-1-8084419** or www.irelandhotels.com

Castlegregory / Cloghane / Dingle (An Daingean)

Harbour House & Leisure Centre

Guesthouse ★ ★ ★ Map 1 C 5

Scraggane Pier, Castlegregory,
Co. Kerry
Tel: +353-66-713 9292
Email: stay@iol.ie
Web: www.maharees.ie
GPS: N +52° 18' 54.40" W -10° 2' 18.00"

Location
Superbly located at the top of Scraggane Pier on the tip of the Maharees Isthmus near Castlegregory Village on the Dingle Peninsula. 35 mins. from Kerry Airport.

Property Highlights
Family-run, Island Restaurant famous for fish and steaks, Fitz's Old World Bar, indoor heated swimming pool, gym & sauna.

Local Attractions
Local amenities include golf, walking, scuba diving, wind surfing, surfing, fishing, horse riding, cycling, etc.

B&B from: €35.00 - €55.00

Host(s): Pat & Ronnie Fitzgibbon

Facilities

Closed 19 December - 03 January

O'Connor's Guesthouse

Guesthouse ★ ★ Map 1 B 5

Cloghane, Dingle Peninsula,
Co. Kerry
Tel: +353-66-713 8113
Email: oconnorsguesthouse@eircom.net
Web: www.cloghane.com
GPS: N +52° 14' 4.86" W -10° 10' 56.38"

Location
At foot of Mount Brandon and on the Dingle Way. Overlooking Brandon Bay.

Property Highlights
Family friendly, on Dingle Way with cosy bar. Home cooked meals served in dining room, with spectacular views of sea and mountains.

Local Attractions
Hiking trails, sea/river fishing, safe beaches, golf courses, horse riding, water sports and boat hire.

B&B from: €37.50 - €50.00

Host(s): Micheal & Elizabeth O'Dowd

Facilities

Closed 01 November - 28 February

Alpine House

Guesthouse ★ ★ ★ Map 1 B 4

Mail Road, Dingle,
Co. Kerry
Tel: +353-66-915 1250
Email: alpinedingle@eircom.net
Web: www.alpineguesthouse.com
GPS: N +52° 8' 15.13" W -10° 16' 8.57"

Location
Two minute stroll to town centre, harbour, restaurants and bus stop. No need for car or taxi. Private parking.

Property Highlights
Bright and spacious en suite bedrooms - TV, hairdryers and central heating. Non smoking. Breakfast is a choice of hot menu and buffet. WiFi available.

Local Attractions
Restaurant & activity reservations available. Drying facilities for walkers and cyclists. Packed lunches. Luggage transfers arranged.

B&B from: €35.00 - €55.00

Host(s): Paul O'Shea

Facilities

Closed 05 January - 03 February

Ireland South   B&B Rates are per Person Sharing per Night incl. Breakfast. Room/Suite Rates are per Room per Night. See also page 08

To Book Call **+353-1-8084419** or www.irelandhotels.com

Co. Kerry

Dingle (An Daingean)

An Bothar Pub

Guesthouse ★★★ Map 1 B 5

Cuas, Ballydavid, Tralee,
Co. Kerry
Tel: +353-66-915 5342
Email: botharpub@eircom.net
Web: www.botharpub.com
GPS: N +52° 13' 35.16"   W -10° 18' 26.29"

Location
We are located north of Dingle at the foot of Mount Brandon approx 1km from the sea.

Property Highlights
We provide locally produced food, much of which is grown or produced on site. Home baking, free range eggs, potatoes from our own garden.

Local Attractions
We are located at the foot of Mount Brandon & on the Dingle Way Walk. Fishing, golfing & horse riding nearby. In the country away from traffic & noise, this is a peaceful and relaxing place to visit.

B&B from: €35.00 - €40.00

Host(s): Maurice & Aileen Walsh

7

Facilities

Closed 24 - 26 December

An Portán

Guesthouse ★★ Map 1 B 4

Dún Chaoin/Dunquin, Trá Lí,
Co. Kerry
Tel: +353-66-915 6212
Email: donn@eircom.net
Web: www.anportan.com
GPS: N +52° 8' 4.19"   W -10° 27' 8.30"

Location
Located in Dún Chaoin, the most westerly village in Ireland, opposite the Blasket Islands. 20 minutes drive from Dingle on N599. Ferry to the Blasket Islands, 1km.

Property Highlights
Award-winning restaurant fully licensed, small conference room, 14 bedrooms each with separate entrance in secluded setting. Private car park.

Local Attractions
Blasket Islands, beaches, golf, hill walking.

B&B from: €40.00 - €45.00

Host(s): Rónán O'Donnchadha

14

Facilities

Closed 01 October - 01 May

Bambury's Guest House

Guesthouse ★★★ Map 1 B 4

Mail Road, Dingle,
Co. Kerry
Tel: +353-66-915 1244
Email: info@bamburysguesthouse.com
Web: www.bamburysguesthouse.com
GPS: N +52° 8' 11.84"   W -10° 16' 9.45"

Location
At the entrance to Dingle Town via N86. We are the first house on the left after roundabout and access to Skellig Hotel.

Property Highlights
Quiet secure setting with private car parking. Just 2 minutes walk to town centre where one can enjoy pubs, restaurants, fishing port and marina.

Local Attractions
Explore Dingle Town, an old fishing port, by foot or the Dingle Peninsula beyond with spectacular views at every turn of the road. Horseriding, angling and golf on local 18 hole golf links.

B&B from: €35.00 - €60.00

Host(s): Bernie Bambury

12

Facilities

Open All Year

B&B Rates are per Person Sharing per Night incl. Breakfast. Room/Suite Rates are per Room per Night. See also page 08

Ireland South   211

Co. Kerry

To Book Call **+353-1-8084419** or www.irelandhotels.com

Dingle (An Daingean)

Coastline Guesthouse

Guesthouse ★ ★ ★ Map 1 B 4

The Wood, Dingle,
Co. Kerry
Tel: +353-66-915 2494
Email: coastlinedingle@eircom.net
Web: www.coastlinedingle.com
GPS: N +52° 8' 26.89"   W -10° 17' 4.39"

Location
Beautiful seafront guesthouse on the shores of Dingle Harbour/Bay. 5 minutes walk from the centre of town. Ideal location to enjoy all Dingle has to offer.

Property Highlights
Wonderful sea views of the harbour, with free WiFi, private parking, DD phone, TV, hairdryer, tea/coffee facilities, all rooms en suite. Excellent breakfast, relaxing guest lounge, ground floor rooms.

Local Attractions
Slea Head drive, horseriding, angling, Dingle Way Walking Route, golf, fishing, cycling.

B&B from: €35.00 - €55.00

Host(s): Vivienne O'Shea

8

Facilities

Closed 20 November - 05 February

Dingle Bay Hotel

Hotel ★ ★ ★ Map 1 B 4

Strand Street, Dingle,
Co. Kerry
Tel: +353-66-915 1231
Email: info@dinglebayhotel.com
Web: www.dinglebayhotel.com
GPS: N +52° 8' 22.30"   W -10° 16' 26.03"

Location
Dingle's newest hotel, located by the pier and marina, in the centre of Dingle Town.

Property Highlights
Paudie's Bar, popular with locals and visitors, is now renowned for its excellent food and live music. Seafood is a speciality.

Local Attractions
Dingle Bay Hotel is ideally situated for local shops, bars, restaurants and the many activities Dingle has to offer.

B&B from: €50.00 - €105.00

Host(s): Kathleen Sheehy

25

Facilities

Closed 19 - 26 December

Dingle Benners Hotel

Hotel ★ ★ ★ Map 1 B 4

Main Street, Dingle,
Co. Kerry
Tel: +353-66-915 1638
Email: info@dinglebenners.com
Web: www.dinglebenners.com
GPS: N +52° 8' 28.90"   W -10° 16' 6.01"

Location
Located in the heart of Dingle Town. Kerry Airport 67km, Shannon 170km, Cork Airport 170km, Tralee train station 50km.

Property Highlights
Great location, unique nostalgic hotel. Character, rustic furnishings, friendly, welcoming, personal service. Accommodating and courteous staff. Dingle's oldest hotel.

Local Attractions
Slea Head, Conor Pass, Inch Beach, Ventry Beach, dolphin trips, Blasket Islands, Dingle Aquarium, Horseriding, archaeology, Irish language & culture activity holidays, walking, cycling, kayaking.

B&B from: €60.00 - €105.00

Host(s): Muireann Nic Giolla Ruaidh

51

Facilities

Closed 18 - 27 December

212 Ireland South   B&B Rates are per Person Sharing per Night incl. Breakfast. Room/Suite Rates are per Room per Night. **See also page 08**

To Book Call **+353-1-8084419** or www.irelandhotels.com

Co. Kerry

Dingle (An Daingean)

Dingle Skellig Hotel

Hotel ★ ★ ★ ★   Map 1 B 4

Dingle,
Co. Kerry
Tel: +353-66-915 0200
Email: reservations@dingleskellig.com
Web: www.dingleskellig.com
GPS: N +52° 8' 1.90"   W -10° 16' 9.90"

Location
On the shores of Dingle Bay, only 40 mins. from Kerry Airport & Tralee Bus & Train Station. On the outskirts of Dingle Town, just a few mins. walk from Main Street.

Property Highlights
Renowned hotel with leisure centre, pool & Peninsula Spa, winner of Yon-Ka Hotel Spa of the Year 2009. Excellent cuisine, stunning views. Established conference & banqueting. Family facilities.

Local Attractions
Lots to do in Dingle, Oceanworld Aquarium, Height Climbing Wall, Dingle Seal Sanctuary. Slea Head Drive with fantastic scenic views. Walking, fishing, beautiful beaches, all in close proximity.

B&B from: €60.00 - €135.00

Host(s): Graham Fitzgerald

113

Activities   **Facilities**

Closed 21 - 27 December

Gorman's Clifftop House and Restaurant

Guesthouse ★ ★ ★ ★   Map 1 B 5

Glaise Bheag, Ballydavid, Dingle Peninsula,
Tralee, Co. Kerry
Tel: +353-66-915 5162
Email: info@gormans-clifftophouse.com
Web: www.gormans-clifftophouse.com
GPS: N +52° 12' 21.88"   W -10° 21' 36.94"

Location
A welcoming 4 star Country House on the scenic Slea Head overlooking the Atlantic on the Dingle Peninsula. Dingle 12km.

Property Highlights
Spectacular views of mountains and sea. Luxurious, spacious rooms include mini-suites with king size beds & jacuzzi. Breathtaking views from our Garden. Kitchen run by owner chef.

Local Attractions
Hiking the Dingle Way, climb Mount Brandon, visit Gallarus Oratory. Irish spoken. Bird watching, water sports, golf.

B&B from: €50.00 - €85.00

Host(s): Vincent & Sile Gorman

9

Facilities

Closed 23 - 26 December

Greenmount House

Guesthouse ★ ★ ★ ★   Map 1 B 4

Upper John Street, Dingle,
Co. Kerry
Tel: +353-66-915 1414
Email: info@greenmounthouse.ie
Web: www.greenmounthouse.ie
GPS: N +52° 8' 17.88"   W -10° 15' 46.47"

Location
At the edge of Dingle Town, within walking distance of all local amenities. Beautiful sea views.

Property Highlights
We have won several breakfast awards, served in a sun room overlooking the town and harbour. Hot tub available for guests.

Local Attractions
Close to the harbour with boat trips & Fungi the Dolphin. Slea Head Drive, Conor Pass. Ancient ruins, Iron Age forts, beehive huts, early Christian oratories. The town boasts many shops & restaurants.

B&B from: €40.00 - €80.00

Host(s): Maria Curran

14

Facilities

Closed 20 - 27 December

B&B Rates are per Person Sharing per Night incl. Breakfast. Room/Suite Rates are per Room per Night. See also page 08   Ireland South   213

Co. Kerry

To Book Call +353-1-8084419 or www.irelandhotels.com

Dingle (An Daingean)

Hillgrove (The)

Guesthouse ★ ★   Map 1 B 4

Spa Road, Dingle,
Co. Kerry
Tel: +353-66-915 1131
Email: info@hillgrovedingle.com
Web: www.hillgrovedingle.com
GPS: N +52° 8' 35.86"   W -10° 15' 46.96"

Location
Ideally located at the foot of Conor Pass. 3 minutes walk from Dingle Town Centre.

Property Highlights
12 en suite bedrooms. Accommodation consists of a range of triples, doubles & twins. We pride ourselves on the care and courtesy that we give our guests.

Local Attractions
Aquarium, angling, Fungi the Dolphin, bowling, horseriding, boat trips.

B&B from: €50.00 - €65.00

Host(s): Kieran Ashe

12

Facilities

Open All Year

Old Pier (The)

Guesthouse ★ ★ ★   Map 1 B 4

An Fheothanach, Ballydavid, Dingle,
Co. Kerry
Tel: +353-66-915 5242
Email: info@oldpier.com
Web: www.oldpier.com
GPS: N +52° 12' 44.05"   W -10° 21' 17.63"

Location
At roundabout west of Dingle Town take the R549 north towards Mount Brandon for 7.1 miles. We are overlooking the majestic views of Smerwick Harbour, west of Feohanagh.

Property Highlights
All rooms en suite. Award-winning restaurant offering a broad range of locally caught seafood & meat dishes. Beautiful sea & mountain vistas. Private parking, pet friendly. Fresh fish available.

Local Attractions
Mountain and cliff walks to suit all abilities. Spectacular beaches, cosy local pubs. Golf links nearby, shore angling. All in the heart of An Ghaeltacht.

B&B from: €35.00 - €45.00

Host(s): Padraig & Jacquie O'Connor

6

Facilities

Open All Year

Pax House

Guesthouse ★ ★ ★ ★   Map 1 B 4

Upper John Street, Dingle,
Co. Kerry
Tel: +353-66-915 1518
Email: info@pax-house.com
Web: www.pax-house.com
GPS: N +52° 8' 1.77"   W -10° 15' 26.14"

Location
One of the most spectacular views in the peninsula, overlooking Blanket Island, Dingle Bay, Ring of Kerry and harbour's entrance.

Property Highlights
The highlights of Pax House are its location and views. A wonderful award winning breakfast.

Local Attractions
Links golf course, horse riding on the beach or mountain, canoeing, swimming with the dolphin, walking and cycling tours to the Blasket Islands.

B&B from: €30.00 - €60.00
Suites from: €100.00 - €140.00

Host(s): John O'Farrell

11

Facilities

Closed 01 November - 01 December

B&B Rates are per Person Sharing per Night incl. Breakfast. Room/Suite Rates are per Room per Night. See also page 08

To Book Call **+353-1-8084419** or www.irelandhotels.com

Co. Kerry
Kenmare

Foleys Townhouse

Guesthouse ★ ★ ★   Map 1 D 3

Henry Street, Kenmare,
Co. Kerry
Tel: +353-64-664 2162
Email: info@foleyskenmare.com
Web: www.foleyskenmare.com
GPS: N +51° 52' 45.78"   W -9° 35' 0.20"

Location
Great town centre location in the heart of it all, a short walk to Kenmare. Finest pubs, restaurants and clubs. Kenmare is the jewel of the Ring of Kerry & Beara.

Property Highlights
Award-winning inn. 10 en suite rooms. 3 star. Live music, great food, owner chef. Free broadband. Great Irish welcome.

Local Attractions
Ring of Kerry, Ring of Beara, Kenmare & Ring of Kerry Golf Clubs, Killarney National Park, Gap of Dunloe. Great pubs & restaurants, Seafari, sea cruises, fishing & sandy beaches.

B&B from: €39.00 - €65.00

Host(s): Marion Foley

10

Facilities

Open All Year

Lansdowne Arms Hotel

Hotel ★ ★ ★   Map 1 D 3

Main Street, Kenmare,
Co. Kerry
Tel: +353-64-664 1368
Email: info@lansdownearms.com
Web: www.lansdownearms.com
GPS: N +51° 52' 44.60"   W -9° 34' 53.93"

Location
Situated in the heart of Kenmare Town.

Property Highlights
Relaxed atmosphere in this bijou hotel with warm & friendly staff. Comfortable rooms, hairdryers, tea/coffee facility, phone & TV. On site parking. Extensive menu in 2 bars & restaurant & live music.

Local Attractions
Quills Woollen Markets, Star Sailing School, Seafari Eco Cruises, Dereen Gardens, Kenmare Heritage Centre, Molly Gallivan's Visitor Centre.

B&B from: €45.00 - €65.00

Host(s): The Quill Family

26

Facilities

Open All Year

KENMARE
Ireland's most spectacular nature experience.

- 2 hour-10 mile cruise around river and islands
- Humourous, Informative and Friendly Guides
- Seal and Wildlife Watching
- Free use of Binoculars, Charts, and Books
- Complimentary Lollipops, Sweets, Snacks, Tea, Coffee, and Rum
- Surprise Entertainment for all ages including Irish Music and Song
- Full Toilet Facilities
- No Seasickness!

FUN ECO NATURE & SEAL WATCHING CRUISE

Reservations Essential
Tel No.: 064 664 2059
www.seafariireland.com
Consult local tourist offices for sailing times

10% Discount on production of this advert

Co. Kerry

To Book Call **+353-1-8084419** or www.irelandhotels.com

Kenmare

O'Donnabhain's Townhouse

Guesthouse ★ ★ ★   Map 1 D 3

Henry Street, Kenmare,
Co. Kerry
Tel: +353-64-664 2106
Email: info@odonnabhain-kenmare.com
Web: www.odonnabhain-kenmare.com
GPS: N +51° 52' 45.50"   W -9° 35' 1.28"

Location
O'Donnabhain's, with its great location provides a memorable and quality experience for your stay in Kenmare, a great base to explore Southern Ireland.

Property Highlights
Family-owned and operated, spacious rooms, town centre location, guest car park, free WiFi, music sessions, tourist/local knowledge.

Local Attractions
Kenmare, Ring of Kerry, Ring of Beara, Lakes of Killarney, Muckross House, Killarney, Glengariff, Bantry, West Cork, Gap of Dunloe, Healy Pass.

B&B from: €30.00 - €55.00

Host(s): Jeremiah Foley

10

Activities   **Facilities**

Open All Year

Sea Shore Farm Guesthouse

Guesthouse ★ ★ ★   Map 1 D 3

Tubrid, Kenmare,
Co. Kerry
Tel: +353-64-664 1270
Email: seashore@eircom.net
Web: www.seashorekenmare.com
GPS: N +51° 52' 38.61"   W -9° 36' 0.69"

Location
Turn left off N71 North immediately out of Kenmare Town, also off Sneem N70 Ring of Kerry Road, one mile from Kenmare Town.

Property Highlights
Stunning setting overlooking Kenmare Bay. Blissful peace/quiet affording unspoilt walks through our farm to shore with abundance of wildlife & sea life.

Local Attractions
Walking/hiking, golf, swimming, angling, deep sea fishing trips, Seafari cruise, horseriding, Heritage Park, waterfall/park, stone circles.

B&B from: €45.00 - €60.00

Host(s): Mary Patricia O'Sullivan

6

Facilities

Closed 01 November - 14 March

Sheen Falls Lodge

Hotel ★ ★ ★ ★ ★   Map 1 D 3

Kenmare,
Co. Kerry
Tel: +353-64-664 1600
Email: info@sheenfallslodge.ie
Web: www.sheenfallslodge.ie
GPS: N +51° 52' 27.45"   W -9° 33' 48.56"

Location
The hotel is located on a 300 acre estate minutes drive from the scenic town of Kenmare, which is located on the Ring of Kerry.

Property Highlights
Bedrooms have views overlooking the waterfalls or Kenmare Bay. The hotel has two restaurants, a bar and one of the largest wine cellars in Ireland. Health club & many activities on the estate.

Local Attractions
Golf, horse riding, scenic drives and water sports within easy reach of the hotel.

Room Rate from: €220.00 - €410.00
Suites from: €340.00 - €1,310.00

Host(s): Alan P Campbell

66

Activities   **Facilities**

Closed 01 January - 04 February

B&B Rates are per Person Sharing per Night incl. Breakfast. Room/Suite Rates are per Room per Night. See also page 08

To Book Call **+353-1-8084419** or www.irelandhotels.com

Co. Kerry
Killarney

Aghadoe Heights Hotel & Spa

Hotel ★ ★ ★ ★ ★   Map 2 E 4

Lakes of Killarney, Killarney,
Co. Kerry
Tel: +353-64-663 1766
Email: info@aghadoeheights.com
Web: www.aghadoeheights.com
GPS: N +52° 3' 33.18"   W -9° 28' 45.14"

Location
Overlooking the Lakes of Killarney and mountain vista. 20 minutes from Kerry Airport, 5 minutes from Killarney Train Station and Killarney Town Centre.

Property Highlights
Award-winning 5* hotel boasting stunning views, luxurious spa, restaurants & bars, indoor pool, gym, tennis court, thermal spa, meeting & conference facilities, free parking, complimentary WiFi.

Local Attractions
Several championship golf courses, The Ring of Kerry Day Trip, Dingle Peninsula Day Trip, 25,000 acre Killarney National Park, Muckross House, Ross Castle, Innisfallen Island Boat Trips.

B&B from: €80.00 - €185.00

Host(s): Marie & Pat Chawke

74

Activities Facilities

Open All Year

Arbutus Hotel

Hotel ★ ★ ★ ★   Map 2 E 4

College Street, Town Centre, Killarney,
Co. Kerry
Tel: +353-64-663 1037
Email: stay@arbutuskillarney.com
Web: www.arbutuskillarney.com
GPS: N +52° 3' 34.44"   W -9° 30' 21.92"

Location
In the heart of Killarney town centre & just a short walk from the bus & rail station. The ideal base to enjoy Killarney National Park, Ring of Kerry, Dingle or many of the great golf links.

Property Highlights
The warmth & intimacy of a townhouse hotel where loving attention to detail is evident in the marvellous Celtic Deco design, home-cooked food, service and personal tips. A truly special hotel.

Local Attractions
Killarney National Park, Killarney's Lakes, Golf, The Gap of Dunloe, INEC, Muckross House & Gardens, Ross Castle, St. Mary's Cathedral and Football stadium.

B&B from: €60.00 - €90.00

Host(s): Buckley Family

30

Facilities

Closed 20 December - 08 February

Ashville House

Guesthouse ★ ★ ★   Map 2 E 4

Rock Road, Killarney,
Co. Kerry
Tel: +353-64-663 6405
Email: info@ashvillekillarney.com
Web: www.ashvillekillarney.com
GPS: N +52° 3' 48.65"   W -9° 30' 44.86"

Location
2 minutes from Killarney Town Centre. 8 minutes walk from bus and train stations. 16km from Kerry Airport. 100km from Cork Airport and ferry.

Property Highlights
Town centre location. WiFi and internet access. Spacious bedrooms. Tea/coffee facilities. Free private car park. Extensive breakfast menu. Tours arranged. Many awards achieved.

Local Attractions
Top restaurants, great shopping, Killarney National Park, Ireland's best golf courses, mountain climbing & hiking, Ring of Kerry, Dingle Peninsula.

B&B from: €30.00 - €55.00

Host(s): Declan & Elma Walsh

12

Facilities

Closed 01 November - 01 March

B&B Rates are per Person Sharing per Night incl. Breakfast. Room/Suite Rates are per Room per Night. See also page 08

Ireland South   217

Co. Kerry

To Book Call **+353-1-8084419** or www.irelandhotels.com

Killarney

Best Western Eviston House Hotel

Hotel ★ ★ ★   Map 2 E 4

New Street, Killarney,
Co. Kerry
Tel: +353-64-663 1640
Email: info@evistonhouse.com
Web: www.evistonhouse.com
GPS: N +52° 3' 31.71" W -9° 30' 38.31"

Location
Located in the heart of Killarney. Minutes from train & bus stations. Kerry Airport 16km, Cork Airport 87km, Shannon Airport 123km.

Property Highlights
Luxurious rooms, excellent value standard & superior rooms. De luxe with king bed & whirlpool bath. Fitness suite, sauna & hot tub. Free WiFi. Dine in our famous "Danny Mann" Pub with live trad music.

Local Attractions
Minutes from Killarney National Park, Muckross House & championship golf. Our reception staff will gladly book tours, golf & activities.

Room Rate from: €78.00 - €136.00

Host(s): Edward Eviston

103

Facilities

Closed 23 - 25 December

Brook Lodge Hotel

Hotel ★ ★ ★ ★   Map 2 E 4

O'Flaherty Road, High Street, Killarney,
Co. Kerry
Tel: +353-64-663 1800
Email: brooklodgekillarney@eircom.net
Web: www.brooklodgekillarney.com
GPS: N +52° 3' 38.81" W -9° 30' 45.00"

Location
Ideally located in Killarney Town Centre off the street on its own grounds with private parking. 2 minutes walk to shops, pubs, restaurants. 15 minutes from Kerry Airport.

Property Highlights
Family-run with friendly, personal service. Large rooms, tea/coffee making facilities in bedrooms, free WiFi, lift & wheelchair facilities, golfers/walkers drying room, food served up to 8pm in bar.

Local Attractions
8 minute walk to Killarney National Park, golfing, cycling, boating, horseriding, touring The Ring of Kerry and Dingle Peninsula.

B&B from: €45.00 - €90.00
Suites from: €150.00 - €200.00

Host(s): Joan Counihan

24

Facilities

Closed 01 November - 01 April

Cahernane House Hotel

Hotel ★ ★ ★ ★   Map 2 E 4

Muckross Road, Killarney,
Co. Kerry
Tel: +353-64-663 1895
Email: info@cahernane.com
Web: www.cahernane.com
GPS: N +52° 2' 36.01" W -9° 30' 36.95"

Location
20 minutes from Kerry Airport. 5 minutes from Killarney Town Centre, beside the National Park on the Muckross Road.

Property Highlights
Quiet & peaceful location, tucked away from all the noise yet within easy reach of all amenities. Nice situation, scenic surrounds, excellent food, tennis & croquet.

Local Attractions
Killarney and surrounds, Muckross House & Park, Killarney National Park, Ladies View, Ross Castle, Torc Waterfall, Ring of Kerry, Dingle Peninsula, Beara Peninsula.

B&B from: €65.00 - €95.00
Suites from: €240.00 - €320.00

Host(s): Jimmy Browne

38

Facilities

Closed 01 November - 01 March

B&B Rates are per Person Sharing per Night incl. Breakfast. Room/Suite Rates are per Room per Night. See also page 08

Your Local Airport

KERRY AIRPORT

Business or Pleasure ...
Bringing People
Closer Together

From any of our international hub airports you can connect to over 300 worldwide destinations.

Direct Flights To/From:

- DUBLIN
- LONDON (STANSTED)
- LONDON (LUTON)
- FRANKFURT (HAHN)
- DUSSELDORF (WEEZE)
- FARO
- ALICANTE
- MANCHESTER

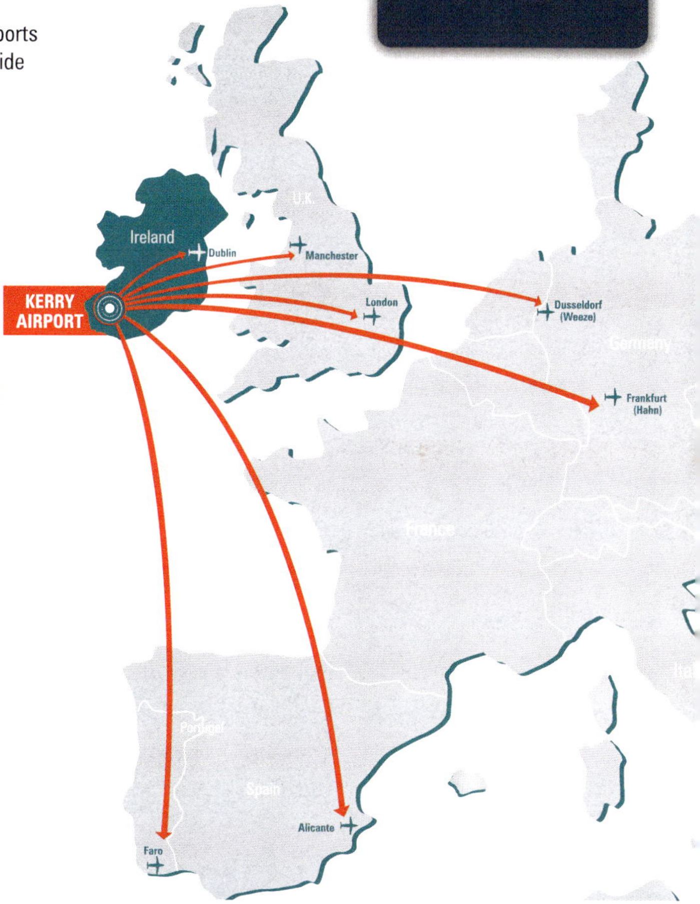

RYANAIR
www.ryanair.com

www.aerarann.com

Kerry Airport, Farranfore, Co. Kerry
T: +353 (0) 66 9764644 • E: info@kerryairport.ie

www.kerryairport.ie

Co. Kerry

To Book Call **+353-1-8084419** or www.Irelandhotels.com

Killarney

Castlerosse Hotel and Golf Resort

Hotel ★ ★ ★   Map 2 E 4

Lower Lake, Killarney,
Co. Kerry
Tel: +353-64-663 1144
Email: res@castlerosse.ie
Web: www.castlerosse.ie
GPS: N +52° 3' 57.49"   W -9° 32' 23.91"

Location
Castlerosse is located on the lakeshore just 2km from Killarney Town Centre on The Ring of Kerry Road.

Property Highlights
9 hole golf course, 20m pool, gym, sauna, steam room, jacuzzi, kiddies playground, tennis court, basketball & football court.

Local Attractions
Direct access to Killarney National Park, neighbours to Killarney Golf & Fishing Club.

B&B from: €45.00 - €90.00

Host(s): Danny Bowe
120

Activities   **Facilities**

Closed 01 November - 01 April

Crystal Springs

Guesthouse ★ ★ ★   Map 2 E 4

Woodlawn Rd (Off N71), Ballycasheen, Killarney,
Co. Kerry
Tel: +353-64-663 3272
Email: crystalsprings@eircom.net
Web: www.crystalspringsbb.com
GPS: N +52° 3' 10.47"   W -9° 29' 15.77"

Location
Overlooking the banks of the peaceful River Flesk. Just a short walk from Killarney Town Centre, Bus & Train Stations, I.N.E.C. 1km. Ample, safe parking.

Property Highlights
Justifiably holding an outstanding reputation for quality & service, a warm welcome awaits you. AA 4*, spacious en suite rooms. Some 4 poster beds overlooking the water. Family & ground floor rooms.

Local Attractions
Fishing on location from our garden. Close to Killarney National Park, Ross Castle, Muckross House, Torc Waterfalls, on the Ring of Kerry Route. Golf, Horse Riding, Mountain/Hill Walking, Bike Hire.

B&B from: €35.00 - €58.00

Host(s): Eileen & Tim Brosnan
8

Facilities

Closed 22 - 27 December

Darby O'Gill's Country House Hotel

Hotel ★ ★ ★   Map 2 E 4

Mallow Road(N72), Lissivigeen, Killarney,
Co. Kerry
Tel: +353-64-663 4168
Email: darbyogill@eircom.net
Web: www.darbyogillshotel.com
GPS: N +52° 3' 8.24"   W -9° 26' 55.20"

Location
Darby O'Gill's is located in the countryside overlooking Torc Mountain, just a short drive from Killarney Town Centre.

Property Highlights
The hotel offers live music including traditional sessions, country bands & set dancing ceilis. Proper venue for weddings, functions and meetings. A great national hotel.

Local Attractions
Close to Killarney National Park, Muckross House and Gardens, Torc Waterfall, Ring of Kerry, Gap of Dunloe, Killarney Golf & Fishing Club & Ross Castle.

Room Rate from: €49.00 - €129.00

Host(s): Pat Gill
43

Facilities

Closed 24 - 25 December

Ireland South   B&B Rates are per Person Sharing per Night incl. Breakfast. Room/Suite Rates are per Room per Night.   See also page 08

To Book Call **+353-1-8084419** or www.irelandhotels.com

Co. Kerry
Killarney

Dromhall Hotel

Hotel ★ ★ ★   Map 2 E 4

Muckross Road, Killarney,
Co. Kerry
Tel: +353-64-663 9300
Email: info@dromhall.com
Web: www.dromhall.com
GPS: N +52° 3' 11.92"   W -9° 30' 22.63"

Location
Perfectly located, a 5 minute stroll from Killarney's Town Centre & near the INEC. On the Muckross Road, Killarney's Golden Mile, en route to the National Park.

Property Highlights
Spacious bedrooms including interconnecting & family rooms. Choice of bars & restaurants, Leisure Club & Zen Day Spa, free private parking & Wi-Fi. Meeting & banquet facilities.

Local Attractions
On the Ring of Kerry, near Killarney Racecourse, Muckross House & Gardens, Ross Castle & Torc Waterfall. With some of the world's leading championship golf courses close by, it is a golfer's paradise.

B&B from: €55.00 - €119.00

Host(s): Bernadette Randles

69

Facilities

Closed 19 - 27 December

Earls Court House

Hotel ★ ★ ★   Map 2 E 4

Woodlawn Road, Off Muckross Rd, Killarney,
Co. Kerry
Tel: +353-64-663 4009
Email: info@killarney-earlscourt.ie
Web: www.killarney-earlscourt.ie
GPS: N +52° 3' 6.03"   W -9° 30' 17.13"

Location
Elegant 4* hotel located on its own grounds in a quiet peaceful suburb, 100m off Muckross Rd, 7 minute walk to Killarney town centre, 5 minute walk to National Park.

Property Highlights
A family run hotel, spacious rooms graced with antiques, king beds, winner of the Irish Classic Award 2009, Ireland's Best Breakfast Award 2006 and Romantic Elegance Reward, WiFi & free parking.

Local Attractions
Central to all the main attractions in Killarney, National Park, Lakes of Killarney, Muckross House and Gardens, Ring of Kerry, Dingle, Gap of Dunloe, 6 championship golf courses.

B&B from: €40.00 - €70.00
Suites from: €120.00 - €160.00

Host(s): Emer & Ray Moynihan

30

Facilities

Closed 07 November - 01 February

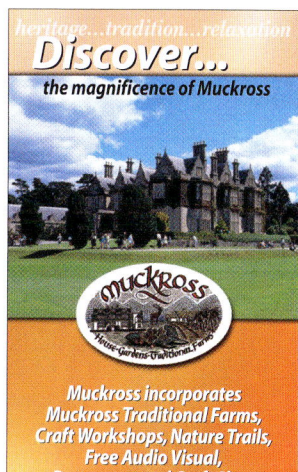

Discover...
the magnificence of Muckross

Muckross incorporates Muckross Traditional Farms, Craft Workshops, Nature Trails, Free Audio Visual, Restaurant and Craft Shop

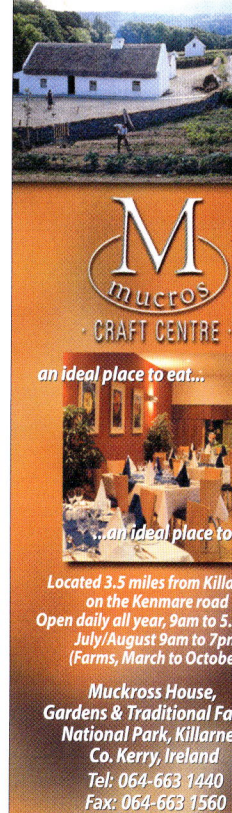

mucros CRAFT CENTRE

an ideal place to eat...

...an ideal place to shop

**Located 3.5 miles from Killarney on the Kenmare road
Open daily all year, 9am to 5.30pm,
July/August 9am to 7pm
(Farms, March to October)**

**Muckross House,
Gardens & Traditional Farms,
National Park, Killarney,
Co. Kerry, Ireland
Tel: 064-663 1440
Fax: 064-663 1560
Email: info@muckross-house.ie
Web: www.muckross-house.ie**

B&B Rates are per Person Sharing per Night incl. Breakfast. Room/Suite Rates are per Room per Night. **See also page 08**

Co. Kerry

To Book Call **+353-1-8084419** or www.irelandhotels.com

Killarney

Europe Hotel & Resort (The)

Hotel ★ ★ ★ ★ ★ Map 2 E 4

Fossa, Killarney,
Co. Kerry
Tel: +353-64-667 1300
Email: reservations@theeurope.com
Web: www.theeurope.com
GPS: N +52° 4' 1.10"   W -9° 34' 24.89"

Location
3 miles from Killarney town & train station. 20 minutes from Kerry Airport, Cork 75 minutes, Shannon 90 minutes. Ample free car parking & Heli Pad.

Property Highlights
Stunning lakeshore spa – all guests enjoy complimentary access to 20m lap pool, indoor & outdoor vitality pools, thermal suites, relaxation areas and techno-gym.

Local Attractions
Overlooking the Lakes of Killarney & MacGillycuddy Mountains. Ideally located to visit the Ring of Kerry and Dingle Peninsula, Killarney National Park, Muckross House & Gardens.

B&B from: €110.00 - €145.00
Suites from: €400.00 - €1,500.00

Host(s): Michael W. Brennan

187

Facilities

Closed 31 October - 16 March

Failte Hotel

Hotel ★ ★ Map 2 E 4

College Street, Killarney,
Co. Kerry
Tel: +353-64-663 3404
Email: failtehotel@eircom.net
Web: www.failtekillarney.com
GPS: N +52° 3' 33.86"   W -9° 30' 24.58"

Location
Situated in the heart of the town close to all amenities, 5 minutes walk to railway station, 20 minutes drive to Kerry Airport.

Property Highlights
Our award-winning hotel is very popular with visitors & locals. The menu includes the delights of the sea & land with attentive service. Enjoy a drink in one of Kerry's popular bars, music nightly.

Local Attractions
Boat trips, golfing, fishing, jaunting cars, walking, mountain climbing, shopping, sightseeing.

B&B from: €45.00 - €75.00

Host(s): Dermot & Eileen O'Callaghan

15

Facilities

Closed Christmas Day & Good Friday

Fairview Guesthouse

Guesthouse ★ ★ ★ ★ Map 2 E 4

Michael Collins Place, College Street, Killarney,
Co. Kerry
Tel: +353-64-663 4164
Email: info@killarneyfairview.com
Web: www.killarneyfairview.com
GPS: N +52° 3' 35.95"   W -9° 30' 23.18"

Location
A landmark building superbly located in the heart of Killarney Town, less than a minute's walk to bus and train stations. Functionality meets fabulous.

Property Highlights
Luxurious boutique style guesthouse, unique in quality, location, service & elegance. Spacious rooms with optional jacuzzi suites, mini-suites & penthouses. Elevator access. Winner of several awards.

Local Attractions
A place for all seasons, and an ideal place for touring the South West, Ring of Kerry, Gap of Dunloe, Dingle, Killarney National Park, Muckross House & Gardens, Ross Castle & Torc Waterfall.

B&B from: €38.00 - €69.00

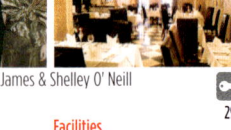

Host(s): James & Shelley O' Neill

29

Facilities

Closed 24 - 26 December

B&B Rates are per Person Sharing per Night incl. Breakfast. Room/Suite Rates are per Room per Night. **See also page 08**

To Book Call **+353-1-8084419** or www.irelandhotels.com

Co. Kerry
Killarney

Foley's Townhouse & Restaurant

Guesthouse ★ ★ ★ ★   Map 2 E 4

23 High Street, Killarney,
Co. Kerry
Tel: +353-64-663 1217
Email: info@foleystownhouse.com
Web: www.foleystownhouse.com
GPS: N +52° 3' 38.93"   W -9° 30' 35.67"

Location
Town centre location, on right hand side of the high street, going north. Close to all amenities. 1km from the railway station, 16km from local airport.

Property Highlights
Third generation & family run. Award-winning seafood/steak restaurant downstairs. Secure private car parking at rear. AA 5 Diamond Award. Michelin listed.

Local Attractions
Centre of Killarney's famed beauty spot & National Park , gateway to Ring of Kerry, many local amenities e.g. Ross Castle, Muckross House, Gap of Dunloe, boat trips, mountain trekking.

B&B from: €65.00 - €90.00
Suites from: €220.00 - €300.00

Host(s): Carol Hartnett

28

Activities

Facilities

Closed 01 December - 01 March

Friars Glen

Guesthouse ★ ★ ★ ★   Map 2 E 4

Mangerton Road, Muckross, Killarney,
Co. Kerry
Tel: +353-64-663 7500
Email: friarsglen@eircom.net
Web: www.friarsglen.ie
GPS: N +52° 01' 14"   W -9° 29' 21"

Location
Located 300mtrs off N71, 4km south of Killarney at Muckross & within Killarney National Park.

Property Highlights
4**** country house set in 27 acres offering personal service, genuine Irish hospitality, and the highest standards of accommodation and service.

Local Attractions
Ideal base for exploring Ireland's Southwest, Killarney National Park, Lakes of Killarney, Muckross House. Hiking - Kerry Way. World renowned golf courses. Day trips; Dingle, Ring of Kerry, Beara.

B&B from: €45.00 - €65.00

Host(s): Mary Fuller

10

Facilities

Closed 24 October - 07 March

DEROS COACH TOURS
And Limousine Service

Daily Tours from Killarney.

Ring of Kerry. Gap of Dunloe. Dingle & Slea Head. Killarney Lakes & National Park.

* All Vehicle Sizes Available.
* Extended Coach Tours Organised On Request.
* Conference & Incentives Group Our Speciality.
* Golf Tours Arranged.
* Private Tours arranged
* Airport Transfers

Deros Coaches,
Main Street,
Killarney,
Co. Kerry,
Ireland.
Phone:
(064) 6631251 & 6631567
Fax:
(064) 6634077
Email:
info@derostours.com
Web:
www.derostours.com

B&B Rates are per Person Sharing per Night incl. Breakfast. Room/Suite Rates are per Room per Night. **See also page 08**

Co. Kerry

To Book Call **+353-1-8084419** or www.irelandhotels.com

Killarney

Fuchsia House

Guesthouse ★ ★ ★   Map 2 E 4

Muckross Road, Killarney,
Co. Kerry
Tel: +353-64-663 3743
Email: fuchsiahouse@eircom.net
Web: www.fuchsiahouse.com
GPS: N +52° 3' 3.3"   W -9° 30' 25.91"

Location
Set well back from the Muckross Road (N71) in mature leafy gardens. Close to restaurants, pubs, leisure centres & only 7 mins. walk from Killarney Town Centre.

Property Highlights
Enjoy the elegance of an earlier age. Spacious rooms with bath & shower. Separate guest kitchen with tea/coffee. Free WiFi. Parking. Irish & vegetarian menus. Recommended by all leading guide books.

Local Attractions
Ideal base for touring the Ring of Kerry, Dingle Peninsula, Gap of Dunloe, Muckross House & Gardens, Ross Castle, Beara Peninsula, Golfing, Walking, Fishing.

B&B from: €38.00 - €60.00

Host(s): Neil & Marie Burke

Activities
Facilities

Closed 01 November - 01 April

Gleann Fia Country House

Guesthouse ★ ★ ★   Map 2 E 4

Lower Coolcorcoran, Kilcummin Road, Killarney,
Co. Kerry
Tel: +353-64-663 5035
Email: info@gleannfia.com
Web: www.gleannfia.com
GPS: N +52° 4' 30.14"   W -9° 30' 23.43"

Location
2km from Killarney Town & situated on acres of gardens with woodland & river walks! All guestrooms tastefully decorated, some with antiques & all with pleasant views.

Property Highlights
What our guests say: "breakfast at its best", "comfortable accommodation", "peaceful & relaxing", "a wonderful charming house", " so warm, so touching, so professionally managed".

Local Attractions
The National Park, Muckross House & Gardens, Muckross Abbey, Ross Castle, The Gap of Dunloe, Ring of Kerry, Dingle. Activities include golf, hill walking, outdoor adventure.

B&B from: €30.00 - €65.00

Host(s): Bridget & Conor O'Connell

Activities
Facilities

Open All Year

Heights Hotel Killarney (The)

Hotel ★ ★ ★   Map 2 E 4

Cork Road, Killarney,
Co. Kerry
Tel: +353-64-663 1158
Email: info@killarneyheights.ie
Web: www.killarneyheights.ie
GPS: N +52° 3' 33.15"   W -9° 28' 45.13"

Location
Situated less than a mile from the town centre and the train station, 15 minutes from Kerry Airport and 1 hour from Cork Airport.

Property Highlights
71 bedrooms, conference and function facilities. Mill Restaurant and Old Mill Bar provide delicious meals and great music and entertainment. Ideal wedding venue.

Local Attractions
The perfect base to explore the Ring of Kerry, Killarney Lakes, Ross Castle, Gap of Dunloe, Muckross House & Gardens, Torc Waterfall & The Killarney National Park.

B&B from: €40.00 - €80.00

Host(s): Collette Andre O'Riordan

Activities
Facilities

Closed 24 - 26 December

B&B Rates are per Person Sharing per Night incl. Breakfast. Room/Suite Rates are per Room per Night. See also page 08

To Book Call **+353-1-8084419** or www.irelandhotels.com

Co. Kerry
Killarney

Holiday Inn Killarney

Hotel ★ ★ ★ Map 2 E 4

Muckross Road, Killarney,
Co. Kerry
Tel: +353-64-663 3000
Email: info@holidayinnkillarney.com
Web: www.holidayinnkillarney.com
GPS: N +52° 2' 58.41" W -9° 30' 26.64"

Location
Holiday Inn Killarney enjoys a quiet but central location close to Killarney Town centre.

Property Highlights
Spacious en suite rooms, tastefully decorated to the highest standards. Fully equipped leisure centre, Library Point Restaurant serving finest local cuisine & Saddlers Pub with live entertainment.

Local Attractions
Walk, Climb, Cycle, Boat & Fish or Horse Trek your way through beauty, nature & history. Visit the wonderful Killarney lakes, Killarney National Park, Kenmare Heritage Centre or The Gap of Dunloe.

Room Rate from: €69.00 - €189.00
Suites from: €99.00 - €219.00

Host(s): Misja Herfurt

100

Facilities

Closed 24 - 25 December

Hotel Dunloe Castle

Hotel ★ ★ ★ ★ Map 2 E 4

Killarney,
Co. Kerry
Tel: +353-64-664 4111
Email: reservations@thedunloe.com
Web: www.thedunloe.com
GPS: N +52° 3' 34.85" W -9° 37' 38.65"

Location
5 miles from Killarney town & train station, 20 minutes from Kerry Airport, Cork 75 minutes, Shannon 90 minutes. Ample free car parking & Heli Pad

Property Highlights
Unrivalled complimentary leisure facilities include 25m indoor pool, steam, sauna, fishing, horse riding, indoor tennis, children's adventure playground & movie nights.

Local Attractions
Overlooking the Gap of Dunloe. Perfect base from which to explore Killarney town, Muckross House & Gardens, Ring of Kerry and Dingle Peninsula.

B&B from: €85.00 - €130.00
Suites from: €600.00 - €600.00

Host(s): Mr. Jason Clifford

98

Facilities

Closed 16 October - 22 April

B&B Rates are per Person Sharing per Night incl. Breakfast. Room/Suite Rates are per Room per Night. See also page 08

Ireland South

Co. Kerry

To Book Call **+353-1-8084419** or www.irelandhotels.com

Killarney

International Hotel Killarney

Hotel ★ ★ ★ Map 2 E 4

Kenmare Place, Killarney,
Co. Kerry
Tel: +353-64-663 1816
Email: inter@iol.ie
Web: www.killarneyinternational.com
GPS: N +52° 3' 29.65" W -9° 30' 27.27"

Location
Set at the heart of Killarney Town adjacent to rail & bus station, Killarney National Park and just 17km from Kerry Airport.

Property Highlights
Hannigans Award-Winning Bar & Restaurant, Live Music, In-House 3D Golf Simulator, exceptional comfort with Jacuzzi Baths, memory foam mattresses & newly refurbished rooms.

Local Attractions
Stroll to the National Park, Ross Castle, Lakes of Killarney, Cinema, Outlet Centre, selection of bars & restaurants, St. Mary's Cathedral.

B&B from: €49.00 - €99.00
Suites from: €150.00 - €250.00

Host(s): Terence Mulcahy

90

Activities
Facilities

Closed 22 - 26 December

Inveraray Farm Guesthouse

Guesthouse ★ ★ Map 2 E 4

Coolmagort, Beaufort,
Killarney
Tel: +353-64-664 4224
Email: inver@indigo.ie
Web: www.inver-aray.com
GPS: N +52° 3' 52.76" W -9° 38' 5.19"

Location
Situated 9km west of Killarney off N72. 10 minutes to Killarney Town/train/bus station. 25 minutes to Kerry Airport, 80 minutes to Cork Airport, 2 hrs Shannon Airport.

Property Highlights
Breathtaking views of Killarney Mountains, Lakes, Gap of Dunloe from our landscaped garden. Some rooms with door to garden. Free WiFi, home cooking, fish, baking, playground & patio. Friendly service.

Local Attractions
Restaurants & pubs 5 minutes walk. National Park, Ross Castle, Gap of Dunloe, mountain climbing, golf, free fishing on River Laune.

B&B from: €35.00 - €45.00

Host(s): Noel & Eileen Spillane

9

Activities
Facilities

Closed 20 November - 20 February

Kathleens Country House

Hotel ★ ★ ★ ★ Map 2 E 4

Tralee Road, Killarney,
Co. Kerry
Tel: +353-64-663 2810
Email: info@kathleens.net
Web: www.kathleens.net
GPS: N +52° 4' 51.89" W -9° 31' 0.60"

Location
Immersed in mature landscaped gardens. 1km north of Killarney Town in peaceful tranquil green area. Private free car park. Tour Ring of Kerry/Dingle here.

Property Highlights
Traditional hospitality, attentiveness & welcome. Elegant decor. Free WiFi. Sumptuous breakfasts. All rooms en suite. Itineraries, golf tee times arranged. Singles welcome.

Local Attractions
Visit Killarney National Park, Ross Castle, Ring of Kerry & Dingle Peninsula. A golfers paradise within driving distance of Killarney, Waterville, Dooks, Tralee, Ballybunion golf courses.

B&B from: €39.50 - €67.50

Host(s): Kathleen O'Regan-Sheppard

17

Activities
Facilities

Closed 01 October - 30 April

226 Ireland South   B&B Rates are per Person Sharing per Night incl. Breakfast. Room/Suite Rates are per Room per Night. **See also page 08**

To Book Call **+353-1-8084419** or www.irelandhotels.com

Co. Kerry
Killarney

Killarney Avenue Hotel

Hotel ★ ★ ★ ★   Map 2 E 4

Town Centre, Killarney,
Co. Kerry
Tel: +353-64-663 2522
Email: info@killarneyavenue.com
Web: www.killarneyavenue.com
GPS: N +52° 3' 26.07" W -9° 30' 21.64"

Location
This boutique 4**** hotel has an idyllic setting in the heart of Killarney.

Property Highlights
Well appointed rooms provide guests with every care & comfort. Druids Restaurant provides a perfect blend of local & classical cuisine. The Kenmare Rooms is a distinctly different hotel bar.

Local Attractions
Guests are welcome to use the leisure facilities of our sister hotel (Killarney Towers Hotel), 100m away. Close to shopping, vistor attractions and Kerry's premier golf courses.

B&B from: €50.00 - €75.00

Host(s): Denis McCarthy

Facilities

66

Open All Year

Killarney Lodge

Guesthouse ★ ★ ★ ★   Map 2 E 4

Countess Road, Killarney,
Co. Kerry
Tel: +353-64-663 6499
Email: klylodge@iol.ie
Web: www.killarneylodge.net
GPS: N +52° 3' 23.81" W -9° 30' 21.19"

Location
Killarney Town Centre. Property in its own private gardens. Kerry Airport - 15 minutes. Bus & Rail Stations - 3 minute walk.

Property Highlights
Private car park. 16 en suite, air conditioned bedrooms. Free Wireless Internet Access. Power showers. Extensive breakfast menu. Highly recommended by Trip Advisor.

Local Attractions
Adjacent to Killarney National Park. Ideal base for touring Ring of Kerry, Dingle, etc. 7 championship golf courses nearby.

B&B from: €50.00 - €72.00

Host(s): Catherine Treacy

Activities

Facilities

16

Closed 01 November - 01 March

Killarney Park Hotel

Hotel ★ ★ ★ ★ ★   Map 2 E 4

Town Centre, Killarney,
Co. Kerry
Tel: +353-64-663 5555
Email: info@killarneyparkhotel.ie
Web: www.killarneyparkhotel.ie
GPS: N +52° 3' 27.94" W -9° 30' 17.13"

Location
Town centre, Killarney. 4 minutes walk from train station. 17kms to Kerry Airport. 87kms from Cork Airport.

Property Highlights
Award-winning afternoon tea daily. Award-winning Park Restaurant. Irish whiskey tasting menu available. Golf drying room, children's play area & hotel gardens.

Local Attractions
Ring of Kerry - 110 miles of beautiful scenery. Gap of Dunloe - most varied & exciting tour in Ireland. Muckross House & Gardens. Ross Castle 15th century.

B&B from: €125.00 - €175.00
Suites from: €295.00 - €450.00

Host(s): Niamh O'Shea

Activities

Facilities

68

Closed 24 - 26 December

B&B Rates are per Person Sharing per Night incl. Breakfast. Room/Suite Rates are per Room per Night. See also page 08

Co. Kerry

To Book Call **+353-1-8084419** or www.irelandhotels.com

Killarney

Killarney Plaza Hotel & Spa

Hotel ★ ★ ★ ★ Map 2 E 4

Town Centre, Killarney,
Co. Kerry
Tel: +353-64-662 1100
Email: info@killarneyplaza.com
Web: www.killarneyplaza.com
GPS: N +52° 3' 27.75"   W -9° 30' 31.93"

Location
The Killarney Plaza & Molton Brown Spa reigns over the town of Killarney with grace and glamour.

Property Highlights
The Killarney Plaza successfully blends gracious hospitality, quality service and amenities in such a way that guests, using the hotel for business or pleasure, feel at ease.

Local Attractions
The leisure area and Molton Brown Spa allow guests to unwind and relax in luxurious surroundings.

B&B from: €60.00 - €100.00
Suites from: €200.00 - €350.00

Host(s): Edith Kirk

198

Closed 19 December - 11 February

Killarney Royal Hotel

Hotel ★ ★ ★ ★ Map 2 E 4

College Street, Killarney,
Co. Kerry
Tel: +353-64-663 1853
Email: reception@killarneyroyal.ie
Web: www.killarneyroyal.ie
GPS: N +52° 3' 36.18"   W -9° 30' 20.14"

Location
Town centre location, 250m from train & bus station, 16km from Kerry Airport.

Property Highlights
Luxurious accommodation, restaurant, bistro & bar with renowned afternoon tea. Friendly Irish hospitality with a staff who posses a genuine desire to please.

Local Attractions
All Kerry highlights including Killarney National Park, Ring of Kerry & Muckross. Also in close proximity golf, water-sports, cycling, walking, riding and the very best fishing.

B&B from: €55.00 - €160.00
Suites from: €150.00 - €360.00

Host(s): Claire & Brian Scally

29

Closed 23 - 27 December

Killarney Towers Hotel & Leisure Centre

Hotel ★ ★ ★ ★ Map 2 E 4

Town Centre, Killarney,
Co. Kerry
Tel: +353-64-663 1038
Email: info@killarneytowers.com
Web: www.killarneytowers.com
GPS: N +52° 3' 31.10"   W -9° 30' 25.48"

Location
The Killarney Towers Hotel enjoys a dominant position in the town centre. All of the attractions of this vibrant town are on your doorstep.

Property Highlights
Having undergone a €10 million refurbishment in 2008, our hotel provides guests with the very best in comfort and modern services.

Local Attractions
Whether one is looking for a midweek or weekend getaway or flying into Kerry on business, the Killarney Towers is the perfect place to stay.

B&B from: €50.00 - €75.00

Host(s): Giles Casey

182

Closed 31 October - 01 February

228   Ireland South   B&B Rates are per Person Sharing per Night incl. Breakfast. Room/Suite Rates are per Room per Night. **See also page 08**

To Book Call **+353-1-8084419** or www.irelandhotels.com

Co. Kerry
Killarney

Killeen House Hotel

Hotel ★ ★ ★   Map 2 E 4

Aghadoe, Lakes of Killarney,
Co. Kerry
Tel: +353-64-663 1711
Email: charming@indigo.ie
Web: www.killeenhousehotel.com
GPS: N +52° 4' 33.12"   W -9° 34' 16.30"

Location
Set in the beautiful Aghadoe area of the famous Lakes of Killarney, 5 minutes drive from the town centre. Very close to Killarney Golf & Fishing Club.

Property Highlights
Be assured of a memorable stay in our truly charming hotel, with only 23 rooms, set in landscaped gardens. Elegant dining in Rozzers famous restaurant. Relax in the unique DIY Golf Pub.

Local Attractions
The ideal base for touring the magical Kingdom of Kerry. Stunning scenery, world-class golf and fishing superb beaches and mountain trails.

B&B from: €70.00 - €120.00

Host(s): Geraldine & Michael Rosney

23

Facilities

Closed 21 October - 20 April

Kingfisher Lodge Guesthouse

Guesthouse ★ ★ ★   Map 2 E 4

Lewis Road, Killarney,
Co. Kerry
Tel: +353-64-663 7131
Email: info@kingfisherlodgekillarney.com
Web: www.kingfisherlodgekillarney.com
GPS: N +52° 3' 48.86"   W -9° 30' 20.78"

Location
On Ring of Kerry Route, 4 minutes walk to Killarney Town Centre, bus/rail station 6 minutes, Kerry Airport 15km.

Property Highlights
Award-winning, Lonely Planet and Michelin recommended luxury guesthouse AA****. Private parking, free WiFi, gardens, en suite rooms, satellite TV, phone, tea/coffee.

Local Attractions
26,000 acre Killarney National Park, lakes, mountains, golfing, fishing, walking, climbing, horse riding, boating, bus tour, tee-times, walks arranged by Donal (qualified guide).

B&B from: €30.00 - €60.00

Host(s): Ann & Donal Carroll

11

Activities

Facilities

Closed 13 December - 11 February

Lake Hotel (The)

Hotel ★ ★ ★ ★   Map 2 E 4

On the Lake Shore, Muckross Road, Killarney,
Co. Kerry
Tel: +353-64-663 1035
Email: info@lakehotel.com
Web: www.lakehotel.com
GPS: N +52° 3' 4.67"   W -9° 30' 22.33"

Location
The Lake Hotel is situated 1km from Killarney on the Muckross road, off the N72 road.

Property Highlights
The Lake Hotel is a family owned & run hotel which offers a unique setting on the lakeshore & a warm Irish welcome. Also lakeside dining & an outdoor hot tub overlooking the lakes & mountains.

Local Attractions
Adjacent to Killarney National Park with 25,000 acres for hiking, walking, kayaking, boating, cycling & horse riding. Also Ring of Kerry, Gap of Dunloe, Kenmare, Dingle, Derrynane & the Skelligs.

B&B from: €52.00 - €100.00

Host(s): Niall Huggard

131

Activities   Facilities

Closed 06 December - 03 February

B&B Rates are per Person Sharing per Night incl. Breakfast. Room/Suite Rates are per Room per Night. See also page 08

Ireland South

Co. Kerry

To Book Call **+353-1-8084419** or www.irelandhotels.com

Killarney

Malton (The)

Hotel ★ ★ ★ ★   Map 2 E 4

Town Centre, Killarney,
Co. Kerry
Tel: +353-64-663 8000
Email: res@themalton.com
Web: www.themalton.com
GPS: N +52° 3' 31.97"   W -9° 30' 13.23"

Location
Town centre, adjacent to train station. Close to Kerry Airport. Walking distance from Killarney National Park.

Property Highlights
6 acres of landscaped gardens, leisure centre, outdoor playground, tennis courts, conference centre, banqueting suites, private dining, à la carte restaurant & Punchbowl Bar serving food.

Local Attractions
Killarney National Park, Muckross House & traditional farms, Gap of Dunloe, Molls Gap, MacGillycuddy Reeks.

B&B from: €70.00 - €140.00
Suites from: €300.00 - €500.00

172

Host(s): Conor Hennigan

Activities   Facilities

Open All Year

McSweeney Arms Hotel

Hotel ★ ★ ★   Map 2 E 4

College Street, Killarney,
Co. Kerry
Tel: +353-64-663 1211
Email: mcsweeneyarms@eircom.net
Web: www.mcsweeneyarms.com
GPS: N +52° 3' 36.10"   W -9° 30' 21.55"

Location
5 minutes walk from Killarney's bus & train station. 20 minutes drive to Kerry Airport. Within 2 hours from both Cork & Shannon Airport.

Property Highlights
26 beautifully appointed guest rooms. Family-run hotel that makes their guest feel right at home. Traditional & lively sports bar. Restaurant offers excellent local produce. Private dining facilities.

Local Attractions
Killarney's National Park, Ross Castle, Muckross House & Gardens, three 18 hole parkland championship golf courses, historic churches, cinema, shopping outlet centre.

B&B from: €50.00 - €85.00

26

Host(s): Tony McSweeney

Facilities

Closed 06 December - 04 March

Muckross Park Hotel & Cloisters Spa

Hotel ★ ★ ★ ★ ★   Map 2 E 4

Lakes of Killarney, Killarney,
Co. Kerry
Tel: +353-64-662 3400
Email: info@muckrosspark.com
Web: www.muckrosspark.com
GPS: N +52° 1' 29.29"   W -9° 29' 23.32"

Location
In the heart of the National Park, a few miles from Killarney & minutes from the Lakes of Muckross House.

Property Highlights
Exceptional Cloisters Spa, a sanctuary for mind & body. Molly Darcy's Pub with food available all day & GB Shaws Restaurant for an exquisite dining experience.

Local Attractions
Muckross House & Abbey, National Park, Torc Waterfall on the Ring of Kerry, Gap of Dunloe & Black Valley.

B&B from: €60.00 - €110.00
Suites from: €250.00 - €1,000.00

68

Host(s): Niall Kerins

Activities   Facilities

Closed 03 January - 10 February

230   Ireland South   B&B Rates are per Person Sharing per Night incl. Breakfast. Room/Suite Rates are per Room per Night. **See also page 08**

To Book Call **+353-1-8084419** or www.irelandhotels.com

Co. Kerry
Killarney

Murphy's of Killarney

Guesthouse ★ ★ ★   Map 2 E 4

18 College Street, Killarney,
Co. Kerry
Tel: +353-64-663 1294
Email: info@murphysofkillarney.com
Web: www.murphysofkillarney.com
GPS: N +52° 3' 34.05"   W -9° 30' 22.32"

Location
Murphy's is located in Killarney Town Centre adjacent to the bus station. Located only 15 minutes from Kerry Airport.

Property Highlights
Murphy's offers quality accommodation in a prime location incorporating Lord Kenmare's Restaurant. Murphy's traditional bar & Squire Pub. Food served daily.

Local Attractions
Local amenities include golf, fishing, horse riding, walking. Killarney is an outdoor paradise, whatever your pursuit. Home to Ireland's finest National Park.

B&B from: €40.00 - €70.00

Host(s): Sean Murphy

20

Facilities

Closed 22 - 29 December

Old Weir Lodge

Guesthouse ★ ★ ★ ★   Map 2 E 4

Muckross Road, Killarney,
Co. Kerry
Tel: +353-64-663 5593
Email: oldweirlodge@eircom.net
Web: www.oldweirlodge.com
GPS: N +52° 3' 5.04"   W -9° 30' 26.07"

Location
On main road towards National Park & 500m from town centre. Ross Golf Club nearby.

Property Highlights
Multi-channel TV, ice, hairdryers, 2 lounges, home baking. Traditional, coeliac & vegetarian breakfast. Totally non-smoking. Tours arranged.

Local Attractions
National park, Muckross House, Ross Castle, Torc Waterfall, Killarney Lakes. 5 minutes walk from town centre, Gap of Dunloe, 4 golf clubs in close proximity.

B&B from: €40.00 - €70.00

Host(s): Maureen & Dermot O'Donoghue

30

Facilities

Closed 20 December - 28 December

Randles Court Hotel

Hotel ★ ★ ★ ★   Map 2 E 4

Muckross Road, Killarney,
Co. Kerry
Tel: +353-64-663 5333
Email: info@randlescourt.com
Web: www.randlescourt.com
GPS: N +52° 3' 14.17"   W -9° 30' 23.23"

Location
Only 5 minutes stroll from Killarney's Town Centre yet pleasantly secluded from it all. Very close to Irelands National Events Centre (INEC) & National Park.

Property Highlights
Luxurious rooms incl. Upgraded Junior Suites. Choice of fine dining restaurants, leisure club, Zen Day Spa, free private parking & WiFi access. Golf drying & storage room, meeting & event facilities.

Local Attractions
On the famous Ring of Kerry, near INEC, Racecourse, Muckross House & National Park, Ross Castle & Torc Waterfall. Superb mountain view of the McGillycuddy Reeks & Carrauntoohil, our highest peak.

B&B from: €65.00 - €180.00
Suites from: €130.00 - €450.00

Host(s): Tom Randles

68

Facilities

Closed 19 - 27 December

B&B Rates are per Person Sharing per Night incl. Breakfast. Room/Suite Rates are per Room per Night. **See also page 08**

Co. Kerry
Killarney

Ross (The)

Hotel ★★★★　　　　　　　　　Map 2 E 4

Town Centre, Killarney,
Co. Kerry
Tel: +353-64-663 1855
Email: info@theross.ie
Web: www.theross.ie
GPS: N +52° 3' 29.16"   W -9° 30' 28.04"

Location
3 minute walk to railway station, town centre Killarney. 24kms from Kerry Airport, 87kms from Cork Airport, 135kms from Shannon Airport.

Property Highlights
Cellar One Restaurant - Great wine, great food. Home to the popular local bar in town, "Lane's Café Bar". Cocktail Bar.

Local Attractions
Muckross House & Gardens. Ring of Kerry - 110 miles of beautiful scenery. 15th century Ross Castle. National Park, 25,000 acres. Lakes of Killarney.

B&B from: €80.00 - €110.00
Suites from: €180.00 - €275.00

Host(s): Padraig & Janet Treacy

29

Facilities

Closed 24 - 26 December

Scotts Hotel Killarney

Hotel ★★★　　　　　　　　　Map 2 E 4

Scotts Street, Killarney,
Co. Kerry
Tel: +353-64-663 1060
Email: info@scottshotelkillarney.com
Web: www.scottshotelkillarney.com
GPS: N +52° 3' 33.46"   W -9° 30' 22.67"

Location
Located in Killarney Town Centre, opposite the bus & railway station.

Property Highlights
With 120 en suite bedrooms including de luxe suites & plush apartments, 3 bars, a fabulous restaurant plus an exclusive underground car park.

Local Attractions
Scott's is an ideal base to explore Killarney National Park, enjoy a cruise with the M.V. Pride of the Lakes & is in close proximity to the INEC. Excellent golf courses in close proximity.

B&B from: €49.00 - €95.00
Suites from: €130.00 - €240.00

Host(s): Maurice Eoin O'Donoghue

120

Activities

Facilities

Closed 24 - 25 December

Victoria House Hotel

Hotel ★★★　　　　　　　　　Map 2 E 4

Muckross Road, Killarney,
Co. Kerry
Tel: +353-64-663 5430
Email: info@victoriahousehotel.com
Web: www.victoriahousehotel.com
GPS: N +52° 2' 36.00"   W -9° 30' 0.17"

Location
Located at the gateway to Killarney National Park, next door to the INEC. 1.5km from Killarney town on the N71.

Property Highlights
This family run, charming boutique hotel offers an exceptional welcoming and personal service. De luxe upgrades available. WiFi available.

Local Attractions
Muckross House and Gardens, National Park, Torc Waterfall, Gap of Dunloe, Kerry Way, Lakes of Killarney, Ross Castle.

B&B from: €40.00 - €110.00
Suites from: €150.00 - €260.00

Host(s): John Courtney

35

Facilities

Closed 01 December - 01 February

To Book Call **+353-1-8084419** or www.irelandhotels.com

Co. Kerry

Killorglin / Portmagee / Sneem

Bianconi (The)

Guesthouse ★ ★ ★   Map 1 D 4

Annadale Road, Lower Bridge St. Killorglin,
Ring of Kerry, Co. Kerry
Tel: +353-66-976 1146
Email: info@bianconi.ie
Web: www.bianconi.ie
GPS: N +52° 6′ 21.82″   W -9° 47′ 5.45″

Location
20 minutes from Kerry Airport, 25 minutes from Killarney Railway Station. On the Ring of Kerry, beside rivers, lakes and mountains and beaches.

Property Highlights
Homely atmosphere. Excellent chef serves the highest quality fish, Hereford Beef and Kerry Highland Lamb. Snacks served all day. Comfortable rooms with all facilities.

Local Attractions
Boating on Caragh Lake, mountain climbing on the Reeks, fishing on the River Laune, golf at Killorglin. Friendly local people. Close to all beaches.

B&B from: €45.00 - €65.00

14

Host(s): Ray Sheehy

Facilities

Closed 23 - 28 December

Moorings (The)

Guesthouse ★ ★ ★   Map 1 B 3

Portmagee,
Co. Kerry
Tel: +353-66-947 7108
Email: moorings@iol.ie
Web: www.moorings.ie
GPS: N +51° 53′ 8.54″   W -10° 21′ 57.21″

Location
Located in fishing village of Portmagee. Just off the Ring of Kerry (R565). The Moorings overlooks the village's busy working harbour.

Property Highlights
Stylish bedrooms including four superior sea view mini suites. Dine in our renowned seafood restaurant & relax with some traditional Irish music in the Bridge Bar.

Local Attractions
Main departure point for boats to the Skelligs. Dramatic scenery, history & culture await you. Our delightful gift shop Cois Cuain offers a selection of quality gifts.

B&B from: €45.00 - €50.00

16

Host(s): Patricia & Gerard Kennedy

Facilities

Closed 24 - 25 December

Parknasilla Resort

Hotel ★ ★ ★ ★   Map 1 C 3

Sneem,
Co. Kerry
Tel: +353-64-667 5600
Email: info@parknasillahotel.ie
Web: www.parknasillahotel.ie
GPS: N +51° 48′ 56.44″   W -9° 52′ 29.25″

Location
Overlooking Kenmare Bay, surrounded by the Kerry Mountains & situated within 500 acres of parkland.

Property Highlights
Full Day Spa, outdoor hot tubs, swimming pool, thermal suites, clay pigeon shooting, archery, fishing, 12 hole golf course.

Local Attractions
Ring of Kerry, Derrynane Walk, Staigue Fort, Derreen Gardens. Sailing, horse riding, sea, river & lake fishing, 7 mapped walks, guided walking tours, horse & carriage tours.

B&B from: €50.00 - €170.00
Suites from: €250.00 - €2,000.00

83

Host(s): Jim Feeney

Activities

Facilities

Closed 02 January - 16 March

B&B Rates are per Person Sharing per Night incl. Breakfast. Room/Suite Rates are per Room per Night. See also page 08

Co. Kerry

To Book Call **+353-1-8084419** or www.irelandhotels.com

Sneem / Tahilla / Tarbert

Sneem Hotel

Hotel ★ ★ ★ ★   Map 1 C 3

**Goldens Cove, Sneem, Ring of Kerry,
Co. Kerry**
Tel: +353-64-667 5100
Email: information@sneemhotel.com
Web: www.sneemhotel.com
GPS: N +51° 50' 17.40"   W -9° 53' 57.45"

Location
Newly opened 4 star hotel, located in a quiet, perfect cove. On the N70 Ring of Kerry in the village of Sneem. 64km from Kerry Airport, 50km from Killarney.

Property Highlights
Family run. Spectacular sea views & views of the Kerry Mts. On the Ring of Kerry. Ideal wedding & conference venue. Luxury bedrooms, self-catering apartments & suites. Free WiFi. Free bikes & kayaks.

Local Attractions
Ring of Kerry, Derrynane Beach & water sports, Staigue Fort, The Skelligs, Waterville Golf Course, Ring of Kerry Golf Course, Skellig Golf Course, Carrauntoohil Mountain, The Kerry Way Walks.

B&B from: €65.00 - €95.00
Suites from: €190.00 - €250.00

Host(s): Nicola Duggan

69

Activities

Facilities

Closed 24 - 25 December

Tahilla Cove Country House

Guesthouse ★ ★ ★   Map 1 D 3

**Tahilla, Near Sneem,
Co. Kerry**
Tel: +353-64-664 5204
Email: tahillacove@eircom.net
Web: www.tahillacove.com
GPS: N +51° 49' 50.78"   W -9° 48' 19.89"

Location
Located on "Ring of Kerry" seashore. On N7, 16km west of Kenmare, 7km east of Sneem.

Property Highlights
Spectacular seashore setting, gardens, pier, en suite bedrooms with TV, hairdryers, ironing, tea/coffee facilities. Log fires, bar, lounge, evening meals.

Local Attractions
Ideal touring base for Ring of Kerry, Beara, Kenmare, Killarney, Skellig Islands, Garnish & Derreen Gardens, golfing & fishing.

B&B from: €50.00 - €75.00

Host(s): James/Deirdre/Chas Waterhouse

9

Facilities

Closed 20 October - 01 April

Kirby's Lanterns Hotel

Hotel ★ ★ ★   Map 5 E 7

**Glin / Tarbert Coast Road, Tarbert,
Co. Kerry**
Tel: +353-68-36210
Email: reservations@thelanternshotel.ie
Web: www.thelanternshotel.ie
GPS: N +52° 34' 4.45"   W -9° 20' 45.79"

Location
Overlooking the River Shannon on the Kerry Limerick border. 40 minutes from Limerick City on the N69 and 30 minutes from Tralee.

Property Highlights
A traditional Irish welcome in this intimate family-run hotel where a home from home experience awaits you from your hosts Fergal and Marie.

Local Attractions
15 minutes from world-renowned Ballybunion Golf Links. Close to Foynes Flying Boat Museum and minutes away from the Tarbert Killimer Car Ferry.

B&B from: €30.00 - €90.00

Host(s): Marie Kirby / Fergal Meade

22

Facilities

Closed 25 December

234   Ireland South   B&B Rates are per Person Sharing per Night incl. Breakfast. Room/Suite Rates are per Room per Night.   See also page 08

To Book Call **+353-1-8084419** or www.irelandhotels.com

Co. Kerry
Tralee

Ballygarry House Hotel & Spa

Hotel ★ ★ ★ ★   Map 1 D 5

Killarney Road, Tralee,
Co. Kerry
Tel: +353-66-712 3322
Email: info@ballygarryhouse.com
Web: www.ballygarryhouse.com
GPS: N +52° 15' 39.92"   W -9° 39' 35.65"

Location
In 6 acres of mature gardens, against the backdrop of the Kerry Mountains on the outskirts of Tralee Town .Kerry Airport 15 minutes drive, train station 10 minutes.

Property Highlights
A warm welcome, luxurious guest rooms, library and drawing room, Brooks Restaurant and Nádúr Spa combine to create the perfect country house experience.

Local Attractions
Tralee is bursting with all-weather attractions - Aqua Dome, Siamsa Tíre, Blennerville Windmill - and perfectly located for touring the Ring of Kerry and Dingle Peninsula.

B&B from: €55.00 - €90.00
Suites from: €150.00 - €220.00

Host(s): Padraig McGillicuddy

64

Activities

Facilities

Closed 21 - 28 December

Ballyseede Castle Hotel

Hotel ★ ★ ★ ★   Map 1 D 5

Ballyseede, Tralee,
Co. Kerry
Tel: +353-66-712 5799
Email: info@ballyseedecastle.com
Web: www.ballyseedecastle.com
GPS: N +52° 15' 23.51"   W -9° 38' 48.06"

Location
Fifteen minutes from Kerry Airport, 30 minutes from Killarney, 10 minutes from Tralee, 10 minutes from Bus & Train station.

Property Highlights
The only castle hotel in the South West. Family-owned and operated hotel and set on 30 acres of woodland. Fine dining.

Local Attractions
Easy access to the Ring of Kerry & Dingle Peninsula. Near Championship Golf Courses, Ballybunion, Tralee, Killarney.

B&B from: €65.00 - €110.00

Host(s): Marnie Corscadden & Rory O'Sullivan

22

Facilities

Closed 20 December - 01 March

Brook Manor Lodge

Guesthouse ★ ★ ★ ★   Map 1 D 5

Fenit Road, Tralee,
Co. Kerry
Tel: +353-66-712 0406
Email: brookmanor@eircom.net
Web: www.brookmanorlodge.com
GPS: N +52° 17' 0.75"   W -9° 44' 46.77"

Location
Brook Manor Lodge is situated on the Fenit Road (R558), approx 2km from Tralee. Ideal base for touring Dingle Peninsula and Killarney.

Property Highlights
Free internet access, laptop & printer for guest use. Free WiFi. Cable TV in bedrooms.

Local Attractions
Golfing, Fishing, Sightseeing, Beaches. Dingle Peninsula 45 minutes drive & Killarney 35 minutes drive.

B&B from: €45.00 - €70.00
Suites from: €130.00 - €160.00

Host(s): Sandra Lordan

8

Facilities

Closed 21 - 31 December

B&B Rates are per Person Sharing per Night incl. Breakfast. Room/Suite Rates are per Room per Night. See also page 08

Co. Kerry

To Book Call **+353-1-8084419** or www.irelandhotels.com

Tralee

Carlton Hotel Tralee

Hotel ★ ★ ★ ★   Map 1 D 5

Dan Spring Rd, Tralee,
Co. Kerry
Tel: +353-66-719 9100
Email: reservations.tralee@carlton.ie
Web: www.carlton.ie/tralee
GPS: N +52° 15' 49.06"   W -9° 42' 2.43"

Location
7 minutes walk to town centre, 5 minutes to Aquadome, 15 minutes to Kerry Airport, 25 minutes to Killarney. Only 10 minutes from beaches.

Property Highlights
Home to Rose of Tralee International Festival. Free entry to Aquadome, free entry to Kingdom Greyhound Stadium, Kids Club during holidays, sauna, steam room, gym.

Local Attractions
Aqua Dome, Indoor Water World, Dingle Peninsula, Banna Strand & other sandy beaches, Blennerville Windmill, Toby World, Siamsa Tire, Kerry County Museum.

B&B from: €59.00 - €200.00

Host(s): Thys Vogels

165

Closed 23 - 26 December

Grand Hotel

Hotel ★ ★ ★   Map 1 D 5

Denny Street, Tralee,
Co. Kerry
Tel: +353-66-712 1499
Email: info@grandhoteltralee.com
Web: www.grandhoteltralee.com
GPS: N +52° 16' 8.16"   W -9° 42' 17.82"

Location
Located in the town centre beside the town park, taxi rank, etc. 15km from Kerry Airport, 1km from train / bus station.

Property Highlights
Facilities include 43 contemporary guest rooms with complimentary WiFi. Samuel's Restaurant, Pikeman Bar, choice of meeting rooms.

Local Attractions
Siamsa Tire, Aqua Dome, Town Park, Kerry Museum, Blennerville Windmill, Toby World, Greyhound Stadium, numerous Golf Courses, Ring of Kerry route, designated walking.

B&B from: €55.00 - €85.00

Host(s): Dick Boyle

43

Closed 24 - 26 December

Meadowlands Hotel

Hotel ★ ★ ★ ★   Map 1 D 5

Oakpark, Tralee,
Co. Kerry
Tel: +353-66-718 0444
Email: info@meadowlandshotel.com
Web: www.meadowlandshotel.com
GPS: N +52° 16' 34.36"   W -9° 41' 28.72"

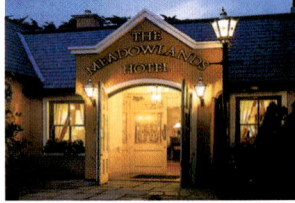

Location
Located just 1km from Tralee Town centre. Within walking distance of railway station. On its own 2 acres of landscaped gardens.

Property Highlights
The food is exceptional - fish caught daily on owner's own trawler and presented in our award-winning restaurant.

Local Attractions
Nearby attractions include: golf courses (links), greyhound racing, beaches & mountains. Tralee attractions including The Windmill, Aquadome, Geraldine Experience, Siamsa Tire.

B&B from: €45.00 - €140.00
Suites from: €200.00 - €450.00

Host(s): Padraig & Peigi O'Mathuna

57

Closed 23 - 27 December

---

236   Ireland South   B&B Rates are per Person Sharing per Night incl. Breakfast. Room/Suite Rates are per Room per Night. **See also page 08**

To Book Call **+353-1-8084419** or www.irelandhotels.com

Co. Kerry
Waterville

Butler Arms Hotel

Hotel ★ ★ ★ ★   Map 1 B 3

**Waterville,
Co. Kerry
Tel:** +353-66-947 4144
Email: reservations@butlerarms.com
Web: www.butlerarms.com
GPS: N +51° 49' 39.97"   W -10° 10' 20.29"

Location
The Butler Arms Hotel is situated in the centre of Waterville. Our nearest airport is Kerry and the nearest train station is Killarney.

Property Highlights
The Butler Arms Hotel has been family-run for over 4 generations by the Huggard Family. The hotel serves high quality food in our restaurant & bar.

Local Attractions
Local attractions include Skelligs Rock, Lough Currane and Waterville Golf Links, plus the new course Skellig Bay.

B&B from: €60.00 - €100.00
Suites from: €200.00 - €400.00

Host(s): Louise & Paula Huggard

36

Activities   **Facilities**

Closed 31 October - 31 March

Smugglers Inn

Guesthouse ★ ★ ★   Map 1 B 3

**Cliff Road, Waterville,
Co. Kerry
Tel:** +353-66-947 4330
Email: info@thesmugglersinn.ie
Web: www.thesmugglersinn.ie
GPS: N +51° 50' 13.73"   W -10° 11' 41.89"

Location
Situated on Ring of Kerry, overlooking the Atlantic Ocean and long sandy beach at the gates of Waterville Golf Links.

Property Highlights
Comfortable en suite bedrooms with sea or mountain views, complete with tea/coffee facilities, hairdryer, TV, WiFi and award-winning gourmet restaurant.

Local Attractions
18 Hole Championship Waterville Golf Links Course, Lough Currane for Salmon and Sea Trout Fishing, Skellig Mhichíl World Heritage Site.

B&B from: €35.00 - €75.00

Host(s): Henry Hunt

14

Activities   **Facilities**

Closed 01 November - 31 March

B&B Rates are per Person Sharing per Night incl. Breakfast. Room/Suite Rates are per Room per Night. See also page 08   Ireland South   237

Co. Kilkenny

To Book Call **+353-1-8084419** or www.irelandhotels.com

Graiguenamanagh / Kilkenny City

Waterside

Guesthouse ★ ★ ★   Map 7 M 7

The Quay, Graiguenamanagh,
Co. Kilkenny
Tel: +353-59-972 4246
Email: info@watersideguesthouse.com
Web: www.watersideguesthouse.com
GPS: N +52° 32' 25.39"   W -6° 57' 13.63"

Location
Waterside is located on the banks of the River Barrow in the Medieval River Town of Graiguenamanagh in scenic South Kilkenny.

Property Highlights
Waterside is a carefully converted 19th century granite corn store with feature wooden beams and superb stonework housing an excellent restaurant and cosy rooms with river views.

Local Attractions
Graiguenamanagh is base camp for all who enjoy outdoors life around the Barrow River & Blackstairs Mountains. Hillwalkers, fishers & boaters mingle in the traditional pubs with music & craic all year.

B&B from: €35.00 - €55.00

Host(s): Brigid & Brian Roberts

10

Facilities

Closed 23 December - 01 February

Bailey (The)

Guesthouse   Map 7 L 7

9-11 Parliament Street,
Kilkenny
Tel: +353-56-777 0422
Email: reservations.thebailey.kilkenny@gmail.com
GPS: N +52° 39' 14.73"   W -7° 15' 15.20"

Location
Situated in the heart of Kilkenny. Directly across from the Court House and 5 minutes from the train station.

Property Highlights
All rooms en suite, tea and coffee making facilities, hairdryers & TVs in each room.

Local Attractions
Historic Court House, St. Canice's Cathedral, St. Mary's Cathedral, Kilkenny Castle, Design Centre, Smithwick's Brewery, Watergate Theatre.

B&B from: €50.00 - €120.00

Host(s): Joanne Cooney

10

Facilities

Open All Year

Bridge Court House

Guesthouse ★ ★ ★   Map 7 L 7

Greensbridge,
Kilkenny
Tel: +353-56-776 2998
Email: anegan@eircom.net
Web: www.kilkennybridgecourt.com
GPS: N +52° 39' 27.73"   W -7° 15' 17.76"

Location
City centre location, approximately 10 minutes from the train station, within easy walking distance of all major tourist attractions, areas and shopping areas.

Property Highlights
Bridge Court House is a modern comfortable family-run 3* guesthouse offering excellent value in a great city centre location. Complimentary parking and free broadband access. A cosy TV room awaits.

Local Attractions
Kilkenny Castle is within 10 minutes walk from our home, St. Canice's Tower is a 3 minute walk and right beside us there are 2 lovely walks beside the River Nore.

B&B from: €35.00 - €40.00

Host(s): Don & Niamh Egan

9

Facilities

Closed 20 - 30 December

238   Ireland South   B&B Rates are per Person Sharing per Night incl. Breakfast. Room/Suite Rates are per Room per Night.   **See also page 08**

To Book Call **+353-1-8084419** or www.irelandhotels.com

Co. Kilkenny
Kilkenny City

Butler House

Guesthouse ★ ★ ★ ★   Map 7 L 7

16 Patrick Street,
Kilkenny
Tel: +353-56-776 5707
Email: res@butler.ie
Web: www.butler.ie
GPS: N +52° 38' 55.82"   W -7° 15' 3.39"

Location
Butler House is situated in the centre of Kilkenny City. Butler House is the only property with direct access to Kilkenny Castle via its walled garden and the Castle Yard.

Property Highlights
This 18th century Dower House of Kilkenny Castle is the most unique residence at which to reside when visiting Kilkenny. A property of immense historical significance in a prime location.

Local Attractions
Local attractions include the medieval city of Kilkenny, Kilkenny Castle, Kilkenny Design Centre, St Canice's Cathedral, Rothe House, Kilkenny Craft workshops & much more.

B&B from: €49.50 - €100.00
Suites from: €150.00 - €250.00

Host(s): Gabrielle Hickey

13

Closed 23 - 29 December

Club House Hotel

Hotel ★ ★   Map 7 L 7

Patrick Street,
Kilkenny
Tel: +353-56-772 1994
Email: info@clubhousehotel.com
Web: www.clubhousehotel.com
GPS: N +52° 38' 57.65"   W -7° 15' 6.49"

Location
Situated in the heart of Mediaeval Kilkenny, adjacent to Kilkenny Castle, shopping, pubs & restaurants. Complimentary on site parking.

Property Highlights
Kilkenny's vintage hotel - homely, intimate atmosphere where old values of guest satisfaction, comfort and value for money prevail.

Local Attractions
Discover Kilkenny's various festivals, golf, equestrian hunting, racing, fishing, parks and gardens, fine dining, vibrant pubs and clubs, craft trail.

B&B from: €45.00 - €125.00

Host(s): James P. Brennan / Ian Brennan

28

Closed 24 - 29 December

The 'Footprints in Coal' exhibition and interpretive centre tells the intriguing tale of the pre-dinosaur fossils found deep in the Castlecomer coal mines. This multi media exhibition brings to life the fossils, found in only six other places in the world! The Jarrow Café and a gift shop are also located in the visitor centre. Visitors can explore woodland walks, fishing lakes, the design craft yard and children's adventure playground. Open all year round. Please visit the website for information on seasonal events.

Opening Times:
May to Aug 9.30am – 5.30pm.
Sep, Oct, Mar & Apr 10am – 5pm.
Nov to Feb, 10.30am – 4.30pm.
Last admission 45 mins before closing. Opens out of hours for groups by appointment.

Admission Rates:
Adult €8, Children under 4 Free, Child 4-12 €5, Student / Senior €6, Family (2+1) €18, each additional child with family €2.

For Further Information:
Castlecomer Discovery Park.
The Estate Yard, Castlecomer,
Co. Kilkenny.
Tel: + 353 56 444 0707
Email: info@discoverypark.ie
Web: www.discoverypark.ie

Co. Kilkenny

To Book Call **+353-1-8084419** or www.irelandhotels.com

Kilkenny City

Fanad House

Glendine Inn

Hotel Kilkenny

Guesthouse ★ ★ ★ Map 7 L 7

**Castle Road,
Kilkenny**
Tel: +353-56-776 4126
Email: fanadhouse@hotmail.com
Web: www.fanadhouse.com
GPS: N +52° 38' 48.02"   W -7° 14' 32.30"

Guesthouse ★ ★ Map 7 L 7

**Castlecomer Road,
Kilkenny**
Tel: +353-56-772 1069
Email: info@glendineinn.com
Web: www.glendineinn.com
GPS: N +52° 40' 1.63"   W -7° 15' 10.51"

Hotel ★ ★ ★ ★ Map 7 L 7

**College Road,
Kilkenny**
Tel: +353-56-776 2000
Email: reservations@hotelkilkenny.ie
Web: www.hotelkilkenny.ie
GPS: N +52° 38' 35.22"   W -7° 15' 40.65"

Location
Situated close to Kilkenny Castle. We are a five minute walk to the city centre.

Location
We are ideally located for golf (course 200m away). The railway station and the historic City of Kilkenny are only 1.5km away.

Location
Hotel Kilkenny - located 90 minutes from Dublin and also easily accessible by train and bus services.

Property Highlights
All rooms are en suite with bath/shower, tea/coffee facilities, multi-channel TV, hairdryer & DD phone. Free private parking, free WiFi.

Property Highlights
The Glendine Inn has been a licensed tavern for over 200 years.

Property Highlights
The perfect 4* location for all your wedding, conference and family leisure needs.

Local Attractions
Overlooking Kilkenny Castle Park. Ideal base to visit Ireland's Medieval Capital & tour the South East.

Local Attractions
Kilkenny Golf Club, Castlecomer Discovery Park, Kilkenny City 1.5km, Jenkinstown, Dunmore Caves.

Local Attractions
A short stroll to the Medieval City. Golf and Racing are also available close by.

B&B from: €35.00 - €100.00

B&B from: €35.00 - €85.00

B&B from: €65.00 - €85.00
Suites from: €180.00 - €220.00

Host(s): Pat Wallace

Host(s): The Phelan Family

Host(s): Michael Griffin

Facilities

Facilities

Activities   **Facilities**

Open All Year

Closed 25 - 27 December

Open All Year

To Book Call **+353-1-8084419** or www.irelandhotels.com

Co. Kilkenny
Kilkenny City

Kilford Arms Hotel

Hotel ★ ★ ★   Map 7 L 7

John Street,
Kilkenny
Tel: +353-56-776 1018
Email: info@kilfordarms.ie
Web: www.kilfordarmskilkenny.com
GPS: N +52° 39' 14.58"   W -7° 14' 52.16"

Location
City centre hotel, just yards from train/bus station. Within walking distance of all the major sights and attractions Kilkenny has to offer.

Property Highlights
O'Faolain's Super Bar is Kilkenny's most vibrant bar. This fantastic venue features 3 levels of stunning architecture, creating a wonderful ambience. Truly a must see on your next trip to Kilkenny.

Local Attractions
New McDonagh Shopping Centre, Kilkenny Castle, Rothe House, St. Canice's Cathedral, Castlecomer Discovery Park, Dunmore Caves.

B&B from: €40.00 - €130.00

Host(s): Pius Phelan

60

Facilities

Open All Year

Kilkenny House Hotel

Hotel ★ ★ ★   Map 7 L 7

Freshford Road, Talbot's Inch,
Kilkenny
Tel: +353-56-777 0711
Email: kilkennyhouse@eircom.net
Web: www.kilkennyhousehotel.ie
GPS: N +52° 40' 2.23"   W -7° 16' 0.09"

Location
Located on the R693 road to M8 and Cashel. Located between the city's two main hospitals - St Luke's General and Aut Even Private. Short walk to town.

Property Highlights
Enter the warmth & style of the hotel. Spacious, tastefully decorated bedrooms with power showers, 21" satellite TV, free WiFi & bottled water. Situated on 2 acres with 100 car spaces. Owner operated.

Local Attractions
Guests can walk in 5 mins. to St. Luke's General / Aut Even Private Hospitals, Kilkenny Greyhound Track - Wed & Fri Racing, Nore Linear Park & River Walk. Kilkenny City 4 mins. by car or short walk.

B&B from: €25.00 - €65.00

Host(s): Ted Dore

30

Facilities

Closed 16 December - 01 April

Kilkenny Ormonde Hotel

Hotel ★ ★ ★ ★   Map 7 L 7

Ormonde Street,
Kilkenny
Tel: +353-56-775 0200
Email: info@kilkennyormonde.com
Web: www.kilkennyormonde.com
GPS: N +52° 38' 58.56"   W -7° 15' 11.69"

Location
In the very heart of vibrant Kilkenny is the syylish Ormonde Hotel. Minutes from the Mc Donagh Train Station and just over an hour from Dublin. Explore the city by foot from the hotel doorstep.

Property Highlights
Leisure facilities include a 21m pool, kids pool, sauna, steam room & jacuzzi. Free Kids Club daily in July/August. Luxurious KO Elemis Spa on site offers discount to residents.

Local Attractions
Within walking distance of top city landmarks such as Kilkenny Castle, St. Canice's Cathedral & only a few steps from the High St. shopping paradise, theatre, restaurants & bars.

B&B from: €99.00 - €299.00
Suites from: €169.00 - €399.00

Host(s): Colin Ahern

118

Activities   **Facilities**

Closed 23 - 27 December

B&B Rates are per Person Sharing per Night incl. Breakfast. Room/Suite Rates are per Room per Night. **See also page 08** Ireland South   241

Co. Kilkenny

To Book Call **+353-1-8084419** or www.irelandhotels.com

Kilkenny City

Kilkenny River Court

Hotel ★★★★ Map 7 L 7

The Bridge, John Street,
Kilkenny
Tel: +353-56-772 3388
Email: info@rivercourthotel.com
Web: www.rivercourthotel.com
GPS: N +52° 39' 5.55" W -7° 14' 57.37"

Location
Located in Kilkenny City centre, resting on the banks of the River Nore, directly overlooked by Kilkenny's 12th century castle.

Property Highlights
Leisure and treatment rooms. Exquisite cuisine by Gerard Dunne, Executive Head Chef formerly of the QE2. Al fresco dining options.

Local Attractions
Kilkenny City offers superb shopping - high fashion clothing, crafts, jewels. There's also Kilkenny Castle, Rothe House, St. Canice's and Swithwicks Brewery.

B&B from: €45.00 - €130.00
Suites from: €180.00 - €400.00

Host(s): Patrick Joyce
90

Activities Facilities

Closed 19 - 26 December

Langton House Hotel

Hotel ★★★ Map 7 L 7

69 John Street,
Kilkenny
Tel: +353-56-776 5133
Email: reservations@langtons.ie
Web: www.langtons.ie/www.set.ie
GPS: N +52° 39' 11.93" W -7° 14' 53.48"

Location
Designed to a 4* standard & situated on vibrant John Street in Kilkenny City Centre, a moment's walk from the Train & Bus Station. Only 80 minutes to Dublin.

Property Highlights
Boasting 34 beautifully appointed guestrooms incorporating a collection of suites, all designed with your comfort in mind. Our award-winning bars & restaurants are renowned for their high standards.

Local Attractions
Beautiful, ancient county where history, modern living & rich culture are fused in an unspoiled landscape. Visit the many historical sites from Rothe House to St. Canice's Cathedral & Kilkenny Castle.

B&B from: €45.00 - €110.00
Suites from: €100.00 - €250.00

Host(s): Sean Read
34

Activities Facilities

Closed 25 December

Laurels

Guesthouse ★★★ Map 7 L 7

College Road,
Kilkenny
Tel: +353-56-776 1501
Email: laurels@eircom.net
Web: www.thelaurelskilkenny.com
GPS: N +52° 38' 40.97" W -7° 15' 39.17"

Location
6 - 10 minutes walk from city centre. Close to the Ring Road and Kilkenny's main tourist attractions. Located opposite Hotel Kilkenny.

Property Highlights
All rooms include a hospitality tray, have a TV, hairdryer & wireless broadband. There is secure parking for all guests. Some rooms have Super King-size beds & whirlpool baths.

Local Attractions
Kilkenny Castle - 6-10 minutes walk. Kilkenny Tourist Office - 6-10 minutes walk. Thomastown, Inistioge & Gorman are all within a 30 minute drive.

B&B from: €30.00 - €50.00

Host(s): Brian & Betty McHenry
9

Facilities

Open All Year

---

242 Ireland South   B&B Rates are per Person Sharing per Night incl. Breakfast. Room/Suite Rates are per Room per Night. See also page 08

Co. Kilkenny
Kilkenny City

Website

Mobile App

Printed Guide

facebook.com/irelandhotels

irelandhotels.com/onlineguide

Lyrath Estate Hotel & Convention Centre

Hotel ★ ★ ★ ★ ★   Map 7 L 7

Dublin Road,
Kilkenny
Tel: +353-56-776 0088
Email: info@lyrath.com
Web: www.lyrath.com
GPS: N +52° 38' 52"   W -7° 11' 48"

Location
Ideally located just 1.2km from the heart of Kilkenny City and just over 1 hour's drive south of Dublin.

Property Highlights
Boating, cycling, walking amid 170 acres, the Oasis Spa, leisure facilities, bars, restaurants all situated around Lyrath's 17th century house.

Local Attractions
Kilkenny is renowned for arts & crafts including Chesneau Leather, Nicholas Mosse. There's also quad biking, golfing, horse riding and fishing.

B&B from: €60.00 - €150.00
Suites from: €210.00 - €999.00

Host(s): Patrick Joyce

137

Activities   **Facilities**

Closed 19 - 26 December

Newpark Hotel

Hotel ★ ★ ★ ★   Map 7 L 7

Castlecomer Road,
Kilkenny
Tel: +353-56-776 0500
Email: reservations@newparkhotel.com
Web: www.flynnhotels.com
GPS: N +52° 39' 51.71"   W -7° 15' 1.69"

Location
Set in 20 acres of parkland, yet only a short stroll from the mediaeval city of Kilkenny. Train station close by.

Property Highlights
129 superior rooms & suites, full conference & banqueting facilities. Escape Health Club & Aveda Spa with outdoor Infinity Pool. Wide range of dining options.

Local Attractions
Adjacent to Kilkenny Golf Club and in close proximity to Kilkenny Castle, St. Canice's Cathedral, Rothe House & Dominican Black Abbey.

B&B from: €55.00 - €95.00
Suites from: €250.00 - €400.00

Host(s): John & Allen Flynn

129

Activities   **Facilities**

Closed 24 - 26 December

Co. Kilkenny

To Book Call **+353-1-8084419** or www.irelandhotels.com

Kilkenny City / Knocktopher

Rosquil House

Guesthouse ★ ★ ★ ★   Map 7 L 7

**Castlecomer Road,
Kilkenny**
Tel: +353-56-772 1419
Email: info@rosquilhouse.com
Web: www.rosquilhouse.com
GPS: N +52° 39' 45.38"   W -7° 15' 3.39"

Location
Located a short walk from the centre of the medieval Kilkenny City, 1km from bus & railway station. 1.5 hours from Dublin Airport.

Property Highlights
Rosquil House offers the ambience of a hotel with the best traditions of Irish hospitality. AA Guesthouse of the Year 2009/2010.

Local Attractions
Close to al the historic sights of the city: Kilkenny Castle, St. Canice's Cathedral, Rothe House, St. Mary's Cathedral, Black Abbey. Golf, Horse Riding, Walking & Cycling Trails. Bicycles for hire.

B&B from: €40.00 - €55.00

Host(s): Jenny Nolan

7

Facilities

Open All Year

Springhill Court Hotel, Conference, Leisure & Spa

Hotel ★ ★ ★   Map 7 L 7

**Waterford Road,
Kilkenny**
Tel: +353-56-772 1122
Email: reservations@springhillcourt.com
Web: www.brennanhotels.com
GPS: N +52° 37' 55.91"   W -7° 15' 4.78"

Location
The hotel is located on the ring road and within walking distance of town. 1 hour from Dublin & ease of access to Waterford Motorway. Bus & train access.

Property Highlights
Leisure centre and Spa. Free parking. Free Kids Club during school holidays. Kids share free B&B.

Local Attractions
Kilkenny Medieval City, several heritage sites including Kilkenny Castle & Jerpoint Abbey. Great options for shopping & socialising. Gowran Racecourse. Several golf courses. Extensive walks.

B&B from: €40.00 - €100.00

Host(s): Seamus O'Carroll

85

Facilities

Open All Year

Carrolls Hotel

Hotel ★ ★   Map 7 L 6

**Knocktopher,
Co. Kilkenny**
Tel: +353-56-776 8082
Email: info@carrollsknocktopher.com
Web: www.carrollshotel.com
GPS: N +52° 29' 9.08"   W -7° 13' 3.96"

Location
Situated between Kilkenny and Waterford. The hotel is located just off the M9 at exit 10 in the village of Knocktopher.

Property Highlights
Enjoy the excellent service, warmth & luxury of our family-run hotel. Rooms are en suite with TV & DD phone. Sionnach Sioc Restaurant has an excellent reputation. Live music 2 nights a week.

Local Attractions
Golfing, karting, fishing, horse riding and shooting are available nearby. Jerpoint Abbey, Jerpoint Park, Mount Juliet, Inistioge, Famine Gardens (Newmarket).

B&B from: €40.00 - €60.00

Host(s): Padraig Carroll

10

Facilities

Closed 24 - 26 December

B&B Rates are per Person Sharing per Night incl. Breakfast. Room/Suite Rates are per Room per Night. See also page 08

To Book Call **+353-1-8084419** or www.irelandhotels.com **Co. Kilkenny - Co. Tipperary**

Mullinavat / Cahir

Rising Sun

Guesthouse ★ ★ ★ Map 4 L 6

Mullinavat, Via Waterford,
Co. Kilkenny
Tel: +353-51-898173
Email: info@therisingsun.ie
Web: www.therisingsun.ie
GPS: N +52° 22' 15.02"   W -7° 10' 18.81"

Location

Located on the N9 Waterford Kilkenny road, 200 metres off the M9 Motorway at Junction 11. Centrally located to Waterford (12km) & Kilkenny (30km).

Property Highlights

Built in 1644 & restored in keeping with the history of that time. We have 10 spacious en suite rooms, full Bar & A la Carte Restaurant. Serving food all day.

Local Attractions

9 & 18 hole golf courses on our doorstep. Close to Rivers Nore, Barrow & Suir for all fishing & outdoor activities. Bishops Mountain clay pigeon range 5 miles away. Close to Tramore & Dunmore East.

B&B from: €40.00 - €60.00

Host(s): Patricia Phelan

10

Facilities

Open All Year

Cahir House Hotel

Hotel ★ ★ ★ Map 3 J 6

The Square, Cahir,
Co. Tipperary
Tel: +353-52-744 3000
Email: info@cahirhousehotel.ie
Web: www.cahirhousehotel.ie
GPS: N +52° 22' 27.77"   W -7° 55' 27.96"

Location

Located just off the M8 from Dublin to Cork. Central to all in Munster at crossroads in Ireland.

Property Highlights

Traditional bar offering snugs, a quiet library area and plenty of home-grown hospitality. The Bistro serves snacks & 3 course meals. On site beauty salon. Traditional music and other entertainment.

Local Attractions

Cahir Castle, The Swiss Cottage & The Rock of Cashel. Hiking in spectacular mountain ranges overlooking Cahir. Golf in Cahir Park Golf Club. Fishing, horse racing & greyhound racing locally also.

B&B from: €55.00 - €140.00

Host(s): Robert Scannell

40

Activities

Facilities

Closed 25 - 26 December

Kilcoran Lodge Hotel

Hotel ★ ★ ★ Map 3 J 6

Kilcoran, Cahir,
Co. Tipperary
Tel: +353-52-744 1288
Email: info@kilcoranlodge.com
Web: www.kilcoranlodgehotel.com
GPS: N +52° 20' 52.09"   W -8° 0' 55.49"

Location

1km from Exit 11 on the M8 Motorway travelling Northbound or Southbound 6km from Cahir Town. Bus & train station located in town centre.

Property Highlights

Kilcorcan Lodge Hotel is steeped in old world charm & character. A welcome retreat with warm & friendly staff, blazing fires, excellent food, world-class Irish Coffees. Leisure centre & gym.

Local Attractions

Cahir Castle, Swiss Cottage, Rock of Cashel, Mitchelstown Caves, Parson's Green, Hill Walking, Fishing, golf, horse riding, cycling.

B&B from: €49.50 - €60.00
Suites from: €100.00 - €150.00

Host(s): Liam Duffy

22

Facilities

Open All Year

B&B Rates are per Person Sharing per Night incl. Breakfast. Room/Suite Rates are per Room per Night. *See also page 08*

Co. Tipperary

Carrick-on-Suir / Cashel

Carraig Hotel

Hotel ★ ★ ★   Map 3 K 5

Main Street, Carrick-on-Suir,
Co. Tipperary
Tel: +353-51-641455
Email: info@carraighotel.com
Web: www.carraighotel.com
GPS: N +52° 20' 43.96"   W -7° 24' 45.10"

Location
Located in Carrick-on-Suir on N24. Waterford 25 minutes away & Kilkenny 45 minutes. Clonmel 20 minutes. Waterford Airport 17 miles, Rosslare 68 miles away.

Property Highlights
Conference & Banquet facilities for small meetings/gatherings & larger functions/conferences. The Front Bar is more than a local, a great meeting place for coffee/lunch. Restaurant wine & dine menu.

Local Attractions
River Suir & Marina, Ormonde Castle & Tudor Manor House, Heritage Centre all 2 mins. walk. Carrick-on-Suir 18 Hole Golf Course. Curraghmore House, home of Marquis of Waterford & ancestors since 1170.

B&B from: €40.00 - €75.00

Host(s): Paul Norris

24

Facilities

Closed 24 - 26 Dec

Aulber House

Guesthouse ★ ★ ★   Map 3 J 6

Deerpark, Golden Road, Cashel,
Co. Tipperary
Tel: +353-62-63713
Email: info@aulberhouse.com
Web: www.aulberhouse.com
GPS: N +52° 30' 52.95"   W -7° 53' 56.79"

Location
On the N74 Road, on the outskirts of the historical town of Cashel. 5 minutes walk to the Main St. Close to pubs and restaurants. Set on 1 acre of landscaped gardens.

Property Highlights
Purpose built guesthouse. Spacious rooms with modern comforts. Parking, broadband, facilities for persons with mobility impairment. AA****. Good old fashioned hospitality in luxurious surroundings.

Local Attractions
The world famous Rock of Cashel. 5 golf courses within 20 minutes of Aulber. Fishing locally, horse riding, Pitch & Putt, forest walks & tourist trails, mountains, caves, Brú Ború Cultural Centre.

B&B from: €40.00 - €70.00

Host(s): Bernice & Sean Alley

12

Facilities

Closed 01 December - 01 February

Baileys Hotel Cashel

Hotel ★ ★ ★ ★   Map 3 J 6

42 Main Street, Cashel,
Co. Tipperary
Tel: +353-62-61937
Email: info@baileyshotelcashel.com
Web: www.baileyshotelcashel.com
GPS: N +52° 30' 56.84"   W -7° 53' 24.01"

Location
In the heart of Cashel Town, halfway between Dublin and Cork off the N8, an hour from Shannon Airport.

Property Highlights
Elegant rooms provide free hi-speed internet, interactive TV and air con. Cellar Bar serves food daily and superb dining is available in Restaurant No. 42.

Local Attractions
The Rock of Cashel, Dominic's Abbey, Pubs & Shops are within a short stroll. Golf, Fishing & Racing are all nearby.

B&B from: €55.00 - €80.00
Suites from: €160.00 - €220.00

Host(s): Phil Delaney

20

Facilities

Closed 22 December - 02 January

---

246   Ireland South   B&B Rates are per Person Sharing per Night incl. Breakfast. Room/Suite Rates are per Room per Night. **See also page 08**

To Book Call **+353-1-8084419** or www.irelandhotels.com

Co. Tipperary
Cashel / Clonmel

Cashel Palace Hotel

Hotel ★ ★ ★ ★ Map 3 J 6

Main Street, Cashel,
Co. Tipperary
Tel: +353-62-62707
Email: reception@cashel-palace.ie
Web: www.cashel-palace.ie
GPS: N +52° 31' 2.46"   W -7° 53' 21.29"

Location
Built in 1730 as the Bishop's Palace, situated on 28 acres of gardens in the centre of the town of Cashel. 2 hours from Dublin, 1 hour from Cork, Shannon and Waterford.

Property Highlights
Cashel Palace is complemented by tranquil walled gardens and 21 beautifully appointed en suite bedrooms. Light snacks, lunch & dinner served every day. Groups very welcome.

Local Attractions
A private path through the garden leads to the famous Rock of Cashel, as well as Brú Ború - a National Cultural Centre at the Rock's foot. Fishing, Short Walks, Horse Riding & Golf all local.

B&B from: €65.00 - €88.00
Suites from: €199.00 - €234.00

Host(s): Susan & Patrick Murphy

21

Activities   Facilities

Closed 23 - 26 December

Dundrum House Hotel, Golf & Leisure Resort

Hotel ★ ★ ★ Map 3 I 7

Dundrum, Cashel,
Co. Tipperary
Tel: +353-62-71116
Email: reservations@dundrumhouse.ie
Web: www.dundrumhousehotel.com
GPS: N +52° 32' 58.97"   W -8° 1' 47.27"

Location
10 minutes from Cashel and Tipperary Towns. 2 hours from Dublin, 1 hour from Cork, 1 hour from Shannon.

Property Highlights
64 bedroomed Manor Hotel. 4 star self-catering holiday homes. Championship golf course, leisure centre, fine dining all day.

Local Attractions
Rock of Cashel, Cahir Castle, Glen of Aherlow, Clonmel and the picturesque mountains and beautiful forest walks.

B&B from: €49.00 - €69.00

Host(s): The Crowe Family

64

Activities   Facilities

Closed 19 - 26 December

Clonmel Park Conference Leisure & Spa Hotel

Hotel ★ ★ ★ ★ Map 3 K 5

Cahir Road Roundabout, Clonmel,
Co. Tipperary
Tel: +353-52-618 8700
Email: reservations@clonmelparkhotel.com
Web: www.brennanhotels.com
GPS: N +52° 21' 23.67"   W -7° 44' 19.63"

Location
On Cahir roundabout. 30 minutes from Waterford, 2 hours from Dublin & 40 minutes from Kilkenny. Public transport outside hotel.

Property Highlights
Leisure facilities & Spa. Free Kids Club during school holidays. Kids share free B&B.

Local Attractions
Clonmel Race Track, Rock of Cashel, Swiss Cottage, St. Patrick's Well, excellent walks.

B&B from: €45.00 - €110.00

Host(s): Michael Boyle

99

Facilities

Open All Year

B&B Rates are per Person Sharing per Night incl. Breakfast. Room/Suite Rates are per Room per Night. See also page 08

Co. Tipperary

Clonmel / Glen of Aherlow

To Book Call **+353-1-8084419** or www.irelandhotels.com

Fennessy's Hotel

Hotel ★ ★   Map 3 K 5

Gladstone Street, Clonmel,
Co. Tipperary
Tel: +353-52-612 3680
Email: info@fennessyshotel.com
Web: www.fennessyshotel.com
GPS: N +52° 21' 16.53"   W -7° 42' 7.69"

Location
Right in the centre of Clonmel, this beautiful Georgian building is easily located on Gladstone St. opposite the town's main church.

Property Highlights
All bedrooms are en suite and have security safes, DD phone, multi channel TV, hairdryer, tea/coffee facilities, some with jacuzzis. Family-run hotel. Elegant ambience throughout.

Local Attractions
Main shopping area, swimming pool, leisure centre, riverside walks are a stone's throw from our front door. Golf, hill walking, fishing, pony trekking. After your visit, you will wish to return.

B&B from: €35.00 - €50.00

Host(s): Richard & Esther Fennessy

Facilities

Open All Year

Hotel Minella & Leisure Club

Hotel ★ ★ ★ ★   Map 3 K 5

Coleville Road, Clonmel,
Co. Tipperary
Tel: +353-52-612 2388
Email: frontdesk@hotelminella.ie
Web: www.hotelminella.ie
GPS: N +52° 21' 10.30"   W -7° 41' 12.15"

Location
5 minutes from Clonmel Town Centre. Approx. 1 hour from Cork Airport, 1.5 hours from Shannon Airport, 2 hours from Dublin Airport, 1.5 hours from Rosslare Harbour.

Property Highlights
Family owned & operated, noted for personal service. 4 superior suites, with balcony overlooking grounds & river. 2 have outdoor hot tubs. Club Minella: 20m pool & kids pool, outdoor Canadian Hot Tub.

Local Attractions
Rock of Cashel, Cahir Castle, Swiss Cottage, Ormonde Castle, scenic drives e.g. The Vee.

B&B from: €55.00 - €130.00
Suites from: €200.00 - €300.00

Host(s): John Nallen

Activities   Facilities

Closed 22 - 29 December

Aherlow House Hotel and Lodges

Hotel ★ ★ ★   Map 3 I 6

Glen of Aherlow,
Co. Tipperary
Tel: +353-62-56153
Email: reservations@aherlowhouse.ie
Web: www.aherlowhouse.ie
GPS: N +52° 25' 28.78"   W -8° 11' 32.19"

Location
Take the main road from Cork to Dublin (N8). At the Cahir traffic circle take the Limerick road (N24) to Tipperary Town.
Garmin Sat Nav: Q5C-11-X24.

Property Highlights
Hunting lodge converted into an exquisitely furnished hotel & 4* self catering lodges. We welcome you to a peaceful atmosphere enhanced by a fine reputation for hospitality. Overlooks Glen of Aherlow.

Local Attractions
Walking, horseriding, cycling, rambling and fishing. Lowland walks follow the River Aherlow along the valley floor. More adventurous walkers will be tempted by the Galtee range.

B&B from: €60.00 - €70.00
Suites from: €200.00 - €200.00

Host(s): Ferghal & Helen Purcell

Facilities

Open All Year

To Book Call **+353-1-8084419** or www.irelandhotels.com

Co. Tipperary

Horse and Jockey / Nenagh / Templemore

Horse and Jockey Hotel

Hotel ★★★★　　　Map 7 J 7

Horse and Jockey,
Co. Tipperary
Tel: +353-504-44192
Email: info@horseandjockeyhotel.com
Web: www.horseandjockeyhotel.com
GPS: N +52° 36' 56.19"　W -7° 46' 32.64"

Location
Located 600m from Exit 6 off new M8 Cork-Dublin Motorway. 6km from major train station, Thurles within 1.5 hours of all major Irish cities.

Property Highlights
67 spacious & modern bedrooms. 10 dedicated & fully equipped conference rooms. Luxurious leisure centre & pool area & Elemis Spa with 7 treatment rooms. Renowned "Gift Horse Gallery" Gift Shop.

Local Attractions
Semple Stadium - GAA, Rock of Cashel, Cahir Castle, Coolmore Stud, 3 National Hunt Racecourses (Tipperary, Thurles & Clonmel), Thurles Golf Club.

B&B from: €75.00 - €90.00
Suites from: €190.00 - €220.00

Host(s): Tom Egan

Closed 25 - 26 December

Abbey Court Hotel, Lodges & Trinity Leisure Spa

Hotel ★★★　　　Map 6 I 8

Dublin Road, Nenagh,
Co. Tipperary
Tel: +353-67-41111
Email: info@abbeycourt.ie
Web: www.abbeycourt.ie
GPS: N +52° 51' 52.92"　W -8° 11' 24.37"

Location
Hotel located 5 minutes off N7, 30 minutes from Limerick, 45 minutes from Shannon, 90 minutes from Dublin.

Property Highlights
82 superior rooms, 25 4-star lodges, indoor pool, spa, crèche, extensive conference & meeting facilities, renowned for weddings, extensive gardens, landmark location. A Great National Hotel.

Local Attractions
Within 1 hour's drive of Lough Derg, Rock of Cashel, Limerick City, Bunratty Castle, County Cork, Shannon Airport. With golf, fishing & horse riding all nearby.

B&B from: €50.00 - €139.00

Host(s): Matthias Muller

Open All Year

Templemore Arms Hotel

Hotel ★★　　　Map 7 J 8

Main Street, Templemore,
Co. Tipperary
Tel: +353-504-31423
Email: info@templemorearms.com
Web: www.templemorearms.com
GPS: N +52° 47' 50.21"　W -7° 49' 59.93"

Location
Located at the foot of the Devil's Bit, the Templemore Arms Hotel is the ideal location for your perfect breakaway.

Property Highlights
The family-owned Templemore Arms Hotel is Tipperary's leading wedding venue and is famed for its weekly social dancing nights.

Local Attractions
The hotel is located at the foot of the Devil's Bit, 30 minutes away from the Rock of Cashel and Holycross Abbey.

B&B from: €40.00 - €55.00
Suites from: €99.00 - €139.00

Host(s): Dan Ward

Closed Christmas Day & Good Friday

B&B Rates are per Person Sharing per Night incl. Breakfast. Room/Suite Rates are per Room per Night. **See also page 08**

Co. Tipperary

To Book Call **+353-1-8084419** or www.irelandhotels.com

Thurles / Tipperary Town

Anner Hotel & Leisure Centre

Hotel ★ ★ ★   Map 7 J 7

Dublin Road, Thurles,
Co. Tipperary
Tel: +353-504-21799
Email: info@annerhotel.ie
Web: www.theannerhotel.ie
GPS: N +52° 40' 43.32"   W -7° 47' 46.74"

Location
Located on the outskirts of Thurles on the Dublin Road with train station 1km away.

Property Highlights
We offer guests a warm welcome, excellent food & friendly service in comfortable surroundings. Superb leisure centre, 18m pool, kiddies' pool, jacuzzi, steam room, sauna & gym. Conference facilities.

Local Attractions
Rock of Cashel, Lar Na Pairc, Holycross Abbey, Farney Castle, Silvermines. Ideal base for touring, golf, walking and leisure breaks.

B&B from: €60.00 - €95.00

Host(s): Michael Cleary

64

Facilities

Closed 25 - 27 December

Ballyglass Country House

Hotel ★ ★   Map 3 I 6

Glen of Aherlow Road,
Tipperary Town
Tel: +353-62-52104
Email: info@ballyglasshouse.com
Web: www.ballyglasshouse.com
GPS: N +52° 26' 31.23"   W -8° 9' 56.28"

Location
Ballyglass House is located 3km from Tipperary Town and just 3km from the breathtaking Glen of Aherlow.

Property Highlights
We are family-run, serving home cooked, locally sourced produce. Free internet access for our guests.

Local Attractions
The Glen of Aherlow Nature Park is just 3km away, Tipperary Golf Club 2km, Hillwalking 5km.

B&B from: €45.00 - €50.00

Host(s): The Byrne Family

10

Facilities

Closed 24 - 28 December

Ballykisteen Hotel & Golf Resort

Hotel ★ ★ ★ ★   Map 6 I 6

Limerick Junction,
Co. Tipperary
Tel: +353-62-33333
Email: info@ballykisteenhotel.com
Web: www.ballykisteenhotel.com
GPS: N +52° 30' 7.65"   W -8° 13' 0.45"

Location
Ballykisteen Hotel is centrally located. Dublin 2.5 hours, Galway 2 hours, Cork 1.5 hours, Limerick 30 mins. Just a short distance from Limerick Junction Railway Station, close to Tipperary Town.

Property Highlights
Situated amidst 170 acres of the former Ballykisteen Stud, the perfect haven of peace & tranquillity. Championship Golf Course, Serenity Day Spa & Kids Club. Adjacent to Railway Station & Racecourse.

Local Attractions
Tipperary Racecourse, Glen of Aherlow, Rock of Cashel, Thomond Park, Cahir Castle, Mitchelstown Caves.

B&B from: €50.00 - €76.50
Suites from: €125.00 - €178.00

Host(s): Stephen O'Connor

40

Activities   Facilities

Closed 25 - 26 December

---

250   Ireland South   B&B Rates are per Person Sharing per Night incl. Breakfast. Room/Suite Rates are per Room per Night. **See also page 08**

To Book Call **+353-1-8084419** or www.irelandhotels.com

Co. Waterford
Ardmore

Cliff House Hotel

Hotel ★ ★ ★ ★ Map 3 K 3

Ardmore,
Co. Waterford
Tel: +353-24-87800
Email: info@thecliffhousehotel.com
Web: www.thecliffhousehotel.com
GPS: N +52° 9' 8.72" W -7° 9' 46.45"

Location
Stunningly located on the side of a cliff overlooking Ardmore Bay, just on the edge of Ardmore Village in beautiful West Waterford.

Property Highlights
All bedrooms and public areas overlook the gorgeous views of Ardmore Bay - lovely outdoor terraces offering delicious food.

Local Attractions
St. Declan's Well, Ardmore. Lismore Castle, Lismore. Jameson Midleton Distillery, Cork. Waterford Crystal, Waterford. 5 beautiful beaches within walking distance and our own cliff walk.

B&B from: €90.00 - €122.50
Suites from: €300.00 - €450.00

Host(s): Adriaan Bartels

39

Facilities

Closed 24 - 27 December

Newtown Farm

Guesthouse ★ ★ ★ Map 3 K 3

Newtown, Grange, Ardmore, Via Youghal,
Co. Waterford
Tel: +353-24-94143
Email: farm@newtownfarm.com
Web: www.newtownfarm.com
GPS: N +51° 59' 48" W -7° 43' 30"

Location
Located just off N25 at Grange. The farm is 12 minutes from Youghal, 15 minutes from Dungarvan, 8 mins. from Ardmore. Cork Airport 40 mins., Waterford 40 mins.

Property Highlights
Hard Tennis Court, Steam Room. Set on its own land with a view of the Atlantic Ocean and the surrounding country side.

Local Attractions
Beach, Cliff Walk, Fishing, Golf.

B&B from: €36.00 - €40.00

Host(s): Teresa O'Connor

7

Facilities

Closed 31 October - 01 March

Round Tower Hotel (The)

Hotel ★ ★ Map 3 K 3

College Road, Ardmore,
Co. Waterford
Tel: +353-24-94494
Email: rth@eircom.net
GPS: N +51° 57' 1.86" W -7° 43' 37.41"

Location
Hotel on right before entering Main St. Ardmore. From Dungarvan: Follow N25, signposted Cork, turn left onto R673. From Youghal: Follow N25, signposted Waterford.

Property Highlights
Located within walking distance of village, historical sites and beaches. Ample parking and child friendly garden. Regular music sessions take place.

Local Attractions
A historical seaside village. Oldest Christian settlement in Ireland with 12th century round tower & cathedral. Annual Pattern Festival on 24th July. Close to beautiful sandy beaches for bathing.

B&B from: €45.00 - €65.00

Host(s): Aidan & Patricia Quirke

12

Facilities

Closed 20 December - 04 January

B&B Rates are per Person Sharing per Night incl. Breakfast. Room/Suite Rates are per Room per Night. See also page 08

Co. Waterford

To Book Call **+353-1-8084419** or www.irelandhotels.com

Ballymacarbry / Cappoquin / Dungarvan

Hanoras Cottage

Guesthouse ★ ★ ★ ★   Map 3 K 5

**Nire Valley, Ballymacarbry,
Co. Waterford**
Tel: +353-52-613 6134
Email: hanorascottage@eircom.net
Web: www.hanorascottage.com
GPS: N +52° 16' 38.62"   W -7° 38' 2.13"

Location
Located between Clonmel and Dungarvan in the Nire Valley, Ballymacarbry, Co. Waterford, Ireland.

Property Highlights
Understated luxury is the hallmark of our 4 star guesthouse accommodation. All of our bedrooms are spacious, thoughtfully furnished, with individual décor and all have jacuzzi baths.

Local Attractions
Ideal location for walkers of all grades, hill, forest or country road. Our 4* accommodation is a favourite with bird watchers, photographers & nature lovers. Golf nearby. Perfect for small weddings.

B&B from: €70.00 - €100.00

Host(s): The Wall Family

10

Facilities

Closed 20 - 28 December

Richmond House

Guesthouse ★ ★ ★ ★   Map 3 J 4

**Cappoquin,
Co. Waterford**
Tel: +353-58-54278
Email: info@richmondhouse.net
Web: www.richmondhouse.net
GPS: N +52° 8' 21.34"   W -7° 50' 48.15"

Location
Half mile outside Cappoquin. Private grounds with picturesque gardens. The River Blackwater is a half mile away and is famous for its fishing. Canoeing arranged.

Property Highlights
Richmond House was built in 1704 by the Earl of Cork. Richmond is now a 4* guesthouse & restaurant. All rooms are en suite with period finishings. Our restaurant uses mainly local produce.

Local Attractions
We are a 4 mins. drive from the Heritage Town of Lismore, 10 minutes from Mt. Mellerary, 15 minutes from the beautiful Vee Gap. We have fabulous fishing on the Blackwater. 18 hole golf courses nearby.

B&B from: €60.00 - €80.00

Host(s): Paul & Claire Deevy

9

Facilities

Closed 23 December - 15 January

Clonea Strand Hotel, Golf & Leisure

Hotel ★ ★ ★   Map 3 K 4

**Clonea, Dungarvan,
Co. Waterford**
Tel: +353-58-45555
Email: info@clonea.com
Web: www.clonea.com
GPS: N +52° 5' 39.93"   W -7° 32' 46.59"

Location
Our hotel overlooks the Blue Flag Clonea Strand, close to several mapped cycle routes and 3km from the market town of Dungarvan.

Property Highlights
It uniquely has 10 pin bowling and a spectacular golf course. The menus are dominated by fresh seafood.

Local Attractions
Ideally located to visit Lismore Castle, Waterford Crystal, the Comeragh Mountains, Round Tower in Ardmore, Cork and Waterford City.

Room Rate from: €59.00 - €129.00

Host(s): Mark Knowles

59

Facilities

Closed 23 - 25 December

252   Ireland South   B&B Rates are per Person Sharing per Night incl. Breakfast. Room/Suite Rates are per Room per Night. See also page 08

To Book Call **+353-1-8084419** or www.irelandhotels.com

Co. Waterford

Dungarvan / Dunmore East

Park Hotel, Leisure Centre & Holiday Homes

Hotel ★ ★ ★ Map 3 K 4

Shandon, Dungarvan,
Co. Waterford
Tel: +353-58-42899
Email: reservations@parkhoteldungarvan.com
Web: www.flynnhotels.com
GPS: N +52° 5' 40.52"   W -7° 37' 24.51"

Location
5 minutes from Dungarvan Town. On main Cork & Waterford Road. 20 minutes from Waterford Airport.

Property Highlights
Leisure Centre, WiFi, Holiday Homes, family friendly, kids club, exceptional food, Irish welcome, special offers.

Local Attractions
Blue Flag Beaches, 5 minutes walk from town centre, super golf courses, fishing, hill walking, pubs & clubs, shopping centre.

B&B from: €59.00 - €85.00

Host(s): Pierce Flynn

86

Activities **Facilities**

Closed 24 - 26 December

Seaview Guest House

Guesthouse ★ ★ ★ Map 3 K 4

Windgap, N25/Youghal Road, Dungarvan,
Co. Waterford
Tel: +353-58-41583
Email: info@seaviewdungarvan.com
Web: www.seaviewdungarvan.com
GPS: N +52° 2' 54.67"   W -7° 39' 39.08"

Location
Located on the road from Waterford to Cork.

Property Highlights
Our 8 rooms are large & bright, all en suite with TV, tea & coffee making facilities & DD telephone & wireless internet access & some with views over Dungarvan Bay. Ground floor rooms available.

Local Attractions
Visit miles of uncrowded beaches, climb local glacially carved mountains & lakes. Dungarvan, Gold Coast & West Waterford Golf Clubs nearby. Marine Bar with authentic Irish music, Famine Graveyard.

B&B from: €35.00 - €45.00

Host(s): Nora Fahey

8

Facilities

Closed 01 December - 31 January

Beach Guest House

Guesthouse ★ ★ ★ ★ Map 4 M 5

Lower Village, Dunmore East,
Co. Waterford
Tel: +353-51-383316
Email: beachouse@eircom.net
Web: www.dunmorebeachguesthouse.com
GPS: N +52° 9' 18.98"   W -6° 59' 42.52"

Location
Located by the beach in the centre of the village. Take first left in the village to the strand and we are on the left facing the sea.

Property Highlights
Luxury 4**** property with sea views, private car park, free WiFi, close to all amenities. Breakfast menu has an extensive choice.

Local Attractions
Picturesque fishing village with neat rows of thatched cottages, superb walks and sporting amenities. Championship golf courses within 10 miles.

B&B from: €35.00 - €45.00

Host(s): Breda Battles

7

Facilities

Closed 01 November - 28 February

B&B Rates are per Person Sharing per Night incl. Breakfast. Room/Suite Rates are per Room per Night. See also page 08

Ireland South 253

Co. Waterford

To Book Call **+353-1-8084419** or www.irelandhotels.com

Faithlegg / Lismore / Tramore

Faithlegg House Hotel | Lismore House Hotel | Beach Haven House

Hotel ★ ★ ★ ★ Map 4 M 5	Hotel ★ ★ ★ Map 3 J 4	Guesthouse ★ ★ ★ Map 4 L 5
Faithlegg, Co. Waterford	Main Street, Lismore, Co. Waterford	Tivoli Terrace, Waterford Road, Tramore, Co. Waterford
Tel: +353-51-382000	Tel: +353-58-72966	Tel: +353-51-390208
Email: reservations@fhh.ie	Email: info@lismorehousehotel.com	Email: beachhavenhouse@eircom.net
Web: www.faithlegg.com	Web: www.lismorehousehotel.com	Web: www.beachhavenhouse.com
GPS: N +52° 15' 29.17" W -7° 1' 30.99"	GPS: N +52° 8' 15.03" W -7° 55' 57.37"	GPS: N +52° 9' 56.52" W -7° 8' 43.74"

Location

Faithlegg House Hotel is located on the already renowned 18 hole championship golf course, overlooking the estuary of the River Suir.

Location

Lismore House Hotel is located in the centre of Lismore and is just 1 hour from Cork City and Wateford City.

Location

Located in Tramore just a few minutes walk to the beach, town centre, Splashworld and Racecourse. 7 miles from Waterford City.

Property Highlights

82 bedrooms, including 14 master rooms in the original house. A health and beauty club, comprehensive meeting, conference and event facilities.

Property Highlights

Built in 1797, the hotel has been completely restored & refurbished to retain the glory of its Georgian old-world style & charm and reflects the heritage of Lismore Castle and surrounds.

Property Highlights

Luxurious home with warm and friendly atmosphere. Free parking & WiFi. Extensive breakfast menu. All rooms en suite with TV, tea & coffee.

Local Attractions

Located six miles outside Waterford City, Faithlegg has a range of self catering holiday homes on site. An FBD Hotel, AA 4 star approved.

Local Attractions

Lismore Castle, Gardens and Heritage Centre and so much more are just minutes from our doorstep.

Local Attractions

5 miles of Beach, Amusement Park, 27 Hole Championship Golf Course, 4 Surf Schools, Horse Riding, many Restaurants & Pubs.

B&B from: €79.00 - €109.00
Suites from: €199.00 - €278.00

B&B from: €35.00 - €60.00

B&B from: €30.00 - €40.00

Host(s): Alison Redmond   82

Host(s): Pierce Connell   29

Host(s): Avery & Niamh Coryell   8

Activities   Facilities

Facilities

Closed 20 - 27 December

Open All Year

Open All Year

254   Ireland South   B&B Rates are per Person Sharing per Night incl. Breakfast. Room/Suite Rates are per Room per Night. **See also page 08**

Co. Waterford

Tramore

Grand Hotel

Hotel ★ ★ ★   Map 4 L 5

Tramore,
Co. Waterford
Tel: +353-51-381414
Email: thegrandehotel@eircom.net
Web: www.grand-hotel.ie
GPS: N +52° 9' 39.56" W -7° 9' 6.69"

Location
Located in the town centre overlooking Tramore Bay with shops, pubs and restaurants minutes walk away. 6kms from Waterford Airport, 9kms from Waterford City.

Property Highlights
Award-winning Doneraile Restaurant with sea views, Two Bars, Live Music, Family Friendly with Kids Club in Summer. Function & Conference centre.

Local Attractions
Discounts available with all attractions golf, surfing, leisure centre, horse riding, tennis courts, fishing trips – all are minutes away.

B&B from: €30.00 - €80.00

Host(s): Tom & Anna Treacy

70

Facilities

Open All Year

Top Two Visitor Attractions
Lismore, Co. Waterford.

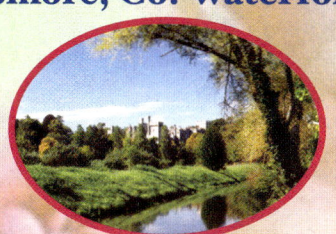

Lismore Castle Gardens & Lismore Castle Arts

Prince John first built a castle in Lismore in 1185, and a round tower, dating from the 13th century still stands today. Within the defensive walls of the castle, the gardens at Lismore provide spectacular views, and the herbaceous border gives an impressive show of colour throughout summer. There is also a fine selection of specimen magnolias, camellias, and rhododendrons, and a remarkable yew walk where Edmund Spenser is said to have written the 'Faerie Queen'. While wandering the gardens, visitors are invited to enjoy several pieces of contemporary sculpture, and encouraged to visit Lismore Castle Arts, which shows works by some of the worlds leading contemporary artists, providing a vibrant programme to be enjoyed by the local community and tourists alike. Visitors to the gardens are welcome to visit the gallery free of charge. Lismore Castle is the Irish home of the Duke of Devonshire and his family and, when not in residence, the castle may be rented, fully staffed, to guests.

Tel: 058 54424 Fax: 058 54896
E-mail: lismoreestates@eircom.net
Website: www.lismorecastle.com
www.lismorecastlearts.com
Open Daily 11am to 4pm from Mid April to 30th September

Admission charges:
€8 per Adult
€4 per Child
Special Rates for students, OAP's and Groups of 20 or more

Lismore Heritage Centre

Situated in the centre of the town, is a must for those who wish to experience the rich history of the town and its surroundings. Your host Brother Declan (alias Niall Toibin) will take you on a fascinating journey through time in "The Lismore Experience" – an exciting audio-visual presentation which tells the story of the town since St. Carthages arrival in 636AD. Also exhibition galleries on Monastic, Norman and Medieval Lismore and a science exhibition room on the life and works of Robert Boyle, 'the Father of Modern Chemistry' who was born at Lismore Castle. Guided tours of this monastic town leave the Heritage Centre at appointed times each day. New for 2011 Lismore Family Fun Experience Pack – Explore the natural environment in a fun way.

Open 9.30am – 5.30pm
Monday – Friday (year round)
10am – 5.30pm Saturday
(April – September)
12noon – 5.30pm Sunday
(April – September)

Closed 1pm – 2pm
(October – April)

Admission charges:
€5 per Adult
Kids go Free
Special rates for students and OAPs

Tel: 058 54975 Fax: 058 53009
e-mail: info@lismoreheritage.ie
www.discoverlismore.com

Co. Waterford

To Book Call **+353-1-8084419** or www.irelandhotels.com

Tramore / Waterford City

Majestic Hotel

Hotel ★ ★ ★   Map 4 L 5

Tramore,
Co. Waterford
Tel: +353-51-381761
Email: info@majestic-hotel.ie
Web: www.majestic-hotel.ie
GPS: N +52° 9' 47.20"   W -7° 8' 54.23"

Location
Located in Ireland's premier seaside resort, overlooking Tramore Bay and its 5km Beach. 10km Waterford City, 5km Waterford Airport.

Property Highlights
Award-winning 3* hotel recently refurbished to 4* standard. Family friendly with leisure facilities at Splashworld opposite hotel. Free car parking.

Local Attractions
Beautiful scenic walks and drives along the coast. Surfing, sailing, fishing, horse riding and tennis. Championship 27 hole golf course.

Room Rate from: €79.00 - €99.00

Host(s): Annette & Danny Devine   60

Activities   **Facilities**

Closed 24 - 26 December

O'Shea's Hotel

Hotel ★ ★ ★   Map 4 L 5

Strand Street, Tramore,
Co. Waterford
Tel: +353-51-381246
Email: info@osheas-hotel.com
Web: www.osheas-hotel.com
GPS: N +52° 9' 35.54"   W -7° 9' 1.03"

Location
Our hotel is located on the beach in downtown Tramore. 12km to Waterford Airport, 11km to Waterford City, 90km to Rosslare Harbour.

Property Highlights
Family friendly, owner managed, old world charm, renowned for good food. Same owners for 43 years. Great pub atmosphere. All rooms tastefully decorated with tea/coffee, TV, irons, hairdryers.

Local Attractions
Tramore Golf Club, Waterford Crystal Visitor Centre, Pony Trekking, Water Sports, Horse Racing, Angling, Greyhound Racing, Scenic Drives, The Beach.

B&B from: €40.00 - €75.00

Host(s): Joe & Noreen O'Shea   29

Activities   **Facilities**

Closed 24 - 26 December

Arlington Lodge Town House & Restaurant

Hotel ★ ★ ★ ★   Map 4 L 5

John's Hill,
Waterford City
Tel: +353-51-878584
Email: info@arlingtonlodge.com
Web: www.arlingtonlodge.com
GPS: N +52° 14' 58.89"   W -7° 6' 17.24"

Location
Located in Waterford City, 14km from Waterford Airport and 82km from Rosslare Europort. Cork 125km, Shannon 152km, Dublin 157km.

Property Highlights
Georgian surroundings with complementary broadband in every room. Maurice and his team make the perfect hosts for a memorable stay. Renowned restaurant.

Local Attractions
Arlington Lodge is the perfect base for touring the south east. The area boasts some of the most beautiful countryside in Ireland, with splendid scenery and miles of spectacular coastline.

B&B from: €55.00 - €95.00
Suites from: €170.00 - €220.00

Host(s): Maurice Keller   20

Facilities

Closed 24 December - 02 January

256   Ireland South   B&B Rates are per Person Sharing per Night incl. Breakfast. Room/Suite Rates are per Room per Night. **See also page 08**

To Book Call **+353-1-8084419** or www.irelandhotels.com

Co. Waterford
Waterford City

Athenaeum House Hotel

Hotel ★ ★ ★ ★   Map 4 L 5

Christendom, Ferrybank,
Waterford
Tel: +353-51-833999
Email: info@athenaeumhousehotel.com
Web: www.athenaeumhousehotel.com
GPS: N +52° 15' 38.56"   W -7° 5' 52.56"

Location
On the banks of the River Suir overlooking Waterford Harbour on 6 acres of lawn and woodland.

Property Highlights
Boutique Hotel with 29 bedrooms in garden and woodland setting with outdoor patio. Red Rosette awarded restaurant, meeting rooms, luxurious bedroom suites.

Local Attractions
Waterford Crystal is one of the highlights of Trail to Waterford, The Viking Triangle, Reginald's Tower. 10 golf courses within 20 minutes drive. Beautiful Coastline, Beaches & Comeragh Mountains.

B&B from: €40.00 - €75.00
Suites from: €140.00 - €240.00

Host(s): Mailo & Stan Power

29

Closed 01 January - 10 February

Coach House (The)

Guesthouse ★ ★ ★   Map 4 L 5

Butlerstown Castle, Butlerstown,
Cork Road, Waterford
Tel: +353-51-384656
Email: coachhse@iol.ie
Web: www.butlerstowncastle.com
GPS: N +52° 13' 41.36"   W -7° 11' 1.10"

Location
Situated in quiet countryside on the L4047, just off R680, 5 minutes from Waterford City. Airport 15 minutes, train station 10 minutes away.

Property Highlights
Historic country house set in secluded gardens including Victorian walled garden & ruins of 13th century tower house. "Butlerstown Castle" authorised for civil weddings/partnership ceremonies.

Local Attractions
Waterford Crystal, Mount Congreve Gardens, Waterford Viking Quarter, 5 Golf Courses, Beaches, Horse Trekking, Surfing, Water Sports, Megalithic Dolmens are all close by.

Room Rate from: €40.00 - €165.00

Host(s): Des O'Keeffe

7

Closed 01 November - 01 April

Dooley's Hotel

Hotel ★ ★ ★   Map 4 L 5

The Quay,
Waterford
Tel: +353-51-873531
Email: hotel@dooleys-hotel.ie
Web: www.dooleys-hotel.ie
GPS: N +52° 15' 46.46"   W -7° 6' 56.99"

Location
This family-run & managed hotel is located in the heart of historic Waterford City overlooking the waterfront. Close to bus and train station.

Property Highlights
Close to all amenities, catering for corporate & leisure guests. Enjoy the style & comfort of the Dry Dock Bar & New Ship Restaurant. Long tradition of hospitality, good food and friendliness.

Local Attractions
House of Waterford Crystal, Waterford Museum of Treasures, Waterford City Walking Tours, Reginald's Tower, Edmund Rice Heritage centre, Christ Church Cathedral, Bishop's Palace, Medieval Under Crofts.

B&B from: €35.00 - €99.00

Host(s): Tina & Margaret Darrer

113

Closed 24 - 28 December

B&B Rates are per Person Sharing per Night incl. Breakfast. Room/Suite Rates are per Room per Night. **See also page 08**   Ireland South   257

Co. Waterford

To Book Call **+353-1-8084419** or www.irelandhotels.com

Waterford City

Fitzwilton Hotel

Hotel ★ ★ ★ ★   Map 4 L 5

**Bridge Street,
Waterford**
Tel: +353-51-846900
Email: info@fitzwiltonhotel.ie
Web: www.fitzwiltonhotel.ie
GPS: N +52° 15' 47.78"   W -7° 7' 12.63"

Location
Located in the very heart of Waterford City. Only 2 minutes walk from the train station, bus station and city centre.

Property Highlights
Waterford City's only 4 star hotel, offers 88 rooms & suites, beauty salon, gym, restaurant Chez-K's, Met Bar Café, free on-site parking & WiFi.

Local Attractions
Walking distance from Waterford Crystal, Reginald's Tower, Waterford Museum, Christ Church Cathedral, John Robert's Square, city centre shopping & entertainment district.

B&B from: €42.50 - €85.00
Suites from: €179.00 - €349.00

Host(s): Aiden Fleming

88

Facilities

Closed 23 - 26 December

Granville Hotel

Hotel ★ ★ ★   Map 4 L 5

**Meagher Quay,
Waterford**
Tel: +353-51-305555
Email: stay@granville-hotel.ie
Web: www.granville-hotel.ie
GPS: N +52° 15' 43.58"   W -7° 6' 43.87"

Location
Prestigious city centre hotel overlooking the River Suir. In the heart of the city's historic, cultural, business & shopping centre. Close to bus & train stations.

Property Highlights
This family run hotels one of Ireland's oldest with significant historical connections. Friendliness, hospitality & good food are all part of a stay here.

Local Attractions
Waterford is blessed with a variety of landscape & environment, where every activity, sport, historic & cultural can be enjoyed against a backdrop of wonderful & exciting scenery.

B&B from: €40.00 - €110.00

Host(s): Ann & Liam Cusack

98

Activities **Facilities**

Closed 24 - 27 December

Portree House

Guesthouse ★ ★   Map 4 L 5

**10-11 Mary Street, Waterford City,
Co. Waterford**
Tel: +353-51- 874574
Email: info@portreeguesthouse.ie
Web: www.portreeguesthouse.ie
GPS: N +52° 15' 50.25"   W -7° 7' 15.06"

Location
Located just 3 minutes walk from both the train & bus stations.
Just 5 minutes walk to the city centre and its shops and attractions.

Property Highlights
From the moment you arrive at Portree House you will be greeted with a sense of warmth and luxury, Elegance exudes throughout this Georgian property. We also have hostel type accommodation available.

Local Attractions
The world famous Waterford Crystal Centre is just a stroll away. Easy reach of 4 top class golf courses. Fishing, equestrian & surfing activities are all close by.

Room Rate from: €39.00 - €99.00

Host(s): Christopher Walker

20

Facilities

Open All year

B&B Rates are per Person Sharing per Night incl. Breakfast. Room/Suite Rates are per Room per Night. **See also page 08**

HOUSE OF WATERFORD CRYSTAL

SPARK OF
CREATION

The House of Waterford Crystal
- Guided Tour of Prestige Factory
- Fascinating Visitor Centre
- Opulent Retail Store
- Coffee Shop

Exquisite pieces of crystal…
Created before your very eyes.

House of Waterford Crystal
The Mall, Waterford City, Ireland
Call: +353 (0)51 317 000
Email: houseofwaterfordcrystal@wwrd.com

www.waterfordvisitorcentre.com

Co. Waterford

To Book Call **+353-1-8084419** or www.irelandhotels.com

Waterford City

St. Albans Guesthouse

Guesthouse ★ ★ Map 4 L 5

**Cork Road,
Waterford**
Tel: +353-51-358171 / 379393
Email: stalbansbandb@yahoo.com
Web: www.stalbansbandb.com
GPS: N +52° 15' 5.43"   W -7° 7' 0.87"

Location
Ideally located minutes walk from Waterford City centre and Waterford Crystal. Close to Waterford Airport.

Property Highlights
Our very spacious superbly appointed rooms are all en suite with multi-channel TV, tea/coffee facilities and hairdryer. Secure parking at rear of premises. 4 championship golf courses in vicinity.

Local Attractions
Horse riding 3km. Tennis courts, swimming pool 2 minutes. Several local beaches and breathtaking scenery.

B&B from: €35.00 - €35.00

Host(s): Helen & Tom Mullally

8

Closed 20 - 30 December

Tower Hotel & Leisure Centre

Hotel ★ ★ ★ Map 4 L 5

**The Mall,
Waterford**
Tel: +353-51-862300
Email: reservations@thw.ie
Web: www.towerhotelwaterford.com
GPS: N +52° 15' 36.27"   W -7° 6' 17.97"

Location
Within walking distance of the train & bus station. Waterford Airport is approximately 12km from the hotel.

Property Highlights
Renu Treatment Rooms, complimentary WiFi throughout the hotel, car parking, leisure facilities, 20m pool, 3 dining options, Kids Club for Bank Holiday weekends & summer season.

Local Attractions
2 minutes walk from the newly opened 'House of Waterford Crystal' Visitor Centre. 15km from picturesque Dunmore East. Copper Coast Mini Farm, Suir Valley Railway, Dunmore East Adventure Centre.

B&B from: €35.00 - €100.00
Suites from: €110.00 - €250.00

Host(s): Alicia Maguire

135

Closed 24 - 28 December

Waterford Marina Hotel

Hotel ★ ★ ★ Map 4 L 5

**Canada Street,
Waterford**
Tel: +353-51-856600
Email: info@waterfordmarinahotel.com
Web: www.waterfordmarinahotel.com
GPS: N +52° 15' 30.03"   W -7° 6' 6.23"

Location
City Centre. 10 minutes walk to bus station. Short drive to train station, 15 minutes to Waterford Airport. 45 minutes Rosslare Harbour. Cork Airport 130km (N25). Dublin Airport 175km (M9).

Property Highlights
Nestled on the banks of the River Suir, with free on site parking. 81 guest rooms with WiFi. The Waterfront Bar & Restaurant are situated on the riverside offering wide, varied menus for all to enjoy.

Local Attractions
Minutes from the New House of Waterford Crystal & Viking Triangles plus great shopping and nightlife all on our doorstep. Also you can explore Tramore & Dunmore East within 15 minutes drive.

B&B from: €39.00 - €120.00

Host(s): Karen Dollery

81

Closed 18 - 29 December

260 Ireland South

B&B Rates are per Person Sharing per Night incl. Breakfast. Room/Suite Rates are per Room per Night. **See also page 08**

To Book Call **+353-1-8084419** or www.irelandhotels.com **Co. Waterford - Co. Wexford**

Waterford City / Barntown / Bunclody

Woodlands Hotel

Hotel ★ ★ ★   Map 4 L 5

Dunmore Road,
Waterford
Tel: +353-51-392700
Email: info@woodlandshotel.ie
Web: www.woodlandshotel.ie
GPS: N +52° 14' 21.11"   W -7° 3' 51.92"

Location
Located on the Dunmore Rd. In close proximity to all amenities. 5 minutes from Waterford City Centre. Close to all National Roads.

Property Highlights
Ample free car parking, wheelchair accessible, recently refurbished, superb leisure centre, spacious bedrooms, renowned wedding & conference venue.

Local Attractions
Dunmore East, Premier Golf Courses, close to Waterford Airport, Waterford Regional Hospital, House of Waterford Crystal, Tall Ships 2011.

Room Rate from: €49.00 - €100.00

Host(s): Barry Howard

47

Facilities

Closed 24 - 25 December

Stanville Lodge Hotel

Hotel ★ ★ ★   Map 4 N 6

Barntown,
Co. Wexford
Tel: +353-53-913 4300
Email: info@stanville.ie
Web: www.stanville.ie
GPS: N +52° 20' 24.92"   W -6° 34' 49.52"

Location
5km from Wexford Town, 25km from Rosslare, 40 minutes from Waterford, 50 minutes from Kilkenny.

Property Highlights
Exceptional Wedding Banquet Room. Relaxing reception with open fire and Italian marble floor. Kiddies play area.

Local Attractions
Irish National Heritage Park, Dunbrody Famine Ship, Johnstown Castle & Gardens, JFK Arboretum, Hook Lighthouse, Wexford Wildfowl Reserve, South East Coastal Drive.

B&B from: €27.50 - €70.00

Host(s): Anne Marie Neville

30

Facilities

Closed 25 - 27 December

Carlton Millrace Hotel & C-Spa

Hotel ★ ★ ★ ★   Map 8 N 7

Riversedge, Bunclody,
Co. Wexford
Tel: +353-53-937 5100
Email: reservations.millrace@carlton.ie
Web: www.carlton.ie/millrace
GPS: N +52° 39' 18.99"   W -6° 39' 21.21"

Location
On the edge of the Bunclody Golf & Fishing Club & the River Slaney. 75 minutes from M9/N11, 1 hour from Rosslare, local beaches 30 minutes, 15 minutes from train.

Property Highlights
60 well appointed bedrooms, Lady Lucy's fine dining rooftop restaurant, C-Spa with relaxing room & heated loungers, Kid's Club, free parking, 18m pool, gym, Carlton Rewards, entertainment on weekends.

Local Attractions
Bunclody Golf & Fishing Club, Mount Leinster Hill Walking, Altamont Gardens, Hook Lighthouse, JKF Park & Arboretum, sandy beaches, tennis courts, playground, sports centre, Rathood Centre.

B&B from: €49.00 - €129.00
Suites from: €180.00 - €310.00

Host(s): Edward Scally

60

Facilities

Closed 23 - 26 December

B&B Rates are per Person Sharing per Night incl. Breakfast. Room/Suite Rates are per Room per Night. *See also page 08*

Ireland South

Co. Wexford

To Book Call **+353-1-8084419** or www.irelandhotels.com

Curracloe / Enniscorthy / Foulksmills

Hotel Curracloe

Hotel ★ ★ Map 4 O 6

Curracloe,
Co. Wexford
Tel: +353-53-913 7308
Email: hotelcurracloe@eircom.net
Web: www.hotelcurracloe.com
GPS: N +52° 23' 36.53" W -6° 23' 38.17"

Location
Hotel Curracloe is situated only 5 minutes from Wexford Town and the train station.

Property Highlights
Our 29 rooms are en suite with modern facilities and our award-winning Blake Restaurant and Bar serve the best of home produce.

Local Attractions
We are located only minutes' drive from Blue and Green Flag Beaches and central to Golfing, Angling and Horse Riding Amenities.

B&B from: €35.00 - €60.00

Host(s): John & Margaret Hanrahan

29

Facilities

Open All Year

Riverside Park Hotel and Leisure Club

Hotel ★ ★ ★ ★ Map 4 N 6

The Promenade, Enniscorthy,
Co. Wexford
Tel: +353-53-923 7800
Email: info@riversideparkhotel.com
Web: www.riversideparkhotel.com
GPS: N +52° 29' 51.10" W -6° 34' 0.98"

Location
Picturesquely situated on the banks of the River Slaney on the edge of the bustling market town of Enniscorthy, only a short stroll from bus & train stations.

Property Highlights
Set in a scenic location & featuring a spectacular penthouse suite, luxurious bedrooms, Moorings & Alamo Restaurants, the Riverside Leisure Club, Conference & Banqueting Facilities, Promenade Bar.

Local Attractions
The Riverside Park Hotel & Leisure Club provides an excellent base for exploring the Sunny South East, with The National 1798 Centre, Irish National Heritage Park, Johnstown Castle & Golf all nearby.

B&B from: €47.50 - €80.00
Suites from: €150.00 - €200.00

Host(s): Jim Maher

60

Activities **Facilities**

Closed 24 - 26 Dec & 10 - 27 Jan

Horse and Hound Hotel

Hotel ★ ★ ★ Map 4 N 5

Ballinaboola, Foulksmills,
Co. Wexford
Tel: +353-51-428482
Email: info@horseandhoundhotel.ie
Web: www.horseandhoundhotel.ie
GPS: N +52° 22' 9.85" W -6° 50' 13.62"

Location
Set in Ballinaboola a picturesque village on the N25 from Rosslare, 5 miles from New Ross.

Property Highlights
Enjoy a meal in our locally renowned restaurant or a stay in tastefully decorated bedrooms.

Local Attractions
J.F. Kennedy Park, dunbrody Famine Ship, Ros Tapestry, Kennedy Homestead, Hook Lighthouse, Heritage Centre Wexford, Johnstown Castle & Gardens.

B&B from: €40.00 - €90.00

Host(s): Brendan & Christy Murphy

26

Facilities

Closed 24 - 26 December

B&B Rates are per Person Sharing per Night incl. Breakfast. Room/Suite Rates are per Room per Night. **See also page 08**

To Book Call **+353-1-8084419** or www.irelandhotels.com

Co. Wexford

Gorey

Amber Springs Hotel & Health Spa

Hotel ★ ★ ★ ★   Map 8 0 7

Wexford Road, Gorey,
Co. Wexford
Tel: +353-53-948 4000
Email: info@amberspringshotel.ie
Web: www.amberspringshotel.ie
GPS: N +52° 40' 5.28" W -6° 17' 25.16"

Location
Situated on the Sunny South east Coast, 50 minutes from Dublin, 120 minutes from Airport, walking distance from both the town centre and railway station.

Property Highlights
Designed to a superior 4* de luxe standard. 69 de luxe rooms, 11 executive suites. Outdoor play area, swings, slide, football pitch. Free parking. Full leisure centre & spa on site.

Local Attractions
10 minutes from Courtown Beach, Seal Sanctuary, Gravity Extreme Pirates Cove, Kia Ora Mini Farm.

B&B from: €85.00 - €115.00

Host(s): Sandra Wogan
80
Activities Facilities

Closed 24 - 27 December

Ashdown Park Hotel Conference

Hotel ★ ★ ★ ★   Map 8 0 7

Coach Road, Gorey,
Co. Wexford
Tel: +353-53-948 0500
Email: info@ashdownparkhotel.com
Web: www.ashdownparkhotel.com
GPS: N +52° 40' 44.01" W -6° 17' 5.40"

Location
Situated in Gorey, Co. Wexford, we are walking distance from local bus stop and train station and only 50 minutes from Dublin.

Property Highlights
We offer a pool, sauna, steam room, gym, kids' club, babysitters, DVD players, fridges, cots, camp beds. Award-winning restaurant, live traditional Irish music every Wed & live bands every Wed & Sun.

Local Attractions
Beaches, Kia Ora Mini Farm, Cinema, Quadding, Golf Courses, Horse Riding, Heritage Park, Woollen Mills, Amusements, Bowling, Crazy Golf, Shopping Centre.

B&B from: €55.00 - €99.00
Suites from: €160.00 - €295.00

Host(s): Liam Moran
79
Activities Facilities

Closed 24 - 26 December

Marlfield House

Hotel ★ ★ ★ ★   Map 8 0 7

Courtown Road R742, Gorey,
Co. Wexford
Tel: +353-53-942 1124
Email: info@marlfieldhouse.ie
Web: www.marlfieldhouse.com
GPS: N +52° 40' 06" W -6° 16' 46"

Location
Marlfield House is located 1 hour south of Dublin, outside Gorey on the Courtown Road R742.

Property Highlights
Beautifully restored country house on 36 acres of fine gardens & grounds. Rooms are fitted with beautiful antiques, paintings, flowers & marble bathrooms. 6 grand state rooms open onto the lake.

Local Attractions
Close to many Golf Courses including Courtown, Druids Glen, The European & Woodenbridge. Marlfield is a short drive from the monastic settlement at Glendalough, Powerscourt and 1 hour from Kilkenny.

B&B from: €90.00 - €125.00
Suites from: €180.00 - €350.00

Host(s): Mary, Ray, Margaret & Laura Bowe
19
Facilities

Closed 02 January - 04 March

Co. Wexford

To Book Call **+353-1-8084419** or www.irelandhotels.com

New Ross / Newbawn / Rosslare

Brandon House Hotel & Solas Croí Eco Spa

Hotel ★ ★ ★ ★   Map 4 M 6

New Ross,
Co. Wexford
Tel: +353-51-421703
Email: info@brandonhousehotel.ie
Web: www.brandonhousehotel.ie
GPS: N +52° 23' 13.39"   W -6° 56' 40.11"

Location
We are conveniently situated on the N25 in New Ross, between Waterford & Wexford - central to all attractions in the South East.

Property Highlights
Solas Croí Spa, Celtic Gardens, Five Senses Walk, Brandon Woods, Health & Leisure Club.

Local Attractions
Dunbrody Famine Ship, Ros Tapestry, JFK Arboretum, Hook Light House, JFK Homestead, Duncannon Fort, Tintern Abbey.

Room Rate from: €59.00 - €149.00
Suites from: €120.00 - €249.00

Host(s): Bettie-Marie Burger-Smit

79

Activities

Facilities

Closed 19 - 26 December

Cedar Lodge Hotel & Restaurant

Hotel ★ ★ ★ ★   Map 4 N 6

Carrigbyrne, Newbawn, (Near New Ross),
Co. Wexford
Tel: +353-51-428386
Email: info@cedarlodgehotel.ie
Web: www.cedarlodgehotel.ie
GPS: N +52° 21' 51.34"   W -6° 46' 25.80"

Location
Located in Carrigbyrne, County Wexford on the N25 primary route approximately halfway between Wexford town & New Ross. 30 minutes drive from Rosslare ferry port.

Property Highlights
The Cedar Lodge is a 20 bedroom four star hotel. The hotel restaurant is recommended by most good food guides. Fine food is complemented by our extensive wine list.

Local Attractions
Local hill walking, Wexford Opera Festival, Irish National Heritage Park, Wexford Beaches, John F. Kennedy Arboretum, Enniscorthy Greyhound Track, Wexford Racecourse and Tintern Abbey.

B&B from: €80.00 - €100.00

Host(s): Thomas Martin

20

Facilities

Closed 25 December - 01 February

Danby Lodge Hotel

Hotel ★ ★ ★   Map 4 O 5

Rosslare Road, Killinick,
Co. Wexford
Tel: +353-53-915 8191
Email: info@danbylodge.ie
Web: www.danbylodge.ie
GPS: N +52° 15' 28.29"   W -6° 26' 48.03"

Location
Situated in the sunny south-east of Ireland. Danby Lodge is located 5 minutes from Rosslare Euro Port & 10 minutes from Wexford Town.

Property Highlights
From the moment you walk through the door you receive a warm welcome, gracious hospitality & personal service that is 2nd to none. Beautifully appointed bedrooms, conference facilities, function room.

Local Attractions
Golf courses, horse riding, walking, Heritage Parks, beaches, fishing, angling.

B&B from: €45.00 - €60.00

Host(s): Aoife Sambou

29

Facilities

Open All Year

264   Ireland South   B&B Rates are per Person Sharing per Night incl. Breakfast. Room/Suite Rates are per Room per Night. See also page 08

To Book Call **+353-1-8084419** or www.irelandhotels.com

Co. Wexford
Rosslare / Rosslare Harbour

Kelly's Resort Hotel & Spa

Hotel ★ ★ ★ ★   Map 4 O 5

Rosslare,
Co. Wexford
Tel: +353-53-913 2114
Email: info@kellys.ie
Web: www.kellys.ie
GPS: N +52° 16' 31.77"   W -6° 23' 16.09"

Location
Located on Rosslare beach, only 5 minutes walk from Rosslare Strand and Station. Set in the heart of Rosslare village, only 20 minutes from Wexford Town.

Property Highlights
Enjoy numerous indoor/outdoor amenities, choice of local championship golf courses, luxurious "SeaSpa" with Thermal Suite hosting an array of heat & steam experiences & choice of holistic treatments.

Local Attractions
Johnstown Castle Gardens, Ferrycarrig Heritage Park, JFK Trust, Dunbrody Ship, Saltee Islands. Also golf, fishing, windsurfing & water sports centre.

B&B from: €88.00 - €104.00
Suites from: €390.00 - €460.00

Host(s): Bill Kelly

Activities   **Facilities**

Closed 05 December - 18 February

Ferryport House

Guesthouse ★ ★ ★   Map 4 O 5

Rosslare Harbour,
Co. Wexford
Tel: +353-53-913 3933
Email: info@ferryporthouse.com
Web: www.ferryporthouse.com
GPS: N +52° 14' 56.74"   W -6° 20' 36.49"

Location
Only a 2 minute drive from Rosslare Harbour, ferry & train terminal. 15 minutes from Wexford Town.

Property Highlights
Spacious en suite rooms, modern decor, excellent Fusion Restaurant offering a taste of the orient as well as fresh local seafood, steaks & vegetarian dishes.

Local Attractions
Numerous golf courses, horse riding, walking trails, cycling tracks, heritage parks, beaches adjacent, fishing & angling all close by.

B&B from: €30.00 - €45.00

Host(s): William & Patricia Roche

Facilities

Closed 24 - 26 December

Irish National Heritage Park
Ferrycarrig, Co. Wexford

Tel: +353 53 9120733
Fax: +353 53 9120911
Email: info@inhp.com
Web: www.inhp.com

"Over 9000 years of History"

Stroll through the park with its homesteads, places of ritual, burial modes and long forgotten remains.

Opening Times
May-Aug 9.30am-6.30pm
Sept-Apr 9.30am-5.30pm

Facilities:
• Guided Tours
• Restaurant
• Gift & Craft Shop
• Free car / coach parking

B&B Rates are per Person Sharing per Night incl. Breakfast. Room/Suite Rates are per Room per Night. See also page 08

Co. Wexford

To Book Call **+353-1-8084419** or www.irelandhotels.com

Rosslare Harbour / Wexford Town

Harbour View Hotel

Hotel ★ ★ ★   Map 4 O 5

Rosslare Harbour,
Co. Wexford
Tel: +353-53-916 1450
Email: info@harbourviewhotel.ie
Web: www.harbourviewhotel.ie
GPS: N +52° 15' 3.77"   W -6° 20' 31.53"

Location
Situated on the N25 close to ferries, trains & coaches - an ideal base for touring the sunny south east or stop-over.

Property Highlights
24 beautifully appointed guest rooms all en suite with modern facilities, some providing sea views. Gift shop, off licence within hotel and ample car parking facilities.

Local Attractions
Local amenities include golf, angling, horse riding and sandy beaches.

B&B from: €45.00 - €60.00

Host(s): James & Grace Chan

24

Facilities

Open All Year

Hotel Rosslare

Hotel ★ ★ ★   Map 4 O 5

Rosslare Harbour,
Co. Wexford
Tel: +353-53-913 3110
Email: reservations@hotelrosslare.ie
Web: www.hotelrosslare.ie
GPS: N +52° 14' 59.95"   W -6° 20' 11.97"

Location
Situated in Rosslare Harbour, we are the ideal base for touring the sunny south east and for ferry travel.

Property Highlights
Family-run hotel with many rooms with private balcony & sea view. Health & Beauty Salon and hairdressers on site. Seafood Restaurant & weekend entertainment.

Local Attractions
Angling, golf & horse riding nearby. Visit Kilmore Quay, Hook Lighthouse & Johnstown Castle.

B&B from: €40.00 - €75.00

Host(s): Deirdre Kelly

25

Facilities

Closed 24 - 26 December

Drinagh Court Hotel

Hotel ★ ★ ★   Map 4 N 6

Drinagh, near Wexford Town,
Co. Wexford
Tel: +353-53-914 3295
Email: info@drinaghcourthotel.com
Web: www.drinaghcourthotel.com
GPS: N +52° 18' 27.60"   W -6° 27' 25.27"

Location
The hotel is situated 1.5 miles from Wexford Town & 8 miles from Rosslare Ferryport.

Property Highlights
Family run hotel with a good reputation for friendly hospitality, good service & good food, at reasonable prices.

Local Attractions
Situated on the outskirts of Wexford Town & 15 mins. drive to Rosslare Ferryport. Within walking distance of cinema, bowling alley & pitch & putt course.

B&B from: €49.00 - €60.00

Host(s): Daniel & Susan Finnerty

21

Facilities

Closed 24 - 27 December

266 Ireland South   B&B Rates are per Person Sharing per Night incl. Breakfast. Room/Suite Rates are per Room per Night. See also page 08

To Book Call **+353-1-8084419** or www.irelandhotels.com

Co. Wexford
Wexford Town

Faythe Guest House

Guesthouse ★ ★ ★   Map 4 O 6

**The Faythe, Swan View,
Wexford**
Tel: +353-53-912 2249
Email: damian@faytheguesthouse.com
Web: www.faytheguesthouse.com
GPS: N +52° 19' 59"   W -6° 27' 25"

Location
We are located in Wexford town centre, 100km Dublin Airport, 40km Waterford Airport, 15km Rosslare Ferry Port. Toll bridge payment facility available.

Property Highlights
Motorbike friendly, breakfast cooked to order. Private family occasions & special dietary needs catered for. BBQ area, utensils provided. Early breakfast on request. Private off-road car park.

Local Attractions
National Heritage Park, Johnstown Castle, Hook Lighthouse, Kilmore Quay, Dunbrody Famine Ship, Wexford Opera House, 1798 Visitor Centre, Bowling, Children's Play Zones, Pools, Daily Walking Tours.

B&B from: €30.00 - €45.00

Host(s): Damian & Siobhan Lynch

10

Facilities

Closed 23 - 28 December

Ferrycarrig Hotel

Hotel ★ ★ ★ ★   Map 4 N 6

**Ferrycarrig,
Wexford**
Tel: +353-53-912 0999
Email: reservations@ferrycarrighotel.com
Web: www.ferrycarrighotel.ie
GPS: N +52° 20' 59.24"   W -6° 30' 16.28"

Location
One of the most scenic locations of any hotel in Ireland, overlooking the River Slaney, on the main Dublin Road (N11), 3kms outside of Wexford Town.

Property Highlights
All rooms offer spectacular views over the river. Outdoor dining for breakfast & bar food available (seasonal). 5* health & fitness club, 20m pool onsite. Health & Beauty Lodge, Hair Salon, Kids Club.

Local Attractions
Ferrycarrig Castle, River Slaney, Irish National Heritage Park.

B&B from: €65.00 - €150.00
Suites from: €250.00 - €350.00

Host(s): Jeanette O'Keeffe

102

Activities   **Facilities**

Open All Year

Maldron Hotel Wexford

Hotel ★ ★ ★   Map 4 O 6

**Ballindinas, Barntown,
Wexford**
Tel: +353-53-917 2000
Email: info.wexford@maldronhotels.com
Web: www.maldronhotels.com
GPS: N +52° 20' 14.94"   W -6° 30' 51.20"

Location
Located outside Wexford town en route to Rosslare Europort at the junction of the N11 and N25.

Property Highlights
Contemporary hotel boasting spacious guest rooms, pool and gymnasium, crèche and outdoor playground.

Local Attractions
Miles and miles of sandy beaches, picturesque fishing villages and a Viking maritime town.

B&B from: €49.00 - €109.00

Host(s): Rory Fitzpatrick

108

Facilities

Closed 21 - 27 December

B&B Rates are per Person Sharing per Night incl. Breakfast. Room/Suite Rates are per Room per Night. See also page 08

Co. Wexford

To Book Call **+353-1-8084419** or www.irelandhotels.com

Wexford Town

Newbay Country House

Guesthouse ★ ★ ★   Map 4 0 6

Newbay,
Wexford
Tel: +353-53-914 2779
Email: newbay@newbayhouse.com
Web: www.newbaycountryhouse.com
GPS: N +52° 19' 41.53"   W -6° 30' 50.10"

Location
Just 5 minutes drive from Wexford Town Centre, just off N11 / N25.

Property Highlights
Beautiful Georgian guesthouse in an idyllic countryside setting, with tennis courts, bouncy castles, gardens and a forest.

Local Attractions
Opera Festival, golf, angling, beaches (Blue Flag), Johnstown Castle & Agricultural Museum, National Heritage Park.

B&B from: €29.95 - €49.95

Host(s): Alex Scallan Jr

11

Activities Facilities

Closed 25 December

Riverbank House Hotel

Hotel ★ ★ ★   Map 4 0 6

The Bridge,
Wexford
Tel: +353-53-912 3611
Email: info@riverbankhousehotel.com
Web: www.riverbankhousehotel.com
GPS: N +52° 20' 40.52"   W -6° 27' 18.61"

Location
Located on private grounds at the foot of Wexford bridge, a short stroll from the bustling streets of Wexford town centre, the hotel gazes onto the River Slaney.

Property Highlights
The River Bar's beautiful views & spectacular sunsets offers a room of superb elegance. 'Windows' restaurant, in the professional charge of David Furlong offers an exciting à la carte menu.

Local Attractions
Local activities include golf, beaches, horse riding, angling, Europe's oldest lighthouse at Hook Head, The Irish National Heritage Park, replica famine ship at New Ross, restaurants & nightlife.

B&B from: €39.00 - €85.00

Host(s): Colm Campbell

23

Activities Facilities

Closed 25 December & Good Friday

St. George Guest House

Guesthouse ★ ★   Map 4 0 6

Upper Georges Street,
Wexford
Tel: +353-53-914 3474
Email: info@stgeorgeguesthouse.com
Web: www.stgeorgeguesthouse.com
GPS: N +52° 20' 22.14"   W -6° 28' 0.40"

Location
5 minutes walk to bus & train station. 90 minutes to Dublin, 40 minutes to Waterford, 15 minutes to Rosslare, 5 minutes walk to the town centre, 5 minutes to opera house.

Property Highlights
The building retains some of its 100 year old history. All rooms are modern with multi-channel TV, tea & coffee making facilities, WiFi & free car parking available.

Local Attractions
Wexford Opera House, venue for regular shows & concerts. Nearby many good fishing spots, local knowledge available. 4 attractive golf course within 20 minutes drive.

B&B from: €35.00 - €45.00

Host(s): Michael Power

10

Facilities

Closed 20 December - 20 January

268 Ireland South   B&B Rates are per Person Sharing per Night incl. Breakfast. Room/Suite Rates are per Room per Night. **See also page 08**

To Book Call **+353-1-8084419** or www.irelandhotels.com

Co. Wexford
Wexford Town

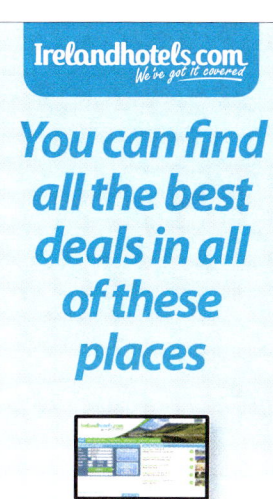

Website

Mobile App

Printed Guide

facebook.com/irelandhotels

irelandhotels.com/onlineguide

Talbot Hotel Conference and Leisure Centre

Hotel ★ ★ ★ ★   Map 4 0 6

On The Quay,
Wexford Town
Tel: +353-53-912 2566
Email: sales@talbothotel.ie
Web: www.talbothotel.ie
GPS: N +52° 20' 8.53"   W -6° 27' 26.38"

Location
Overlooking the Marina in the heart of Wexford Town, the Talbot Hotel dates back to 1905 and offers all that is best in traditional hospitality.

Property Highlights
Luxurious guestrooms. Ballast Bank Bar & Grill with live music. Award-winning Oyster Lane Restaurant. Conference Centre, Quay leisure Centre.

Local Attractions
Complimentary guest parking. Perfect for visiting Wexford's Opera House, Quayfront, Johnstown Castle & Gardens, Hook Lighthouse, Dunbrody Famine Ship and many shops & restaurants.

B&B from: €49.00 - €90.00

Host(s): Declan Moriarty

107

Activities   Facilities

Closed 24 - 26 December

Whites of Wexford

Hotel ★ ★ ★ ★   Map 4 0 6

Abbey Street,
Wexford
Tel: +353-53-912 2311
Email: info@whitesofwexford.ie
Web: www.whitesofwexford.ie
GPS: N +52° 20' 25.28"   W -6° 27' 50.68"

Location
Centrally located in historic Wexford Town, Whites is an ideal location to explore the sunny South East, within close proximity to bus & Wexford train station & Rosslare Europort.

Property Highlights
157 luxury bedrooms, tranquillity spa, leisure centre, cryotherapy clinic, outdoor courtyard, Terrace Restaurant, Library Bar & car parking. Something for everyone!

Local Attractions
Local attractions include Wexford Opera House, Wexford Arts Centre, Wexford Heritage Park, Dunbrody Famine Ship, Hook Lighthouse, sandy beaches & quay front walks.

B&B from: €55.00 - €105.00
Suites from: €250.00 - €450.00

Host(s): Peter Wilson

157

Facilities

Closed 24 - 26 December

B&B Rates are per Person Sharing per Night incl. Breakfast. Room/Suite Rates are per Room per Night. See also page 08

Enjoy SMITHWICK'S Sensibly. Visit drinkaware.ie

Judge it for yourself.

The international judges awarded Smithwick's Superior Irish Ale a Gold Medal in the 2010 Monde Selection Awards. Why not judge it for yourself?

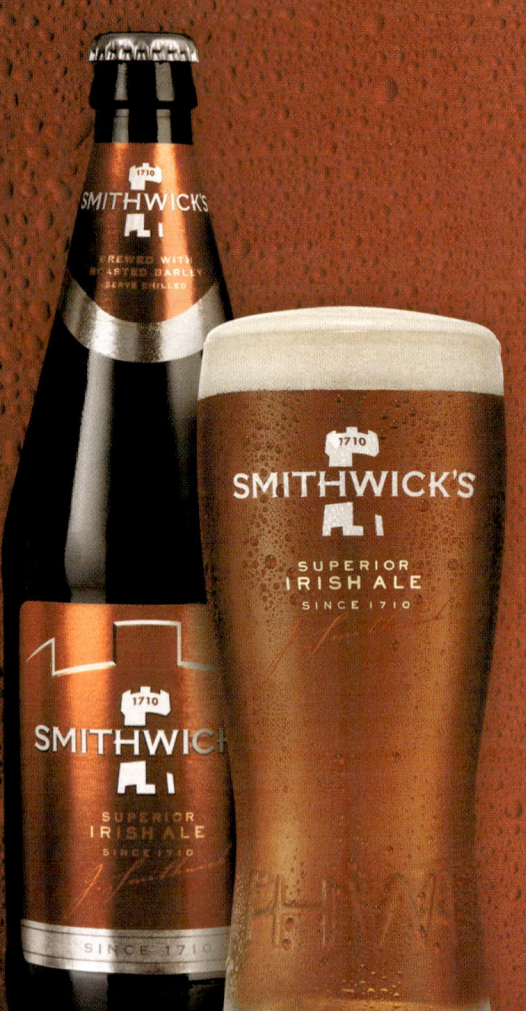

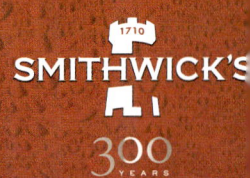

Golf
2011

As competitors and worldwide audiences discovered at the Ryder Cup in 2006 and the Walker Cup in 2007, golfing in Ireland is not quite like golfing in any other place on earth. Here, the game has long been part of the national culture and is for everyone - that includes you! With its rugged landscape, Ireland provides great golf courses in magnificent locations, with many links courses perched on the edge of the Atlantic Ocean. And they are relatively uncrowded.

So get in the swing - come golfing in Ireland!

Irelandhotels.com
We've got it covered

Golfing In Ireland
...where to stay when you play!

We invite you to sample the golf, the countryside and the friendship of the Irish people and then to stay in some of Ireland's most charming accommodation. We have listed a range of hotels and guesthouses which are either situated on or close to a golf course. Your host will assist you if necessary in arranging your golfing requirements including tee reservations and green fee charges. A full description of the hotels and guesthouses may be seen by consulting the relevant page number below.
Listings are by Region, County, Premises Name in alphabetical order.

Ireland West
Co. Clare

Dough Mor Lodge
Lahinch, Co. Clare
Tel: +353-65-708 2063 ....Page 42
Arrangements with Golf Courses:
Lahinch Golf Club (36 holes), Doonbeg Golf Club, Kilrush, Kilkee, East Clare, Shannon, Dromoland Castle
Facilities available:

Halpin's Townhouse Hotel
Kilkee, Co. Clare
Tel: +353-65-905 6032 ....Page 40
Arrangements with Golf Courses:
Ballybunion, Lahinch, Kilkee, Doonbeg, Woodstock, Shannon
Green Fees from: €40.00
Facilities available:

Sancta Maria Hotel
Lahinch, Co. Clare
Tel: +353-65-708 1041 ....Page 43
Arrangements with Golf Courses:
Lahinch Championship Golf Links, Lahinch Castle, Doonbeg, Woodstock, Dromoland, Spanish Point
Green Fees from: €40.00
Facilities available:

Temple Gate Hotel
Ennis, Co. Clare
Tel: +353-65-682 3200 ....Page 39
Arrangements with Golf Courses:
Woodstock, Ennis, Lahinch, East Clare, Doonbeg, Dromoland
Green Fees from: €20.00
Facilities available:

Vaughan Lodge and Seafood Restaurant
Lahinch, Co. Clare
Tel: +353-65-708 1111 ....Page 44
Arrangements with Golf Courses:
Lahinch, Doonbeg, Spanish Point, Dromoland, Kilrush, Ennis
Green Fees from: €100.00
Facilities available:

Co. Donegal

Arnolds Hotel
Dunfanaghy, Co. Donegal
Tel: +353-74-913 6208 ....Page 49
Arrangements with Golf Courses:
Dunfanaghy 18 Hole Links, Cloughaneely 9 Hole Parkland, Rosapenna 36 Hole Links, Cruit Island 9 Hole Links, Portsalon 18 Hole Links, Letterkenny 18 Hole Parkland
Green Fees from: €26.00
Facilities available:

Best Western Milford Inn Hotel & Natural Wellness
Letterkenny, Co. Donegal
Tel: +353-74-915 3313 ....Page 52
Arrangements with Golf Courses:
Portsalon, Rosapenna, Letterkenny, Dunfanaghy, Ballyliffin, Letterkenny
Green Fees from: €35.00
Facilities available:

Castle Grove Country House Hotel
Letterkenny, Co. Donegal
Tel: +353-74-915 1118 ....Page 52
Arrangements with Golf Courses:
Portsalon, Letterkenny, Rosapenna, Ballyliffin, Murvagh
Green Fees from: €50.00
Facilities available:

Downings Bay Hotel
Downings, Co. Donegal
Tel: +353-74-915 5586 ....Page 49
Arrangements with Golf Courses:
Rosapenna Links, Dunfanaghy, Portsalon, Letterkenny
Green Fees from: €25.00
Facilities available:

Great Northern Hotel
Bundoran, Co. Donegal
Tel: +353-71-984 1204 ....Page 47
Golf Course(s) On Site:
1 x 18 Hole Golf Course(s)
Arrangements with Golf Courses:
Donegal, Strandhill, Rosses Point
Green Fees from: €35.00
Facilities available:

Jackson's Hotel, Conference & Leisure Centre
Ballybofey, Co. Donegal
Tel: +353-74-913 1021 ....Page 45
Arrangements with Golf Courses:
Ballybofey and Stranorlar, Murvagh, Cruit Island, Portsalon, Dunfanaghy
Green Fees from: €20.00
Facilities available:

 All inclusive Golf Package
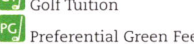 Golf Tuition
 Golf Cart
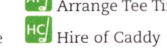 Arrange Tee Times
Hire Of Clubs
Preferential Green Fees
Transport To Course
Hire of Caddy

Golfing In Ireland
...where to stay when you play!

Solis Lough Eske Castle
Donegal Town, Co. Donegal
Tel: +353-74-972 5100 ....Page 49
Arrangements with Golf Courses:
Donegal (Murvagh), Narin/Portnoo, Ballyliffin
Green Fees from: €35.00
Facilities available:

Waters Edge (The)
Rathmullan, Co. Donegal
Tel: +353-74-915 8182 ....Page 54
Arrangements with Golf Courses:
Portsalon, Letterkenny, Rosapenna, Dunfanaghy, Ballyliffin
Green Fees from: €35.00
Facilities available:

Co. Galway

Claregalway Hotel (The)
Galway City, Co. Galway
Tel: +353-91-738300 ....Page 62
Arrangements with Golf Courses:
Cregmore Park Golf Course
Green Fees from: €35.00
Facilities available:

Lady Gregory Hotel, Conference & Leisure Club
Gort, Co. Galway
Tel: +353-91-632333 ....Page 70
Arrangements with Golf Courses:
Gort
Green Fees from: €30.00
Facilities available:

Lough Rea Hotel & Spa
Loughrea, Co. Galway
Tel: +353-91-880088 ....Page 73
Arrangements with Golf Courses:
Lough Rea Golf Club
Green Fees from: €15.00
Facilities available:
GP CH PG TC

Raheen Woods Hotel Tranquillity Spa & Kardio Kidz
Athenry, Co. Galway
Tel: +353-91-875888 ....Page 55
Arrangements with Golf Courses:
Athenry Golf Club, Cregmore Park Golf Club
Green Fees from: €35.00
Facilities available:

Shannon Oaks Hotel & Country Club
Portumna, Co. Galway
Tel: +353-90-974 1777 ....Page 75
Arrangements with Golf Courses:
Portumna Golf Course, Birr Golf Club, Glasson Golf Club, East Clare, Galway Bay, Nenagh Golf Course
Green Fees from: €25.00
Facilities available:

Twelve (The)
Galway City, Co. Galway
Tel: +353-91-597000 ....Page 69
Arrangements with Golf Courses:
Barna Golf Course
Green Fees from: €35.00
Facilities available:
GP AT PG

Co. Leitrim

Landmark Hotel
Carrick-on-Shannon, Co. Leitrim
Tel: +353-71-962 2222 ....Page 78
Arrangements with Golf Courses:
Carrick Golf Club
Green Fees from: €20.00
Facilities available:

Co. Limerick

Fitzgeralds Woodlands House Hotel & Spa
Adare, Co. Limerick
Tel: +353-61-605100 ....Page 79
Arrangements with Golf Courses:
Adare Manor Golf Club, Adare Golf Club, Newcastle West, Charleville, Limerick County Golf Club, Castletroy Golf Club
Green Fees from: €32.00
Facilities available:

Co. Mayo

Ashford Castle
Cong, Co. Mayo
Tel: +353-94-954 6003 ....Page 87
Golf Course(s) On Site:
1 x 9 Hole Golf Course(s)
Facilities available:
GT GC CH

Castlecourt Hotel Spa, Leisure, Conference
Westport, Co. Mayo
Tel: +353-98-55088 ....Page 90
Arrangements with Golf Courses:
Westport, Ballinrobe, Castlebar, Belmullet, Clew Bay, Enniscrone
Green Fees from: €30.00
Facilities available:

Downhill House Hotel & Eagles Leisure Club
Ballina, Co. Mayo
Tel: +353-96-21033 ....Page 84
Arrangements with Golf Courses:
Ballina, Enniscrone, Carne (Belmullet), Rosses Point, Strandhill, Westport, Claremorris, Ballinrobe, Castlebar, Tubbercurry, Swinford
Green Fees from: €35.00
Facilities available:

 All inclusive Golf Package
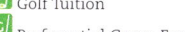 Golf Tuition
 Golf Cart
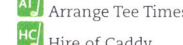 Arrange Tee Times
CH Hire Of Clubs
PG Preferential Green Fees
TC Transport To Course
HC Hire of Caddy

Golfing In Ireland
...where to stay when you play!

Co. Mayo CONTINUED

Healys Restaurant & Fishing Lodge
Pontoon, Co. Mayo
Tel: +353-94-925 6443 ....Page 89
Arrangements with Golf Courses:
Castlebar, Ballina, Westport, Enniscrone, Carne, Swinford
Green Fees from: €20.00
Facilities available:

Mill Times Hotel Westport
Westport, Co. Mayo
Tel: +353-98-29200 ....Page 92
Arrangements with Golf Courses:
Westport Golf Club, Carne Golf Club, Enniscrone Golf Club, Connemara Golf Club, Ballinrobe & Castlebar
Green Fees from: €25.00
Facilities available:

Mount Falcon
Ballina, Co. Mayo
Tel: +353-96-74472 ....Page 84
Arrangements with Golf Courses:
Enniscrone, Carne Belmullet, Rosses Point, Ballinrobe, Westport and Castlebar
Green Fees from: €55.00
Facilities available:

Sea Rod Inn
Belmullet, Co. Mayo
Tel: +353-97-86767 ....Page 85
Arrangements with Golf Courses:
Carne, Belmullet, New Doohoma Par 3
Green Fees from: €50.00
Facilities available:

Westport Plaza Hotel
Spa, Leisure, Conference
Westport, Co. Mayo
Tel: +353-98-51166 ....Page 93
Arrangements with Golf Courses:
Westport, Ballinrobe, Belmullet, Clew Bay, Enniscrone, Castlebar
Green Fees from: €30.00
Facilities available:

Westport Woods Hotel & Spa
Westport, Co. Mayo
Tel: +353-98-25811 ....Page 93
Arrangements with Golf Courses:
Westport, Castlebar, Ballinrobe, Clew Bay, Carne (Belmullet)
Green Fees from: €35.00
Facilities available:

Wyatt Hotel
Westport, Co. Mayo
Tel: +353-98-25027 ....Page 93
Arrangements with Golf Courses:
Westport Golf Club, Castlebar Golf Club, Ballinrobe Golf Club, Carne Golf Links
Green Fees from: €35.00
Facilities available:

Co. Sligo

Castle Dargan Golf Hotel Wellness
Ballygawley, Co. Sligo
Tel: +353-71-911 8080 ....Page 94
Golf Course(s) On Site:
1 x 18 Hole Golf Course(s)
Arrangements with Golf Courses:
County Sligo Golf Club, Rosses Point
Green Fees from: €40.00
Facilities available:

Diamond Coast Hotel
Enniscrone, Co. Sligo
Tel: +353-96-26000 ....Page 95
Arrangements with Golf Courses:
Enniscrone Golf Club, Carne Golf Links, Sligo Golf Club
Green Fees from: €40.00
Facilities available:

Radisson Blu Hotel & Spa Sligo
Sligo Town, Co. Sligo
Tel: +353-71-914 0008 ....Page 96
Arrangements with Golf Courses:
Co. Sligo Golf Club, Rosses Point
Green Fees from: €40.00
Facilities available:

Yeats Country Hotel, Spa & Leisure Club
Rosses Point, Co. Sligo
Tel: +353-71-917 7211 ....Page 96
Arrangements with Golf Courses:
Co. Sligo, Strandhill, Enniscrone, Bundoran, Castle Dargan, Murvagh
Green Fees from: €50.00
Facilities available:

Northern Ireland

Co. Antrim

Bayview Hotel
Bushmills, Co. Antrim
Tel: +44-28-2073 4100 ......Page 103
Arrangements with Golf Courses:
Royal Portrush, Rathmore, Portstewart, Castlerock, Ballycastle, Bushfoot
Green Fees from: £20.00
Facilities available:

Bushmills Inn Hotel
Bushmills, Co. Antrim
Tel: +44-28-2073 3000 ......Page 104
Arrangements with Golf Courses:
Royal Portrush, Portstewart, Castlerock, Ballycastle, Bushfoot, Gracehill
Facilities available:

274

 All inclusive Golf Package
Hire Of Clubs
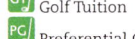 Golf Tuition
Preferential Green Fees
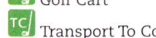 Golf Cart
Transport To Course
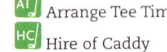 Arrange Tee Times
Hire of Caddy

Golfing In Ireland
...where to stay when you play!

Hilton Templepatrick
Templepatrick, Co. Antrim
Tel: +44-28-9443 5500 ......Page 105
Golf Course(s) On Site:
1 x 18 Hole Golf Course(s)
Green Fees from: £25.00
Facilities available:

Ramada Portrush
Portrush, Co. Antrim
Tel: +44-28-7082 6100 ......Page 104
Arrangements with Golf Courses:
Royal Portrush, Portstewart,
Castlerock, Ballycastle, Bushfoot,
Gracehill, Galgorm Castle
Green Fees from: £60.00
Facilities available:

Belfast City

Malone Lodge Hotel & Apartments
Belfast City
Tel: +44-28-9038 8000 ......Page 106
Arrangements with Golf Courses:
Malone Golf Club
Green Fees from: £40.00
Facilities available:

Co. Derry

Radisson Blu Roe Park Resort
Limavady, Co. Derry
Tel: +44-28-7772 2222 ......Page 108
Golf Course(s) On Site:
1 x 18 Hole Golf Course(s)
Arrangements with Golf Courses:
Roe Park Golf Club, Radisson Blu
Roe Park Resort
Green Fees from: £25.00
Facilities available:

Co. Down

Burrendale Hotel, Country Club & Spa
Newcastle, Co. Down
Tel: +44-28-4372 2599 ......Page 109
Arrangements with Golf Courses:
Royal County Down, Kilkeel,
Downpatrick, Ardglass, Spa, Bright
Facilities available:

Co. Fermanagh

Mahon's Hotel
Irvinestown, Co. Fermanagh
Tel: +44-28-6862 1656 ......Page 110
Arrangements with Golf Courses:
Castle Hume Golf Course,
Enniskillen Golf Club, Murvagh
Golf Club, Nick Faldo's Course at
Lough Erne Resort
Facilities available:

Dublin & Ireland East

Co. Cavan

Crover House Hotel & Golf Club
Mountnugent, Co. Cavan
Tel: +353-49-854 0206 ......Page 118
Golf Course(s) On Site:
1 x 9 Hole Golf Course(s)
Green Fees from: €15.00
Facilities available:

Radisson Blu Farnham Estate Hotel
Cavan Town, Co. Cavan
Tel: +353-49-437 7700 ......Page 118
Golf Course(s) On Site:
1 x 18 Hole Golf Course(s)
Green Fees from: €35.00
Facilities available:

Slieve Russell Hotel Golf & Country Club
Ballyconnell, Co. Cavan
Tel: +353-49-952 6444 ......Page 117
Golf Course(s) On Site:
1 x 18 Hole Golf Course(s)
1 x Par 3 Golf Course(s)
Green Fees from: €30.00
Facilities available:

Co. Dublin

Aberdeen Lodge
Dublin City, Co. Dublin
Tel: +353-1-283 8155 ....Page 122
Arrangements with Golf Courses:
St. Margarets, Portmarnock,
K Club, Elm Park, Carton House,
Druids Glen
Green Fees from: €60.00
Facilities available:

Castleknock Hotel and Country Club
Dublin City, Co. Dublin
Tel: +353-1-640 6300 ....Page 129
Golf Course(s) On Site:
1 x 18 Hole Golf Course(s)
Arrangements with Golf Courses:
Luttrellstown, Carton House,
Citywest, Castleknock Golf
Course, Westmanstown,
St. Margarets
Green Fees from: €40.00
Facilities available:

Charleville Lodge
Dublin City, Co. Dublin
Tel: +353-1-838 6633 ....Page 130
Arrangements with Golf Courses:
St. Margaret's, Luttrellstown, The
Links, Portmarnock, The Island
Golf Links
Green Fees from: €70.00
Facilities available:

 All inclusive Golf Package   Golf Tuition   Golf Cart    Arrange Tee Times

Hire Of Clubs   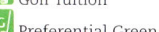 Preferential Green Fees   Transport To Course   Hire of Caddy

...where to stay when you play!

Co. Dublin CONTINUED

Clontarf Castle Hotel
Dublin City, Co. Dublin
Tel: +353-1-833 2321 ....Page 131
Arrangements with Golf Courses:
Royal Dublin, St. Margaret's,
Portmarnock, St. Anne's, Clontarf,
Malahide
Green Fees from: €50.00
Facilities available:

Deer Park Hotel Golf & Spa
Howth, Co. Dublin
Tel: +353-1-832 2624 ....Page 147
Golf Course(s) On Site:
2 x 9 Hole Golf Course(s)
1 x 18 Hole Golf Course(s)
1 x Par 3 Golf Course(s)
Green Fees from: €10.00
Facilities available:

Grand Hotel
Malahide, Co. Dublin
Tel: +353-1-845 0000 ....Page 149
Arrangements with Golf Courses:
Portmarnock GC, Malahide GC,
The Island GC, Swords GC,
St. Margarets, Royal Dublin
Green Fees from: €60.00
Facilities available:

Gresham (The)
Dublin City, Co. Dublin
Tel: +353-1-874 6881 ....Page 135
Arrangements with Golf Courses:
Royal Dublin, Portmarnock,
St. Margaret's, The Island,
St. Anne's, Malahide
Facilities available:

Redbank House Guesthouse & Restaurant
Skerries, Co. Dublin
Tel: +353-1-849 1005 ....Page 150
Arrangements with Golf Courses:
Skerries, Laytown, Bettystown,
Baltray, Portmarnock,
St. Margaret's, Donabate
Green Fees from: €30.00
Facilities available:

Waterside House Hotel & Signal Restaurant
Donabate, Co. Dublin
Tel: +353-1-843 6153 ....Page 119
Arrangements with Golf Courses:
Donabate, Turvey, Beaverstown,
Balcarrick, The Island Links,
St. Margaret's
Green Fees from: €35.00
Facilities available:

Co. Kildare

K Club (The)
Straffan, Co. Kildare
Tel: +353-1-601 7200 ....Page 156
Golf Course(s) On Site:
2 x 18 Hole Golf Course(s)
Green Fees from: €95.00
Facilities available:

Maudlins House Hotel
Naas, Co. Kildare
Tel: +353-45-896999 ....Page 154
Arrangements with Golf Courses:
Naas Golf Club, The Heritage
Killenard, Craddockstown Golf
Club, Knockanally Golf Club,
Palmerstown House, K Club,
Straffan
Green Fees from: €50.00
Facilities available:

Westgrove Hotel
Clane, Co. Kildare
Tel: +353-45-989900 ....Page 152
Arrangements with Golf Courses:
Millicent GC, Killeen GC,
Craddockstown GC, Knockanally
GC, K Club, Carton House
Facilities available:

Co. Laois

Heritage Golf & Spa Resort (The)
Killenard, Co. Laois
Tel: +353-57-864 5500 ......Page 157
Golf Course(s) On Site:
1 x 9 Hole Golf Course(s)
1 x 18 Hole Golf Course(s)
Green Fees from: €40.00
Facilities available:

Co. Longford

Annaly Hotel
Longford Town, Co. Longford
Tel: +353-43-334 3690 ......Page 158
Arrangements with Golf Courses:
Longford, Ballyconnell, Glasson,
Mullingar, Roscommon
Facilities available:

Longford Arms Hotel, Spa & Leisure Centre
Longford Town, Co. Longford
Tel: +353-43-334 6296 ......Page 158
Arrangements with Golf Courses:
Longford, Glasson, Ballyconnell,
Carrick-on-Shannon,
Roscommon, Mullingar
Facilities available:

Co. Louth

Ballymascanlon House Hotel
Dundalk, Co. Louth
Tel: +353-42-935 8200 ......Page 161
Golf Course(s) On Site:
1 x 18 Hole Golf Course(s)
Green Fees from: €25.00
Facilities available:

276   All inclusive Golf Package   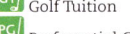 Golf Tuition    Golf Cart   Arrange Tee Times
 Hire Of Clubs   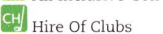 Preferential Green Fees   Transport To Course   Hire of Caddy

Golfing In Ireland
...where to stay when you play!

d (The)
Drogheda, Co. Louth
Tel: +353-41-987 7700 ......Page 160
Arrangements with Golf Courses:
Baltray (County Louth), Seapoint, Bettystown & Laytown, Dundalk
Green Fees from: €40.00
Facilities available:

Co. Meath

Headfort Arms
Kells, Co. Meath
Tel: +353-818-222800 ......Page 164
Arrangements with Golf Courses:
Headfort Golf Course - 36 Holes, Royal Tara, Navan Race Course, Delvin Castle, Ballinlough Castle
Green Fees from: €35.00
Facilities available:

Knightsbrook Hotel, Spa & Golf Resort
Trim, Co. Meath
Tel: +353-46-948 2100 ......Page 165
Golf Course(s) On Site:
1 x 18 Hole Golf Course(s)
Arrangements with Golf Courses:
Kileen Castle, Headfort, Rathcore, Royal Tara, Co. Louth
Green Fees from: €35.00
Facilities available:

Station House Hotel and Signal Restaurant
Kilmessan, Co. Meath
Tel: +353-46-902 5239 ......Page 164
Arrangements with Golf Courses:
Royal Tara, Blackbush, Headfort, The K Club, The Island Links, Carton House
Green Fees from: €35.00
Facilities available:

Trim Castle Hotel
Trim, Co. Meath
Tel: +353-46-948 3000 ......Page 165
Arrangements with Golf Courses:
Royal Tara, Headfort Old and New, Rathcore
Green Fees from: €45.00
Facilities available:

Co. Offaly

Bridge House Hotel
Tullamore, Co. Offaly
Tel: +353-57-932 5600 ......Page 168
Arrangements with Golf Courses:
Esker Hills & Tullamore Golf Clubs both 5 minutes away, Castle Barna Golf Club 12km away, Glasson, Virtual Reality Golf Facility on site
Green Fees from: €35.00
Facilities available:

Tullamore Court Hotel
Tullamore, Co. Offaly
Tel: +353-57-934 6666 ......Page 170
Arrangements with Golf Courses:
Tullamore, Esker Hills, Castle Barna, Mount Temple, Glasson, Birr, The Heritage at Killenard
Green Fees from: €35.00
Facilities available:

Co. Westmeath

Glasson Country House Hotel and Golf Club
Athlone, Co. Westmeath
Tel: +353-90-648 5120 ......Page 171
Golf Course(s) On Site:
1 x 18 Hole Golf Course(s)
Arrangements with Golf Courses:
Glasson Golf Hotel and Country Club, Athlone Golf Club, Mount Temple Golf Club, Esker Hills, Moate Golf Club, Tullamore
Green Fees from: €60.00
Facilities available:

Greville Arms Hotel
Mullingar, Co. Westmeath
Tel: +353-44-934 8563 ......Page 173
Arrangements with Golf Courses:
Mullingar, Glasson, Mount Temple, Tullamore, Longford, Esker Hills
Green Fees from: €30.00
Facilities available:

Prince of Wales Hotel
Athlone, Co. Westmeath
Tel: +353-90-647 6666 ......Page 171
Arrangements with Golf Courses:
Mount Temple, Athlone, Glasson, Esker Hills
Green Fees from: €25.00
Facilities available:

Sheraton Athlone Hotel
Athlone, Co. Westmeath
Tel: +353-90-645 1000 ......Page 172
Arrangements with Golf Courses:
Glasson Golf Course, Athlone Golf Course, Moate Golf Course, Mount Temple, Esker Hills
Green Fees from: €25.00
Facilities available:

Co. Wicklow

Glendalough Hotel
Glendalough, Co. Wicklow
Tel: +353-404-45135 ......Page 176
Arrangements with Golf Courses:
The European Club, Woodenbridge, Charlesland, Druid's Glen, Blainroe, Roundwood
Green Fees from: €35.00
Facilities available:

Grand Hotel
Wicklow Town, Co. Wicklow
Tel: +353-404-67337 ......Page 178
Arrangements with Golf Courses:
Druids Glen, Wicklow Golf Club, Blainroe Golf Club, Arklow Links, Delgany Golf Club, Druids Heath
Green Fees from: €35.00
Facilities available:

 All inclusive Golf Package
 Golf Tuition
 Golf Cart
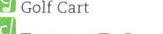 Arrange Tee Times
 Hire Of Clubs
Preferential Green Fees
Transport To Course
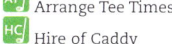 Hire of Caddy

Golfing In Ireland
...where to stay when you play!

Co. Wicklow CONTINUED

Martello Hotel (The)
Bray, Co. Wicklow
Tel: +353-1-286 8000 ....Page 176
Arrangements with Golf Courses:
Bray, Woodbrook, Old Conna, Powerscourt, Greystones, Druid's Glen
Green Fees from: €50.00
Facilities available:

The Ritz-Carlton, Powerscourt
Enniskerry, Co. Wicklow
Tel: +353-1-274 8888 ....Page 176
Golf Course(s) On Site:
2 x 18 Hole Golf Course(s)
Arrangements with Golf Courses:
Powerscourt Golf Club
Green Fees from: €60.00
Facilities available:

Yew Tree @ The Chester Beatty Inn
Ashford, Co. Wicklow
Tel: +353-404-40206 ....Page 175
Arrangements with Golf Courses:
Druid's Glen, Woodenbridge, Blainroe, European, Powerscourt, Wicklow Golf Club
Green Fees from: €30.00
Facilities available:

Ireland South

Co. Carlow

Mount Wolseley Hotel, Spa & Country Club
Tullow, Co. Carlow
Tel: +353-59-918 0100 ....Page 184
Golf Course(s) On Site:
1 x 18 Hole Golf Course(s)
Green Fees from: €40.00
Facilities available:

Talbot Hotel Carlow
Carlow Town, Co. Carlow
Tel: +353-59-915 3000 ......Page 184
Arrangements with Golf Courses:
Carlow Golf Club, Mount Juliet, Gowran, The Heritage
Green Fees from: €50.00
Facilities available:

Co. Cork

Actons Hotel
Kinsale, Co. Cork
Tel: +353-21-477 9900 ......Page 202
Arrangements with Golf Courses:
Kinsale, Old Head of Kinsale, Fota Island, Bandon, Harbour Point, Little Island
Green Fees from: €30.00
Facilities available:

Blarney Castle Hotel
Blarney, Co. Cork
Tel: +353-21-438 5116 ......Page 188
Arrangements with Golf Courses:
Muskerry, Lee Valley, Fota Island, Harbour Point, Mallow, Monkstown, Blarney, Kinsale
Green Fees from: €30.00
Facilities available:

Blarney Golf Resort
Blarney, Co. Cork
Tel: +353-21-438 4477 ......Page 188
Golf Course(s) On Site:
1 x 18 Hole Golf Course(s)
Arrangements with Golf Courses:
Lee Valley, Cork Golf Club, Fota Island, Douglas Golf Club, Bantry Golf Club
Green Fees from: €30.00
Facilities available:

Blue Haven Kinsale (The)
Kinsale, Co. Cork
Tel: +353-21-477 2209 ......Page 202
Arrangements with Golf Courses:
Kinsale Golf Club, Old Head Golf Club, Fota
Green Fees from: €50.00
Facilities available:

Commodore Hotel
Cobh, Co. Cork
Tel: +353-21-481 1277 ......Page 192
Arrangements with Golf Courses:
Cobh - 18 Hole Course, Water Rock Golf Course, East Cork, Midleton
Green Fees from: €25.00
Facilities available:

Dunmore House Hotel
Clonakilty, Co. Cork
Tel: +353-23-883 3352 ......Page 191
Golf Course(s) On Site:
1 x 9 Hole Golf Course(s)
Arrangements with Golf Courses:
Macroom, Bandon, Skibbereen, Old Head of Kinsale, The Island and Fota Island
Green Fees from: €25.00
Facilities available:

Fota Island Resort
Fota Island, Co. Cork
Tel: +353-21-488 3700 ......Page 200
Golf Course(s) On Site:
3 x 18 Hole Golf Course(s)
Arrangements with Golf Courses:
Old Head Kinsale, Cork Golf Club, Lee Valley, Cobh Golf Club
Green Fees from: €60.00
Facilities available:

Gresham Metropole
Cork City, Co. Cork
Tel: +353-21-464 3700 ......Page 196
Arrangements with Golf Courses:
Fota Island, Little Island, Harbour Point, Muskerry, Kinsale, Douglas Golf Club, Monkstown Golf Club
Facilities available:

Maryborough Hotel & Spa
Cork City, Co. Cork
Tel: +353-21-436 5555 ......Page 198
Arrangements with Golf Courses:
Douglas, Fota Island, Cork, Kinsale Old Head, Harbour Point, Monkstown
Green Fees from: €45.00
Facilities available:

| GP | All inclusive Golf Package | GT | Golf Tuition | GC | Golf Cart | AT | Arrange Tee Times |
| CH | Hire Of Clubs | PG | Preferential Green Fees | TC | Transport To Course | HC | Hire of Caddy |

Golfing In Ireland
...where to stay when you play!

Old Bank House (The)
Kinsale, Co. Cork
Tel: +353-21-477 4075 ......Page 203
Arrangements with Golf Courses:
Old Head of Kinsale, Kinsale - Farrangalway, Fota Golf Course, Cork Golf Club, Ballybunion, Waterville
Green Fees from: €50.00
Facilities available:
GP GT AT CH PG TC HC

Westlodge Hotel
Bantry, Co. Cork
Tel: +353-27-50360 ....Page 187
Arrangements with Golf Courses:
Bantry Bay Golf Club - guaranteed times, 18 hole Championship Course
Green Fees from: €40.00
Facilities available:
GP GT GC AT CH PG TC HC

White House
Kinsale, Co. Cork
Tel: +353-21-477 2125 ......Page 204
Arrangements with Golf Courses:
Kinsale 18 Hole and 9 Hole, Old Head, Bandon, Carrigaline, Muskerry
Green Fees from: €25.00
Facilities available:
AT CH PG

Co. Kerry

Aghadoe Heights Hotel & Spa
Killarney, Co. Kerry
Tel: +353-64-663 1766 ......Page 217
Arrangements with Golf Courses:
Waterville, Ballybunion, Killarney, Beaufort, Tralee, Dooks, Old Head of Kinsale
Green Fees from: €45.00
Facilities available:
GP GT GC AT CH PG TC HC

Butler Arms Hotel
Waterville, Co. Kerry
Tel: +353-66-947 4144 ......Page 237
Arrangements with Golf Courses:
Waterville, Dooks, Killarney, Tralee, Ring of Kerry, Skellig Bay
Green Fees from: €60.00
Facilities available:
GP GT GC AT CH PG TC HC

Castlerosse Hotel and Golf Resort
Killarney, Co. Kerry
Tel: +353-64-663 1144 ......Page 220
Golf Course(s) On Site:
1 x 9 Hole Golf Course(s)
Arrangements with Golf Courses:
Killarney's Mahony's Point, Killeen, Lackabane, Dooks, Beaufort
Green Fees from: €20.00
Facilities available:
GP GC AT CH PG

Dingle Skellig Hotel
Dingle (An Daingean), Co. Kerry
Tel: +353-66-915 0200 ......Page 213
Arrangements with Golf Courses:
Dingle Golf Links, Ceann Sibéal, Castlegregory
Green Fees from: €29.00
Facilities available:
GP GC AT CH PG

Foley's Townhouse & Restaurant
Killarney, Co. Kerry
Tel: +353-64-663 1217 ......Page 223
Arrangements with Golf Courses:
Killarney, Barrow, Beaufort, Dooks, Ballybunion, Waterville
Facilities available:
AT

Fuchsia House
Killarney, Co. Kerry
Tel: +353-64-663 3743 ......Page 224
Arrangements with Golf Courses:
Killarney, Tralee, Ballybunion, Waterville, Dooks, Beaufort
Green Fees from: €30.00
Facilities available:
GT GC AT CH PG TC HC

Gleann Fia Country House
Killarney, Co. Kerry
Tel: +353-64-663 5035 ......Page 224
Arrangements with Golf Courses:
Killarney, Beaufort, Tralee, Ballybunion, Dooks, Waterville, Ring of Kerry Golf Course, Kenmare, Old Head, Kinsale, Skellig Bay
Green Fees from: €50.00
Facilities available:
GP GT GC AT CH PG TC HC

Grand Hotel
Tralee, Co. Kerry
Tel: +353-66-712 1499 ......Page 236
Arrangements with Golf Courses:
Tralee, Ballybunion, Waterville, Dingle, Dooks, Killarney
Green Fees from: €75.00
Facilities available:
GP GT GC AT CH PG TC HC

Heights Hotel Killarney (The)
Killarney, Co. Kerry
Tel: +353-64-663 1158 ......Page 224
Arrangements with Golf Courses:
3 in Killarney Golf Club, Beaufort, Dooks, Killorglin
Green Fees from: €40.00
Facilities available:
GP AT CH PG HC

International Hotel Killarney
Killarney, Co. Kerry
Tel: +353-64-663 1816 ......Page 226
Arrangements with Golf Courses:
Killarney Golf & Fishing Club (Killeen), Mahony's Point, Lackabane, Beaufort
Green Fees from: €35.00
Facilities available:
GP GC AT CH PG HC

Inveraray Farm Guesthouse
Killarney, Co. Kerry
Tel: +353-64-664 4224 ......Page 226
Arrangements with Golf Courses:
Beaufort, Dunloe, Killarney, Ross, Killorglin, Dooks
Green Fees from: €35.00
Facilities available:
GT GC AT CH TC HC

GP All inclusive Golf Package GT Golf Tuition GC Golf Cart AT Arrange Tee Times
CH Hire Of Clubs PG Preferential Green Fees TC Transport To Course HC Hire of Caddy

279

Golfing In Ireland
...where to stay when you play!

Co. Kerry CONTINUED

Kathleens Country House
Killarney, Co. Kerry
Tel: +353-64-663 2810 ......Page 226
Arrangements with Golf Courses:
Killarney, Dooks, Ballybunion, Tralee, Waterville, Ceann Sibéal, Dingle
Green Fees from: €45.00
Facilities available:
GP / AT / PG / TC / HC

Killarney Lodge
Killarney, Co. Kerry
Tel: +353-64-663 6499 ......Page 227
Arrangements with Golf Courses:
Killarney GC, Tralee, Waterville, Dooks, Old Head, Ballybunion
Green Fees from: €50.00
Facilities available:
GT / GC / AT / CH / PG / TC / HC

Killarney Park Hotel
Killarney, Co. Kerry
Tel: +353-64-663 5555 ......Page 227
Arrangements with Golf Courses:
Killarney, Ballybunion, Tralee, Waterville, Dooks, Ring of Kerry
Green Fees from: €70.00
Facilities available:
GT / GC / AT / CH / PG / TC

Killarney Plaza Hotel & Spa
Killarney, Co. Kerry
Tel: +353-64-662 1100 ......Page 228
Arrangements with Golf Courses:
Killarney Golf & Fishing Club, Waterville, Ballybunion, Dooks, Tralee, Old Head of Kinsale
Green Fees from: €55.00
Facilities available:
GP / AT / CH / HC

Killarney Royal Hotel
Killarney, Co. Kerry
Tel: +353-64-663 1853 ......Page 228
Arrangements with Golf Courses:
Killarney, Tralee, Dooks, Waterville, Beaufort, Ross
Green Fees from: €60.00
Facilities available:
GT / GC / AT / CH / PG / TC

Kingfisher Lodge Guesthouse
Killarney, Co. Kerry
Tel: +353-64-663 7131 ......Page 229
Arrangements with Golf Courses:
Beaufort, Killarney, Killorglin, Waterville, Ballybunion, Tralee
Green Fees from: €20.00
Facilities available:
GP / GT / GC / AT / CH / PG / TC / HC

Lake Hotel (The)
Killarney, Co. Kerry
Tel: +353-64-663 1035 ......Page 229
Arrangements with Golf Courses:
Killarney (3 courses), Beaufort, Dooks, Ballybunion, Waterville, Tralee, Ross, Castlerosse, Ring of Kerry, Skellig Bay
Green Fees from: €30.00
Facilities available:
GP / GT / GC / AT / CH / PG / TC / HC

Meadowlands Hotel
Tralee, Co. Kerry
Tel: +353-66-718 0444 ......Page 236
Arrangements with Golf Courses:
Ballybunion, Tralee (Barrow), Killarney, Dooks, Killorglin, Waterville
Green Fees from: €70.00
Facilities available:
GT / GC / AT / CH / PG / HC

O'Donnabhain's Townhouse
Kenmare, Co. Kerry
Tel: +353-64-664 2106 ......Page 216
Arrangements with Golf Courses:
Kenmare, Ring of Kerry, Bantry, Dooks, Waterville
Green Fees from: €30.00
Facilities available:
GP / AT / PG / TC

Parknasilla Resort
Sneem, Co. Kerry
Tel: +353-64-667 5600 ......Page 233
Golf Course(s) On Site:
1 x 9 Hole Golf Course(s)
Green Fees from: €20.00
Facilities available:
GP / AT / CH / PG

Scotts Hotel Killarney
Killarney, Co. Kerry
Tel: +353-64-663 1060 ......Page 232
Arrangements with Golf Courses:
Killarney, Ross, Beaufort, Ring of Kerry, Dooks, Ballybunion
Green Fees from: €40.00
Facilities available:
GP / AT / CH / PG / TC / HC

Sheen Falls Lodge
Kenmare, Co. Kerry
Tel: +353-64-664 1600 ......Page 216
Arrangements with Golf Courses:
Kenmare, Ring of Kerry
Green Fees from: €45.00
Facilities available:
GP / GT / GC / AT / CH / PG / TC / HC

Smugglers Inn
Waterville, Co. Kerry
Tel: +353-66-947 4330 ......Page 237
Arrangements with Golf Courses:
Waterville (2 Courses), Killarney (2 Courses), Dooks, Tralee, Ballybunion, Kenmare, Parknasilla
Green Fees from: €70.00
Facilities available:
AT

Sneem Hotel
Sneem, Co. Kerry
Tel: +353-64-667 5100 ......Page 234
Arrangements with Golf Courses:
Ring of Kerry Golf Course, Waterville, Parknasilla, Killeen & Mahonys Golf Courses Killarney, Old Head Golf Links Kinsale
Green Fees from: €50.00
Facilities available:
GP / AT / CH / TC / HC

Co. Kilkenny

Butler House
Kilkenny City, Co. Kilkenny
Tel: +353-56-776 5707 ......Page 239
Arrangements with Golf Courses:
Kilkenny, Mount Juliet, Carlow, Killerig Castle, Kilkea Castle, Gowran Park
Green Fees from: €30.00
Facilities available:
GT / GC / AT / CH / PG / TC / HC

---

280 | GP All inclusive Golf Package | GT Golf Tuition | GC Golf Cart | AT Arrange Tee Times
CH Hire Of Clubs | PG Preferential Green Fees | TC Transport To Course | HC Hire of Caddy

Golfing In Ireland
...where to stay when you play!

Kilkenny River Court
Kilkenny City, Co. Kilkenny
Tel: +353-56-772 3388 ......Page 242
Arrangements with Golf Courses:
Gowran Park, Kilkenny
Green Fees from: €30.00
Facilities available:
GP AT CH PG TC HC

Langton House Hotel
Kilkenny City, Co. Kilkenny
Tel: +353-56-776 5133 ......Page 242
Arrangements with Golf Courses:
Mount Juliet, Kilkenny Golf Club, Gowran Park, Castlecomer Golf Club
Green Fees from: €90.00
Facilities available:
GP AT CH PG TC HC

Lyrath Estate Hotel & Convention Centre
Kilkenny City, Co. Kilkenny
Tel: +353-56-776 0088 ......Page 243
Arrangements with Golf Courses:
Gowran Park, Kilkenny
Green Fees from: €30.00
Facilities available:
GP AT CH PG TC HC

Co. Tipperary

Abbey Court Hotel, Lodges & Trinity Leisure Spa
Nenagh, Co. Tipperary
Tel: +353-67-41111 ....Page 249
Arrangements with Golf Courses:
Nenagh, Roscrea, Birr, Portumna, Thurles, Castletroy
Green Fees from: €25.00
Facilities available:
GP GT GC AT CH PG TC HC

Ballykisteen Hotel & Golf Resort
Tipperary Town, Co. Tipperary
Tel: +353-62-33333 ....Page 250
Golf Course(s) On Site:
1 x 18 Hole Golf Course(s)
Green Fees from: €25.00
Facilities available:
GP GT GC AT CH PG HC

Cahir House Hotel
Cahir, Co. Tipperary
Tel: +353-52-744 3000 ......Page 245
Arrangements with Golf Courses:
Cahir Park, Carrick-on-Suir, Clonmel, Ballykisteen, Dundrum, Tipperary, Thurles, Mount Juliet
Green Fees from: €30.00
Facilities available:
GP GT GC AT CH PG TC HC

Dundrum House Hotel, Golf & Leisure Resort
Cashel, Co. Tipperary
Tel: +353-62-71116 ....Page 247
Golf Course(s) On Site:
1 x 18 Hole Golf Course(s)
Arrangements with Golf Courses:
All Club Choice Ireland Courses
Green Fees from: €30.00
Facilities available:
GP GT GC AT CH PG TC HC

Co. Waterford

Dooley's Hotel
Waterford City, Co. Waterford
Tel: +353-51-873531 ....Page 257
Arrangements with Golf Courses:
Waterford, Tramore, Faithlegg, Waterford Castle, Mount Juliet, Carrick-on-Suir
Green Fees from: €45.00
Facilities available:
GP GT GC AT CH PG TC HC

Lismore House Hotel
Lismore, Co. Waterford
Tel: +353-58-72966 ....Page 254
Arrangements with Golf Courses:
Gold Coast Golf Club, Dungarvan Golf Club, Lismore Golf Club
Green Fees from: €25.00
Facilities available:
GP AT PG TC

Majestic Hotel
Tramore, Co. Waterford
Tel: +353-51-381761 ....Page 256
Arrangements with Golf Courses:
Tramore, Waterford, Faithlegg, Waterford Castle, Mount Juliet, Dunmore East
Green Fees from: €30.00
Facilities available:
GP GT GC AT CH PG TC HC

O'Shea's Hotel
Tramore, Co. Waterford
Tel: +353-51-381246 ....Page 256
Arrangements with Golf Courses:
Tramore, Faithlegg, Waterford Castle, Waterford, Dungarvan
Green Fees from: €25.00
Facilities available:
GP GT GC AT CH PG TC HC

Park Hotel, Leisure Centre & Holiday Homes
Dungarvan, Co. Waterford
Tel: +353-58-42899 ....Page 253
Arrangements with Golf Courses:
Dungarvan Golf Club, West Waterford Golf Club, Gold Coast Golf Club
Green Fees from: €25.00
Facilities available:
GP GT GC AT CH PG TC

Tower Hotel & Leisure Centre
Waterford City, Co. Waterford
Tel: +353-51-862300 ....Page 260
Arrangements with Golf Courses:
Waterford Castle, Waterford, Faithlegg, Tramore
Green Fees from: €25.00
Facilities available:
GP GT GC AT CH PG HC

    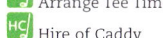

GP — All inclusive Golf Package
GT — Golf Tuition
GC — Golf Cart
AT — Arrange Tee Times
CH — Hire Of Clubs
PG — Preferential Green Fees
TC — Transport To Course
HC — Hire of Caddy

...where to stay when you play!

Co. Wexford

**Amber Springs Hotel
& Health Spa**
Gorey, Co. Wexford
Tel: +353-53-948 4000 ......Page 263
Arrangements with Golf Courses:
Seafield, Courtown, Coollattin,
Ballymoney
Green Fees from: €36.00
Facilities available:

**Ashdown Park Hotel
Conference
& Leisure Centre**
Gorey, Co. Wexford
Tel: +353-53-948 0500 ......Page 263
Arrangements with Golf Courses:
Courtown, Ballymoney, Coolattin,
Enniscorthy, Woodenbridge,
Seafield, Bunclody
Green Fees from: €30.00
Facilities available:

Kelly's Resort Hotel & Spa
Rosslare, Co. Wexford
Tel: +353-53-913 2114 ......Page 265
Arrangements with Golf Courses:
Rosslare Golf Club, St. Helen's Bay
Golf & Country Club, Wexford Golf
Club
Green Fees from: €30.00
Facilities available:

**Riverside Park Hotel and
Leisure Club**
Enniscorthy, Co. Wexford
Tel: +353-53-923 7800 ......Page 262
Arrangements with Golf Courses:
Enniscorthy Golf Club, Rosslare
Golf Club, Wexford Golf Club, New
Ross Golf Club, Seafield Golf Club,
St. Helen's Golf Club
Green Fees from: €25.00
Facilities available:

**Talbot Hotel Conference
and Leisure Centre**
Wexford Town, Co. Wexford
Tel: +353-53-912 2566 ......Page 269
Arrangements with Golf Courses:
St. Helen's, Wexford, Rosslare,
Enniscorthy, Courtown
Green Fees from: €25.00
Facilities available:

Did you know?

Year round golfing in Ireland is perfectly feasible - provided you have suitable wet weather gear! - but conditions are best between April and October.

During these months you can expect to be able to play up to 7pm in the evening at least, with many courses playable until 10pm or 11pm. During the months of June-August you may even fit two games into a single day.

For best value, aim to play as early as possible in the day and preferably on a week day. In many golf clubs there are few if any tee times available to visitors at weekends during the summer, so if you must play at the weekend book well in advance.

---

282      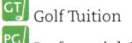      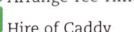

Angling 2011

Ireland is accepted as being the outstanding angling holiday resort in Europe. Whether you are a competition angler, a serious specimen hunter, or just fishing while on holiday, you are sure to enjoy yourself here. With over 14,000km of rivers feeding over 4,000 lakes and with no part of Ireland over 112km from the sea, Ireland can, in truth, be called an angler's dream!

So come on and get hooked!

Irelandhotels.com
We've got it covered

Angling In Ireland
...where to stay when you're Angling!

We invite you to sample the fishing, the countryside and the friendship of the Irish people and then to stay in some of Ireland's most charming accommodation. We have listed a range of hotels and guesthouses which are either situated with or near angling facilities. Your host will assist you in arranging your angling itinerary. A full description of the hotels and guesthouses may be seen by consulting the relevant page number below.

Listings are by Region, County, Premises Name in alphabetical order.

Ireland West

Co. Clare

Ardilaun Guesthouse
Ennis, Co. Clare
Tel: +353-65-682 2311 .... Page 37
Coarse Angling:
Pike, Perch
Game Angling:
Trout, Salmon
Facilities available:
DR, PL, FR

Falls Hotel & Spa
Ennistymon, Co. Clare
Tel: +353-65-707 1004 .... Page 40
Coarse Angling:
Bream, Tench, Pike
Facilities available:
PL

Co. Donegal

Downings Bay Hotel
Downings, Co. Donegal
Tel: +353-74-915 5586 .... Page 49
Sea Angling:
Pollock, Mackerel, Tuna, Ling, Skate, Cod, Haddock
Facilities available:
BH, PL

Jackson's Hotel, Conference & Leisure Centre
Ballybofey, Co. Donegal
Tel: +353-74-913 1021 .... Page 45
Sea Angling:
Pollock, Mackerel, Herring
Game Angling:
Salmon, Trout
Facilities available:
BT, PL, FR, PR

Solis Lough Eske Castle
Donegal Town, Co. Donegal
Tel: +353-74-972 5100 .... Page 49
Coarse Angling:
Bream, Roach, Pike
Sea Angling:
Mackerel, Pollock
Game Angling:
Salmon, Sea Trout, Grilse, Char, Brown Trout
Facilities available:
BT, BH, DR, PL, GI, FR, PR

Co. Galway

Anglers Rest Hotel
Headford, Co. Galway
Tel: +353-93-35528 .... Page 71
Game Angling:
Brown Trout, Salmon
Facilities available:
BH, DR, PL, GI, FR

Ballynahinch Castle Hotel
Ballynahinch, Co. Galway
Tel: +353-95-31006 .... Page 56
Sea Angling:
Charter Available
Game Angling:
Salmon, Brown Trout, Sea Trout
Facilities available:
BT, BH, DR, PL, GI, TR, FR, PR

Ben View House
Clifden, Co. Galway
Tel: +353-95-21256 .... Page 58
Sea Angling:
Cod, Herring, Whiting, Pollock, Plaice
Game Angling:
Salmon, Trout
Facilities available:
BT, BH, DR, FR, PR

Claregalway Hotel (The)
Galway City, Co. Galway
Tel: +353-91-738300 .... Page 62
Coarse Angling:
Pike
Game Angling:
Brown Trout, Salmon
Facilities available:
BT, DR, PL, GI, TR, FR, PR

Corrib Wave Guest House
Oughterard, Co. Galway
Tel: +353-91-552147 .... Page 74
Coarse Angling:
Pike, Perch
Game Angling:
Brown Trout, Salmon
Facilities available:
BT, BH, DR, PL, GI, TR, FR

Doonmore Hotel
Inishbofin Island, Co. Galway
Tel: +353-95-45814 .... Page 71
Sea Angling:
Pollock, Mackerel, Plaice
Facilities available:
BH, DR, PL, FR

Fairhill House Hotel
Clonbur (An Fháirche), Co. Galway
Tel: +353-94-954 6176 .... Page 61
Coarse Angling:
Pike, Roach, Perch, Bream, Eel
Sea Angling:
Dogfish, Cod, Ray, Shark, Pollock
Game Angling:
Salmon, Wild Brown Trout
Facilities available:
BT, BH, DR, PL, GI, TR, FR, PR

Inishbofin House Hotel
Inishbofin Island, Co. Galway
Tel: +353-95-45809 .... Page 72
Sea Angling:
Pollock, Ray, Plaice, Mackerel, Gurnard, Tope
Facilities available:
BT, BH, DR, PL, FR

Park Lodge Hotel
Spiddal, Co. Galway
Tel: +353-91-553159 .... Page 76
Sea Angling:
Mackerel, Cod, Pollock
Facilities available:
DR, PL

Shannon Oaks Hotel & Country Club
Portumna, Co. Galway
Tel: +353-90-974 1777 .... Page 75
Coarse Angling:
Bream, Roach, Tench, Perch, Pike
Facilities available:
BT, BH, PL, GI, FR, PR

---

284  Bait & Tackle  Boats For Hire  Drying Room 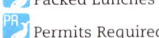 Packed Lunches
GI Gillie TR Tackle Room FR Freezer For Storage Of Catch PR Permits Required

Angling In Ireland
...where to stay when you're Angling!

Co. Limerick

Fitzgeralds Woodlands House Hotel & Spa
Adare, Co. Limerick
Tel: +353-61-605100 ....Page 79
Coarse Angling:
Pike
Game Angling:
Trout, Salmon
Facilities available:
BT, BH, DR, PL, GI, FR, PR

Co. Mayo

Ashford Castle
Cong, Co. Mayo
Tel: +353-94-954 6003 ....Page 87
Coarse Angling:
Pike
Game Angling:
Salmon, Trout
Facilities available:
BT, BH, DR, PL, GI, FR, PR

Ballina Manor Hotel
Ballina, Co. Mayo
Tel: +353-96-80900 ....Page 83
Game Angling:
Salmon, Trout
Facilities available:
BT, DR, PL, GI, TR, FR, PR

Castlecourt Hotel Spa, Leisure, Conference
Westport, Co. Mayo
Tel: +353-98-55088 ....Page 90
Coarse Angling:
Pike, Perch, Roach, Bream, Tench, Hybrids
Sea Angling:
Cod, Shark, Pollock, Plaice, Dogfish, Conger Eels, Whiting, Monkfish
Game Angling:
Trout, Salmon
Facilities available:
BT, BH, DR, PL, GI, FR, PR

Healys Restaurant & Fishing Lodge
Pontoon, Co. Mayo
Tel: +353-94-925 6443 ....Page 89
Coarse Angling:
Pike, Perch
Sea Angling:
Blue Shark, Pollock, Mackerel, Cod, Sole, Brill, Turbot, Plaice, Conger Eel
Game Angling:
Salmon, Brown Trout, Rainbow Trout, Sea Trout
Facilities available:
BT, BH, DR, PL, GI, TR, FR, PR

Mount Falcon
Ballina, Co. Mayo
Tel: +353-96-74472 ....Page 84
Game Angling:
Salmon, Rainbow Trout
Facilities available:
BT, DR, PL, GI, TR, FR, PR

Sea Rod Inn
Belmullet, Co. Mayo
Tel: +353-97-86767 ....Page 85
Sea Angling:
Pollock, Skate, Dogfish, Cod, Mackerel
Facilities available:
BH, PL, FR

Westport Plaza Hotel Spa, Leisure, Conference
Westport, Co. Mayo
Tel: +353-98-51166 ....Page 93
Coarse Angling:
Pike, Perch, Roach, Bream, Tench, Hybrids
Sea Angling:
Cod, Shark, Pollock, Plaice, Dogfish, Conger Eels, Whiting, Monkfish
Facilities available:
BT, BH, DR, PL, GI, FR, PR

Co. Sligo

Radisson Blu Hotel & Spa Sligo
Sligo Town, Co. Sligo
Tel: +353-71-914 0008 ....Page 96
Coarse Angling:
Bream, Pike, Perch, Hybrids
Sea Angling:
Cod, Ling, Mackerel, Pollock, Sea Bass, Shark
Game Angling:
Salmon, Sea Trout, Trout
Facilities available:
PL

Did you know?

Ireland is recognised as being the outstanding angling destination in Europe. The vast variety & quality of our fishing has given the country a reputation of which we are justly proud.

The Irish climate is well suited to sport angling. It is temperate and kind to the angler with moderate summers, mild winters and adequate rainfall throughout the year.

BT Bait & Tackle   BH Boats For Hire   DR Drying Room   PL Packed Lunches
GI Gillie   TR Tackle Room   FR Freezer For Storage Of Catch   PR Permits Required

Angling In Ireland
...where to stay when you're Angling!

Dublin & Ireland East

Co. Cavan

Crover House Hotel & Golf Club
Mountnugent, Co. Cavan
Tel: +353-49-854 0206 ......Page 118
Coarse Angling:
Pike
Game Angling:
Trout
Facilities available:

Keepers Arms
Ballyconnell, Co. Cavan
Tel: +353-49-952 3318 ......Page 117
Coarse Angling:
Bream, Pike, Roach, Tench
Facilities available:

Lakeside Manor Hotel
Virginia, Co. Cavan
Tel: +353-49-854 8200 ......Page 119
Coarse Angling:
Bream, Hybrids, Roach, Perch, Pike
Game Angling:
Trout
Facilities available:

Co. Kildare

K Club (The)
Straffan, Co. Kildare
Tel: +353-1-601 7200 ....Page 156
Coarse Angling:
Bream, Tench, Roach, Rudd, Carp
Game Angling:
Rainbow Trout, Brown Trout
Facilities available:

Maudlins House Hotel
Naas, Co. Kildare
Tel: +353-45-896999 ....Page 154
Coarse Angling:
Roach, Perch, Rudd, Pike, Tench
Game Angling:
Rainbow Trout, Brown Trout, Salmon
Facilities available:

Co. Longford

Annaly Hotel
Longford Town, Co. Longford
Tel: +353-43-334 3690 ......Page 158
Coarse Angling:
Pike, Bream, Tench
Facilities available:

Longford Arms Hotel, Spa & Leisure Centre
Longford Town, Co. Longford
Tel: +353-43-334 6296 ......Page 158
Coarse Angling:
Pike, Bream
Facilities available:

Co. Louth

McKevitt's Village Hotel
Carlingford, Co. Louth
Tel: +353-42-937 3116 ......Page 160
Sea Angling:
Cod, Sea Bass, Mackeral, Pollock
Facilities available:

Co. Monaghan

Castle (The) at Castle Leslie Estate
Glaslough, Co. Monaghan
Tel: +353-47-88100 ....Page 166
Coarse Angling:
Pike
Facilities available:

Co. Westmeath

Glasson Country House Hotel and Golf Club
Athlone, Co. Westmeath
Tel: +353-90-648 5120 ......Page 171
Coarse Angling:
Pike, Perch, Roach, Bream
Game Angling:
Brown Trout
Facilities available:

Ireland South

Co. Cork

Munster Arms Hotel
Bandon, Co. Cork
Tel: +353-23-884 1562 ......Page 187
Game Angling:
Salmon, Sea Trout, Brown Trout
Facilities available:

West Cork Hotel
Skibbereen, Co. Cork
Tel: +353-28-21277 ....Page 207
Sea Angling:
Mackerel, Cod, Pollock
Game Angling:
Trout, Salmon
Facilities available:

Co. Kerry

Butler Arms Hotel
Waterville, Co. Kerry
Tel: +353-66-947 4144 ......Page 237
Sea Angling:
Bass, Pollock, Cod, Shark, Mackerel, Whiting
Game Angling:
Salmon, Sea Trout
Facilities available:

Dingle Skellig Hotel
Dingle (An Daingean), Co. Kerry
Tel: +353-66-915 0200 ......Page 213
Sea Angling:
Pollock, Garfish, Blue Shark, Tope, Dogfish, Ling, Whiting, Ray
Facilities available:

Inveraray Farm Guesthouse
Killarney, Co. Kerry
Tel: +353-64-664 4224 ......Page 226
Sea Angling:
Sea Trout
Game Angling:
Brown Trout, Salmon
Facilities available:

Killarney Royal Hotel
Killarney, Co. Kerry
Tel: +353-64-663 1853 ......Page 228
Game Angling:
Brown Trout, Salmon
Facilities available:

BT Bait & Tackle	BH Boats For Hire	DR Drying Room	PL Packed Lunches
GI Gillie	TR Tackle Room	FR Freezer For Storage Of Catch	PR Permits Required

Angling In Ireland
...where to stay when you're Angling!

Lake Hotel (The)
Killarney, Co. Kerry
Tel: +353-64-663 1035 ......Page 229
Sea Angling:
Sea Trout, Pollock, Shark
Game Angling:
Salmon, Brown Trout
Facilities available:
BT, BH, DR, PL, GI, FR, PR

Sheen Falls Lodge
Kenmare, Co. Kerry
Tel: +353-64-664 1600 ......Page 216
Sea Angling:
Shark, Mackerel, Pollock, Skate, Conger Eel, Dogfish
Game Angling:
Salmon, Trout
Facilities available:
BT, BH, DR, PL, GI, TR, FR, PR

Smugglers Inn
Waterville, Co. Kerry
Tel: +353-66-947 4330 ......Page 237
Sea Angling:
Cod, Bass, Mackerel, Tuna, Plaice, Sole
Game Angling:
Salmon, Sea Trout, Brown Trout
Facilities available:
BH, DR, PL, GI, FR

Sneem Hotel
Sneem, Co. Kerry
Tel: +353-64-667 5100 ......Page 234
Sea Angling:
Conger, Pollock, Ray
Game Angling:
Rainbow Trout, Brown Trout, Salmon
Facilities available:
BT, BH, DR, PL, GI, TR, PR

Co. Kilkenny

Kilkenny River Court
Kilkenny City, Co. Kilkenny
Tel: +353-56-772 3388 ......Page 242
Coarse Angling:
Shad, Bream
Game Angling:
Trout, Salmon
Facilities available:
BT, BH, DR, PL, GI, TR, PR

Lyrath Estate Hotel & Convention Centre
Kilkenny City, Co. Kilkenny
Tel: +353-56-776 0088 ......Page 243
Coarse Angling:
Shad, Bream
Game Angling:
Salmon, Trout
Facilities available:
BT, BH, DR, PL, GI, TR, FR, PR

Co. Tipperary

Cahir House Hotel
Cahir, Co. Tipperary
Tel: +353-52-744 3000 ......Page 245
Coarse Angling:
Perch, Pike
Game Angling:
Trout, Salmon
Facilities available:
PL, GI, FR, PR

Cashel Palace Hotel
Cashel, Co. Tipperary
Tel: +353-62-62707 ....Page 247
Coarse Angling:
Perch
Game Angling:
Salmon, Brown Trout, Grilse
Facilities available:
BT, DR, PL, GI, FR, PR

Co. Waterford

Lismore House Hotel
Lismore, Co. Waterford
Tel: +353-58-72966 ....Page 254
Game Angling:
Salmon, Sea Trout
Facilities available:
BT, DR, PL, GI, FR, PR

BT — Bait & Tackle
BH — Boats For Hire
DR — Drying Room
PL — Packed Lunches
GI — Gillie
TR — Tackle Room
FR — Freezer For Storage Of Catch
PR — Permits Required

Direct low rates and great special offers guaranteed

Irelandhotels.com
We've got it covered

You can find all the best deals in all of these places

Website | Mobile App | Printed Guide |
facebook.com/irelandhotels | irelandhotels.com/onlineguide

Conference 2011

Small meetings or large conferences are part and parcel of life in Irish hotels and guesthouses. What makes Ireland special as a venue is the warmth of the welcome you will receive, coupled with excellent facilities which can be tailored to your needs.

Our venues will tick all your boxes!

Irelandhotels.com
We've got it covered

Conference Facilities
...Select A Venue For your Agenda!

We will be glad to see you and work with you to make your meeting or conference a successful one. Choose from the wide selection of special facilities throughout the country as shown here. A full description of the hotels and guesthouses may be seen by consulting the relevant page number below.

Listings are by Region, County, Premises Name in alphabetical order

Ireland West
Co. Clare

Bunratty Castle Hotel
Bunratty, Co. Clare
Tel: +353-61-478700 ....Page 35
Contact Person:
Marguerite Curran
Number of Meeting/Conference Rooms: 4
Number of Delegates catered for in any one room:
Minimum: 10 Maximum: 500
Facilities available:

Falls Hotel & Spa
Ennistymon, Co. Clare
Tel: +353-65-707 1004 ......Page 40
Contact Person:
Joanne Clancy
Number of Meeting/Conference Rooms: 5
Number of Delegates catered for in any one room:
Minimum: 2 Maximum: 350
Facilities available:

Temple Gate Hotel
Ennis, Co. Clare
Tel: +353-65-682 3300 ......Page 39
Contact Person:
Paul Madden
Number of Meeting/Conference Rooms: 6
Number of Delegates catered for in any one room:
Minimum: 2 Maximum: 200
Facilities available:

Co. Donegal

Creevy Pier Hotel
Ballyshannon, Co. Donegal
Tel: +353-71-985 8355 ......Page 46
Contact Person:
Jason Horkan
Number of Meeting/Conference Rooms: 1
Number of Delegates catered for in any one room:
Minimum: 20 Maximum: 120
Facilities available:

Downings Bay Hotel
Downings, Co. Donegal
Tel: +353-74-915 5586 ......Page 49
Contact Person:
Eileen Rock
Number of Meeting/Conference Rooms: 3
Number of Delegates catered for in any one room:
Minimum: 10 Maximum: 300
Facilities available:

Great Northern Hotel
Bundoran, Co. Donegal
Tel: +353-71-984 1204 ......Page 47
Contact Person:
Philip McGlynn
Number of Meeting/Conference Rooms: 5
Number of Delegates catered for in any one room:
Minimum: 2 Maximum: 1000
Facilities available:

Jackson's Hotel, Conference & Leisure Centre
Ballybofey, Co. Donegal
Tel: +353-74-913 1021 ......Page 45
Contact Person:
Ankush Shingal
Number of Meeting/Conference Rooms: 8
Number of Delegates catered for in any one room:
Minimum: 2 Maximum: 1000
Facilities available:

Mill Park Hotel, Conference Centre & Leisure Club
Donegal Town, Co. Donegal
Tel: +353-74-972 2880 ......Page 48
Contact Person:
Conference & Banqueting Manager
Number of Meeting/Conference Rooms: 5
Number of Delegates catered for in any one room:
Minimum: 2 Maximum: 400
Facilities available:

Solis Lough Eske Castle
Donegal Town, Co. Donegal
Tel: +353-74-972 5100 ......Page 49
Contact Person:
Michele McConalogue
Number of Meeting/Conference Rooms: 4
Number of Delegates catered for in any one room:
Minimum: 2 Maximum: 400
Facilities available:

 Black Out Facilities  Air-Conditioning  Interpreting Equipment  Audio Visual

Conference Facilities
...Select A Venue For your Agenda!

Co. Galway

Carlton Hotel Galway
Galway City, Co. Galway
Tel: +353-91-381200 ....Page 62
Contact Person:
Dunna Mannion
Number of Meeting/Conference
Rooms: 9
Number of Delegates catered for
in any one room:
Minimum: 2 Maximum: 120
Facilities available:

Claregalway Hotel (The)
Galway City, Co. Galway
Tel: +353-91-738300 ....Page 62
Contact Person:
Tommy Normoyle
Number of Meeting/Conference
Rooms: 5
Number of Delegates catered for
in any one room:
Minimum: 2 Maximum: 350
Facilities available:

Connemara Coast Hotel
Furbo, Co. Galway
Tel: +353-91-592108 ....Page 61
Contact Person:
Ann Downey
Number of Meeting/Conference
Rooms: 7
Number of Delegates catered for
in any one room:
Minimum: 30 Maximum: 500
Facilities available:

Delphi Mountain Resort
Leenane, Co. Galway
Tel: +353-95-42208 ....Page 72
Contact Person:
John Sullivan
Number of Meeting/Conference
Rooms: 2
Number of Delegates catered for
in any one room:
Minimum: 4 Maximum: 40
Facilities available:
AV

Doonmore Hotel
Inishbofin Island, Co. Galway
Tel: +353-95-45814 ....Page 71
Contact Person:
Aileen Murray
Number of Meeting/Conference
Rooms: 2
Number of Delegates catered for
in any one room:
Minimum: 20 Maximum: 80
Facilities available:
BO IE AV

Flannery's Hotel
Galway City, Co. Galway
Tel: +353-91-755111 ....Page 64
Contact Person:
Emma Mooney
Number of Meeting/Conference
Rooms: 4
Number of Delegates catered for
in any one room:
Minimum: 2 Maximum: 100
Facilities available:

g Hotel (The)
Galway City, Co. Galway
Tel: +353-91-865200 ....Page 65
Contact Person:
Eilish Wall
Number of Meeting/Conference
Rooms: 6
Number of Delegates catered for
in any one room:
Minimum: 2 Maximum: 120
Facilities available:
BO AC IE AV

Hotel Meyrick
Galway City, Co. Galway
Tel: +353-91-564041 ....Page 66
Contact Person:
Duty Manager
Number of Meeting/Conference
Rooms: 5
Number of Delegates catered for
in any one room:
Minimum: 2 Maximum: 350
Facilities available:
BO AC AV

Inishbofin House Hotel
Inishbofin Island, Co. Galway
Tel: +353-95-45809 ....Page 72
Contact Person:
C&B Coordinator
Number of Meeting/Conference
Rooms: 1
Number of Delegates catered for
in any one room:
Minimum: 2 Maximum: 120
Facilities available:
BO AC AV

Lady Gregory Hotel, Conference & Leisure Club
Gort, Co. Galway
Tel: +353-91-632333 ....Page 70
Contact Person:
Brian Morrissey
Number of Meeting/Conference
Rooms: 3
Number of Delegates catered for
in any one room:
Minimum: 10 Maximum: 350
Facilities available:
BO AC IE AV

Lough Rea Hotel & Spa
Loughrea, Co. Galway
Tel: +353-91-880088 ....Page 73
Contact Person:
Helen Leddy
Number of Meeting/Conference
Rooms: 7
Number of Delegates catered for
in any one room:
Minimum: 1 Maximum: 400
Facilities available:
BO AC IE AV

Meadow Court Hotel
Loughrea, Co. Galway
Tel: +353-91-841051 ....Page 74
Contact Person:
Tom Corbett Jnr
Number of Meeting/Conference
Rooms: 2
Number of Delegates catered for
in any one room:
Minimum: 1 Maximum: 325
Facilities available:
BO AC AV

BO Black Out Facilities   AC Air-Conditioning   IE Interpreting Equipment   AV Audio Visual

Conference Facilities
...Select A Venue For your Agenda!

Co. Galway CONTINUED

Park Lodge Hotel
Spiddal, Co. Galway
Tel: +353-91-553159 ....Page 76
Contact Person:
Jane Marie Foyle
Number of Meeting/Conference Rooms: 1
Number of Delegates catered for in any one room:
Minimum: 40 Maximum: 60
Facilities available:

Sullivan's Royal Hotel
Gort, Co. Galway
Tel: +353-91-631257/401 ..Page 71
Contact Person:
John Sullivan
Number of Meeting/Conference Rooms: 2
Number of Delegates catered for in any one room:
Minimum: 2 Maximum: 80
Facilities available:

Twelve (The)
Galway City, Co. Galway
Tel: +353-91-597000 ....Page 69
Contact Person:
Fergus O'Halloran
Number of Meeting/Conference Rooms: 4
Number of Delegates catered for in any one room:
Minimum: 2 Maximum: 110
Facilities available:

Co. Leitrim

Bush Hotel
Carrick-on-Shannon, Co. Leitrim
Tel: +353-71-967 1000 ......Page 77
Contact Person:
Joseph Dolan
Number of Meeting/Conference Rooms: 6
Number of Delegates catered for in any one room:
Minimum: 4 Maximum: 350
Facilities available:

Lough Rynn Castle
Mohill, Co. Leitrim
Tel: +353-71-963 2700 ......Page 78
Contact Person:
Ruth Conlon
Number of Meeting/Conference Rooms: 5
Number of Delegates catered for in any one room:
Minimum: 2 Maximum: 450
Facilities available:

Co. Limerick

Dunraven Arms Hotel
Adare, Co. Limerick
Tel: +353-61-605900 ....Page 79
Contact Person:
Louis Murphy
Number of Meeting/Conference Rooms: 4
Number of Delegates catered for in any one room:
Minimum: 12 Maximum: 200
Facilities available:

Fitzgeralds Woodlands House Hotel & Spa
Adare, Co. Limerick
Tel: +353-61-605100 ....Page 79
Contact Person:
David or Bríd
Number of Meeting/Conference Rooms: 3
Number of Delegates catered for in any one room:
Minimum: 2 Maximum: 500
Facilities available:

Co. Mayo

Ashford Castle
Cong, Co. Mayo
Tel: +353-94-954 6003 ......Page 87
Contact Person:
Monica Feeney
Number of Meeting/Conference Rooms: 2
Number of Delegates catered for in any one room:
Minimum: 35 Maximum: 120
Facilities available:

Ballina Manor Hotel
Ballina, Co. Mayo
Tel: +353-96-80900 ....Page 83
Contact Person:
Sinead Costello
Facilities available:

Castlecourt Hotel
Spa, Leisure, Conference
Westport, Co. Mayo
Tel: +353-98-55088 ....Page 90
Contact Person:
Sinead Hopkins
Number of Meeting/Conference Rooms: 7
Number of Delegates catered for in any one room:
Minimum: 10 Maximum: 750
Facilities available:

 Black Out Facilities   Air-Conditioning   Interpreting Equipment   Audio Visual

Conference Facilities
...Select A Venue For your Agenda!

Harlequin Hotel
Castlebar, Co. Mayo
Tel: +353-94-928 6200 ......Page 86
Contact Person:
Caroline Leonard
Number of Meeting/Conference Rooms: 4
Number of Delegates catered for in any one room:
Minimum: 8 Maximum: 50
Facilities available:

Hotel Westport
Westport, Co. Mayo
Tel: +353-98-25122 ....Page 91
Contact Person:
Declan Heneghan / Eithne Cosgrove / Rhona Chambers
Number of Meeting/Conference Rooms: 7
Number of Delegates catered for in any one room:
Minimum: 5 Maximum: 300
Facilities available:

Knock House Hotel
Knock, Co. Mayo
Tel: +353-94-938 8088 ......Page 88
Contact Person:
Brian Crowley
Number of Meeting/Conference Rooms: 3
Number of Delegates catered for in any one room:
Minimum: 2 Maximum: 130
Facilities available:

McWilliam Park Hotel (The)
Claremorris, Co. Mayo
Tel: +353-94-937 8000 ......Page 87
Contact Person:
Lesley Joyce/David Glynn
Number of Meeting/Conference Rooms: 5
Number of Delegates catered for in any one room:
Minimum: 10 Maximum: 600
Facilities available:

Mount Falcon
Ballina, Co. Mayo
Tel: +353-96-74472 ....Page 84
Contact Person:
Della Boland
Number of Meeting/Conference Rooms: 4
Number of Delegates catered for in any one room:
Minimum: 2 Maximum: 300
Facilities available:

Mulranny Park Hotel
Mulranny, Co. Mayo
Tel: +353-98-36000 ....Page 89
Contact Person:
Events Manager
Number of Meeting/Conference Rooms: 3
Number of Delegates catered for in any one room:
Minimum: 2 Maximum: 350
Facilities available:

Park Hotel Kiltimagh
Kiltimagh, Co. Mayo
Tel: +353-94-937 4922 ......Page 88
Contact Person:
Conference Sales Manager
Number of Meeting/Conference Rooms: 2
Number of Delegates catered for in any one room:
Minimum: 2 Maximum: 400
Facilities available:

TF Royal Hotel & Royal Theatre
Castlebar, Co. Mayo
Tel: +353-94-902 3111 ......Page 86
Contact Person:
Carmel Kelly
Number of Meeting/Conference Rooms: 9
Number of Delegates catered for in any one room:
Minimum: 2 Maximum: 1000
Facilities available:

Westport Plaza Hotel
Spa, Leisure, Conference
Westport, Co. Mayo
Tel: +353-98-51166 ....Page 93
Contact Person:
Sinead Hopkins
Number of Meeting/Conference Rooms: 1
Number of Delegates catered for in any one room:
Minimum: 2 Maximum: 100
Facilities available:

Wyatt Hotel
Westport, Co. Mayo
Tel: +353-98-25027 ....Page 93
Contact Person:
Barney Clarke
Number of Meeting/Conference Rooms: 3
Number of Delegates catered for in any one room:
Minimum: 2 Maximum: 300
Facilities available:

 Black Out Facilities    Air-Conditioning   Interpreting Equipment   Audio Visual

Conference Facilities
...Select A Venue For your Agenda!

Co. Sligo

Radisson Blu Hotel & Spa Sligo
Sligo Town, Co. Sligo
Tel: +353-71-914 0008 ......Page 96
Contact Person:
Arlene Gibbs
Number of Meeting/Conference Rooms: 10
Number of Delegates catered for in any one room:
Minimum: 4 Maximum: 750
Facilities available:

Sligo Park Hotel & Leisure Club
Sligo Town, Co. Sligo
Tel: +353-71-919 0400 ......Page 97
Contact Person:
Bernadette Coffey, Sales Manager
Number of Meeting/Conference Rooms: 7
Number of Delegates catered for in any one room:
Minimum: 2 Maximum: 550
Facilities available:

Northern Ireland

Co. Antrim

Bushmills Inn Hotel
Bushmills, Co. Antrim
Tel: +44-28-2073 3000 ....Page 104
Contact Person:
Alan Walls
Number of Meeting/Conference Rooms: 5
Number of Delegates catered for in any one room:
Minimum: 6 Maximum: 45
Facilities available:

Hilton Templepatrick
Templepatrick, Co. Antrim
Tel: +44-28-9443 5500 ....Page 105
Contact Person:
Laura Nixon
Number of Meeting/Conference Rooms: 10
Number of Delegates catered for in any one room:
Minimum: 1 Maximum: 500
Facilities available:

Londonderry Arms Hotel
Carnlough, Co. Antrim
Tel: +44-28-2888 5255 ....Page 104
Contact Person:
Frank O'Neill & Annette Bonnar
Number of Meeting/Conference Rooms: 4
Number of Delegates catered for in any one room:
Minimum: 1 Maximum: 150
Facilities available:

Ramada Portrush
Portrush, Co. Antrim
Tel: +44-28-7082 6100 ....Page 104
Contact Person:
Mary O'Neill
Number of Meeting/Conference Rooms: 4
Number of Delegates catered for in any one room:
Minimum: 5 Maximum: 100
Facilities available:

Belfast City

Fitzwilliam Hotel Belfast (The)
Belfast City
Tel: +44-28-9044 2080 ....Page 105
Contact Person:
Elissa Gallagher
Number of Meeting/Conference Rooms: 4
Number of Delegates catered for in any one room:
Minimum: 6 Maximum: 55
Facilities available:

Hilton Belfast
Belfast City
Tel: +44-28-9027 7000 ....Page 105
Contact Person:
Gareth Milligan
Number of Meeting/Conference Rooms: 11
Number of Delegates catered for in any one room:
Minimum: 1 Maximum: 450
Facilities available:

  Black Out Facilities    Air-Conditioning    Interpreting Equipment    Audio Visual

Conference Facilities

...Select A Venue For your Agenda!

La Mon Hotel & Country Club
Belfast City
Tel: +44-28-9044 8631 ....Page 106
Contact Person:
Denise Maghie (Duty Manager)
Number of Meeting/Conference Rooms: 14
Number of Delegates catered for in any one room:
Minimum: 10 Maximum: 600
Facilities available:

Malone Lodge Hotel & Apartments
Belfast City
Tel: +44-28-9038 8000 ....Page 106
Contact Person:
Conference Co-Ordinator
Number of Meeting/Conference Rooms: 4
Number of Delegates catered for in any one room:
Minimum: 2 Maximum: 120
Facilities available:

Co. Derry

Best Western White Horse Hotel
Derry City, Co. Derry
Tel: +44-28-7186 0606 ....Page 108
Contact Person:
Claire Fawl
Number of Meeting/Conference Rooms: 5
Number of Delegates catered for in any one room:
Minimum: 2 Maximum: 400
Facilities available:

Radisson Blu Roe Park Resort
Limavady, Co. Derry
Tel: +44-28-7772 2222 ....Page 108
Contact Person:
Samantha Ferguson
Number of Meeting/Conference Rooms: 7
Number of Delegates catered for in any one room:
Minimum: 1 Maximum: 450
Facilities available:

Co. Down

Burrendale Hotel, Country Club & Spa
Newcastle, Co. Down
Tel: +44-28-4372 2599 ....Page 109
Contact Person:
Fiona O'Hare
Number of Meeting/Conference Rooms: 7
Number of Delegates catered for in any one room:
Minimum: 2 Maximum: 400
Facilities available:

Canal Court Hotel
Newry, Co. Down
Tel: +44-28-3025 1234 ....Page 109
Contact Person:
Conference & Banqueting Office
Number of Meeting/Conference Rooms: 10
Number of Delegates catered for in any one room:
Minimum: 2 Maximum: 500
Facilities available:

Co. Fermanagh

Killyhevlin Hotel
Enniskillen, Co. Fermanagh
Tel: +44-28-6632 3481 ....Page 110
Contact Person:
Mandy Vance
Number of Meeting/Conference Rooms: 6
Number of Delegates catered for in any one room:
Minimum: 2 Maximum: 600
Facilities available:

Manor House Resort Hotel
Enniskillen, Co. Fermanagh
Tel: +44-28-6862 2200 ....Page 110
Contact Person:
Sinead Stewart
Number of Meeting/Conference Rooms: 7
Number of Delegates catered for in any one room:
Minimum: 1 Maximum: 400
Facilities available:

BO Black Out Facilities **AC** Air-Conditioning **IE** Interpreting Equipment **AV** Audio Visual

295

Conference Facilities
...Select A Venue For your Agenda!

Dublin & Ireland East

Co. Cavan

Hotel Kilmore
Cavan Town, Co. Cavan
Tel: +353-49-433 2288 ....Page 118
Contact Person:
Roisín McFadden
Number of Meeting/Conference Rooms: 4
Number of Delegates catered for in any one room:
Minimum: 5 Maximum: 800
Facilities available:

Radisson Blu Farnham Estate Hotel
Cavan Town, Co. Cavan
Tel: +353-49-437 7700 ....Page 118
Contact Person:
Patsy Mooney
Number of Meeting/Conference Rooms: 11
Number of Delegates catered for in any one room:
Minimum: 2 Maximum: 380
Facilities available:

Slieve Russell Hotel Golf & Country Club
Ballyconnell, Co. Cavan
Tel: +353-49-952 6444 ....Page 117
Contact Person:
Órlaith Donohoe
Number of Meeting/Conference Rooms: 9
Number of Delegates catered for in any one room:
Minimum: 2 Maximum: 1200
Facilities available:

Co. Dublin

Ashling Hotel
Dublin City, Co. Dublin
Tel: +353-1-677 2324 ......Page 123
Contact Person:
Conference Coordinator
Number of Meeting/Conference Rooms: 10
Number of Delegates catered for in any one room:
Minimum: 2 Maximum: 220
Facilities available:

Best Western Dublin Skylon Hotel
Dublin City, Co. Dublin
Tel: +353-1-884 3900 ......Page 123
Contact Person:
Deirdre McENiff
Number of Meeting/Conference Rooms: 4
Number of Delegates catered for in any one room:
Minimum: 2 Maximum: 100
Facilities available:

Bewley's Hotel Ballsbridge
Dublin City, Co. Dublin
Tel: +353-1-668 1111 ......Page 124
Contact Person:
Barbara Dunne
Number of Meeting/Conference Rooms: 8
Number of Delegates catered for in any one room:
Minimum: 2 Maximum: 300
Facilities available:

Bewley's Hotel Dublin Airport
Dublin Airport, Co. Dublin
Tel: +353-1-871 1000 ......Page 120
Contact Person:
Valerie Abbot
Number of Meeting/Conference Rooms: 16
Number of Delegates catered for in any one room:
Minimum: 2 Maximum: 300
Facilities available:

Bewley's Hotel Leopardstown
Dublin City, Co. Dublin
Tel: +353-1-293 5000 ......Page 124
Contact Person:
Helen Ryan
Number of Meeting/Conference Rooms: 11
Number of Delegates catered for in any one room:
Minimum: 2 Maximum: 158
Facilities available:

Bewley's Hotel Newlands Cross
Dublin City, Co. Dublin
Tel: +353-1-464 0140 ......Page 124
Contact Person:
Grainne McKeown
Number of Meeting/Conference Rooms: 10
Number of Delegates catered for in any one room:
Minimum: 2 Maximum: 18
Facilities available:

Blakes Hotel & Spa
Dublin City, Co. Dublin
Tel: +353-1-668 8324 ......Page 126
Contact Person:
Pat Halpin
Number of Meeting/Conference Rooms: 2
Number of Delegates catered for in any one room:
Minimum: 5 Maximum: 80
Facilities available:

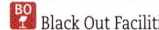 Black Out Facilities    Air-Conditioning   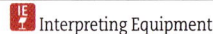 Interpreting Equipment    Audio Visual

Conference Facilities
...Select A Venue For your Agenda!

Bracken Court Hotel
Balbriggan, Co. Dublin
Tel: +353-1-841 3333 ......Page 119
Contact Person:
Aisling Eccles
Number of Meeting/Conference Rooms: 6
Number of Delegates catered for in any one room:
Minimum: 2 Maximum: 450
Facilities available:
BO AC IE AV

Brooks Hotel
Dublin City, Co. Dublin
Tel: +353-1-670 4000 ......Page 126
Contact Person:
Claire Fitzpatrick
Number of Meeting/Conference Rooms: 4
Number of Delegates catered for in any one room:
Minimum: 2 Maximum: 60
Facilities available:
BO AC IE AV

Burlington (The)
Dublin City, Co. Dublin
Tel: +353-1-618 5600 ......Page 126
Contact Person:
Richard Huggard
Number of Meeting/Conference Rooms: 24
Number of Delegates catered for in any one room:
Minimum: 10 Maximum: 1,500
Facilities available:
BO AC IE AV

Buswells Hotel
Dublin City, Co. Dublin
Tel: +353-1-614 6500 ......Page 127
Contact Person:
Dee McCabe
Number of Meeting/Conference Rooms: 7
Number of Delegates catered for in any one room:
Minimum: 1 Maximum: 80
Facilities available:
AC IE AV

Camden Court Hotel
Dublin City, Co. Dublin
Tel: +353-1-475 9666 ......Page 128
Contact Person:
Denise Corboy
Number of Meeting/Conference Rooms: 12
Number of Delegates catered for in any one room:
Minimum: 2 Maximum: 250
Facilities available:
BO AC IE AV

Cassidys Hotel
Dublin City, Co. Dublin
Tel: +353-1-878 0555 ......Page 128
Contact Person:
Maeve Sankey
Number of Meeting/Conference Rooms: 6
Number of Delegates catered for in any one room:
Minimum: 2 Maximum: 100
Facilities available:
BO AC IE AV

Castleknock Hotel and Country Club
Dublin City, Co. Dublin
Tel: +353-1-640 6300 ......Page 129
Contact Person:
Dearbhla Sheridan, Events Manager
Number of Meeting/Conference Rooms: 15
Number of Delegates catered for in any one room:
Minimum: 2 Maximum: 500
Facilities available:
BO AC IE AV

Charleville Lodge
Dublin City, Co. Dublin
Tel: +353-1-838 6633 ......Page 130
Contact Person:
Paul Stenson
Number of Meeting/Conference Rooms: 1
Number of Delegates catered for in any one room:
Minimum: 1 Maximum: 10
Facilities available:
AV

Cliff Town House (The)
Dublin City, Co. Dublin
Tel: +353-1-638 3939 ......Page 131
Contact Person:
Laetitia Tricard Wilde
Number of Meeting/Conference Rooms: 1
Number of Delegates catered for in any one room:
Minimum: 2 Maximum: 120
Facilities available:
AV

Clontarf Castle Hotel
Dublin City, Co. Dublin
Tel: +353-1-833 2321 ......Page 131
Contact Person:
Nadiene Sheridan
Number of Meeting/Conference Rooms: 10
Number of Delegates catered for in any one room:
Minimum: 2 Maximum: 600
Facilities available:
BO AC IE AV

Conrad Dublin
Dublin City, Co. Dublin
Tel: +353-1-602 8900 ......Page 132
Contact Person:
Pamela McGrath
Number of Meeting/Conference Rooms: 9
Number of Delegates catered for in any one room:
Minimum: 2 Maximum: 350
Facilities available:
BO AC IE AV

Finnstown Country House Hotel
Lucan, Co. Dublin
Tel: +353-1-601 0700 ......Page 148
Contact Person:
Edwina King
Number of Meeting/Conference Rooms: 7
Number of Delegates catered for in any one room:
Minimum: 2 Maximum: 300
Facilities available:
BO AC AV

BO Black Out Facilities   AC Air-Conditioning   IE Interpreting Equipment   AV Audio Visual

Conference Facilities
...Select A Venue For your Agenda!

Co. Dublin CONTINUED

Fitzpatrick Castle Hotel
Killiney, Co. Dublin
Tel: +353-1-230 5400 ......Page 148
Contact Person:
Eilish Kealy
Number of Meeting/Conference Rooms: 10
Number of Delegates catered for in any one room:
Minimum: 2 Maximum: 600
Facilities available:

Grand Hotel
Malahide, Co. Dublin
Tel: +353-1-845 0000 ......Page 149
Contact Person:
Hilary Fogarty
Number of Meeting/Conference Rooms: 14
Number of Delegates catered for in any one room:
Minimum: 2 Maximum: 500
Facilities available:

Gresham (The)
Dublin City, Co. Dublin
Tel: +353-1-874 6881 ......Page 135
Contact Person:
Michelle Costelloe
Number of Meeting/Conference Rooms: 21
Number of Delegates catered for in any one room:
Minimum: 1 Maximum: 350
Facilities available:

Hilton Dublin
Dublin City, Co. Dublin
Tel: +353-1-402 9988 ......Page 137
Contact Person:
Natasha Sevrugina
Number of Meeting/Conference Rooms: 4
Number of Delegates catered for in any one room:
Minimum: 1 Maximum: 400
Facilities available:

Hilton Dublin Airport
Dublin Airport, Co. Dublin
Tel: +353-1-866 1800 ......Page 120
Contact Person:
events.dublinairport@hilton.com
Number of Meeting/Conference Rooms: 9
Number of Delegates catered for in any one room:
Minimum: 1 Maximum: 350
Facilities available:

Hotel Isaacs
Dublin City, Co. Dublin
Tel: +353-1-813 4700 ......Page 137
Contact Person:
Finuala Caffrey
Number of Meeting/Conference Rooms: 7
Number of Delegates catered for in any one room:
Minimum: 1 Maximum: 100
Facilities available:

Lansdowne Hotel
Dublin City, Co. Dublin
Tel: +353-1-668 2522 ......Page 138
Contact Person:
Helen Quinn
Number of Meeting/Conference Rooms: 2
Number of Delegates catered for in any one room:
Minimum: 50 Maximum: 80
Facilities available:

Mercer Hotel
Dublin City, Co. Dublin
Tel: +353-1-478 2179 ......Page 141
Contact Person:
Darelle Van Jaarsveld
Number of Meeting/Conference Rooms: 3
Number of Delegates catered for in any one room:
Minimum: 2 Maximum: 100
Facilities available:

Radisson Blu St Helen's Hotel
Dublin City, Co. Dublin
Tel: +353-1-218 6000 ......Page 143
Contact Person:
Rebecca Whitehead
Number of Meeting/Conference Rooms: 11
Number of Delegates catered for in any one room:
Minimum: 8 Maximum: 350
Facilities available:

Red Cow Moran Hotel
Dublin City, Co. Dublin
Tel: +353-1-459 3650 ......Page 143
Contact Person:
Deborah O'Brien
Number of Meeting/Conference Rooms: 15
Number of Delegates catered for in any one room:
Minimum: 2 Maximum: 700
Facilities available:

Royal Marine Hotel
Dun Laoghaire, Co. Dublin
Tel: +353-1-230 0030 ......Page 147
Contact Person:
Brenda Killeen
Number of Meeting/Conference Rooms: 14
Number of Delegates catered for in any one room:
Minimum: 2 Maximum: 600
Facilities available:

Sandymount Hotel (formerly Mount Herbert Hotel)
Dublin City, Co. Dublin
Tel: +353-1-614 2000 ......Page 144
Contact Person:
Michelle Sweeney
Number of Meeting/Conference Rooms: 9
Number of Delegates catered for in any one room:
Minimum: 2 Maximum: 100
Facilities available:

 Black Out Facilities   AC Air-Conditioning   IE Interpreting Equipment    Audio Visual

Conference Facilities

...Select A Venue For your Agenda!

Shelbourne Hotel (The)
Dublin City, Co. Dublin
Tel: +353-1-663 4500 ......Page 144
Contact Person:
Caitriona O'Neill
Number of Meeting/Conference Rooms: 13
Number of Delegates catered for in any one room:
Minimum: 1 Maximum: 500
Facilities available:

Stillorgan Park Hotel
Dublin City, Co. Dublin
Tel: +353-1-200 1800 ......Page 144
Contact Person:
Lorna Lambert
Number of Meeting/Conference Rooms: 20
Number of Delegates catered for in any one room:
Minimum: 2 Maximum: 500
Facilities available:

Tara Towers Hotel
Dublin City, Co. Dublin
Tel: +353-1-269 4666 ......Page 145
Contact Person:
Darelle Van Jaarsveld
Number of Meeting/Conference Rooms: 4
Number of Delegates catered for in any one room:
Minimum: 2 Maximum: 300
Facilities available:

Temple Bar Hotel
Dublin City, Co. Dublin
Tel: +353-1-677 3333 ......Page 145
Contact Person:
Paul Donnelly
Number of Meeting/Conference Rooms: 5
Number of Delegates catered for in any one room:
Minimum: 2 Maximum: 70
Facilities available:

Waterside House Hotel & Signal Restaurant
Donabate, Co. Dublin
Tel: +353-1-843 6153 ......Page 119
Contact Person:
Paul Slattery
Number of Meeting/Conference Rooms: 2
Number of Delegates catered for in any one room:
Minimum: 2 Maximum: 400
Facilities available:

Westin Dublin
Dublin City, Co. Dublin
Tel: +353-1-645 1000 ......Page 147
Contact Person:
Marlene Buckridge
Number of Meeting/Conference Rooms: 9
Number of Delegates catered for in any one room:
Minimum: 2 Maximum: 270
Facilities available:

Co. Kildare

Clanard Court Hotel
Athy, Co. Kildare
Tel: +353-59-864 0666 ....Page 151
Contact Person:
Sandra Foy / Clare Dunne
Number of Meeting/Conference Rooms: 6
Number of Delegates catered for in any one room:
Minimum: 1 Maximum: 450
Facilities available:

Courtyard Hotel Leixlip
Leixlip, Co. Kildare
Tel: +353-1-629 5100 ......Page 152
Contact Person:
Lynda Roche
Number of Meeting/Conference Rooms: 4
Number of Delegates catered for in any one room:
Minimum: 2 Maximum: 120
Facilities available:

Derby House Hotel
Kildare Town, Co. Kildare
Tel: +353-45-522144........Page 152
Contact Person:
Cecilia Lau
Number of Meeting/Conference Rooms: 2
Number of Delegates catered for in any one room:
Minimum: 2 Maximum: 200
Facilities available:

K Club (The)
Straffan, Co. Kildare
Tel: +353-1-601 7200 ......Page 156
Contact Person:
Fiona Devane
Number of Meeting/Conference Rooms: 9
Number of Delegates catered for in any one room:
Minimum: 2 Maximum: 460
Facilities available:

Keadeen Hotel
Newbridge, Co. Kildare
Tel: +353-45-431666........Page 156
Contact Person:
Pauline Barry
Number of Meeting/Conference Rooms: 10
Number of Delegates catered for in any one room:
Minimum: 2 Maximum: 800
Facilities available:

Maudlins House Hotel
Naas, Co. Kildare
Tel: +353-45-896999........Page 154
Contact Person:
David Fagan
Number of Meeting/Conference Rooms: 5
Number of Delegates catered for in any one room:
Minimum: 2 Maximum: 130
Facilities available:

Black Out Facilities   Air-Conditioning   Interpreting Equipment   Audio Visual

299

Conference Facilities
...Select A Venue For your Agenda!

Co. Kildare CONTINUED

Westgrove Hotel
Clane, Co. Kildare
Tel: +353-45-989900 ....Page 152
Contact Person:
Clodagh McDonnell
Number of Meeting/Conference Rooms: 10
Number of Delegates catered for in any one room:
Minimum: 2 Maximum: 500
Facilities available:

Co. Laois

Portlaoise Heritage Hotel
Portlaoise, Co. Laois
Tel: +353-57-867 8588 ....Page 157
Contact Person:
Sandra Brennan
Number of Meeting/Conference Rooms: 13
Number of Delegates catered for in any one room:
Minimum: 5 Maximum: 300
Facilities available:

Co. Longford

Annaly Hotel
Longford Town, Co. Longford
Tel: +353-43-334 3690 ....Page 158
Contact Person:
Duty Manager
Number of Meeting/Conference Rooms: 4
Number of Delegates catered for in any one room:
Minimum: 10 Maximum: 450
Facilities available:

Longford Arms Hotel, Spa & Leisure Centre
Longford Town, Co. Longford
Tel: +353-43-334 6296 ....Page 158
Contact Person:
Duty Manager
Number of Meeting/Conference Rooms: 6
Number of Delegates catered for in any one room:
Minimum: 10 Maximum: 450
Facilities available:

Co. Louth

Ballymascanlon House Hotel
Dundalk, Co. Louth
Tel: +353-42-935 8200 ....Page 161
Contact Person:
Chris Brayden
Number of Meeting/Conference Rooms: 8
Number of Delegates catered for in any one room:
Minimum: 8 Maximum: 300
Facilities available:

d (The)
Drogheda, Co. Louth
Tel: +353-41-987 7700 ....Page 160
Contact Person:
Margaret Caherty
Number of Meeting/Conference Rooms: 6
Number of Delegates catered for in any one room:
Minimum: 2 Maximum: 250
Facilities available:

McKevitt's Village Hotel
Carlingford, Co. Louth
Tel: +353-42-937 3116 ....Page 160
Contact Person:
Dermot O'Farrell
Number of Meeting/Conference Rooms: 1
Number of Delegates catered for in any one room:
Minimum: 40 Maximum: 100
Facilities available:

Westcourt Hotel
Drogheda, Co. Louth
Tel: +353-41-983 0965 ....Page 160
Contact Person:
Thomas Gavan
Number of Meeting/Conference Rooms: 3
Number of Delegates catered for in any one room:
Minimum: 1 Maximum: 400
Facilities available:

Co. Meath

CityNorth Hotel
Gormanston, Co. Meath
Tel: +353-1-690 6666 ......Page 163
Contact Person:
Marianne Fanning
Number of Meeting/Conference Rooms: 13
Number of Delegates catered for in any one room:
Minimum: 2 Maximum: 650
Facilities available:

Knightsbrook Hotel, Spa & Golf Resort
Trim, Co. Meath
Tel: +353-46-948 2100 ....Page 165
Contact Person:
Clara Clarke
Number of Meeting/Conference Rooms: 14
Number of Delegates catered for in any one room:
Minimum: 2 Maximum: 1100
Facilities available:

Newgrange Hotel
Navan, Co. Meath
Tel: +353-46-907 4100 ....Page 164
Contact Person:
Caroline Hegarty
Number of Meeting/Conference Rooms: 6
Number of Delegates catered for in any one room:
Minimum: 2 Maximum: 500
Facilities available:

 Black Out Facilities    Air-Conditioning   Interpreting Equipment   Audio Visual

Conference Facilities

...Select A Venue For your Agenda!

Station House Hotel and Signal Restaurant
Kilmessan, Co. Meath
Tel: +353-46-902 5239 ....Page 164
Contact Person:
Denise Slattery
Number of Meeting/Conference Rooms: 4
Number of Delegates catered for in any one room:
Minimum: 2 Maximum: 350
Facilities available:

Trim Castle Hotel
Trim, Co. Meath
Tel: +353-46-948 3000 ....Page 165
Contact Person:
Jillian O'Brien
Number of Meeting/Conference Rooms: 8
Number of Delegates catered for in any one room:
Minimum: 2 Maximum: 500
Facilities available:

Co. Monaghan

Castle (The) at Castle Leslie Estate
Glaslough, Co. Monaghan
Tel: +353-47-88100 ....Page 166
Contact Person:
Karen Matthews
Number of Meeting/Conference Rooms: 5
Number of Delegates catered for in any one room:
Minimum: 2 Maximum: 250
Facilities available:

Co. Offaly

Bridge House Hotel
Tullamore, Co. Offaly
Tel: +353-57-932 5600 ....Page 168
Contact Person:
Denise Brereton
Number of Meeting/Conference Rooms: 7
Number of Delegates catered for in any one room:
Minimum: 10 Maximum: 600
Facilities available:

Tullamore Court Hotel
Tullamore, Co. Offaly
Tel: +353-57-934 6666 ....Page 170
Contact Person:
Michelle Peake
Number of Meeting/Conference Rooms: 14
Number of Delegates catered for in any one room:
Minimum: 5 Maximum: 750
Facilities available:

Co. Westmeath

Glasson Country House Hotel and Golf Club
Athlone, Co. Westmeath
Tel: +353-90-648 5120 ....Page 171
Contact Person:
Gareth Jones / Fidelma Reid
Number of Meeting/Conference Rooms: 5
Number of Delegates catered for in any one room:
Minimum: 4 Maximum: 200
Facilities available:

Radisson Blu Hotel Athlone
Athlone, Co. Westmeath
Tel: +353-90-644 2600 ....Page 172
Contact Person:
Meetings and Events Department
Number of Meeting/Conference Rooms: 10
Number of Delegates catered for in any one room:
Minimum: 10 Maximum: 600
Facilities available:

Sheraton Athlone Hotel
Athlone, Co. Westmeath
Tel: +353-90-645 1000 ....Page 172
Contact Person:
Gemma Hynes
Number of Meeting/Conference Rooms: 11
Number of Delegates catered for in any one room:
Minimum: 2 Maximum: 850
Facilities available:

Co. Wicklow

Glendalough Hotel
Glendalough, Co. Wicklow
Tel: +353-404-45135 ....Page 176
Contact Person:
Alan Groarke
Number of Meeting/Conference Rooms: 3
Number of Delegates catered for in any one room:
Minimum: 5 Maximum: 200
Facilities available:

Glenview Hotel & Leisure Cub
Glen-O-The-Downs, Co. Wicklow
Tel: +353-1-287 3399 ......Page 177
Contact Person:
Deirdre Flanagan
Number of Meeting/Conference Rooms: 8
Number of Delegates catered for in any one room:
Minimum: 1 Maximum: 300
Facilities available:

 Black Out Facilities  Air-Conditioning  Interpreting Equipment  Audio Visual

Conference Facilities
...Select A Venue For your Agenda!

Co. Wicklow CONTINUED

Grand Hotel
Wicklow Town, Co. Wicklow
Tel: +353-404-67337 ....Page 178
Contact Person:
Wendy Murphy
Number of Meeting/Conference Rooms: 4
Number of Delegates catered for in any one room:
Minimum: 5 Maximum: 380
Facilities available:

Martello Hotel (The)
Bray, Co. Wicklow
Tel: +353-1-286 8000 ......Page 176
Contact Person:
Frances Lamb / Donal Byrne
Number of Meeting/Conference Rooms: 1
Number of Delegates catered for in any one room:
Minimum: 20 Maximum: 100
Facilities available:

The Ritz-Carlton, Powerscourt
Enniskerry, Co. Wicklow
Tel: +353-1-274 8888 ......Page 176
Contact Person:
Jens Flugge
Number of Meeting/Conference Rooms: 10
Number of Delegates catered for in any one room:
Minimum: 10 Maximum: 600
Facilities available:

Ireland South
Co. Carlow

Lord Bagenal Inn
Leighlinbridge, Co. Carlow
Tel: +353-59-977 4000 ....Page 184
Contact Person:
Sue Baldwin
Number of Meeting/Conference Rooms: 4
Number of Delegates catered for in any one room:
Minimum: 2 Maximum: 450
Facilities available:

Mount Wolseley Hotel, Spa & Country Club
Tullow, Co. Carlow
Tel: +353-59-918 0100 ....Page 184
Contact Person:
Anne Marie Hayes
Number of Meeting/Conference Rooms: 15
Number of Delegates catered for in any one room:
Minimum: 2 Maximum: 800
Facilities available:

Talbot Hotel Carlow
Carlow Town, Co. Carlow
Tel: +353-59-915 3000 ....Page 184
Contact Person:
Niamh Whelan
Number of Meeting/Conference Rooms: 5
Number of Delegates catered for in any one room:
Minimum: 2 Maximum: 400
Facilities available:

Co. Cork

Abbey Hotel
Ballyvourney, Co. Cork
Tel: +353-26-45324 ....Page 186
Contact Person:
John Buckley
Number of Meeting/Conference Rooms: 1
Number of Delegates catered for in any one room:
Minimum: 2 Maximum: 200
Facilities available:

Actons Hotel
Kinsale, Co. Cork
Tel: +353-21-477 9900 ....Page 202
Contact Person:
Mary Kirby
Number of Meeting/Conference Rooms: 3
Number of Delegates catered for in any one room:
Minimum: 2 Maximum: 250
Facilities available:

Blarney Golf Resort
Blarney, Co. Cork
Tel: +353-21-438 4477 ....Page 188
Contact Person:
Caroline Nyhan
Number of Meeting/Conference Rooms: 7
Number of Delegates catered for in any one room:
Minimum: 20 Maximum: 350
Facilities available:

Commons Inn Hotel
Cork City, Co. Cork
Tel: +353-21-421 0300 ....Page 194
Contact Person:
Ashley Colson
Number of Meeting/Conference Rooms: 3
Number of Delegates catered for in any one room:
Minimum: 2 Maximum: 300
Facilities available:

 Black Out Facilities    Air-Conditioning   Interpreting Equipment   Audio Visual

...Select A Venue For your Agenda!

Fitzgeralds Vienna Woods Hotel Cork
Cork City, Co. Cork
Tel: +353-21-455 6800 ....Page 195
Contact Person:
Maryann Wholly
Number of Meeting/Conference Rooms: 6
Number of Delegates catered for in any one room:
Minimum: 1 Maximum: 300
Facilities available:

Fota Island Resort
Fota Island, Co. Cork
Tel: +353-21-488 3700 ....Page 200
Contact Person:
Clodagh Kelleher (Events Manager)
Number of Meeting/Conference Rooms: 6
Number of Delegates catered for in any one room:
Minimum: 12 Maximum: 400
Facilities available:

Garryvoe Hotel
Shanagarry, Co. Cork
Tel: +353-21-464 6718 ....Page 206
Contact Person:
Stephen Belton
Number of Meeting/Conference Rooms: 5
Number of Delegates catered for in any one room:
Minimum: 2 Maximum: 300
Facilities available:

Gresham Metropole
Cork City, Co. Cork
Tel: +353-21-464 3700 ....Page 196
Contact Person:
Ann McCarthy
Number of Meeting/Conference Rooms: 12
Number of Delegates catered for in any one room:
Minimum: 1 Maximum: 350
Facilities available:

Hayfield Manor Hotel
Cork City, Co. Cork
Tel: +353-21-484 5900 ....Page 196
Contact Person:
Úna O'Shea
Number of Meeting/Conference Rooms: 4
Number of Delegates catered for in any one room:
Minimum: 2 Maximum: 120
Facilities available:

Hotel Isaacs
Cork City, Co. Cork
Tel: +353-21-450 0011 ....Page 196
Contact Person:
Paula Lynch
Number of Meeting/Conference Rooms: 2
Number of Delegates catered for in any one room:
Minimum: 1 Maximum: 50
Facilities available:

Inchydoney Island Lodge & Spa
Clonakilty, Co. Cork
Tel: +353-23-883 3143 ....Page 191
Contact Person:
Helen Deakin / Amy Dorgan
Number of Meeting/Conference Rooms: 4
Number of Delegates catered for in any one room:
Minimum: 1 Maximum: 250
Facilities available:

Maryborough Hotel & Spa
Cork City, Co. Cork
Tel: +353-21-436 5555 ....Page 198
Contact Person:
Mary Bernard
Number of Meeting/Conference Rooms: 10
Number of Delegates catered for in any one room:
Minimum: 2 Maximum: 500
Facilities available:

Oriel House Hotel, Leisure Club & Spa
Ballincollig, Co. Cork
Tel: +353-21-420 8400 ....Page 185
Contact Person:
Ann Shanahan
Number of Meeting/Conference Rooms: 5
Number of Delegates catered for in any one room:
Minimum: 2 Maximum: 400
Facilities available:

Silver Springs Moran Hotel
Cork City, Co. Cork
Tel: +353-21-450 7533 ....Page 199
Contact Person:
Caroline White
Number of Meeting/Conference Rooms: 8
Number of Delegates catered for in any one room:
Minimum: 2 Maximum: 1500
Facilities available:

Springfort Hall Hotel
Mallow, Co. Cork
Tel: +353-22-21278 ....Page 205
Contact Person:
Paul Walsh
Number of Meeting/Conference Rooms: 7
Number of Delegates catered for in any one room:
Minimum: 1 Maximum: 300
Facilities available:

West Cork Hotel
Skibbereen, Co. Cork
Tel: +353-28-21277 ....Page 207
Contact Person:
Karen Buchanan
Number of Meeting/Conference Rooms: 3
Number of Delegates catered for in any one room:
Minimum: 10 Maximum: 300
Facilities available:

 Black Out Facilities    Air-Conditioning   Interpreting Equipment   Audio Visual

Conference Facilities
...Select A Venue For your Agenda!

Co. Cork CONTINUED

Westlodge Hotel
Bantry, Co. Cork
Tel: +353-27-50360..........Page 187
Contact Person:
Eileen M. O'Shea or Annette McCarthy
Number of Meeting/Conference Rooms: 3
Number of Delegates catered for in any one room:
Minimum: 20 Maximum: 300
Facilities available:

Co. Kerry

Aghadoe Heights Hotel & Spa
Killarney, Co. Kerry
Tel: +353-64-663 1766 ....Page 217
Contact Person:
Jacinta Prendergast
Number of Meeting/Conference Rooms: 4
Number of Delegates catered for in any one room:
Minimum: 6 Maximum: 120
Facilities available:

Dingle Skellig Hotel
Dingle (An Daingean), Co. Kerry
Tel: +353-66-915 0200 ....Page 213
Contact Person:
Karen Byrnes
Number of Meeting/Conference Rooms: 2
Number of Delegates catered for in any one room:
Minimum: 10 Maximum: 200
Facilities available:

Grand Hotel
Tralee, Co. Kerry
Tel: +353-66-712 1499 ....Page 236
Contact Person:
Eileen Egan
Number of Meeting/Conference Rooms: 8
Number of Delegates catered for in any one room:
Minimum: 2 Maximum: 300
Facilities available:

Heights Hotel Killarney (The)
Killarney, Co. Kerry
Tel: +353-64-663 1158 ....Page 224
Contact Person:
Noreen O'Leary
Number of Meeting/Conference Rooms: 3
Number of Delegates catered for in any one room:
Minimum: 20 Maximum: 400
Facilities available:

Lake Hotel (The)
Killarney, Co. Kerry
Tel: +353-64-663 1035 ....Page 229
Contact Person:
Heather MacIver / Aoife Hickey
Number of Meeting/Conference Rooms: 4
Number of Delegates catered for in any one room:
Minimum: 1 Maximum: 110
Facilities available:

Malton (The)
Killarney, Co. Kerry
Tel: +353-64-663 8000 ....Page 230
Contact Person:
Emer Corridan/Dawn Fitzell
Number of Meeting/Conference Rooms: 15
Number of Delegates catered for in any one room:
Minimum: 2 Maximum: 1000
Facilities available:

Meadowlands Hotel
Tralee, Co. Kerry
Tel: +353-66-718 0444 ....Page 236
Contact Person:
Siobhan O' Mahony
Number of Meeting/Conference Rooms: 6
Number of Delegates catered for in any one room:
Minimum: 20 Maximum: 250
Facilities available:

Muckross Park Hotel & Cloisters Spa
Killarney, Co. Kerry
Tel: +353-64-662 3400 ....Page 230
Contact Person:
Niall Kerins
Number of Meeting/Conference Rooms: 4
Number of Delegates catered for in any one room:
Minimum: 2 Maximum: 230
Facilities available:

Sneem Hotel
Sneem, Co. Kerry
Tel: +353-64-667 5100 ....Page 234
Contact Person:
Nicola Duggan
Number of Meeting/Conference Rooms: 3
Number of Delegates catered for in any one room:
Minimum: 10 Maximum: 500
Facilities available:

Co. Kilkenny

Butler House
Kilkenny City, Co. Kilkenny
Tel: +353-56-776 5707 ....Page 239
Contact Person:
Gabrielle Hickey
Number of Meeting/Conference Rooms: 3
Number of Delegates catered for in any one room:
Minimum: 1 Maximum: 100
Facilities available:

Black Out Facilities   Air-Conditioning   Interpreting Equipment   Audio Visual

Conference Facilities

...Select A Venue For your Agenda!

Hotel Kilkenny
Kilkenny City, Co. Kilkenny
Tel: +353-56-776 2000 ....Page 240
Contact Person:
Alva Kenny
Number of Meeting/Conference Rooms: 11
Number of Delegates catered for in any one room:
Minimum: 5 Maximum: 700
Facilities available:

Kilkenny Ormonde Hotel
Kilkenny City, Co. Kilkenny
Tel: +353-56-775 0200 ....Page 241
Contact Person:
Deirdre Twomey
Number of Meeting/Conference Rooms: 10
Number of Delegates catered for in any one room:
Minimum: 2 Maximum: 450
Facilities available:

Kilkenny River Court
Kilkenny City, Co. Kilkenny
Tel: +353-56-772 3388 ....Page 242
Contact Person:
Kerry Foreman
Number of Meeting/Conference Rooms: 6
Number of Delegates catered for in any one room:
Minimum: 2 Maximum: 260
Facilities available:

Langton House Hotel
Kilkenny City, Co. Kilkenny
Tel: +353-56-776 5133 ....Page 242
Contact Person:
Sean Reád
Number of Meeting/Conference Rooms: 1
Number of Delegates catered for in any one room:
Minimum: 10 Maximum: 400
Facilities available:

Lyrath Estate Hotel & Convention Centre
Kilkenny City, Co. Kilkenny
Tel: +353-56-776 0088 ....Page 243
Contact Person:
Dervla / Mary Áine
Number of Meeting/Conference Rooms: 10
Number of Delegates catered for in any one room:
Minimum: 2 Maximum: 1500
Facilities available:

Newpark Hotel
Kilkenny City, Co. Kilkenny
Tel: +353-56-776 0500 ....Page 243
Contact Person:
yguilfoyle@newpark.com
Number of Meeting/Conference Rooms: 7
Number of Delegates catered for in any one room:
Minimum: 5 Maximum: 500
Facilities available:

Co. Tipperary

Abbey Court Hotel, Lodges & Trinity Leisure Spa
Nenagh, Co. Tipperary
Tel: +353-67-41111..........Page 249
Contact Person:
Joanne O' Dwyer
Number of Meeting/Conference Rooms: 12
Number of Delegates catered for in any one room:
Minimum: 2 Maximum: 450
Facilities available:

Ballykisteen Hotel & Golf Resort
Tipperary Town, Co. Tipperary
Tel: +353-62-33333..........Page 250
Contact Person:
Sales Team
Number of Meeting/Conference Rooms: 6
Number of Delegates catered for in any one room:
Minimum: 2 Maximum: 350
Facilities available:

Cashel Palace Hotel
Cashel, Co. Tipperary
Tel: +353-62-62707..........Page 247
Contact Person:
Elaine Corstin
Number of Meeting/Conference Rooms: 3
Number of Delegates catered for in any one room:
Minimum: 2 Maximum: 10
Facilities available:

Dundrum House Hotel, Golf & Leisure Resort
Cashel, Co. Tipperary
Tel: +353-62-71116..........Page 247
Contact Person:
Deirdre Crowe
Number of Meeting/Conference Rooms: 3
Number of Delegates catered for in any one room:
Minimum: 2 Maximum: 350
Facilities available:

Horse and Jockey Hotel
Horse and Jockey, Co. Tipperary
Tel: +353-504-44192........Page 249
Contact Person:
Caroline Egan
Number of Meeting/Conference Rooms: 10
Number of Delegates catered for in any one room:
Minimum: 2 Maximum: 200
Facilities available:

BO Black Out Facilities   **AC** Air-Conditioning   **IE** Interpreting Equipment   **AV** Audio Visual

305

Conference Facilities
...Select A Venue For your Agenda!

Co. Tipperary CONTINUED

Hotel Minella & Leisure Club
Clonmel, Co. Tipperary
Tel: +353-52-612 2388 ....Page 248
Contact Person:
John Nallen
Number of Meeting/Conference Rooms: 10
Number of Delegates catered for in any one room:
Minimum: 2 Maximum: 500
Facilities available:
BO AC IE AV

Templemore Arms Hotel
Templemore, Co. Tipperary
Tel: +353-504-31423 ....Page 249
Contact Person:
Dan Ward
Number of Meeting/Conference Rooms: 2
Number of Delegates catered for in any one room:
Minimum: 2 Maximum: 350
Facilities available:
AC AV

Co. Waterford

Dooley's Hotel
Waterford City, Co. Waterford
Tel: +353-51-873531 ....Page 257
Contact Person:
Clare O'Mahony
Number of Meeting/Conference Rooms: 3
Number of Delegates catered for in any one room:
Minimum: 2 Maximum: 300
Facilities available:
BO AC AV

Granville Hotel
Waterford City, Co. Waterford
Tel: +353-51-305555 ....Page 258
Contact Person:
Richard Hurley
Number of Meeting/Conference Rooms: 4
Number of Delegates catered for in any one room:
Minimum: 1 Maximum: 200
Facilities available:
BO AC AV

Park Hotel, Leisure Centre & Holiday Homes
Dungarvan, Co. Waterford
Tel: +353-58-42899 ....Page 253
Contact Person:
David Livingstone
Number of Meeting/Conference Rooms: 17
Number of Delegates catered for in any one room:
Minimum: 2 Maximum: 500
Facilities available:
BO AC IE AV

Tower Hotel & Leisure Centre
Waterford City, Co. Waterford
Tel: +353-51-862300 ....Page 260
Contact Person:
Catherina Hurley
Number of Meeting/Conference Rooms: 7
Number of Delegates catered for in any one room:
Minimum: 2 Maximum: 450
Facilities available:
BO AC IE AV

Waterford Marina Hotel
Waterford City, Co. Waterford
Tel: +353-51-856600 ....Page 260
Contact Person:
Linda Bennett
Number of Meeting/Conference Rooms: 1
Number of Delegates catered for in any one room:
Minimum: 2 Maximum: 50
Facilities available:
BO IE AV

Co. Wexford

Amber Springs Hotel & Health Spa
Gorey, Co. Wexford
Tel: +353-53-948 4000 ....Page 263
Contact Person:
Sandra Wogan
Number of Delegates catered for in any one room:
Minimum: 2 Maximum: 600
Facilities available:
BO AC IE AV

Ashdown Park Hotel Conference & Leisure Centre
Gorey, Co. Wexford
Tel: +353-53-948 0500 ....Page 263
Contact Person:
Liam Moran
Number of Meeting/Conference Rooms: 5
Number of Delegates catered for in any one room:
Minimum: 5 Maximum: 500
Facilities available:
BO AC IE AV

Brandon House Hotel & Solas Croí Eco Spa
New Ross, Co. Wexford
Tel: +353-51-421703 ....Page 264
Contact Person:
Moira Carroll
Number of Meeting/Conference Rooms: 4
Number of Delegates catered for in any one room:
Minimum: 2 Maximum: 400
Facilities available:
AC IE AV

BO Black Out Facilities   AC Air-Conditioning   IE Interpreting Equipment   AV Audio Visual

306

...Select A Venue For your Agenda!

Ferrycarrig Hotel
Wexford Town, Co. Wexford
Tel: +353-53-912 0999 ....Page 267
Contact Person:
Áine Byrne
Number of Meeting/Conference Rooms: 4
Number of Delegates catered for in any one room:
Minimum: 2 Maximum: 450
Facilities available:

Riverbank House Hotel
Wexford Town, Co. Wexford
Tel: +353-53-912 3611 ....Page 268
Contact Person:
Caroline Byrne
Number of Meeting/Conference Rooms: 2
Number of Delegates catered for in any one room:
Minimum: 10 Maximum: 350
Facilities available:

Riverside Park Hotel and Leisure Club
Enniscorthy, Co. Wexford
Tel: +353-53-923 7800 ....Page 262
Contact Person:
Joy Rothwell - Conference & Banqueting Manager
Number of Meeting/Conference Rooms: 5
Number of Delegates catered for in any one room:
Minimum: 2 Maximum: 700
Facilities available:

Newbay Country House
Wexford Town, Co. Wexford
Tel: +353-53-914 2779 ....Page 268
Contact Person:
Áine Frizelle
Number of Meeting/Conference Rooms: 2
Number of Delegates catered for in any one room:
Minimum: 10 Maximum: 120
Facilities available:

Black Out Facilities    Air-Conditioning    Interpreting Equipment    Audio Visual

Direct low rates and great special offers guaranteed

Irelandhotels.com
We've got it covered

You can find all the best deals in all of these places

Website | Mobile App | Printed Guide |
facebook.com/irelandhotels | irelandhotels.com/onlineguide

Spa & Leisure
2011

Ireland is rapidly developing its spa market, with a selection of destination, day, health and resort spas to choose from, as well as superb leisure facilities - all in the wonderful surroundings that make Ireland a unique holiday destination. The following pages will provide a flavour of some of the facilities and treatments on offer in many of the hotels and guesthouses featured in this guide.

So come on and get pampered!

Irelandhotels.com
We've got it covered

Spa & Leisure In Ireland
...Let us pamper you, while you stay!

We invite you to Ireland to enhance your precious leisure time. Relax in the perfect sanctuary of the oasis that is Ireland! Our philosophy is to enable you to leave us fully refreshed and restored by experiencing some of the wonderful spa & leisure treatments available in the unique and warm facilities on offer in the hotels and guesthouses listed in this section. A full description of the hotels and guesthouses can be had by looking up the appropriate page number.

Listings are by Region, County, Premises Name in alphabetical order.

Ireland West
Co. Clare

Bunratty Castle Hotel
Bunratty, Co. Clare
Tel: +353-61-478700 .... Page 35
Name of Spa:
Angsana Spa
No. of Treatments: 20
No. of Treatment Rooms: 5
Treatments Offered:
Massage, Body Polish, Facial, Indian Head Massage, Skin Enhancer, Hands Paraffin, Feet Paraffin, 1/2 Day & Full Day Pamper Packages
Facilities available:
Sauna, Steam Room, Vitality Pool, Relaxation Balcony, Relaxation Suite, Jacuzzi, Fully Equipped Gym, Personal Training Facilities

Falls Hotel & Spa
Ennistymon, Co. Clare
Tel: +353-65-707 1004 .... Page 40
Name of Spa:
River Spa
Type of Spa:
Hotel with Selective Spa
No. of Treatments: 50
No. of Treatment Rooms: 12
Treatments Offered:
Facials, Body Massage, Mens' Treatments, Dry Floats, Wraps, Mud Treatments, Couples Treatments, Body Polish, 1/2 and Full Day Packages and much more
Facilities available:
20m Swimming Pool, Outdoor Hot Tub, Jacuzzi, Steam Room, Sauna, Gymnasium, Jet Pool and Childrens Pool

Kilkee Thalassotherapy Centre & Guesthouse
Kilkee, Co. Clare
Tel: +353-65-905 6742 .... Page 42
Name of Spa:
Kilkee Thalassotherapy Centre
Type of Spa:
Seaweed Baths
No. of Treatments: 18
No. of Treatment Rooms: 6
Treatments Offered:
Natural Seaweed Baths, Balneotherapy, Swedish Massage, Body Scrub, Seaweed Body Wrap, Frigi-Thalgo, Facials, Manicures, Pedicures, Aromatherapy, Massage, Reflexology, Hot Stone Massage
Facilities available:
Sauna, Steam Room, Manicure/Pedicure Room, 6 Treatment Rooms. Relaxation area. Winner, Best Day Spa 2004 (Irish Beauty Industry)

Co. Donegal

Jackson's Hotel, Conference & Leisure Centre
Ballybofey, Co. Donegal
Tel: +353-74-913 1021 .... Page 45
Name of Spa:
Health Suite
No. of Treatments: 10
No. of Treatment Rooms: 3
Treatments Offered:
Full Body Massage, Indian Head Massage, Reflexology, Facials, Manicures, Pedicures, Yoga
Facilities available:
22m Swimming Pool, Jacuzzi, Steam Cabin, Sauna, Massage Rooms, Spa Bath, Sun Beds, Hot Tub, Aqua Lounger

Kee's Hotel, Leisure & Wellness Centre
Ballybofey, Co. Donegal
Tel: +353-74-913 1018 .... Page 46
Name of Spa:
Eternal Beauty
No. of Treatments: 15
No. of Treatment Rooms: 1
Treatments Offered:
Facials, Waxing, Tinting, Reflexology, Hopi Ear Candle, Hot Stone Therapy Massage, Aromatherapy Massage, Make-up, Manicure & Pedicure, Tanning
Facilities available:
Swimming Pool, Gym, Sauna, Jacuzzi, Steam Room, Massage Room

Mill Park Hotel, Conference Centre & Leisure Club
Donegal Town, Co. Donegal
Tel: +353-74-972 2880 .... Page 48
Name of Spa:
The Wellness Centre
No. of Treatments: 20
No. of Treatment Rooms: 4
Treatments Offered:
Massage, Waxing, Make up, Manicure, Pedicure, Facials, Body Wraps, Holistic Treatments, Hopi Candle, Hot Stone Therapy Treatments
Facilities available:
Massage Room, Beauty Treatment Room, Nail Bar, Heated Swimming Pool, Fitness Room, Steam Room, Jacuzzi, Solarium

---

Did you know?
Reflexology
The physical act of applying pressure to the feet & hands without the use of oil or lotion. It is based on a system of zones & reflex areas that reflect an image of the body on the feet and hands with a premise that such work effects a physical change to the body.

...Let us pamper you, while you stay!

Spa & Leisure In Ireland
...Let us pamper you, while you stay!

Shandon Hotel
Spa and Wellness
Dunfanaghy, Co. Donegal
Tel: +353-74-913 6137 ....Page 50
Name of Spa:
OCEAN SPA
Type of Spa:
Hotel with Comprehensive Spa
No. of Treatments: 60
No. of Treatment Rooms: 10
Treatments Offered:
Spa Experience, Peppermint Sea Twist, Seascape Stone Massage, Reflexology, Aromatherapy, Four Layer Facial, Turkish Body Scrub, Full Body Massage, Indian Head Massage, Seaweed Body Treatment
Facilities available:
Hydro Vitality Pool, Heated Loungers, Foot Spa, Salt Grotto, Herb Sauna, Ice Fountain, Lifestyle Showers, Outdoor Canadian Hot Tub, Dry Floatation, Balneotherapy Bath

Silver Tassie Hotel & Spa
Letterkenny, Co. Donegal
Tel: +353-74-912 5619 ....Page 53
Name of Spa:
Seascape Spa
No. of Treatments: 30
No. of Treatment Rooms: 6
Treatments Offered:
Seaweed Bath, Massage Treatments, Facials, Beauty Treatments, Pedicure, Make-Up, Spray Tan
Facilities available:
Treatment Rooms, Aroma Steam Room, Cocoon Meditation Room, Seaweed Bath, Spray Tanning Room, Hair Salon, Double Treatment Room, Snooze Relaxation Room

Solis Lough Eske Castle
Donegal Town, Co. Donegal
Tel: +353-74-972 5100 ....Page 49
Name of Spa:
Spa Solis
Type of Spa:
Resort Spa
No. of Treatments: 40
No. of Treatment Rooms: 7
Treatments Offered:
Facial Therapy, Bodycare Therapy, Massage Therapy, Pregnancy Therapy, Ultimate Rituals, Hand Therapy, Foot Therapy
Facilities available:
Hydrotherapy Pool, Sanarium, Tropical Rain Showers, Swimming Pool, Ice Fountain, Couples Suites, Singles Suites, Relaxation Room, Fitness Centre

Co. Galway

Abbeyglen Castle Hotel
Clifden, Co. Galway
Tel: +353-95-21201 ....Page 57
Name of Spa:
Abbeyglen Beauty & Relaxation Centre
No. of Treatments: 16
No. of Treatment Rooms: 3
Treatments Offered:
Escale Beauté, Le Grand Classique, Optimiser, Pamper Package, De luxe Jessica Manicure, Jessica Zen Spa Pedicure, Spray Tanning
Facilities available:
Sauna, Jacuzzi, Pedicure Station, Relaxation Room, Nail Bar

Clifden Station House Hotel
Clifden, Co. Galway
Tel: +353-95-21699 ....Page 59
Name of Spa:
Renew Spa
Type of Spa:
Hotel with Leisure Club Spa
No. of Treatments: 18
No. of Treatment Rooms: 4
Treatments Offered:
Body Scrubs, Mud Wraps, Facials, Massages, Reflexology, Deep Cleanse, Retreat Ritual
Facilities available:
Swimming Pool, Kiddies' Paddling Pool, Jacuzzi, Sauna, Steam Room, Gymnasium

Courtyard Marriott Galway
Galway City, Co. Galway
Tel: +353-91-513200 ....Page 64
Name of Spa:
The Spa
Type of Spa:
Hotel with Extensive Spa
No. of Treatments: 60
No. of Treatment Rooms: 7
Treatments Offered:
Signature Baths & Scrubs, Facials, Thermal Therapies, Body, Mens Treatments, IPL Rejuvenation
Facilities available:
Thermal Suite, Relaxation Loungers, Relaxation Room, Finnish Sauna, Aroma Steam Cabin, Feature Showers, Glass Ice Cave

Delphi Mountain Resort
Leenane, Co. Galway
Tel: +353-95-42208 ....Page 72
Name of Spa:
Delphi Mountain Resort Spa
Type of Spa:
Resort Spa
No. of Treatments: 20
No. of Treatment Rooms: 4
Treatments Offered:
Facials, Seaweed Baths, Wraps, Massages, Manicure, Pedicure
Facilities available:
Sauna, Steamroom, Jacuzzi

Did you know?

'CACI' Quantum:

Non-Surgical Face & Body Lifts
The CACI Quantum is the most advanced face and body treatment system available. Using specific facial techniques in conjunction with a combination of slimming and toning applications, it restores and re-defines facial muscles, reducing lines and wrinkles while simultaneously tightening body muscles.

...Let us pamper you, while you stay!

Spa & Leisure In Ireland

...Let us pamper you, while you stay!

Co. Galway CONTINUED

g Hotel (The)
Galway City, Co. Galway
Tel: +353-91-865200 ....Page 65
Name of Spa:
ESPA at the g
Type of Spa:
Hotel with Comprehensive Spa
No. of Treatments: 50
No. of Treatment Rooms: 12
Treatments Offered:
ESPA Super Active Facials, ESPA Aromatherapy Massage, ESPA Body Massages, ESPA Body Wraps, ESPA Chakra Balancing Treatments with Hot Stones, ESPA Holistic Back, Face & Scalp Massage with Hot Stones, Purva Karma Four Hand Massage, Dosha Specific Body Ritual, ESPA Hand & Arm Treatment with Hot Stones, ESPA Foot & Leg Treatment with Hot Stones, ESPA Pre & Post Natal Indulgence
Facilities available:
Vitality Pool, Crystal Steam Room, Lifestyle Shower, Rain Shower, Rock Sauna, Ice Fountain, Heated Loungers, Water Wall Feature, Glass Pavilion Relaxation Room, Secret Rooftop Zen Garden, 8 Treatment Rooms, 4 Beauty Suites

Hotel Meyrick
Galway City, Co. Galway
Tel: +353-91-564041 ....Page 66
Name of Spa:
The Square Spa
No. of Treatments: 40
No. of Treatment Rooms: 5
Treatments Offered:
Dermalogica Facial, Dermalogica Body Wrap, De luxe Manicure, Indian Head Massage, Swedish Full Body Massage, De luxe Pedicure, Platinum Detox, Hot Stone Massage, Detoxifying Sea Mud Wrap
Facilities available:
Jacuzzi, Steam Room, Relaxation Room, Hydrotherapy Bath, Fitness Suite, Outdoor Canadian Hot Tub

Inishbofin House Hotel
Inishbofin Island, Co. Galway
Tel: +353-95-45809 ....Page 72
Name of Spa:
Marine Spa
No. of Treatments: 12
No. of Treatment Rooms: 7
Treatments Offered:
Variety of Treatments and Beauty Therapy available

Lady Gregory Hotel, Conference & Leisure Club
Gort, Co. Galway
Tel: +353-91-632333 ....Page 70
Name of Spa:
Claddagh Heart
No. of Treatments: 36
No. of Treatment Rooms: 5
Treatments Offered:
Massage, Facials, Pedicures, Manicures, Tanning, Body Wraps, Waxing, Tinting, Ear Candling, Lazer Teeth Whitening
Facilities available:
Hydro Bath, Dry Floatation Bed, Foam Bath, Manicure Table, Tanning Room, 2 Bathrooms, 3 Showers, Pedicure Chair

Lough Rea Hotel & Spa
Loughrea, Co. Galway
Tel: +353-91-880088 ....Page 73
Name of Spa:
Shore Island Spa
No. of Treatments: 40
No. of Treatment Rooms: 10
Treatments Offered:
Massage, Hot Stone, Reflexology, Indian Head Massage, Facial
Facilities available:
Sauna, Steamroom, Sanarium, Jacuzzi, Light & Dark Relaxation Room

Raheen Woods Hotel
Tranquillity Spa & Kardio Kidz
Athenry, Co. Galway
Tel: +353-91-875888 ....Page 55
Name of Spa:
Tranquillity
No. of Treatments: 50
No. of Treatment Rooms: 6
Treatments Offered:
Germaine De Cappucini Facials, Dermalogica Facial, Body Wraps including Chocolate Wrap, Massage, Waxing, Pedicures, Manicures, Spa Days, Spray Tan, Make Up
Facilities available:
20m Heated Indoor Pool, Gymnasium, Sauna and Steam Room, Hydrotherapy Bath, Jacuzzi, Kiddies Pool, Crèche, Kardio Kidz Activity Centre

Co. Limerick

Absolute Hotel & Spa
Limerick City, Co. Limerick
Tel: +353-61-463600 ....Page 80
Name of Spa:
Escape Spa
Type of Spa:
Hotel with Extensive Spa
No. of Treatments: 20
No. of Treatment Rooms: 6
Treatments Offered:
Active Glow Facial, Total Indulgence Facial, Absolute Harmony Facial, Inchwrap, White Chocolate Body Wrap, Yummy Mummy Body Wrap, Hot Stone Massage
Facilities available:
5 Treatment Rooms, Thermal Suite which includes Jacuzzi, Sauna, Steam Room, Ice Drench, Feature Showers, Heated Loungers, Gem Stone Room, Relaxation Area, Male/Female Changing Rooms

---

Did you know?

Hot Stone Massage

Is a specialty massage that uses smooth, heated stones. They are often basalt, a black volcanic rock that absorbs and retains heat well. It is a deeply soothing, relaxing form of massage. The heat helps tight muscles release.

...Let us pamper you, while you stay!

Spa & Leisure In Ireland
...Let us pamper you, while you stay!

Fitzgeralds Woodlands House Hotel & Spa
Adare, Co. Limerick
Tel: +353-61-605100 ....Page 79
Name of Spa:
Revas Hair Salon, Beauty & Relaxation Spa
Type of Spa:
Hotel with Extensive Spa
No. of Treatments: 100
No. of Treatment Rooms: 18
Treatments Offered:
Hot Stone Massage Therapy, Body Polish, Platinum Detox, Non-Surgical Lyposculpture, Ocean Chleir Seaweed Envelopment Wrap, Genesis Inch Loss Wrap, Stimulating & Oxygenerating Facial, GM Collin Skin Care
Facilities available:
Thermal Suite, Herb Sauna, Crystal Steam Room, Experience Showers, Rasul Mud Chamber, Foot Baths, Relaxation Area, Rock Pool, Hair Salon, Balneotherapy Bath, Dining Area

No 1 Pery Square, Hotel & Spa
Limerick City, Co. Limerick
Tel: +353-61-402402 ....Page 82
Name of Spa:
The Spa @ No1
No. of Treatments: 30
No. of Treatment Rooms: 8
Treatments Offered:
Voya Facial, Voya Massage, Pre Natal & Post Natal Massage, Mom & Me Treatments, Seaweed Bathing Ritual, Body Wraps, Couples Treatments, Manicure & Pedicure, Make Up, Hot Towel Shave & Man Maintenence Facial
Facilities available:
Full Thermal Suite, Herbal Cocoon, Aroma Steam, Sauna with Coals, Foot Pools, Snooze Room, Zen Garden, Irish Mist Showers

Co. Mayo

Ashford Castle
Cong, Co. Mayo
Tel: +353-94-954 6003 ....Page 87
Name of Spa:
Health & Beauty Rooms
No. of Treatments: 10
No. of Treatment Rooms: 2
Treatments Offered:
Grand Classique Facial, Body Detox, Lavish Foot Treatment, Aroma-Stone Massage, Swedish Full Body Massage, Deep Tissue Massage, Head to Toe Revive, Reflexology, Tanning Treatment, Back Massage
Facilities available:
Jacuzzi, Steam Room, Sauna, Fitness Room

Castlecourt Hotel Spa, Leisure, Conference
Westport, Co. Mayo
Tel: +353-98-55088 ....Page 90
Name of Spa:
Spa Sula
No. of Treatments: 32
No. of Treatment Rooms: 10
Treatments Offered:
Rasul Mud Treatment, Dry Floatation Bath, Hydrotherapy Bath, Aromatherapy, Reflexology & Indian Head Massage, Body Treatments, Facials
Facilities available:
Thermal Suites, Rasul Mud Chamber, Dry Floatation, Outdoor Hot Tub, Rock Sauna, Relaxation Area

Hotel Westport
Westport, Co. Mayo
Tel: +353-98-25122 ....Page 91
Name of Spa:
Ocean Spirit Spa
Type of Spa:
Hotel with Selective Spa
No. of Treatments: 70
No. of Treatment Rooms: 10
Treatments Offered:
Cleopatra Bath, Body Peels & Wraps, Facials, Massages, Manicures, Pedicures, Spray Tan, Waxing, Tinting, Make Up
Facilities available:
5 Individual Treatment Rooms, Hamam, Cleopatra Bath, Serail, Relaxation Room, Pedicure & Manicure Room, Spray Tan Room, Sauna, Jacuzzi, Steam Room

McWilliam Park Hotel (The)
Claremorris, Co. Mayo
Tel: +353-94-937 8000 ....Page 87
No. of Treatments: 53
No. of Treatment Rooms: 3
Treatments Offered:
Facials, Massage, Manicure, Pedicures, Waxing, Tinting, Body Treatments, Tan & Sunbed, Pregnancy Treatments, Hydrotherapy Treatments, Make Up
Facilities available:
Hydrotherapy Machine, Sunbed, 3 Luxury Massage Rooms, 2 Nail Bars, Make Up Studio, Showers, Reception/Waiting Area, Spray Tan Room, Toilet Facilities

Mount Falcon
Ballina, Co. Mayo
Tel: +353-96-74472 ....Page 84
Name of Spa:
The Spa @ Mount Falcon
Type of Spa:
Hotel with Leisure Club Spa
No. of Treatments: 60
No. of Treatment Rooms: 4
Treatments Offered:
Facials, Massage, Body Treatments
Facilities available:
Sauna, 17m Swimming Pool, Jacuzzi, Steam Room, Air Conditioned Gym

Westport Plaza Hotel Spa, Leisure, Conference
Westport, Co. Mayo
Tel: +353-98-51166 ....Page 93
Name of Spa:
Spa Sula
Type of Spa:
Hotel with Comprehensive Spa
No. of Treatments: 32
No. of Treatment Rooms: 9
Treatments Offered:
Rasul Mud Treatment, Dry Floatation Bath, Hydrotherapy Bath, Aromatherapy, Reflexology & Indian Head Massage, Body Treatments, Facials
Facilities available:
Thermal Suites, Rasul Mud Chamber, Dry Floatation, Outdoor Hot Tub, Rock Sauna, Relaxation Area

Spa & Leisure In Ireland

...Let us pamper you, while you stay!

Co. Mayo CONTINUED

Wyatt Hotel
Westport, Co. Mayo
Tel: +353-98-25027 ....Page 93
Name of Spa:
Wellness Suite
No. of Treatments: 12
No. of Treatment Rooms: 1
Treatments Offered:
Therapeutic Massage, Indian Head Massage, De-Stress Pamper Package, Anti-Ageing Facial Treatment, Acne/Purifying Facial, Eyelash Tinting, Manicure & Pedicure
Facilities available:
Wellness Suite

Co. Roscommon

Kilronan Castle Estate & Spa
Ballyfarnon, Co. Roscommon
Tel: +353-71-961 8000 ....Page 94
Name of Spa:
Kilronan Castle Estate & Spa
Type of Spa:
Hotel with Extensive Spa
No. of Treatments: 75
No. of Treatment Rooms: 10
Treatments Offered:
Kimia Perfection Facial, SPC Soothing Eyes Treatment, Body Therapy Massage, Hot Stone Therapy, Rasul Treatment, Floatation Treatment, Pregnancy Treatments, Scrubs & Wraps, Waxing, Manicures, Pedicures
Facilities available:
14m Pool, Sauna, Steam Room, Jacuzzi, Gym, Fitness Studio, Nail Bar, Relaxation Room, Juice Bar, Thermal Suite

Co. Sligo

Castle Dargan Golf Hotel Wellness
Ballygawley, Co. Sligo
Tel: +353-71-911 8080 ....Page 94
Name of Spa:
Icon Spa
Type of Spa:
Hotel with Comprehensive Spa
No. of Treatments: 47
No. of Treatment Rooms: 4
Treatments Offered:
Facials, Body Wraps & Scrubs, Microdermabrasion, Balneotherapy, Floatation Therapy, Beauty Treatments, Mens' Treatments, Touch Therapies, Mother-To-Be Treatments – Mama Mio
Facilities available:
HydroSpa, Steam Room, Ice Fountain, Herb Sauna, Hydrotherapy Pool/Suite, Relaxation Suite, Touch Therapy Suite, Nail Bar

Pier Head Hotel, Spa and Leisure Centre
Mullaghmore, Co. Sligo
Tel: +353-71-916 6171 ....Page 96
Name of Spa:
Pier Head Spa & Leisure Centre
No. of Treatment Rooms: 2
Treatments Offered:
Hot Stone Therapy, Reflexology, Swedish Massage, Full Range of Dermalogica Facials available, Waxing, Manicures and many other beauty treatments
Facilities available:
Seaweed Bath & Steam Room, Outdoor Canadian Hot Tub, Indoor Heated Swimming Pool, Sea-Facing Gym, Sauna & Massage Room

Radisson Blu Hotel & Spa Sligo
Sligo Town, Co. Sligo
Tel: +353-71-914 0008 ....Page 96
Name of Spa:
Solas Spa
Type of Spa:
Hotel with Extensive Spa
No. of Treatments: 50
No. of Treatment Rooms: 7
Treatments Offered:
Thermal Suite & Rasul, ESPA Facials, Body Massage, Body Wraps, Pre & Post Natal Treatments, Reflexology, Holistic Treatments, Manicure & Pedicure, Full & Half Day Package
Facilities available:
Balneotherapy Bath, Thermal Suite & Rasul, 7 Treatment Rooms, Dry Floatation Tank, Relaxation Suite

Yeats Country Hotel, Spa & Leisure Club
Rosses Point, Co. Sligo
Tel: +353-71-917 7211 ....Page 96
Name of Spa:
Eros Health Spa
Type of Spa:
Hotel with Extensive Spa
No. of Treatments: 35
No. of Treatment Rooms: 6
Treatments Offered:
Seaweed Baths, Hydrotherapy Bath, Reiki, Reflexology, Aromatherapy, Swedish Massage, Hot Stone Treatments, Yon-ka Paris Beauty Treatments, Manicure, Waxing
Facilities available:
Relaxation Suite, Double Treatment Room, Single Treatment Room, Double Seaweed Bath Suite, Single Seaweed Bath Suite, Hydrotherapy Suite, Day Packages & Vouchers available

Did you know?

Pressotherapy
This is an exclusive detoxifying treatment, which through effective lymphatic drainage, helps to promote the body's natural toxin clearing functions. The revitalization and oxygenation of the tissue helps to slim and redefine the legs, stomach and arms while enhancing skin tone.

Reiki
Reiki practitioners channel energy in a particular pattern to heal and harmonize. Unlike other healing therapies based on the premise of a human energy field, Reiki seeks to restore order to the body whose vital energy has become unbalanced. It brings about deep relaxation, destroys energy blockages, detoxifies the system.

...Let us pamper you, while you stay!

Spa & Leisure In Ireland
...Let us pamper you, while you stay!

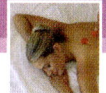

Northern Ireland

Co. Derry

Radisson Blu Roe Park Resort
Limavady, Co. Derry
Tel: +44-28-7772 2222 ......Page 108
Name of Spa:
The Roe Spa
No. of Treatments: 60
No. of Treatment Rooms: 12
Treatments Offered:
Hot Stone Massage, Seaweed Body Wraps, Skin Specific Facials, Anti-Ageing & Advanced Performance Facials, Jessana Spa Pedicure & Manicure, Elemis Bathing Ceremonies, Exotic Rasul, Aqua Veda Exfoliation Treatment, Specific Mens' Treatments, Glow Minerals Make Up
Facilities available:
Champagne Bath, Rasul Mud Chamber, Aqua Veda Exfoliation, Pedicure Suite & Nail Clinic, Aqua Meditation Chamber, Relaxation Suite, Refreshment Centre & Leisure Facilities - Leisure Pool, Sauna & Steam Room

Co. Down

Burrendale Hotel, Country Club & Spa
Newcastle, Co. Down
Tel: +44-28-4372 2599 ......Page 109
Name of Spa:
Burrendale Spa
No. of Treatments: 50
No. of Treatment Rooms: 8
Treatments Offered:
Facial, Massage, Make Up, Body Wrap, Reflexology, Manicure, Pedicure, Waxing, Nail Art, Hot Stone Therapy, Full Body Treatments, Reiki, Aromatherapy, Floatation Treatment, Body Exfoliation, Treatments for Men, Full Spa, Day & Weekend Pampering Packages
Facilities available:
Hairdressers, Relaxation Room, Treatment Rooms, Swimming Pool, Spa Bath, Sauna, Solarium, Gym & Fitness Suite

Dublin & Ireland East

Co. Cavan

Radisson Blu Farnham Estate Hotel
Cavan Town, Co. Cavan
Tel: +353-49-437 7700 ......Page 118
Name of Spa:
Farnham Estate Health Spa
Type of Spa:
Resort Spa
No. of Treatments: 80
No. of Treatment Rooms: 19
Treatments Offered:
Yonka Product Range, Le Grande Classique Facial, Aroma Luxe Massage, Pregnancy Treatments, Mens' Treatments
Facilities available:
Gymnasium, Indoor/Outdoor Infinity Pool, Thermal Suite, 19 Treatment Rooms, 7km of Walkways, Relaxation Rooms, Yoga Studio

Slieve Russell Hotel Golf & Country Club
Ballyconnell, Co. Cavan
Tel: +353-49-952 6444 ......Page 117
Name of Spa:
Ciúin Spa and Wellness Centre
Type of Spa:
Resort Spa
No. of Treatments: 44
No. of Treatment Rooms: 17
Treatments Offered:
Full Range of Elemis Treatments - Elemis Mothers To Be Massage, Elemis Body Sculpting Cellulite & Colon Therapy, Elemis Aromastone Therapy, Ciúin Signature Body Treatment, Full and Half Day Rituals, O.P.I. and Bare Mineral Make-up for finishing touches, Holistic Therapy, Microdermabrasion
Facilities available:
Hammam (Traditional Turkish Bath), Herb Sauna, Salt Grotto, Floatation Tank, Relaxation Room, Rasul, Adventure and Health Showers, Hydrotherapy Pool, 17 Treatment rooms

Co. Dublin

Blakes Hotel & Spa
Dublin City, Co. Dublin
Tel: +353-1-668 8324 ....Page 126
Name of Spa:
Blakes Spa
No. of Treatments: 10
No. of Treatment Rooms: 8
Treatments Offered:
Full Body Massage, Manual Lymphatic Drainage, Feet Reflexology Massage, Oil-Seasalt Massage, Shiatsu, La Stone-Therapy, Indian Head Massage, Beauty Treatments, Ayurvedic Treatment
Facilities available:
Aroma Steam Bath, Herbal Bath, Finnish Sauna, Laconium, Ice Fountain, Crystal Sound Meditation Room, Relaxation Area, Jacuzzi, Colour Therapy, Feet Reflexology Walk

Castleknock Hotel and Country Club
Dublin City, Co. Dublin
Tel: +353-1-640 6300 ....Page 129
Name of Spa:
Tonic Health & Day Spa
No. of Treatments: 19
No. of Treatment Rooms: 4
Treatments Offered:
Facials, Massage, Reflexology, Body Treatments, Manicures, Pedicures, Waxing, False Tan Application, Beauty Treatments
Facilities available:
Sauna, Steam Room, Spa Jacuzzi, 18m Swimming Pool, Gymnasium, Aerobics Studio, Childrens' Pool

Did you know?

Rasul

An Oriental ceremony for body care involving a cleansing seaweed soap shower, medicinal muds and an invigorating herbal steam bath.

...Let us pamper you, while you stay!

...Let us pamper you, while you stay!

Co. Dublin CONTINUED

Deer Park Hotel Golf & Spa
Howth, Co. Dublin
Tel: +353-1-832 2624 ....Page 147
Name of Spa:
DP Spa
Type of Spa:
Hotel with Selective Spa
No. of Treatments: 65
No. of Treatment Rooms: 6
Treatments Offered:
Hot Stone Massage, Balneotherapy Bath, Hydro Lifting Facial, Moor Mud Body Mask, Full Body Spray Tan, Full Body Massage
Facilities available:
Single Treatment Rooms, Double Treatment Rooms, Relaxation Room, Balneotherapy Bath Room, Spray Tan Room

Royal Marine Hotel
Dun Laoghaire, Co. Dublin
Tel: +353-1-230 0030 ....Page 147
Name of Spa:
Sansana Spa
Type of Spa:
Hotel with Comprehensive Spa
No. of Treatments: 50
No. of Treatment Rooms: 9
Treatments Offered:
Dry Floatation, Hydrotherapy, Razul, Massage, Hot Stone Therapy, Tanning, Manicure & Pedicure, Body Wraps, Body Scrubs, Voya Face & Body Rituals, Dermalogica Facials
Facilities available:
18m Infinity Pool, Jacuzzi, Treatment Rooms, Gymnasium, Rock Sauna, Aroma Steam, Drench Shower, Experience Shower, Ice Font, Aqua Relaxation Room

Stillorgan Park Hotel
Dublin City, Co. Dublin
Tel: +353-1-200 1800 ....Page 144
Name of Spa:
White Pebble Spa
Type of Spa:
Hotel with Extensive Spa
No. of Treatments: 30
No. of Treatment Rooms: 7
Treatments Offered:
8 Facials including Le Grand Classique & Alpha Vital, Tanning, Eyes, Hands & Feet, Reflexology, Body Treatments, Waxing, Stone Massage
Facilities available:
Relaxation Room, Steam Room, Changing Rooms, Gym

Co. Kildare

K Club (The)
Straffan, Co. Kildare
Tel: +353-1-601 7200 ....Page 156
Name of Spa:
The K Spa
Type of Spa:
Resort Spa
No. of Treatments: 100
No. of Treatment Rooms: 12
Treatments Offered:
Facials, Massages, Wraps, Wet Treatments
Facilities available:
Jacuzzi, Sauna, Aerobic Studio, Wet Treatmant Area, Gym, Hairdressers

Maudlins House Hotel
Naas, Co. Kildare
Tel: +353-45-896999 ....Page 154
Name of Spa:
Maudlins Hair Salon
No. of Treatments: 34
No. of Treatment Rooms: 2
Treatments Offered:
Full Hair Salons
Facilities available:
Massaging Chairs for Hair Treatments

Westgrove Hotel
Clane, Co. Kildare
Tel: +353-45-989900 ....Page 152
Name of Spa:
Spa Haven
Type of Spa:
Hotel with Extensive Spa
No. of Treatments: 20
No. of Treatment Rooms: 7
Treatments Offered:
Elemis Facials, Deep Tissue Massage, Hot Stone Therapy, Elemis Body Wraps, Hydrotherapy Bath, Rasul Mud Chamber, Hammam Body Cleansing
Facilities available:
Fully Equipped Gym, 20m Pool, Sauna, Steam Room, Jacuzzi, Kids Pool, Aerobics Suite

Co. Laois

Heritage Golf & Spa Resort (The)
Killenard, Co. Laois
Tel: +353-57-864 5500 ......Page 157
Name of Spa:
The Spa at the Heritage
Type of Spa:
Resort Spa
No. of Treatments: 70
No. of Treatment Rooms: 20
Treatments Offered:
Massage, Wraps, Hydrotherapy, Facials, Mud Wraps, Stone Therapy, Manicure, Sports & Body Therapy, Mens Treatments, Eye/Lip Treatments
Facilities available:
Sanarium, Tepidarium, Hydrotherapy Pool, Tropical Showers, Hammam, Steam Bath, Sauna, Foot Bath, Mud Chamber, Ice Fountain

Portlaoise Heritage Hotel
Portlaoise, Co. Laois
Tel: +353-57-867 8588 ......Page 157
Name of Spa:
Ealu Spa
No. of Treatments: 40
No. of Treatment Rooms: 7
Treatments Offered:
Hot Stone Massage, Facial Glow Therapeutics, Teeth Whitening, Tan Organic Spray Tanning
Facilities available:
22 Metre Pool, 2 Jacuzzis, Sauna, Steam Room, Gymnasium

Did you know?

Aromatherapy
Aromatherapy is a form of alternative medicine that uses volatile liquid plant materials, known as essential oils (EOs), and other scented compounds from plants for the purpose of affecting a person's mood or health.

...Let us pamper you, while you stay!

Spa & Leisure In Ireland
...Let us pamper you, while you stay!

Co. Longford

Annaly Hotel
Longford Town, Co. Longford
Tel: +353-43-334 3690 ......Page 158
Name of Spa:
Life Health & Fitness
Treatments Offered:
Indian Head massage, Swedish/Maternity Deep Tissue Massage, Aromatherapy, Manicures, Pedicures
Facilities available:
20m Pool, Large Gym, Sauna, Steam Room, Jacuzzi

Longford Arms Hotel, Spa & Leisure Centre
Longford Town, Co. Longford
Tel: +353-43-334 6296 ......Page 158
Name of Spa:
Longford Arms Hotel and Spa
No. of Treatments: 15
No. of Treatment Rooms: 3
Treatments Offered:
Indian Head Massage, Swedish/Maternity/Infant Deep Tissue Massage, Hot Stone Massage, Aromatherapy, Manicures & Pedicures
Facilities available:
Sauna, Steam Room, Jacuzzi, 22 Metre Salt Pool, Large Gym

Co. Meath

CityNorth Hotel
Gormanston, Co. Meath
Tel: +353-1-690 6666 ......Page 163
Name of Spa:
Lavender Treatment Room
No. of Treatments: 15
No. of Treatment Rooms: 1
Treatments Offered:
The Dermalogical Facial, Swedish Massage, Tanning, Threading Hair Removal, Body Waxing, Spa Manicure, Deluxe Manicure, Spa Pedicure, Special Makeup

Dunboyne Castle Hotel & Spa
Dunboyne, Co. Meath
Tel: +353-1-801 3500 ......Page 162
Name of Spa:
Seoid
Type of Spa:
Hotel with Comprehensive Spa
No. of Treatments: 80
No. of Treatment Rooms: 18
Treatments Offered:
Balneotherapy, Dry Floatation, Hydrojet Water Massage Bed, Rasul, Anne Sémonin product range, Voya product range
Facilities available:
18 Treatment Rooms including Hydrotherapy Pool, Heat Rooms, Experience Showers, Fitness Suite, Outdoor Hot Tub, Relaxation Rooms

Knightsbrook Hotel, Spa & Golf Resort
Trim, Co. Meath
Tel: +353-46-948 2100 ......Page 165
Name of Spa:
The River Spa
Type of Spa:
Hotel with Extensive Spa
No. of Treatments: 8
No. of Treatment Rooms: 17
Treatments Offered:
Holistic Therapies, Facials, Body Treatments, Rasul, Massage
Facilities available:
Gym, 16m Swimming Pool, Herb Sauna, Rasul Bath, Salt Grotto, Steam Room, Jacuzzi, Foot Spas, Spa Treatment Rooms

Co. Monaghan

Castle (The) at Castle Leslie Estate
Glasslough, Co. Monaghan
Tel: +353-47-88100 ....Page 166
Name of Spa:
The Victorian Treatment Rooms
No. of Treatment Rooms: 7
Treatments Offered:
Wraps, Facials, Spa Manicures & Pedicures, Stimulating Deep Tissue Massage, Relaxing & Soothing Massage, Revitalising & Detoxifying Massage, Indian Head Massage, Reiki, Reflexology, Auricular Ear Coning, Day Experience Packages, Men Only Treatments
Facilities available:
Outdoor Hot Tub, Victorian Steam Boxes, Relaxation Room, Day Experience Packages

Hillgrove Hotel Leisure & Spa
Monaghan Town, Co. Monaghan
Tel: +353-47-81288 ....Page 167
Name of Spa:
Lir Spa & Wellness Centre
Type of Spa:
Hotel with Comprehensive Spa
No. of Treatments: 85
No. of Treatment Rooms: 8
Treatments Offered:
Facials, Massage, Body Wraps, Exfoliation, Water Treatments, Alternative Therapies, Tanning Treatments, Beauty Treatments, Nail Bar & Hair Salon
Facilities available:
Thermal Spa Area, Rasul, Floatation Bed, Hydrotherapy Pool, Herbal Sauna, Pedi Spas, Ice Fountain, Monsoon Showers, Relaxation Room, Hair Salon

---

Did you know?

Body Wraps
Improve elimination of toxins in the body while remineralizing the body with the nutrients it needs. Wraps can have toning, relaxing, or stimulating effects and can provide relief from pain due to improper removal of metabolic waste products.

...Let us pamper you, while you stay!

Spa & Leisure In Ireland
...Let us pamper you, while you stay!

Co. Offaly

Bridge House Hotel
Tullamore, Co. Offaly
Tel: +353-57-932 5600 ......Page 168
Name of Spa:
Sanctuary Spa
Type of Spa:
Hotel with Selective Spa
No. of Treatments: 50
No. of Treatment Rooms: 7
Treatments Offered:
Spray Tan, Sports Massage, Indian Head Massage, Facials, Hot Stone Therapy, Reflexology, Seaweed Treatments, Nail Bar, Hydrotherapy Treatments, Relaxation Chambers, Beauty Treatments
Facilities available:
Sauna, Steam Room, Jacuzzi, Outdoor Hydrotherapy Pool, Swimming Pool, State of the Art Health Club, Fitness/ Aerobic Studio, Power Plate Vibration Training System, Cardio Theatre, Spinning, Boxercise, Personal Trainers, Virtual Golf

Co. Westmeath

Glasson Country House Hotel and Golf Club
Athlone, Co. Westmeath
Tel: +353-90-648 5120 ......Page 171
Name of Spa:
Glasson Treatment Centre
No. of Treatments: 5
No. of Treatment Rooms: 1
Treatments Offered:
Aromatherapy Massage, Full Body Massage, Indian Head Massage, Back, Neck & Shoulder Massage, Hot Lava Shell Massage
Facilities available:
Sauna & Steam Room, Fitness Suite, Treatment Room

Sheraton Athlone Hotel
Athlone, Co. Westmeath
Tel: +353-90-645 1000 ......Page 172
Name of Spa:
Sirana Spa
Type of Spa:
Hotel with Comprehensive Spa
No. of Treatments: 50
No. of Treatment Rooms: 7
Treatments Offered:
Body Wraps, Aromatherapy, Massage, Hot Stone Treatments, Full Body Polish, Head Massage, Facials, Hand & Foot Treatments, Sirana Fresh Facial, Bamboo Massage, Coconut Rub & Milk Ritual by Elemis, Leighton Denny Manicures & Pedicures
Facilities available:
Swimming Pool, Sauna, Steam Room, Relaxation Suite, Rasul, Laconium, Hair & Beauty Studios, Jacuzzi, Tepidarium & Serenity Area, Sheraton Fitness offering the latest life fitness technology

Temple Country Retreat & Spa
Moate, Co. Westmeath
Tel: +353-57-933 5118 ......Page 172
Name of Spa:
Temple Country Retreat & Spa
Type of Spa:
Destination Spa
No. of Treatments: 80
No. of Treatment Rooms: 18
Treatments Offered:
Massage, Reflexology, Hot Stone Massage, Detox Herbal Massage, Chocotherapy, Vinotherapy, Jessana Manicure, Jessana Pedicure, Floatation
Facilities available:
Vitality Pool, Sauna, Steam Room, Experience Showers, Foot Spa, Yoga Studio, Gym, Juice Bar, Tranquillity Room, Daily Programme of Yoga, Walking, Fitness & Relaxation Classes, Pilates & Chi-Kung Classes, One-to-One Personal Training, Nutritionist & Lifestyle Coach by Appointment

Co. Wicklow

Glenview Hotel & Leisure Cub
Glen-O-The-Downs, Co. Wicklow
Tel: +353-1-287 3399 ....Page 177
Name of Spa:
The Haven Beauty Salons
No. of Treatments: 26
No. of Treatment Rooms: 3
Treatments Offered:
Dermalogica Body Wrap, Body Polish, Dermalogica Facials, Full Body Massage, St. Tropez Spray Tan, Shellac Manicure & Pedicure, full day packages - Brides & Mums to Be
Facilities available:
Swimming Pool, Sauna, Steam Room, Jacuzzi, Outdoor Hot Tub, Fully Equipped Gymnasium

The Ritz-Carlton, Powerscourt
Enniskerry, Co. Wicklow
Tel: +353-1-274 8888 ....Page 176
Name of Spa:
ESPA at The Ritz-Carlton, Powerscourt
Type of Spa:
Hotel with Comprehensive Spa
No. of Treatments: 50
No. of Treatment Rooms: 21
Treatments Offered:
ESPA at Ritz-Carlton Treatments Rituals, ESPA Ayurvedic influenced Treatments, ESPA Advanced Facials, Comprehensive Spa - Fáilte Ireland
Facilities available:
Fitness Suite with Technogym Equipment, Chi Studio, Indoor Swimming Pool, Spa Café, 21 Treatment Rooms

Did you know?

Hammam

It means "spreader of warmth". It is the word given to the sensual bathing retreat that evolved over thousands of years and traces its roots back to the Roman Thermae.

...Let us pamper you, while you stay!

Spa & Leisure In Ireland
...Let us pamper you, while you stay!

Ireland South

Co. Carlow

Mount Wolseley Hotel, Spa & Country Club
Tullow, Co. Carlow
Tel: +353-59-918 0100 ......Page 184
Name of Spa:
Sanctuary Spa
Type of Spa:
Resort Spa
No. of Treatments: 56
No. of Treatment Rooms: 14
Treatments Offered:
Facials: De Luxe Collagen Face, Eyes & Neck Treatment, Total Rehydration Treatment
Body Therapies: Total Body Polish, Balneotherapy, Cellutox Ocean Wrap Specialist Therapies: Thalgomince Pregnancy Therapy. Elemis & Thalgo products used in our treatments, Hot & Cold Stone Massage
Facilities available:
Oval Spa Pool with Waterfalls, Experience Showers, Rasul Room, Steam Room & Dry Air Room, Floatation Chambers, Sabiamed Light Treatment, Relaxation Room

Talbot Hotel Carlow
Carlow Town, Co. Carlow
Tel: +353-59-915 3000 ......Page 184
Name of Spa:
Classic Beauty at the Talbot Hotel
No. of Treatments: 25
No. of Treatment Rooms: 4
Treatments Offered:
Bodywraps, Aromatherapy Massage, Manicure, Pedicure, Mens Skincare Treatment, Intensive Moisture Facial, Revitalising Eye Rescue Treatment, Teeth Whitening, Reflexology
Facilities available:
Treatment Rooms, Nail Bar, Make Up Room, Sauna, Spa Pool, Steam Room

Co. Cork

Blarney Golf Resort
Blarney, Co. Cork
Tel: +353-21-438 4477 ......Page 188
Name of Spa:
Blarney Golf Resort and Spa
Type of Spa:
Hotel with Leisure Club Spa
No. of Treatments: 40
No. of Treatment Rooms: 5
Treatments Offered:
Hot Stone Massage, Deep Pore Cleansing Facial, Eye Crystal Treatment, De Luxe Manicure, Seaweed Wrap, Yonka & Matis Products
Facilities available:
Sauna, 20m Swimming Pool, Gym, Jacuzzi, Steam Room, Childrens' Pool

Fota Island Resort
Fota Island, Co. Cork
Tel: +353-21-488 3700 ......Page 200
Name of Spa:
Fota Island Spa
Type of Spa:
Resort Spa
No. of Treatments: 60
No. of Treatment Rooms: 18
Treatments Offered:
Cold Marine Leg Wrap, Spa Packages, Hot Stones, Marine Body Polish, Chocolate Sensualite Wrap, Green Tea Silhouette Therapy, Lushly Polynesian Hand/Foot Ritual, Comfort Zone Facials
Facilities available:
Fitness Suite, Indoor Swimming Pool, 18 Treatment Rooms, Hydrotherapy Area, Thermal Area, Juice Bar, Relaxation Area, Garden

Did you know?

Thalassotherapy

This is a traditional, holistic marine-based therapy that uses natural ocean elements to restore wellness and to unveil one's pure, natural beauty.

Hayfield Manor Hotel
Cork City, Co. Cork
Tel: +353-21-484 5900 ......Page 196
Name of Spa:
The Beautique
Type of Spa:
Hotel with Selective Spa
No. of Treatments: 24
No. of Treatment Rooms: 6
Treatments Offered:
Facials, Massage, Body Wraps, Manicures, Pedicures, Spray Tan, Hot Stone Therapy
Facilities available:
Indoor Swimming Pool, Gym, Steam Room, Outdoor Hot Tub, Lounge Area, Nail Bar, Personal Trainer

Inchydoney Island Lodge & Spa
Clonakilty, Co. Cork
Tel: +353-23-883 3143 ......Page 191
Name of Spa:
Island Spa
Type of Spa:
Thalassotherapy Resort
No. of Treatments: 25
No. of Treatment Rooms: 17
Treatments Offered:
Island Spa Tropical Ritual (new), Rasul, Slimming Algotherapy, Spa Manicure, Facial, Cryotherapy, Chocolate Ritual, Aroma Stone Massage
Facilities available:
Thalassotherapy Pool, Hammam, Sauna, Relaxation Room, Gymnasium, Seawater Pool

Maryborough Hotel & Spa
Cork City, Co. Cork
Tel: +353-21-436 5555 ......Page 198
Name of Spa:
Maryborough Spa
Type of Spa:
Hotel with Comprehensive Spa
No. of Treatments: 38
No. of Treatment Rooms: 10
Treatments Offered:
Hot Stone Therapy, Massage, Ayurvedic Rituals, Facials, Body Wraps, Full & 1/2 Day Programmes
Facilities available:
Relaxation Rooms, Vitality (Male & Female), Thermal Suites, 10 Treatment Rooms, Spa Café, Finishing Touches Studio

...Let us pamper you, while you stay!

Spa & Leisure In Ireland

...Let us pamper you, while you stay!

Co. Cork CONTINUED

**Oriel House Hotel,
Leisure Club & Spa**
Ballincollig, Co. Cork
Tel: +353-21-420 8400 ......Page 185
Name of Spa:
The Oriel Bijoux Spa
Type of Spa:
Hotel with Extensive Spa
No. of Treatments: 24
No. of Treatment Rooms: 7
Treatments Offered:
Oriel Collagen Facial, Nurturing Pregnancy Treatment, Oxygenating Rose Quartz Facial, Scentao of Asia Hot Stone Massage, Indian Head Massage, Vitamin Body Cocoon.
Facilities available:
7 Treatment Rooms, 4 Person Rasul, Aroma Steam Room, Hammam Table, Relaxation Area.

Westlodge Hotel
Bantry, Co. Cork
Tel: +353-27-50360 ....Page 187
No. of Treatments: 7
No. of Treatment Rooms: 2
Treatments Offered:
Reflexology, Full Body Massage, Aromatherapy Massage, Indian Head Massage, Sports Massage, Reiki, Top'n'Tail, Hot Stones Massage
Facilities available:
Heated Swimming Pool, Sauna, Steam Room, Jacuzzi, Fully equipped Gym, Squash Court

Co. Kerry

Aghadoe Heights Hotel & Spa
Killarney, Co. Kerry
Tel: +353-64-663 1766 ......Page 217
Name of Spa:
The Spa at The Heights
Type of Spa:
Resort Spa
No. of Treatments: 58
No. of Treatment Rooms: 10
Treatments Offered:
Futuresse Face & Body Treatments, Biodroga Wraps, Aveda Face & Body Treatments, Manicure, Pedicure, Indian Head Massage, Reflexology & Thermal Suite, Neom Treatments & Products
Facilities available:
Hammam, Rock Sauna, Laconium, Aroma Grotto, Tropical Rain Shower, Cold Fog Shower, Heated Loungers, Relaxation Room, Slipper Bath, Serail, Swimming Pool, Jacuzzi, Fitness Suite, Tennis Court, Yoga, Pilates, Hair Salon

Ballygarry House Hotel & Spa
Tralee, Co. Kerry
Tel: +353-66-712 3322 ......Page 235
Name of Spa:
Nádúr
Type of Spa:
Hotel with Extensive Spa
No. of Treatments: 40
No. of Treatment Rooms: 7
Treatments Offered:
Hydrotherapy & Seaweed Treatments, USPA Concept Facials, Holistic Therapies, Herbal & Mud Body Wrap, Hot Stone Massage, Ritual Body Massage, Beauty & Tanning, Maternity Massage & Body Treatments
Facilities available:
Beauty Suite, Glass Sauna, Crystal Steam Room, Outdoor Canadian Hot Tub, Vitality Showers, Tanning Suite, Hydrotherapy Bath, Relaxation Room, Hair Stylist

**Castlerosse Hotel
and Golf Resort**
Killarney, Co. Kerry
Tel: +353-64-663 1144 ......Page 220
Type of Spa:
Hotel with Leisure Club Spa
No. of Treatments: 21
No. of Treatment Rooms: 2
Treatments Offered:
The non-surgical face lift, Opus Belle Facial, Hydro Lypio, Dr Grandle A.C.E., Eye Lift Rejuvenation Treatment, Clinical Facials, Variety of Body Treatments, Hot Stone Massage, Swedish Massage, Indian Head Massage, Reflexology, Ear Candling, Manicure, Pedicure
Facilities available:
2 Treatment Rooms

Dingle Skellig Hotel
Dingle (An Daingean), Co. Kerry
Tel: +353-66-915 0200 ......Page 213
Name of Spa:
The Peninsula Spa
Type of Spa:
Seaweed Baths
No. of Treatments: 55
No. of Treatment Rooms: 7
Treatments Offered:
Yon-ka Aroma Stone, Yon-ka Face & Body Treatments, Peninsula Spa Face & Body Treatments, Massage, Hydrotherapy, Body Wraps, Sports Injury, Tanning, Nail Treatments, Makeovers, Selection of unique "Irish" treatments from local Organic Products & Ingredients
Facilities available:
Outdoor Hot Tub overlooking Dingle Harbour, Relaxation Suite with Refreshments Bar, Hydrotherapy Suite, Sauna, Steam Room, Beauty Salon, Outdoor Relaxation Balcony, 17m Pool, Childrens' pool, Jacuzzi in Leisure Club

---

Did you know?

Rasul:
An Oriental ceremony for body care involving a cleansing seaweed soap shower, medicinal muds and an invigorating herbal steam bath.

Reflexology
The physical act of applying pressure to the feet & hands without the use of oil or lotion. It is based on a system of zones & reflex areas that reflect an image of the body on the feet and hands with a premise that such work effects a physical change to the body.

...Let us pamper you, while you stay!

Killarney Park Hotel
Killarney, Co. Kerry
Tel: +353-64-663 5555 ......Page 227
Name of Spa:
The Spa at the Killarney Park Hotel
Type of Spa:
Hotel with Extensive Spa
No. of Treatments: 45
No. of Treatment Rooms: 8
Treatments Offered:
Eve Lom Facial, Elemis Aroma Stone Therapy, Elemis Japanese Silk Booster Facial, Elemis Well Being Massage, Elemis Fennel Cleansing Cellulite and Colon Therapy, Healing Bath Ceremony, Elemis Musclease Aroma Spa Ocean Wrap
Facilities available:
8 Custom-built Private Treatment Suites, specially designed Relaxation Room, Hydrotherapy Suite, Caldarium, Couples Suite, Juice Bar

Killarney Plaza Hotel & Spa
Killarney, Co. Kerry
Tel: +353-64-662 1100 ......Page 228
Name of Spa:
Molton Brown Spa
No. of Treatments: 20
No. of Treatment Rooms: 8
Treatments Offered:
Selection of Molton Brown Body & Facial, Hand & Feet Therapies
Facilities available:
Private Leisure Club with Pool, Sauna, Gym, Molton Brown Spa

Lake Hotel (The)
Killarney, Co. Kerry
Tel: +353-64-663 1035 ......Page 229
Name of Spa:
Muckross Fitness Centre & Lake Beauty & Treatment Rooms
No. of Treatments: 14
No. of Treatment Rooms: 3
Treatments Offered:
Massages, Facials, Manicures, Pedicures
Facilities available:
Gym, Sauna, Steam Room, Outdoor Hot Tub overlooking Lake, Three Beauty Treatment Rooms

Malton (The)
Killarney, Co. Kerry
Tel: +353-64-663 8000 ......Page 230
Name of Spa:
Innisfallen Health & Beauty Rooms
Type of Spa:
Hotel with Leisure Club Spa
No. of Treatments: 20
No. of Treatment Rooms: 3
Treatments Offered:
Hydrotherapy Bath, Facials, Manicures, Pedicures, Hot Stone Massage, Lomi Lomi Massage, Body Treatments, Waxing and Tinting
Facilities available:
Indoor Heated Swimming Pool, Jacuzzi, Steam Room, Gym, Sauna, Tennis Courts, Hydrotherapy Bath

Muckross Park Hotel & Cloisters Spa
Killarney, Co. Kerry
Tel: +353-64-662 3400 ......Page 230
Name of Spa:
Cloisters Spa
Type of Spa:
Resort Spa
No. of Treatments: 50
No. of Treatment Rooms: 12
Treatments Offered:
Massage, Facials, Microdermabrasion, Manicure, Pedicure, Hot Shaves, Hydrotherapy Baths, Energy Healing, Reflexology
Facilities available:
Thermal Suite, Vitality Pool, Herb Sauna, Ice Fountain, Salt Grotto, Eucalyptus Mist, Mud Rasul, Relaxation Suite, Heated Loungers, UV Sonacare Camera

Parknasilla Resort
Sneem, Co. Kerry
Tel: +353-64-667 5600 ......Page 233
Type of Spa:
Hotel with Leisure Club Spa
No. of Treatments: 52
No. of Treatment Rooms: 12
Treatments Offered:
Exotic Ritual for Hands, Indian Head Massage, Exotic Ginger & Lime Salt Glow, Aroma Stone Massage, Skin IQ Facial, Elemis Skin Special Facial
Facilities available:
Aromatherapy Steam Room, Hydrotherapy Foot Spas, Heated Lounges, Pool, Laconium, Herb Sauna, Salt Inhalation Steam Cabin

Co. Kilkenny

Hotel Kilkenny
Kilkenny City, Co. Kilkenny
Tel: +353-56-776 2000 ......Page 240
Name of Spa:
Lilac Lodge Spa
No. of Treatments: 40
No. of Treatment Rooms: 4
Treatments Offered:
Dermalogica Facial Treatments, Yon-ka Facial Treatments, Aroma Hot Stone Massage, Phyto-Marine Slimming Treatment, Reflexology, Sports Therapy Massage, Waxing, Tanning, Body Treatments
Facilities available:
Luxury Relaxation Room, 4 Treatment Rooms, Complimentary off-street Parking

---

Did you know?

Abhyanga

Abhyanga massage is a gentle but firm whole body massage from head to toe using warm medicated oils. Oils are chosen according to the prakruti (psychosomatic constitution) and the illness. The massage is done in a soft rhythmic way with one or two persons massaging at the same time for forty five to sixty minutes.

...Let us pamper you, while you stay!

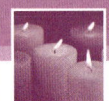

Spa & Leisure In Ireland
...Let us pamper you, while you stay!

Co. Kilkenny CONTINUED

Kilkenny Ormonde Hotel
Kilkenny City, Co. Kilkenny
Tel: +353-56-775 0200 ......Page 241
Name of Spa:
KO Spa
No. of Treatments: 38
No. of Treatment Rooms: 7
Treatments Offered:
Elemis Advanced Anti-Ageing Facials, Pro-Collagen Quartz Lift Facial, SOS Purifying Facial, Absolute Spa Ritual, Deep Tissue Muscle Massage, Solo Delight Grooming for Feet, Exotic Lime & Ginger Salt Glow, Exotic Coconut Rub and Milk Ritual Wrap, Exotic Frangipani Body Nourish Wrap, Solar Oil Mini Manicure
Facilities available:
21m Swimming Pool, Kids Pool, Extensive Gym Area, Aerobics Studio, Children's Crèche Facility, Sauna, Jacuzzi, Steam Room, 7 Spa Treatment Rooms, Relaxation Room

Kilkenny River Court
Kilkenny City, Co. Kilkenny
Tel: +353-56-772 3388 ......Page 242
Type of Spa:
Hotel with Leisure Club Spa
No. of Treatments: 10
No. of Treatment Rooms: 3
Treatments Offered:
Aromatherapy, Massage, Sports Massage, Reiki, Reflexology
Facilities available:
Treatment Rooms, Gymnasium, 17m Swimming Pool, Geyser Pool, Jacuzzi, Steam Room

Did you know?

Pressotherapy

This is an exclusive detoxifying treatment, which through effective lymphatic drainage, helps to promote the body's natural toxin clearing functions. The revitalization and oxygenation of the tissue helps to slim and redefine the legs, stomach and arms while enhancing skin tone.

Lyrath Estate Hotel & Convention Centre
Kilkenny City, Co. Kilkenny
Tel: +353-56-776 0088 ......Page 243
Name of Spa:
Oasis Spa
Type of Spa:
Hotel with Comprehensive Spa
No. of Treatments: 47
No. of Treatment Rooms: 10
Treatments Offered:
European Deep Cleanse Facial, Spirulina Wrap, Bora Body Mud Wrap, Reflexology, Reiki, Caviar Facial, Indian Head Massage, Rasul, Hot Stones
Facilities available:
Male Relaxation Area, Female Relaxation Area, Hydro Pool - both indoor & outdoor, Sauna, Steam Room, Gym, Tropical Showers, Couples Suite, 17m infinity Swimming Pool, Treatment Rooms

Newpark Hotel
Kilkenny City, Co. Kilkenny
Tel: +353-56-776 0500 ......Page 243
Name of Spa:
Escape Health Club & Spa
No. of Treatments: 40
No. of Treatment Rooms: 4
Treatments Offered:
Carribean Glow Body Scrub, Pure Focus Facial, Elemental Nature Massage, Aveda Luxury Spa Pedicure, Carribean Therapy Hand Treatment, Revitalizing Eye Treatment, Green Science Anti Ageing Facial
Facilities available:
Relaxation Suite, Outdoor Infinity Pool

Co. Tipperary

Abbey Court Hotel, Lodges & Trinity Leisure Spa
Nenagh, Co. Tipperary
Tel: +353-67-41111 ....Page 249
Name of Spa:
Trinity Leisure Spa
No. of Treatments: 20
No. of Treatment Rooms: 8
Treatments Offered:
Swedish Massage, Decleor Facials, Jessica Pedicure, Manicure, Make-up, Waxing, Self-Tan, Universal Contour Wrap
Facilities available:
Balneotherapy Bath, Sun Room

Ballykisteen Hotel & Golf Resort
Tipperary Town, Co. Tipperary
Tel: +353-62-33333 ....Page 250
Name of Spa:
Serenity Day Spa
No. of Treatments: 38
No. of Treatment Rooms: 5
Treatments Offered:
Hot Stone Massage, Crystal Eye Treatment, Creative Manicure, Zen Spa Pedicure, Indian Head Massage, California Spray Tan, Vita Liberata Make-up, Yon-ka Signature Facial
Facilities available:
Swimming Pool, Sauna, Jacuzzi, Steam Room, Gym, Kids Club

Cahir House Hotel
Cahir, Co. Tipperary
Tel: +353-52-744 3000 ......Page 245
Name of Spa:
Cahir House Hotel Health & Beauty Spa
No. of Treatments: 36
No. of Treatment Rooms: 4
Treatments Offered:
Facials, Manicure, Pedicure, Reflexology, Hydrotherapy Bath, Body Treatments, Sunbeds, Indian Head Massage, Pamper Days
Facilities available:
Steam Room, Sauna, Sun Beds

Hotel Minella & Leisure Club
Clonmel, Co. Tipperary
Tel: +353-52-612 2388 ......Page 248
Name of Spa:
Club Minella
No. of Treatments: 14
No. of Treatment Rooms: 2
Treatments Offered:
Massage, Reflexology, Micronized Marine Algae Wrap, Toning Body Wrap, Marine Facial, Waxing, Manicure, Body Polish
Facilities available:
Treatment Rooms, Jacuzzi, Relaxation Room, Outdoor Hot Tub, 20m Pool, Outdoor Tennis Court, Sauna, Steam Room, Gym, Gardens

...Let us pamper you, while you stay!

Spa & Leisure In Ireland
...Let us pamper you, while you stay!

Co. Waterford

Park Hotel, Leisure Centre & Holiday Homes
Dungarvan, Co. Waterford
Tel: +353-58-42899 ....Page 253
Name of Spa:
The Park Hotel & Leisure Centre
No. of Treatments: 5
No. of Treatment Rooms: 2
Treatments Offered:
Swedish & Deep Tissue Massage, Reflexology, Therapeutic Massage
Facilities available:
20m Swimming Pool, Gym, Sauna, Steam Room, Whirlpool, Jacuzzi, Kids Pool, Chartered Physiotherapist, Kids Club

Co. Wexford

Amber Springs Hotel & Health Spa
Gorey, Co. Wexford
Tel: +353-53-948 4000 ......Page 263
Name of Spa:
Cocoon Health & Beauty Spa
Type of Spa:
Hotel with Extensive Spa
No. of Treatment Rooms: 11
Treatments Offered:
Massage, Facials, Waxing, Manicure, Body Wraps, Balneo Treatment, Dry Floatation, Relaxation Room
Facilities available:
18m Indoor Pool, Jacuzzi, Steam Room, Sauna, Hydro Therapy Pool, Fitness Centre, Kiddies Pool & Games Room, Supervised playzone.

Ashdown Park Hotel Conference & Leisure Centre
Gorey, Co. Wexford
Tel: +353-53-948 0500 ......Page 263
Name of Spa:
Ashdown Club & Beauty Studio
No. of Treatments: 8
No. of Treatment Rooms: 1
Treatments Offered:
Massage Treatments
Facilities available:
18m Swimming Pool, Kids' Pool, Jacuzzi, Steam Room, Sauna, Gym

Brandon House Hotel & Solas Croí Eco Spa
New Ross, Co. Wexford
Tel: +353-51-421703 ....Page 264
Name of Spa:
Solas Croí Eco Spa
Type of Spa:
Hotel with Selective Spa
No. of Treatments: 70
No. of Treatment Rooms: 8
Treatments Offered:
Complete Tri-Dosha Ayurvedic Treatments, Reflexology, Hot Stone Massage, Elemis Products, Mamamio Maternity Treatments, Cosmetic Therapies
Facilities available:
20m Swimming Pool, Swimming Lessons, Sauna, Aerobics, Gym, Hydro Therapy Grotto, Kids Swimming Pool

Ferrycarrig Hotel
Wexford Town, Co. Wexford
Tel: +353-53-912 0999 ......Page 267
Name of Spa:
Health & Beauty at The Lodge
No. of Treatments: 45
No. of Treatment Rooms: 4
Treatments Offered:
Facials, Aromatherapy, Massage, Reflexology, Hot Stone Therapy, Indian Head Massage, Manicures & Pedicures, Makeovers, Body Treatments, Pamper Days, Bridal Packages
Facilities available:
Intense Pulsed Light, Platinum Detox, Relaxation and Reception Area

Kelly's Resort Hotel & Spa
Rosslare, Co. Wexford
Tel: +353-53-913 2114 ......Page 265
Name of Spa:
SeaSpa
Type of Spa:
Resort Spa
No. of Treatments: 34
No. of Treatment Rooms: 12
Treatments Offered:
Aromatherapy & Holistic Massages, Body Wraps, Facials, Ayurvedic Hot Stone Treatments, Reflexology, Reiki, Sports Therapy Massage, Manicure & Pedicure, Candling, Acupuncture
Facilities available:
Serail Mud Room, Seaweed Baths, Rock Sauna, Heated Loungers, Sea Water Vitality Pool, Rain Forest Showers, Pebble Walk Way, Salt Infused Steam Rooms, Relaxation Rooms, Laconium Sauna

---

Did you know?

Thalassotherapy

This is a traditional, holistic marine-based therapy that uses natural ocean elements to restore wellness and to unveil one's pure, natural beauty.

Reiki

Reiki practitioners channel energy in a particular pattern to heal and harmonize. Unlike other healing therapies based on the premise of a human energy field, Reiki seeks to restore order to the body whose vital energy has become unbalanced. It brings about deep relaxation, destroys energy blockages, detoxifies the system.

HeritageISLAND
IRELAND'S VISITOR ATTRACTIONS

Ireland's Visitor Attractions offer a fascinating and fun day out for all the family. Visit www.heritageisland.com to book online and discover medieval castles, historic houses, museums, folk parks, distilleries and much more.

Heritage Island attractions include Dublin & Belfast Zoo, Guinness Storehouse, the House of Waterford Crystal, Blarney Castle, Cliffs of Moher, Belleek Pottery and many more. A full listing of all the attractions can be found on www.heritageisland.com and are shown on the maps at the back of the this guide.

To be kept up to date with events and activies taking place throughout Ireland visit:

- www.heritageisland.com
- www.facebook.com/heritageisland
- www.BookAnAttraction.com for discounted tickets

HeritageISLAND
IRELAND'S VISITOR ATTRACTIONS

DISCOUNT PASS

Visit www.heritageisland.com to purchase a Ireland's Visitor Attraction Guide and recieve great discounts to Ireland's leading tourist attractions.

IRISH HOTELS FEDERATION

KEY TO MAPS

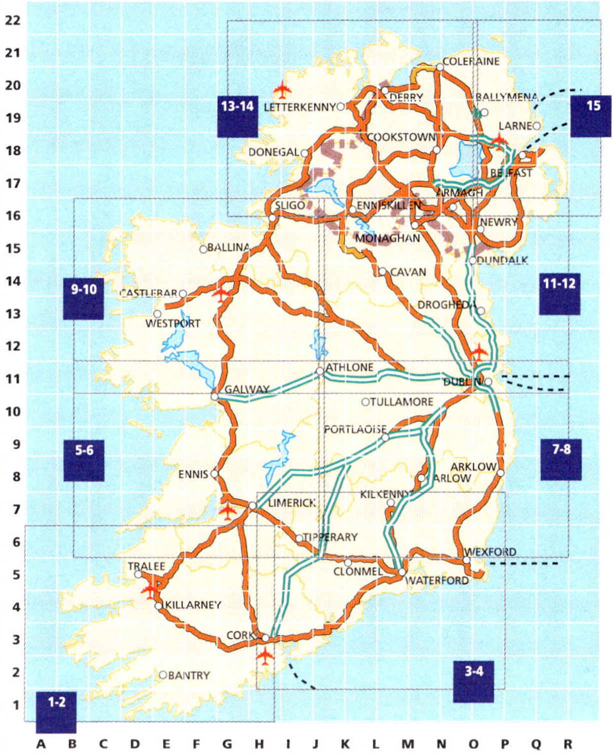

LEGEND

- M50 — Motorway
- N7 — Dual Carriageway
- N2 — National Primary Routes
- N69 — National Secondary Routes
- Regional Routes
- Other Roads
- ●——14——● Distances Between Centres (in Kilometres)
- County Boundary
- Northern Ireland/Republic of Ireland Border
- SHANNON AIRPORT ✈ Airports
- Holyhead ——— Ferries

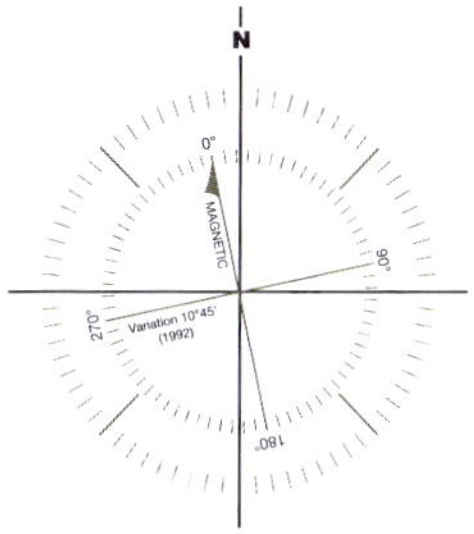

DISTANCE CHART
in Kilometres

ARMAGH	ATHLONE	BELFAST	CARLOW	CLIFDEN	CORK	DERRY	DUBLIN	DUNDALK	ENNISKILLEN	GALWAY	KILKENNY	KILLARNEY	LARNE	LIMERICK	PORTLAOISE	ROSSLARE HARBOUR	SHANNON AIRPORT	SLIGO	TRALEE	WATERFORD	WEXFORD	WICKLOW
159																						
66	224																					
211	108	248																				
316	171	370	256																			
380	219	423	187	287																		
114	225	118	309	303	460																	
129	124	167	82	296	256	233																
45	142	82	166	314	340	158	84															
81	127	135	240	237	346	98	175	101														
238	92	303	177	79	206	277	216	233	192													
245	121	282	39	248	148	335	114	200	242	169												
388	229	430	235	295	89	480	303	348	356	214	196											
105	264	40	287	411	462	122	206	121	174	343	320	470										
279	119	320	138	184	101	369	192	238	245	105	114	109	356									
208	71	250	37	229	174	287	82	167	192	150	50	221	285	109								
282	201	320	93	348	206	385	151	237	324	269	100	272	356	204	130							
293	134	345	163	172	126	357	216	261	261	93	138	134	380	24	134	229						
148	116	203	224	167	336	142	213	171	68	142	237	345	240	235	187	319	224					
382	222	423	242	288	121	472	296	341	349	208	216	32	460	103	213	291	127	338				
285	167	324	74	296	126	383	156	240	290	217	48	192	359	124	97	81	148	283	211			
264	184	301	76	330	187	365	132	219	306	250	81	254	338	187	113	19	209	299	272	61		
185	138	222	61	311	256	293	56	140	221	232	100	303	259	193	82	118	216	238	296	135	100	

SCALE 1 : 625 000

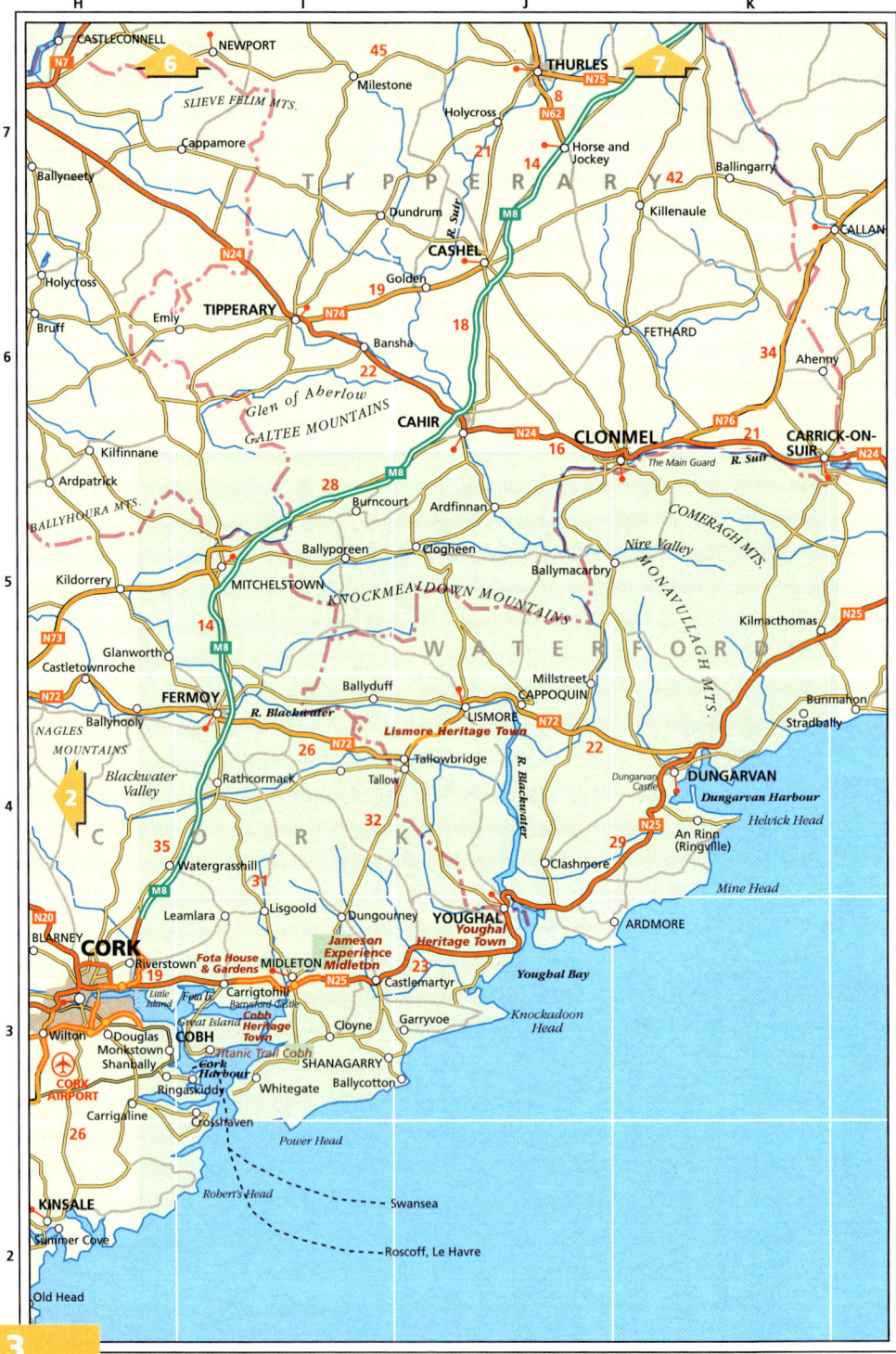

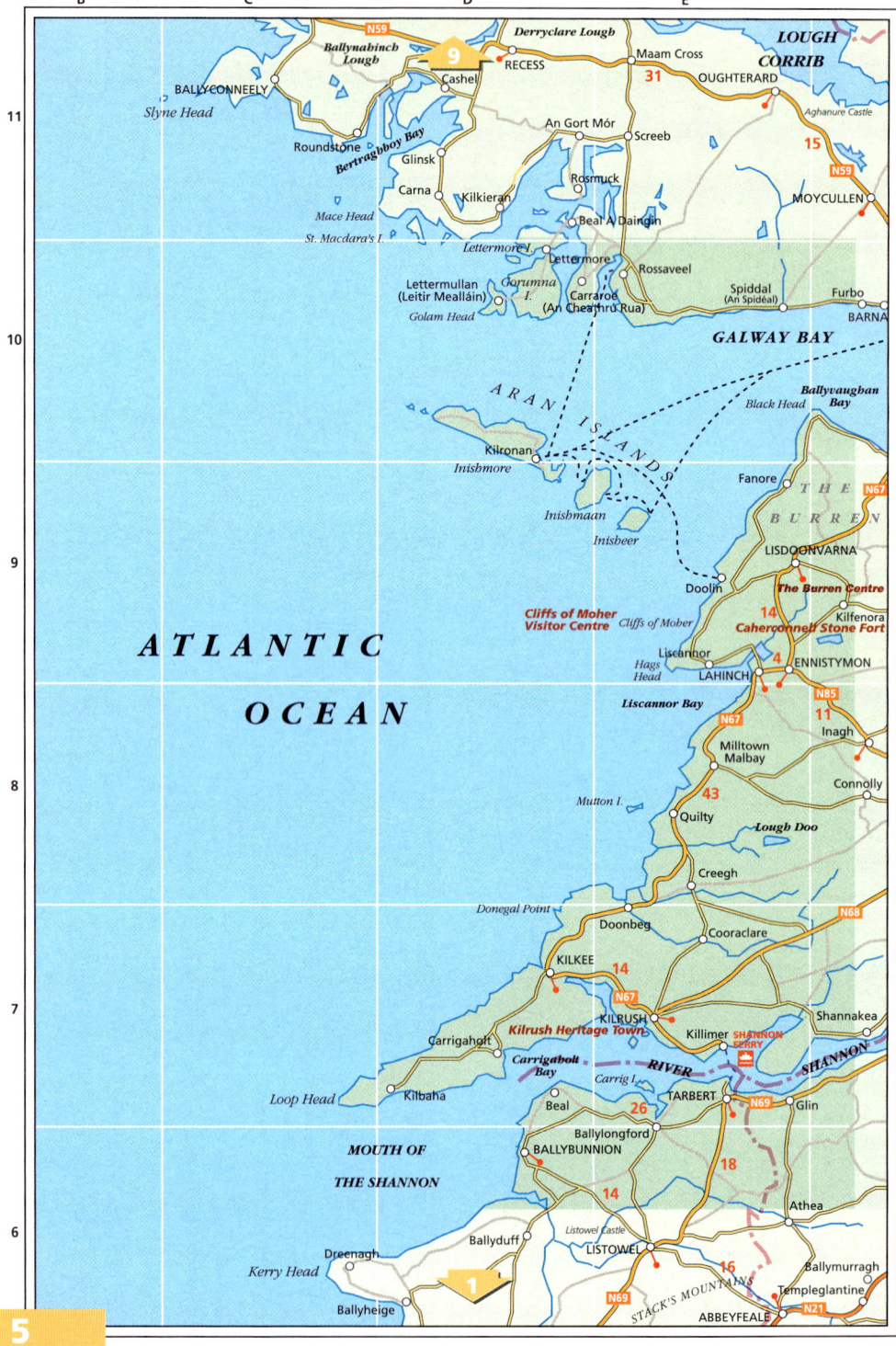

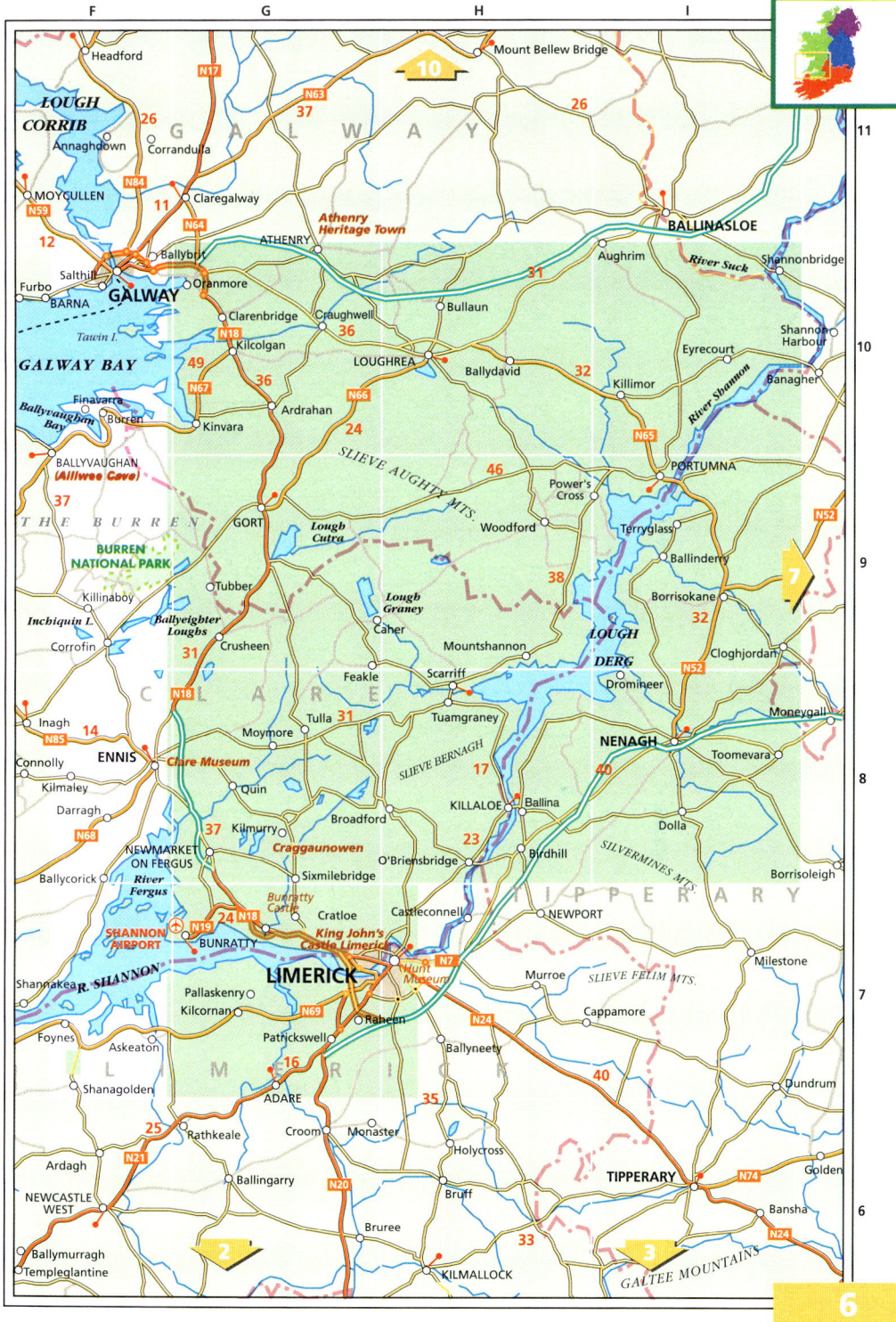

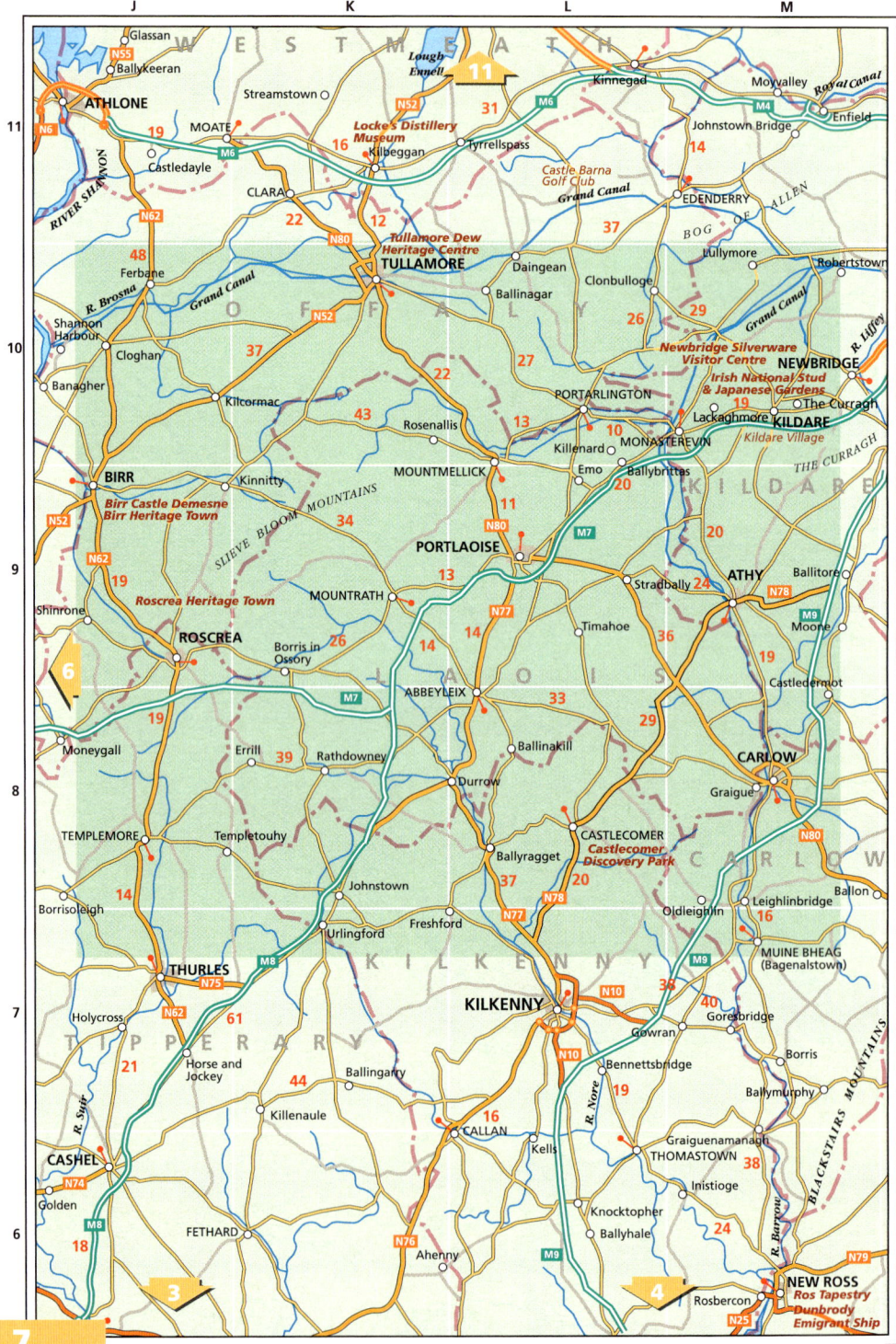

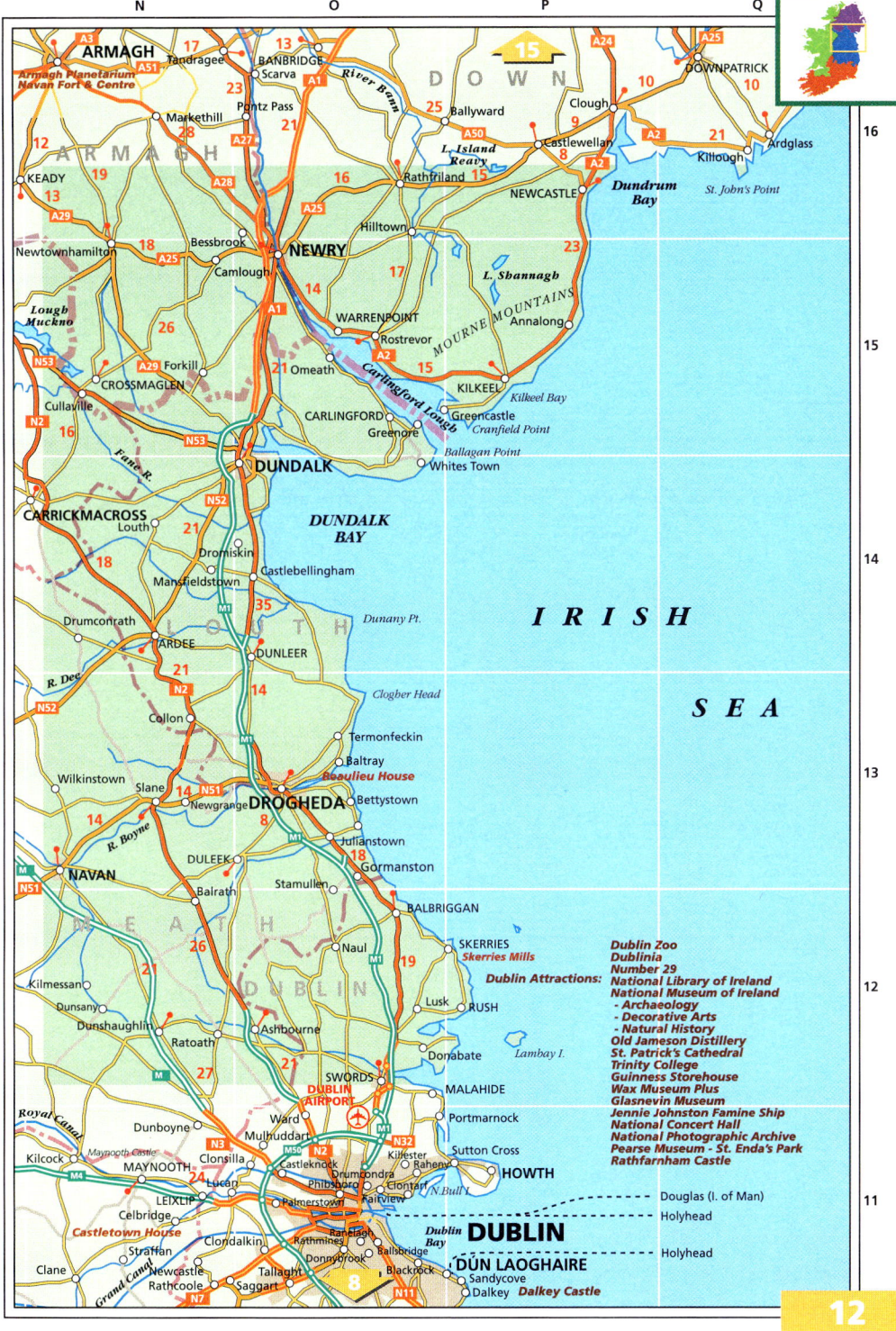

Index of Hotels and Guesthouses

A

Aaron House
Birr, Co. Offaly 168
☎ +353-57-913 7040

Abbey Court Hotel, Lodges & Trinity Leisure Spa
Nenagh, Co. Tipperary 249
☎ +353-67-41111

Abbey Hotel
Ballyvourney, Co. Cork........................186
☎ +353-26-45324

Abbeyglen Castle Hotel
Clifden, Co. Galway 57
☎ +353-95-21201

Abbott Lodge
Dublin City, Co. Dublin 121
☎ +353-1-836 5548

Aberdeen Lodge
Dublin City, Co. Dublin 122
☎ +353-1-283 8155

Absolute Hotel & Spa
Limerick City, Co. Limerick 80
☎ +353-61-463600

Achill Cliff House Hotel
Achill Island, Co. Mayo 82
☎ +353-98-43400

Achill House
Cork City, Co. Cork 193
☎ +353-21-427 9447

Actons Hotel
Kinsale, Co. Cork 202
☎ +353-21-477 9900

Aghadoe Heights Hotel & Spa
Killarney, Co. Kerry......................217
☎ +353-64-663 1766

Aherlow House Hotel and Lodges
Glen of Aherlow, Co. Tipperary 248
☎ +353-62-56153

Aherne's Townhouse & Seafood Restaurant
Youghal, Co. Cork 208
☎ +353-24-92424

Aisleigh Guest House
Carrick-on-Shannon, Co. Leitrim 77
☎ +353-71-962 0313

Aisling Guest House
Ashbourne, Co. Meath......................162
☎ +353-1-835 0359

All The Twos Guesthouse
Clifden, Co. Galway 58
☎ +353-95-22222

Alpine House
Dingle (An Daingean), Co. Kerry 210
☎ +353-66-915 1250

Ambassador Hotel & Health Club
Cork City, Co. Cork 193
☎ +353-21-453 9000

Amber Springs Hotel & Health Spa
Gorey, Co. Wexford 263
☎ +353-53-948 4000

An Bothar Pub
Dingle (An Daingean), Co. Kerry 211
☎ +353-66-915 5342

An Chúirt, (Gweedore Court Hotel) & Earagail Health Club
Gweedore, Co. Donegal 51
☎ +353-74-953 2900

An Crúiscín Lán Hotel
Spiddal, Co. Galway......................76
☎ +353-91-553148

An Glen Guesthouse
Dublin City, Co. Dublin 122
☎ +353-1-855 1374

An Portán
Dingle (An Daingean), Co. Kerry 211
☎ +353-66-915 6212

Anglers Rest Hotel
Headford, Co. Galway 71
☎ +353-93-35528

Annaly Hotel
Longford Town, Co. Longford 158
☎ +353-43-334 3690

Anner Hotel & Leisure Centre
Thurles, Co. Tipperary......................250
☎ +353-504-21799

Aran View House Hotel & Restaurant
Doolin, Co. Clare 36
☎ +353-65-707 4061

Arbutus Hotel
Killarney, Co. Kerry......................217
☎ +353-64-663 1037

Árd Einne Guesthouse
Aran Islands, Co. Galway 54
☎ +353-99-61126

Ard Na Breátha
Donegal Town, Co. Donegal 47
☎ +353-74-972 2288

Ardagh House
Dublin City, Co. Dublin 122
☎ +353-1-497 7068

Ardilaun Guesthouse
Ennis, Co. Clare......................37
☎ +353-65-682 2311

Ardilaun Hotel Conference Centre & Leisure Club
Galway City, Co. Galway 61
☎ +353-91-521433

Ard-Na-Sidhe Country House
Caragh Lake, Co. Kerry 209
☎ +353-66-976 9105

Arklow Bay Conference, Leisure & Spa Hotel
Arklow, Co. Wicklow 174
☎ +353-402-32309

Arlington Lodge Town House & Restaurant
Waterford City, Co. Waterford 256
☎ +353-51-878584

Arnolds Hotel
Dunfanaghy, Co. Donegal......................49
☎ +353-74-913 6208

Ashbourne Marriott Hotel
Ashbourne, Co. Meath......................162
☎ +353-1-835 0800

Ashdown Park Hotel Conference & Leisure Centre
Gorey, Co. Wexford 263
☎ +353-53-948 0500

Ashford Castle
Cong, Co. Mayo 87
☎ +353-94-954 6003

Ashford Court Boutique Hotel
Ennis, Co. Clare 38
☎ +353-65-689 4444

Ashlee Lodge
Blarney, Co. Cork 188
☎ +353-21-438 5346

Ashley Hotel
Cork City, Co. Cork 194
☎ +353-21-450 1518

Ashling Hotel
Dublin City, Co. Dublin 123
☎ +353-1-677 2324

Ashville House
Killarney, Co. Kerry......................217
☎ +353-64-663 6405

Athenaeum House Hotel
Waterford City, Co. Waterford 257
☎ +353-51-833999

Atlantic Guesthouse
Donegal Town, Co. Donegal 48
☎ +353-74-972 1187

Atlantic View Guesthouse
Galway City, Co. Galway 62
☎ +353-91-582109

Auburn Lodge Hotel & Leisure Centre
Ennis, Co. Clare 38
☎ +353-65-682 1247

Augusta Lodge
Westport, Co. Mayo......................89
☎ +353-98-28900

Aulber House
Cashel, Co. Tipperary 246
☎ +353-62-63713

B

Bailey (The)
Kilkenny City, Co. Kilkenny 238
☎ +353-56-777 0422

Baileys Hotel Cashel
Cashel, Co. Tipperary 246
☎ +353-62-61937

Bailie Hotel
Bailieborough, Co. Cavan......................117
☎ +353-42-966 5334

Ballina Manor Hotel
Ballina, Co. Mayo......................83
☎ +353-1890-238400

Ballinalacken Castle Country House & Restaurant
Doolin, Co. Clare 36
☎ +353-65-707 4025

Ballygarry House Hotel & Spa
Tralee, Co. Kerry......................235
☎ +353-66-712 3322

Index of Hotels and Guesthouses   GUINNESS

Ballyglass Country House
Tipperary Town, Co. Tipperary 250
☎ +353-62-52104

Ballykisteen Hotel & Golf Resort
Tipperary Town, Co. Tipperary 250
☎ +353-62-33333

Ballyknocken House & Cookery School
Ashford, Co. Wicklow 174
☎ +353-404-44627

Ballymascanlon House Hotel
Dundalk, Co. Louth 161
☎ +353-42-935 8200

Ballynahinch Castle Hotel
Ballynahinch, Co. Galway 56
☎ +353-95-31006

Ballyseede Castle Hotel
Tralee, Co. Kerry 235
☎ +353-66-712 5799

Ballyvaughan Lodge
Ballyvaughan, Co. Clare 35
☎ +353-65-707 7292

Bambury's Guest House
Dingle (An Daingean), Co. Kerry 211
☎ +353-66-915 1244

Barrowville Town House
Carlow Town, Co. Carlow 183
☎ +353-59-914 3324

Bay View Hotel & Leisure Centre
Killybegs, Co. Donegal 51
☎ +353-74-973 1950

Bayview Hotel
Ballycotton, Co. Cork 185
☎ +353-21-464 6746

Bayview Hotel
Bushmills, Co. Antrim 103
☎ +44-28-2073 4100

Beach Guest House
Dunmore East, Co. Waterford 253
☎ +353-51-383316

Beach Haven House
Tramore, Co. Waterford 254
☎ +353-51-390208

Beaufort House
Carlingford, Co. Louth 159
☎ +353-42-937 3879

Beech Hill Country House Hotel
Derry City, Co. Derry 107
☎ +44-28-7134 9279

Bel-Air Hotel
Ashford, Co. Wicklow 175
☎ +353-404-40109

Belleek Castle
Ballina, Co. Mayo 83
☎ +353-96-22400

Belvedere Hotel Parnell Square
Dublin City, Co. Dublin 123
☎ +353-1-873 7700

Ben View House
Clifden, Co. Galway 58
☎ +353-95-21256

Best Western Dublin Skylon Hotel
Dublin City, Co. Dublin 123
☎ +353-1-884 3900

Best Western Eviston House Hotel
Killarney, Co. Kerry 218
☎ +353-64-663 1640

Best Western Milford Inn Hotel & Natural Wellness
Letterkenny, Co. Donegal 52
☎ +353-74-915 3313

Best Western Pery's Hotel
Limerick City, Co. Limerick 80
☎ +353-61-413822

Best Western White Horse Hotel
Derry City, Co. Derry 108
☎ +44-28-7186 0606

Bewley's Hotel Ballsbridge
Dublin City, Co. Dublin 124
☎ +353-1-668 1111

Bewley's Hotel Dublin Airport
Dublin Airport, Co. Dublin 120
☎ +353-1-871 1000

Bewley's Hotel Leopardstown
Dublin City, Co. Dublin 124
☎ +353-1-293 5000

Bewley's Hotel Newlands Cross
Dublin City, Co. Dublin 124
☎ +353-1-464 0140

Bianconi (The)
Killorglin, Co. Kerry 233
☎ +353-66-976 1146

Blakes Hotel & Spa
Dublin City, Co. Dublin 126
☎ +353-1-668 8324

Blarney Castle Hotel
Blarney, Co. Cork 188
☎ +353-21-438 5116

Blarney Golf Resort
Blarney, Co. Cork 188
☎ +353-21-438 4477

Blarney Stone
Cork City, Co. Cork 194
☎ +353-21-427 0083

Blarney Woollen Mills Hotel
Blarney, Co. Cork 189
☎ +353-21-438 5011

Bloomfield House Hotel
Mullingar, Co. Westmeath 173
☎ +353-44-934 0894

Blue Haven Kinsale (The)
Kinsale, Co. Cork 202
☎ +353-21-477 2209

Boffin Lodge
Westport, Co. Mayo 90
☎ +353-98-26092

Bracken Court Hotel
Balbriggan, Co. Dublin 119
☎ +353-1-841 3333

Brandon House Hotel & Solas Croí Eco Spa
New Ross, Co. Wexford 264
☎ +353-51-421703

Bridge Court House
Kilkenny City, Co. Kilkenny 238
☎ +353-56-776 2998

Bridge Hotel
Arklow, Co. Wicklow 174
☎ +353-402-31666

Bridge House Hotel
Tullamore, Co. Offaly 168
☎ +353-57-932 5600

Brook Lodge Hotel
Killarney, Co. Kerry 218
☎ +353-64-663 1800

Brook Manor Lodge
Tralee, Co. Kerry 235
☎ +353-66-712 0406

Brooks Hotel
Dublin City, Co. Dublin 126
☎ +353-1-670 4000

Brown Trout Golf & Country Inn
Aghadowey, Co. Derry 107
☎ +44-28-7086 8209

Bunratty Castle Hotel
Bunratty, Co. Clare 35
☎ +353-61-478700

Bunratty Grove
Bunratty, Co. Clare 36
☎ +353-61-369579

Burlington (The)
Dublin City, Co. Dublin 126
☎ +353-1-618 5600

Burrendale Hotel, Country Club & Spa
Newcastle, Co. Down 109
☎ +44-28-4372 2599

Bush Hotel
Carrick-on-Shannon, Co. Leitrim 77
☎ +353-71-967 1000

Bushmills Inn Hotel
Bushmills, Co. Antrim 104
☎ +44-28-2073 3000

Bushtown Hotel
Coleraine, Co. Derry 107
☎ +44-28-7035 8367

Buswells Hotel
Dublin City, Co. Dublin 127
☎ +353-1-614 6500

Butler Arms Hotel
Waterville, Co. Kerry 237
☎ +353-66-947 4144

Butler House
Kilkenny City, Co. Kilkenny 239
☎ +353-56-776 5707

Butlers Town House
Dublin City, Co. Dublin 127
☎ +353-1-667 4022

Buttermilk Lodge
Clifden, Co. Galway 58
☎ +353-95-21951

C

Cahernane House Hotel
Killarney, Co. Kerry 218
☎ +353-64-663 1895

Cahir House Hotel
Cahir, Co. Tipperary 245
☎ +353-52-744 3000

Index of Hotels and Guesthouses

Camden Court Hotel
Dublin City, Co. Dublin 128
☎ +353-1-475 9666

Canal Court Hotel
Newry, Co. Down 109
☎ +44-28-3025 1234

Carlton Abbey Hotel & C-Spa
Athy, Co. Kildare 151
☎ +353-59-863 0100

Carlton Atlantic Coast Hotel & Ayurveda C Spa
Westport, Co. Mayo 90
☎ +353-98-29000

Carlton Castletroy Park Hotel
Limerick City, Co. Limerick 81
☎ +353-61-335566

Carlton Dublin Airport Hotel
Dublin Airport, Co. Dublin 120
☎ +353-1-866 7500

Carlton Hotel & C-Spa Kinsale
Kinsale, Co. Cork 202
☎ +353-21-470 6000

Carlton Hotel Galway
Galway City, Co. Galway 62
☎ +353-91-381200

Carlton Hotel Tralee
Tralee, Co. Kerry 236
☎ +353-66-719 9100

Carlton Millrace Hotel & C-Spa
Bunclody, Co. Wexford 261
☎ +353-53-937 5100

Carlton Redcastle Hotel & C-Spa
Moville, Co. Donegal 53
☎ +353-74-938 5555

Carlton Shearwater Hotel & C-Spa
Ballinasloe, Co. Galway 56
☎ +353-909-630400

Carna Bay Hotel
Carna, Co. Galway 57
☎ +353-95-32255

Carraig Hotel
Carrick-on-Suir, Co. Tipperary 246
☎ +353-51-641155

Carrig Country House
Caragh Lake, Co. Kerry 209
☎ +353-66-976 9100

Carrigaline Court Hotel & Leisure Centre
Carrigaline, Co. Cork 189
☎ +353-21-485 2100

Carrolls Hotel
Knocktopher, Co. Kilkenny 244
☎ +353-56-776 8082

Carroll's Pierhouse Hotel
Skerries, Co. Dublin 149
☎ +353-1-849 1033

Casey's Hotel
Glengarriff, Co. Cork 200
☎ +353-27-63010

Casey's of Baltimore
Baltimore, Co. Cork 186
☎ +353-28-20197

Cashel House Hotel
Cashel, Co. Galway 57
☎ +353-95-31001

Cashel Palace Hotel
Cashel, Co. Tipperary 247
☎ +353-62-62707

Cassidys Hotel
Dublin City, Co. Dublin 128
☎ +353-1-878 0555

Castle (The)
Castletownshend, Co. Cork 190
☎ +353-28-36180

Castle (The) at Castle Leslie Estate
Glaslough, Co. Monaghan 166
☎ +353-47-88100

Castle Arms Hotel
Durrow, Co. Laois 156
☎ +353-57-873 6117

Castle Dargan Golf Hotel Wellness
Ballygawley, Co. Sligo 94
☎ +353-71-911 8080

Castle Grove Country House Hotel
Letterkenny, Co. Donegal 52
☎ +353-74-915 1118

Castle Hotel
Dublin City, Co. Dublin 128
☎ +353-1-874 6949

Castle Oaks House Hotel & Country Club
Castleconnell, Co. Limerick 79
☎ +353-61-377666

Castlecourt Hotel Spa, Leisure, Conference
Westport, Co. Mayo 90
☎ +353-98-55088

Castleknock Hotel and Country Club
Dublin City, Co. Dublin 129
☎ +353-1-640 6300

Castlemartyr Resort
Castlemartyr, Co. Cork 190
☎ +353-21-4219000

Castlemurray House Hotel
Dunkineely, Co. Donegal 50
☎ +353-74-973 7022

Castlerosse Hotel and Golf Resort
Killarney, Co. Kerry 220
☎ +353-64-663 1144

Cawley's Guesthouse
Tubbercurry, Co. Sligo 97
☎ +353-71-918 5025

Cedar Lodge Hotel & Restaurant
Newbawn, Co. Wexford 264
☎ +353-51-428386

Celtic Lodge Guesthouse
Dublin City, Co. Dublin 129
☎ +353-1-878 8732

Celtic Ross Hotel
Rosscarbery, Co. Cork 206
☎ +353-23-884 8722

Charleville Lodge
Dublin City, Co. Dublin 130
☎ +353-1-838 6633

Charleville Park Hotel & Leisure Club
Charleville, Co. Cork 191
☎ +353-63-33700

CityNorth Hotel
Gormanston, Co. Meath 163
☎ +353-1-690 6666

Ciúin House & Chungs Asian Restaurant
Carrick-on-Shannon, Co. Leitrim 78
☎ +353-71-967 1488

Clanard Court Hotel
Athy, Co. Kildare 151
☎ +353-59-864 0666

Clanree Hotel Conference & Leisure Centre
Letterkenny, Co. Donegal 52
☎ +353-74-912 4369

Claregalway Hotel (The)
Galway City, Co. Galway 62
☎ +353-91-738300

Clarence (The)
Dublin City, Co. Dublin 130
☎ +353-1-407 0800

Clayton Hotel Galway
Galway City, Co. Galway 63
☎ +353-91-721900

Clew Bay Hotel
Westport, Co. Mayo 91
☎ +353-98-28088

Clifden Guesthouse
Dublin City, Co. Dublin 130
☎ +353-1-874 6364

Clifden Station House Hotel
Clifden, Co. Galway 59
☎ +353-95-21699

Cliff House Hotel
Ardmore, Co. Waterford 251
☎ +353-24-87800

Cliff Town House (The)
Dublin City, Co. Dublin 131
☎ +353-1-638 3939

Clifton House
Limerick City, Co. Limerick 81
☎ +353-61-451166

Clonea Strand Hotel, Golf & Leisure
Dungarvan, Co. Waterford 252
☎ +353-58-45555

Clonmel Park Conference Leisure & Spa Hotel
Clonmel, Co. Tipperary 247
☎ +353-52-618 8700

Clontarf Castle Hotel
Dublin City, Co. Dublin 131
☎ +353-1-833 2321

Club House Hotel
Kilkenny City, Co. Kilkenny 239
☎ +353-56-772 1994

Coach House (The)
Waterford City, Co. Waterford 257
☎ +353-51-384656

Coastline Guesthouse
Dingle (An Daingean), Co. Kerry 212
☎ +353-66-915 2494

Index of Hotels and Guesthouses

Commodore Hotel
Cobh, Co. Cork 192
☎ +353-21-481 1277

Commons Inn Hotel
Cork City, Co. Cork 194
☎ +353-21-421 0300

Connemara Coast Hotel
Furbo, Co. Galway 61
☎ +353-91-592108

Connemara Country Lodge
Clifden, Co. Galway 59
☎ +353-87-992 5777 / 095-22112

Conrad Dublin
Dublin City, Co. Dublin 132
☎ +353-1-602 8900

Coolcower House
Macroom, Co. Cork 204
☎ +353-26-41695

Corrib Haven Guest House
Galway City, Co. Galway 63
☎ +353-91-524171

Corrib Wave Guest House
Oughterard, Co. Galway 74
☎ +353-91-552147

Corthna-Lodge Guesthouse
Schull, Co. Cork 206
☎ +353-28-28517

County Arms Hotel & Leisure Club
Birr, Co. Offaly 168
☎ +353-57-912 0791

Courthouse (The)
Ballyhaunis, Co. Mayo 85
☎ +353-94-963 0068

Courtmacsherry Hotel & Coastal Cottages
Courtmacsherry, Co. Cork 199
☎ +353-23-884 6198

Courtyard Hotel Leixlip
Leixlip, Co. Kildare 152
☎ +353-1-629 5100

Courtyard Marriott Galway
Galway City, Co. Galway 64
☎ +353-91-513200

Creevy Pier Hotel
Ballyshannon, Co. Donegal 46
☎ +353-71-985 8355

Creggan Court Hotel
Athlone, Co. Westmeath 170
☎ +353-90-647 7777

Crofton Bray Head Inn
Bray, Co. Wicklow 175
☎ +353-1-286 7182

Croke Park Hotel (The)
Dublin City, Co. Dublin 132
☎ +353-1-871 4444

Crover House Hotel & Golf Club
Mountnugent, Co. Cavan 118
☎ +353-49-854 0206

Crystal Springs
Killarney, Co. Kerry 220
☎ +353-64-663 3272

Cullinan's Seafood Restaurant & Guesthouse
Doolin, Co. Clare 37
☎ +353-65-707 4183

D

d (The)
Drogheda, Co. Louth 160
☎ +353-41-987 7700

Danby Lodge Hotel
Rosslare, Co. Wexford 264
☎ +353-53-915 8191

Darby O'Gill's Country House Hotel
Killarney, Co. Kerry 220
☎ +353-64-663 4168

Deebert House Hotel
Kilmallock, Co. Limerick 80
☎ +353-63-31200

Deer Park Hotel Golf & Spa
Howth, Co. Dublin 147
☎ +353-1-832 2624

Delphi Mountain Resort
Leenane, Co. Galway 72
☎ +353-95-42208

Derby House Hotel
Kildare Town, Co. Kildare 152
☎ +353-45-522144

Dergvale Hotel
Dublin City, Co. Dublin 132
☎ +353-1-874 4753

Derrynane Hotel & Holiday Homes
Caherdaniel, Co. Kerry 209
☎ +353-66-947 5136

Diamond Coast Hotel
Enniscrone, Co. Sligo 95
☎ +353-96-26000

Dingle Bay Hotel
Dingle (An Daingean), Co. Kerry..........212
☎ +353-66-915 1231

Dingle Benners Hotel
Dingle (An Daingean), Co. Kerry..........212
☎ +353-66-915 1638

Dingle Skellig Hotel
Dingle (An Daingean), Co. Kerry..........213
☎ +353-66-915 0200

Dooley's Hotel
Waterford City, Co. Waterford 257
☎ +353-51-873531

Doonmore Hotel
Inishbofin Island, Co. Galway 71
☎ +353-95-45814

Dorrians Imperial Hotel
Ballyshannon, Co. Donegal 46
☎ +353-71-985 1147

Dough Mor Lodge
Lahinch, Co. Clare 42
☎ +353-65-708 2063

Downhill House Hotel & Eagles Leisure Club
Ballina, Co. Mayo 84
☎ +353-96-21033

Downhill Inn
Ballina, Co. Mayo 84
☎ +353-96-73444

Downings Bay Hotel
Downings, Co. Donegal 49
☎ +353-74-915 5586

Drinagh Court Hotel
Wexford Town, Co. Wexford................266
☎ +353-53-914 3295

Dromhall Hotel
Killarney, Co. Kerry 221
☎ +353-64-663 9600

Dromoland Castle
Newmarket-on-Fergus, Co. Clare 45
☎ +353-61-368144

Drury Court Hotel
Dublin City, Co. Dublin 133
☎ +353-1-475 1988

Dun Ri Guesthouse
Clifden, Co. Galway 60
☎ +353-95-21625

Dunboyne Castle Hotel & Spa
Dunboyne, Co. Meath 162
☎ +353-1-801 3500

Dundrum House Hotel, Golf & Leisure Resort
Cashel, Co. Tipperary 247
☎ +353-62-71116

Dunmore House Hotel
Clonakilty, Co. Cork 191
☎ +353-23-883 3352

Dunraven Arms Hotel
Adare, Co. Limerick 79
☎ +353-61-605900

Dylan Hotel
Dublin City, Co. Dublin 133
☎ +353-1-660 3000

E

Eagle Lodge
Ballybunion, Co. Kerry 208
☎ +353-68-27224

Earls Court House
Killarney, Co. Kerry 221
☎ +353-64-663 4009

Egan's Guesthouse
Dublin City, Co. Dublin 133
☎ +353-1-830 3611

Europe Hotel & Resort (The)
Killarney, Co. Kerry 222
☎ +353-64-667 1300

Eyre Square Hotel
Galway City, Co. Galway 64
☎ +353-91-569633

F

Failte Hotel
Killarney, Co. Kerry 222
☎ +353-64-663 3404

Fairhill House Hotel
Clonbur (An Fháirche), Co. Galway.......61
☎ +353-94-954 6176

Fairview Guesthouse
Killarney, Co. Kerry 222
☎ +353-64-663 4164

Faithlegg House Hotel
Faithlegg, Co. Waterford 254
☎ +353-51-382000

Falls Hotel & Spa
Ennistymon, Co. Clare 40
☎ +353-65-707 1004

Index of Hotels and Guesthouses

Fanad House
Kilkenny City, Co. Kilkenny 240
☎ +353-56-776 4126

Faythe Guest House
Wexford Town, Co. Wexford 267
☎ +353-53-912 2249

Fennessy's Hotel
Clonmel, Co. Tipperary 248
☎ +353-52-612 3680

Ferrycarrig Hotel
Wexford Town, Co. Wexford 267
☎ +353-53-912 0999

Ferryport House
Rosslare Harbour, Co. Wexford 265
☎ +353-53-913 3933

Ferryview Guesthouse
Dublin City, Co. Dublin 134
☎ +353-1-833 5893

Finnstown Country House Hotel
Lucan, Co. Dublin 148
☎ +353-1-601 0700

Fir Grove Hotel
Mitchelstown, Co. Cork 205
☎ +353-25-24111

Fitzgeralds Vienna Woods Hotel Cork
Cork City, Co. Cork 195
☎ +353-21-455 6800

Fitzgeralds Woodlands House Hotel & Spa
Adare, Co. Limerick 79
☎ +353-61-605100

Fitzpatrick Castle Hotel
Killiney, Co. Dublin 148
☎ +353-1-230 5400

Fitzsimons Hotel
Dublin City, Co. Dublin 134
☎ +353-1-677 9315

Fitzwilliam Hotel Belfast (The)
Belfast City, Belfast City 105
☎ +44-28-9044 2080

Fitzwilton Hotel
Waterford City, Co. Waterford 258
☎ +353-51-846900

Flannery's Hotel
Galway City, Co. Galway 64
☎ +353-91-755111

Foleys Townhouse
Kenmare, Co. Kerry 215
☎ +353-64-664 2162

Foley's Townhouse & Restaurant
Killarney, Co. Kerry 223
☎ +353-64-663 1217

Fort Royal Country House
Rathmullan, Co. Donegal 54
☎ +353-74-915 8100

Fota Island Resort
Fota Island, Co. Cork 200
☎ +353-21-488 3700

Four Seasons Hotel & Leisure Club
Monaghan Town, Co. Monaghan 167
☎ +353-47-81888

Four Seasons Hotel Dublin
Dublin City, Co. Dublin 134
☎ +353-1-665 4000

Foyles Hotel
Clifden, Co. Galway 60
☎ +353-95-21801

Friars Glen
Killarney, Co. Kerry 223
☎ +353-64-663 7500

Friar's Lodge
Kinsale, Co. Cork 203
☎ +353-21-477 7384

Fuchsia House
Killarney, Co. Kerry 224
☎ +353-64-663 3743

G

g Hotel (The)
Galway City, Co. Galway 65
☎ +353-91-865200

Gables Guesthouse & Leisure Centre
Newbridge, Co. Kildare 154
☎ +353-45-435330

Galgorm Resort & Spa
Ballymena, Co. Antrim 103
☎ +44-28-2588 1001

Galway Bay Hotel, Conference & Leisure Centre
Galway City, Co. Galway 65
☎ +353-91-520520

Garnish House
Cork City, Co. Cork 195
☎ +353-21-427 5111

Garryvoe Hotel
Shanagarry, Co. Cork 206
☎ +353-21-464 6718

Glassdrumman Lodge
Annalong, Co. Down 108
☎ +44-28-4376 8451

Glasson Country House Hotel and Golf Club
Athlone, Co. Westmeath 171
☎ +353-90-648 5120

Gleann Fia Country House
Killarney, Co. Kerry 224
☎ +353-64-663 5035

Gleesons Townhouse & Restaurant
Roscommon Town, Co. Roscommon 94
☎ +353-90-662 6954

Glendalough Hotel
Glendalough, Co. Wicklow 176
☎ +353-404-45135

Glendarragh Valley Inn
Enniskillen, Co. Fermanagh 109
☎ +44-28-6863 2777

Glendine Inn
Kilkenny City, Co. Kilkenny 240
☎ +353-56-772 1069

Glengarriff Park Hotel
Glengarriff, Co. Cork 200
☎ +353-27-63000

Glenlo Abbey Hotel
Galway City, Co. Galway 65
☎ +353-91-526666

Glenluce Lodge
Ballycastle, Co. Antrim 103
☎ +44-28-2076 2914

Glenogra House
Dublin City, Co. Dublin 135
☎ +353-1-668 3661

Glenview Guesthouse
Ballinamore, Co. Leitrim 77
☎ +353-71-964 4157

Glenview Hotel & Leisure Cub
Glen-O-The-Downs, Co. Wicklow 177
☎ +353-1-287 3399

Glenwood House
Carrigaline, Co. Cork 190
☎ +353-21-437 3878

Gorman's Clifftop House and Restaurant
Dingle (An Daingean), Co. Kerry 213
☎ +353-66-915 5162

Gougane Barra Hotel
Gougane Barra, Co. Cork 201
☎ +353-26-47069

Grand Central Hotel
Bundoran, Co. Donegal 47
☎ +353-71-984 2722

Grand Hotel
Wicklow Town, Co. Wicklow 178
☎ +353-404-67337

Grand Hotel
Malahide, Co. Dublin 149
☎ +353-1-845 0000

Grand Hotel
Tralee, Co. Kerry 236
☎ +353-66-712 1499

Grand Hotel
Tramore, Co. Waterford 255
☎ +353-51-381414

Granville Hotel
Waterford City, Co. Waterford 258
☎ +353-51-305555

Great Northern Hotel
Bundoran, Co. Donegal 47
☎ +353-71-984 1204

Greenmount House
Dingle (An Daingean), Co. Kerry 213
☎ +353-66-915 1414

Grennans Country House & Cottages
Tullamore, Co. Offaly 169
☎ +353-57-935 5893

Gresham (The)
Dublin City, Co. Dublin 135
☎ +353-1-874 6881

Gresham Metropole
Cork City, Co. Cork 196
☎ +353-21-464 3700

Greville Arms Hotel
Mullingar, Co. Westmeath 173
☎ +353-44-934 8563

Grovemount House
Ennistymon, Co. Clare 40
☎ +353-65-707 1431

See also Index to Location pages 14 - 15

Index of Hotels and Guesthouses   GUINNESS

H

Halpin's Townhouse Hotel
Kilkee, Co. Clare..........................40
☎ +353-65-905 6032

Hampton Hotel
Dublin City, Co. Dublin 135
☎ +353-1-668 0995

Hanoras Cottage
Ballymacarbry, Co. Waterford ...252
☎ +353-52-613 6134

Harbour Hotel & Restaurant
Naas, Co. Kildare 154
☎ +353-45-879145

Harbour House & Leisure Centre
Castlegregory, Co. Kerry 210
☎ +353-66-713 9292

Harbour View Hotel
Rosslare Harbour, Co. Wexford ..266
☎ +353-53-916 1450

Harcourt Hotel
Dublin City, Co. Dublin 136
☎ +353-1-478 3677

Harlequin Hotel
Castlebar, Co. Mayo 86
☎ +353-94-928 6200

Harrington Hall
Dublin City, Co. Dublin 136
☎ +353-1-475 3497

Harvey's Guest House
Dublin City, Co. Dublin 136
☎ +353-1-874 8384

Harvey's Point Hotel
Donegal Town, Co. Donegal 48
☎ +353-74-972 2208

Hayfield Manor Hotel
Cork City, Co. Cork 196
☎ +353-21-484 5900

Hazel Hotel
Monasterevin, Co. Kildare 153
☎ +353-45-525373

Headfort Arms
Kells, Co. Meath 164
☎ +353-818-222800

Healys Restaurant & Fishing Lodge
Pontoon, Co. Mayo 89
☎ +353-94-925 6443

Heights Hotel Killarney (The)
Killarney, Co. Kerry 224
☎ +353-64-663 1158

Heritage Golf & Spa Resort (The)
Killenard, Co. Laois 157
☎ +353-57-864 5500

Highlands Hotel
Glenties, Co. Donegal 50
☎ +353-74-955 1111

Hillgrove (The)
Dingle (An Daingean), Co. Kerry ...214
☎ +353-66-915 1131

Hillgrove Hotel Leisure & Spa
Monaghan Town, Co. Monaghan ...167
☎ +353-47-81288

Hillview House
Lusk, Co. Dublin 149
☎ +353-1-843 8218

Hilton Belfast
Belfast City, Belfast City 105
☎ +44-28-9027 7000

Hilton Dublin
Dublin City, Co. Dublin 137
☎ +353-1-402 9988

Hilton Dublin Airport
Dublin Airport, Co. Dublin 120
☎ +353-1-866 1800

Hilton Templepatrick
Templepatrick, Co. Antrim 105
☎ +44-28-9443 5500

Hodson Bay Hotel
Athlone, Co. Westmeath 171
☎ +353-90-644 2000

Holiday Inn Killarney
Killarney, Co. Kerry 225
☎ +353-64-663 3000

Horse and Hound Hotel
Foulksmills, Co. Wexford 262
☎ +353-51-428482

Horse and Jockey Hotel
Horse and Jockey, Co. Tipperary ...249
☎ +353-504-44192

Hotel Curracloe
Curracloe, Co. Wexford 262
☎ +353-53-913 7308

Hotel Dunloe Castle
Killarney, Co. Kerry 225
☎ +353-64-664 4111

Hotel Isaacs
Cork City, Co. Cork 196
☎ +353-21-450 0011

Hotel Isaacs
Dublin City, Co. Dublin 137
☎ +353-1-813 4700

Hotel Kilkenny
Kilkenny City, Co. Kilkenny 240
☎ +353-56-776 2000

Hotel Kilmore
Cavan Town, Co. Cavan.............118
☎ +353-49-433 2288

Hotel Meyrick
Galway City, Co. Galway 66
☎ +353-91-564041

Hotel Minella & Leisure Club
Clonmel, Co. Tipperary 248
☎ +353-52-612 2388

Hotel Rosslare
Rosslare Harbour, Co. Wexford ..266
☎ +353-53-913 3110

Hotel Westport
Westport, Co. Mayo 91
☎ +353-98-25122

House Hotel (The)
Galway City, Co. Galway 66
☎ +353-91-538900

Huntsman Inn
Galway City, Co. Galway 66
☎ +353-91-562849

Hyland's Burren Hotel
Ballyvaughan, Co. Clare 35
☎ +353-65-707 7037

I

Imperial Hotel with Escape Salon and Spa
Cork City, Co. Cork 197
☎ +353-21-427 4040

Inchydoney Island Lodge & Spa
Clonakilty, Co. Cork...................191
☎ +353-23-883 3143

Inishbofin House Hotel
Inishbofin Island, Co. Galway 72
☎ +353-95-45809

Inishmore House
Galway City, Co. Galway 67
☎ +353-91-582639

Innishannon House Hotel
Innishannon, Co. Cork 201
☎ +353-21-477 5121

International Hotel Killarney
Killarney, Co. Kerry 226
☎ +353-64-663 1816

Inveraray Farm Guesthouse
Killarney, Co. Kerry 226
☎ +353-64-664 4224

J

Jackson's Hotel, Conference & Leisure Centre
Ballybofey, Co. Donegal 45
☎ +353-74-913 1021

Jim Edwards
Kinsale, Co. Cork 203
☎ +353-21-477 2541

K

K Club (The)
Straffan, Co. Kildare...................156
☎ +353-1-601 7200

Kathleens Country House
Killarney, Co. Kerry 226
☎ +353-64-663 2810

Keadeen Hotel
Newbridge, Co. Kildare 156
☎ +353-45-431666

Keepers Arms
Ballyconnell, Co. Cavan 117
☎ +353-49-952 3318

Kee's Hotel, Leisure & Wellness Centre
Ballybofey, Co. Donegal 46
☎ +353-74-913 1018

Kelly's Resort Hotel & Spa
Rosslare, Co. Wexford 265
☎ +353-53-913 2114

Kennys Guest House
Castlebar, Co. Mayo 86
☎ +353-94-902 3091

Kilcoran Lodge Hotel
Cahir, Co. Tipperary 245
☎ +353-52-744 1288

Kilford Arms Hotel
Kilkenny City, Co. Kilkenny 241
☎ +353-56-776 1018

Index of Hotels and Guesthouses

Kilkee Thalassotherapy Centre & Guesthouse
Kilkee, Co. Clare 42
☎ +353-65-905 6742

Kilkenny House Hotel
Kilkenny City, Co. Kilkenny 241
☎ +353-56-777 0711

Kilkenny Ormonde Hotel
Kilkenny City, Co. Kilkenny 241
☎ +353-56-775 0200

Kilkenny River Court
Kilkenny City, Co. Kilkenny 242
☎ +353-56-772 3388

Killarney Avenue Hotel
Killarney, Co. Kerry 227
☎ +353-64-663 2522

Killarney Guest House
Cork City, Co. Cork 197
☎ +353-21-427 0290

Killarney Lodge
Killarney, Co. Kerry 227
☎ +353-64-663 6499

Killarney Park Hotel
Killarney, Co. Kerry 227
☎ +353-64-663 5555

Killarney Plaza Hotel & Spa
Killarney, Co. Kerry 228
☎ +353-64-662 1100

Killarney Royal Hotel
Killarney, Co. Kerry 228
☎ +353-64-663 1853

Killarney Towers Hotel & Leisure Centre
Killarney, Co. Kerry 228
☎ +353-64-663 1038

Killeen House Hotel
Killarney, Co. Kerry 229
☎ +353-64-663 1711

Killyhevlin Hotel
Enniskillen, Co. Fermanagh 110
☎ +44-28-6632 3481

Kilmurry Lodge Hotel
Limerick City, Co. Limerick 81
☎ +353-61-331133

Kilronan Castle Estate & Spa
Ballyfarnon, Co. Roscommon 94
☎ +353-71-961 8000

Kingfisher Lodge Guesthouse
Killarney, Co. Kerry 229
☎ +353-64-663 7131

Kirby's Lanterns Hotel
Tarbert, Co. Kerry 234
☎ +353-68-36210

Knightsbrook Hotel, Spa & Golf Resort
Trim, Co. Meath 165
☎ +353-46-948 2100

Knock House Hotel
Knock, Co. Mayo 88
☎ +353-94-938 8088

Knockranny House Hote & Spa
Westport, Co. Mayo 92
☎ +353-98-28600

L

La Mon Hotel & Country Club
Belfast City, Belfast City 106
☎ +44-28-9044 8631

La Stampa Hotel
Dublin City, Co. Dublin 138
☎ +353-1-677 4444

Lady Gregory Hotel, Conference & Leisure Club
Gort, Co. Galway 70
☎ +353-91-632333

Lahinch Golf & Leisure Hotel
Lahinch, Co. Clare 43
☎ +353-65-708 1100

Lake Hotel (The)
Killarney, Co. Kerry 229
☎ +353-64-663 1035

Lakeside Manor Hotel
Virginia, Co. Cavan 119
☎ +353-49-854 8200

Landmark Hotel
Carrick-on-Shannon, Co. Leitrim 78
☎ +353-71-962 2222

Langton House Hotel
Kilkenny City, Co. Kilkenny 242
☎ +353-56-776 5133

Lansdowne Arms Hotel
Kenmare, Co. Kerry 215
☎ +353-64-664 1368

Lansdowne Hotel
Dublin City, Co. Dublin 138
☎ +353-1-668 2522

Laurels
Kilkenny City, Co. Kilkenny 242
☎ +353-56-776 1501

Leenane Hotel
Leenane, Co. Galway 73
☎ +353-95-42249

Lisdonagh House
Caherlistrane, Co. Galway 56
☎ +353-93-31163

Lisloughrey Lodge
Cong, Co. Mayo 88
☎ +353-94- 954 5400

Lismar Guesthouse
Dundalk, Co. Louth 161
☎ +353-42-935 7246

Lismore House Hotel
Lismore, Co. Waterford 254
☎ +353-58-72966

Lodge (The) at Castle Leslie Estate
Glaslough, Co. Monaghan 166
☎ +353-47-88100

Londonderry Arms Hotel
Carnlough, Co. Antrim 104
☎ +44-28-2888 5255

Longford Arms Hotel, Spa & Leisure Centre
Longford Town, Co. Longford 158
☎ +353-43-334 6296

Lord Bagenal Inn
Leighlinbridge, Co. Carlow 184
☎ +353-59-977 4000

Lough Rea Hotel & Spa
Loughrea, Co. Galway 73
☎ +353-91-880088

Lough Rynn Castle
Mohill, Co. Leitrim 78
☎ +353-71-963 2700

Lynham's Hotel
Glendalough, Co. Wicklow 177
☎ +353-404-45345

Lyrath Estate Hotel & Convention Centre
Kilkenny City, Co. Kilkenny 243
☎ +353-56-776 0088

M

Mahon's Hotel
Irvinestown, Co. Fermanagh 110
☎ +44-28-6862 1656

Majestic Hotel
Tramore, Co. Waterford 256
☎ +353-51-381761

Maldron Hotel Cardiff Lane
Dublin City, Co. Dublin 138
☎ +353-1-643 9500

Maldron Hotel Citywest
Dublin City, Co. Dublin 139
☎ +353-1-461 9900

Maldron Hotel Cork
Cork City, Co. Cork 198
☎ +353-21-452 9200

Maldron Hotel Galway
Galway City, Co. Galway 67
☎ +353-91-792244

Maldron Hotel Limerick
Limerick City, Co. Limerick 82
☎ +353-61-436100

Maldron Hotel Parnell Square
Dublin City, Co. Dublin 139
☎ +353-1-871 6800

Maldron Hotel Portlaoise
Portlaoise, Co. Laois 157
☎ +353-57-869 5900

Maldron Hotel Smithfield
Dublin City, Co. Dublin 139
☎ +353-1-485 0900

Maldron Hotel Tallaght
Dublin City, Co. Dublin 140
☎ +353-1-468 5400

Maldron Hotel Wexford
Wexford Town, Co. Wexford 267
☎ +353-53-917 2000

Malin Hotel
Malin, Co. Donegal 53
☎ +353-74-937 0606

Malone Lodge Hotel & Apartments
Belfast City, Belfast City 106
☎ +44-28-9038 8000

Malton (The)
Killarney, Co. Kerry 230
☎ +353-64-663 8000

Index of Hotels and Guesthouses   GUINNESS

Manor House Resort Hotel
Enniskillen, Co. Fermanagh 110
☎ +44-28-6862 2200

Maple Hotel
Dublin City, Co. Dublin 140
☎ +353-1-855 5442

Marian Guest House
Dublin City, Co. Dublin 140
☎ +353-1-874 4129

Marian Lodge Guesthouse
Galway City, Co. Galway 68
☎ +353-91-521678

Marine Hotel
Sutton, Co. Dublin 150
☎ +353-1-839 0000

Markree Castle
Collooney, Co. Sligo 95
☎ +353-71-916 7800

Marlfield House
Gorey, Co. Wexford 263
☎ +353-53-942 1124

Martello Hotel (The)
Bray, Co. Wicklow 176
☎ +353-1-286 8000

Maryborough Hotel & Spa
Cork City, Co. Cork 198
☎ +353-21-436 5555

Maudlins House Hotel
Naas, Co. Kildare 154
☎ +353-45-896999

McCormack's Guesthouse
Mullingar, Co. Westmeath 173
☎ +353-44-934 1483

McKevitt's Village Hotel
Carlingford, Co. Louth 160
☎ +353-42-937 3116

McSweeney Arms Hotel
Killarney, Co. Kerry 230
☎ +353-64-663 1211

McWilliam Park Hotel (The)
Claremorris, Co. Mayo 87
☎ +353-94-937 8000

Meadow Court Hotel
Loughrea, Co. Galway 74
☎ +353-91-841051

Meadowlands Hotel
Tralee, Co. Kerry 236
☎ +353-66-718 0444

Menlo Park Hotel
Galway City, Co. Galway 68
☎ +353-91-761122

Mercer Hotel
Dublin City, Co. Dublin 141
☎ +353-1-478 2179

Merriman Inn & Restaurant
Kinvara, Co. Galway 72
☎ +353-91-638222

Merrion Hotel (The)
Dublin City, Co. Dublin 141
☎ +353-1-603 0600

Mespil Hotel
Dublin City, Co. Dublin 141
☎ +353-1-488 4600

Metro Hotel Dublin Airport
Dublin Airport, Co. Dublin 121
☎ +353-1-866 9500

Mill Park Hotel, Conference Centre & Leisure Club
Donegal Town, Co. Donegal 48
☎ +353-74-972 2880

Mill Times Hotel Westport
Westport, Co. Mayo 92
☎ +353-98-29200

Moat Lodge
Lucan, Co. Dublin 148
☎ +353-1-624 1584

Moorings (The)
Portmagee, Co. Kerry 233
☎ +353-66-947 7108

Moorland Guesthouse
Laghey, Co. Donegal 51
☎ +353-74-973 4319

Mount Falcon
Ballina, Co. Mayo 84
☎ +353-96-74472

Mount Wolseley Hotel, Spa & Country Club
Tullow, Co. Carlow 184
☎ +353-59-918 0100

Mountain View Guest House
Oughterard, Co. Galway 74
☎ +353-91-550306

Moy House
Lahinch, Co. Clare 43
☎ +353-65-708 2800

Muckross Park Hotel & Cloisters Spa
Killarney, Co. Kerry 230
☎ +353-64-662 3400

Mulranny Park Hotel
Mulranny, Co. Mayo 89
☎ +353-98-36000

Munster Arms Hotel
Bandon, Co. Cork 187
☎ +353-23-884 1562

Murphy's of Killarney
Killarney, Co. Kerry 231
☎ +353-64-663 1294

Muskerry Arms
Blarney, Co. Cork 189
☎ +353-21-438 5200

N

Newbay Country House
Wexford Town, Co. Wexford 268
☎ +353-53-914 2779

Newgrange Hotel
Navan, Co. Meath 164
☎ +353-46-907 4100

Newpark Hotel
Kilkenny City, Co. Kilkenny 243
☎ +353-56-776 0500

Newtown Farm
Ardmore, Co. Waterford 251
☎ +353-24-94143

No 1 Pery Square, Hotel & Spa
Limerick City, Co. Limerick 82
☎ +353-61-402402

Number 31
Dublin City, Co. Dublin 142
☎ +353-1-676 5011

O

O'Connors Guesthouse
Doolin, Co. Clare 37
☎ +353-65-707 4498

O'Connor's Guesthouse
Cloghane, Co. Kerry 210
☎ +353-66-713 8113

O'Donnabhain's Townhouse
Kenmare, Co. Kerry 216
☎ +353-64-664 2106

O'Donovan's Hotel
Clonakilty, Co. Cork 192
☎ +353-23-883 3250

Old Bank House Kinsale (The)
Kinsale, Co. Cork 203
☎ +353-21-477 4075

Old Ground Hotel
Ennis, Co. Clare 38
☎ +353-65-682 8127

Old Pier (The)
Dingle (An Daingean), Co. Kerry 214
☎ +353-66-915 5242

Old Weir Lodge
Killarney, Co. Kerry 231
☎ +353-64-663 5593

Oranmore Lodge Hotel, Conference & Leisure Centre
Galway City, Co. Galway 68
☎ +353-91-794400

Oriel House Hotel, Leisure Club & Spa
Ballincollig, Co. Cork 185
☎ +353-21-420 8400

O'Sheas Hotel
Dublin City, Co. Dublin 142
☎ +353-1-836 5670

O'Shea's Hotel
Tramore, Co. Waterford 256
☎ +353-51-381246

Óstán Oileán Acla
Achill Island, Co. Mayo 83
☎ +353-98-45138

P

Palmerstown Lodge
Dublin City, Co. Dublin 142
☎ +353-1-623 5494

Park Hotel Kiltimagh
Kiltimagh, Co. Mayo 88
☎ +353-94-937 4922

Park Hotel, Leisure Centre & Holiday Homes
Dungarvan, Co. Waterford 253
☎ +353-58-42899

Park Lodge Hotel
Spiddal, Co. Galway 76
☎ +353-91-553159

GUINNESS — Index of Hotels and Guesthouses

Parknasilla Resort
Sneem, Co. Kerry 233
☎ +353-64-667 5600

Pax House
Dingle (An Daingean), Co. Kerry 214
☎ +353-66-915 1518

**Pier Head Hotel,
Spa and Leisure Centre**
Mullaghmore, Co. Sligo 96
☎ +353-71-916 6171

Pier House
Aran Islands, Co. Galway 55
☎ +353-99-61417

Portlaoise Heritage Hotel
Portlaoise, Co. Laois 157
☎ +353-57-867 8588

Portree House
Waterford City, Co. Waterford 258
☎ +353-51- 874574

Prince of Wales Hotel
Athlone, Co. Westmeath 171
☎ +353-90-647 6666

Q

**Quality Hotel & Leisure
Centre Youghal**
Youghal, Co. Cork 208
☎ +353-24-93050

Quay House (The)
Clifden, Co. Galway 60
☎ +353-95-21369

Quay West
Westport, Co. Mayo 92
☎ +353-98-27863

R

Radisson Blu Farnham Estate Hotel
Cavan Town, Co. Cavan 118
☎ +353-49-437 7700

**Radisson Blu Hotel &
Spa Sligo**
Sligo Town, Co. Sligo 96
☎ +353-71-914 0008

Radisson Blu Hotel Athlone
Athlone, Co. Westmeath 172
☎ +353-90-644 2600

Radisson Blu Roe Park Resort
Limavady, Co. Derry 108
☎ +44-28-7772 2222

Radisson Blu St Helen's Hotel
Dublin City, Co. Dublin 143
☎ +353-1-218 6000

**Raheen Woods Hotel Tranquillity
Spa & Kardio Kidz**
Athenry, Co. Galway 55
☎ +353-91-875888

Ramada Portrush
Portrush, Co. Antrim 104
☎ +44-28-7082 6100

Randles Court Hotel
Killarney, Co. Kerry 231
☎ +353-64-663 5333

Rathbaun Hotel
Lisdoonvarna, Co. Clare 44
☎ +353-65-707 4009

Red Cow Moran Hotel
Dublin City, Co. Dublin 143
☎ +353-1-459 3650

**Redbank House Guesthouse &
Restaurant**
Skerries, Co. Dublin 150
☎ +353-1-849 1005

Redclyffe Guest House
Cork City, Co. Cork 198
☎ +353-21-427 3220

Renvyle House Hotel
Renvyle, Co. Galway 75
☎ +353-95-43511

Richmond House
Cappoquin, Co. Waterford 252
☎ +353-58-54278

Richmond Inn Guesthouse
Cloondara, Co. Longford 158
☎ +353-43-332 6126

Rising Sun
Mullinavat, Co. Kilkenny 245
☎ +353-51-898173

River Lee Hotel (The)
Cork City, Co. Cork 199
☎ +353-21-425 2700

Riverbank House Hotel
Wexford Town, Co. Wexford 268
☎ +353-53-912 3611

Riverside Guesthouse
Charlestown, Co. Mayo 87
☎ +353-94-925 4200

**Riverside Park Hotel and
Leisure Club**
Enniscorthy, Co. Wexford 262
☎ +353-53-923 7800

Roganstown Hotel & Country Club
Swords, Co. Dublin 150
☎ +353-1-843 3118

Rosleague Manor
Letterfrack, Co. Galway 73
☎ +353-95-41101

Rosquil House
Kilkenny City, Co. Kilkenny 244
☎ +353-56-772 1419

Ross (The)
Killarney, Co. Kerry 232
☎ +353-64-663 1855

Ross Lake House Hotel
Oughterard, Co. Galway 75
☎ +353-91-550109

Round Tower Hotel (The)
Ardmore, Co. Waterford 251
☎ +353-24-94494

Roundstone House Hotel
Roundstone, Co. Galway 76
☎ +353-95-35864

Royal Marine Hotel
Dun Laoghaire, Co. Dublin 147
☎ +353-1-230 0030

S

Salthill Hotel
Galway City, Co. Galway 69
☎ +353-91-522711

Sancta Maria Hotel
Lahinch, Co. Clare 43
☎ +353-65-708 1041

**Sandymount Hotel (formerly Mount
Herbert Hotel)**
Dublin City, Co. Dublin 144
☎ +353-1-614 2000

Scotts Hotel Killarney
Killarney, Co. Kerry 232
☎ +353-64-663 1060

Sea Dew Guesthouse
Tullamore, Co. Offaly 170
☎ +353-57-935 2054

Sea Rod Inn
Belmullet, Co. Mayo 85
☎ +353-97-86767

Sea Shore Farm Guesthouse
Kenmare, Co. Kerry 216
☎ +353-64-664 1270

Sea View Guest House
Allihies, Co. Cork 185
☎ +353-27-73004

Seaview Guest House
Dungarvan, Co. Waterford 253
☎ +353-58-41583

Seaview House Hotel
Ballylickey, Co. Cork 186
☎ +353-27-50073

Seven Oaks Hotel
Carlow Town, Co. Carlow 183
☎ +353-59-913 1308

**Shandon Hotel
Spa and Wellness**
Dunfanaghy, Co. Donegal 50
☎ +353-74-913 6137

**Shannon Oaks Hotel
& Country Club**
Portumna, Co. Galway 75
☎ +353-90-974 1777

Sheedy's Country House Hotel
Lisdoonvarna, Co. Clare 44
☎ +353-65-707 4026

Sheen Falls Lodge
Kenmare, Co. Kerry 216
☎ +353-64-664 1600

Shelbourne Hotel (The)
Dublin City, Co. Dublin 144
☎ +353-1-663 4500

Sheraton Athlone Hotel
Athlone, Co. Westmeath 172
☎ +353-90-645 1000

Shirley Arms Hotel
Carrickmacross, Co. Monaghan 166
☎ +353-42-967 3100

Silver Springs Moran Hotel
Cork City, Co. Cork 199
☎ +353-21-450 7533

Silver Tassie Hotel & Spa
Letterkenny, Co. Donegal 53
☎ +353-74-912 5619

Silverbirch Hotel
Omagh, Co. Tyrone 111
☎ +44-28-8224 2520

Index of Hotels and Guesthouses   GUINNESS

Skeffington Arms Hotel
Galway City, Co. Galway 69
☎ +353-91-563173

Slieve Russell Hotel Golf & Country Club
Ballyconnell, Co. Cavan 117
☎ +353-49-952 6444

Sligo City Hotel
Sligo Town, Co. Sligo 97
☎ +353-71-914 4000

Sligo Park Hotel & Leisure Club
Sligo Town, Co. Sligo 97
☎ +353-71-919 0400

Smugglers Inn
Waterville, Co. Kerry 237
☎ +353-66-947 4330

Sneem Hotel
Sneem, Co. Kerry 234
☎ +353-64-667 5100

Solis Lough Eske Castle
Donegal Town, Co. Donegal 49
☎ +353-74-972 5100

Springfort Hall Hotel
Mallow, Co. Cork 205
☎ +353-22-21278

Springhill Court Hotel, Conference, Leisure & Spa Hotel
Kilkenny City, Co. Kilkenny 244
☎ +353-56-772 1122

St. Albans Guesthouse
Waterford City, Co. Waterford 260
☎ +353-51-358171 / 379393

St. George Guest House
Wexford Town, Co. Wexford 268
☎ +353-53-914 3474

Stanville Lodge Hotel
Barntown, Co. Wexford 261
☎ +353-53-913 4200

Station House Hotel and Signal Restaurant
Kilmessan, Co. Meath 164
☎ +353-46-902 5239

Stillorgan Park Hotel
Dublin City, Co. Dublin 144
☎ +353-1-200 1800

Strand Guest House
Kilkee, Co. Clare 42
☎ +353-65-905 6177

Sullivan's Royal Hotel
Gort, Co. Galway 71
☎ +353-91-631257/401

T

Tahilla Cove Country House
Tahilla, Co. Kerry 234
☎ +353-64-664 5204

Talbot Hotel Carlow
Carlow Town, Co. Carlow 184
☎ +353-59-915 3000

Talbot Hotel Conference and Leisure Centre
Wexford Town, Co. Wexford 269
☎ +353-53-912 2566

Tara Towers Hotel
Dublin City, Co. Dublin 145
☎ +353-1-269 4666

Temple Bar Hotel
Dublin City, Co. Dublin 145
☎ +353-1-677 3333

Temple Country Retreat & Spa
Moate, Co. Westmeath 172
☎ +353-57-933 5118

Temple Gate Hotel
Ennis, Co. Clare 39
☎ +353-65-682 3300

Templemore Arms Hotel
Templemore, Co. Tipperary 249
☎ +353-504-31423

Ten Square Hotel
Belfast City, Belfast City 106
☎ +44-28-9024 1001

TF Royal Hotel & Royal Theatre
Castlebar, Co. Mayo 86
☎ +353-94-902 3111

The Ritz-Carlton, Powerscourt
Enniskerry, Co. Wicklow 176
☎ +353-1-274 8888

Tierney's Guest House
Kinsale, Co. Cork 204
☎ +353-21-477 2205

Tigh Fitz
Aran Islands, Co. Galway 55
☎ +353-99-61213

Tinakilly House Hotel
Rathnew, Co. Wicklow 178
☎ +353-404-69274

Tower Hotel & Leisure Centre
Waterford City, Co. Waterford 260
☎ +353-51-862300

Trim Castle Hotel
Trim, Co. Meath 165
☎ +353-46-948 3000

Trinity Capital Hotel
Dublin City, Co. Dublin 145
☎ +353-1-648 1000

Tullamore Court Hotel
Tullamore, Co. Offaly 170
☎ +353-57-934 6666

Tullylagan Country House Hotel
Cookstown, Co. Tyrone 111
☎ +44-28-8676 5100

Twelve (The)
Galway City, Co. Galway 69
☎ +353-91-597000

U

Uppercross House
Dublin City, Co. Dublin 146
☎ +353-1-497 5486

V

Vaughan Lodge and Seafood Restaurant
Lahinch, Co. Clare 44
☎ +353-65-708 1111

Victoria Hotel
Galway City, Co. Galway 70
☎ +353-91-567433

Victoria House Hotel
Killarney, Co. Kerry 232
☎ +353-64-663 5430

Viewmount House
Longford Town, Co. Longford 159
☎ +353-43-334 1919

W

Waterford Marina Hotel
Waterford City, Co. Waterford 260
☎ +353-51-856600

Waterfront (The)
Baltimore, Co. Cork 187
☎ +353-28-20600

Waterloo House
Dublin City, Co. Dublin 146
☎ +353-1-660 1888

Waters Edge (The)
Rathmullan, Co. Donegal 54
☎ +353-74-915 8182

WatersEdge Hotel
Cobh, Co. Cork 192
☎ +353-21-481 5566

Waterside
Graiguenamanagh, Co. Kilkenny 238
☎ +353-59-972 4246

Waterside House Hotel & Signal Restaurant
Donabate, Co. Dublin 119
☎ +353-1-843 6153

West Cork Hotel
Skibbereen, Co. Cork 207
☎ +353-28-21277

Westbury Hotel (The)
Dublin City, Co. Dublin 146
☎ +353-1-679 1122

Westcourt Hotel
Drogheda, Co. Louth 160
☎ +353-41-983 0965

Westgrove Hotel
Clane, Co. Kildare 152
☎ +353-45-989900

Westin Dublin
Dublin City, Co. Dublin 147
☎ +353-1-645 1000

Westlodge Hotel
Bantry, Co. Cork 187
☎ +353-27-50360

Westport Plaza Hotel Spa, Leisure, Conference
Westport, Co. Mayo 93
☎ +353-98-51166

Westport Woods Hotel & Spa
Westport, Co. Mayo 93
☎ +353-98-25811

Westwood Hotel (The)
Galway City, Co. Galway 70
☎ +353-91-521442

White House
Kinsale, Co. Cork 204
☎ +353-21-477 2125

Index of Hotels and Guesthouses

Whites of Wexford
Wexford Town, Co. Wexford...................269
☎ +353-53-912 2311

Woodenbridge Hotel & Lodge
Woodenbridge, Co. Wicklow...................178
☎ +353-402-35146

Woodhill House
Ardara, Co. Donegal 45
☎ +353-74-954 1112

Woodlands Hotel
Waterford City, Co. Waterford...............261
☎ +353-51-392700

Wyatt Hotel
Westport, Co. Mayo.....................93
☎ +353-98-25027

Y

Yeats Country Hotel, Spa & Leisure Club
Rosses Point, Co. Sligo 96
☎ +353-71-917 7211

Yew Tree @ The Chester Beatty Inn
Ashford, Co. Wicklow................................175
☎ +353-404-40206

Notes

Direct low rates and great special offers guaranteed

Irelandhotels.com
We've got it covered

You can find all the best deals in all of these places

Website | Mobile App | Printed Guide |
facebook.com/irelandhotels | irelandhotels.com/onlineguide

Irelandhotels.com
We've got it covered